QUESTIONS
OF EVIDENCE

QUESTIONS
OF EVIDENCE

Proof, Practice, and Persuasion across the Disciplines

EDITED BY

JAMES CHANDLER, ARNOLD I. DAVIDSON,
AND HARRY HAROOTUNIAN

THE UNIVERSITY OF CHICAGO PRESS

Chicago and London

The essays in this volume originally appeared in various issues of
Critical Inquiry. Acknowledgment of the original publication date
may be found on the first page of each essay.

The University of Chicago Press, Chicago, 60637
The University of Chicago Press, Ltd., London
© 1991, 1992, 1993, 1994 by the University of Chicago
All rights reserved. Published 1994
Printed in the United States of America
ISBN (cl.) 0-226-10082-0
ISBN (pa.) 0-226-10083-9

98 97 96 95 94   5 4 3 2 1

Library of Congress Cataloging-in-Publication Data

Questions of evidence : proof, practice, and persuasion across the
    disciplines / edited by James Chandler, Arnold I. Davidson, and Harry
    Harootunian.
        p. cm.
    Contains 12 essays originally published in three consecutive issues of
    Critical Inquiry (Summer 1991 to Winter 1992), an essay by Mary
    Poovey (Winter 1993), responses to the essays by various faculty mem-
    bers of the University of Chicago, and replies to the responses by the
    authors of the essays.
    Includes bibliographical references and index.
    ISBN 0-226-10082-0 (cloth).—ISBN 0-226-10083-9 (pbk.)
    1. Evidence. 2. Critical theory. 3. Interdisciplinary research.
I. Chandler, James K. II. Davidson, Arnold Ira. III. Harootunian,
Harry D., 1929–.
BD181.Q47 1994
121'.65—dc20   94-12897
                                                    CIP

The paper used in this publication meets the minimum requirements of
American National Standard for Information Sciences—Permanence of
Paper for Printed Library Materials, ANSI Z39.48-1984.♾

Contents

History and the Uses of Inquiry

Experience and the Disciplines of Proof

Editors' Introduction

James Chandler, Arnold I. Davidson,
and Harry Harootunian

The topic of evidence is so central for research and scholarship that it is extraordinary how little direct attention it has received. The best-known exception to this rule of neglect is probably still R. G. Collingwood's defense of the humanities in *The Idea of History* (1946), which argued that only "history," in Collingwood's expanded sense, could address enlightenment aspirations to a "science" of human nature. What distinguished history from science, on this account, was the operation of an "a priori imagination" that governed the activity of historical construction; what distinguished historical imagination from the artistic imagination was its respect for evidence. Collingwood's landmark discussion of "Historical Evidence" offered a powerful critique of what he called the "scissors-and-paste" model of history, and a compelling case for the notion of the historian's constitutive dialogue with the human past—a notion newly recuperated in the work of recent theorists.[1] Question and evidence are therefore "correlative" in the strong sense that facts can only become evidence in response to some particular question.

Yet despite its range and acuity, Collingwood's discussion of evidence suffers from two related shortcomings that severely qualify its continuing usefulness. Its science-history distinction is drawn with a sharpness that seems misleading in the light of the last half-century's work in many fields, especially in the philosophy of science. Hence the difficulty Collingwood's defenders have had in maintaining his sharp distinction between the (historically apprehended) "inside" of an event and its (scien-

---

1. See, for example, Dominick La Capra, "Rethinking Intellectual History and Reading Texts," *Rethinking Intellectual History: Texts, Contexts, Language* (Ithaca, N.Y., 1983), pp. 23–71 and "Intellectual History and Critical Theory," *Soundings in Critical Theory* (Ithaca, N.Y., 1989), pp. 182–209, for a critique of what he calls "cut-and-paste" historicism (p. 193).

tifically explained) "outside." Both the theory of historical reenactment and the doctrine of *Einfühlung*, which derive from the German hermeneutic tradition, have come under strong attack for related reasons, and from positions as diverse as those of the logical positivists and the poststructuralists. Second, within the vast realm of what he calls "history," Collingwood did not respect distinctions among disciplines and thus could not attend to differences among the ways in which evidence figures in various humanistic practices of inquiry and argument. In short, while Collingwood's line of analysis helped scholars to see that evidence always responds to questions, it did not register how complicated the questions of evidence prove to be.

We think the present moment is a timely one for examining the relation between evidentiary protocols and academic disciplines, for investigating the entire range of questions provoked by the status and function of evidence. Since academic practices for constituting and deploying evidence tend to be discipline-specific, the much-discussed crisis of the disciplines in recent years—what Clifford Geertz has called the "blurring" of the disciplinary genres—has given rise to a series of controversies about the status of evidence in current modes of investigation and argument: deconstruction, gender studies, New Historicism, cultural studies, new approaches to the history and philosophy of science, the critical legal studies movement, and so on. Unfortunately, these controversies too often devolve into oversimplified debates about who has the evidence and who does not, who did their homework and who did not, or about the dangers of an ill-defined academic relativism. Attention needs to be better and otherwise directed: toward the configuration of the fact-evidence distinction in different disciplines and historical moments, for example; or toward the relative function of such notions as "self-evidence," "ex-

James Chandler, professor of English at the University of Chicago, is the author of *Wordsworth's Second Nature* (1984). He is currently completing *England in 1819,* studies in and of romantic case history. **Arnold I. Davidson,** the executive editor of *Critical Inquiry,* is professor of philosophy and a member of the Committee on the Conceptual Foundations of Science at the University of Chicago. Appointed a fellow at the Wissenschaftskolleg, Berlin for 1994–95, he has recently published a series of essays on the tradition of spiritual exercises in philosophy and is completing a book on the history of horror and wonder. **Harry Harootunian,** a coeditor of *Critical Inquiry* and Max Palevsky Professor of History and East Asian Languages and Civilizations at the University of Chicago, is the author of *Things Seen and Unseen: Discourse and Ideology in Tokugawa Nativism* (1988) and editor, with Masao Miyoshi, of *Postmodernism and Japan* (1989) and *Japan in the World* (1993).

perience," "test," "testimony," and "textuality" in various academic discourses; or toward the ways in which the invoked "rules of evidence" are themselves the products of historical developments, and themselves undergo redifferentiation and reformulation.

Unfortunately, the force with which such second-order questions of evidence seem to intrude themselves has been matched by a corresponding reluctance to confront them head on. We can illustrate this point by reference to one of the books that set the direction of much work in the humanities in the 1980s, Stephen Greenblatt's important study *Renaissance Self-Fashioning* (1981). This book is perhaps the most widely cited example of the range of new work in humanities that goes under the name of the New Historicism. Its many readers will recall that while it discusses More, Tyndall, Spenser, and Donne, its capstone is the ingenious and controversial final chapter, an analysis of Shakespeare's *Othello* in the context of Tudor-Stuart imperialism. The chapter moves from an examination of memoirs of English explorers in the New World to a suggestion that what characterizes the particular talent of these explorers is a developed capacity for "improvisation," which proves to be a mode of nonviolent conquest through assimilation of a people's language and manners. Greenblatt cites Daniel Lerner's description of the colonial encounters as generating the theory and practice of Western empathy, and Greenblatt wants to connect this emergence, as Lerner himself does, to the modern critical tradition (in which Collingwood stands) that grounds interpretation in *Einfühlung*. But, for Greenblatt, the improviser is no empathizer; he is above all a conqueror and his learning about the Other is a small act of appropriation in the service of a larger one. Having established so much, Greenblatt turns to *Othello* to argue the bold thesis that "what Professor Lerner calls 'empathy,' Shakespeare calls 'Iago.'"[2] Greenblatt then develops an interpretation of the play (for us) that centers in Iago's interpretation of the world (for Othello). Iago emerges as the figure of the theatrical improviser-appropriator, a counterpart in domestic affairs, as it were, for the English explorer abroad. Empathy, then, is cultural appropriation.

But since this argument implicates the motives underlying the critical tradition that has defended itself under the banner of interpretative empathy, it also has implications for Greenblatt's own critical procedures: for the improviser Iago is to Othello as the improviser Greenblatt is to us. This analogy in Greenblatt's work between figures in his essays and the figure of himself as essayist is yet more pronounced in his more recent work, where he comments on those sixteenth-century go-betweens who report back to their European home bases in now-obscure diaries and

---

2. Stephen Greenblatt, *Renaissance Self-Fashioning: From More to Shakespeare* (Chicago, 1980), p. 225. See Daniel Lerner, *The Passing of Traditional Society: Modernizing the Middle East* (1958; New York, 1964).

journals on the wonders discovered in the New World; for these are clearly stand-ins for the Greenblatt who reports to us on the wonders of these almost completely unread texts. Insofar as the analogy holds, however, it becomes remarkable that the thematics of evidence, so conspicuous in the exchanges between Othello and Iago—the famous line, "Give me the ocular proof," belongs to an elaborate system of such references in the play—are so little explored by Greenblatt. Specifically, Othello's appetite for evidence and Iago's falsification of it (with the planting of the handkerchief) are not acknowledged as having implications for the handling of evidence in the counterpart relationship of the critic (Greenblatt) and his readers. We thus come upon the repressed question of evidence in Greenblatt's book: is there an equivalent of the planted handkerchief in the argument of *Renaissance Self-Fashioning?*

It is an unseemly question but one which the logic of the work itself calls for. We offer this detailed comment on Greenblatt's brilliant analysis as an exemplum. On the basis of this book, he has rightly taken his place at or near the head of a generation of scholars challenging old forms of evidentiary practices in the humanities. He is dealing with one of the classic texts on the theme of evidence in our tradition. He is constructing an analogy that leads right to the point of making the connection between evidence in interpretation and evidence in one's own interpretation. While he himself does not make it, his readers now must if they wish to come to terms with the potential challenge such new work poses to our assumed rules of evidence.

A related matter of relevance can be explicated by returning to Geertz. If the blurring he discusses has prompted a widespread crossing of boundaries, it has also put into question, in fields such as history and some of the "softer" social sciences, the very object of inquiry. This questioning has often led to recognizing the indeterminacy of disciplinary divisions and the all-too-contingent nature of the conventions that motivate their practice. In historical studies, the status of evidence has invariably been bonded to the certainty of an object of study, which has been the past. To secure that object, severe distinctions were necessarily made between primary (archival) sources and secondary materials. The former tended to privilege documentary materials belonging to (or contemporary with) the past under study, while the latter were classified as later writings and accounts on the particular subject. In addition to this differentiation of evidence, historians grappled with the need to establish a stable referent external to the actual reconstruction that was supposed to authenticate the historical veracity of a past or an event "guaranteed by the 'real.'"

As a result of this task, historians believed it was possible to reconstruct the past by employing archival and documentary materials that were, in some way, outside of signification. Under these circumstances, the evaluation of evidence concentrated on determining, through a num-

ber of techniques and tests, the reliability of the source as a true reflection
of a past rather than its status as a representation and its conditions of
production. In this operation the document was seen as a reflection of a
determinant reality rather than as a constituent agent in the reconstruction of a conception of the real. But once the status of the referent was
problematized and shown to be not on the other side of signification but
inside the historian's discourse that posits it as a referent, the status of
evidence was altered. In place of appealing to evidence as a dictation of
reality that authorized a reconstruction of the past, it was necessary to
view materials as evidence for the constitutive role they played in shaping
the image of the past. After it was recognized that the authority of the
past as an object had become problematic, the crossing of boundaries
invited a vast broadening or diversification of materials that might be
consulted, a kind of "dehierarchicization" of evidence, the abandonment
of ironclad and often arbitrary differentiation between primary sources
and secondary literature and the gradual acknowledgment of a discursive
practice more constructive than reconstructive.

We have seen the beginnings of attempts to address the new questions—in recent Modern Language Association, American History Association, and American Philosophy Association sessions, and in the recent
exchange in the American Historical Association Forum over Natalie
Zemon Davis's *The Return of Martin Guerre*—but they need to be met yet
more directly and on a larger scale.[3] In widening the horizon of analysis
for the new history—as well as the New Historicism and other related
developments—it is not enough to consider the different and changing
roles of evidence in the humanities, even when we extend *humanities* to
include what used to be called the human sciences more broadly. The
altered configuration of the disciplines with which we must now come to
terms is altered across the board. No attempt to address it can afford to
leave entirely out of account, for example, what has happened in recent
work in the philosophy of science.

With the decline of the positivist tradition in the philosophy of science that sought to ground scientific claims in a theory-independent observation language, the status of scientific rationality was profoundly
problematized. The resulting emphasis on the primacy of theory, combined with the attempt to give sociological accounts of science that put
"good" and "bad" science on completely equal footing, threatened to reduce the role of evidence, facts, and proof to the point of nonexistence.
The history of these positivism/antipositivism and realism/antirealism debates in the history and philosophy of science have made us acutely aware
of the need to reconceptualize the whole set of notions that have structured these debates, that have been in play on both sides of the issues. In

3. See Robert Finlay, "The Refashioning of Martin Guerre," and Natalie Zemon Davis,
"On the Lame," *American Historical Review* 93 (June 1988): 553–603.

rethinking the nature of scientific evidence, questions of evidence in the sciences and the humanities have been brought together again so as to reopen the divisions so firmly established in earlier discussions.

In its attack on these large and vexing problems, this book must be understood as the culmination of several years of diverse kinds of work by diverse hands. It grew out of a plan for a special issue of *Critical Inquiry* in which essays would be solicited to consider such questions of evidence as we have just outlined. To this scheme was eventually joined another, a plan for a major conference at the University of Chicago on the same themes with the same scholars. Once the Centennial Committee of the university guaranteed us support for such a conference, we were free to experiment with the standard conference format in the humanities. The wide readership of *Critical Inquiry* made it possible to plan preconference publication of work by the scholars we wished to involve from out-side Chicago; prospective members of the audience for the conference were admonished by prior advertisement to familiarize themselves with these essays in advance of the event. The aim was to devote less confer-ence time to reading papers and more to discussing the issues they raise. The sessions at the conference thus took place around a series of rela-tively formal exchanges between designated respondents and the authors of the essays in question. The respondents were chosen from among the university faculty at Chicago, including many of the editors of *Critical Inquiry* who had the advantage of having already vetted all of the prepub-lished papers. In most cases, these assignments were made slightly askew of conventionally defined field expertise, even when more straightfor-ward arrangements were possible. We asked the respondents to generate a text, readable in about fifteen minutes, that might be sent to the author of the essay in question some weeks before the conference. We asked the authors to prepare a fifteen-minute rejoinder to that response to be read or extemporized in the session.

Since these responses were meant to be read to an audience that had *not* just heard (though they were expected to have read) the papers under discussion, we specifically charged respondents with the task of initial syn-opsis. One of the reasons we tended to choose respondents somewhat out of field was to foster discursive bridge building between different disci-plinary idioms and between different areas of expertise. We sought, that is, to use the responses to enable both the conference and the volume to work on more than one level: they serve both as introductions to each essay for the newcomer to the field in question and as an in-depth inter-rogation of that paper's argument. The problem of demonstration in ar-gument becomes, in this sense, both the volume's subject matter and one of the keys to its construction. In any case, the presence of the responses relieves us of one duty normally incurred by editors asked to introduce such collections: the summary of the papers' central arguments.

The present volume, then, includes the following items: the twelve originally commissioned essays, collected together from the three consecutive issues of *Critical Inquiry* (Summer 1991 to Winter 1992) in which they first appeared; a thirteenth essay, by Mary Poovey, who graciously agreed to participate in the conference on relatively late notice; responses to all thirteen essays by faculty from a variety of departments and disciplines at Chicago; and the rejoinders to these responses by the authors of the essays. It is our hope that just as the initial essays represented the matter, so the printed texts of these exchanges might capture the energy of the extraordinary two-day event on the Chicago campus. We also hope these newly published materials will suggest how a language began to be formed for talking about these issues across disciplines but with exceptional trenchancy and sophistication. They indeed constitute the main evidence of what happened at the conference, apart from hearsay reports and the set of seven audio diskettes on which the proceedings were recorded. Since we cannot include the dozens of hours of discussions that comprise the audio record of the event, we will let the following exchange, which captures the enthusiasm, engagement, and spirit of the conference, serve as evidence for the other discussions. In response to Richard Lewontin's argument that biology does not consist of genuine laws and that therefore there are no real biological anomalies, this marvelous exchange occurred:

LORRAINE DASTON: *(to R. C. Lewontin)*	Are you saying, then, that, since all biological laws reduce merely to ad hoc lists, there could be no such thing as a biological anomaly?
LEWONTIN:	There might be anomalies that involve organisms but that might be otherwise classified. If I began to levitate toward the ceiling at this moment, that would be an anomaly in physics but not in biology.
CARLO GINZBURG:	Would you count an instance of personal immortality as an anomaly in biology?
LEWONTIN:	Yes, only it would be impossible to produce the evidence for such a case.

We have many institutions and many persons to thank for support, encouragement, and advice in the long unfolding of this project. Tom Mitchell responded to a casual proposal four years ago with characteristic energy and savvy. Kinaret Jaffe and the Centennial Committee of the University of Chicago made an early commitment to us and stood by it, even after we were refused funding by the Division of Research Programs at a National Endowment for the Humanities over which Lynn Cheney then presided. We received crucial additional funding from the new Chicago Humanities Institute under its acting director, Norma Field, and have also received subsequent help from the institute under Arjun Appadurai, its current director, to defray some of the costs of producing this volume. Philip Gossett, dean of the Division of the Humanities, got behind our efforts at an early stage and helped to mediate various bureaucratic problems as they arose. Celia Homans's assistance with budgetary work was timely and absolutely invaluable. Lorraine Brochu-Mudloff (administrative assistant to CHI), together with Jeffrey Mash, John Chaimov, and Deborah Weiss, handled innumerable details along the way. Jay Williams, David A. Schabes, and Ann Hobart edited the manuscripts at a level of professional excellence that is their trademark. Together with John O'Brien, Jessica Burstein, Peter Struck, and David Grubbs they proofread and prepared the manuscripts for publication. Finally, we thank our friends and colleagues in the Chicago community for their advice and support. For them, our wish is that they may all be as robust at the age of one hundred as is their university.

THE SUBJECT
OF EVIDENCE

Contagious Folly: *An Adventure* and Its Skeptics

Terry Castle

What to make of someone who sees a ghost? In his 1830 attack on superstition, *Letters on Demonology and Witchcraft,* Sir Walter Scott was forthright: anyone who claimed to see an apparition was either mad or on the way to becoming so. Since ghosts, according to Scott, did not exist, to maintain that one had seen one was to be pathetically unbalanced—the victim of some "lively dream, a waking reverie, the excitation of a powerful imagination, or the misrepresentation of a diseased organ of sight." The skeptic was not to be deceived by the air of apparent reasonableness with which the ghost-seer typically described his or her visions: in the case of every such person he had met with, Scott wrote, "shades of mental aberration have afterwards occurred, which sufficiently accounted for the supposed apparitions, and will incline me always to feel alarmed in behalf of the continued health of a friend, who should conceive himself to have witnessed such a visitation."[1]

But what if *two* people claim to see a ghost? If specters are indeed to be understood, as Scott thought, psychologically—as hallucinatory products of an abnormally excited or "diseased" imagination—how then to account for an apparition seen by two people at once? Are we to conclude that hallucinations can be shared? Or that spectral delusions, like the germs of a virus, can somehow be transmitted from the brain of one person to another? What sort of psychical mechanism would explain such a

1. Sir Walter Scott, *Letters on Demonology and Witchcraft, Addressed to J. G. Lockhart, Esq.,* 2d ed. (London, 1831), pp. 344–45.

This essay originally appeared in *Critical Inquiry* 17 (Summer 1991).

strangely infectious brand of folly? Scott himself avoids the issue by refusing to allow that simultaneous sightings ever occur. Yet the omission is clearly tactical: for to acknowledge such a possibility, let alone debunk it, the resolute skeptic would have to work twice as hard, if only to remain half-convincing.

The question of the so-called collective hallucination (as it has come to be known to psychical researchers) is neither as arcane nor as irrelevant to everyday life as it might first appear. On the contrary, it illuminates a much larger philosophical issue. In *Group Psychology and the Analysis of the Ego,* his 1921 book devoted to the relationship between individual and group psychology, Sigmund Freud lamented that there was still "no explanation of the nature of suggestion, that is, of the conditions under which influence without adequate logical foundation takes place."[2] What the science of psychology lacked, in other words, was an understanding of ideological transference—the process by which one individual imposed his or her beliefs and convictions on another. How did an idea spread, so to speak, from one person to the next, resulting in the formation of a group consciousness? The phenomenon of the collective hallucination puts the issue starkly—if ambiguously—in relief. If a ghost or apparition can be said to represent, in Freud's terms, an idea "without adequate logical foundation," a *delusion,* then the process by which two people convince each other that they have seen one—and in turn attempt to convince others—might be taken to epitomize the formation of ideology itself.

In what follows I shall examine a case of collective hallucination—certainly the most notorious and well documented in the annals of modern psychical research—precisely as a way of spotlighting this larger problem. My goal in so doing is not so much to expose the folly of people who claim to see ghosts (though the notion of folly will play a crucial part in what I have to say) but the difficulty that inevitably besets anyone who attempts to debunk such claims on supposedly rationalist grounds. For in the absence of any satisfying explanation of how such "folly" spreads—how a private delusion becomes a *folie à deux* (or *trois* or *quatre*)—the labors of the skeptic are doomed to result only in a peculiar rhetorical and epistemological impasse.

The case I wish to resurrect—at some risk, I realize, of exciting

2. Sigmund Freud, *Group Psychology and the Analysis of the Ego,* trans. and ed. James Strachey (New York, 1959), p. 22.

Terry Castle is professor of English at Stanford University and the author of *Masquerade and Civilization: The Carnivalesque in Eighteenth-Century English Culture and Fiction* (1986). She has just published a new study entitled *The Apparitional Lesbian: Female Homosexuality and Modern Culture* (1993).

readerly mirth—is that of the "Ghosts of Versailles." The case dates from 1911. In that year two eminent English women academics, Charlotte Anne Moberly and Eleanor Jourdain, the principal and vice-principal, respectively, of St. Hugh's College, Oxford, published under the pseudonyms "Miss Morison" and "Miss Lamont" a book entitled *An Adventure* in which they asserted that while on a sightseeing tour of the gardens of the Petit Trianon near Versailles on 10 August 1901, they had encountered the apparitions of Marie Antoinette and several members of her court precisely as they had existed in the year 1789. After jointly researching the matter for nearly ten years in the French national archives, Moberly and Jourdain wrote, they had been forced to conclude that they had travelled backwards in time—perhaps by entering telepathically into "an act of memory" performed by Marie Antoinette herself during her incarceration following the sacking of the Tuileries. In the central chapters of *An Adventure* (which quickly became a best-seller) they laid out this bizarre theory in detail, along with a mass of so-called historical and topographical evidence supposedly confirming it.

What prompted Moberly and Jourdain—the respectable daughters of clergymen both—to make such a fantastic claim? The story behind *An Adventure,* though a convoluted one, is worth relating in some detail. At the time of their fateful trip to Versailles in the summer of 1901, Miss Moberly and Miss Jourdain, who were subsequently to live and work together for twenty-three years, were only slightly acquainted. Charlotte Anne Moberly (1846–1937), the older and better connected of the two (her father was the bishop of Salisbury), had been principal of the small Oxford women's college, St. Hugh's, since its founding in 1886. Eleanor Jourdain (1864–1924) was an Oxford graduate in history and the headmistress of a girls' school in Watford. When Jourdain was recommended for the vacant post of vice-principal at St. Hugh's, Moberly agreed to meet with her in Paris (where Jourdain was staying) to see if the two of them could work together compatibly. The trip to Versailles, a place neither woman had visited before, came at the end of several days of sightseeing together in the French capital.[3]

As the two recount it in the opening chapter of *An Adventure,* they set off by train for Versailles on 10 August. After touring the main palace (which left them unimpressed) they decided to venture out into the grounds in search of the Petit Trianon. At the time—or so they claimed—

3. In synopsizing the background to *An Adventure* I have drawn on Lucille Iremonger's *Ghosts of Versailles: Miss Moberly and Miss Jourdain and Their Adventure: A Critical Study* (London, 1957), hereafter abbreviated *GV;* and Joan Evans's "End to *An Adventure:* Solving the Mystery of the Trianon," *Encounter* 47 (Oct. 1976): 33–47, hereafter abbreviated "E." Moberly's family memoir, *Dulce Domum: George Moberly, His Family and Friends* (London, 1911), provides additional information about her upbringing and milieu; further information about Eleanor Jourdain can be found in Hilary Spurling's *Ivy: The Life of I. Compton-Burnett* (New York, 1984), pp. 312–19.

Fig. 2.—Eleanor Jourdain (1864–1924)

Fig. 1.—Charlotte Anne Moberly (1846–1937)

neither one of them knew much about French history, or indeed about the Trianon itself, except that it had been the favorite retreat of the ill-fated queen, Marie Antoinette, before the French Revolution. The day was pleasant, however, and both were in the mood for a walk. Soon after passing an imposing building at the bottom of the Long Water—the Grand Trianon—the two women got lost. They wandered for a while at random, passing a deserted farmhouse where Jourdain noticed a peculiar-looking old plough and began to feel (as she put it later) as if "something were wrong."[4] Moberly was surprised that Jourdain did not ask the way from a woman shaking a cloth out the window of one of the outbuildings, but concluded that her companion knew where she was going. Turning down a lane, they espied two men dressed in "long greyish-green coats with small three-cornered hats." Moberly remembered seeing "a wheelbarrow of some kind close by" and assumed that the men were gardeners, or else "dignified officials" of some kind (*A*, p. 4). Here Miss Jourdain did ask the way, and they were instructed to go down a path in front of them. As they began to walk forward, Jourdain saw a cottage on her right in front of which a woman and a girl were standing. Both were dressed unusually, with "white kerchiefs tucked into the bodice." The woman handed the girl a jug, and for a moment they seemed to pause, like figures "in a *tableau vivant*" (*A*, pp. 17, 18n).

As they continued down the path, Moberly and Jourdain next came upon something resembling a garden kiosk, shaded by trees. A man was sitting nearby. Moberly was instantly overtaken by an "extraordinary" sensation of depression. "Everything suddenly looked unnatural, therefore unpleasant; even the trees behind the building seemed to have become flat and lifeless, *like a wood worked in tapestry.* There were no effects of light and shade, and no wind stirred the trees. It was all intensely still" (*A*, pp. 4, 5). Jourdain had similar sensations—she had a feeling of "heavy dreaminess" as if she were walking in her sleep—but neither woman shared her forebodings with the other at the time. These feelings of distress intensified when the man by the kiosk looked up at them. According to Moberly he was "repulsive" in appearance: his complexion was "dark and rough," and despite the heat, he wore a heavy black cloak and a slouch hat (*A*, p. 5). Jourdain remembered him as "dark" with an "evil and yet unseeing" expression: she thought his face had been pitted by smallpox (*A*, p. 18). Both were relieved when a "red-faced" man wearing "buckled shoes" suddenly rushed up behind them, warned them (in oddly accented French) that they were going the wrong way, and then ran off in another direction.

4. Elizabeth Morison and Frances Lamont [Charlotte Moberly and Eleanor Jourdain], *An Adventure*, 2d ed. (London, 1913), p. 17; hereafter abbreviated *A*. *An Adventure* went through five editions in all—in 1911, 1913, 1924, 1931, and 1955. Each edition was also reprinted. The different editions vary considerably: some, for instance, include the appendices and "A Rêverie," while others do not.

Quickly they set off after him, crossed over a small bridge with a stream under it, and at last came in view of what they presumed to be the Petit Trianon. At this point Moberly saw a fair-haired woman sitting on a stool with her back to the house, apparently sketching. The woman wore a large white summer hat and a curiously old-fashioned dress "arranged on her shoulders in handkerchief fashion" (*A*, p. 8). The dress, which Moberly thought unusual at the time, was covered with a pale green fichu. As she and Jourdain went up the steps of the terrace to the house, Moberly, looking back at the sketching woman, had once again an unaccountable feeling of gloom. Suddenly a young man dressed like a footman came out of a second building opening out onto the terrace. Slamming a door behind him, he hurried towards them with a "peculiar smile" and told them that the main entrance was on the other side of the house (*A*, p. 20). Accordingly, they went around to the front of the house where a French wedding party was waiting to tour the rooms. Recovering their spirits, Moberly and Jourdain attached themselves to the happy group and the rest of the day passed off uneventfully. They returned to Paris that evening.

For a week neither woman alluded to the afternoon at the Trianon. One day, however, as Miss Moberly began to write about it in a letter to her sister, her uneasiness returned:

> As the scenes came back one by one, the same sensation of dreamy unnatural oppression came over me so strongly that I stopped writing, and said to Miss Lamont [Jourdain], "Do you think that the Petit Trianon is haunted?" Her answer was prompt, "Yes, I do." I asked her where she felt it, and she said, "In the garden where we met the two men, but not only there." She then described her feeling of depression and anxiety which began at the same point as it did with me, and how she tried not to let me know it. [*A*, pp. 11–12]

There the matter rested, however, until both returned to England. That November, three months after their visit, Miss Jourdain (who in the meantime had accepted Moberly's offer of the St. Hugh's vice-principalship) came to stay with her new friend and the two took up the subject again. In the course of their conversation Moberly referred in passing to the "sketching lady" and was shocked to discover that Jourdain had not seen her. "I exclaimed that it was impossible that she should not have seen the individual; for we were walking side by side and went straight up to her, passed her and looked down upon her from the terrace." Having uncovered this new "element of mystery" (*A*, p. 13), each resolved to write a separate, detailed account of what she had seen, to be shown to the other later. Moberly completed her account on 25 November; Jourdain hers on 28 November.

Comparing narratives, the two soon noticed more eerie discrepancies. Besides the sketching lady, Miss Moberly had seen a woman shaking a cloth out of a window—Miss Jourdain had seen neither. Moberly in turn had not seen Jourdain's "woman and girl with a jug," even though, according to Jourdain, they had walked right past them. But this was not all: Jourdain had also discovered two startling pieces of information. While turning over a set of school lessons on the French Revolution, she had suddenly realized that the day on which they had visited the Trianon, 10 August, was the anniversary of the sacking of the Tuileries. On that day in 1792, Louis XVI and Marie Antoinette had witnessed the massacre of their Swiss Guards and been imprisoned in the Hall of the Assembly. Struck by this ominous coincidence, Jourdain immediately asked a French friend if she had ever heard anything about the Petit Trianon being haunted. To her amazement the friend confirmed that indeed, "on a certain day in August," Marie Antoinette was regularly seen in the Trianon garden, wearing a light flapping hat and a pink dress. The queen's servants and courtiers also appeared in the vicinity, reenacting their distinctive "occupations and amusements" for a day and a night (*A*, p. 22).

At once they started to wonder (in Moberly's words)

> whether we had inadvertently entered within an act of the Queen's memory when alive, and whether this explained our curious sensation of being completely shut in and oppressed. What more likely, we thought, than that during those hours in the Hall of the Assembly, or in the Conciergerie, she had gone back in such vivid memory to other Augusts spent at Trianon that some impress of it was imparted to the place? [*A*, pp. 23–24]

They began reading up on the life of Marie Antoinette—with thrilling results. Leafing through Gustave Desjardins's *Petit Trianon* (1885), Moberly found a portrait of the doomed queen by Wertmüller in which, astonishingly, she recognized the face of the sketching lady. The clothes were also identical. Could the lady, Jourdain asked her friend, have been an apparition of the queen herself? Conjecture turned to conviction after Jourdain made a second visit to Versailles in January 1902. Not only was she unable to retrace their steps, all the grounds around the Trianon seemed mysteriously altered. (Nowhere, for example, could she find the strange "kiosk," or the bridge with the stream under it.)[5] She did gather, however, another crucial bit of information: on her last day at the

---

5. There were uncanny moments during this second visit: Jourdain remembered feeling "the swish of a dress" close by her at one point, and later thought she heard eighteenth-century music being played somewhere by an unseen orchestra. She wrote down twelve bars of this music from memory afterwards and in 1907 showed them to an unnamed "musical expert" who said they dated from "about 1780." After researching the matter further at the Conservatoire de Musique in Paris, Jourdain concluded that "the twelve bars represented the chief motives of the light opera of the eighteenth century" and could be

Fig. 3.—Miss Moberly in youth and in middle age

Trianon—supposedly 5 October 1789—Marie Antoinette had been sitting in her garden when a page ran towards her with a message that a mob from Paris would be at the gates in an hour's time. Suddenly, the two women realized, it all made sense. While imprisoned in the Hall of the Assembly in 1792, Marie Antoinette must undoubtedly have thought back to that day in 1789 when she first heard the awful news that her crown was in danger. This would indeed explain the terrible "depression" both of them had experienced in the grounds. The "red-faced" man who had run past them in such a hurry near the kiosk, they concluded, was probably the very messenger running to the queen with the news: they had literally stepped "into" her memory.

Exalted by their discovery, Moberly and Jourdain sent a letter to the Society for Psychical Research asserting that the Trianon was haunted and including their written accounts from 1901 as evidence. To their chagrin the accounts were returned as unworthy of investigation. They realized they would have to put their case more compellingly. What better way to

---

found, in different variations, in the works of "Sacchini, Philidor, Monsigny, Grétry and Pergolesi" (*A*, pp. 94–95). Her findings were rudely satirized by a writer in the *Musical Times* of 1 September 1912, who pointed out that she had conveniently neglected to print the "ubiquitous twelve bars" in *An Adventure*. In a subsequent letter about *An Adventure* to the same journal, the distinguished music critic Ernest Newman—referring to "those wildly ludicrous pages dealing with the phantom music"—dismissed Jourdain's musicological claims as "grotesque" (quoted in *GV*, pp. 293–94).

Fig. 4.—Miss Jourdain in youth and in middle age

do so, they surmised, than to demonstrate that everything they had seen at the Trianon—from the moment they found themselves lost to the moment they joined the wedding party—had in fact *only* existed in the year 1789? Accordingly, they set out to do just this. For the next nine years, in libraries, historical archives, and at the Trianon itself, they carried out an elaborate, if not obsessional, search for evidence. In 1911, convinced they had found just the proofs they needed, they published the fruits of their research in the pages of *An Adventure*.

In their central chapter—"Summary of Results of Research"—the two laid out this "proof" in surreal detail. They began with the first object they had seen, the peculiar-looking plough noticed by Miss Jourdain just after they had lost their way. Questioning a gardener at the Trianon in 1905, they reported, they had learned that no ploughs had been kept there in 1901, there being "no need of one" (*A*, p. 41). Some time later, in 1908, another gardener told them that the shape of ploughs had "entirely altered in character since the Revolution" (*A*, pp. 41–42) and that the one seen by Miss Jourdain was definitely of an "old type" no longer found anywhere in France. True, they conceded, on a document they had uncovered in "the Archives Nationales" listing all the gardening tools bought for the Trianon between 1780 and 1789, there had been no mention of a plough. But as they had learned "from Desjardins's book," during the reign of Louis XVI, "an old plough used in his predecessor's reign had been preserved at the Petit Trianon and sold with the king's other properties during the Revolution" (*A*, p. 42). The implication was obvious: Miss

Jourdain had seen a plough that could only have emanated from the eighteenth century.

Other objects received similar glosses. The cottage, for example, in front of which they had seen the woman and the girl with the jug, they argued, most closely resembled a structure "not now in existence" shown on an old map from 1783 found in the Trianon archives in 1907 (*A*, p. 47). The mysterious kiosk—nowhere to be seen in the present garden—was identical, they had discovered, to a lost "ruine" pictured on another old eighteenth-century plan (*A*, p. 48). As for the little bridge with a stream under it, this corresponded to an obscure "*'pont rustique'*" mentioned by the Comte D'Hezecques in his *Souvenirs d'un page de la cour de Louis XVI* (1873)—also no longer in existence. It was definitely *not*, they asserted, the more famous (and obvious) Rocher Bridge, which, according to calculations they had carried out on the spot, was "too high above the lakes" to be the same one they had crossed (*A*, p. 67). Most eerily perhaps, the door they thought they had heard slamming as they went up the steps of the Trianon terrace—the door from which the footman with the "peculiar smile" had emerged—led only to a ruined chapel that had never been used, according to a guide, "since it was used by the Court." Indeed, when Miss Jourdain attempted to open the door from the inside, some time in 1906, she found it "bolted, barred, and cobwebbed over from age and disuse" (*A*, p. 81).

Their evidence relating to people, however, was no less extensive. The two men in "greenish-grey coats" to whom they had first spoken, they contended, were members of Marie Antoinette's famed *gardes Suisses:* only royal bodyguards from the 1780s, they had learned, ever wore liveries of this color at the Trianon. Indeed, they had concluded, they were probably "two of the three Bersy brothers," said to have been on duty on the fateful day of 5 October 1789 (*A*, p. 46). The woman and the girl with the jug were identified as the wife and daughter of one of Marie Antoinette's undergardeners: the girl was the same age as "Marion," a gardener's child they had read about in Julie Lavergne's 1879 *Légendes de Trianon* (*A*, p. 54). The sinister pockmarked "kiosk man," in turn, was none other than the wicked Comte de Vaudreuil, who had acted "an enemy's part" toward the queen by encouraging her to permit a performance of Beaumarchais's politically dangerous play *Le Mariage de Figaro* in 1784. Vaudreuil was a Creole and marked by smallpox: this explained the kiosk man's "dark and rough" complexion. The fact that the latter wore a large slouch hat and heavy black cloak on a hot summer's day confirmed the identification: according to Pierre de Nolhac's *La Reine Marie-Antoinette* (1890), they noted, Vaudreuil had himself once taken the role of Count Almaviva in Beaumarchais's drama, dressing for it in "a large dark cloak and Spanish hat," and often wore his costume on other occasions (*A*, p. 52). In a similar fashion, the "running man" was identified as Marie Antoinette's page De Bretagne (his Breton origins supposedly explained his unusual French accent), and the "chapel man" as a footman named Lagrange, who in 1789 had had rooms near the Trianon terrace (*A*, pp. 65, 85).[6]

But Moberly and Jourdain's crowning proofs, not surprisingly, had to do with the sketching lady seen by Miss Moberly. The Wertmüller portrait had made them suspect from the start of course that the lady might be the queen herself: the features were identical, they confirmed, right down to the short nose and somewhat "square" face (*A*, p. 74). This particular portrait, moreover, had always been considered, they had found, the truest likeness of the queen. But their clinching piece of evidence once again was sartorial. In 1908, looking into the journals of Madame Éloffe, Marie Antoinette's *modiste*, they had discovered to their amazement that in July and September of 1789 Madame Éloffe had made for the queen "two green silk bodices" and several "white fichus." This information "agreed exactly" with the dress worn by the sketching lady in 1901. What Miss Moberly remembered as the lady's unusual-looking "pale green fichu," they realized triumphantly, was actually one of Madame Éloffe's green bodices, with a light-colored "muslin, or gauze" fichu over it (*A*, pp. 75–76). The lady was none other than Marie Antoinette herself.

After completing these demonstrations, all of which were supplemented with numerous scholarly footnotes, appendices, and diagrams, Moberly and Jourdain concluded with something they called, rather more lyrically, "A Rêverie." Subtitled, "A Possible Historical Clue," "A Rêverie" was actually an imaginary account—composed in a suitably pathetic, pseudo-Carlylian manner—of the supposed meditations of Marie Antoinette during her imprisonment with Louis XVI and the Dauphin following the sacking of the Tuileries on 10 August 1792. In the course of this florid narration (which Moberly and Jourdain clearly intended as a kind of royalist apologia as well as an explanatory coda to their "adventure" itself) the much-abused queen, worn out by her sufferings at the hands of the revolutionary mob, is depicted sinking into a trancelike state in which she sees a series of phantom images of her beloved Trianon: an "old plough" from her husband's boyhood, two of her loyal bodyguards,

6. Moberly and Jourdain drew most of their basic historical information about Marie Antoinette and her court from various late nineteenth-century popular histories: Pierre de Nolhac's *La Reine Marie-Antoinette* (Paris, 1890), Julie Lavergne's *Légendes de Trianon, Versailles et Saint-Germain* (Paris, 1879), Gustave Adolphe Desjardins's *Le Petit Trianon: Histoire et description* (Versailles, 1885), and the Comte de Reiset's *Modes et usages du temps de Marie Antoinette* (Paris, 1885). That these sources gave a somewhat romantic, unscholarly, and anecdotal picture of life at the Trianon was pointed out by several of Moberly and Jourdain's critics. "What is Julie Lavergne's *Légendes de Trianon*," asked Iremonger dismissively, "but a charming imaginative creation, built upon the bones of fact perhaps, but the merest rainbow tissue of flights of fantasy? What is de Nolhac's *Marie Antoinette the Queen* but a gorgeous picture-book with all the difficulties of considering France under the Revolution made easy and engaging, a chocolate éclair for a serious student?" (*GV*, p. 286).

Fig. 5.—The Petit Trianon, west front, showing the terrace from which Miss Moberly espied the "sketching lady"

the Bersy brothers, in "long green coats," the "rustic cottage" where the gardener's daughter Marion and her mother lived, the Comte de Vaudreuil in his "Spanish" costume, and so on. What she hallucinates, in short, is everything seen by Moberly and Jourdain in 1901—with one significant addition. Thinking back to her last day at the Trianon, and how she sat sketching on the lawn, she suddenly remembers "the two strangers" who walked past her "onto the terrace." Thus did Moberly and Jourdain, imagining the doomed queen imagining them, seek to lend telepathic credibility to their own richly phantasmagorical vision.[7]

Dare one call *An Adventure* preposterous? Certainly most people who read the book in 1911 thought so. From the start *An Adventure* provoked both extraordinary public interest (11,000 copies had been sold by 1913) and an extraordinary number of skeptical attacks. The first and most wounding of these assaults was unquestionably the review published in the journal of the Society for Psychical Research by Mrs. Henry Sidgwick, the

7. Both Iremonger and Evans credited the effusions of "A Rêverie" to Moberly; her prose style was purportedly more "emotional" than Jourdain's. Moberly's brother Robert, it is worth noting, won the Newdigate Prize in 1867 for a poem about Marie Antoinette, the lachrymose sentimentality of which may well have influenced "A Rêverie":

> In simple peace she moves; more joyously
> Here 'mid the shame, and on the road to die—
> Than when of old her royal beauty shone
> Mid the triumphant splendour of a throne. . . .
> —Naught rests but heaven:—no form of woman this—
> It is a spirit divine that moves to bliss.
>
> [quoted in *GV*, p. 287]

Fig. 7.—A plate from the journal of Madame Éloffe, dressmaker to Marie Antoinette, showing a transparent fichu worn over a bodice, as described by Moberly

Fig. 6.—The Wertmüller portrait of Marie Antoinette

wife of the Society's president, late in 1911. Not only did she find Moberly and Jourdain's voluminous "evidence" ridiculous, Mrs. Sidgwick (who was the sister of Lord Balfour) took a distinctly satirical attitude toward the ladies themselves. Citing one "M. Sage," a French associate of the society who had walked over the Trianon gardens with *An Adventure* in hand, she maintained that Moberly and Jourdain ("who at best do not seem to be very good at topography") had simply gotten lost in the grounds and then misidentified what they had seen—after the fact. What they encountered there, she argued, were merely "real persons and things" from 1901, which they had subsequently "decked out by tricks of memory (and after the idea of haunting had occurred to them) with some additional details of costume suitable to the times of Marie Antoinette."[8] Her factotum M. Sage provided examples: Moberly and Jourdain's two "Swiss guards," for instance, were undoubtedly ordinary Trianon gardeners; the latter wore little caps, or *képis*, which could easily be mistaken for parts of a uniform. Likewise, all the buildings and objects they had seen could be correlated with existing structures in the Trianon grounds—the Temple of Love, the Belvédère, the Rocher bridge, and so forth.

But other attacks soon followed. In a chapter on apparitions in his book *Psychical Research,* also from 1911, W. F. Barrett, a physicist and Fellow of the Royal Society, declared that Moberly and Jourdain's visions were the result of "lively imagination stimulated by expectancy" and lacked "any real evidential value."[9] Interestingly, he wondered whether the two had been influenced by a 1907 account in the *Journal of the Society for Psychical Research* of a young woman who claimed to have been in communication with the spirit of Marie Antoinette since girlhood. He also reminded his readers of another recent case of Marie Antoinette-obsession: that of the celebrated medium Hélène Smith, who believed herself to be a reincarnation of the queen. Smith's bizarre accomplishments, which included being able to produce bits of automatic writing in Marie Antoinette's hand, had been exhaustively documented in a book published in 1900 by the Swiss psychologist Theodore Flournoy.[10]

Meanwhile Moberly and Jourdain were not silent. In 1913 they

8. Mrs. Sidgwick's anonymous review appeared in the June 1911 supplement to the *Proceedings of the Society for Psychical Research.* It is also reprinted in full in chapter 12 of *GV.*

9. W. F. Barrett, *Psychical Research* (London, 1911), pp. 200, 201.

10. The first case mentioned by Barrett is described in the *Journal of the Society for Psychical Research* 13 (June 1907): 90–96. The young woman in question had nightly visions of Marie Antoinette during her childhood and subsequently developed such an obsession with the dead queen that she spent most of her waking hours at the South Kensington Museum "gazing at Marie Antoinette's bust, examining her toilet table with its little rouge pots, etc." On the renowned Swiss medium Hélène Smith, who claimed to be the reincarnation not only of Marie Antoinette but also of Cagliostro, several "Hindoo" sheiks and princesses, and a mysterious personage from Mars named "Pouzé Ramié," see Theodore Flournoy, *From India to the Planet Mars: A Study of a Case of Somnambulism,* trans. Daniel B. Vermilye (1900; New York, 1963).

issued a revised edition of *An Adventure* including a section called "Answers to Questions We Have Been Asked," designed to deflect such assaults. Here they reiterated their belief that they had indeed seen people from the eighteenth century—and not unusually dressed gardeners, tourists, or people in masquerade costume, as Sidgwick and others had suggested. No "historical fetes" had taken place at the Trianon on 10 August 1901, they had discovered, nor had any "cinematographs" in which costumed actors might have appeared been filmed on the grounds that day (see *A,* pp. 111–17). Responding to Barrett's insinuation that they had been influenced by stories of other apparitions, the two denied any morbid interest in spiritualism or the occult ("we are the daughters of English clergymen, and heartily hold and teach the faith of our fathers") and stoutly reaffirmed their native good sense (*A,* p. 101). Finally, by way of rejoinder to those who thought the whole thing a hoax, they now reproduced the "original" accounts each had written—supposedly independently —in November 1901, along with two "fuller" accounts, composed a few weeks later for the benefit of readers "unfamiliar" with the Trianon grounds.[11]

Yet these gambits seemed merely to inflame the skeptics further. For the next sixty years, in fact, books and articles disputing the claims of *An Adventure* (which itself went through three more editions) continued to appear. Neither the death of Jourdain in 1924, nor that of Moberly in 1937, did anything to stop the flow: indeed, the posthumous revelation that the pseudonymous "Miss Morison" and "Miss Lamont" were in fact two distinguished Oxford lady dons only intensified popular fascination with the case.[12] J. R. Sturge-Whiting published a book-length study *The Mystery of Versailles* in 1938, shortly after the death of Moberly; David Landale Johnston's *Trianon Case, A Review of the Evidence* appeared in 1945. In 1950 W. H. Salter's detailed examination of the supposedly "original" 1901 accounts—" 'An Adventure': A Note on the Evidence"— was published in the *Journal of the Society for Psychical Research,* followed in 1952 by the first French article on the subject, Léon Rey's "Promenade hors du temps" in the *Revue de Paris.* (An annotated French translation of

11. In the appendix to the 1913 edition Moberly and Jourdain called their original accounts, respectively, "A1" and "A2" and the subsequent "fuller" accounts "B1" and "B2." Confusingly, later writers—following W. H. Salter—referred to the first accounts as "M1" and "J1" and the second as "M2" and "J2." In this obsession with alphabetical nomenclature, *Adventure* scholarship often reads like a parody of biblical textual scholarship.

12. Moberly and Jourdain's authorship was publicly revealed for the first time in the fourth edition of *An Adventure,* ed. Edith Olivier, with a note by J. W. Dunne (London, 1931). Yet the fact of their authorship was already by then widely known. Moberly and Jourdain had told officials at the Society for Psychical Research about the Trianon apparitions in 1902; in later years they shared their story with virtually anyone who would listen. Thus Evans's assertion—in the preface to the 1955 edition of *An Adventure*—that even in 1911 the identity of the book's authors was largely a *"secret de Polichinelle"* (p. 20), that is to say, no secret at all.

An Adventure, complete with sardonic preface by Jean Cocteau, appeared in 1959.)[13] Perhaps the most damning as well as most exhaustive assault on the book came in 1957—in the shape of Lucille Iremonger's 300-page *ad feminam* attack, *The Ghosts of Versailles: Miss Moberly and Miss Jourdain and Their Adventure.* But even twenty years later the Trianon case was still arousing controversy: seventy-five years after Moberly and Jourdain's first encounter with the "sketching lady" and her ilk, Joan Evans, Eleanor Jourdain's literary executor and holder of the copyright to *An Adventure,* put forth her own debunking explanation of the Trianon apparitions in an essay entitled "An End to *An Adventure:* Solving the Mystery of the Trianon" in *Encounter* in 1976.[14]

Few of Moberly and Jourdain's numerous critics, to be sure, explicated the Trianon "ghosts" in precisely the same way. Most were convinced, certainly, that there had to be some commonplace explanation for what the two women had seen—the likeliest being that Moberly and Jourdain had simply mistaken ordinary people and objects from 1901 for those of the ancien régime. But given the intricacies of the case, there was little agreement on specific details—whether the kiosk was "really" the Temple of Love or "really" the Belvédère, whether the men in greenish coats were gardeners or officials, and so on. Certain features of the case became much-debated cruxes—the mysterious "chapel door," for instance, to which Sturge-Whiting (whose on-the-spot investigations became as tireless as Moberly and Jourdain's own) devoted an entire chapter of *The Mystery of Versailles.*[15]

Opinion was also divided on the subject of Moberly and Jourdain themselves. The chivalrous Sturge-Whiting, writing in the 1930s, was inclined to see the authors of *An Adventure* in relatively flattering terms, as a pair of eccentric spinsters, harmlessly caught up in a sentimental flight

13. See Moberly and Jourdain, *Les Fantômes de Trianon (Une Aventure),* trans. Julliette and Pierre Barrucand (Monaco, 1959). As well as the preface by Cocteau, the French edition includes a lengthy (mostly skeptical) introduction by Robert Amadou.

14. Moberly and Jourdain were not entirely without defenders: following the unexpected death of Jourdain in 1924, Olivier, a former protegée of Moberly's from St. Hugh's, took on the task of preparing the third edition of *An Adventure* and remained a lifelong partisan. A few scientific writers were also sympathetic: Dunne, the author of *An Experiment with Time* (New York, 1927), suggested that Moberly and Jourdain's story confirmed Einstein's theory of relativity; G. N. M. Tyrrell, an electrical engineer and later president of the Society for Psychical Research, reviewed the case, apparently seriously, in a book on apparitions in 1942. Rather more tongue-in-cheek was the advocacy of Cocteau: in the preface to the 1959 French translation of *An Adventure,* he eulogized "les dames d'Oxford" (Moberly had died in 1937) for their futuristic assault on conventional notions of space and time. Despite the fact that Moberly and Jourdain hailed from "Grande Bretagne"—"ou les histoires de fantômes abondent"—their book, Cocteau wrote, constituted "une manière de scandale non conformiste de la plus haute valeur" (*Les Fantômes de Trianon,* p. 9).

15. See J. R. Sturge-Whiting, *The Mystery of Versailles: A Complete Solution* (London, 1938), pp. 125–34.

of fancy. Though their claim to have encountered Marie Antoinette was nothing more—in his view—than a "pathetic illusion," they had elaborated it, he thought, in perfectly good faith: he saw no reason to question their integrity. Far from intending to deceive anyone, the "brave ladies," he gallantly intoned, had simply been swept away by a conception of the greatest "beauty and pathos."[16]

Others were less sure. Salter, writing in 1950, suspected—as Mrs. Sidgwick had done earlier—that Moberly and Jourdain had in fact tampered with the "evidence" in order to make their time-travel story more convincing. Salter was particularly dubious about the two sets of "original" accounts—supposedly written in November and December of 1902—printed in the 1913 edition of *An Adventure*. How reliable could such eyewitness accounts be, he asked, when they had been produced almost three months after the events described? What proof was there that Moberly and Jourdain had not collaborated on them? Most damagingly, he presented evidence, gleaned from the abortive correspondence between Moberly and Jourdain and the Society for Psychical Research in 1901, that the second, "fuller," or more elaborate set of accounts—which Moberly and Jourdain claimed to have composed only a week or two after the first set—had not been written in 1901 at all, but possibly as late as 1906.[17] Since a number of crucial details in Moberly and Jourdain's story—that the chapel door had been "slammed," for example—only appeared in the longer accounts, much of the so-called proof for their identifications suddenly became suspect. To claim in 1901 that they had heard the door slam was one thing: it made the subsequent discovery, several years later, that the chapel door had been "barred and bolted" all the more exciting and remarkable. But if the slamming sound was a

16. Ibid., pp. 147, 158, 146.

17. See W. H. Salter, "'An Adventure': A Note on the Evidence," *Journal of the Society for Psychical Research* 35 (Jan.–Feb. 1950): 178–87. His findings are also reviewed at length in *GV*. Salter's reasoning was as follows: in the second edition of *An Adventure* (1913), the first edition in which all four of the accounts were published, Moberly and Jourdain claimed that the first accounts (M1 and J1) had been written on "November 25" and "November 28," and the second (M2 and J2) in "November 1901" and "December 1901," respectively. Yet, he observed, when the two of them wrote to Mrs. Henry Sidgwick at the Society for Psychical Research about the Versailles apparitions in October 1902, they sent only M1 and J1 as evidence. Why, he asked, if the more detailed accounts M2 and J2 were already then in existence, having supposedly been written "'for those who had not seen the place'" (p. 181), had Moberly and Jourdain not sent them instead? When asked later what had happened to the original manuscripts of M2 and J2, Moberly and Jourdain said only that they had destroyed them, after copying them along with "a few introductory sentences" into an exercise book in 1906. Concluded Salter, as summed up by Iremonger, "it does look rather as if M2 and J2, instead of having been written, as Miss Moberly claims, a matter of days after M1 and J1, were written *at best a year afterwards,* and perhaps much later than that!" (*GV,* pp. 190–91). Tellingly, almost all of the additional information provided in M2 and J2 served to strengthen Moberly and Jourdain's claim that they had seen eighteenth-century personages.

superaddition from 1906, after they had already gone back and *seen* the door, then it began to look as though Moberly and Jourdain had been embellishing—for dramatic effect—all along.

Still even Salter was reluctant to say anything directly incriminating about two long-deceased and "much respected" ladies. No such scruples inhibited Iremonger, author of *The Ghosts of Versailles* (1957). Iremonger had been a student at St. Hugh's, where memories of Moberly and Jourdain loomed large. She was also a descendant of the Comte de Vaudreuil—the "repulsive-looking" kiosk man—and may have wished to vindicate her unprepossessing ancestor, for her book is without question the most gossipy attack on *An Adventure,* being largely devoted to compromising rumors and anecdotes about its authors' private lives. Among Iremonger's more provocative findings was that despite their protestations to the contrary, both Moberly and Jourdain had had paranormal experiences before and after the Trianon visit, and that Moberly in particular was prone to aural and visual hallucinations. As a child she had heard the words "PINNACLED REALITY" as she stared at the spires of Winchester Cathedral; on the day her father, the bishop, died in 1885, she had seen two strange birds with dazzling white feathers and immense wings fly over the cathedral into the west. In Cambridge in 1913 she saw a procession of medieval monks; and at the Louvre the following year, she saw a man "six or seven feet high" in a crown and togalike dress whom she at first took to be Charlemagne, but later decided was an apparition of the Roman emperor Constantine (*GV,* pp. 40–45).

But Iremonger's most sensational revelations had to do with Moberly and Jourdain's relationship itself. That the two were lesbians, and hence morally and psychologically suspect, was one of Iremonger's barely concealed assumptions. After they had "joined forces" following their experience at Versailles (*GV,* p. 89), she declared, their relationship was that of "'husband and wife.'" In the beginning Miss Moberly—the older, shyer, and plainer of the two—was the "husband" and Miss Jourdain the "wife":

> The shy woman liked the sociable one; the rugged woman liked the smooth one; the plain unfeminine creature warmed to the little charmer, flowery hats, silken ankles and all. The clumsy Miss Moberly fell for the airs and graces of 'French' Miss Jourdain. [*GV,* p. 86]

Very quickly, however, the roles reversed. Jourdain was the more powerful personality, according to Iremonger, and over the years came to dominate her friend more and more, especially after 1915, when Moberly retired and Jourdain succeeded her as principal. Jourdain ruled over Moberly and St. Hugh's in equally peremptory fashion, becoming increasingly subject to paranoid delusions. During the war she became convinced a German spy was hiding somewhere in the college; later, in a fit of megalomaniac pique, she accused several members of the St. Hugh's faculty of plotting against her and Moberly. She dropped dead of a heart attack—literally—during the resulting scandal, and Moberly was left to mourn her for the next thirteen years. Given such pathological goings-on, Iremonger insinuated, it was not hard to see the Trianon ghost story as symptomatic—of the "unhealthy" emotional tie that existed between its perpetrators.[18]

Iremonger's exposé prompted a rebuttal; reviewing the literature surrounding the *Adventure* case in 1976, Joan Evans—who as a child had known both Moberly and Jourdain and was herself a distinguished don of English literature—censured Iremonger for being indiscreet and "less than generous to Miss Jourdain" ("E," p. 42n). Evans's own explanation of the Trianon mystery was in part a not-so-subtle attempt to defend Moberly and Jourdain against the suggestions of double-dealing and sexual deviance. Evidence had come to light, she wrote, that, while failing to substantiate the time-travel thesis, nonetheless "vindicated" the two women and confirmed "the accuracy of their observations" ("E," p. 45). What this "evidence" turned out to be was a 1965 biography of Robert de Montesquiou (1855–1921), the wealthy dandy and aesthete on whom Marcel Proust modeled his character of the Baron de Charlus, in which it was alleged that Montesquiou had at one time lived in a house at Versailles and held fancy-dress parties there.[19] Though it was not clear in what year Montesquiou's parties had taken place, or whether he had ever held one near the Trianon, this did not stop Evans from indulging in a fairly elaborate fantasy of her own. Moberly and Jourdain had inadvertently wandered into a "rehearsal" for a kind of homosexual garden fete, she maintained, in which Montesquiou, his young lover Gabriel Yturri (formerly "a salesman in a smart tie shop") and various male friends were "trying out" their costumes. The two men in "greenish coats" were probably Montesquiou and Yturri; the others were probably members of the Montesquiou clique. The "sketching lady" was most likely a transvestite: "the well-bred Miss Moberly," Evans noted, had thought "she showed 'a good deal of leg.'" Evans was not exactly sure who the repulsive "kiosk man" was, but she was confident that Moberly and Jourdain's discomfort

---

18. Though she never once used the word *lesbian* to describe them, Iremonger's interest in her subjects' emotional predilections verged on the prurient. Quoting an unnamed St. Hugh's source, she described Jourdain's "unhealthy" relationships with various students in the college, who reciprocated by falling in love with their principal. "An illuminating punning phrase which had currency at that time," wrote Iremonger, "was, 'Have you crossed Jordan yet?' In other words, have you fallen under the sway of this woman who is acknowledged to be consciously exercising her charm to bind students to her?" According to "the Mistress of Girton," Iremonger noted, "'a lot of kissing went on'" (*GV*, p. 88).

19. See Philippe Jullian, *Robert de Montesquiou, un prince 1900* (Paris, 1965); trans. John Haylock and Francis King, under the title *Prince of Aesthetes: Count Robert de Montesquiou, 1855–1921* (New York, 1968).

in his presence was "a credit to their morals and their breeding" ("E," p. 46). Neither woman had any previous knowledge of "the more decadent aspects of the aristocratic, plutocratic and artistic classes in '*la belle époque*,'" nor of "the London world of Oscar Wilde and Aubrey Beardsley"; hence the disgust they felt toward the kiosk man, Evans concluded, "may well have arisen from the instinctive reaction of a decent woman to a pervert" ("E," pp. 45, 47).

What to make of these theories and countertheories? To the reader confronting them for the first time the controversies surrounding *An Adventure* are likely to seem as bizarre as *An Adventure* itself. For in their own way the skeptics were as bewitched by the Trianon apparitions as Moberly and Jourdain were. The task of proving Moberly and Jourdain wrong became for many of them a compulsion—a kind of *idée fixe*. In a revealing aside in *The Ghosts of Versailles*, Iremonger warned of the "*Adventure-manie*" that so often overtook those (like herself) who began delving too deeply into the details of the case. "There have been many enthusiastic amateurs," she wrote,

> who, coming to it often as believers in *An Adventure*, but unable to overlook its weaknesses, have permitted themselves what Nietzsche called the luxury of scepticism, and have submerged themselves in its intricacies almost to the abandonment of a sense of proportion. No doubt many more will do so in the future, for interest in this story can grow first into an absorbing hobby and then into a real *Adventure-manie*. [*GV*, p. 298]

The prime symptom of *Adventure*-mania was a passion for invoking "evidence"—often of a strikingly dubious sort.[20] Yet in this Moberly and Jourdain's critics simply followed in the footsteps of the ladies themselves. If Moberly and Jourdain, rummaging through archives, had fallen victims to a kind of hermeneutic *folie*—a befuddling obsession with proving themselves right at any cost—it was precisely this obsession which, like an infection, they succeeded in transmitting to their critics.

---

20. *An Adventure*'s critics were especially fond of invoking racial or occupational stereotypes as evidence. Iremonger, for example, attributed Moberly's mystical and excitable streak to the fact that she was supposedly of Russian extraction. (Moberly claimed to be descended from Peter the Great.) Moberly's face, wrote Iremonger, was "perfectly Slavonic. She might have been Mr Molotov's twin sister" (*GV*, p. 59). Somewhat differently, though equally disparagingly, Evans described Moberly as having "the narrow square head often found in the middle ranks of the Anglican clergy"—thus explaining, presumably, her lack of critical intelligence (Evans, preface, *An Adventure*, p. 14). Even the commonsensical Salter was inclined toward ruminations of this nature: explaining, in 1950, the strange clothing worn by the people described in *An Adventure*, he spoke of the typically "French" predilection for unusual uniforms. Likewise he added, "the cloaks and sombreros (or slouch hats) of the sitting and running men were, unless my recollection of that period is wholly wrong, an attire much affected by contemporary artists" (Salter, "A Note on the Evidence," p. 185).

At the same time the skeptics were strangely oblivious to what now seems the most intriguing psychological aspect of the case. The peculiar fervor, the near-hysteric nature of the response generated by *An Adventure* can only be explained, it seems to me, by the fact that the book was the work of *two* authors—and two women at that. The "united front" presented by Moberly and Jourdain, their openly collaborative intellectual and emotional relationship, served without question as a subliminal goad to their critics. As female dons, Moberly and Jourdain represented a new and hitherto unprecedented generation of independent educated women; as single women living their lives together (in however enigmatic a dyad) they stood as a threat to conventional sexual arrangements as well. In a society in which masculine prestige was under assault on a number of fronts, the spectacle of two eminent women speaking, uncannily, "as one"—even on so fantastical a theme—must have seemed unusually disturbing to those concerned with upholding patriarchal values. To prove such women wrong—to show them up as victims of the most comical and exquisite folly—was also to validate reactionary sexual and intellectual hierarchies.[21]

And yet it was precisely this "conglomerate" aspect of *An Adventure* that the skeptics seemed unprepared—or unable—to elucidate. There was, if not exactly a logical flaw, what one might call a theoretical absence at the heart of the skeptical point of view. If it were true (as even hostile critics such as Iremonger allowed) that Moberly and Jourdain were women of at least some dignity and intelligence, then why had neither one of them ever once questioned the judgment of the other? If it were possible (barely) to imagine one of them inventing the Marie Antoinette fantasy, how had the other one gotten sucked into it, too? How to explain the bizarre mutuality of their conviction, the intense, self-perpetuating, seemingly symbiotic exchange of illusion that must have taken place between them for nearly twenty-five years? While obsessed with what they regarded as Moberly and Jourdain's "folly," what the skeptics failed to explain, paradoxically, was its most curious feature—its spectacularly collaborative nature.

---

21. Even some of Moberly and Jourdain's defenders, paradoxically, managed to discredit them. In "Is There a Case for Retrocognition?" a bizarre essay published in the *Journal of the American Society for Psychical Research* 44 (Apr. 1950): 43–64, W. H. W. Sabine—while willing to accept Moberly and Jourdain's story whole hog—argued that they had not in fact gone back in time: they had simply had a "precognition," or foreglimpse, of the results of their future research. Their "hallucinatory visions," he maintained, "did not contain any information not ascribable to clairvoyant awareness of documents and books, and/or precognition of the coming experience of looking them up" (p. 63). Why, then, were their visions specifically of Marie Antoinette? Because, Sabine argued, they suffered from "lingering schoolgirl sentimentality" (p. 61). They were already obsessed with the dead queen in 1901; they "precognized" the future researches they would undertake regarding her; and through a kind of maudlin, back-to-front ESP, thought they *saw* her.

At this point a brief authorial confession is in order. When I first began to think of writing about *An Adventure* I was convinced—perhaps as a result of my own creeping "*Adventure*-mania"—that I could in fact clarify this most bewildering aspect of the Trianon case.[22] What, I asked myself, was the partnership of Moberly and Jourdain—so intimate and yet so bizarre—if not but an instance of the psychological phenomenon known as *folie à deux*? Wasn't a *folie à deux* precisely a kind of "double" or "shared" delusion? But even as I invoked the concept, doubts assailed me: I realized I had only the vaguest notion of how a *folie à deux* actually worked, and no idea at all when the term itself originated. My ignorance led me to a perusal of the psychoanalytic writing on the subject—with problematic results. For if here indeed was a theory of collective folly, it was hardly one to resolve the enigmas of *An Adventure*. On the contrary, far from "explaining" Moberly and Jourdain, the concept of the *folie à deux* merely reinstated the theoretical problem in a new way.

What is a *folie à deux*? The term, which literally means "psychosis of two," was coined in the late nineteenth century by two French psychiatrists, Charles Lasègue and J. Falret, whose 1877 paper, "La Folie à deux (ou folie communiquée)," is still regarded as the classic clinical description of the phenomenon.[23] Clinicians in the early part of the century had been much puzzled by something they usually referred to, for want of a better term, as "infectious insanity" or "insanity by contagion": the apparent transmission of delusional ideas between two persons. Heredity alone, it seemed, was not sufficient to explain such cases: though two family members were sometimes involved, numerous instances of shared insanity had been documented between persons who were unrelated to one another.[24] Lasègue and Falret were the first writers to explain "contagious insanity" as a function of interpersonal dynamics. Of course, as they were quick to point out, under ordinary circumstances insanity was *not* contagious; nurses in asylums, after all, seldom contracted lunatic ideas from their

22. In April of 1990 this "mania" led me, like Sturge-Whiting and others before me, to visit the Trianon and retrace Moberly and Jourdain's steps in the hope—unrealized—of seeing an apparition.

23. See Charles Lasègue and J. Falret, "La Folie à deux (ou folie communiquée)," *Annales Medico-Psychologiques* 18 (Nov. 1877); trans. Richard Michaud, under the original title, *American Journal of Psychiatry (Suppl.)* 121 (Oct. 1964): 1–23; hereafter abbreviated "F."

24. The alienist D. Hack Tuke was the first British clinician to appropriate Lasègue and Falret's term; see his essay "Folie à Deux," *Brain: A Journal of Neurology* (Jan. 1888): 408–21. On the subsequent history of the concept, see Alexander Gralnick, "Folie à Deux—The Psychosis of Association: A Review of 103 Cases and the Entire English Literature," *Psychiatric Quarterly* 16 (Apr. 1942): 230–63, 491–520; Berchmans Rioux, "A Review of Folie à Deux, the Psychosis of Association," *Psychiatric Quarterly* 37 (July 1963): 405–28; and Robert A. Faguet and Kay F. Faguet, "La Folie à Deux," in *Extraordinary Disorders of Human Behavior*, ed. Claude T. H. Friedmann and Robert Faguet (New York, 1982), pp. 1–14.

patients. But under pathological conditions, they warned, "delusional conceptions" could in fact spread—exactly like an infectious disease—from one person to another, resulting in the syndrome of *folie à deux.*

A *folie à deux,* wrote Lasègue and Falret, necessarily involved an active and a passive partner.[25] The active partner—that is, the one "carrying," or initiating the delusion—typically suffered from some sort of hereditary insanity. The passive partner, though not insane in a social or legal sense, was usually a person of somewhat "low intelligence, better disposed to passive docility than to independence" ("F," p. 4). Close proximity over a long period of time was essential for the delusional conception to spread from one partner to the other: the two almost always lived together in relative isolation, away from other friends or family. In isolation, the passive partner gradually yielded to the unremitting "moral pressure" applied by the actively insane partner. Women who lived alone together (often sisters or mothers and daughters) were especially prone to *folie à deux,* though the syndrome was known to affect married couples as well.

Crucial to Lasègue and Falret's analysis was that the delusion itself be of what they called a "moderate" or semi-plausible nature. Grossly lunatic fancies were not easily transmissible, they thought, only those that had a certain probability inherent in them already. "The less preposterous the insanity," they noted, "the easier it becomes communicable." Typically, the delusion related to some past or future event and thus was difficult to disprove on evidentiary grounds:

> If the insane person gives persuasive and lengthy details about these events, it is difficult to prove either to him or to one's self that this event has not taken place. The deluded person has developed his ideas so consistently and logically that no gaps are apparent. His topical memory excludes everything except his morbid ideas. He is never caught at fault, whatever the date of the event he describes, and the more monotonous and circumscribed his persuasive description becomes, the more likely that his listener will be convinced. ["F," p. 4]

The delusion had also to strike a "sentimental" chord in the passive partner, reinforcing existing hopes or fears. Delusions regarding lost legacies, or persecution by hidden enemies, were common. Among the case histories related by Lasègue and Falret was one involving a poverty-stricken mother and daughter who moved to Paris under the delusion (initiated by the daughter) that they were about to inherit a huge legacy; another involved an elderly spinster who persuaded her orphaned niece that someone was attempting to poison them. In the case of the twin

---

25. Later clinicians sometimes substituted the terms *parasite* and *infected one, inductor* and *inductee, transmitter* and *receiver, activator* and *victim, aggressor* and *recipient,* or *sadist* and *masochist* for Lasègue and Falret's *active* and *passive* partners. See Gralnick, "Folie à Deux—The Psychosis of Association," pp. 235, 237.

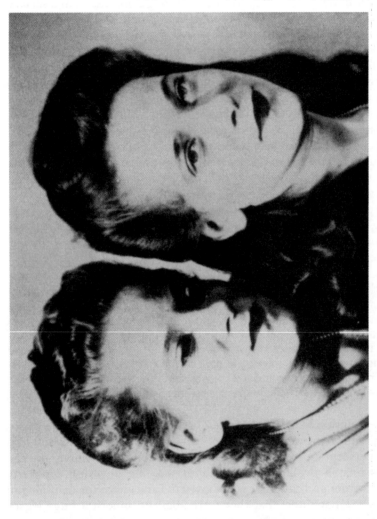

Fig. 8.——The twins, "Marie and Maria," suffering from *folie à deux*, 1950s. From Berchmans Rioux, "A Review of Folie à Deux, the Psychosis of Association," *Psychiatric Quarterly* 37 (July 1963): 405–28

sisters, "Joséphine" and "Lucille," Joséphine's conviction that police were threatening to "expose" her and her sister for living together resulted in a joint suicide attempt.[26] Admittedly, wrote Lasègue and Falret, the passive partner sometimes resisted, yet this initial resistance only prompted the active partner to modify the delusion so as to make it more plausible to his or her associate. The passive partner gave way by gradual stages, "fighting at first, giving in little by little, and finally identifying himself completely with the conceptions that he has slowly assimilated" ("F," p. 8). At that point, after countless rehearsals and much discussion of "evidence," the delusion became their "common cause," "to be repeated to all in an almost identical fashion." The only therapeutic indication in such cases was to separate the partners, in the hope that at least one of them might recover, especially the passive partner, who would be thereby "cut off from his source of delusions" ("F," p. 18).

Subsequent studies of *folie à deux* seemed to confirm Lasègue and Falret's clinical observations. Though Freud did not write about the phenomenon of *folie à deux*, several of his protégés, including A. A. Brill, C. P. Oberndorf, and Helene Deutsch, did.[27] Deutsch, in a 1938 article, was the first to connect the syndrome explicitly with homosexuality, especially between women. The paranoid nature of most shared delusions could almost always be attributed, she thought, to strong homosexual bonds between the two partners, and offered two case histories—one involving a mother and daughter, and the other, a pair of sisters—to demonstrate the

---

26. The theme of double suicide, usually between sisters, crops up frequently in the *folie à deux* literature. Tuke in 1887 described the case of the baronesses Anna and Louisa Guttenburg, who "committed suicide by drowning themselves in the Starnberg Lake, on the identical spot where the King of Bavaria was found dead eleven months before" and were discovered the next day "in the soft clay, firmly clasped in each other's arms" (Tuke, "Folie à Deux," pp. 414–15). A case of sororal double suicide (with distinctly lesbian overtones) occurred, interestingly enough, in the family of Compton-Burnett, the novelist and companion of Margaret Jourdain, Eleanor Jourdain's younger sister. Compton-Burnett's sisters Primrose and Topsy committed suicide together in 1917 by taking an overdose of Veronal. Later it was suggested that the two had been involved in an incestuous affair, having been found dead in one another's arms in the bed they always shared. See Spurling, *Ivy*, pp. 234–36.

27. Freud's silence on the subject of *folie à deux* is intriguing. The closest he came to touching on it was in a striking passage on identification in *Group Psychology and the Analysis of the Ego.* "Supposing," he wrote,

> that one of the girls in a boarding school has had a letter from someone with whom she is secretly in love which arouses her jealousy, and that she reacts to it with a fit of hysterics; then some of her friends who know about it will catch the fit, as we say, by mental infection. The mechanism is that of identification based upon the possibility or desire of putting oneself in the same situation. The other girls would like to have a secret love affair too, and under the influence of a sense of guilt they also accept the suffering involved in it. [P. 39]

Later psychoanalytic writers inevitably cited this passage when explaining *folie à deux.* "Freud's basic example of the mechanism of identification," wrote Oberndorf, "concerns

point.[28] Reviewing the clinical literature on *folie à deux* in 1942, Alexander Gralnick reiterated the connection: not only did most reported cases of *folie à deux* involve female couples, "the impression one gets from reading the cases in the literature is that homosexual drives are often present in a marked degree. If the Freudian-minded are correct," he wrote, "homosexuality must be a large element in these cases, because persecutory ideas are so prominent."[29]

With a little imagination, much here obviously could be made to apply to Moberly and Jourdain. If we take the Trianon story to be the sign of a *folie à deux*, then the "active" partner, it seems clear, would have had to have been Jourdain: she was the first to introduce the all-important figure of Marie Antoinette into the discussions of the Versailles events; she was the first to make the crucial connection between 10 August 1901 and 10 August 1789; she was the more enthusiastic of the two in the subsequent search for "evidence." Moreover throughout her adult life—at least according to the muckraking Iremonger—she seems to have suffered from increasingly vehement paranoid fantasies.[30] Jourdain's sister, the furniture historian Margaret Jourdain, always referred to the Trianon case as "my sister's folly"; the novelist Ivy Compton-Burnett, Margaret Jourdain's companion for over thirty years, said she could not think of anyone more likely than Eleanor "to delude herself into believing *An Adventure.*"[31]

But much about the Trianon story itself—quite apart from the obsessional manner in which Moberly and Jourdain defended it—also suggests the classic *folie*. If we accept, in however etiolated a form, the rumor that Moberly and Jourdain were lesbians, then the Trianon "delu-

---

related hysterical manifestations involving several boarding-school girls when one of their number goes through a crisis in a blighted love affair. Such a group situation, transient and evanescent in its character, bears a psychological resemblance to the more profound and continued disturbances grouped under *folie à deux*" (C. P. Oberndorf, "Folie à Deux," *International Journal of Psycho-Analysis* 15 [Jan. 1934]: 15). What the Freudian paradigm also reinforced, obviously, was the longstanding psychiatric connection between "mental infection" and women—particularly women living in all-female environments.

28. Helene Deutsch, "Folie à Deux," *Psychoanalytic Quarterly* 7 (Apr. 1938): 307–18; reprt. Deutsch, *Neuroses and Character Types: Clinical Psychoanalytic Studies* (New York, 1965), pp. 237–47; hereafter abbreviated "FD."

29. Gralnick, "Folie à Deux—The Psychosis of Association," pp. 239–40.

30. Jourdain was the first of the two women to return to the Trianon—in January 1902. Unlike Moberly, Jourdain spoke some French and had something of an obsession (disavowed in *An Adventure*) with French history and culture. That she had imposed her fancies on Moberly was clearly Iremonger's conclusion: Iremonger quoted a St. Hugh's source who remembered Jourdain saying that she had difficulty distinguishing between "the dream world and reality" and that she believed in second sight and auras (quoted in *GV*, p. 99).

31. Spurling, *Ivy*, p. 314.

sion," with its incriminating admixture of romantic and paranoid elements, seems almost too good to be true. How else, one might ask, might two repressed female homosexuals express their relationship than through such a story? Whether or not Moberly and Jourdain were aware of the lingering rumors regarding Marie Antoinette's own lesbianism (rumors that persisted well into the early twentieth century) the choice of Marie Antoinette—a sentimental emblem both of female sexuality and unjust persecution—seems inspired.[32] Indeed the whole Trianon "adventure" might be read as a sexual allegory—a kind of Freudian dream quest—symbolizing, through the imagery of the queen and her court, the formation of a female-female erotic bond. The wandering through mysterious wooded glades, the two male guides (would-be suitors?) who give wrong directions, the encounter with, and subsequent flight from, the repulsive-looking man, the revelatory vision of the sketching lady, the final meeting up with the joyful wedding party (celebrating Moberly and Jourdain's own symbolic marriage?) outside the gynocentric pavilion of the Petit Trianon itself—all suggest a turning away from masculine sexuality toward a world of female-female love and ritual.[33] It is worth noting, perhaps, that the Wertmüller portrait of Marie Antoinette, in which Moberly and Jourdain took such an interest, depicts the queen with her two children—combining the themes of maternal love and erotic triangulation. For Moberly and Jourdain to have triangulated their relationship

32. In his 1933 biography of the queen, Stefan Zweig discussed rumors about her "Sapphic inclinations" at length. Owing to Louis XVI's inability "to gratify her physiological requirements," as Zweig quaintly put it, Marie Antoinette turned to female companions to "relieve her spiritual and bodily tensions." " 'There have very generally been ascribed to me two tastes,'" she was supposed to have written to her mother, " 'that for women and that for lovers.'" The Comtesse de Polignac was her most notorious favorite: Zweig described their passion as "a sudden and overwhelming interest, a clap of thunder, a sort of superheated falling in love" (Zweig, *Marie Antoinette: The Portrait of an Average Woman*, trans. Eden and Cedar Paul [New York, 1933], pp. 119–21). The rumors about Marie Antoinette have always had particular currency among lesbians: an early issue of *The Ladder*, the underground lesbian periodical published in the United States between 1956 and 1972, contained an essay about the relationship between Marie Antoinette and the Comtesse de Polignac. See Lennox Strong, "The Royal Triangle: Marie Antoinette and the Duchesse de Polignac," in *Lesbian Lives: Biographies of Women from "The Ladder"*, ed. Barbara Grier and Coletta Reid (Oakland, Calif., 1976), pp. 180–85.

33. Sabine hinted at a psychoanalytic interpretation when he spoke of *An Adventure*'s dreamlike, "story-book" aspects: "This definitely 'bad man' [the kiosk man] who is awaiting the women in a lonely spot has to be escaped from. So—as though in response to the wish—on the scene runs the young and handsome page, quite an incipient story-book hero, and the two ladies are saved from a most disagreeable encounter" (Sabine, "Is There a Case for Retrocognition?" p. 54). What Sabine's reading neglects, however, is precisely the "feminocentric" pull of the story—toward the queen and her symbol, the Petit Trianon. On the role of the "pavilion" as an emblem of female erotic and intellectual independence in eighteenth- and nineteenth-century fiction, see Nancy K. Miller, "Writing from the Pavilion: George Sand and the Novel of Female Pastoral," *Subject to Change: Reading Feminist Writing* (New York, 1988), pp. 204–28.

with one another, so to speak, through the figure of the dead queen does not seem so improbable when one considers other similarly "spiritualizing" triangles between women in the period, such as that between Radclyffe Hall, Lady Una Troubridge, and Hall's deceased ex-lover, "Ladye," Mabel Batten, with whom she and Troubridge communicated regularly through a spirit medium for over twenty years.[34]

And yet how much does the diagnosis of *folie à deux* really tell us? As even its earliest formulators seemed to realize, the concept is something of an ambiguous one. Lasègue and Falret, for example, were clearly troubled by the clinical difficulties involved in identifying the syndrome at all—so deceptively "probable" were the stories often told by their patients. "How often the doctor, even an experienced one," they wrote, "asks himself whether the original fact reported has not really happened rather than being imaginary, and hesitates between an exaggeration and an emotional aberration" ("F," p. 4). Precisely because *folie à deux* was a form of mental alienation "sitting," as they put it, "between reason and confirmed insanity," the clinician often found himself in the position of the passive partner—on the verge of being persuaded himself of the supposedly "lunatic" idea ("F," p. 9).

In several telling passages Lasègue and Falret associated the delusions of *folie à deux* with the seductive fantasies of literature. The case histories of *folie à deux*, they wrote, were "intimate tragedies" of a sort "familiar to physicians, unknown to novelists" ("F," p. 16). (Their own case histories, replete with quasi-novelistic details of life in the less salubrious environs of late nineteenth-century Paris, often recall Émile Zola.) Couples suffering from shared delusions typically elaborated their tales with "the apparent sincerity with which one relates the events of a romantic novel" ("F," p. 10). The clinician was put into the role of literary critic: on the lookout for those palpably "imaginative" touches by which the maddened pair revealed their joint alienation. The danger, of course, was that he might fall under the narrative spell himself, transforming the *folie à deux* into a *folie à trois*.

In an attempt to allay the problem (which was at bottom an epistemological one) later clinicians sought to clarify the interpsychic mechanism by which the so-called *folie* spread from one person to another. In her much-cited essay on the subject, Deutsch proposed that *folie à deux* was a pathological form of "identification" in which each partner sought through fantasy to reconstitute a "lost object" from his or her psychic past.

---

34. See Michael Baker, *Our Three Selves: The Life of Radclyffe Hall* (New York, 1985), pp. 84–97. Hall and Troubridge's relationship paralleled Moberly and Jourdain's in interesting ways. Not least was the fact that both couples felt themselves profoundly susceptible to occult influences: in Brighton in 1920, Hall, in the company of Troubridge, saw the apparition of a mutual friend inspecting an automobile in a garage. The two published an account of their experience in the *Journal of the Society for Psychical Research* 20 (Apr. 1921): 78–88.

The contagion metaphor was somewhat misleading, she thought: in cases of true *folie à deux*, it was not so much that one partner "infected" the other, but that "both already possessed in common, repressed psychic contents which broke out earlier in one and later in the other." "Close living together, apart from others," did not induce the *folie à deux*; it was merely the first expression of those "unconscious bonds" which later brought both parties to similar delusional ideas ("FD," p. 316).

But at the same time Deutsch's invocation of unconscious forces made the underlying diagnostic problem more glaring. The same process of identification at work in a *folie à deux*, she noted, "can also be found in a psychic state so universally human that its character of 'normality' cannot be denied: 'being in love.'" On a grander scale, at the level of mass psychology, the same process also explained the behavior of "large groups of men, entire nations and generations." It was necessary, she concluded, to

> distinguish here as with individuals between hysterical, libidinally determined mass influences, and schizophrenic ideas held in common; likewise between mass liberations of instincts under the guise of ideals, and paranoid projections, etc. Many things have their place in these *folies en masse* and the approval or disapproval of the surrounding world is often the sole criterion as to whether a particular action is deemed a heroic deed or an act of madness. ["FD," p. 318]

But how to distinguish them? If the psychic process behind *folie à deux* was identical to that behind supposedly "normal" phenomena—such as falling in love or sharing in some collective social ideal—what made the *folie à deux* pathological? Deutsch's cryptic final sentence gave it away: only the "approval or disapproval of the surrounding world."

Yet if society alone decided which shared beliefs were "normal" and which were not, it was not hard to see how the diagnosis of *folie à deux* might be exploited for social and political ends: to demonize relationships between persons in whom intellectual or emotional solidarity was suspect. It is not perhaps accidental that what might be called the "invention" of *folie à deux* coincided with the rise of a number of emancipation movements in Europe and the United States—notably the women's suffrage movement, the organized labor movement, and the incipient homosexual emancipation movement.[35] How better to discredit new and threatening political associations than by labeling their proponents—in advance—as prone to shared insanity? A number of early writers on *folie à deux* displayed their animating prejudices quite openly. In an essay on *folie à deux*

35. The British socialist and freethinker Edward Carpenter (1844–1929) was one of the first writers to call for homosexual emancipation: his pamphlet *Homogenic Love, and Its Place in a Free Society* appeared in England in 1894. In Germany the homosexual emancipation movement developed under the leadership of the sexologist Magnus Hirschfeld (1868–1935), who founded a group called the Scientific-Humanitarian Committee in

in the *Journal of Mental Science* from 1910, for instance, the psychiatrist Arthur W. Wilcox took as his prime example of "contagious political insanity" the "unlawful and in every way extraordinary conduct of the suffragettes."[36] Later clinicians associated *folie à deux* not only with women and homosexuals—always the primary target groups—but also with other "dangerous" minorities, including the laboring poor, immigrants, and blacks.[37]

To be sure, in many of the cases related in the annals of *folie à deux* one is hard pressed to say what role social or political determinants may have played in the diagnosis, so patently "mad" do the beliefs involved seem to be. To read Oberndorf's 1934 case history about a husband and wife, Mr. and Mrs. V., who refused to leave their house for two years because both experienced an uncontrollable sensation of "whirling" and "fear of slipping" when they did so, is to feel oneself in the presence of a deep-seated and ultimately obscure mental aberration. (This same couple, wrote Oberndorf, also practiced "an unusual sexual perversion—a compulsion which involved the plunging of Mrs. V. fully dressed into a bath tub of water.")[38] Yet in other cases, such as that of the famous "silent twins" June and Jennifer Gibbons—two black twins who grew up in an immigrant West Indian family in Wales in the 1970s, invented their own private language, wrote novels and stories together, and refused to communicate

---

Berlin in 1897. His periodical devoted to the homosexual cause, *Yearbook for Sexual Intermediate Types,* appeared between 1899 and 1923. On the involvement of lesbians in Hirschfeld's movement, see *Lesbians in Germany: 1890's–1920's,* ed. Lillian Faderman and Brigitte Eriksson (Tallahassee, Fla., 1990).

36. Arthur W. Wilcox, "Communicated Insanity," *Journal of Mental Science* 56 (July 1910): 481. Along the same lines, at the conclusion of his 1887 essay on the subject, Tuke warned that "we should discourage susceptible young women, and especially hysterical ones, from associating with persons having delusions, or even entertaining wild eccentric notions short of insane delusions" (Tuke, "Folie à Deux," p. 421).

37. In "A Study of *Folie à Deux*," *Journal of Mental Science* 85 (Nov. 1939): 1212–23, Stanley M. Coleman and Samuel L. Last argued that economic distress was "the ground upon which *folie à deux* flourishes. . . . [It] is a most potent reason for causing dissatisfaction with reality." This same "dissatisfaction with reality" on a grander scale, they argued, led to the creation of "new creeds and religions" and political ideologies such as "Communism and fascism" (p. 1220). On the association between *folie à deux* and blacks, see J. W. Babcock, "Communicated Insanity and Negro Witchcraft," *American Journal of Insanity* 51 (Apr. 1895): 518–23. Babcock, who was the superintendent of the South Carolina Lunatic Asylum in Columbia, described a case in which a white man, "B. S.," became "infected" with religious delusions after meeting a black faith healer, "Doctor" George Darby, who claimed to effect magical cures with the assistance of "Little Solomon," a bundle of roots tied up in cloth. B. S. in turn passed his delusions on to his wife and brother and "five negro men." After B. S. was committed to an asylum, his wife and brother recovered; the five black men apparently did not. What is especially striking about the case history is the author's implicit assumption that blacks are more prone to collective delusions than whites, and that once infected, become incurable.

38. Oberndorf, "Folie à Deux," p. 17.

with adults—one senses that much of their so-called madness was in fact merely an adaptive response to intolerable social alienation and emotional deprivation.[39]

To invoke the concept of the *folie à deux* as a way of discrediting Moberly and Jourdain, therefore, is to involve oneself, at the very least, in rhetorical and epistemological difficulties. To dismiss "les dames d'Oxford" (as Cocteau called them) as crazy is clearly not enough: the challenge, as we have seen, is to explain how the two of them could have been "crazy" in exactly the same way. Yet the only possible psychological explanation—that Moberly and Jourdain suffered from some kind of "contagious insanity" or psychosis by association—is fraught with ideological problems. From the start the theory of *folie à deux* reinscribed a host of late nineteenth-century cultural prejudices—that women were more "delusional" than men, that pairs of women were untrustworthy, that women exhibiting "morbid" sexual tendencies (lesbians, in other words) were the least trustworthy of all. Nor have modern-day psychiatrists and clinicians entirely dispensed with these problematical assumptions: most recent studies of *folie à deux* have continued to rely, uncritically, on the antiquated etiological principles established by Lasègue and Falret over a hundred years ago.[40]

Have we thus arrived at a backhanded vindication of the authors of *An Adventure?* After a fashion, perhaps. True, the skeptic will still object, it remains difficult to credit Moberly and Jourdain's most pressing claim— that on 10 August 1901 at the Petit Trianon, they "entered into an act of memory" and encountered Marie Antoinette and her court. The so-called evidence marshalled on behalf of this claim—the business of antique ploughs, footmens' liveries, unusually buckled shoes, pockmarked faces, garden kiosks, and green fichus—will remain for most of us, perhaps, eternally unconvincing: a testament to folly alone.

And yet skepticism too has its pitfalls. Skepticism is liable, as we have seen, to its own kind of folly—that debunking "mania," or compulsion to disprove, so ruefully acknowledged by Iremonger in *The Ghosts of Versailles.* To disbelieve—at least in the case of *An Adventure*—is to risk losing oneself in an alienating welter of evidence and counterevidence. But more troublingly, skepticism is silent on what one might suppose to be the central issue of the case: how a belief ostensibly as "delusional" as Moberly and Jourdain's should have grown up between the two of them in the first place. Rationalism holds, above all, that delusions are a disease of subjectivity—that they come about, as Deutsch put it, when an individual

39. See Marjorie Wallace, *The Silent Twins* (New York, 1986).
40. See Faguet and Faguet's "La Folie à Deux," in *Extraordinary Disorders of Human Behavior.* The authors, both professors of psychiatry at the University of California, Los Angeles, repeat without dispute Lasègue and Falret's one-hundred-year-old observation that women suffer from *folie à deux* more than men (p. 7; see "F," p. 16).

fails to separate "inner content" from "perception." "It is a complicated developmental process," she observed,

> to be able to distinguish inner content from perception. The simplest criterion is: perception is that which others accept as perception. A contact with the surrounding world is indispensable in applying this criterion. A psychotic individual has not only given up the differentiation of the inner world from the world of reality, but he has given up the need for confirmation from the latter by destroying the bridge between himself and other objects. The ego then takes its delusion for reality and professes it as truth. ["FD," p. 317]

Yet according to such logic, we notice, Moberly and Jourdain were not delusional. Neither one gave up her "contact" with the surrounding world; indeed, precisely in their contact with one another, each found the primordial confirmation that she needed.

Here, then, is the impasse into which skepticism leads: it becomes impossible to distinguish so-called normal collective convictions from pathological ones. If folly is contagious, paradoxically, then it can no longer be folly; for folly is defined by the very fact that it is *not* contagious. Indeed, at the collective level, one might argue, folly ceases to exist: it is transformed into ideology. Were Moberly and Jourdain the victims of *folie à deux* or the inventors of a new romantic ideology? Were they "insane" or were they "in love"? And how to dismiss them, or even to begin to dismiss them, without revealing one's own ideological presumptions and prejudices? As long as skepticism is unable to answer such questions—to make, in short, any coherent distinction between collective dogma and collective hallucination—*An Adventure* will remain what Moberly and Jourdain intended it to be: a rebuke to scoffers, a challenge to the incredulous.

For Your Eyes Only: Ghost Citing

Françoise Meltzer

I will begin with an annotated, so to speak, summary of Terry Castle's essay "Contagious Folly: *An Adventure* and Its Skeptics" (pp. 11–42). It begins by asking how an idea spreads and whether delusions can be contagious like viruses. The corollary question here is whether such a transfer of ideas might not serve as the formation of ideology itself, resulting in group consciousness. The assumption is that such a transfer of ideas entails a "collective hallucination." The paper immediately cites Freud's lament that there is insufficient data on the power of suggestion, that is, in Freud's words, "the conditions under which influence without adequate logical foundation takes place" (quoted, p. 112). Such conditions are present for Castle in the case of the "Ghosts of Versailles," the story told in the book *An Adventure,* published in 1911 by two women using pseudonyms.

These two English women, Charlotte Moberly and Eleanor Jourdain, were by all accounts well educated and proper: "the principal and vice-principal, respectively, of St. Hugh's College, Oxford." They were "the respectable daughters of clergymen both," and yet their book made the "fantastic claim" that "while on a sightseeing tour of the gardens of the Petit Trianon near Versailles on 10 August 1901," they had met the apparition of Marie Antoinette and several members of her court (p. 13). Here is, then, the collective hallucination or delusion grounded "without adequate logical foundation."

Thus the paper's first question, "But what if *two* people claim to see a ghost?" has already been circumscribed within the limits of a delusionary or hallucinatory psychic economy (p. 11). The question is not what would qualify as evidence for the sighting of a ghost but rather how two people could share the same delusion and how skeptics will be helpless to respond conclusively concerning the *reasons* for such an example of collective hallucination. Moreover, by using Freud as part of its grounding, Castle's essay gives us a model for evidence that relies on adequacy between reality and testimony. Castle from the beginning, then, resorts to the positivistic logic that the rest of her paper will brilliantly debunk. On the other hand, nothing brings out positivism more quickly than what we are talking about here: ghosts.

The paper can be roughly divided into three parts. The first consists of the introductory remarks I have summarized plus the details of this fascinating case. Here we learn how the women themselves reconstruct their experience through ten years of serious archival work on the France of 1789 and on the Petit Trianon. In detectivelike fashion, in other words, Moberly and Jourdain seek to recast their experience in the language and "proofs" of scholarship. Their research will give them the accuracy of detail (historical, architectural, temporal, and sartorial) that for them, clearly, will supply the evidence of their truth-telling.

The second part of Castle's essay provides the history of *An Adventure*'s reception, the attacks on and defenses of the two authors. These responses are intriguing not only because of the various tactics they undertake but also, as Castle points out, because they are at least as ludicrous as the ghost story inspiring them. One skeptic saw the women as laboring under a "pathetic illusion" (quoted, p. 27) but in good faith (they were swept away). Another claimed, on the other hand, that they had tampered with the "evidence," that is, with the two narratives that they had written separately shortly after the incident. They had done this to compare their experiences, since they had earlier discovered that there were discrepancies: they did not see the same things or the same people (only Moberly, for example, saw the person she later identified as Marie Antoinette). Thus the question of "original" narrative and possible fraudulence is introduced. Yet another response occurred in 1957 in the form of a book by one Lucille Iremonger. This work, Castle tells us, is vicious. Iremonger claims that Jourdain and especially Moberly had had many previous such visions and that they were lesbians. This becomes evidence for Iremonger (a wonderful name under the circumstances) that any claims by the two must be suspect (indeed, the story is "symptomatic" of

---

Françoise Meltzer is professor of romance languages and literature at the University of Chicago. A coeditor of *Critical Inquiry* and editor of *The Trial(s) of Psychoanalysis* (1987), she is the author of *Salomé and the Dance of Writing: Portraits of Mimesis in Literature* (1987) and *Hot Property: The Stakes and Claims of Literary Originality* (1994).

such an unnatural union [p. 29]). Finally, in 1976 the two women are defended by Joan Evans who writes that the Count de Montesquiou used to hold costume parties at the Petit Trianon, and so through no fault of their own, they were the victims of a trompe l'oeil. (I should add that Evans turns the lesbian motif around, claiming that the two well-bred women sensed perversion when they saw it—Montesquiou was homosexual—and so instinctively recoiled from one particular man in their vision, a man who for Evans could be none other than the Count.)

In the next part of her essay, Castle asks what can be made of these charges and defenses. She suggests that the contagion spread to the critics to whom Jourdain and Moberly seemed to have transmitted their hermeneutic madness. The essay here spends quite a bit of time on the notion of *folie à deux* (which Helene Deutsch, for example, connected with lesbianism) and on the meaning of *folly*. Castle shows that the notion of *folie à deux* is gendered; its formulation coincides with the gradual emancipation of women in Europe and the United States, and it can be read as gynophobic. (*Folie à deux* is also articulated in terms of class; it is associated with the poor, immigrants, and blacks.) The "'united front'" presented by Moberly and Jourdain's narrative was galling to the guardians of patriarchal values (p. 31). Since nothing could explain in any convincing way their collaborative folly, the hysteria spread to the critics who, confronted with what Castle calls "epistemological difficulties," grew testy (p. 41).

Castle herself gets caught up in the repetition compulsion, and by her own admission. She goes to the Petit Trianon in 1990 in hopes of seeing an apparition and gets pulled into trying to solve the mystery. She concludes by noting that it is hard to make the distinction between collective dogma and collective hallucination. *An Adventure* remains an enigma.

I have spent a long time recapitulating the argument of this fascinating article because it is rich in both the problematics and assumptions of evidentiary logic. In the remarks that follow, I try to raise some of the questions that seem to me to demand acknowledgement and just a very few of the possible implications.

1. What is the status of psychoanalysis here? Castle quickly moves to discuss the Versailles event in terms of mental instability: *delusion, hysteria, hallucination, folie à deux,* and *folly* are some of the words used to describe Jourdain and Moberly's experience, thus placing it within the bounds of psychoanalytic discourse. She notes that Freud's silence on *folie à deux* is "intriguing" and gives a quotation from *Group Psychology and the Analysis of the Ego* as "the closest he came to touching on it" (p. 35 n. 27). Significantly, the passage quoted has to do with hysteria spreading in a girls' boarding school, which Freud sees in terms of identification with another's desire. Indeed, it is Freud who uses the language of contagion to describe such an occurrence: other girls will "catch the fit" from the first "by mental infection" (quoted, ibid). As I have mentioned, Castle keeps to this medical vocabulary of contagion herself in her article, so that one

question might be how the secondary infection of psychoanalytic jargon and its baggage are functioning in her own text. It is worth noting, moreover, that the female of the species is imagined by the patriarchal texts of psychoanalysis as succumbing more easily to the disease of hysteria, so that the cadre of the girls' boarding school in the Freud quotation cited by Castle is a consciously gendered example on Freud's part. More dirtily, perhaps, it should be remembered that women living together menstruate together. I need not, I am sure, elaborate on how this defilement of the female (which Freud specifically mentions in his discussion of the *mikvah* for example) is a mysterious form of contagion that spreads from woman to woman. I would suggest that beneath the female gendering of *folie à deux* (as in Deutsch, for example) lies this subtext of synchronized defilement that was itself used as evidence in nineteenth-century Europe of female susceptibility to contagion at the biological level (the psychic being merely an extension of such a susceptibility). My argument then would run something like this: The insistence, in the "definition" of *folie à deux,* upon "close proximity over a long period of time" (p. 33) for producing a delusional conception is a displacement of synchronized menstruation, which does in fact occur under those circumstances and which creates a fear more atavistic, if less specific, than does (even) the new generation of educated and independent women.[1]

1. The following footnote is to be read as a parallel text (rather than subtext, for example) to these comments. In 1969, a Wellesley undergraduate named Martha McClintock was a summer intern at Jackson Laboratory. During a lunch table discussion, she mentioned to her male colleagues that women who live together menstruate together. The men, all scientists, did not believe her: they wanted *evidence.* Anecdotal evidence—indeed, experience—was judged insufficient. It had already been established (scientifically) that in mice the presence of a male could trigger ovulation. But McClintock was arguing that in humans synchronized menstruation seemed to be unaffected by males and seemed rather to be a female/female interaction. To settle this argument, she wrote her first research paper, "Menstrual Synchrony and Suppression," *Nature,* 22 Jan. 1971, pp. 244–45. The study worked from roommates and "close friend groups" living in the same dormitory. The paper concludes that in humans "there is some interpersonal physiological process which affects the menstrual cycle," one which cannot be solely explained (if at all) by "exposure to males." What seems rather to account for the synchrony is "that the individuals of the group spend time together" (p. 245). Why remained unclear.

The lunch table argument that she lacked (scientifically acceptable) evidence became McClintock's career. From her graduate work at Harvard University to her professorship at the University of Chicago, she has continued working on synchronized menstruation. Her initial work with college women shifted almost immediately to mice, which have been the subject of her laboratory work for nearly twenty years. As a result of her work, scientific study is returning to animals to examine McClintock's findings; that synchronization in *animals* is also the result of interaction among females. Moreover, synchronization affects much more than the advent of the menstrual cycle. Synchronization directly affects the timing (including the suppression and enhancement) of fertility and senescence, and it synchronizes (and thus optimizes) births. See McClintock, "A Functional Approach to the Behavioral Endocrinology of Rodents," in *Psychobiology of Reproductive Behavior: An Evolutionary Perspective,* ed. David Crews (Englewood Cliffs, N.J., 1987), pp. 176–203. See also Julie A. Mennella, Mark S. Blumberg, McClintock, H. Molzt, "Inter-litter Competition and Com-

2. Evidence in itself, of course, contains the idea of vision [*videre*]. Part of the difficulty in this tale lies in the privileging of sight as the obvious means of establishing the truth. What, in other words, did Moberly and Jourdain really *see*, if anything? And to what extent does what they saw mean the same thing as the truth? (We are back to the problem of the *adaequatio*.) Here we come to a problem the occult shares with religion and psychoanalysis: How do you produce evidence for what is normally invisible (ghosts, God, the unconscious respectively)? What is acceptable as evidence in such a paradox? What does an eyewitness mean here? These are the questions implicit in *An Adventure,* its epistemological impasse.

As Lorraine Daston points out in her essay in this volume (pp. 273–74), facts become evidence when put in the service of a claim. She notes that in the seventeenth century, Protestant theologians debunked sacramental miracles by insisting on "a public and visible demonstration" (quoted, p. 264). Private occurrences were disallowed. It is important to note that in the story of the women, two boils down somehow still to one; their plurality (and thus the "publicness" of the event) is denied. The suggestion that they are lesbians seeks to neutralize their difference; they are really only one and the same person saying the same thing, redundantly. The real ghosts in the story then are the women, whose vision is rejected on the grounds that two women do not constitute a public. How many women would it take to move out of a "private" and attain a "public" realm? The notion of private/public is so gendered, in other words, that for this kind of thinking, two means one.

This is a logic to which Freud himself turns in a 1906 paper entitled

---

munal Nursing among Norway Rats: Advantages of Birth Synchrony," *Behavioral Ecology and Sociobiology* 27 (1990): 183–90.

For the last few years, McClintock's lab at Chicago has returned to human subjects and is now able to make similar claims concerning human synchrony. In the meantime, anthropology has caught on to all of this. Two recent books attest to such an interest: *Blood Magic: The Anthropology of Menstruation,* ed. Thomas Buckley and Alma Gottlieb (Berkeley, 1988), and Christopher Knight, *Blood Relations: Menstruation and the Origins of Culture* (New Haven, Conn. 1991); the latter argues that synchrony is the root of culture. Here we have gone full circle—that is, we are strangely almost in the same place as in the beginning (the lunch table). From a denial that menstruation can be synchronized by anything besides a male presence, we are encountering such a sweeping ("anthropological") claim for synchrony that the power of female/female interaction is broadened ad infinitum and thus becomes once again easily dismissable as a claim. In fact, McClintock says, synchrony is just one of many manifestations of social control of fertility among women. It is not, McClintock told me recently, "the root of culture" but rather the tusk of an elephant that is only beginning to be understood. Are we bumping into a gendered epistemology? epistemo-phobia (the root metaphor) as against -philia (enjoying approaching an as-yet-unimaginable elephant)? The fear of what females can do when they live together is one that sees synchrony as *evidence* of (as a symptom of) the power of women in crowds, of many women acting as one. It is a fear that can only function from a perspective which is not "female"; which uses "folly à deux" as a model that both acknowledges and attempts to excise synchrony.

"Psycho-analysis and the Establishment of the Facts in Legal Proceedings." Here Freud, addressing lawyers and judges, says he "must draw an analogy between the criminal and the hysteric." Both have a secret, with one difference: the criminal knows his; the hysteric doesn't. Thus the therapist has the same task as the examining magistrate, except that the therapist will know before the hysteric what her secret is (she may never know at all).[2] Freud's tale of epistemological detective work genders knowledge. He will decide the difference between fiction and the real and between the imagination and the intellect. Thus the therapeutic situation itself corresponds to the definitions given by Castle for *folie à deux:* in "close proximity over a long period of time," an active partner convinces a passive one of the accuracy of his delusional conception. The case of Dora seems to me to be striking evidence of this claim.

Let us not forget that it is Freud who rejects intellectual uncertainty as a triggering mechanism for the uncanny. Intellectual uncertainty, Freud says following Jentsch's definition, is the inability to discern whether something is animate or inanimate, living or dead. Ghosts seem to me to fit such a category. It is amazing, Freud notes in the "Delusions and Dreams in Jensen's *Gradiva*" (which begins as a ghost story and ends as a doubled one), how easily even people possessed of "the most powerful intelligence" will believe in something absurd "provided it satisfies powerful emotional impulses." He knew a doctor once, he says, who lost a female patient to Graves disease. The doctor felt guilty for her death. When a woman resembling the dead one entered his office several years later, "he could frame only a single thought: 'So after all it's true that the dead can come back to life.'" Not until the woman introduced herself as the sister of the dead one did the doctor's dread give way to shame (for having been fooled). Freud ends the anecdote with an astonishing punch line: "The doctor to whom this occurred," he says, "was, however, none other than myself."[3] He therefore openly identifies with the protagonist of Jensen's *Gradiva* who believes that he has seen a ghost from the time of Pompeii. What I am suggesting here, then, is twofold. First, the status of *folie à deux* is unclear in psychoanalysis, although hysteria by contagion is clearly gendered female (and the therapeutic situation can be seen as such a *folie*). Second, an epistemological quandary for an evidentiary logic is magnificently provided by any ghost story: eyewitnessing is insufficient, and the *adaequatio* breaks down entirely. It is for this reason, perhaps, that the skeptics remain as ludicrous in dismissing the story as the authors, for example, in telling it. How do we talk about ghosts qua ghosts? What is the evidence for demonstrating that they do not exist?

3. This brings me to the rhetorical angle. Castle (understandably)

2. Sigmund Freud, "Psycho-analysis and the Establishment of the Facts in Legal Proceedings," *The Standard Edition of the Complete Psychological Works of Sigmund Freud*, trans. and ed. James Strachey, 24 vols. (London, 1953–74), 9:108.

3. Freud, "Delusions and Dreams in Jensen's *Gradiva*," in *Standard Edition*, 9:71, 71–72.

uses distancing terms in discussing the ghost sightings. But what is the valence of words such as "claimed," "supposedly," "presumed," "so-called," in Castle's discourse, and where does she assume her readers stand in relation to them? What is Castle's position when she says that the "so-called evidence" provided by the women "will remain for most of us, perhaps, eternally unconvincing" (p. 41)? Who is this "us"? Is Castle herself trying (in Carlo Ginzburg's terms) to homogenize all the narratives so that they "fit" with the facts? What is the evidentiary status of the photos that appear with her article? Is the rhetoric of ekphrasis that characterizes Jourdain and Moberly's account meant to serve (for them, or for Castle, or for both) as evidence that these were indeed ghosts?

4. In closing, I would like to turn to a text by Marx in which ghosts walk fairly constantly, *The Eighteenth Brumaire of Louis Bonaparte*. There he gives us the best anecdote for evidence as vested in the eyewitness account (I'll believe it when I see it), one that is found in Hegel's *Philosophy of Right* as well. It is taken from a fable by Aesop, in which a man brags that he has eyewitnesses to prove that he once jumped very high in Rhodes. His interlocutor responds to this boast by reminding him that this is Rhodes, so he might as well jump now to prove his feat: "Hic Rhodus, hic salta!"[4]

I would suggest that this is a challenge Castle's text poses to the ghosts of Versailles as well as to the eyewitnesses Moberly and Jourdain. Her journey to the Petit Trianon is a "hic Rhodus, hic salta" to the ghosts, of course, but also to the women themselves. It is a challenge that betrays a belief in evidence as necessarily ocular, and in an *adaequatio*, as I have said, between events and reality for demonstrating the truth. Ghosts, then, can indeed serve, as Marx points out, to glorify the struggle of a new revolution, and this may be precisely how Marie Antoinette functions here: conservative in the French revolution but radical for the cause of the emancipation of women. But ghosts also function as the blind spot in the logic of ocular evidence, haunting its Enlightenment assumptions with a presence for which there is no counterevidence. As such, then, ghosts may be seen as the index of doubt, or the limits of any apodictic theory for which, as we know, the demand for evidence ceaselessly yearns.

4. Karl Marx, *The Eighteenth Brumaire of Louis Bonaparte* (1852; New York, 1963), p. 19.

A Rejoinder to Françoise Meltzer

Terry Castle

I have—if I have interpreted Françoise Meltzer's challenge correctly ("For Your Eyes Only: Ghost Citing" [pp. 43–49])—been asked to fess up: am I a positivist or an idealist, a skeptic or a believer, a Freudian or a non-Freudian, an analyst or a would-be analysand? (Referring to my own Moberly-and-Jourdainish trip to Versailles, Meltzer diagnoses me as suffering from a "repetition compulsion" [p. 45].) Do I see myself as a neutral retailer of historical "facts"—a kind of tourist-photographer in the world of turn-of-the-century occultism—or do I have perhaps my own intellectual or ideological stake in the issues raised by *An Adventure* and its interpretations?

On the crucial matter of evidence—whether any so-called evidence can in fact provide access to what we commonly refer to as truth— Meltzer seems to be suggesting (again if I read her right) that I am of two minds. On the one hand, I ridicule the "positivistic" search for proofs and counterproofs carried out by Charlotte Moberly and Eleanor Jourdain and their would-be debunkers; on the other, I rely on a kind of "positivistic" evidentiary logic when it suits me, as, for example, when I provide photographs of Moberly and Jourdain, of the Petit Trianon, and so on, in order to confer a certain verisimilitude and authority on my own reconstruction of the "facts" of the case. Am I *really* a thoroughgoing skeptic on the subject of evidence, or am I not myself perhaps a closet "evidence-monger," with more than a little resemblance to the unfortunately named (yet perversely entertaining) Lucille Iremonger? I cannot, I find, answer any of these questions definitively, or at least not in the space allowed, but I will nonetheless try to get at them (in an ire-mongering fashion) by offering a kind of confessional ghost-commentary to my original text.

Meltzer's central question—a question she restates in different ways—has to do with what she calls the "status of psychoanalysis" in my essay. She notes that I use words such as *delusion, hysteria, hallucination, folie à deux,* and *folly* to describe the experience of the women, "thus placing it within the bounds of psychoanalytic discourse" (p. 45). Subsequently, when I take up the history of the "'mental infection'" theories of the later nineteenth century, Meltzer wonders "how the secondary infection of psychoanalytic jargon and its baggage are functioning in [my] own text" (p. 46). I can only respond here by describing what I *thought* I was doing—though I find now I may have been doing more things in the essay than I realized, or consciously intended, at the time I was writing. One thing I wanted to do was to ironize the language of psychological explanation itself. That is, I wanted to take up some of the terms conventionally used to explain away the apparitional (*hallucination, delusion,* and so forth), use them in the seemingly colloquial or vernacular or positivistic sense, and yet at the same time, as I proceeded through the "story" of *An Adventure* and its aftermath, to use them in such a way that their inadequacy as explanatory terms would become increasingly obvious. The goal was to destabilize or estrange the meaning of terms such as *hallucination, folie, delusion*—even, paradoxically, as I invoked them myself.

Why do this? I had for some time been haunted by the problem of the apparitional. I work in eighteenth-century studies, and the problem of ghosts and specters (what are they? where do they come from?) is writ large in eighteenth-century literature—especially in the gothic fiction of the 1780s and 1790s. It has always seemed to me that one of the central innovations of the Enlightenment, though one that most educated people tend now to take for granted, was precisely what one might call the rationalization of the spectral—the reinterpretation of the apparitional as a psychological rather than pneumatological phenomenon. Traditional Christian dogma—the system of belief that prevailed throughout much of Western civilization from the Middle Ages to roughly the end of the seventeenth century—held that there was in fact an invisible world out there somewhere, populated by ethereal beings (spirits, demons, or souls of the dead) who could materialize on occasion and reveal themselves to the living. What gradually took over—crucially, I think, during the later eighteenth century—was a new belief: spirits and apparitions were

---

Terry Castle is professor of English at Stanford University and the author of *Masquerade and Civilization: The Carnivalesque in Eighteenth-Century English Culture and Fiction* (1986). She has just published a new study entitled *The Apparitional Lesbian: Female Homosexuality and Modern Culture* (1993).

merely projections from within, or *hallucinations,* and usually resulted from some mental or physiological disorder.

Yet one thing that has always disturbed me about this so-called rationalization of the spectral is how intimately it has always been bound up with the cultural humiliation of women. In the antipneumatological writings of the sixteenth and seventeenth centuries—in Reginald Scot's *Discoverie of Witchcraft* (1584), say, or Locke's *Essay Concerning Human Understanding* (1690)—it was inevitably women who were seen as being particularly susceptible to the hallucinatory. (Locke blamed superstitious "nursemaids," for example, for instilling the fear of ghosts in the minds of their young charges.) And in eighteenth- and nineteenth-century skeptical literature the same misogynistic bias is much in evidence. Out of a kind of perverse female chauvinism, I felt myself animated by a creeping urge to debunk the debunkers, to one-up or embarrass the would-be explainers. Freud, of course, is one of the most important of these "explainers" in our own era, although he is also already a fairly late figure in the history of rationalist reinterpretation. I would argue that the claim that Freud makes—most memorably perhaps in *The Interpretation of Dreams*— that ghosts and specters are in fact projections from the unconscious— expressions of repressed material in the psyche of the perceiver—is simply a later and technically more refined version of the "hallucination" or "projection" theory already extant in late eighteenth- and early nineteenth-century psychology.

From one angle, if the attempt to ironize psychological language works, my essay might be considered an anti-Freudian statement. From the "female chauvinist" standpoint, Freud is undoubtedly one of the most galling of modern thinkers precisely because he reinscribes so obsessively the putative connection between femininity and the delusional—the celebrated Dora case history being the most glaring case in point. But I also intended the essay to be antipsychological in a much broader sense. By critiquing some of the characteristic moves of eighteenth- , nineteenth- , and indeed twentieth-century skeptics, I wanted, implicitly at least, to preserve a notional space for the numinous—for *le monde irréale*—and by extension save a space for women and even, perhaps, for a kind of female visionary authority.

In launching my critique of hallucination theory I found myself employing a strategy often employed by nineteenth-century spiritualists: I focused on a case of so-called collective apparition-seeing. Historically speaking, apparitions seen by two or more individuals have played a tremendously important part in debates about the supernatural—notably in the debates between spiritualists and nonbelievers around the turn of this century—for the simple reason that (assuming one accepts the truth-value of eyewitness testimony and one's witnesses are not lying) so-called collective apparitions are the most difficult to explain away in strictly psychological terms.

This is not to say that there have not been psychological attempts to account for them. According to the miasma theory of the early nineteenth century, for example, as set forth by Sir Walter Scott in his *Letters on Demonology and Witchcraft* (1830), collective apparitions could sometimes be caused by "bad air" acting on the brains of perceivers: when ships approached the harbor of Cadiz, Scott wrote, with its famously unhealthy miasma, sailors often reported sharing group hallucinations. The later nineteenth-century concept of contagious insanity, or *folie à deux*, was in a way simply a more subtle and personalized version of the miasma theory: here, not a noxious gas, but the "infectious" nearby presence of someone else suffering from delusions was enough to cause hallucinations in a susceptible individual.

In retracing the history of the *folie à deux*, I hoped to show, not only that the idea of contagious insanity was a fairly recent one (the term *folie à deux* itself dates from the 1870s), but also that it was troubled from the start by what one might call a kind of ideological static. From the start the theory depended upon a host of nineteenth-century social prejudices: those considered most liable to "infection" (women, homosexuals, the poor, blacks, immigrants) were precisely those groups most feared and despised by the ruling classes of the age. A diagnosis of *folie à deux* could easily be used, I suggested, against those in whom "intellectual or emotional solidarity was suspect" (p. 39). Nor have twentieth-century clinicians dispensed with such prejudicial notions. In laying out my critique, I took particular pleasure in taking some rude swipes at Helene Deutsch, who might be considered—again from the "female chauvinist" position—as one of the most irritating collaborators in the Freudian business of stigmatizing women (and especially lesbians) for their supposedly inherent delusionary tendencies.

I was gratified in reading Meltzer's remarks to see that I had to some degree "infected" her with my own way of thinking. The connection she makes between the way the *folie à deux* is supposed to work and the way that the Freudian transference is supposed to work (both processes involving close proximity between two people over a drawn out period, an "active" partner and a "passive" partner, and a process by which the active partner persuades the passive one of a certain "truth") is a fascinating one and deserves further study. (In outlining the theory of *folie à deux*, I left it to the reader to see the obvious irony in the fact that the theory itself was the brainchild of *two* male psychiatrists, Lasègue and Falret, who wrote as an indivisible pair. To the degree that Lasègue and Falret present themselves, through their collaboration, as coproducers of the same idea—or "cothinkers" of the same thoughts—they might themselves be considered an en-*folie*-ated couple.)

Meltzer's suggestion that the association made in the nineteenth century between women and contagious insanity may point to an "atavistic" fear of "synchronized defilement"—the synchronization of the menstrual cycle that occurs when pairs or groups of women live in close proximity—is likewise an intriguing one (p. 46). It also resonates uncannily with nineteenth-century biographical traditions concerning Marie Antoinette. Immediately after finishing "Contagious Folly," I began looking in greater detail into nineteenth-century writing about Marie Antoinette, especially the numerous biographies of her produced in England and France between 1850 and 1900. I wanted to see why it was that Moberly and Jourdain picked her, as it were, to "see." One detail Marie Antoinette's nineteenth-century biographers almost inevitably linger over, to great pathetic effect, was the fact that during her imprisonment in the Conciergerie in the last six months before her execution, she suffered from a kind of persistent fluxing or supermenorrhaghia. Countless witnesses at her trial and execution commented on her "spectral" or "ghostly" appearance—the result, undoubtedly, of the extreme anemia from which she was suffering in the last weeks of her life. I'm not quite sure what to do with this oblique connection with the theme of menstruation, but I think it worth noting that Marie Antoinette (as Moberly and Jourdain undoubtedly would have known from their reading) was in a sense a chronically "bleeding woman" and that her fluxing was in turn immediately linked, metaphorically, with her "apparitionality."

Yet it was also precisely as I began to look further into the cultural background to Moberly and Jourdain's *An Adventure* that I found my own ideological stake in the case (and my own very thinly disguised crypto-Freudianism) becoming painfully clear. I subsequently wrote a second essay, a kind of sequel to "Contagious Folly," in which I took up the historical question, Why Marie Antoinette? What I discovered while researching the case was that Moberly and Jourdain were not the only women at the turn of the century who were obsessed with the French queen. Many women shared their obsession; at least two also claimed publicly to have seen her apparition. (In the 1890s the celebrated Swiss medium "Hélène Smith" held seances at which she pretended to speak in the queen's voice and reproduce her handwriting.) Along with these supplementary cases of outright Marie Antoinette obsession, I found a huge hagiographical literature, largely produced by women, about the queen and her various trials and misfortunes.[1]

What inspired this collective fixation, I became convinced, was in fact a kind of sublimated homoeroticism. (And already, the reader will notice, I cannot begin to describe this second project without falling immediately into a Freudian language.) The queen was notorious during her lifetime for her intense friendships with women and may indeed have had sexual liaisons with two women at her court, the Princesse de Lamballe and the

---

1. See Terry Castle, *The Apparitional Lesbian: Female Homosexuality and Modern Culture* (New York, 1993), pp. 107–49.

Comtesse de Polignac. At the time of the Revolution, her enemies repeat-edly accused her of being a "Sapphist" and circulated hundreds of porno-graphic pamphlets in which her putative "tribadism" was a prominent theme. After her death, and in the first half of the nineteenth century, various royal apologists, including the Goncourt brothers, attempted to defend her against the allegations by stressing the "spiri-tual" or platonic nature of these friendships. The idea seems to have been to salvage her reputation by romanticizing or idealizing her intimacies with other women. But the net result was to keep the rumor of her homo-sexuality alive. Over the course of the nineteenth century Marie An-toinette gradually became a recognized icon of female-female erotic bonding and by the early twentieth century a sort of underground lesbian heroine.

What I found myself arguing, as I analyzed various instances of Marie Antoinette obsession, was that the queen's visionary image or "ap-parition" functioned as a way for women at the turn of the century to symbolize otherwise unconscious or inadmissible lesbian desires. She be-came, I suggested, a kind of enabling figure, a trope or imaginative topos: a way of representing an emotion, or expressing a fantasy, which could not be expressed in any other way. Peculiar as it may sound, it was easier in 1890 to admit to having seen the ghost of Marie Antoinette than it was to admit to desiring another woman.

If this seems to dovetail perfectly (and horribly) with Helene Deutsch's idea that cases of "shared obsession" are particularly likely to occur between women with homosexual tendencies, I'm afraid that it does. Not only did I find myself, in this sequel, falling back into a com-pletely nonironic Freudian explanatory language, I found that in order to posit (as I wanted to) the existence of a kind of lesbian Imaginary, or a sort of unconscious lesbian "cultural poetics" at work in the nineteenth and early twentieth century—a hidden tropology of lesbian desire—I had to resuscitate some of the very arguments I pretended so heartily to disdain in "Contagious Folly." I have been since forced to conclude that what drew me to *An Adventure* in the first place, though I tried as hard as I could to disguise or deny it, was precisely its "psychological meaning"—not the "question of evidence" at all, which I happily retreated from as soon as I could, but the question of sexual identity.

Self Evidence

Simon Schaffer

> To turn and fix . . . ones attention upon oneself, is not perhaps itself
> entirely without its effects. There is so intimate a connection . . .
> between the volitions of the soul and the motions of the body, that it is
> not easy to prescribe limits to the influence of attention. . . . The first
> thing therefore, to which the commissioners were bound to attend,
> was not to observe too minutely what passed within them.
> —*Report of the Commissioners on Animal Magnetism*, 1785

There seems to be an important historical connexion between changes in
the concept of evidence and that of the person capable of giving evidence. Michel Foucault urged that during the classical age the relationship between evidence and the person was reversed: scholasticism derived
statements' authority from that of their authors, while scientists now hold
that matters of fact are the most impersonal of statements.[1] In a similar
vein, Ian Hacking defines a kind of evidence which 'consists in one thing
pointing beyond itself', and claims that until the early modern period 'testimony and authority were primary, and things could count as evidence
only insofar as they resembled the witness of observers and the authority
of books'.[2] This captures a rather familiar theme of the ideology of early
modern natural philosophy. *Nullius in verba* was the Royal Society of

1. See Michel Foucault, *L'Ordre du discours: Leçon inaugurale au Collège de France
prononcée le 2 décembre 1970* (Paris, 1971).
2. Ian Hacking, *The Emergence of Probability: A Philosophical Study of Early Ideas about
Probability, Induction and Statistical Inference* (Cambridge, 1975), pp. 34, 33.

This essay originally appeared in *Critical Inquiry* 18 (Winter 1992).

London's motto. Robert Boyle, doyen of the Society's experimental philosophers, tried to build up the credit of laboratory objects at the expense of untrustworthy humans. He reckoned that 'inanimate bodies . . . are not capable of prepossessions, or giving us partial informations', while 'vulgar men may be influenced by predispositions, and so many other circumstances, that they may easily give occasion to mistakes'. So an inanimate body's deeds could function as signs of some other state of affairs in a way that the stories of vulgar humans could not.[3]

Not all were so condemned. The vulgar could not be trusted to know themselves, but a privileged group was potentially capable of giving evidence. Its formation was of fundamental significance for the conduct of natural philosophy. This paper explores this collective body of reliable providers of evidence. Two notions of evidence were in play here. Hacking picks out one of these: evidence as a gesture beyond the fact to some other state of affairs. But evidence also carries the rhetorical sense of vividness, a gesture which refers to the immediate appeal of the fact itself. An early use of evidence as self-reference is to be found in Boyle's *Occasional Reflections upon Several Subjects* (1665). The book gathered together a series of essays which Boyle began in the 1640s. Drawing both on the literature of Anglican apologetics and on the courtesy literature of polite performance, Boyle set out a programme for the contemplation and transcription of commonplace and artificial experiences viewed as emblems. The metaphor of the inscription, of hieroglyphics, was fundamental. In the imagined solitude of his laboratory, Boyle was able to read and then write down the meanings of God's nature. Hence self-evidence became a primary quality of the Christian virtuoso's world, both because he could descry the meanings of nature's signs and because in so doing he fashioned his moral character. One such meditation was transcribed at Leighs Priory, the house of his pious sister Mary Rich, where he kept a glowworm in a crystal glass. Boyle's meditation prompted the thought that the creature's light had been its undoing, since otherwise it would not have been shut up. So great wit was often a burden, for 'Men allow . . . much praise, but little Rest'. But it also suggested the impossibility of confining truth: 'there are certain Truths, that have in them so much of native

---

3. Quoted in Steven Shapin and Simon Schaffer, *Leviathan and the Air Pump* (Princeton, N.J., 1985), p. 218. See also Peter Dear, '*Totius in verba:* Rhetoric and Authority in the Early Royal Society', *Isis* 76 (June 1985): 145–61.

Simon Schaffer lectures in history and philosophy at the University of Cambridge. He is the coauthor (with Steven Shapin) of *Leviathan and the Air-Pump: Hobbes, Boyle, and the Experimental Life* (1985) and coauthor (with David Gooding and Trevor Pinch) of *The Uses of Experiment: Studies in the Natural Sciences* (1989).

Light or Evidence, that . . . in spight of Prisons, it shines freely'.[4] Self-evidence emerged in company with the transition from privacy to publicity, from meditation to reputation.

Boyle helped define the difference between the false light of Wit, the delusions of the Vulgar, and the true light of Philosophy. True philosophers knew themselves. They could be trusted to tell what had happened to them. Since the Fall, men's senses had been dimmed. Experimental philosophy could restore knowledge to its prelapsarian state. This was especially apparent when natural philosophers proffered their own bodies in evidence. They often did. They blinded themselves with sunlight, gassed themselves into states of ecstasy and insensibility, and electrified their limbs into paralysis or spasm. In celebrated episodes of the 1660s, for example, Isaac Newton poked brass plates and bodkins between his eyeball and the bone to test the relation between will and vision; Arthur Coga, a 'very freakish and extravagant' Cambridge divinity student, was paid a guinea so that fellows of the Royal Society could transfuse twelve ounces of sheep's blood into his veins, and in return presented them with a Latin account of his experience.[5] The aim was to establish matters of fact in optics, physiology, pneumatics, or electricity. This enterprise of experimentation on the self raises interesting questions about the polity of natural philosophy. Experimenters' bodies were integrated into collective bodies of practitioners. They were equipped with the technologies of instrumentation, literary reportage, and social organisation to warrant reports of artificial experience.

In his account of the fortunes of the body as a site of knowledge, Foucault suggested that instead of viewing knowledge solely as the result of subjects' activity one could document the processes which invested the body and determined the forms of knowledge to which it was subject. The paper which follows can be seen as a contribution to this 'political anatomy' of experimental philosophy.[6] Here evidence is treated both as the result of certain theatrical rituals through which the person of the experimenter was integrated into public performances, and also as the result of the accreditation of experimenters' stories by the public community of natural philosophy. Bodies are treated both as the objects on which experimenters worked and as the collective to which they belonged and from

4. Robert Boyle, *Occasional Reflections upon Several Subjects with a Discourse about such kind of thoughts* (1665; Oxford, 1848), p. 310. For the background to this text, see Shapin, '"The Mind Is Its Own Place": Science and Solitude in Seventeenth-Century England', *Science in Context* 4 (Spring 1991): 143–70. For evidence as vividness, see Carlo Ginzburg, 'Montrer et citer: La Vérité de l'histoire', *Le Débat* 56 (Sept.–Oct. 1989): 43–54.

5. For Newton, see J. E. McGuire and Martin Tamny, *Certain Philosophical Questions: Newton's Trinity Notebook* (Cambridge, 1983), pp. 438, 482. For Coga, see Marjorie Hope Nicolson, *Pepys' Diary and the New Science* (Charlottesville, Va., 1965), pp. 77–82, 167–69.

6. Foucault, *Discipline and Punish: The Birth of the Prison*, trans. Alan Sheridan (1975; Harmondsworth, 1979), p. 28.

which they drew authority. These links between the privacy of the experimental trial on the individual body and the public warrant of collective authority can be clarified through the concept of *evidential context*, the proper implications of some trial.[7] Experimenters who used their own bodies tried to shift the evidential context from the body itself to some wider natural philosophical concern. The episodes considered below are Stephen Gray's efforts in the 1730s to build an electrical model of the solar system; Italian work of the 1740s to demonstrate the diffusion of medicinal fluids through electrified glass tubes; and Parisian commissions of the 1780s on animal magnetism. Evidential contexts for these trials included the motions of the planets or of universally diffused electrical and magnetic fluids. Critics who denied these implications tried to shift the evidential context back to the experimenter's body. Trials which some reckoned revealed truths about the universe were judged by others to reveal much about the movements of Gray's hands, Italian servingmen's bellies, or Charles Deslon's eyes. Stabilizing an evidential context relied on the power and authority of the collective body of experimental philosophy. Winning that body's assent was a condition of making evidence. I will close with a brief account of the fate of these trials after the transformation of the collective at the end of the *ancien régime*. If the politics of the King's body was a victim of that transformation, so too was the court culture of the corporations of natural philosophers. We see a shift from the rituals of public performance towards the figure of the disembodied scientific genius; and we see the new insistence on the importance of self-registering material devices and instrumentation. These two changes are associated with each other. The disembodiment of the scientist and the embodiment of skill within the scientific instrument are both results of the process of making evidence out of the person of the experimenter.

The Gestures of Experiment

In early modern natural philosophy, the management of the practitioner's body was involved in the establishment of his credit. Trust and honour developed through the face-to-face interactions of this patrician culture were immensely dependent on the apparently trivial and superficial marks of comportment and behaviour. Norbert Elias reminds us that the society of orders bred an 'extraordinarily sensitive feeling for the status and importance that should be attributed to a person in society on the basis of his bearing, speech, manner or appearance'. He also argues that this culture of restraint and self-control accompanied the emergence of

7. See Trevor J. Pinch, 'Towards an Analysis of Scientific Observation: The Externality and Evidential Significance of Observational Reports in Physics', *Social Studies of Science* 15 (Feb. 1985): 3–35.

the modern polity. Good society provided many public and private sites where, according to Elias, members' 'individual market value, their reputations, their prestige, in a word their personal social power . . . were exalted, abased or lost'.[8] Natural philosophers could help themselves to these codes to show how to interpret their performances. They paid much attention to the means by which experiments tried in private spaces, backstage, could be made to transit to the public settings of polite culture. Privacy was suspect and the stage was little better. Distinctions between trials and shows mattered most in a natural philosophy much addicted to histrionics. The comparison with the dress codes of the stage is close. In mid-eighteenth-century plays, public dress was customary even in allegedly private scenes, while plebeian costume was typically displaced by a more fanciful and pastoral costume even for servants and the urban poor. What seemed most intimate might be seen as public action. Humble actors could be represented as public personages.[9] Hence the force of Montesquieu's joke in *Lettres persanes* (1721) that while in a theatre 'the main action is on a platform, called the *stage*', yet in the boxes too one could see 'men and women acting out scenes together' and 'eventually everyone goes off to a room where they act a special sort of play: it begins with bows and continues with embraces. . . . The place seems to breed affection'.[10]

Thus cultural conventions did not provide unambiguous instruction for natural philosophers aiming at the production of credit. There were no universally effective means for reading bodily gesture. Early modern genteel bodies were treated as objects to be decorated in a deceitful or playful manner; judgment of others' status was persistently subverted in masquerades, streets, and courts. Terry Castle points out that 'masquerade dress demystified the sartorial code by exposing its arbitrariness'.[11] Critics of the Georgian theatre, such as the Jacobite poet and physician John Byrom and his friend the novelist and printer Samuel Richardson, were also hostile to the theatricality of experimental philosophy. Richardson condemned the lecturers' audiences as 'gay people, who, if they have white teeth, hear [the lecturer] with open mouths, though perhaps shut hearts'. Byrom also focussed on the physiognomy of performance. In 1746 he composed a vicious satire of contemporary efforts to encode the means actors should use to represent emotion, efforts which Byrom reckoned were designed to show 'the muscular Effect of Thought / In Looks and Features, Nerves and Sinews, wrought,—/ For

8. Norbert Elias, *The Court Society*, trans. Edmund Jephcott (Oxford, 1983), pp. 55, 96.

9. See Shapin, 'The House of Experiment in Seventeenth-Century England', *Isis* 79 (Sept. 1988): 373–404.

10. Montesquieu, *Persian Letters*, trans. C. J. Betts (1721; Harmondsworth, 1973), p. 79. See also Richard Sennett, *The Fall of Public Man: The Forces Eroding Public Life and Burdening the Modern Psyche with Roles It Cannot Perform* (New York, 1977), pp. 65–72, 110.

11. Terry Castle, *Masquerade and Civilization: The Carnivalesque in Eighteenth-Century English Culture and Fiction* (London, 1986), p. 57.

what? To teach his Buskin-footed Fools / How to belie their Want of Sense by Rules!'[12] Public fascination with the arts of physiognomy, especially in the version propounded by the Swiss pastor Johann Lavater, was a consequence of, and a contribution to, this trouble of recognition. Lavater's friendly satirist, the natural philosopher and dramatic critic Georg Lichtenberg, wrote pithily in the late 1760s of the link between magnetic, ideographic, and physiognomic signs: 'We can see nothing whatever of the soul unless it is visible in the expression of the countenance; one might call the faces at a large assembly of people a history of the human soul written in a kind of Chinese ideograms. As the magnet arranges iron filings, so the soul arranges around itself the facial features'.[13]

Analogies between these puzzles of public expression and the commonplaces of eighteenth-century experimental philosophy were ubiquitous. Thus Jean-Georges Noverre, a collaborator of David Garrick at Drury Lane in the 1750s, wrote that actors must 'trap the public with the force of *illusion*', while at the same time the '*truth* . . . which characterises the great Actor . . . is, if I may so express myself, the image of the electric shock: it is a fire which is rapidly communicated, which instantly embraces the spectators' imagination'.[14] There was a complex relationship between the discourse of public illusion and that of public experiment. Showmen deployed their wares, such as electric fire, in the marketplace of natural philosophy, making them evident by multiplying the places where they could appear and perform reliably. Benjamin Martin, a leading public lecturer, and many like him made such entities real by distributing the practices and instruments which could realise them. Martin promised his audience a visit 'to a Gentleman's House, who has a proper apparatus for that purpose, and will be extremely pleased with an Opportunity to satisfy your Curiosity, in a most entertaining and innocent Manner. . . . These Things may possibly salute your Eyes and Ears at the same Time as you are sitting with him at the Tea-Table'.[15] The new instrumentation of the mid-eighteenth century included the high-powered glass globes or cylinders rotated against the hand or a leather stop to excite them; the so-called

12. Samuel Richardson, *Correspondence,* ed. Anna Laetitia Barbauld, 6 vols. (London, 1804), 3:319; John Byrom, 'The Art of Acting', 11. 15–18, *The Poems of John Byrom,* ed. A. W. Ward, 2 vols. (Manchester, 1894–95), 1:261.

13. Georg Lichtenberg, *Aphorisms,* trans. and ed. R. J. Hollingdale (Harmondsworth, 1990), p. 31. For Lavater's debate with Lichtenberg, see Johann Lavater, 'Remarks on an Essay upon Physiognomy', *Essays on Physiognomy,* 7th ed. (1793–94; London, 1850), pp. 266–92.

14. Jean-Georges Noverre, *Lettres sur la danse et sur les ballets* (Lyon, 1760), pp. 285–86; my emphasis; all translations my own except where noted. See also Marian Hobson, *The Object of Art: The Theory of Illusion in Eighteenth-Century France* (Cambridge, 1982), pp. 194–97, and Leigh Woods, *Garrick Claims the Stage: Acting as Social Emblem in Eighteenth-Century England* (Westport, Conn., 1984), p. 95.

15. Benjamin Martin, *The Young Gentleman and Lady's Philosophy,* 2d ed., 2 vols. (1759; London, 1772), 1:318–19.

Leyden jar, a glass bottle filled with water which could receive the electric fluid and give off shocks when held in the hand; or the orrery, an elegant machine which displayed the motions of the heavenly bodies. Domestication of such machines in salons and schoolrooms was always difficult. Customers and students had to indulge in new bodily routines if they wished to repeat the public experimental shows. The mathematics teacher John Ryland proposed 'a living orrery, made with sixteen school-boys', substituting human bodies for the metallic models of celestial ones. 'Half an hour spent in this play once a week will in the compass of a year fix such clear and sure ideas of the solar system as they can never forget to the last hour of life'.[16] Ryland's scheme was characteristic of a culture which linked the disciplined body and the disciplined understanding. Electrical philosophers made the same point because electrical shows often involved remarkable bodily gestures. The prominent Parisian lecturer Jean Antoine Nollet described *'beatifying electricity'*, when sparks were drawn from victims' hair; the fashionable *Gentleman's Magazine* carried stories 'that a lady's finger, that her whale-bone petticoat, should send forth flashes of true lightening, and that such charming lips could set on fire a house'. 'Brilliant assemblies' were supposed to witness new electrical displays which would work only if subjects carefully followed the instructions philosophers proposed for their bodies.[17]

A range of troubles governed the ability of electrical performers to manage and replicate their public trials. First, *enculturation:* the trials were fragile and dependent on the experimenter's body. In the 'beatification' the insulated subject was to sit exactly beneath a pointed metal crown under an electrified plate. In the 'electrical Venus' a number of electrified suitors were arranged round an insulated lady: 'each person should bend a little forwards, and lean their heads towards the same shoulder so as to prevent any other parts beside the lips coming within the sphere of the electrical effluvia'. Nollet stated that in trials on the effect of electricity on perspiration one must make sure that 'the people one uses are always in the same circumstances, that they maintain a uniform diet, that they are weighed and electrified at the same hour for the same period of time'.[18] All this looked like artifice. Electrical fire would become natural only if these patterns of conduct could become tacit, and understood as self-evident. This is a familiar lesson of recent sociology of scientific knowl-

---

16. John Ryland, *An Easy Introduction to Mechanics, Geometry, Plane Trigonometry, Measuring Heights and Distances, Optics, Astronomy* (London, 1768), pp. xix, xxi–xxii.

17. Jean Antoine Nollet to E. F. Dutour, 27 Apr. 1745; quoted in J. L. Heilbron, *Electricity in the Seventeenth and Eighteenth Centuries: A Study of Early Modern Physics* (Berkeley, 1979), p. 282; [Albrecht von Haller], 'An historical account of the wonderful discoveries, made in Germany, etc. concerning Electricity', *Gentleman's Magazine* 15 (Apr. 1745): 194.

18. John Neale, *Directions for Gentlemen who have Electrical Machines* (London, 1747), p. 30; Nollet, *Recherches sur les causes particulieres des phénoménes électriques* (Paris, 1749), pp. 386–87.

edge. The repetition of a trial relies on the transmission of craft skills which cannot be completely specified in explicit instructions and must be acquired through shared culture. The purveyors of electrical experiments needed to propagate a new cultural practice in which strange bodily deportment could be learnt and then judged natural. They could not rely on formal rules alone.

Second, *calibration:* the tenets of this shared culture were challenged when replication was troubled. A reliable experiment depended on a competent performance. The criterion of such competence was just the right outcome of the trial. But often trials were staged to check what the outcome should be. When the outcome was in question, there could be no unambiguous criterion of adequate replication. This is what H. M. Collins calls the 'experimenters regress'.[19] The regress could be closed by calibrating the experimental setup. This would give an independent indication of the competence of some trial. Calibration worked because the culture supplied a similarity relation between a surrogate phenomenon and the phenomenon in question. Electrical calibrations relied on specific bodily skills. A mid-eighteenth-century electrician knew that a body was electrified if he could draw a spark via his finger. He followed the fire's path by tracing the shock through his body. Self-inspection was crucial: the Surrey divine Henry Miles noticed that if someone approached 'the electrified Person with his Hand near his Shoulder, the said Gentleman felt a very pungent Stroke on his Flesh, thro' his Coat and Waistcoat'. Miles's colleagues worked out ways of calibrating the 'Stroke' so as to judge likenesses between varying trials.[20] So the electrician's body became an instrument on which surrogate phenomena for the unknown electrical fire could be played out.

Third, *ontology:* these techniques were underwritten by electrical ontology, since it was widely agreed that electrical fluids governed the behaviour of living matter. This reflexivity is a commonplace. Instruments' credit is built up by suggesting that their structure matches that of the nature to be investigated. Ontologies support practices when users indicate that some artifice is a good model of a natural system; practices support ontologies when it is argued that this artifice gives reliable information about that system. John Desaguliers moved from instructions for rubbing the glass tube to an analogy with the effect of winds on trees, and thence to the claim that pollenation was an electrical process, and finally that the behaviour of light bodies near the tube explained how pollenation worked. Eighteenth-century electricians built models of electric fish out of Leyden jars to show that electricity functioned in the same way in the

19. H. M. Collins, *Changing Order: Replication and Induction in Scientific Practice* (London, 1985), pp. 84, 100–103.

20. Henry Miles, 'Extracts of Two Letters . . . containing several Electrical Experiments', *Philosophical Transactions* 44 (Jan.–Feb. 1746): 55.

natural and artificial worlds.[21] The spinning electric globe was analogised with the body, since both pumped vitality around the material system. William Watson, doyen of London electricians in the 1740s, reckoned that 'the Office of the Globes exactly tallies with that of the Heart in Animals', and so it could give information about the way the animal economy worked.[22] The formation of the electrical philosophy, with its talk of active fluids diffused in space and governing both animate and inanimate behaviour, depended on the formation of electrical expertise. The formation of the person of the expert relied on the formation of a new pattern of bodily behaviour.

'A Secret Motion of the Hand': Gray's Electrical Planetarium

These behaviours worked by entering and disappearing into the culture of the experimental philosophical community. Tacit skills like these become evident again, however, during moments of controversy. Protagonists brought forth hitherto unnoticed features of deportment in order to explain, or explain away, apparent differences in the outcome of trials. Making the experimenter's body visible was just to make the oddity of the experiment apparent. The orrery, in its electrical form, provides a good case. During the early 1730s Stephen Gray, in collaboration with the Cambridge don and country gentleman Granville Wheler, tried a series of experiments to communicate an 'attractive vertue' from a rubbed flint glass rod along lines made up of a range of substances, including, notoriously, the body of a schoolboy suspended from strong silk threads. Gray had resided in London at the Charterhouse since 1712, having briefly worked at the observatory in Trinity College Cambridge and with Desaguliers's public lectures in Westminster. The new experiments made his London reputation. Gray was widely credited with 'a particular knack of exciting this property by friction with his hand':[23] evidently both the knack and the property revealed by these 'surprising' trials spread to Europe from the Royal Society. They were replicated and extended in

21. See John Desaguliers, 'Some thoughts concerning Electricity', Royal Society Manuscripts Letters and Papers XVIII (2) no. 34, ff399–400 (3 June 1731); and Henry Cavendish, 'An Account of some Attempts to imitate the Effects of the Torpedo by Electricity', *Philosophical Transactions* 66, no. 1 (1776): 196–225.

22. William Watson, 'A Sequel to the Experiments and Observations tending to illustrate the Nature and Properties of Electricity', *Philosophical Transactions* 44 (Oct.–Dec. 1747): 728.

23. William Stukeley, quoted in I. Bernard Cohen, 'Neglected Sources for the Life of Stephen Gray', *Isis* 45 (May 1954): 43. For Gray, see D. H. Clark and Lesley Murdin, 'The Enigma of Stephen Gray: Astronomer and Scientist (1666–1736)', *Vistas in Astronomy* 23, no. 4 (1974): 351–404, and Michael Ben-Chaim, 'Social Mobility and Scientific Change: Stephen Gray's Contribution to Electrical Research', *British Journal for the History of Science* 23 (Mar. 1990): 3–24.

Paris by the Intendant of the Jardin du Roi, Charles Dufay, who reported back to London on his own work on the various types of electricity, on the relation between electrical repulsion and attraction, and on the behaviour of electrical shocks and sparks drawn from the body.[24]

Gray had shown the electrical virtue in a human body by suspending a boy from silk threads, exciting him, and then allowing pieces of leaf metal to jump towards the boy's body. Dufay went one better: he had himself so suspended precisely to check this phenomenon. The substitution of a proficient for innocent victim proved crucial. Dufay was able to report that near another person 'there immediately issues from my Body one or more pricking Shoots, with a crackling Noise, that causes to that Person as well as to my self, a little Pain resembling that from the sudden Prick of a Pin'.[25] In 1733 Dufay came to London and may have met the electrical workers. During 1734 Gray and Wheler studied these trials with sparks and shocks on 'animal and inanimate bodies', tried to catalogue the pains and lights they generated, and set up a trial in which a suspended boy gave an electric shock and spark to a man standing on a cake of wax or resin. This enterprise drew their attention towards the deportment of human bodies near electrified ones. Gray started using a 'pendulous thread' to estimate the electrical state of the body.[26] Public repetitions of these trials drew appreciative London audiences. Gray reported that 'I have now and then some Companys of Gentlemen and Ladys come to me to be entertained with my Electrical Experiments'.[27] Then, just before his death in February 1736, Gray found what he reckoned were remarkable affinities between electrical and planetary motions 'and he did not doubt but in a short Time to be able to astonish the World with a new Sort of *Planetarium* never before thought of, and that from these Experiments might be established a certain Theory for accounting for the Motions of the Grand *Planetarium* of the Universe'. Gray was a proficient astronomer: he had been a close collaborator of the Astronomer Royal John Flamsteed and had printed papers in the *Philosophical Transactions* on halos, eclipses, and sunspots. In any case, linkage between electricity and astronomy was a prize worth winning in the period of Newtonian hegemony.[28]

24. See Charles Dufay, 'A Letter . . . to his Grace Charles Duke of Richmond and Lennox, concerning Electricity', trans. T. S., *Philosophical Transactions* 38 (Jan.–Mar. 1734): 258–66.

25. Ibid., pp. 261–62.

26. See Stephen Gray, 'Experiments and Observations upon the Light that is produced by communicating Electrical Attraction to animal or inanimate Bodies', *Philosophical Transactions* 39 (Jan.–Mar. 1735): 16–24, and 'A Letter . . . containing some Experiments relating to Electricity', *Philosophical Transactions* 39 (Oct.–Dec. 1735): 166–70.

27. Gray, dictated to Mortimer, 14 Feb. 1736, Royal Society Manuscript Letters G.II no. 31. See also Ben-Chaim, 'Social Mobility and Scientific Change', p. 16, for other reports of visitors.

28. Cromwell Mortimer, 'An Account of some Electrical Experiments intended to be communicated to the Royal Society by Mr. Stephen Gray', *Philosophical Transactions* 39

This was what Gray and his acolyte Wheler did: in a careful ritual derived from their previous work with suspended humans, they took a circular cake of resin, excited it by 'clapping it three or four times with the Hands', rested a small iron sphere on the resin, and above the sphere suspended a small cork from a thread, 'which hold between your Finger and Thumb'. The experimenters found that the cork would revolve round the globe in the same direction as the planets round the sun, and that the cork would move elliptically if the globe were placed eccentrically on the resin. The trial would work if the iron were substituted by black marble, and if the resin were replaced by a rubbed glass hoop; without either glass or resin the orbit would be much slower and smaller. Gray said that the orbit depended on the thread being held by some animal substance: a human hand, a chicken leg, raw meat. He also suggested that the trials were closely linked with well-known peculiarities of the interaction between human bodies and will. 'If a Man resting his Elbows on his Knees, places his Hands at some small Distance from each other, they will gradually accede to each other, without any Will or Intention of the Man to bring them together; and they will again recede of themselves'.[29]

Wheler's problem was to draw attention away from his body toward the solar system. But he had to give sufficient instruction to make the planetary trials credible, and these details were unavoidably linked to the body. So he tried introducing more controlled instrumentation into his setup. An occasion to show these new protocols arose the year following Gray's death. Wheler read more reports of Dufay's work, including the news that Dufay could not replicate Gray's orbital motions. Wheler contacted the Royal Society to protest his and his colleague's originality in determining the motions of threads away from and towards electrified bodies.[30] Wheler travelled up from Kent to show the Londoners his revisions of Gray's trials with planetary bodies. In May 1737 he took over the whole of the Royal Society's library for two days. Much had changed since the previous year to make sure the orbits worked. Now the large resin cake was placed on a glass receiver a yard high. It had to be warmed in a special way the previous night and was excited by being 'struck perpendicularly all over its Surface with the Hands in parallel Directions'. At midday the following day all was ready. The doyen of London astronomical instrument-makers, George Graham, stood by to watch 'the End of Mr Wheler's Finger'. When Wheler held a small cork over an ivory ball on the resin, it

---

(Nov.–Dec. 1736): 403. See also Gray, 'His last Letter . . . concerning the Revolutions which small pendulous Bodies will, by Electricity, make round larger ones', *Philosophical Transactions* 39 (Apr.–June 1736): 220.

29. Mortimer, 'An Account of some Electrical Experiments', p. 402.

30. Granville Wheler, 'Some Electrical Experiments, chiefly regarding the Repulsive Force of Electrical Bodies', *Philosophical Transactions* 41 (Apr.–June 1739): 98.

dutifully performed its planetary orbit as required. When placed eccentrically it would describe an ellipse, and when substituted by a cut-out paper cylinder it would revolve round its own axis as well. But while the audience was satisfied with Wheler's performance, it emerged that it was crucial that he be the man holding the thread. Neither Francis Hauksbee, nor Graham, nor the Society's secretary, could get the thing to work.[31]

It is characteristic of troubled replication that the author is required to produce ever more details of the necessary accompaniments of his trial. Initially, Wheler proposed that the same man must electrify the resin and hold the cork. This explained why Wheler's servant had as little success as the London savants. 'There was something in the human Hand essential to the Experiment'.[32] In February 1738, two years after their first production, Wheler tried one last time to spell out the recipe for the electric planetarium. The ivory ball and the thread should be wet, the thread must be held in the right hand, and the back of a chair could serve as an arm rest. Under these circumstances, Wheler stated, he could get at least 220 revolutions of the cork. But as he gave these details his attention was ineluctably drawn away from the heavens towards his own body. Many trials were devoted to Wheler's posture. His calibrations were designed to set up equivalences between his own arm and hand and more mechanical devices. The influences of his hand shaking or of his pulse were excluded. At length, he supposed that as his right arm became tired it would insensibly approach his body, and thus produce the motion from west to east. A telescope stand was designed to support his arm and this conjecture. Wheler concluded that 'the Motion . . . must generally have been determined by myself; . . . a Desire of producing a Motion from West to East, was the secret Cause that determined the pendulous Body to that direction'. The key phrase was that 'no Motion sensible even to himself' was responsible. This excused Gray and Wheler of wilful deceit; it shifted the evidential context decisively towards the relation between mind and body. Wheler protested mildly against this shift, claiming that 'it may not be improper for Astronomers to consider' his experiments, and noting the similarity between Gray's electric shocks and celestial fire.[33]

Wheler's body emerged as uncontrollable and its motions insensible, but he still proffered his own testimony as that of a reliable practitioner. The strategy he adopted was characteristic of what may be called the

31. Mortimer, 'An Account of some of the Electrical Experiments made by Granville Wheler, Esq. at the Royal Society's House', *Philosophical Transactions* 41 (Apr.–June 1739): 113, 117.

32. Ibid., p. 117.

33. Wheler, 'A Letter . . . containing some Remarks on the late Stephen Gray and his Electrical Circular Experiment', *Philosophical Transactions* 41 (Apr.–June 1739): 124, 123, 125.

Cartesianism of the genteel: in polite society, members could be treated as capable of separating their disorderly bodies from the cool deliverances of their intellectual judgment. The social meaning of this division was an important theme of enlightened discourse. Hence, for example, David Hume's reflexion, based firmly in contemporary nervous physiology, that 'men of delicate taste . . . are easily to be distinguished in society by the soundness of their understanding, and the superiority of their faculties above the rest of mankind'.[34] The deployment of this superiority in the electrical trials highlighted the ambiguities in the person of the experimental author. First, it was necessary to distance the experiment from the immediate circumstances and person of the original experimenter. The social technology of collective witnessing and replicability was designed to effect this. But Wheler's own person was all too obviously the author of these trials. He conceded 'a secret motion of the hand, which the desire of success imperceptibly gave the pendulous Body'. Second, in literary technology it was important to represent oneself as an unwilling entrant onto the public stage. Wheler recalled that in summer 1733 he had wished to publish via Gray, 'through his Hands, to whom they owe their Being. . . . But, unwilling to be an Author, I deferred the Communication from time to time'. The language linking body and author through techniques of hands and body was characteristic. Polite convention demanded such displays of deference and putative withdrawal. Only thus could the credit of gentlemanly reportage be secured. The Society agreed that Wheler had made the invisible motions of his own body evident, and denied that he had provided evidence of electric astronomy.[35] As fellow and gentleman, Wheler could preserve his credit as an author while describing the unnoticed behaviour of his own body. Not everyone could do this. Hired hands and overwrought spirits were scarcely capable of acting as authors of corporeal reports. They were not widely allowed the capacity to separate their reportage from their bodily condition. This problem mattered when the powers of electrical fire began to be distributed throughout the social body to encompass the poor and the sick.

'A very delicate Choice of Persons': Nollet's Italian Tour

Medical electricity boomed during the 1740s. Throughout Europe, the managers of electrical machines carefully scrutinised the effects of powerful electrification on the bodies of paralytics, consumptives, and the poxy.

34. Hume is cited in Christopher Lawrence, 'The Nervous System and Society in the Scottish Enlightenment', in *Natural Order: Historical Studies of Scientific Culture*, ed. Barry Barnes and Shapin (London, 1979), p. 30.

35. Wheler to Benjamin Wilson, 7 Sept. 1748, British Library Manuscripts ADD 30094 f71.; Wheler, 'Some Electrical Experiments', p. 98.

The therapists had a range of resources available to them: a new technology from spring 1746 embodied in Leyden jars, together with a reasoned cosmology which supposed that animate objects were peculiarly susceptible to electric virtue and which also described electrical instruments in animate terms. Fire, shocks, and sparks both mimicked and transformed the living body. German and French professors canvassed the application of electrical fire to human vitality. English operators could draw 'Streams of fine purple Fire' from electrified trees, and tried to accelerate the flow of blood after a phlebotomy by electrification. Making electric fire vital was part of a campaign which infringed on the boundaries between physic, experimental philosophy, and theatre. The *Gentleman's Magazine* listed a number of experiments 'for a gentleman to perform with plants and animals', including the acceleration of vegetable growth, the restoration of health through the electrification of bedding and apparel, and 'whether by putting a tube into the anus of any animal, the electric vapour mayn't be propagated through . . . the whole animal system?' Electrical fire was realised in the mid-1740s as a universally diffused fluid, whose activities crossed the interests of all sections of polite society.[36]

Since electric fire was so potent, its ownership was a contested prize worth winning. But since it was so universal, the authority over its effects was hard to secure. Electrical philosophers set out to enclose the community which could reliably testify to its effects and yet to multiply those humans who could experience it. Nollet, formerly Dufay's assistant, was a protagonist in this process. His *Essai sur l'électricité des corps,* published in summer 1746, summarised the relationship between the motions of electricity and the behaviour of the new spinning globes.[37] Nollet reckoned that affluent and effluent streams of matter entering and leaving bodies could account for the differences between types of electricity and the behaviour of sparks and shocks when these streams collided. Nollet staged shows at court and in the city to realise these streams and to transmit electric influence through docile bodies, including ranks of soldiers or Carthusian monks. The shocks from the Leyden jar were calibrated through their appalling effects: Johann Winckler, classics professor at Leipzig, reported to London about his and his wife's headaches, fevers, and nosebleeds resulting from a Leyden shock. Winckler also designed a strong electrical machine and used a leather pad, rather than his own hand, to electrify it. Neither Nollet nor the Royal Society credited Winckler's sufferings, preferring to attend to their own, but they used his

36. John Browning, 'Part of a Letter . . . concerning the Effect of Electricity on Vegetables', *Philosophical Transactions* 44 (Jan.–Feb. 1747): 375; Daniel Stephenson, 'Electrical Experiments on Animals, Vegetables, *etc.* Proposed', *Gentleman's Magazine* 17 (Mar. 1747): 141.

37. See Nollet, 'Observations sur quelques nouveaux phénoménes d'électricité', *Mémoires de l'Académie Royale des Sciences* (1746): 1–23.

FIG. 1.—The scene of electric medicine. From Johann Gottlieb Schaeffer, *Die electrische Medicin* (Regensburg, 1766), frontispiece. Reproduced by Whipple Library, Department of History and Philosophy of Science, University of Cambridge.

equipment.[38] 'I do not wish to be taken for someone who has shown you the way to the next world', Nollet explained to the Genevan natural philosopher Jean Jallabert, so 'I have found a means of making the disturbance felt safely by dividing it amongst several persons who hold each other by the hand' (*TE*, pp. 139, 143). Theatricality was as useful as safety. He analogised between his own displays and those of Nature: 'the marvels which we deal with at present on our scale are small imitations of those great effects which terrify us—all depends on the same mechanism'.[39]

Electricity was part of Nollet's stock-in-trade. His possession of material technology helped him control the market. He built and commissioned new electric globes, sold them to his colleagues or to those gentry who attended his lectures, and thus disseminated a standardised repertoire of instrumentation.[40] He also managed those persons who could be allowed to give evidence. Monks and soldiers became objects of display, but the community of reliable electrical philosophers needed more careful definition. This pair of strategies, material and social, came into play in Nollet's work on electrotherapy. In spring 1746, soon after getting a Leyden jar working in Paris, Nollet collaborated with a couple of surgeons to electrify paralytics with little success. He was soon attacked by the medical establishment. The surgeon Antoine Louis wrote that medical knowledge 'of the animal economy, the nature of disease and the electric power' demonstrated that electric fire 'was far from curing, and could only harm, those poor sick who have the willingness to subject themselves to his trials'. Thus, the surgeon concluded, Nollet's work 'can lay down no law for the art of healing'.[41] This was a major challenge to Nollet's rights to control the electricity of the body. He mobilised ministerial support to quash the medics, and between winter 1747 and spring 1748 he decided to develop a new set of resources to reinforce these rights. One resource involved marrying his doctrine of the electrical effluent stream to English and

38. See Johann Winckler, 'Letter . . . concerning the Effects of Electricity upon Himself and his Wife', *Philosophical Transactions* 44 (May–June 1746): 211–12. Nollet's response is in Isaac Benguigui, *Théories électriques du XVIIIᵉ siècle: Correspondance Nollet–Jallabert* (Geneva, 1984), p. 173; hereafter abbreviated *TE*. Winckler's 'heated imagination' is discussed in Watson, 'An Account of Professor Winkler's Experiments', *Philosophical Transactions* 47 (1751–52): 241; hereafter abbreviated 'APW'. For Winckler's new machine and his trials see Willem Dirk Hackmann, *Electricity from Glass: The History of the Frictional Electrical Machine, 1600–1850* (Alphen aan den Rijn, 1978), pp. 73–82, 94–96. For Nollet's system see Heilbron, *Electricity in the Seventeenth and Eighteenth Centuries*, pp. 280–88, and Roderick Weir Home, *The Effluvial Theory of Electricity* (New York, 1981), pp. 103–45.

39. Quoted in Jean Torlais, *L'Abbé Nollet: Un Physicien au siècle des lumières* (Paris, 1954), p. 74.

40. See Maurice Daumas, *Scientific Instruments of the Seventeenth and Eighteenth Centuries and Their Makers*, trans. Mary Holbrook (1972; London, 1989), p. 219, and Hackmann, *Electricity from Glass*, pp. 114–15.

41. Antoine Louis, *Observations sur l'électricité* (Paris, 1747), pp. 81, 138.

FIG. 2.—Nollet's experiments on the electrification of water jets, plants, and animals. From Jean Antoine Nollet, *Recherches sur les causes particuliéres des phénoménes électriques* (Paris, 1749), p. 402. Reproduced by Whipple Library, Department of History and Philosophy of Science, University of Cambridge.

German work on the electrification of capillary flow. In phlebotomy and water-jets, experimenters reported that electrification accelerated and enlivened fluid motion. Since Nollet 'consider'd all organized Bodies as Assemblages of capillary Tubes', he reckoned that these results demonstrated the ways electric fire could accelerate vegetable growth and animal perspiration and 'remove Obstructions from the Pores, or . . . scour them of any noxious Humours which they may happen to contain'.[42]

Nollet bolstered his claims by staging a new trial: during April 1748 he got permission from the war minister to take over a room in the Invalides for an electrical programme on paralytics. He consulted his colleague Jallabert for detailed instructions on the right way to manage the show: Had paralytics allegedly cured electrically in Geneva been on a diet? How many Leyden shocks were needed? Despite his preparations, Nollet's Invalides performance remained indecisive. He had recourse to a repertoire of important caveats about such experiments. They were too local: Genevans might respond differently from Parisians. They were too emotionally striking: impressionable victims would not be appropriate witnesses to electricity's effects. Nollet commented that in Geneva Jallabert had randomly chosen 'common folk' whose pulses would obviously race under the ministrations of the experimenter: 'were one to expose natural philosophers to this experiment, we are convinced that electrification would not alter their pulse in any way' (*TE*, p. 62). Nollet confirmed this conjecture by electrifying one of his surgical colleagues with no effect. He pointed out the significance of the extreme localisation of different effects, and the difference between unreliable plebs and calm natural philosophers.[43]

The problems of localisation and social status came to the fore in a remarkable episode in medical electricity during 1748. The Royal Society learnt from Winckler that Venetian experimenters, led by the advocate Gianfrancesco Pivati, had managed to convey the vapours of several medicines into patients' bodies by coating the inside of a sealed glass tube with a substance such as Peruvian balsam, opium, or a purgative. When the tubes were electrified by friction, a patient holding the tube by hand would imbibe the effluvium of the substance in question. Alternatively, linen soaked in the drug could be wrapped round an iron bar. When the bar was electrified, the patient, gripping a ball chained to the bar, would benefit from the effluvium transmitted via the bar. Winckler reported that sulphur or cinnamon could be made to bathe his room, and that 'any person, who was perfectly ignorant of what was doing, would immedi-

42. Nollet, 'Part of a Letter . . . concerning Electricity', *Philosophical Transactions* 45 (Feb.–Mar. 1748): 189, 194. See also Nollet, *Recherches sur les causes particulieres des phénomènes électriques*, pp. 323–29, 366–72.

43. See Nollet, *Recherches sur les causes particulieres des phénomènes électriques*, pp. 406–13.

ately smell the balsam therein. The man, who was electrified, said, that his tea next morning had a finer taste than usual' ('APW', p. 233). The analogy with Nollet's earlier work on the acceleration of perspiration was close. There were confirmed replications in Turin by the anatomist Giovanni Battista Bianchi. Furthermore, remarkable success with the electrification of paralytics was reported by the Bolognese natural philosopher Giovangiuseppe Veratti. The Londoners judged these reports 'extravagant and whimsical', and would not yet authorise them. However, since human bodies conducted electric effluvia, the trial with medicated tubes, 'romantic as it may seem, should not be absolutely condemned without a fair Tryal'.[44]

During the rest of the year, both Watson in London and Nollet in Paris strove to replicate these trials, with no success. Nollet recognised that his own authority was in question; he had been cited by the Italians. The trials seemed to promise major medical reform: 'we have heard of nothing less than . . . purging all Sorts of Persons in a manner of all others the most proper to avoid the Repugnance and Disgust we naturally have to medical Potions'.[45] Even the pox could apparently be cured if the tube were coated with mercury. Nollet observed that Parisian ladies would be especially interested in a therapy 'so easy to manage and fitted to their delicacy' (*TE*, p. 183). The working of his own electrical devices was at issue, since were glass permeable to such fluids then its behaviour in the Leyden jar would also be called into question. Most important, the problems of trust and locality were raised here. 'Respectable Witnesses' in Italy seemed to give good testimony, but Nollet wanted to know 'what fate has reserved these miracles to Italy?'[46] So in spring 1749 he decided to cross the Alps to see 'succeed, in the Hands of those who had said they had, those Phaenomena in Electricity' ('E', p. 374).

Nollet's Italian tour was a remarkable exercise in the political geography of calibration. This calibration required that Nollet make it evident that his body counted as the equivalent of an Italian one, and that his testimony could count instead of those of the experimenters themselves. His strategy was to insist on personal management of the Italians' instruments; choice of Nollet's own candidates for trial, including himself; and demands for explicit recipes for replication. Such visits to the original sites of challenging phenomena are often destructive. They are to be distinguished from the genteel visits to which Gray, Watson, or Nollet himself were willingly subject. The distinction between trying and showing exper-

44. Henry Baker, 'A Letter . . . concerning several Medical Experiments of Electricity', *Philosophical Transactions* 45 (Feb.–Mar. 1748): 274, 275.

45. Nollet, 'An Examination of certain Phaenomena in Electricity, published in Italy', *Philosophical Transactions* 46 (Jan.–Apr. 1750): 370; hereafter abbreviated 'E'.

46. Nollet, 'Expériences et observations faites en différens endroits en Italie', *Histoire et mémoires de l'Académie Royale des Sciences* (1749): 444–88.

iments is fundamental in the establishment of workable matters of fact. When the boundary between privacy and the public is breached, authors may have recourse to a host of features which explain away failures during absurdly public visitations.[47] Thus Nollet confronted conventions of privacy and of gesture in his inspection of Italian sites during the summer of 1749. The vocabulary of the Grand Tour was important here. The knowing ultramontane savant would see through catchpenny tourist attractions. Nollet told the English virtuosi about Vesuvius, Neapolitan grottoes, and the glow of the Venetian lagoon. In most cases, Nollet insinuated, Italian wonders proved to be 'temporary Shadows': just as the lagoon glowed because of insects, and the grottoes' airs were explicable through conventional pneumatics, so the Italian medicated tubes were powerful solely on 'any one, upon whom the Love of the Marvellous can make a victorious Impression' ('E', pp. 383, 397; see also p. 369).[48] Nollet's demystifying tour thus involved the construction of three ideal roles: the witness, the subject, and the practitioner. Each must be invulnerable to the marvellous; each must separate mind from body.

Nollet set out to make himself the perfect witness to the electric cures. The task was hard. He certainly took a sceptical attitude with him: 'I really fear that I have nothing to purge here except imagination'. Despite his protestations that reliable electrical medication would have proved the reality of his favourite effluent matter, and thus that he had no interest in demolishing Italian claims, the Italians themselves judged otherwise. They reported that Nollet was 'a Man so prejudiced against Facts, that the strongest could not make [him] believe'. When Nollet arrived in Venice in August 1749, Pivati summoned a large assembly of notables who, so Nollet believed, were 'called together to be an Evidence of my Conviction' ('E', p. 384). In response, Nollet fashioned himself as an impartial judge. The dilemma he faced was to seem a member competent enough to interpret electrical work, and yet a stranger invulnerable to prejudice. This was part of his strategy for the management of the proper electrical subject. At Turin, in May 1749, he put this strategy into effect. He proffered himself to Bianchi's electrical tubes, initially without issue, and then again some days later, when, so Nollet reported, 'I was troubled with an Indigestion, and felt Pains of the Colic'. The Turinese alleged that Nollet had been electrically purged but would not admit it. Nollet replied that 'during my whole Life I have had a weak Stomach', and that Piedmontese food had disagreed with him ('E', p. 381). Nollet's diet was

47. For breaches of laboratory privacy, see Mary Jo Nye, 'N-rays: An Episode in the History and Psychology of Science', *Historical Studies in the Physical Sciences* 11, pt. 1 (1980): 125–56. For visitation, see Collins and Pinch, *Frames of Meaning: The Social Construction of Extraordinary Science* (London, 1982).

48. For the rhetoric of the tour, see Percy G. Adams, *Travelers and Travel Liars 1660–1800* (Berkeley, 1962).

one problem; the testimony of plebs was another. Amongst the Turin subjects were two servants, one hired by Nollet, the other employed by
Bianchi. Both men reported that the electric tubes had worked, but Nollet
discovered that one had previously taken strong medicine, and failed to
report it, while the other had boasted of his trial all over town. Lack of
candour and love of the marvellous, Nollet reckoned, were endemic
amongst such menials:

> This, I say, made me very delicate in the Choice of the Persons who I
> was desirous should be admitted to our Experiments. I declared that I
> was not willing to receive thereto either Children, Servants, or People
> of the lower Class; but only that reasonable People should be admit-
> ted, and of an Age sufficient to leave nothing to be feared of the
> Truth of what they might depose. ['E', p. 377]

Nollet repeatedly limited those who could give evidence of the state
of their own bodies. They could not even be sick, since invalids were 'prejudiced perhaps by too great Hope, and possessed by a kind of Enthusiasm'
('E', p. 383). When Veratti told him that electrical trials had been performed on 'his servants, that is a valet and two servingwomen', Nollet
sternly counselled that these trials must be repeated 'on people of a solid
brain, incapable of fear, and who would have nothing to gain from whatever happened to them' (*TE*, p. 178). Nollet recognised that his 'extreme
Circumspection' limited the possible scope of the evidence the Italians
might present him. The Italians responded that such conditions simply
prevented replication. This set up a potentially vicious circle, akin to the
experimenters regress, for while Nollet reckoned that no competent trial
could involve the sick or the poor, the Italians insisted that under these
conditions the electrified tubes could not be expected to work. Pivati
stated that 'now there was too much Company; that it was too hot, and, in
consequence, that the Electricity would be too weak for it' ('E', p. 385). In
order to break this regress, Nollet tried yet a third strategy, alongside
those of making himself authoritative and excluding the invalid. This was
a judgment on the persons of the experimenters themselves. He told his
correspondents that Pivati was 'a man completely new in physics, unaccustomed to perform experiments, rather devoted to the marvellous and
believing on very light grounds'. He was 'an ignoramus and a charlatan'
(*TE*, pp. 177, 180). Nollet also mobilised reports from a friendly Turin
physician to confirm this character assassination. Furthermore, Nollet
alleged, the Italians simply used bad instruments, 'a glass Tube, *which was
cracked from one End to the other*', or weak electrical machines ('E', p. 392).
Thus a range of strategies was available to the French critic: he could
explain away any effects on his own person; he could deny the legitimacy
of any female or servant testimony; he could damage the gentlemanly
standing of the experimenter; finally, he could explain the cures as simple

instances of electrification, conformable to his own theory, rather than evidence of the strange transmission of medical odours. This last strategy, for example, was his chosen ruse in Bologna, where he credited Veratti's honour just so as to make the Bolognese cures count as support for the Nollet system of efflux.

Nollet's reports from Italy back to the bodies of natural philosophers in London and Paris were crucial resources in making medical tubes count as evidence of popular enthusiasm and sober electricity. When the great Montpellier physician François Boissier de Sauvages reported successful electrifications of cases of sciatica and gout, Nollet baldly stated that 'I am always afraid when I see such extraordinary facts multiplied on people who are poor, and who will know that they will be helped so long as they have fixed upon them the attention of men of place' (*TE*, p. 186). Similarly, the Londoners rapidly set out to scotch all remaining evidence for electrotherapy through medical tubes. Winckler's testimony, and similar stories from Prague, were hauled before the Royal Society. The Leipzig professor tried sending his own tubes to London to get replication going there. Indeed, a minor trade started in medicated tubes. Henry Miles picked up some of Pivati's tubes from a Mediterranean merchant; they worked 'as well as any of ours'.[49] Winckler gave very detailed recipes to accompany his present. Only silk or woollen cloth would work to rub the tube, while the witness's nose must be at most two inches away. Watson tried these instruments before the president, vice-president, and secretary of the Society. They were joined by one of Winckler's friends, and by 'a person well-skilled in these odours', presumably a perfumer ('APW', p. 238). John Canton and William Watson could get nothing to work. So although, as they conceded, 'every gentleman has a right to perform his experiments in his own way', it seemed implausible to the Londoners that 'our noses are not so good as those of the gentlemen at Leipsic' ('APW', pp. 239, 240). Watson drew the appropriate moral. He straightforwardly reinforced the contrast between 'Prejudice' and 'Credulity'—the property of plebeians, the sick, womenfolk, and Italians—and good judgment, reserved to the 'gentlemen' of the Royal Society and Nollet, their 'worthy Brother'.[50]

The Italian episode both supported and dramatised key conventions to which the body of electrical philosophers subscribed. Nollet's tour helped clarify the status of natural philosophical gentlemen and exclude from the republic of learning those incapable of giving evidence of their

49. Miles, letter to Wilson, 29 Nov. 1750, British Library Manuscripts ADD 30094 f76.

50. Watson, 'A Letter . . . declaring that he as well as many others have not been able to make Odours pass thro' Glass by means of Electricity', *Philosophical Transactions* 46 (Jan.–Apr. 1750): 349, 350. Compare Watson, 'An Account of Dr. Bohadsch's Treatise', *Philosophical Transactions* 47 (1751–52): 345–51.

own bodily condition. These conventions were realised in such episodes, and their propagation depended on making the tacit explicit. Furthermore, different groups within the social body set out to make trials serve different evidential purposes. It was thus, for example, that an aspiring candidate for admission to this body, Benjamin Franklin, learnt of the Italian episode when he began work on electricity in the late 1740s. Franklin was told of these trials by his London correspondent Peter Collinson, who reported Nollet's failure to discover the 'Knack' the Italians seemed to possess. Franklin swiftly built these results into his own account of the Leyden jar. It was a fundamental premise of his story that glass be impermeable to electricity, and he interpreted the results of Nollet's tour as proving this truth. In a series of clever trials, reported to Watson in London, Franklin reinforced the lesson that since cinnamon could not be smelt when inside a sealed electrified tube, glass was really impermeable and thus objects like the Leyden jar must work by being earthed. This was a further move in the evidential context of the medical tubes: what had initially counted as evidence for the motion of topical medicines now testified to the ultimate source of electrical fluid and became a sign of the effects of the power of overwrought imagination.[51]

'We are all really Puppets': Mesmerism on Trial

Contemporaries held that the later decades of the eighteenth century witnessed a 'moral epidemic' fuelled by the imagination. The waspish Paris journalist Louis-Sébastien Mercier used just the same phrase as that of Nollet: 'the love of the marvellous always seduces us'. He diagnosed a disease of the public body. What an isolated individual would promptly reject, the collective would rapidly endorse. 'Such is the people: they don't believe that they can be mistaken as a body'.[52] The solution was to form public groups in which individuals could escape the plague of unreason. Nothing was self-evidently illusory—it had to be demonstrated to be so. The most striking episode was that surrounding the French commissions of enquiry into animal magnetism. Franklin had discussed animal magnetic cures in 1779, and in early 1784 he stated that although such therapy was a case of 'a disposition in mankind to deceive themselves', 'delusion may however in some cases be of use', since animal magnetism

51. See Peter Collinson to Benjamin Franklin, 25 Apr. 1750, and Franklin to Cadwallader Colden, 28 June 1750, *The Papers of Benjamin Franklin*, ed. L. W. Labaree, William B. Willcox, and Claude A. Lopez, 27 vols. (New Haven, Conn., 1959–   ), 3:476, 483. Watson discussed Franklin's work in his 'Account of Mr. Benjamin Franklin's Treatise', *Philosophical Transactions* 47 (1751–52): 202–11.

52. Louis-Sébastien Mercier, *Le Tableau de Paris*, ed. Jeffry Kaplow (1781–88; Paris, 1979), p. 268.

would prevent hypochondriacs from overdoses.[53] In March 1784, Franklin was named by the minister of the Department of Paris, Breteuil, to serve alongside notables such as Antoine Lavoisier and Jean-Sylvain Bailly, representing the Academy of Sciences, and Jean Darcet and Joseph Guillotin from the medical faculty. A second commission, drawn from the Royal Society of Medicine, was also instructed to investigate the astonishingly fashionable animal magnetic therapies developed by the Viennese physician Franz Mesmer, who had reached Paris six years earlier.[54] The specific target of the group's studies was a middle-aged medical practitioner, Charles Deslon, Mesmer's best-known and most controversial interpreter. Deslon's treatment highlights the social construction of subjects' capacity to treat their own bodies as observable and separable from their minds.

Mesmerists' careers were dominated by the politics of the body, both private and public. The pre-Revolutionary conjuncture exacerbated and illuminated the tensions in bodily repertoire provided by Enlightenment culture. Dorinda Outram demonstrates that politics was construed in terms of the way bodies were seen, and which bodies were to be visible. Such powers, as Nollet showed in Italy, would judge those who could not be made fit members of the community of discourse. The enlightened savants formed corporations, such as the Academy of Sciences or the Royal Society of Medicine, which investigated and invigilated both public belief and public welfare. In a setting rather prone to *grands peurs,* fears of child-stealing or cometary collision, of rabies or of grain shortages, it was important to show that the reason of these tribunals would in principle govern the irrationality of the subordinate. Experimenters and medics began to insist that experts could penetrate the interior of the body and uncover the truth of disease and possession. Electrical trials gave evidence of the real seat of illusion. But these experts celebrated the self-possessed bourgeois as the ideal type of the bearer of knowledge. These features of the natural philosophical predicament were not easily reconciled. Self-possession, with its implication that the body was invulnerable to external coercion or internal and rebellious passion, sat uneasily with the newly intrusive gaze of the medical and experimental savant.[55] A pair of roles

53. Franklin, quoted in Denis I. Duveen and Herbert S. Klickstein, 'Benjamin Franklin and Antoine Laurent Lavoisier: Joint Investigations', *Annals of Science* 11 (Dec. 1955): 288.

54. For mesmerism, see Robert Darnton, *Mesmerism and the End of the Enlightenment in France* (Cambridge, Mass., 1968), pp. 47–81, and Charles Coulston Gillispie, *Science and Polity in France at the End of the Old Regime* (Princeton, N.J., 1980), pp. 261–84. Mesmer's works are gathered in Robert Amadou, *Le Magnétisme animal* (Paris, 1971).

55. See Dorinda Outram, *The Body and the French Revolution: Sex, Class and Political Culture* (New Haven, Conn., 1989), pp. 41–67; Michel Vovelle, *La Mentalité révolutionnaire: Societé et mentalités sous la Revolution française* (Paris, 1985), pp. 31–64; and Arlette Farge and Jacques Ravel, *The Rules of Rebellion: Child Abduction in Paris in 1750*, trans. Claudia Mieville (1988; Cambridge, 1991).

characterised the episodes in which these public bodies set out to manage and regulate animal magnetism: the charlatan and the marionette. The commissioners represented animal magnetisers as quacks, thus placing Deslon within the rich bestiary of charlatanry against which medical vigilance was so strenuously directed. In animal magnetic séances 'individuals in a numerous assembly are more subjected to their senses, and less capable of submitting to the dictates of reason. . . . It has been usual to forbid numerous assemblies in seditious towns, as a means of stopping a contagion so easily communicated. Every where example acts upon the moral part of our frame, mechanical imitation upon the physical part'.[56] Mechanical imitation turned subjects into puppets. According to the commissioners, the mesmeric milieu and the therapy subverted the necessary separation of reason from bodily passion: 'In subduing the imagination by . . . the confidence and enthusiasm inspired by magnificent promises, it is possible to exalt the tone of sensible and nervous fibres, and afterwards to direct, by the application of the hands, their impulse towards certain organs' (*R*, p. 10). The savant's self was identified with his rationality. So mesmerists were depriving citizens of self-possession. The charge went further: it was alleged that any magnetiser who believed that his work was effective was himself under the influence of some irrational power; it was also suggested that patients who entered a state of crisis in mesmeric séances were being twitched hither and thither not by genuine forces but by their own imagination. The commissioners set out to spot the strings which were pulling these puppets around: 'They are entirely under the government of the person who distributes the magnetic virtue' (*R*, p. 27). All this was dependent on, and contrasted with, the self-control of the enquiring savant who could detect the concealed mechanism by putting himself in evidence.

The story gained its plausibility precisely because automata and natural philosophical showmanship were intimately connected with quackery on Paris streets. Puppet shows were highly popular throughout the century both in theatres and at the great fairs. After the decline of the Paris fairs in the 1770s, marionettes and automata spread to the boulevards. These machines were judged to be dangerous by churchmen fighting idolatry or by the police waging war against obscenity and satire. Puppet shows and displays of lifelike automata infringed on social boundaries

---

56. *Report of Dr. Benjamin Franklin, and other Commissioners, charged by the King of France, with the examination of the Animal Magnetism, as now practised at Paris*, trans. William Godwin (London, 1785), pp. 92–94; hereafter abbreviated *R*; Godwin is identified as the translator in a letter from Benjamin Vaughan to Franklin, Oct. 1784, cited in Duveen and Klickstein, 'Benjamin Franklin and Antoine Laurent Lavoisier: Joint Investigations', p. 300. See also Jean-Claude Beaune, 'The Classical Age of Automata: An Impressionistic Survey from the Sixteenth to the Nineteenth Century', trans. Ian Patterson, in *Fragments for a History of the Human Body*, ed. Michel Feher, Ramona Naddaff, and Nadia Tazi, 3 vols. (New York, 1989), 1:430–80.

because of their political use and because they claimed academic warrant. The artifices which duplicated life helped efface, or challenge, the difference between polite and popular cultures. The shows also challenged contemporary notions of status and evidence. As Geoffrey Sutton has argued, some showmen, such as the electrical philosophers Le Dru and Mauduyt, were accepted as licit by the public bodies of medicine, court, and philosophy. They might be trusted by communities at some conjunctures, rejected at others. The same therapies could generate widely different evidence. Credibility hinged on judgments of membership and cultural standing. In the case of animal magnetism, this mutually supportive set of judgments was peculiarly difficult to sustain. It was hard to display mesmerists' victims as deluded peasants. They included the Parisian elite. It was hard to deny the bodily existence of magnetic fluids. Such substances were the commonplaces of established natural philosophy. And it was hard to mark as outsiders well-known members of the medical profession.[57]

A revealing comment on these problems was provided during 1784 by the eminent physician Jean-Jacques Paulet. Paulet was a veteran of several campaigns on behalf of the Royal Society of Medicine. In his vitriolic pamphlet, *L'Antimagnétisme*, Paulet composed a spoof on a mesmerist catechism, outlining the protocols of the ideal séance, including the individual treatment in which the magnetiser would sit facing the patient, 'his back to the north', and run his thumbs over the patient's stomach and ribs while fixing his gaze on the eyes.[58] The effect could be multiplied by connecting patients in chains, or by seating them in a circle around the *baquet*, a barrel of magnetized water with iron rods protruding from it. Paulet noted that mesmerists reckoned that trees could be magnetised by placing iron rods in front of them, and, worryingly, that anyone could magnetise themselves. He wanted to display these practices as alien and antique. But he reckoned that animal magnetism, 'at the moment the most fashionable toy' (*A*, p. 5), had become modish and commonplace. So rather than portray it as straightforwardly distant from polite culture, as were peasant medicines or popular illusions, he demonstrated that mesmerism was now all too intimately ensconced within the Parisian social body:

57. See Robert M. Isherwood, *Farce and Fantasy: Popular Entertainment in Eighteenth–Century Paris* (Oxford, 1986), pp. 43–44, 48–51, and Darnton, *Mesmerism and the End of the Enlightenment in France*, pp. 24–29. Geoffrey Sutton ('Electric Medicine and Mesmerism', *Isis* 72 [Sept. 1981]: 389) notes: 'the very procedures that had convinced at least half a dozen doctors several months earlier [in 1783] were ruled ineffective and fraudulent [in 1784]'.

58. Jean-Jacques Paulet, *L'Antimagnétisme* (London, 1784), p. 115; hereafter abbreviated *A*. Compare Antoine Lavoisier, 'Sur le magnétisme animal', in *Oeuvres de Lavoisier*, 6 vols. (Paris, 1865), 3:506; hereafter abbreviated 'MA'.

> In Paris there exist societies where enormous sums are spent to deal
> with these sciences. It is held that in nature there exist powers, invisi-
> ble spirits, sylphs, which can be made available to men; that most of
> the phenomena of nature, that our actions depend on hidden springs,
> on an order of unknown beings; . . . that fate, indeed destiny is deter-
> mined by particular genies who guide us without our knowledge,
> without our being able to see the strings which hold us; at last that in
> this lower world we are all like real puppets, ignorant and utterly
> blind slaves. They strongly impress in everyone's head that it is time
> to enlighten oneself, that man must enjoy his rights, feel the shock of
> invisible forces, or at least make out the hand which guides him.
> [*A*, pp. 3–4]

Paulet's strategy was highly nuanced. References to puppetry linked mesmerism with the boulevards. Talk of sylphs and genies connected it to
'research into Antiquity' (*A*, p. 3). The search for the invisible springs, and
the demand for human rights, made mesmerism into dangerous subversion. Finally, the 'invisible spirits' which haunted the séances were to be
revealed as the highly visible magnetisers, the prime movers of this threatening charade. Animal magnetism was a threat because it challenged
important boundaries in enlightened culture. Lavoisier stated simply that
'the government could not be indifferent about a question of this kind
which interests the health and life of its citizens'. Were each citizen able to
magnetize himself then 'we would have to shut the schools, change the system of instruction, and destroy those bodies regarded till now as the de-
positaries of medical knowledge' ('MA', 3:514).

These exercises in beating the bounds of propriety and property
provided the milieu of Deslon's career. He sponsored Mesmer's most
important autobiographical text and published a manifesto for the new
therapy. He tried to get influential medics to witness successful cures,
and several reports were presented to the Paris medical faculty. He
insisted above all on his own experience: Mesmer had cured Deslon of
headaches and stomach pains, while acknowledging that the young
Frenchman's body was so far gone that no complete cure would ever be
possible. The strategy was completely unsuccessful. The faculty ruled
that he should cease propagandising, and he was suspended for a year.
Successive efforts in front of the faculty were equally disastrous, ending
in expulsion. Deslon tried lobbying at court, but Mesmer's behaviour
alienated all potential patrons. Indeed, Deslon's relationship with his
erstwhile master was notoriously stormy. Mesmer withdrew from Paris to
the Ardennes, where, in company with radical allies, he concocted plans
for a joint stock company and masonic lodge based on mesmeric teaching. Deslon was excluded from these deliberations, publicly broke with
the Mesmer circle, and established his own clinic. He lobbied Versailles
once again for recognition of the virtues of animal magnetism, and it

FIG. 3.—The commissioners, led by Benjamin Franklin, put the Mesmerists to flight. From *Le Magnétisme dévoulé*, reproduced in Robert Darnton, *Mesmerism and the End of the Enlightenment in France* (Cambridge, Mass., 1968), p. 63.

was his demand which prompted the establishment of the commissions in spring 1784.[59]

Between April and July 1784 the commissioners visited Deslon's clinic and, since Franklin was ill with gout at his suburban house at Passy, Deslon also took his machinery there. Establishing power means governing space. Lavoisier wanted a secure boundary between 'the effects of a real agent and those of imagination' ('MA', 3:509). This was the line between experimental space and Deslon's mesmeric world. Condorcet, the Academy's secretary, set out the same conditions on replication as those Nollet had promulgated: 'if he wishes to convince persons without prejudice, let him open his cabinet to natural philosophers, and there, without the sick, and with no witnesses save those who really wish to be there, let him perform very simple and convincing experiments'.[60] This strategy needed control over the mesmeric milieu. The commissioners could then make themselves subjects, witnesses, and experimenters. The careful protocols of Deslon's theatre ruled out this role play. Hand gestures, music, bodily contact, all mattered. So after a few visits the commissioners shifted to private space, their space, by excluding Deslon's clients and staging their own trials (see *R*, pp. 24–27). Mesmerism damaged moral order. A secret report by Commissioner Bailly detailed the astoundingly erotic orientation of mesmeric bodies. Deslon conceded to the police that such deportment might prompt immorality, hence his insistence that mesmerism should be the prerogative of the faculty. The relations of class and gender were stressed to bring out the relations of power and to control these dangers. Lavoisier and his colleagues noted that 'patients of rank . . . might be displeased with the enquiries of the commissioners; the very act of watching them might appear a nuisance' (*R*, p. 29). Furthermore, since the magnetisers were men, they would always be the puppets of the female patient: 'whatever the state of the illness, it does not deprive us of our sex, it does not entirely allow us to escape from the other's power'. The commissioners must be on guard against imperceptible, irresistible deference and passion. Just as mesmerised women 'could give no account of what they experience, they are ignorant of the state in which they are', so the savant must make a space where he could manage the potent imaginations of the séance, lest he become a mute and female victim.[61]

The commissioners could now calibrate mesmerism by insinuating that there should be a similarity relation between animal and other mag-

59. See Charles Deslon, *Observations sur le magnétisme animal* (London, 1780), pp. 16–22. See also Gillispie, *Science and Polity in France at the End of the Old Regime*, pp. 272–81.

60. Condorcet, 'Raisons qui m'ont empêché jusqu'ici de croire au magnétisme animal', in Darnton, *Mesmerism and the End of the Enlightenment in France*, pp. 191–92.

61. Jean-Sylvain Bailly, 'Rapport secret sur le mésmerisme, ou magnétisme animal', in Duveen and Klickstein, 'Benjamin Franklin and Antoine Lavoisier—Documentation', *Annals of Science* 13 (Mar. 1957): 43, 44.

netisms. Iron needles did not respond to the *baquet*. Solar microscopes and thermometers revealed that witnesses' magnetic fluids were sweat and heat. The commissioners damned 'the public process, where there is neither time nor opportunity of making decisive experiments', and where 'they might themselves have been led into error. It was necessary to have liberty to insulate the effects in order to distinguish the causes' (*R*, p. 99). When, each week, they visited Deslon and were magnetised, they could now explain away the effects as 'the result of perpetual and ordinary variations in the state of their health' (*R*, p. 42). Commissioners used their bodies like other instruments, to calibrate and then destroy the magnetic character of the experimentally mastered events. Another circle was set up: Deslon said the commissioners were ignoring his well-evidenced cures, while the commissioners answered that these reports could not be processed experimentally. The regress was broken because the commissioners had power. They ran the show and defined the available explanatory resources. Deslon and the commissioners agreed that the difference in staging explained the difference in outcome. They disagreed about the legitimacy, and the evidential context, of this difference. The commissioners said that in 'the public processes . . . nature [was] wrought up to the highest pitch', but in private experiments 'the body [was] free from pain, and the mind from anxiety, nature preserving her ordinary course' (*R*, p. 43). Deslon simply denied that the experiments were natural. He said the experimenters could not reliably report their own state, that the magnetic touch must be insensible and that the milieu of the *baquet* mattered much.[62] The commissioners answered that if animal magnetism were physical, then close self-scrutiny would be unnecessary; if it were not, then such examination might be deceitful. 'If the magnetism were a real and operative cause, there was no need that it should be made an object of thought, in order to [perceive] its action and [manifest] itself. It ought . . . to render itself perceptible to a mind that should even be distracted from it by design' (*R*, p. 40). This showed how to select subjects according to Nollet's rules. They 'selected from the polite world such as could not be suspected of sinister views, and whose understanding made them capable of inquiring into and giving a faithful account of their sensations' (*R*, p. 46). Any pleb would be distracted and corrupted by the collective gaze of expert savants. So three types of subject were made up: the commissioners, who carefully avoided self-absorption; patricians, who could give credible witness; and 'persons really diseased', selected 'out of the lower class', on whom tricks were played and whose own reports could rarely be trusted (*R*, p. 44).

The commissioners' dramas made mesmerism incorporeal by using the conventions of moral order. Lavoisier wrote the script: Deslon must be

---

62. See Deslon, *Supplément aux deux rapports de mm. les commissaires* (Amsterdam, 1784), pp. 6–7; hereafter abbreviated *S*.

silent; each commissioner must learn and transcribe his part; the precise words and gestures each must make was specified. 'Each of the sick will be led into a place in the house where they are kept in view, each in a separate room; one may be placed in the salon' ('MA', 3:511). Neither a scrofulous child nor a young convulsive gave evidence of mesmeric effect. The commissioners decided that this showed the 'sound understanding' of the former and the 'idiotism' of the latter (R, p. 53). A blindfolded servant and a learned medic were tricked into giving magnetic responses when untreated, and no response when magnetised. In Franklin's garden, a blindfolded boy was paraded through a cherry grove of which just one tree had been magnetised. When he started sweating near the wrong tree, Deslon retorted that all the trees 'participated of the magnetism' (R, p. 68). The commissioners impersonated Deslon and successfully deluded some patients. Thus it was that a planned deception revealed the truth: 'it must be ascribed to the power of communication possessed by the numerous emotions' (R, p. 72). This 'power' became the reality of the commissioners' trials: 'The imagination is that active and terrible power, by which are operated the astonishing effects, that have excited so much attention to the public process' (R, p. 98). While deconstructing animal magnetism, they reconstructed a new force which penetrated the whole social body. They mobilised much evidence for this principle of imagination, located it in the eyes, 'the source of a very high degree of power', and the uterus, whose 'empire and extensive influence . . . over the animal economy is well known' (R, p. 77). As Thomas Laqueur puts it, in Enlightenment discourses of sexuality, 'a notion of order and coherence is replaced by corporeal wiring'.[63] Bailly indicated that the 'mobility' of women's nerves made them a startling whole: 'In touching them in one part, one might say that one simultaneously touches them everywhere. . . . Women . . . are like sounding strings perfectly tuned in unison'. But the power of imitative imagination was 'imposed upon as a law', and could not be confined to the female. Franklin even worried that the reports of imagination's power would damage faith in true scriptural miracles. Thus the experimenters put their own persons in question. They reported their invulnerability to a power they reckoned was omnipotent. Their claim to represent the natural state of body and mind was compromised by their own claims to an exceptionally robust self-possession.[64]

This moral and political puzzle made the commissioners' reports rather vulnerable. Mesmer denied them by denying that Deslon was an adequate representative of animal magnetism. The commissioners

63. Thomas Laqueur, *Making Sex: Body and Gender from the Greeks to Freud* (Cambridge, Mass., 1990), p. 154.

64. Bailly, 'Rapport secret sur le mésmerisme', p. 43; Franklin to William Temple Franklin, 25 Aug. 1784, *The Writings of Benjamin Franklin*, ed. Albert Henry Smith, 10 vols. (New York, 1905–7), 9:268.

answered that they saw no difference between the two therapies. Deslon's strategy was to reprint long lists of autobiographies from his successful patients, to insist that 'to judge if Magnetism exists, and if it is useful, one need not be an academician or physician' (*S*, p. 1), and, most important, to point out that the commissioners seemed invulnerable to the imagination they alleged affected everyone: 'To understand the Commissioners, imagination would almost be our normal state. If that is so, they should have told us how they made sure of themselves when they were judging Magnetism' (*S*, p. 9). Deslon had a good resource to use to make this point. Unlike other commissioners, the naturalist Antoine-Louis Jussieu had tried to magnetise patients himself, and had succeeded in at least four cases. He attributed his own success to an interaction between animal heat and animal electricity. But Deslon reckoned otherwise and printed the testimony of one of Jussieu's subjects, the military instructor Robert. Robert said that he could not deny the fact of animal magnetism. He had indeed responded when Jussieu began to magnetise him: 'If this is the effect of imagination, there is nothing positive in this world'. And who, 'in an enlightened age', could possibly be terrifed by Deslon's *baquet*, 'unless they had the imaginative powers of a Don Quixote?' (*S*, pp. 54–55).[65]

Mesmeric practices remained credible, if mutable, resources. They survived Mesmer's flight to Swabia and Deslon's death in 1786 while under a magnetic trance. In company with the new enterprises of animal electricity and pneumatics, they made good tools for Jacobin natural philosophy. While mid-eighteenth-century experimenters staged polite shows to dramatise active principles in all bodies, in the 1780s and 1790s radicals drew more attention away from the divine author of these principles to their own persons. Galvanism, pneumatics, and mesmerism were used by philosophical materialists to efface distinctions between mind and body.[66] In his 1785 translation of the commissioners' report, the radical journalist William Godwin stressed that while Deslon was wrong, his story, like any branch of ecclesiastical history, was the 'record of our errors' (*R*, p. xviii). Error was metaphysically and politically crucial because it revealed the powers of the unfettered mind: 'in this field the soul has room enough to expand herself, to display all her boundless faculties' (*R*, pp. xvii–xviii). Writing for the London community of radicals and dissenting Whigs, Godwin stressed that such strategies could yield matters of fact about human reason.

---

65. See Antoine-Louis Jussieu, 'Rapport de l'un des commissaires chargés par le roi de l'examen du magnétisme animal', in Alexandre Bertrand, *Du magnétisme animal en France* (Paris, 1826), pp. 151–206.

66. See Darnton, *Mesmerism and the End of the Enlightenment in France*, pp. 50, 106–25.

Conclusion: Embodiment and Disembodiment in Science

When natural philosophers made inferences from their own bodies to matters of fact, they needed a stable and carefully enclosed community to warrant their actions. These communities were integrated into the culture of the *ancien régime*. While Franklin worried that the social destruction of animal magnetism might also entail damage to faith in miracles, Voltaire satirised the stringency of these privileged cultural formations: 'For a miracle to be well established one would wish it to be performed in the presence of the Académie des Sciences of Paris, or the Royal Society of London, and the faculty of medicine, supported by a detachment of the regiment of guards to control the crowd of people whose indiscretion might prevent the operation of the miracle'.[67] The indiscretions of the people and the collapse of credibility of these institutions during the Revolutionary epoch made it increasingly difficult to stage safely such experimental performances. Foucault has summarised this transformation from the power of the classical age to that of modern discipline: 'traditionally, power was what was seen, what was shown. . . . In discipline, it is the subjects who have to be seen'.[68] This was especially true when experimenters made their own bodies into stage props. In France, the great festivals of the Revolutionary regimes involved this inversion of the gaze, as the state surveyed its own people. Critics reckoned this showed the devilish puppetry of Jacobin tyranny.[69] And just as anti-Jacobins saw Revolutionary rituals as bestial, so they judged the clubs of savants as dangerous coteries of materialist conspiracy. In the 1790s the English Jacobin Thomas Beddoes set up a pneumatic institute in Bristol, and hired Humphry Davy to administer powerful gases to his clients. This materialist pneumatics demonstrated the corporeality of the mind.[70] Auto-experimentation was crucial. Davy's *Researches* (1800) was stocked with autobiographical reports of the inhalation of the gas. Davy 'lost all connection with external things. . . . I existed in a world of newly connected and newly modified ideas. I theorised—I imagined that I made discoveries'. The poet Robert Southey wrote that 'Davy has actually invented a new pleasure for which language has no name'. The unspeakable relationship between the evidence of imagination and the power of a material gas proved too vulnerable a resource at a time of fierce conservative reaction. It was not obvious that the reduction of

67. Voltaire, *Philosophical Dictionary*, trans. and ed. Theodore Besterman (1764; Harmondsworth, 1972), p. 316.

68. Foucault, *Discipline and Punish*, p. 187.

69. See Mona Ozouf, *La Fête révolutionnaire 1789–1799* (Paris, 1976), p. 244.

70. See Dorothy A. Stansfield and Ronald G. Stansfield, 'Dr Thomas Beddoes and James Watt: Preparatory Work 1794–96 for the Bristol Pneumatic Institute', *Medical History* 30 (1986): 276–302.

the experimenter's body to the status of a marionette could carry conviction.[71]

Auto-experimentation precisely required that the experimenter become a puppet master over himself. In Britain, the theme was frequently canvassed in Regency culture. The perfect emblem of the experimenter's body as inanimate subject was surely Jeremy Bentham's notorious 'Auto-icon' (1832), an embalmed corpse designed to propagate confidence both in anatomical bequests and in its possessor's genius. The alternative ethos was expressed in *Frankenstein* (1818), where Mary Shelley, responding both to the materialism of her father William Godwin and to the chemical galvanism touted by Davy, brilliantly explored the tensions inherent in the natural philosophical divorce of moral and physical forces.[72] Elsewhere, romantic writers judged that the materialist version of the philosophic puppeteer was hopelessly compromised. Instead, they forged a more direct and dynamic relationship between external nature and the powers of mind. Here the key new role was that of the genius. Enlightenment philosophers had typically denied the status of genius to the natural philosopher, reckoning that since it was replicable and reasonable, experiment could not be the prerogative of the isolated and elevated individual. But the scientific genius, such as Davy or his German rival the chemical galvanist Johann Ritter, became a romantic commonplace. For such men, autobiography was a preferred means of self-expression, and self-experimentation a favoured research strategy. Hence the significance of the romantic debate on the role of self-consciousness. Heinrich von Kleist's 'Über das Marionettentheater', published in his Berlin newspaper in December 1810, can be read as an intervention in this exchange. In several of his texts from this period, Kleist displayed a grasp of contemporary galvanism, and his dialogue confronts the problem of self-knowledge in the setting of a puppet show. The lesson is that self-consciousness destroys effective performance. The perfect machine and the all-knowing, immaterial deity are both capable of grace, but the savant stands trapped by his own sense of self: 'since we have eaten of the tree of knowledge. . . . We must make the journey around the world to see if maybe there is still some opening from behind'.[73] In the same sense,

71. Humphry Davy, *Researches, Chemical and Philosophical, chiefly concerning Nitrous Oxide*, vol. 3 of *The Collected Works of Sir Humphry Davy*, ed. John Davy (London, 1839), p. 289. Southey is quoted in E. B. Smith, 'A Note on Humphry Davy's Experiments on the Respiration of Nitrous Oxide and Other Gases', in *Science and the Sons of Genius: Studies on Humphry Davy*, ed. Sophie Forgan (London, 1980), p. 233.

72. For Bentham, see Ruth Richardson, *Death, Dissection and the Destitute* (London, 1987), pp. 159–61. On Mary Shelley, see Anne K. Mellor, '*Frankenstein*: A Feminist Critique of Science', in *One Culture: Essays on Science and Literature*, ed. George Levine (Madison, Wis., 1987), pp. 287–312.

73. Heinrich von Kleist, 'On the Marionette Theater', trans. Roman Paska, in *Fragments for a History of the Human Body*, 1:417.

Coleridge argued in his *Biographia Literaria* (1817) that the true genius was defined by his unself-consciousness. A genius's 'sensibility is excited by any other cause more powerfully, than by its own personal interests'. So here was a new role for the natural philosopher, in which the management of nature and of the body would be guaranteed by the *disembodiment* of the intellectual. For Coleridge, for example, this process of disembodiment dominated successful performance. It explained the superiority of theatre, in which 'a species of Animal Magnetism' allowed the audience to '*live* for the time within the dilated sphere of [the performer's] intellectual Being'.[74]

Two anecdotes of romantic auto-experimentation illustrate how disembodiment worked in the interpretation of nature. In 1806 Ritter staged a series of trials in Munich with the philosophers Schelling and von Baader to investigate the powers of a Tyrolese diviner, Campetti. Ritter reckoned that such bodies were exceptionally sensitive detectors of a power he called *Siderismus*, the interaction between the motions of the human body and the cosmos. To make *Siderismus* credible, however, he reckoned it was necessary to replace his body with a machine, just as he had done in the 1790s when he successfully removed any animal from his galvanic circuits. He hoped 'to reproduce these phenomena with devices that do not incorporate anything living and then without requiring any exceptionally sensitive instrument that depends . . . in particular on human nerves'.[75] Ritter's trials on Lichtenberg figures, made by discharging electricity through glass or across metal, were just such devices: 'My aim was to rediscover, or else to find, the original or natural script by means of electricity'.[76] Coleridge, a careful reader of Ritter and of Davy, shared the view that nature was a system of signs, and that investigation of this semiotics could be achieved as part of self-understanding. So, for example, he agreed with Godwin that mesmerism taught much about the power of imagination. Magnetic effects could not be material, since magnetisers never perceived their favoured luminous fluid, but they were real, for they dramatised the potency of excited nerves. In a remarkable letter written at the same time as *Biographia Literaria*, he recalled the

74. Samuel Taylor Coleridge, *Biographia Literaria or Biographical Sketches of My Literary Life and Opinions*, 2 vols., ed. James Engell and W. Jackson Bate, vol. 7 of *The Collected Works of Samuel Taylor Coleridge* (1817; Princeton, N.J., 1983), 1:43, 2:239.

75. Quoted in Keld Nielsen, 'Another Kind of Light: The Work of T. J. Seebeck and His Collaboration with Goethe: Part 1', *Historical Studies in the Physical and Biological Sciences* 20, no. 1 (1989): 133. For electric writing, see Johann Ritter, *Fragmente aus dem Nachlasse eines jungen Physikers*, 2 vols. (Heidelberg, 1810), 2:230. The semiotic theory is discussed in Walter Benjamin, *The Origin of German Tragic Drama*, trans. John Osborne (1963; London, 1977), p. 214.

76. Quoted in Walter Wetzels, *Johann Wilhelm Ritter: Physik im Wirkungsfeld der deutschen Romantik* (Berlin, 1973), pp. 52–53.

aftermath of a drunken party in order to demonstrate the relationship between mesmeric illusion and the act of writing:

> I have myself once seen (i.e. appeared to see) my own body under the Bedcloaths flashing silver Light from whatever part I prest it—and the same proceed from the tips of my fingers. I have thus written, as it were, my name, greek words, cyphers, etc. on my Thigh: and instantly seen them together with the Thigh in brilliant Letters of silver Light. . . . I deduced from the Phaenomenon the existence of an imitative sympathy in the nerves, so that those of the Eye copied instantaneously the impressions made on those of the Limbs.[77]

Coleridge worked hard to read bodily experience as neurotic. The Cartesianism of the genteel gave way to the disembodiment of the intellectual. Romantics held that the world was structured in dialogue with the mind: Ritter's view was that 'man's anatomy and that of the body of the Earth and that of the greater human body are a unity'.[78] Thus disembodiment was one solution to the crisis of authority over the experimental body. But as Coleridge's bodily inscription and Ritter's work with *Siderismus* also showed, there was another solution to the problem of making the body yield evidence. This was to replace humans with machines. New experimental regimes were designed to distract attention from the person of the experimenter by making instruments into inscription devices and by automating the experimental process. New scientific disciplines needed disciplined instrumental techniques and docile bodies. Self-registration became a key goal for modern instrumental design. The nineteenth-century body would be increasingly subject to the vigilance of instruments which were supposed to record and transcribe its real processes.[79] These two formations, self-registrative technology and disembodied genius, may seem completely antagonistic. Yet they were produced together. The lesson of the story of self-evidence may therefore be that there is an intimate relationship between the trust placed in the evidence of self-registering scientific instrumentation and the moral authority of the scientific intellectual.

77. Coleridge to Boosey, May 1817, in John Livingston Lowes, *The Road to Xanadu: A Study in the Ways of the Imagination* (1927; London, 1978), p. 546. See also Trevor H. Levere, 'Coleridge and the Human Sciences: Anthropology, Phrenology and Mesmerism', in *Science, Pseudo-Science and Society*, ed. Marsha P. Hanen, Margaret J. Osler, and Robert G. Weyant (Waterloo, Ont., 1980), pp. 171–92.

78. Ritter, *Fragmente aus dem Nachlasse eines jungen Physikers*, 2:37.

79. For a very good account of Davy's path from pneumatic auto-experimentation to galvanic experimental discipline, see Jan Golinski, 'Humphry Davy and the "Lever of Experiment"', in *Experimental Inquiries: Historical, Philosophical and Social Studies of Experimentation in Science*, ed. H. E. Le Grand (Dordrecht, 1990), pp. 99–136.

Massaging the Evidence

Lawrence Rothfield

In "Self Evidence" (pp. 56–91), Simon Schaffer shows how one might begin to fill a large gap in the well-known story of how modern science, with its strict evidential criteria, emerges in the wake of the epistemological break associated with the name of Descartes. Schaffer takes the outlines of the story for granted, assuming that the Cartesian dream of depersonalizing evidence—the dream of purifying the subject/object relationship by removing bodies, personality, subjectivity, sensibility, and sexuality from experimental situations—has come true, at least since around 1820. But between Descartes's time and the early nineteenth century, Schaffer insists, there lies a murky, and for the most part understudied, transitional phase: a period not of science but of "natural philosophy" (p. 56), in which, far from being disembodied geniuses or pure cogitos, experimenters form part of the experiments upon which they report. Experiment itself, the process through which evidence is made, is in this period not yet completely a matter of "controls" that are objectified and manifested in "self-registering" experimental instruments (p. 59). Rather, eighteenth-century experiment occurs in what Schaffer calls "rituals of public performance" (p. 59) that produce evidence only with the active participation of persons: witnesses, subjects, and experimenters. Within this incompletely disembodied experimental framework, Schaffer shows, one particular group of persons, the natural philosophers, tries to privilege itself as "capable of giving evidence" (p. 57) by emphasizing "displays of deference [towards the audience of natural philosophers] and putative withdrawal" from both experiment and report (p. 68). Whether as witnesses of experiments, subjects in experiments, or experimenters, natural philosophers aim to "distance the experiment from the immediate circumstances and person[s]" involved in it (p. 68). Schaffer strictly distinguishes this distancing, however, from the a priori, absolute disembodiment he takes as characteristic of a later, fully Cartesian science, in which the person is taken out of the experimental loop altogether and isolated as a pure mind contemplating an experimental apparatus. Distancing, in contrast, is a social gesture performed in public, a display or demonstration modeled on the politeness associated with being a gentleman, and invoked ideologically against the vulgar interestedness or lack of self-control associated with what Schaffer describes as "hired hands and overwrought spirits" (p. 68), especially those of women and foreigners.

Science, then, is still in this period a cultural practice with very little autonomy relative to the larger culture's class, gender, and ethnic codes. But Schaffer is less concerned about natural philosophy's lack of autonomy than he is in describing the intricacies of the relations that link natural philosophy, as a practice, with its culture. He shows how what one might call a mutual bricolage obtains between natural philosophy and other discourses that also aim at controlling and explaining the mysteries of staged public demonstrations. While natural philosophers rely on codes of proper, genteel behavior to support their claims to provide trustworthy evidence, theorists of acting and physiognomic analysis support *their* claims about evidence by borrowing analogies from natural philosophy.

Such networks of analogy to some extent prop up natural philosophy, but they also pose a danger to it—the danger that the authority natural philosophers seek for their evidence might instead be disseminated or leaked into the public on one hand and contaminated internally on the other by social codes that, far from buttressing science, might make it appear suspect, a parlor trick or confidence game rather than a trial of truth. As Schaffer's examples show, however, the threat of dissemination is limited in two distinct ways.

(1) By *discursive requirements* that experimental replication imposes on analogies: instruments that produce evidence must be calibrated; skills that perform and interpret experiments must be encultured; and structures inherent in evidence must be ontologized. Each of these requirements named by Schaffer—to calibrate, to enculture, to ontologize—amounts to a demand that analogies be transformed into self-

---

Lawrence Rothfield is associate professor of English at the University of Chicago and author of *Vital Signs: Medical Realism in Nineteenth-Century Fiction* (1992). He is currently working on a book about professionalism and its discontents.

evident, replicable identities or abandoned.[1] To be a natural philosopher is to submit to this demand, even if submitting means disqualifying the evidence provided by one's own body. Schaffer's first example shows how powerful such discursive imperatives can be: a scientist who tries and fails to replicate his results by substituting other people's bodies for his own in the experimental setup can nonetheless maintain his authority as a natural philosopher, his capacity to give evidence, precisely because he has tried to replicate in the first place.[2]

(2) By the *stability of the ideological codes* that scientists use to define themselves and others: insofar as codes define an Englishman or French-man as less credulous than an Italian, a man as less suggestible than a woman, a gentleman as more disinterested than a servant or patient, sci-entists can invoke these distinctions strategically to qualify and disqualify the selves who give, produce, and witness evidence. Schaffer's second ex-ample shows how ideological distinctions can be used to disqualify wit-nesses and experimenter as well as the experimented-on subject. Jean Antoine Nollet, a French electrotherapist, destroys an Italian's claim to have conveyed medicine from a sealed, electrified glass tube into the bod-ies of patients and servants. Nollet disqualifies the Italian's evidence by impugning the patients and servants who serve as experimental subjects (they have a self-interest in being treated by doctors or in pleasing their masters), the witnesses (they are credulous, local yokels willing to enter-tain marvels), and the experimenter (he is an ignoramus).

In distinguishing, as I have just done, between discursive and ideological factors at play in the qualifications of evidence and evidence-givers, I am putting a different spin on Schaffer's evidence than he himself does. Or, rather, Schaffer seems to spin his evidence in two irrec-oncilable ways. I would argue, in fact, that his narrative about evidence is wracked by an unresolved structural tension between two incommensu-rable kinds of analysis. One analytics is genealogical, focusing on the un-expected ways in which discursive strategies come together in a given conjuncture to create original and often unstable knowledges (electro-therapy, animal magnetism, electro-astronomy), "new bodily routines" (p. 62), strange and wonderful pieces of evidence, peculiar and multiple

1. Foucault has argued that this demand that knowledge take shape in terms of identi-ties and differences constitutes the classical episteme (in which presumably natural philoso-phy would have its place). See Michel Foucault, *The Order of Things: An Archaeology of the Human Sciences*, trans. pub. (New York, 1973), pp. 46–211.

2. I think Schaffer is wrong to emphasize Granville Wheler's gentlemanliness as the basis for his maintaining his status as natural philosopher. While Wheler is indeed deferen-tial in witnessing the experiments he performs and subjects himself and others to, it seems clear that what satisfies the community is not that he speaks like a gentleman but that he accepts the need to calibrate. The fact that Wheler is willing to try to calibrate the experi-ment using his own servant implies that what is at stake for him, as for the other scientists in this instance, is the body understood not as a class identity but as an experimental in-strument.

subject-positions. The other analytics is dialectical and teleological, focusing on the ways in which various ideological oppositions—between the polite and the vulgar, the genteel and the disorderly, the mechanical and the human, the interested and the disinterested—can be seen as crude, insufficient versions of a fundamental distinction between the embodied object and the disembodied Cartesian subject, a distinction ultimately realized through the elliptical workings of revolutions both scientific and social.

In "Self Evidence," Schaffer's dialectical tendencies get the better of his genealogical ones, with the consequence that those evidentiary cruxes that might be most interestingly unassimilable to the Cartesian teleology end up being not disqualified or repressed but marginalized, left hanging in relation to the overall story that Schaffer wants to continue to tell. I will briefly point to one aspect of "evidencing" in which I think this happens repeatedly and then conclude with a few questions of a more general cast about the prospects a more rigorously genealogical analysis of evidence might open up.

Schaffer analyzes three instances of natural philosophy in action—Granville Wheler's debunking of his own claims linking electricity with planetary motion, Nollet's debunking of the Italian Gianfrancesco Pivati's electrotherapeutic claims, and the French commission's debunking of Charles Deslon's claims on behalf of animal magnetism—and emphasizes that in each case the same fundamental process of disqualification occurs. But the discursive status of what gets disqualified receives relatively short shrift in Schaffer's story. When Nollet dismisses Pivati and his colleagues as ignoramuses and believers in marvels, he signals not just the destruction of Pivati's evidence but the need to understand it as anthropological evidence of an epistemologically archaic scientific attitude; Carlo Ginzburg or Lorraine Daston might be able to tell us more about this attitude and its conceptualization by nonbelievers. Wheler, on the other hand, disqualifies his own body in quite different terms. He confesses that "'the secret Cause'" (p. 67) that gave rise to the effect he interpreted as evidence was "'a secret motion of the hand, which the desire of success imperceptibly gave the pendulous Body'" (p. 68). The effect, then, is itself now seen as evidence not for a natural philosophical force but a psychological one. One could easily go further, following Eve Sedgwick's lead, to place Wheler's particular self-conceptualization of desire—as impelling the hand to engage in secret motions addressed to a pendulous body—within a history of sexuality not restricted to the sciences (a history perhaps with its own literary correlative to Jane Austen: Wheler's hand reminded me of the end of *Sentimental Journey* and tempted me to write an essay that might be titled "Laurence Sterne and the Fondled Boy").

The serious point here is that evidence never is simply disqualified, never disappears as evidence without a trace. Insofar as it is spoken of, it must be evidence of something. As Schaffer himself points out in passing,

Wheler's odd bodily condition could be accounted for by nervous physiology. But Schaffer then goes on to quote David Hume rather than the physiologists, and then only to qualify Wheler's taste, not his experience of desire, which has its own evidentiary qualifications. Disqualification, in short, is less a matter of negating, of saying this evidence does not count, than of shunting it to other sciences, or at least to other forms of knowledge capable of comprehending the rejected material. Schaffer himself seems to recognize this in relation to his third example: "while deconstructing animal magnetism," he declares, "they [the commissioners] reconstructed a new force," the "principle of imagination" (p. 86). Not physiology or anthropology but psychology here serves as the accredited partner to experimental science. It would be wrong, I think, to argue that a developmental history of the sciences of embodiment parallel and subsidiary to the history of experimental science is involved here: nervous physiology does not found a psychology of the imagination, nor is the evidence allocated to psychology necessarily less secure as evidence than the evidence that remains "physical." The sciences of embodiment undergo their own nonteleological mutations just as the physical sciences do. A general history of evidence would want to study the processes by which an experimental body (call it Humean) once evaluated for evidence of its delicacy and secret motions comes to be displaced by a body (call it Coleridgean or, better, Hegelian) evaluated for evidence of its excitability and power.

Let me try to pose in general terms the questions that I think Schaffer's various examples, and his narrating of these examples, raise for me:

(1) What other discursive constraints besides calibration, enculturation, and ontology are involved in generating scientific evidence and qualifying subjects during the 1700s? Discursive constraints operate not only in the performance of an experiment but in the performance of its report, not least in the genres required for representing scientific experience. At the beginning of his article, for instance, Schaffer points out how Boyle's writing involves both meditation and what Schaffer calls "reputation" (p. 58),[3] and he ends by emphasizing that autobiographical reports become central to scientific research during the romantic period. What are the rhetorical forms governing the reports that are produced during the era of natural philosophy, and what pressure do they put on evidence?

(2) How do the strategies used to qualify and disqualify evidence in natural philosophy compare with the strategies used to help extort evidence in other fields of knowledge and power during this period? What is the status of confession in natural philosophy, for example, in compari-

---

3. This sounds strikingly similar to Foucault's remarks about Descartes's deployment of both meditation and demonstration. See Foucault, "My Body, This Paper, This Fire," trans. Geoff Bennington, *Oxford Literary Review* 4 (Autumn 1979): 9–28.

son with the crucial role it plays during this period in establishing evidence in medicine, law, and sexual science?

(3) If natural philosophy is only one of many scientific practices during the eighteenth century, what is its status vis-à-vis other sciences (rather than disqualified sciences and cultural practices)? What jurisdictional disputes, ceding of epistemological ground, or consolidation with other sciences are in play during a given evidentiary crisis?

(4) If we cannot really speak of natural philosophy as a "stable" community "integrated into the culture of the *ancien régime*" (p. 88) (since there is no such thing as either a unified culture or a singular community, but multiple relations of power and knowledge), what sorts of affiliations can justifiably be hypothesized between scientific, literary, and philosophical domains?

Gestures in Question

Simon Schaffer

In his generous remarks on 'Self Evidence', Lawrence Rothfield gives a rather wide-ranging story in which my arguments might find a home. It is a story of modernisation. The separation of objective judgment from subjective bias, dimly envisioned by early modern metaphysics but postponed in the eighteenth-century murk, was at last realised through the heroism of early Victorian experimental technology. As his remarks on the history of the sciences of embodiment suggest, Rothfield may not subscribe to this story. I certainly do not. Narratives of modernisation are asymmetric between a past of error, where cultural forces allegedly distorted knowledge, and our own time, where the truth of nature stands revealed. 'Self Evidence' recognises the important seventeenth-century proclamations of the new role of the evidence of things and the end of textual or personal authority. The social history of the sciences suggests that trust played, and continues to play, a central role in the assessment and management of knowledge claims. How did a culture which routinely denied its reliance on the authority of the person giving evidence nevertheless establish the worth of testimony about states of affairs in nature? This is the question which dominates my study of eighteenth-century natural philosophers' work. The term *natural philosophy* does not refer to an 'understudied, transitional phase', as Rothfield implies (p. 92), but to the regime of knowledge production which lasted until the end of the classical age. This regime has been more studied by historians of science than any other.

'Self Evidence' stresses the role of bodily gestures and material practices in making facts and the contingency of cultural repertoires from which the indispensable conventions of trust are drawn. Rothfield is right that the paper refuses to distinguish between 'discursive and ideological factors' (p. 94) and right to identify its concern with the genealogy of unexpected, unstable knowledges. But the story does not end in the early nineteenth century with a breathtaking escape from culture and a permanently secure emplacement of natural knowledge. The authorial role of the genius and the material technology of self-registering devices were just as culturally contingent as the gestures of the natural philosophical body within the community of baroque experiment. Self-experimentation, for example, was not new nor, as we shall see, did it cease in the early nineteenth century. Instead, the enterprise of self-experiment is used here to dramatise the historically specific processes through which the person of the natural philosopher could be defined as a reliable site of evidence.

Thus the paper asks about the resources which helped make a human body into an experimentally informative device. In his own important account of tales of Victorian detection, Rothfield defines the 'intellectual technology' of the investigative enterprise, including the assumptions which specify the enquiry's object, 'the embodied person treated as an individuated body'. He also insists that this definition be accompanied by an account of the genealogy and powers of these practices.[1] I agree. I ask about the intellectual technology of experiment and trace how projects such as galvanism and mesmerism both exploited and transformed conventions of polite behaviour and licit experiment. In so doing, the origins of representative power are called into question. Who could represent their own limbs' motions? Rothfield reckons that what mattered in the debate about the electric planetarium, for example, was 'the body understood not as a class identity but as an experimental instrument' (p. 94 n. 2). In Augustan Britain, to understand the body as an experimental instrument was precisely to make a class judgment. Granville Wheler's servants could not be authors of reports about their own bodies. He was their representative. He conceded that he had, initially, failed to produce reliably stable orbits with the electrified body. Maybe the aged Stephen Gray had erred. 'I began to doubt of the fact, imagining that the Involuntary Tremors of the old man gave a projectile force'. Gray's status helped resolve these doubts. 'When I considered the Probity, Caution and Experience of Mr Gray I could not help fearing I did

1. Lawrence Rothfield, *Vital Signs: Medical Realism in Nineteenth-Century Fiction* (Princeton, N.J., 1992), p. 139; hereafter abbreviated *VS*.

Simon Schaffer lectures in history and philosophy at the University of Cambridge. He is the coauthor (with Steven Shapin) of *Leviathan and the Air-Pump: Hobbes, Boyle, and the Experimental* (1985) and coauthor (with David Gooding and Trevor Pinch) of *The Uses of Experiment: Studies in the Natural Sciences* (1989).

him injustice in my suspitions'. In 1732 Charles Dufay announced that live and dead animals responded differently to electricity. Wheler could not produce such a difference. He did not challenge Dufay's reports, 'as we believed [him] to be a man of great honour and worth'. Instead, he recalled that Frenchmen liked their meat well hung and Parisian animals long dead might not be so easy to electrify.[2] Probity, caution, honour, and worth were attributes with a specific cultural geography. So were the matters of fact produced with these resources.

Rothfield is right to demand that these episodes be accompanied by a more general account of the fate of rival forms of knowledge and contested conventions of evidence. The excitable bodies of Charles Deslon's mesmerised subjects, so suspect in the milieux of the Parisian academies, reappeared with greater energy and even more potent social dangers in early Victorian Britain and the spiritualist world of the century's end. As Alison Winter has shown, the mesmeric world of the 1830s and 1840s was not self-evidently marginal to orthodox science. Marginalisation was always a careful and painful accomplishment worked out in a complex of social spaces—theatres, hospital wards, drawing rooms, laboratories— where evidence hinged on rival conventions of trust and bodily comportment, of gender and law.[3] A pamphlet of 1842, satirising prurient attacks on London's leading mesmerist John Elliotson, is mockingly entitled 'An eye witness: *a full discovery* of the strange practices of *Dr Elliotson* On the bodies of his *female patients!* at his house . . . , with all the secret experiments *he makes upon them,* and the *Curious Postures they are put into while sitting or standing, when awake or asleep'.*[4] Rothfield's demands for a general history of evidence encompassing both the irritable and the energetic body are met in Winter's account with a careful history of the behaviour of credible figures such as Harriet Martineau, proffering her own bodily experiences in the mesmeric sickroom as evidence of the power of the female invalid, or Elizabeth O'Key, whose mesmeric trances in Elliotson's hospital wards drew on her own experiences as an Evangelical visionary. Representing one's own body could empower one's self. Self-possession remained a central political issue. Hence the rhetorical question posed at the London Mesmeric Infirmary in 1855 to women in the audience: 'Are you aware of the powers you possess by a few patient waves of your hands?'[5] The key to this project is the problem of the power and locale of evidence.

2. Granville Wheler to Cromwell Mortimer, 19 Apr. 1736, Royal Society Library Manuscript LBC 22, p. 279, and Wheler to Benjamin Wilson, 7 Sept. 1748, British Library Manuscripts ADD 30094 f 71.

3. See Alison Winter, *'The Island of Mesmeria': The Politics of Mesmerism in Early Victorian Britain* (Ph.D. thesis, Cambridge University, 1992).

4. Logie Barrow, *Independent Spirits: Spiritualism and English Plebeians 1850–1910* (London, 1986), p. 299.

5. Ibid., p. 81.

The editors of this symposium invited reflexions on the specific historical contexts of the relation between facts and evidence. It was easy for a social historian of the sciences to respond because local studies have been the focus of much recent research. We also need to see how what works in one place gets to work elsewhere. One answer could involve a primitive form of realism. It might be held that the unconditioned external world is just what all sites have in common, so what works in one place must be efficacious everywhere. Realism thus distracts attention from the hard world of replication and the resources needed to make facts evident. A different answer, with which Rothfield seems more sympathetic, uses notions of discipline. Michel Foucault followed his remarks about the disappearance of the author from scientific texts with the announcement that 'the classical age discovered the body as an object and target of power'. The engrossment of the social sphere by this 'political anatomy of detail' allowed the unprecedentedly widespread distribution of new knowledges. 'Side by side with the major technology of the telescope, the lens and the light beam, which were an integral part of the new physics and cosmology, there were the minor techniques of multiple and intersecting observations'.[6] The problem of the multiplication of places where humans could be known becomes a question for the history of systems of government and power. Rothfield has defined the Victorian sleuth's intellectual technology in terms of Foucault's individualising discourses of detail. He reckons that the body studied by Sherlock Holmes 'is a corpus of isolated discrete elements' comparable with the new objects of fin de siècle semiotics (*VS*, pp. 135, 141). Carlo Ginzburg's study of these objects suggests the ways in which resources from the conjectural practices of popular culture were appropriated by regimes of government, for example, the development of fingerprinting, a vital new system of evidence, by the administrators of the Raj and by Francis Galton from the 1860s.[7] So in answer to one of Rothfield's urgent questions, the changing strategies of evidence were very closely articulated with the strategies of the administration of civil society.

Rothfield's closing catechism rightly juxtaposes natural philosophy with confession, philosophy, literature, science, and other ways of writing. These questions are good because they do not make natural science's place self-evident and because they ask about mediation. I questioned the self-evidence of a particular way of making knowledge. This is why I focussed on calibration; it relies on tacit assumptions of disciplinary and epistemic similarity and difference, thus revealing the cultural resources at play in claiming that a specific deed is evidence or not. These resources are not limited to a dark age of prescientific inquiry. The use of artificial

6. Michel Foucault, *Discipline and Punish: The Birth of the Prison,* trans. Alan Sheridan (New York, 1979), pp. 136, 139, 171.

7. See Carlo Ginzburg, *Clues, Myths, and the Historical Method,* trans. John and Anne Tedeschi (Baltimore, 1989), p. 122.

instruments to calibrate bodies is a crucial development of modern science. I venture further examples, these from the late nineteenth century, the period of Rothfield's 'total application' of 'technologies of identification' (*VS,* p. 143), in order to illustrate other histories of the self-possession of the scientist's own, and others', bodies.

The device in question is the galvanometer, first made in the 1820s to detect small current changes by passing a wire beneath a compass needle. I wish to juxtapose two uses of this instrument in calibrating human bodies. The first is by the Cambridge physics professor James Clerk Maxwell. In the 1870s, Maxwell set out to stage an unprecedentedly detailed replication of some famous experiments of Henry Cavendish, a late eighteenth-century electrical philosopher. Cavendish often used his own hand as an electrical device. To estimate the strength of an electric discharge he fed it through his hand and timed his own pulse. 'We learn . . . that Cavendish was his own galvanometer', Maxwell reported. But Cavendish had no galvanometer. This mattered when Maxwell's results differed from his Georgian predecessor. In characteristic fashion, the Cambridge professor of the 1870s used laboratory assistants to calibrate these eighteenth-century manual tests. Then he quantified them. Maxwell recorded precise numbers for the period of oscillations felt in his skin. He consulted local physiologists for help with nerve electrification and frog preparations to calibrate his own shocks. He found that his results about electric shock disagreed with those of Cavendish. 'I am quite unable to account for the opposite result obtained by Cavendish', Maxwell admitted. 'It is quite impossible that Cavendish could be mistaken in this comparison of the intensity of his sensations, for he had more practice than any other observer in comparing them, and he repeated this experiment many times'.[8] He guessed that Cavendish's hands 'were not so wet, and he went more by the "pricking of his thumbs" than I did'.[9] But he never doubted that 'the accuracy which Cavendish attained in the discrimination of the intensity of the shocks [was] truly marvellous, whether we judge by the consistency of his results with each other, or whether we compare them with the latest results obtained with the aid of the galvanometer'.[10]

In Maxwell's Cambridge laboratory Cavendish's authority was unquestioned. Maxwell accepted the enterprise because he was a realist. Cavendish was treated like Maxwell's contemporary, studying the same phenomena as those Maxwell routinely encountered, his work to be calibrated against modern galvanometry and electrophysiology. The realist assumption did its work, for example, when Maxwell's skin responded

8. James Clerk Maxwell, *The Electrical Researches of the Honourable Henry Cavendish* (Cambridge, 1879), pp. lvii, 443.

9. Maxwell, letter to George Chrystal, 5 Mar. 1879, Cambridge Library Manuscripts ADD 8375, no. 20.

10. Maxwell, *The Electrical Researches of the Honourable Henry Cavendish,* p. lvii.

differently from that of Cavendish. Sociologists of scientific knowledge expect a vicious regress to emerge when replications proceed without prior agreement about the proper outcome. Either Cavendish was wrong and his repute damaged, or else he was right and Maxwell had not adequately followed his predecessor's recipe. But while Maxwell announced that Cavendish was wrong, since he gave the wrong account of oscillating discharge, Maxwell also guessed his procedure had been different and thus preserved Cavendish's heroic status. This defines one pattern of replication, calibration, and evidence: the interesting combination of hagiography and realism, in which great scientists may rely both on pointer readings and sensitive thumbs.

My second example of the use of the galvanometer to calibrate the body is taken from the physical research of one of Victorian Britain's most famous scientists, William Crookes. In her wonderful account of Charlotte Anne Moberly and Eleanor Jourdain's *An Adventure*, Terry Castle reminds us of the use the Society of Psychical Research made of terms such as *tricks of memory* and *lively imagination* to disqualify spirit stories like these. Crookes, president of the Society in the late 1890s, surrounded his subjects with an array of cameras and galvanometers, especially a new version designed by the telegraphist Cromwell Varley, expressly to calibrate the behaviour of mediums. The apparatus of the Victorian physics laboratory was designed to break the circuit of aberrant testimony.[11] The London physicist John Tyndall, a fierce sceptic both of spiritualism and of Maxwellian natural philosophy, saw the point. He reported that at a séance he countered the boasts of the medium, 'a delicate-looking young lady', with his own. 'The medium affirmed that she could see actual waves of light coming from the Sun. I retorted that men of science could tell the exact number of waves emitted in a second'. Eventually 'the spirits were consulted and I was pronounced to be a first-class medium'. Gillian Beer points out that this denouement is unsurprising. Tyndall's remarkable public performances helped ambiguously to support the sciences of the unseen and to establish scientists' capacities by intricate analogy with the seer and the sage.[12] Crookes reckoned that electrotechnology could help redirect this enterprise to study what spirits could do when embodied. In the 1870s, he attached galvanometers to mediums' hands to check whether they moved during the apparitions. 'The galvanometer . . . lets the spectators know the moment that the circuit is broken'. Before eminent witnesses, including both Galton and Maxwell's Cambridge successor Lord Rayleigh, another future president of the Society, Crookes drew attention away from spirit phenomena towards the galvanometer

11. See Janet Oppenheim, *The Other World: Spiritualism and Psychical Research in England 1850–1914* (Cambridge, 1985), pp. 344–47.

12. See John Tyndall, *Fragments of Science*, 6th ed., 2 vols. (London, 1879), 2:497–99, and Gillian Beer, 'Helmholtz, Tyndall, Gerard Manley Hopkins: Leaps of the Prepared Imagination', *Comparative Criticism* 13 (1991): 117–45.

needle; this secured 'the advantage of *absolute certainty*'. But this certainty was never secure. Spectres of fraud, of sexual license, of conspiracy haunted the séances which Crookes tried to invigilate.[13]

Neither in Maxwell's laboratory nor Crookes's drawing room did the use of the galvanometer autonomously generate self-evidence. It was always backed up with a very wide range of conventions of reportage, manners, and, above all, bodily behaviour. Consider what was necessary to make bodies yield reliable information. New accounts of the capacities of bodies worked alongside new techniques for managing them. In both galvanometric episodes, the machine was used to help define what could never be mechanised, whether it be manual sensitivity or spiritual communication. Maxwell appealed to Cavendish's incommunicable skill in order to separate his own failure to replicate discharge trials from Cavendish's heroism. Crookes appealed to the social standing of his witnesses, the morality of his relations with the young female mediums, and the expertise of electrical instrument makers, in order to make the galvanometric calibration stick. Instead of seeing scientists' gestures simply as 'truly marvellous', historians have plentiful resources to treat them as culturally explicable and to link them with other narratives, stories of the politics of work heretofore excluded or denigrated by epistemology. These resources can be drawn from recent histories of the body, gesture, and social action. Ever since Lucien Febvre's wartime appeal for a cultural history of sensibility, an appeal directed against Fascist arguments that human nature provides universal categories which transcend culture, a range of allegedly psychological, sempiternal emotions and habits have been successfully analysed by his followers.[14] Material skills possess a history of their own. To investigate that history is to question the self-evidence of our own conventions of knowledge and trust.

13. Oppenheim, *The Other World*, p. 346.

14. See Lucien Febvre, 'Sensibility and History: How to Reconstitute the Emotional Life of the Past', *A New Kind of History and Other Essays*, trans. K. Folca, ed. Peter Burke (New York, 1973), pp. 12–26.

Jane Austen and the Masturbating Girl

Eve Kosofsky Sedgwick

1

The phrase itself is already evidence. Roger Kimball in *Tenured Radicals*—a treatise on educational "corruption" that must have gone to press before the offending paper was so much as written—cites the title "Jane Austen and the Masturbating Girl" from a Modern Language Association convention program quite as if he were Perry Mason, the six words a smoking gun:[1] the warm gun that, for the journalists who have adopted the phrase as an index of depravity in academe, is happiness—offering the squibby pop (fulmination? prurience? funniness?) that lets absolutely anyone, in the righteously exciting vicinity of the masturbating girl, feel a very pundit.[2]

The project sketched out in this paper has evoked, not only the foreclosing and disavowing responses mentioned in its first paragraph, but encouragement and fellowship as well. Some instances for which I am especially grateful: Michael Moon and Paula Bennett collaborated excitingly with me on the "Muse of Masturbation" proposal and panel. Vernon Rosario and Ed Cohen were kind enough to share unpublished writing. Barbara Herrnstein Smith discussed Kant in a particularly helpful conversation. Jonathan Goldberg made invaluable suggestions on an earlier draft of the essay.

1. See Roger Kimball, *Tenured Radicals: How Politics Has Corrupted Our Higher Education* (New York, 1990), pp. 145–46.

2. See, for a few examples of the phrase's career in journalism, Roger Rosenblatt, "The Universities: A Bitter Attack . . . ," review of *Tenured Radicals*, by Kimball, *New York Times Book Review*, 22 Apr. 1990, pp. 3, 36; letters to the editor, *New York Times Book Review*,

This essay originally appeared in *Critical Inquiry* 17 (Summer 1991).

There seems to be something self-evident—irresistibly so, to judge from its gleeful propagation—about the use of the phrase, "Jane Austen and the Masturbating Girl," as the Q.E.D. of phobic narratives about the degeneracy of academic discourse in the humanities. But what? The narrative link between masturbation itself and degeneracy, though a staple of pre-1920s medical and racial science, no longer has any respectable currency. To the contrary: modern views of masturbation tend to place it firmly in the framework of optimistic, hygienic narratives of all-too-normative individual development. When Jane E. Brody, in a recent "Personal Health" column in the *New York Times,* reassures her readers that, according to experts, it is actually entirely possible for people to be healthy *without* masturbating; "that the practice is not essential to normal development and that no one who thinks it is wrong or sinful should feel he or she must try it"; and that even " 'those who have not masturbated . . . can have perfectly normal sex lives as adults,' " the all but perfectly normal Victorianist may be forgiven for feeling just a little—out of breath.[3] In this altered context, the self-evidence of a polemical link between autoeroticism and narratives of wholesale degeneracy (or, in one journalist's historically redolent term, "idiocy")[4] draws on a very widely discredited body of psychiatric and eugenic expertise whose only direct historical continuity with late twentieth-century thought has been routed straight through the rhetoric and practice of fascism. But it now draws on this body of expertise under the more acceptable gloss of the modern, trivializing, hygienic-developmental discourse, according to which autoeroticism not only is funny—any sexuality of any power is likely to hover near the threshold of hilarity—but also must be relegated to the inarticulable space of (a barely superceded) infantility.

"Jane Austen and the Masturbating Girl"—the paper, not the phrase—began as a contribution to an MLA session that the three of us who proposed it entitled "The Muse of Masturbation." In spite of the half-century-long normalizing rehabilitation of this common form of isometric exercise, the proposal to begin an exploration of literary aspects of autoeroticism seemed to leave many people gasping. That could hardly be

---

20 May 1990, p. 54, including one from Catharine R. Stimpson disputing the evidential status of the phrase; and Richard Bernstein, "The Rising Hegemony of the Politically Correct: America's Fashionable Orthodoxy," *New York Times,* 28 Oct. 1990, sec. 4, pp. 1, 4.

3. Jane E. Brody, "Personal Health," *New York Times,* 4 Nov. 1987.

4. Rosenblatt, "The Universities," p. 3.

Eve Kosofsky Sedgwick is the Newman Ivey White Professor of English at Duke University and the author of *Epistemology of the Closet* (1990), *Tendencies* (1993), and a volume of poetry, *Fat Art, Thin Art* (1994).

because literary pleasure, critical self-scrutiny, and autoeroticism have nothing in common. What seems likelier, indeed, is that to label with the literal-minded and (at least by intention) censorious metaphor "mental masturbation" any criticism one doesn't like, or doesn't understand, is actually to refer to a much vaster, indeed foundational, open secret about how hard it is to circumscribe the vibrations of the highly relational but, in practical terms, solitary pleasure and adventure of writing itself.

As the historicization of sexuality, following the work of Michel Foucault, becomes increasingly involved with issues of representation, different varieties of sexual experience and identity are being discovered both to possess a diachronic history—a history of significant change—and to be entangled in particularly indicative ways with aspects of epistemology and of literary creation and reception.[5] This is no less true of autoeroticism than of other forms of sexuality. For example, the Aesthetic in Kant is substantively indistinguishable from, but at the same time definitionally opposed against, autoerotic pleasure. Sensibility, too—even more tellingly for the example of Austen—named the locus of a similarly dangerous overlap. As John Mullan points out in *Sentiment and Sociability: The Language of Feeling in the Eighteenth Century*, the empathetic allo-identifications that were supposed to guarantee the sociable nature of sensibility could not finally be distinguished from an epistemological solipsism, a somatics of trembling self-absorption, and ultimately—in the durable medical code for autoeroticism and its supposed sequelae—"neurasthenia."[6] Similarly unstable dichotomies between art and masturbation have persisted, culminating in those recurrent indictments of self-reflexive art and critical theory themselves as forms of mental masturbation.

Masturbation itself, as we will see, like homosexuality and heterosexuality, is being demonstrated to have a complex history. Yet there are senses in which autoeroticism seems almost uniquely—or, at least, distinctively—to challenge the historicizing impulse. It is unlike heterosexuality, whose history is difficult to construct because it masquerades so readily as History itself; it is unlike homosexuality, for centuries the *crimen nefandum* or "love that dare not speak its name," the compilation of whose history requires acculturation in a rhetoric of the most pointed preterition. Because it escapes both the narrative of reproduction and (when practiced solo) even the creation of any interpersonal trace, it seems to have an affinity with amnesia, repetition or the repetition-compulsion, and ahistorical or history-rupturing rhetorics of sublimity. Neil Hertz has pointed out how much of the disciplinary discourse around masturbation

---

5. My recent book, *Epistemology of the Closet* (Berkeley, 1990) makes this argument at length in relation to the late nineteenth-century crisis of male homo/heterosexual definition.

6. See John Mullan, *Sentiment and Sociability: The Language of Feeling in the Eighteenth Century* (New York, 1988), esp. pp. 201–40.

has been aimed at discovering or inventing proprietary traces to attach to a practice that, itself relatively traceless, may seem distinctively to threaten the orders of propriety and property.[7] And in the context of hierarchically oppressive relations between genders and between sexualities, masturbation can seem to offer—not least as an analogy to writing—a reservoir of potentially utopian metaphors and energies for independence, self-possession, and a rapture that may owe relatively little to political or interpersonal abjection.

The three participants in "The Muse of Masturbation," like most of the other scholars I know of who think and write about masturbation, have been active in lesbian and gay as well as in feminist studies. This makes sense because thinking about autoeroticism is beginning to seem a productive and necessary switchpoint in thinking about the relations—historical as well as intrapsychic—between homo- and heteroeroticism: a project that has not seemed engaging or necessary to scholars who do not register the anti-heterosexist pressure of gay and lesbian interrogation. Additionally, it is through gay and lesbian studies that the skills for a project of historicizing any sexuality have developed; along with a tradition of valuing nonprocreative forms of creativity and pleasure; a history of being suspicious of the tendentious functioning of open secrets; and a politically urgent tropism toward the gaily and, if necessary, the defiantly explicit.

At the same time, part of the great interest of autoeroticism for lesbian and gay thought is that it is a long-execrated form of sexuality, intimately and invaluably entangled with the physical, emotional, and intellectual adventures of many, many people, that today completely *fails* to constitute anything remotely like a minority identity. The history of masturbation phobia—the astonishing range of legitimate institutions that so recently surveilled, punished, jawboned, imprisoned, terrorized, shackled, diagnosed, purged, and physically mutilated so many people, to prevent a behavior that those same institutions now consider innocuity itself—has complex messages for sexual activism today. It seems to provide the most compelling possible exposure of the fraudulence of the scientistic claims of any discourse, *including medicine,* to say, in relation to human behavior, what constitutes disease. "The mass of 'self-defilement' literature," as Vernon A. Rosario II rather mildly points out, can "be read as a gross travesty of public health education."[8] And queer people have recently needed every available tool of critical leverage, including travesty, against the crushing mass of legitimated discourses showing us to be moribund, mutant, pathetic, virulent, or impossible. Even as it demon-

7. See Neil Hertz, *The End of the Line: Essays on Psychoanalysis and the Sublime* (New York, 1985), pp. 148–49.

8. Vernon A. Rosario II, "The Nineteenth-Century Medical Politics of Self-Defilement and Seminal Economy" (Paper delivered at the Nationalisms and Sexualities Conference, Center for Literary and Cultural Studies, Harvard University, June 1989), p. 18.

strates the absolutely discrediting inability of the "human sciences" to offer any effectual resistance to the most grossly punitive, moralistic hijacking, however, the same history of masturbation phobia can also seem to offer the heartening spectacle of a terrible oppression based on "fear" and "ignorance" that, ultimately, withered away from sheer transparent absurdity. The danger of this view is that the encouragement it offers—an encouragement we can hardly forego, so much need do we have of courage—depends on an Enlightenment narrative that can only relegiti-mate the same institutions of knowledge by which the crime was in the first place done.

Today there is no corpus of law or of medicine about masturbation; it sways no electoral politics; institutional violence and street violence do not surround it, nor does an epistemology of accusation; people who have masturbated who may contract illnesses are treated as people who are sick with specific disease organisms, rather than as revelatory embodiments of sexual fatality. Yet when so many confident jeremiads are spontaneously launched at the explicit invocation of the masturbator, it seems that her power to guarantee a Truth from which she is herself excluded has not lessened in two centuries. To have so powerful a form of *sexuality* run so fully athwart the precious and embattled sexual *identities* whose meaning and outlines we always insist on thinking we know, is only part of the revelatory power of the Muse of masturbation.

2

Bedroom scenes are not so commonplace in Jane Austen's novels that readers get jaded with the chiaroscuro of sleep and passion, wan light, damp linen, physical abandon, naked dependency, and the imperfectly clothed body. *Sense and Sensibility* has a particularly devastating bedroom scene, which begins:

> Before the house-maid had lit their fire the next day, or the sun gained any power over a cold, gloomy morning in January, Marianne, only half-dressed, was kneeling against one of the window-seats for the sake of all the little light she could command from it, and writing as fast as a continual flow of tears would permit her. In this situation, Elinor, roused from sleep by her agitation and sobs, first perceived her; and after observing her for a few moments with silent anxiety, said, in a tone of the most considerate gentleness,
> 'Marianne, may I ask?—'
> 'No, Elinor,' she replied, 'ask nothing; you will soon know all.'
> The sort of desperate calmness with which this was said, lasted no longer than while she spoke, and was immediately followed by a return of the same excessive affliction. It was some minutes before she could go on with her letter, and the frequent bursts of grief which

still obliged her, at intervals, to withhold her pen, were proofs enough of her feeling how more than probable it was that she was writing for the last time to Willoughby.[9]

We know well enough who is in this *bedroom:* two women. They are Elinor and Marianne Dashwood, they are sisters, and the passion and perturbation of their love for each other is, at the very least, the backbone of this powerful novel. But who is in this *bedroom scene?* And, to put it vulgarly, what's their scene? It is the naming of a man, the absent Willoughby, that both marks this as an unmistakably sexual scene, and by the same gesture seems to displace its "sexuality" from the depicted bedroom space of same-sex tenderness, secrecy, longing, and frustration. Is this, then, a hetero- or a homoerotic novel (or moment in a novel)? No doubt it must be said to be both, if love is vectored toward an object and Elinor's here flies toward Marianne, Marianne's in turn toward Willoughby. But what, if love is defined only by its gender of object-choice, are we to make of Marianne's terrible isolation in this scene; of her unstanchable emission, convulsive and intransitive; and of the writing activity with which it wrenchingly alternates?

Even before this, of course, the homo/hetero question is problematic for its anachronism: homosexual identities, and certainly female ones, are supposed not to have had a broad discursive circulation until later in the nineteenth century, so in what sense could heterosexual identities as against them?[10] And for that matter, if we are to trust Foucault, the conceptual amalgam represented in the very term *sexual identity,* the cementing of every issue of individuality, filiation, truth, and utterance *to* some representational metonymy of the genital, was a process not supposed to have been perfected for another half- or three-quarters-century after Austen; so that the genital implication in either "homosexual" *or* "heterosexual," to the degree that it differs from a plot of the procreative or dynastic (as each woman's desire seems at least for the moment to do), may mark also the possibility of an anachronistic gap.[11]

9. Jane Austen, *Sense and Sensibility* (Harmondsworth, 1969), p. 193; hereafter abbreviated *SS*.

10. This is (in relation to women) the argument of, most influentially, Lillian Faderman, *Surpassing the Love of Men: Romantic Friendship and Love between Women from the Renaissance to the Present* (New York, 1981), and Carroll Smith-Rosenberg, "The Female World of Love and Ritual: Relations between Women in Nineteenth-Century America," *Signs* 1 (Autumn 1975): 1–29. A recently discovered journal, published as *I Know My Own Heart: The Diaries of Anne Lister (1791–1840),* ed. Helena Whitbread (London, 1988), suggests that revisions of this narrative may, however, be necessary. It is the diary (for 1817–1823) of a young, cultured, religious, socially conservative, self-aware, land-owning rural Englishwoman—an almost archetypal Jane Austen heroine—who formed her sense of self around the pursuit and enjoyment of genital contact and short- and long-term intimacies with other women of various classes.

11. See Michel Foucault, *The History of Sexuality: An Introduction,* vol. 1 of *The History of Sexuality,* trans. Robert Hurley (New York, 1978).

In trying to make sense of these discursive transitions, I have most before me the model of recent work on Emily Dickinson, and in particular Paula Bennett's discussion of the relation between Dickinson's hetero-erotic and her homoerotic poetics in *My Life, a Loaded Gun* and *Emily Dickinson: Woman Poet.*[12] Briefly, Bennett's accomplishment is to have done justice for the somewhat later, New England figure of Dickinson, to a complex range of intense female-homosocial bonds, including genitally figured ones, in her life and writing—without denying the salience and power of the male-directed eros and expectation that also sound there; without palliating the tensions acted out between the two; and at the same time without imposing an anachronistically reified view of the feminist consistency of these tensions. For instance, the all-too-available rhetoric of the polymorphous, of a utopian bisexual erotic pluralism, has little place in Bennett's account. But neither does she romanticize the female-female bonds whose excitement, perturbation, and pain—including the pain of power struggle, of betrayal, of rejection—she shows to form so much of the primary level of Dickinson's emotional life. What her demanding account does enable her to do, however, is to offer a model for under-standing the bedrock, quotidian, sometimes very sexually fraught, female homosocial networks in relation to the more visible and spectacularized, more narratable, but less intimate, heterosexual plots of pre-twentieth-century Anglo-American culture.

I see this work on Dickinson as exemplary for understandings of such other, culturally central, homosocially embedded women authors as Austen and, for example, the Brontës. (Surely there are important gener-alizations yet to be made about the attachments of sisters, perhaps of any siblings, who live together as adults.) But as I have suggested, the first range of questions yet to be asked properly in this context concerns the emergence and cultural entailments of "sexual identity" itself during this period of the incipience of "sexual identity" in its (still incompletely inter-rogated) modern senses. Indeed, one of the motives for this project is to denaturalize any presumptive understanding of the relation of "hetero" to "homo" as modern sexual identities—the presumption, for instance, of their symmetry, their mutual impermeability, or even of their both func-tioning as "sexual identities" in the same sense; the presumption, as well, that "hetero" and "homo," even with the possible addition of "bi," do effi-ciently and additively divide up the universe of sexual orientation. It seems likely to me that in Austen's time *as in our own,* the specification of any distinct "sexual identity" magnetized and reoriented in new ways the heterogeneous erotic and epistemological energies of everyone in its social vicinity, without at the same time either adequating or descriptively exhausting those energies.

12. See Paula Bennett, *My Life, a Loaded Gun: Female Creativity and Feminist Poetics* (Boston, 1986), pp. 13–94, and *Emily Dickinson: Woman Poet* (London, 1990).

One "sexual identity" that did exist as such in Austen's time, already bringing a specific genital practice into dense compaction with issues of consciousness, truth, pedagogy, and confession, was that of the onanist. Among the sexual dimensions overridden within the past century by the world-historical homo/hetero cleavage is the one that discriminates, in the first place, the autoerotic and the alloerotic. Its history has been illuminated by recent researches of a number of scholars.[13] According to their accounts, the European phobia over masturbation came early in the "sexualizing" process described by Foucault, beginning around 1700 with publication of *Onania,* and spreading virulently after the 1750s. Although originally applied with a relative impartiality to both sexes, anti-onanist discourse seems to have bifurcated in the nineteenth century, and the systems of surveillance and the rhetorics of "confession" for the two genders contributed to the emergence of disparate regulatory categories and techniques, even regulatory worlds. According to Ed Cohen, for example, anxiety about boys' masturbation motivated mechanisms of school discipline and surveillance that were to contribute so much to the late nineteenth-century emergence of a widespread, class-inflected male homosexual identity and hence to the modern crisis of male homo/heterosexual definition. On the other hand, anxiety about girls' and women's masturbation contributed more to the emergence of gynecology, through an accumulated expertise in and demand for genital surgery; of such identities as that of the hysteric; and of such confession-inducing disciplinary discourses as psychoanalysis.

Far from there persisting a minority identity of "the masturbator" today, of course, autoeroticism per se in the twentieth century has been conclusively subsumed under that normalizing developmental model, differently but perhaps equally demeaning, according to which it represents a relatively innocuous way station on the road to a "full," that is, alloerotic, adult genitality defined almost exclusively by gender of object choice. As

13. Useful historical work touching on masturbation and masturbation phobia includes G. J. Barker-Benfield, *The Horrors of the Half-Known Life: Male Attitudes toward Women and Sexuality in Nineteenth-Century America* (New York, 1976); Ed Cohen, *Talk on the Wilde Side* (New York, forthcoming); John D'Emilio and Estelle B. Freedman, *Intimate Matters: A History of Sexuality in America* (New York, 1988); E. H. Hare, "Masturbatory Insanity: The History of an Idea," *Journal of the Mental Sciences* 108 (Jan. 1962): 1–25; Robert H. MacDonald, "The Frightful Consequences of Onanism: Notes on the History of a Delusion," *Journal of the History of Ideas* 28 (July–Sept. 1967): 423–31; John Money, *The Destroying Angel: Sex, Fitness and Food in the Legacy of Degeneracy Theory: Graham Crackers, Kellogg's Corn Flakes and American Health History* (Buffalo, N.Y., 1985); George L. Mosse, *Nationalism and Sexuality: Respectability and Abnormal Sexuality in Modern Europe* (New York, 1985); Robert P. Neuman, "Masturbation, Madness, and the Modern Concepts of Childhood and Adolescence," *Journal of Social History* 8 (Spring 1975): 1–27; Elaine Showalter, *The Female Malady: Women, Madness, and English Culture, 1830–1980* (New York, 1985); Smith-Rosenberg, *Disorderly Conduct: Visions of Gender in Victorian America* (New York, 1986); and Jean Stengers and Anne van Neck, *Histoire d'une grande peur, la masturbation* (Brussels, 1984).

Foucault and others have noted, a lush plurality of (proscribed and regulated) sexual identities had developed by the end of the nineteenth century: even the most canonical late-Victorian art and literature are full of sadomasochistic, pederastic and pedophilic, necrophilic, as well as autoerotic images and preoccupations; while Foucault mentions the hysterical woman and the masturbating child along with "entomologized" sexological categories such as zoophiles, zooerasts, auto-monosexualists, and gynecomasts, as typifying the new sexual taxonomies, the sexual "*specification of individuals*," that he sees as inaugurating the twentieth-century regime of sexuality.[14] Although Foucault is concerned to demonstrate our own continuity with nineteenth-century sexual discourse, however, (appealing to his readers as "We 'Other Victorians'"),[15] it makes a yet-to-be-explored difference that the Victorian multiplication of sexual species has today all but boiled down to a single, bare—and moreover fiercely invidious—dichotomy. Most of us now correctly understand a question about our "sexual orientation" to be a demand that we classify ourselves as a heterosexual or a homosexual, regardless of whether we may or may not individually be able or willing to perform that blank, binarized act of category assignment. We also understand that the two available categories are not symmetrically but hierarchically constituted in relation to each other. The identity of the masturbator was only one of the sexual identities subsumed, erased, or overridden in this triumph of the heterosexist homo/hetero calculus. But I want to argue here that the status of the masturbator among these many identities was uniquely formative. I would suggest that as one of the very earliest embodiments of "sexual identity" in the period of the progressive epistemological overloading of sexuality, the masturbator may have been at the cynosural center of a remapping of individual identity, will, attention, and privacy along modern lines that the reign of "sexuality," and its generic concomitant in the novel and in novelistic point-of-view, now lead us to take for granted. It is of more than chronological import if the (lost) identity of the masturbator was the proto-form of modern sexual identity itself.

Thus it seems likely that in our reimaginings of the history of sexuality "as" (we vainly imagine) "we know it," through readings of classic texts, the dropping out of sight of the autoerotic term is also part of what falsely naturalizes the heterosexist imposition of these books, disguising both the rich, conflictual erotic complication of a homoerotic matrix not yet crystallized in terms of "sexual identity," and the violence of heterosexist definition finally carved out of these plots. I am taking *Sense and Sensibility* as my example here because of its odd position, at once germinal and abjected, in the Austen canon and hence in "the history of the novel"; and because its erotic axis is most obviously the unwavering but difficult love

14. Foucault, *History of Sexuality,* pp. 105, 42–43.
15. Ibid., p. 1.

of a woman, Elinor Dashwood, for a woman, Marianne Dashwood. I don't think we can bring this desire into clear focus until we also see how Marianne's erotic identity, in turn, is not in the first place exactly either a same-sex-loving one or a cross-sex-loving one (though she loves both women and men), but rather the one that today no longer exists *as* an identity: that of the masturbating girl.

Reading the bedroom scenes of *Sense and Sensibility,* I find I have lodged in my mind a bedroom scene from another document, a narrative structured as a case history of "Onanism and Nervous Disorders in Two Little Girls" and dated 1881:

> Sometimes [X . . .'s] face is flushed and she has a roving eye; at others she is pale and listless. Often she cannot keep still, pacing up and down the bedroom, or balancing on one foot after the other. . . . During these bouts X . . . is incapable of anything: reading, conversation, games, are equally odious. All at once her expression becomes cynical, her excitement mounts. X . . . is overcome by the desire to do it, she tries not to or someone tries to stop her. Her only dominating thought is to succeed. Her eyes dart in all directions, her lips never stop twitching, her nostrils flare! Later, she calms down and is herself again. "If only I had never been born," she says to her little sister, "we would not have been a disgrace to the family!" And Y . . . replies: "Why did you teach me all these horrors then?" Upset by this reproach, X . . . says: "If someone would only kill me! What joy. I could die without committing suicide."[16]

If what defines "sexual identity" is the impaction of epistemological issues around the core of a particular genital possibility, then the compulsive attention paid by anti-onanist discourse to disorders *of* attention make it a suitable point of inauguration for modern sexuality. Marianne Dashwood, though highly intelligent, exhibits the classic consciousness-symptoms noted by Samuel Tissot in 1758, including "the impairment of memory and the senses," "inability to confine the attention," and "an air of distraction, embarrassment and stupidity."[17] A surprising amount of the narrative tension of *Sense and Sensibility* comes from the bent bow of

16. Demetrius Zambaco, "Onanism and Nervous Disorders in Two Little Girls," trans. Catherine Duncan, *Semiotext(e)* 4, "Polysexuality" (1981): 30; hereafter abbreviated "O." The letters standing in place of the girls' names are followed by ellipses in the original; other ellipses are mine. In quoting from this piece I have silently corrected some obvious typographical errors; since this issue of *Semiotext(e)* is printed entirely in capital letters, and with commas and periods of indistinguishable shape, I have also had to make some guesses about sentence division and punctuation. Zambaco's case was later published, under less equivocal scholarly auspices, in *A Dark Science: Women, Sexuality, and Psychiatry in the Nineteenth Century,* trans. Jeffrey Mousaieff Masson and Marianne Loring, ed. Masson (New York, 1986), pp. 61–89.

17. Quoted and discussed in Cohen, *Talk on the Wilde Side.*

the absentation of Marianne's attention from wherever she is. "Great," at one characteristic moment, "was the perturbation of her spirits and her impatience to be gone" (*SS*, p. 174); once out on the urban scene, on the other hand,

> her eyes were in constant inquiry; and in whatever shop the party were engaged, her mind was equally abstracted from every thing actually before them, from all that interested and occupied the others. Restless and dissatisfied every where . . . she received no pleasure from any thing; was only impatient to be at home again. [*SS*, p. 180]

Yet when at home, her "agitation increased as the evening drew on. She could scarcely eat any dinner, and when they afterwards returned to the drawing room, seemed anxiously listening to the sound of every carriage" (*SS*, p. 177).

Marianne incarnates physical as well as perceptual irritability, to both pleasurable and painful effect. Addicted to "rapidity" (*SS*, p. 75) and "requiring at once solitude and continual change of place" (*SS*, p. 193), she responds to anything more sedentary with the characteristic ejaculation: "'I could hardly keep my seat'" (*SS*, p. 51). Sitting is the most painful and exciting thing for her. Her impatience keeps her "moving from one chair to another" (*SS*, p. 266) or "[getting] up, and walk[ing] about the room" (*SS*, p. 269). At the happiest moments, she frankly pursues the locomotor pleasures of her own body, "running with all possible speed down the steep side of the hill" (*SS*, p. 74) (and spraining her ankle in a tumble), eager for "the delight of a gallop" when Willoughby offers her a horse (*SS*, p. 88). To quote again from the document dated 1881,

> In addition to the practices already cited, X . . . provoked the voluptuous spasm by rubbing herself on the angles of furniture, by pressing her thighs together, or rocking backwards and forwards on a chair. Out walking she would begin to limp in an odd way as if she were lopsided, or kept lifting one of her feet. At other times she took little steps, walked quickly, or turned abruptly left. . . . If she saw some shrub she straddled it and rubbed herself back and forth. . . . She pretended to fall or stumble over something in order to rub against it. ["O," pp. 26–27]

Exactly Marianne's overresponsiveness to her tender "seat" as a node of delight, resistance, and surrender—and its crucial position, as well, between the homosocial and heterosocial avidities of the plot—is harnessed when Elinor manipulates Marianne into rejecting Willoughby's gift of the horse: "Elinor thought it wisest to touch that point no more. . . . Opposition on so tender a subject would only attach her the more to her own opinion. But by an appeal to her affection for her mother . . . Marianne was shortly subdued" (*SS*, p. 89).

The vision of a certain autoerotic closure, absentation, self-sufficiency in Marianne is radiantly attractive to almost everyone, female and male, who views her; at the same time, the same autoerotic inaccessibility is legible to them through contemporaneous discourses as a horrifying staging of autoconsumption. As was typical until the end of the nineteenth century, Marianne's autoeroticism is not defined in opposition to her alloerotic bonds, whether with men or with women. Rather, it signifies an excess of sexuality altogether, an excess dangerous to others but chiefly to herself: the chastening illness that ultimately wastes her physical substance is both the image and the punishment of the "distracted" sexuality that, continually "forgetting itself," threatens, in her person, to subvert the novel's boundaries between the public and the private.

More from the manuscript dated 1881:

> The 19th [September]. Third cauterisation of little Y . . . who sobs and vociferates.
> In the days that followed Y . . . fought successfully against temptation. She became a child again, playing with her doll, amusing herself and laughing gayly. She begs to have her hands tied each time she is not sure of herself. . . . Often she is seen to make an effort at control. Nonetheless she does it two or three times every twenty-four hours. . . . But X . . . more and more drops all pretense of modesty. One night she succeeds in rubbing herself till the blood comes on the straps that bind her. Another time, caught in the act by the governess and unable to satisfy herself, she has one of her terrible fits of rage, during which she yells: "I want to, oh how I want to! You can't understand, Mademoiselle, how I want to do it!" Her memory begins to fail. She can no longer keep up with lessons. She has hallucinations all the time. . . .
> The 23rd. She repeats: "I deserve to be burnt and I will be. I will be brave during the operation, I won't cry." From ten at night until six in the morning, she has a terrible attack, falling several times into a swoon that lasted about a quarter of an hour. At times she had visual hallucinations. At other times she became delirious, wild eyed, saying: "Turn the page, who is hitting me, etc."
> The 25th I apply a hot point to X . . .'s clitoris. She submits to the operation without wincing, and for twenty-four hours after the operation she is perfectly good. But then she returns with renewed frenzy to her old habits. ["O," pp. 32–33]

As undisciplined as Marianne Dashwood's "abstracted" attention is, the farouche, absent presence of this figure also reorganizes the attention of others: Elinor's rapt attention to her, to begin with, but also, through Elinor's, the reader's. *Sense and Sensibility* is unusual among Austen novels not for the (fair but unrigorous) consistency with which its narrative point of view is routed through a single character, Elinor, but rather for the undeviating consistency with which Elinor's regard in turn is vectored in the direction of her beloved. Elinor's self-imposed obligation to offer social countenance to the restless, insulting, magnetic, and dangerous abstraction of her sister constitutes most of the plot of the novel.

It constitutes more than plot, in fact; it creates both the consciousness and the privacy of the novel. The projectile of surveillance, epistemological demand, and remediation that both desire and "responsibility" constrain Elinor to level at Marianne, immobilized or turned back on herself by the always-newly-summoned-up delicacy of her refusal to press Marianne toward confession, make an internal space—internal, that is, to Elinor, hence to the reader hovering somewhere behind her eyes—from which there is no escape but more silent watching. About the engagement she is said to assume to exist between Marianne and Willoughby, for example, her "wonder"

> was engrossed by the extraordinary silence of her sister and Willoughby on the subject. . . . Why they should not openly acknowledge to her mother and herself, what their constant behaviour to each other declared to have taken place, Elinor could not imagine. . . . For this strange kind of secrecy maintained by them relative to their engagement, which in fact concealed nothing at all, she could not account; and it was so wholly contradictory to their general opinions and practice, that a doubt sometimes entered her mind of their being really engaged, and this doubt was enough to prevent her making any inquiry of Marianne. [*SS*, p. 100]

To Marianne, on the other hand, the question of an engagement seems simply not to have arisen.

The insulation of Marianne from Elinor's own unhappiness, when Elinor is unhappy; the buffering of Marianne's impulsiveness, and the absorption or, where that is impossible, coverture of her terrible sufferings; the constant, reparative concealment of Marianne's elopements of attention from their present company: these activities hollow out a subjectivity for Elinor and the novel that might best be described in the 1980s jargon of "co-dependency," were not the pathologizing stigma of that term belied by the fact that, at least as far as this novel is concerned, the co-dependent subjectivity simply *is subjectivity*. Even Elinor's heterosexual plot with Edward Ferrars merely divides her remedial solicitude (that distinctive amalgam of "tenderness, pity, approbation, censure and doubt" [*SS*, p. 129]) between the sister who remains her first concern, and a second sufferer from *mauvaise honte*, the tell-tale "embarrassment," "settled" "absence of mind" (*SS*, p. 123), unsocializable shyness, "want of spirits, of openness, and of consistency," "the same fettered inclination, the same inevitable necessity of temporizing with his mother" (*SS*, p. 126), and a "desponding turn of mind" (*SS*, p. 128), all consequent on his own servitude to an erotic habit formed in the idleness and isolation of an improperly supervised youth.

The co-dependency model is the less anachronistic as Marianne's and Edward's disorders share with the pre-twentieth-century version of masturbation the property of being structured as addictions. (Here, of course, I'm inviting a meditation on the history of the term *self-abuse*, which referred to masturbation from the eighteenth century until very recently—when it's come, perhaps by analogy to *child-abuse*, to refer to battering or mutilation of oneself. Where that older sense of *abuse* has resurfaced, on the other hand, is in the also very recent coinage, *substance abuse*.) Back to 1881:

> The afternoon of the 14th of September X . . . is in a terribly over-excited state. She walks about restlessly, grinding her teeth. . . . There is foam on her lips, she gasps, repeating, "I don't want to, I don't want to, I can't stop myself, I must do it! Stop me, hold my hands, tie my feet!" A few moments later she falls into a state of prostration, becomes sweet and gentle, begging to be given another chance. "I know I'm killing myself," she says. "Save me." ["O," p. 30]

Although *the addict,* as a medicalized personal identity, was (as Virginia Berridge and Griffith Edwards demonstrate in *Opium and the People*) another product of the latter part of the nineteenth century, the hypostatization of the notion of "will" that would soon give rise to the "addict" identity, and that by the late twentieth century would leave no issue of voluntarity untinged by the concept of addiction, is already in place in *Sense and Sensibility.*[18] A concept of addiction involves understanding something called "the will" as a muscle that can strengthen with exercise or atrophy with disuse; the particular muscle on which "will" is modeled in this novel is a sphincter, which, when properly toned, defines an internal space of private identity by holding some kinds of material inside, even while guarding against the admission of others. Marianne's unpracticed muscle lets her privacy dribble away, giving her "neither courage to speak of, nor fortitude to conceal" (*SS*, p. 333) the anguish she experiences. By contrast, in the moment of Elinor's profoundest happiness, when Marianne is restored from a grave illness, Elinor's well-exercised muscle guarantees that what expands with her joy is the private space that, constituting her self, constitutes it also as the space of narrative self-reflection (not to say hoarding):

> Elinor could not be cheerful. Her joy was a different kind, and led to anything rather than to gaiety. Marianne restored to life, health, friends, and to her doating mother, was an idea to fill her heart with

18. See Virginia Berridge and Griffith Edwards, *Opium and the People: Opiate Use in Nineteenth-Century England* (New Haven, Conn., 1987). For more on the epistemology of addiction, co-dependency, and addiction-attribution, see my "Epidemics of the Will," *Zone* (forthcoming).

sensations of exquisite comfort, and expand it in fervent gratitude;—
but it led to no outward demonstrations of joy, no words, no smiles. All
within Elinor's breast was satisfaction, silent and strong. [*SS*, p. 310]

Such an apparently generalizable ideal of individual integrity, the
unitary self-containment of the strong, silent type, can never be stable, of
course. Elinor has constructed herself in this way around an original lack:
the absentation of her sister, and perhaps in the first place the withholding
from herself of the love of their mother, whom she then compulsively
unites with Marianne, the favorite, in the love-drenched tableaux of her
imagination. In the inappropriately pathologizing but descriptively acute
language of "self-help," Marianne's addiction has mobilized in her sister a
discipline that, posed as against addiction, nonetheless also is one. Elinor's
pupils, those less tractable sphincters of the soul, won't close against the
hapless hemorrhaging of her visual attention-flow toward Marianne; it is
this, indeed, that renders her consciousness, in turn, habitable, inviting,
and formative to readers as "point-of-view."
   But that hypostatization of "will" had always anyway contained the
potential for the infinite regress enacted in the uncircumscribable
twentieth-century epidemic of addiction-attribution: the degenerative
problem of where, if not in some further compulsion, one looks for the
will *to* will, as when Marianne, comparing herself with the more continent
Elinor,

felt all the force of that comparison; but not as her sister had hoped,
to urge her to exertion now; she felt it with all the pain of continual
self-reproach, regretted most bitterly that she had never exerted herself before; but it brought only the torture of penitence, without the
hope of amendment. Her mind was so much weakened that she still
fancied present exertion impossible, and therefore it only dispirited
her more. [*SS*, p. 270]

In addition, the concept of addiction also involves a degenerative perceptual narrative of progressively deadened receptiveness to a stimulus
that therefore requires to be steadily increased—as when Marianne's and
her mother's "agony of grief" over the death of the father, at first over-
powering, was then "voluntarily renewed, was sought for, was created
again and again" (*SS*, p. 42). Paradoxically afflicted, as Marianne is, by
both hyperaesthesia and an emboldening and addiction-producing
absentmindedness ("'an heart hardened against [her friends'] merits, and
a temper irritated by their very attention'" [*SS*, p. 337]), the species of
the masturbating girl was described by Augustus Kinsley Gardner in 1860
as one

in whom the least impression is redoubled like that of a "tam-tam,"
[who seek] for emotions still more violent and more varied. It is this

necessity which nothing can appease, which took the Roman women to the spectacles where men were devoured by ferocious beasts. . . . It is the emptiness of an unquiet and sombre soul seeking some activity, which clings to the slightest incident of life, to elicit from it some emotion which forever escapes; in short, it is the deception and disgust of existence.[19]

The subjectivity hollowed out by *Sense and Sensibility*, then, and made available *as* subjectivity for heterosexual expropriation, is not Marianne's but Elinor's; the novel's achievement of a modern psychological interiority fit for the heterosexual romance plot is created for Elinor through her completely one-directional visual fixation on her sister's specularized, desired, envied, and punished autoeroticism. This also offers, however, a useful model for the chains of reader-relations constructed by the punishing, girl-centered moral pedagogy and erotics of Austen's novels more generally. Austen criticism is notable mostly not just for its timidity and banality but for its unresting exaction of the spectacle of a Girl Being Taught a Lesson—for the vengefulness it vents on the heroines whom it purports to love, and whom, perhaps, it does. Thus Tony Tanner, the ultimate normal and normalizing reader of Austen, structures sentence after sentence: "Emma . . . *has to be tutored* . . . into correct vision and responsible speech. Anne Elliot *has to move*, painfully, from an excessive prudence."[20] "Some Jane Austen heroines *have to learn* their true 'duties.' They all *have to find* their proper homes" (*JA*, p. 33). Catherine "quite literally is in danger of perverting reality, and one of the things she *has to learn* is to break out of quotations" (*JA*, p. 45); she "*has to be disabused* of her naïve and foolish 'Gothic' expectations" (*JA*, p. 48). Elizabeth and Darcy "*have to learn to see* that their novel is more properly called" . . . (*JA*, p. 105). A lot of Austen criticism sounds hilariously like the leering schoolprospectuses or governess-manifestoes brandished like so many birch rods in Victorian sadomasochistic pornography. Thus Jane Nardin:

The discipline that helps create the moral adult need not necessarily be administered in early childhood. Frequently, as we have seen, it is not—for its absence is useful in helping to create the problems with which the novel deals. But if adequate discipline is lacking in childhood, it must be supplied later, and this happens only when the character learns "the lessons of affliction" (*Mansfield Park*, p. 459). Only after immaturity, selfishness, and excessive self-confidence have produced error, trouble, and real suffering, can the adult begin to teach

19. Quoted in Barker-Benfield, *The Horrors of the Half-Known Life*, pp. 273–74.
20. Tony Tanner, *Jane Austen* (Cambridge, Mass., 1986), p. 6; hereafter abbreviated *JA*; emphasis, in each case, added.

himself or herself the habits of criticism and self-control which should have been inculcated in childhood.[21]

How can it have taken this long to see that when Colonel Brandon and Marianne finally get together, their first granddaughter will be Lesbia Brandon?

Even readings of Austen that are not so frankly repressive have tended to be structured by what Foucault calls "the repressive hypothesis"—especially so, indeed, to the degree that their project is avowedly *anti*repressive. And these antirepressive readings have their own way of re-creating the spectacle of the Girl Being Taught a Lesson. Call her, in this case, "Jane Austen." The sight to be relished here is, as in psychoanalysis, the forcible exaction from her manifest text of what can only be the barest confession of a self-pleasuring sexuality, a disorder or subversion, seeping out at the edges of a policial conservatism always presumed and therefore always available for violation. That virginal figure "Jane Austen," in these narratives, is herself the punishable girl who "has to learn," "has to be tutored"—in truths with which, though derived from a reading of Austen, the figure of "Jane Austen" can no more be credited than can, for their lessons, the figures "Marianne," "Emma," or, shall we say, "Dora" or "Anna O."

It is partly to interrupt this seemingly interminable scene of punitive/ pedagogical reading, interminably structured as it is by the concept of repression, that I want to make available the sense of an alternative, passionate sexual ecology—one fully available to Austen for her exciting, productive, and deliberate use, in a way it no longer is to us.

That is to say, it is no longer available to us *as passion*, even as its cynosural figure, the masturbating girl, is no longer visible as possessing a sexual identity capable of redefining and reorganizing her surround. We inherit it only in the residual forms of perception itself, of subjectivity itself, of institution itself. The last time I taught *Sense and Sensibility*, I handed out to my graduate class copies of some pages from the 1981 "Polysexuality" issue of *Semiotext(e)*, pages that reproduce without historical annotation what appears to be a late nineteenth-century medical case history in French, from which I have also been quoting here. I handed it

---

21. Nardin is remarkably unworried about any possible excess of severity:

In this group of characters [in *Mansfield Park*], lack of discipline has the expected effect, while excessive discipline, though it causes suffering and creates some problems for Fanny and Susan Price, does indeed make them into hard-working, extremely conscientious women. The timidity and self-doubt which characterize Fanny, and which are a response to continual censure, seem a reasonable price to pay for the strong conscience that even the unfair discipline she received has nurtured in her. [Jane Nardin, "Children and Their Families in Jane Austen's Novels," in *Jane Austen: New Perspectives*, ed. Janet Todd (New York, 1983), p. 83. (Nardin is using *The Novels of Jane Austen*, ed. R. W. Chapman, 5 vols. [London, 1966])]

out then for reasons no more transparent than those that have induced me to quote from it here—beyond the true but inadequate notation that even eight years after reading it, my memory of the piece wouldn't let up its pressure on the gaze I was capable of levelling at the Austen novel. I hadn't even the new historicist's positivist alibi for perpetuating and disseminating the shock of the violent narratives in which they trade: "Deal," don't they seem tacitly but moralistically to enjoin, "deal with your own terror, your own arousal, your disavowals, in your own way, on your own time, in your own [thereby reconstituted as invisible] privacy; it's not our responsibility, because *these awful things are real.*" Surely I did want to spread around to a group of other readers, as if that would ground or diffuse it, the inadmissibly, inabsorbably complex shock of this document. But the pretext of the real was austerely withheld by the informal, perhaps only superficially, sensationalistic *Semiotext(e)* format, which refused to proffer the legitimating scholarly apparatus that would give any reader the assurance of "knowing" whether the original of this document was to be looked for in an actual nineteenth-century psychiatric archive or, alternatively and every bit as credibly, in a manuscript of pornographic fiction dating from any time—any time including the present—in the intervening century. Certainly plenty of the other pieces in that issue of *Semiotext(e)* are, whatever else they are, freshly minted and joltingly potent pornography; just as certainly, nothing in the 1881 document exceeds in any detail the known practices of late nineteenth-century medicine. And wasn't that part of the shock?—the total plausibility either way of the same masturbatory narrative, the same pruriently cool clinical gaze at it and violating hands and instruments on it, even (one might add) further along the chain, the same assimilability of it to the pseudo-distantiating relish of sophisticated contemporary projects of critique. Toward the site of the absent, distracted, and embarrassed attention of the masturbatory subject, the directing of a less accountable flood of discursive attention has continued. What is most astonishing is its continuing entirely unabated by the dissolution of its object, the sexual identity of "the masturbator" herself.

Through the frame of 1881/1981, it becomes easier to see how most of the love story of *Sense and Sensibility,* no simple one, has been rendered all but invisible to most readers, leaving a dryly static tableau of discrete moralized portraits, poised antitheses, and exemplary, deplorable, or regrettably necessary punishments, in an ascetic heterosexualizing context.[22] This tableau is what we now know as "Jane Austen"; fossilized resi-

---

22. As Mullan's *Sentiment and Sociability* suggests—and not only through the evocation of Austen's novel in its title—the eponymous antithesis "sense" versus "sensibility" is undone by, quite specifically, the way sensibility itself functions as a point of pivotal intersection, and potentially of mutual coverture, between alloerotic and autoerotic investments. Mullan would refer to these as "sociability" versus "isolation," "solipsism," or "hypochondria." He

due of the now-subtracted autoerotic spectacle, "Jane Austen" is the name whose uncanny fit with the phrase "masturbating girl" today makes a *ne plus ultra* of the incongruous.

This history of impoverished "Jane Austen" readings is not the result of a failure by readers to "contextualize historically": a new-historicizing point that you can't understand *Sense and Sensibility* without entering into the alterity of a bygone masturbation phobia is hardly the one I am making. What alterity? I am more struck by how profoundly, how destructively twentieth-century readings are already shaped by the discourse of masturbation and its sequelae: *more* destructively than the novel is, even though onanism per se, and the phobia against it, are living issues in the novel as they no longer are today.

We can be the less surprised by the congruence as we see masturbation and the relations surrounding it as the proto-form of any modern "sexual identity," thus as lending their structure to many vantages of subjectivity that have survived the definitional atrophy of the masturbator as an identity: pedagogic surveillance, as we have mentioned, homo/hetero divides, psychiatry, psychoanalysis, gynecology. The interpretive habits that make it so hard to register the erotics of *Sense and Sensibility* are deeply and familiarly encoded in the therapeutic or mock-therapeutic rhetoric of the 1881 document. They involve the immobilizing framing of an isolated sexual subject (a subject, that is, whose isolation is decreed by her identification with a nameable sexual identity), and her staging as a challenge or question addressed to an audience whose erotic invisibility is guaranteed by the same definitional stroke as their entitlement to intervene on the sexuality attributed to her. That it was this particular, apparently unitary and in some ways self-contained, autoerotic sexual identity that crystallized as the prototype *of* "sexual identity" made that isolating embodiment of "the sexual" easier, and made easier as well a radical natur-

---

ignores specifically antimasturbatory medical campaigns in his discussion of late eighteenth-century medicine, but their relevance is clear enough in, for example, the discussion he does offer of the contemporaneous medical phenomenology of menstruation.

> Menstruation is represented as an irregularity which takes the guise of a regularity; it is especially likely to signify a precarious condition in the bodies of those for whom womanhood does not mean the life of the fertile, domesticated, married female. Those particularly at risk are the unmarried, the aging, and the sexually precocious.

> The paradox, of course, is that to concentrate upon the palpitating, sensitized body of the woman caught in the difficult area between childhood and marriage is also to concede the dangers of this condition—those dangers which feature, in another form, in writings on hysteria. [Mullan, *Sentiment and Sociability,* pp. 226, 228]

In *Epistemology of the Closet* (esp. pp. 141–81), I discuss at some length the strange historical career of the epithets "sentimentality" and "sensibility," in terms of the inflammatory and scapegoating mechanics of vicariation: of the coverture offered by these apparently static nouns to the most volatile readerly interchanges between the allo- and the auto-.

alization and erotic dematerialization of narrative point-of-view concerning it.

And the dropping out of sight in this century of the masturbatory identity has only, it seems, given more the authority of self-evidence to the scientific, therapeutic, institutional, and narrative relations originally organized around it. *Sense and Sensibility* resists such "progress" only in so far as we can succeed in making narratively palpable again, under the pressure of our own needs, the great and estranging force of the homo-erotic longing magnetized in it by that radiant and inattentive presence—the female figure of the love that keeps forgetting its name.

Evidences of Masturbation

Lauren Berlant

Eve Kosofsky Sedgwick's "Jane Austen and the Masturbating Girl" (pp. 105–24) performs an act of critical interference in relations among criticism and chastisement, sexuality and exegesis. It seeks to "interrupt [the] seemingly interminable scene of punitive/pedagogical reading" around Jane Austen, a scene in which critics take much unacknowledged pleasure from what they perceive to be Austen's tweaking and thwacking of ordinary women's improper, excessive desires (p. 121). "Jane Austen and the Masturbating Girl" exploits its own interruption of the sadistic canonizing narrative by introducing at least two other tableaus of sexual identity that course through the ostensibly chaste *Sense and Sensibility,* featuring (a) the masturbator/narcissist, Marianne Dashwood, whose autoerotic sexual identity is no longer an animating possibility in the other-directed or "alloerotic" fetishisms of modern sexuality, and (b) her sister Elinor Dashwood, the loving critic/voyeur, whose "type" apparently becomes the modern heterosexual "woman who loves women." Finally, insofar as Sedgwick posits autoeroticism as the first fully realized minority sexual identity, its current banishment from the alloerotic field of possibilities and practices suggests to her not only *another* painful history of erotic negation but also a utopian scenario, in which (for)getting oneself remains to be thought as a condition of sexual expressivity, of release from the genital/copulative organization of pleasure and identity, of a cleavage, once and for all, from the inevitability of the heterosexual narrative.

But what does the representation of a prehistory of modern sexual identities have to do with what "we" do—criticism? Three critical cultures are brought into proximity by "Jane Austen and the Masturbating Girl," all of which have a different take on this question: the journalistic public sphere, whose castigation of the radical humanities has been a matter of much recent concern; the academic sphere of criticism itself, indicated in Sedgwick's polemic against the New Historicism; and then there is the critical context of gay and lesbian studies, which sustains the project of this essay "under," as she says, "the pressure of our own needs" (p. 124). Our needs are to link the history of sexuality to sexually radical social movements in the present tense; to stage an encounter between intellectual genres and the self-understanding of a sexual public; and to help make audible a lost pulse in the corpus of shame and improvisation that chronicles marginal sexualities and marginal knowledges. These three critical publics require different tasks of criticism in Sedgwick's essay, and they generate different questions of evidence.

My concern is to try to characterize the diverse relations of sexuality to commentary that Sedgwick's essay represents. My task is further complicated by my own desire not to repeat what Sedgwick calls the pseudo-distanciation between authors and their objects of knowledge, which is a relation of erotic mastery—in the bad sense (p. 122). When I speak of Eve here (in her corporeal presence), I relegate her to experiencing her subjectivity and interiority as the shamed or caught autoerotic subject does, and when she gives her rejoinder, we exchange positions. Unless we can manage to perform some other relation of criticism: as the essay ends "magnetized" by "the female figure of the love that keeps forgetting its name," I feel compelled to testify here that she is my friend, and also that I share the project of promoting a criticism where the difficult pleasures of knowledge and politics are all bound up in the problematics of writing in, for, and from "publics" (p. 124). These political matters (of interlocution, of call and response) are, therefore, specifically and intensely professional and personal. To make an *ad feminam* argument in this context is a really tangled thing. Especially since governing the essay's view of authorship, authority, and scandalous pleasure is a self-reflexive emblem that works like one of those boardwalk images in which someone is photographed with her head inserted into a cartoon body. Here Eve Sedgwick, Jane Austen, and Austen's libidinously naughty characters all star as the "Girl Being Taught a Lesson" (p. 121).

But neither Sedgwick nor I was the first to imagine such a hydra-headed female freak. The essay begins meditating on the fate of its

---

Lauren Berlant, a coeditor of *Critical Inquiry*, teaches at the University of Chicago. She writes on the cultural/sexual politics of national identity, and on relations between mass nationality, mass culture, modernity, and postmodernity. She is author of *The Anatomy of National Fantasy: Hawthorne, Utopia, and Everyday Life* (1991).

own title, which has caused far more scandal than its argument. The title "Jane Austen and the Masturbating Girl" stands in Roger Kimball's *Tenured Radicals* as the proverbial smoking gun, proof undeniable that the humanities has become incontinent, degenerate, guilty of bad taste.[1] In writing this title, Kimball suggests, Sedgwick turns Jane Austen into something other than the proper anerotic mistress she is supposed to be: a condensation of pornographic fantasies Kimball cannot forget, producing something like the screaming noises echoing in the soundtrack of *Psycho*—Jane Austen and the Masturbating Girl; Jane Austen as the Masturbating Girl; Jane Austen, the girl who masturbates; Eve Sedgwick starring as Jane Austen in an act of scandalous self-miscasting; and even, once the essay was published, the softly pulsating running title cresting the pages of *Critical Inquiry,* "*Eve Kosofsky Sedgwick The Masturbating Girl.*"[2]

Kimball, in turn, represents in Sedgwick's text the "foreclosing and disavowing responses" of "journalists" who play detective seeking to expose "depravity in academe" (p. 105). But while she suggests that he imputes a charge of mental masturbation to her because he cannot bear to acknowledge how masturbatory writing itself is, and what a legitimate and unacknowledged form of private pleasure authorship can be, I think there is another reason someone aghast at the collapse of criticism's disembodiment might cathect on the indexing of Austen and autoeroticism. This has to do with being in a disenfranchised audience. When some journalists and literary critics discover that there is no longer an inevitable or imaginable continuity between their understanding of the tasks of commentary and yours, they experience the humiliated identity of the social outcast; they experience themselves as specifically undesired by you (you as "Eve," and "you" as the collectivity that speaks from within the sphere of "gay and lesbian studies"). They argue that criticism has lost its communicative function; they mean *with them.* And if you are not communicating with them, you are masturbating. Traditional criticism is in this sense as alloerotic as the most boring heterosexuality. The relation between homophobia and critical nostalgia in these circles is not at all simple.

Yet at least the public sphere pundits understand correctly that their intellectual and sexual intelligibility are all of a piece and that the broad appeal of gay and lesbian studies is, truly, threatening to a certain caste of mind. Such self-understanding is not, in this essay's view, characteristic of the New Historicism, but the problem with New Historicism here is its uncanny resemblance to this essay's project of epistemological transformation. Sedgwick's polemic speaks to the too-easy way in which all scan-

1. See Roger Kimball, *Tenured Radicals: How Politics Has Corrupted Our Higher Education* (New York, 1990).
2. See Eve Kosofsky Sedgwick, "Jane Austen and the Masturbating Girl," *Critical Inquiry* 17 (Summer 1991): 818–37.

dal seems alike in this moment of evidentiary upheaval in the humanities. As many have noticed, many New Historicisms rely on an uncannily Reaganesque deployment of anecdotes, whose local explanatory power is assumed to stand in for truths about reality. But this very essay could be described similarly, to a point.

The strategy of "Jane Austen and the Masturbating Girl" is not to claim comprehensive readings of either the scientific literature on masturbation or *Sense and Sensibility*. It uses these discursive domains to generate a counterhistory of sexuality around autoeroticism. To write this, Sedgwick features an 1881 case study of a female masturbator to provide evidence of the ways in which a woman's roving and unattached emotions and desires were transformed, by ropes, brands, and taxonomies, into a disciplined sexual identity, and then, more diffusely, into a modern personality type: the codependent, the addictive. Sedgwick interlaces paragraphs from this study with paragraphs from *Sense and Sensibility*. She turns the stuttering, stumbling, fainting, fluttering, and other corporeal and mental embarrassments Austen seems to represent as the conventional gestures of heterosexual femininity into evidence of other acts—sensations and memories of sensation whose excess to the usual object-obsessed narratives of sexual identity create horizons of libidinous and conceptual possibility called, for short, "autoeroticism." She freely engages in anachronistic juxtaposition, reading between the texts to open a space for a history organized only by the trace of this object, and this subject, "the masturbator." The unboundedness of the sexual knowledge she generates from the unrealized possibilities in the domains of science and literature raises all sorts of questions about the value—say, the comparability—of the evidence these readings orchestrate. Indeed, she avows that she wants to shock her students by disrupting such scholarly anchorings in order to induce creative thinking about the movements of sexual and epistemological energy in 1813, 1881, 1981, and so on (see p. 122).

But in Sedgwick's view the New Historicists disavow their own implication in "pornotroping": she rejects "the pseudo-distantiating relish of sophisticated contemporary projects of critique" (p. 122). We know from her readings of sexual science and of literary criticism that detached chastisement stands as the ur-condition of political domination in this essay. The task for criticism is to claim its *own* historicity, which means making explicit its *own* erotic investments in bringing power and authority into representation. Without such self-reflexivity, she argues, New Historicism generates morally bad criticism that is merely pseudocreative with history, while remaining wedded to the most traditional pedagogy, authoritarian and consumed by the pleasure of its own "rigor" and self-discipline. It is perhaps for this reason that she counterdisciplines the New Historians by refusing here to utter any specific names of critics, or to give any examples of the craft.

Sedgwick attributes her own critical "proclivities" to the context gay and lesbian studies provides for an autoerotic criticism, that is, a criticism that speaks from the intimacy of its own collectivity, that serves its own public in public, expanding the intellectual and erotic imaginary whose impulses created the urgency for criticism in the first place. *Sense and Sensibility* might have been an apposite vehicle for an expanded opportunity. If it indeed demonstrates incontestably Elinor's love for Marianne, Marianne's uncanny repetition of autoerotic performance, the emergence of heterosexual subjectivity and what we might parodically call heterosexual studies or modern literary criticism, the novel is also a hilarious slapstick on the subject of erotic evidence itself. The detectives are almost always the women—Marianne Dashwood, Elinor Dashwood, Lucy Steele—struggling to survive in some proximity to their evident objects of desire, who are, evidently, men, men for whom the women undergo much pain and suffering, even while the main positive affective experience they have is with women, in whom they confide, to whom they confess. In countless scenes female characters inhabit the anxiety of heterosexual desire, and plot their erotic attachments by hysterically overreading something that might or might not be a clue to the fate of a desire they have deliberately solicited or accidently encountered so that they might be able, after all, to live narratively, in a marriage, where they will be able, after all, to *stop reading*, to become stupid, at least about their own lives. It is single men who have the interiority in this text—secret suffering, sordid pasts, control over master narratives—and single women who desire to enter the paper trail of the heterosexual trajectory and who therefore are obsessed with looking for the signs of its existence. But can we really say that the women in this novel desire to become epistemologically or erotically "like" men who love women? What, in truth, does Sedgwick's essay want to tell us, about the erotic subjectivity of women?

It tells us many things, "under the pressure of our own needs," and leaves a trail of open questions and, I think, productive confusions. The stated critical context for this project was to develop "skills for a project of historicizing any sexuality," "along with a tradition of valuing nonprocreative forms of creativity and pleasure; a history of being suspicious of the tendentious functioning of open secrets; and a politically urgent tropism toward the gaily and, if necessary, the defiantly explicit" (p. 108). That is to say, bringing these diverse intertexts into irritating proximity, and making these different arguments about the necessity to reduce the distance between critics and the kinds of desires and knowledges they promote, the essay seeks to open a space to reimagine criticism and sexuality itself.

I am not confused about how the critical and scientific negation of erotic impulses functions as a site of mourning and rage in this text. But I am confused about the erotics of female amnesia it produces, and about the function of "self-evidence" when it comes to reading the "identities"—lesbian, female—we think we already know. For example, in the theoretical and historical framework of this essay, the masturbator is un-differentiated as to gender. Yet somehow the masturbator gets gendered, female, and titled "The Masturbating Girl." Somehow the heterosexual flirtations of Austen's Marianne and Elinor Dashwood, who are also both but differently autoerotic in their relation to the pain of desiring, become frozen only in moments of Elinor's feminine identification and Mari-anne's autoerotic self-absorption. Somehow the difference between Mari-anne and Elinor, who each experience the loss of their erotic identities, becomes smudged at the end of the essay—in the female figure of the love that keeps forgetting its name. Is this love, which founds the possibil-ity of a female or a lesbian erotic subjectivity, only a field of utopian nega-tivity? Is this love available only in titles, like *Lesbia Brandon*, gay and lesbian studies, or in the couple fantasy of "Jane Austen and the Mastur-bating Girl"? Is paratextuality itself the place of feminine erotic self-evidence? What is the function of gendering in this piece? I take as a final example the phrase, "the female figure of the love that keeps forgetting its name," which closes the act of commemoration this essay ventures. The phrase it revises and joins, "the love that dare not speak its name," famously describes the historico-political condition of gay male subjectiv-ity. But "female figure of the love that keeps forgetting its name" has a less clear relation to the lesbian, just as the difference between "cannot speak" and "keeps forgetting" seems a terribly important and underelab-orated explanatory divergence of the possibilities for gay and lesbian his-tory. The former "love" has a name and condenses a public history of desire and negativity; but for the lesbian, as with the masturbator, the love itself is rapt in the grammatical ambiguity of possession: "the female figure of the love." The female figure of a female, a lesbian love? Or does love remain elsewhere to gender, forgetting and remembering, such that this oscillation becomes a kind of namesake, a female figure of rememora-tion, the muse of masturbation's inheritance?

These are not rhetorical questions. Their answers would touch upon the domains of feminism, of identity politics, of the specificity of lesbi-anism, and of the sexual politics of figuration and its displacements. To close, though, I would like to return to the juncture of criticism and chas-tisement. I have been thinking, recently, that projects of redescription like this have become central to many kinds of critical activity in America. It is not only that in the humanities so many truths universally acknowl-edged have come to seem forces of scandalous violence, such that the very complacent languages of identity—of race, gender, sexuality, nation-ality, and aesthetic value—we have used to describe the courses of power have come to seem performances of their own inevitability. It is also that, as some of us disrupt some critical decorums and promote others, other competing moves to redescribe pain, pleasure, and power are emerging, whose impulses and effects seem actively unprincipled. American busi-nesses, to take one example, have been releasing both blue and white collar workers at an extraordinary rate; but partly to circumvent the language of contracts, and partly to misdirect our attention from the failures of both industrial and managerial capitalism, they have invented new figurative languages to describe what we used to call getting fired. Some of these, such as furloughing and downsizing, are conventional now; but my favorite announcement of layoffs is by the Digital Corporation, which in 1992 announced, astonishingly, its grief at having to submit to "involuntary methodologies."[3] As with the masturbating girl under treatment for her digital compulsion, the experience of duress and the impossibility of consent are evoked here by the aptly named business. And as with Roger Kimball, the melodramatic tableau of a power-saturated figure submitting to involuntariness itself obscures the very power even a failing business has, the power of capital, of reification, of renaming its activity of economic violence an "involuntary methodology."

Thus too the jury at the Rodney King police battery trial, as though it were in film graduate school, became convinced that the video demanded scrutiny, interpretation, figurative displacement; and it concluded, from the perspective of its own overreading, that powerlessness was precisely in the places it seemed not to be. The police, apparently, have had to submit to involuntary methodologies as well, so that a victim's gestures of self-protection and even aggressive survival can look exactly like tableaus of tyranny and can provoke, under the wake of authority's seeming disruption, entirely new semiotic norms. Patricia Williams has suggested that the police defense team characterized Rodney King as a gun; frame by frame the jury viewed the "'cocked leg,'" the arm in a "'trigger position.'"[4] Sedgwick's essay is itself full of guns—the smoking, warm gun of Kimball's attack on academia and the explosively erotic loaded gun of Paula Bennett's Emily Dickinson. The range of reference in this arsenal marks Dickinson's creative sexual ecology as the utopian inversion of the chastising, anerotic authorship imagined by conventional criticism. Rodney King, a victim of violence, turns into violence objectified; by risking overreading in the service of unheard-of modern sexualities, "Jane Austen and the Masturbating Girl" discharges the violence of violated identity and provokes us to imagine explicitly what kind of criticism and what kind of politics can be written in its wake.

3. Janice Castro, "Grapevine: Forward Spin," *Time*, 11 May 1992, p. 9.
4. Patricia J. Williams, "The Rules of the Game," *Village Voice*, 12 May 1992, p. 32.

Against Epistemology

Eve Kosofsky Sedgwick

Doing my laundry, packing, and trying to get psyched for this conference, I told myself that however boring it might turn out to be (not that I expected it to be boring), there would at least be the interest of seeing how many different scholars, disciplines, and methodologies were going to wind up getting blamed for the not guilty verdict in the Rodney King police battery case. Which prosecutor, when all was said and done, would be able to make the indictment stick?

Practically anyone, I feared, would now have an easy time in doing so. Now that American journalists have established that we have only deconstruction to blame for the rise of German fascism in the 1930s, we are all free to turn our attention to deciding which branch of postmodern theory has so vitiated the force of the self-evident that even your average gun-toting retired cop in Simi Valley knows enough not to believe the horror that is staring him right in the face.

You can imagine what a relief it is, then, that at such a very early point in the conference, and so promptly too after the disgraceful verdict in California, my friend Lauren Berlant has already explicitly exonerated *me* for one of practically any responsibility at all for the outcome of the Rodney King case (and has even volunteered not to insist too much on the ugly little matter of those "involuntary methodologies" in the high-tech industries). I suppose I may consider myself, at least for the moment, free on my own recognizance to rejoice rather than, as instructed, to re-join. In truth, and to adopt a less equivocal tone, I am very appreciative that "Jane Austen and the Masturbating Girl" (pp. 105–24) has elicited a response that does so much to articulate and open out what must to many readers have seemed the intolerably impacted motives of this far from transparent essay. It's especially important to me that Lauren chose, graciously, and was able, acutely, to read the essay in the light of several ambitions that were indeed at its heart: the project of fostering and furthering, in some form or forms, the linkage she refers to as knowledge/pleasure; the project, as she puts it, of opening a space—out of the very gaps and misfittings among historical discourses—for an ongoing history that has a place and a use for sexually nonconforming people and our often transverse energies; and the project of using the figure of the masturbator to get some rhetorical as well as historical leverage on what can otherwise, as I've experienced too sharply in some of my own trains of thought, prove the fatally self-replicating triad of sanctioned heterosexual presumption, stigmatized gay male hypersalience, and lesbian invisibility.

I take it as axiomatic that such projects can be best entertained only in writing that, one way or another, actively engages with the performative force of its subjects and itself. On the issue of lesbian invisibility, for example, Terry Castle's essay is eloquent in its demonstration that, constatively read, the ghost story in *An Adventure* invokes "the impasse into which skepticism leads";[1] the book can in that light be seen only as true, which is unlikely, or as evidence that its coauthors share a discrediting diagnosis of mental pathology that is anyway all too available for writing off the utterance and subjectivity of women whose lives exhibit "'morbid' sexual tendencies" ("CF," p. 41). But Castle also suggests the viability of quite a different set of questions from those involved in a constative or propositional reading: "How else," Castle asks, "might two repressed female homosexuals express their relationship than through such a story?" ("CF," p. 37). I take the operative word here to be, not *repressed*, but *express*, for *express* opens the door to a whole different set of questions alternative to the lesbian-eradicating options credulous versus crazy. Instead of asking, How could they possibly have believed this story? or even, Where are we to stand to judge its truth or falsity? Castle seems here to suggest a very different question: belief quite aside, what kind of *act* was it for these two women to write *and publish* this—possibly preposterous— indeed, this possibly flamboyantly, best-sellingly, publicly, and above all *jointly* preposterous monument to their courtship; and to the claim made for a place in public history by the perturbed, gappy, depression-tinged but resolute melding of their subjectivities?

Most of my energy in "Jane Austen and the Masturbating Girl" was

1. Terry Castle, "Contagious Folly: *An Adventure* and Its Skeptics," this volume, p. 142; hereafter abbreviated "CF."

Eve Kosofsky Sedgwick is the Newman Ivey White Professor of English at Duke University and the author of *Epistemology of the Closet* (1990), *Tendencies* (1993), and a volume of poetry, *Fat Art, Thin Art* (1994).

devoted to experimenting with structures and rhetorics that I thought might suggest some new sight lines and relations around the performativity of sex, of literature, of theory. (I mean *performativity* here in a double, a tensely double sense: theatrical performance on the one hand, with all its self-ignorant and amnesiac extroversion, and on the other hand the absorptiveness and introversion that deconstruction attributes to speech-act performativity.) Such writing is necessarily experimental. Emily Dickinson refers to death in one poem as

> the interval
> Experience between
> And most profound experiment
> Appointed unto Men—[2]

The relation of experiment to experience has always been, as Simon Schaffer demonstrates,[3] a slippery and often a mutually discrediting one, mediated, in his fascinating argument, through a cloven and thereby newly constituted "self," through the ambiguous and nonsingular status of the body of the experimenter/experiencer. In conceiving of this writing as experimental (and I think I mean thereby to *distinguish* it from what other people refer to as experiential writing), I seem, as Berlant notes, to conjure up at multiple points of the essay holograms of my own body, among others, that are used to perform a wide variety of allegorizing, prosopopoeic, displacing, distantiating, and otherwise dynamic functions; but the scission of whose claim to be entitled to a unified "experience" is part of the repeated enactment of the inquiry.

Rereading "Jane Austen and the Masturbating Girl" in the context of the other "Questions of Evidence" essays, I am struck, not to say embarrassed, by its difference from most of them in sheer specific gravity. Having already been rechristened *Eve Kosofsky Sedgwick The Masturbating Girl* by *Critical Inquiry*'s system of running heads, I don't want to be the one to say the essay *sticks out like a sore thumb;* but surely you know what I mean. Many scholars, asked to reflect on the topic of evidence, seem to inflect their style toward the "rendered" in the sense of being clarified by the straining out of particulate matter. I guess the same invitation made me want my essay "rendered" in the writerly sense—wrought, maybe verging on wrought up. (I remember how much I cheered up about the depredations of the press around my title when I realized one result was that I could start with a sentence in iambic pentameter: "The phrase itself is already evidence" [p. 105].) I wanted to make it inescapable that the piece *was* writerly.

---

2. Emily Dickinson, poem 822, *The Complete Poems of Emily Dickinson*, ed. Thomas H. Johnson (Boston, 1960), p. 399.

3. See Simon Schaffer, "Self Evidence," this volume, pp. 56–91.

It occurs to me too, rereading it for the conference and at the same time in the aftermath of the Rodney King verdict, how much and how similarly the essay is preoccupied with and structured by two forms of anomalous language—specifically, with writerliness itself and, on the other hand, with the genre of the atrocity story. The essay both *allegorizes* and *performs* the atrocity story even as it does writerliness; and each of these acts depends on the essay's strict refusal to provide conceptual facilities for their analytic integration. The self-attentive, congested, *troublant*, and visibly self-pleasured density of writerliness has an apt enough emblem in the Masturbating Girl; and the relations around her stand well enough for the unacknowledged codependency between the institutions and disciplines of humanist thought, even the chastest of them, and the ostensibly marginalized practice of the florid writerliness of many of their founders, catalysts, and celebrities. There's nothing terribly wrong with this disciplinary ecology (I certainly don't want to moralize against codependency per se)—at least until scapegoating time rolls around, as it has this awful way of doing, when the systems dynamic kicks in with a vengeance and yields up something like pure shaming spectacle, spectacle shorn of the relations and ties that have heretofore enabled its reorganization of the gestalt in which it appears.

As for the atrocity story, the essay's most deliberate and principled structural undertaking is, I hope obviously, to make somehow inescapable the *problem* of the atrocity story. By this I don't mean the problem of the atrocity *story* (for example, because it might be a fabrication) as against the actual atrocity; I mean how problematic is the circulation of the atrocity story true *or* false, the kind of currency it represents and motive it provides, the facts it makes graphic at the cost of the relations it obscures.

Now, clearly, there is no point in reflecting only on the atrocity stories of people and causes one disagrees with—the stations of the cross in the "rape of Kuwait," the narrative poetics of the fetus in the jar. The wasting body of Kimberly Bergalis is an atrocity story; but isn't the wasting body of someone I might see at an airport or in a fundraising letter from Larry Kramer, who reminds me of a friend I don't have any more because of AIDS? I can't just be content to call that latter body, by contrast, the compelling emblem of an enduring rage and true motive, though it is that. Indeed, for many people, probably for a majority of women, people stigmatized by color or poverty, lesbians, and gay men, one or some of the bodies that each of us ourselves inhabits already *is* intermittently legible as the text of an atrocity story—whether battered, raped, bashed, mugged, held hostage, or bearing the scars of one of the diseases or disease treatments that are so shiftingly but compellingly definable as forms of medical, state, environmental, or social violence. The atrocity story now flickers around, cleaving as much as defining, the place of many people's proprioception.

But what is it we want or expect from the self-evidence of the atrocity? The exacerbated rage about the Rodney King verdict depends (as Michele Wallace pointed out to me in a recent conversation) on a privileged and, as it turns out, false presumption about what self-evidence is supposed to get you in the American system of justice—as distinct, presumably, from less "developed" justice systems where even confrontations with ocular evidence would not be assumed to ensure victory. And I've been struck by the way journalists' and intellectuals' analyses of the verdict can't seem to stay away from the epistemology of the film. As though somehow it *must* be, however incredibly, that the ladies and gentlemen of the jury had been persuaded to disbelieve the evidence of their own eyes—as though somehow it *must* have happened that they were persuaded not to see what they did see. But I wonder if South Central L.A.'s reading of the verdict might not be different, less epistemologically exciting, and likelier. Maybe those jurors did see what they did see, but for reasons of their own—systemic racism might be one—they just *didn't mind it very much.*

Part of what the performativity of my essay was aimed at, in a context where the "question of evidence" seemed all but predetermined as the question of evidential truth or credibility, was to de-emphasize the epistemology of evidence and instead stress its erotics—that is, to dramatize how not only *evidence* is part of the currency of a social and libidinal economy, but equally so is the epistemological stress itself.

OBJECTS AND OBJECTIVITIES

Belief and Resistance: A Symmetrical Account

Barbara Herrnstein Smith

Questions of evidence—including the idea, still central to what could be called informal epistemology, that our beliefs and claims are duly corrected by our encounters with autonomously resistant objects (for example, facts, rocks, bricks, and texts-themselves)—are inevitably caught up in views of how beliefs, generally, are produced, maintained, and transformed.[1] In recent years, substantially new accounts of these cognitive dynamics—and, with them, more or less novel conceptions of what we might mean by "beliefs"—have been emerging from various nonphilosophical fields (for example, theoretical biology, cognitive science, and the sociology of knowledge) as well as from within disciplinary epistemology. Because of the distinctly reflexive nature of these developments—that is,

My thanks to David Austin, Andy Pickering, David Sanford, and Joe Valente for useful tips and significant resistances.

1. Literary theorists instructed in traditional epistemology readily assimilate the supposedly autonomous corrective force of brute facts to the supposedly autonomous corrective agency of "the text itself." Thus Christopher Norris, invoking a questionable interpretation of Paul de Man's essay, "The Resistance to Theory," argues, "*contra* [Stanley] Fish" and others that "the rhetorical structures" of literary texts offer "inbuilt resistance" to (certain) critical theories and interpretations, and remarks that "there is nothing absurd about the analogy between bumping up against recalcitrant facts in the realm of empirical knowledge and bumping up against anomalous details in the reading of familiar texts" (Christopher Norris, *What's Wrong with Postmodernism: Critical Theory and the Ends of Philosophy* [Baltimore, 1990], p. 115). The absurdity or difficulty is not, of course, in the analogy per se.

This essay originally appeared in *Critical Inquiry* 18 (Autumn 1991).

new conceptions of concepts, revised beliefs about belief, invocations of evidence said to challenge the operation of evidence, quasi-logical refutations of the authority of logic, and so on—the deployment of positions and arguments becomes extremely difficult here, as does even the description of the relevant events in intellectual history. Indeed, since we are dealing here not merely with shifts of, as it is sometimes put, "vocabulary," but, often enough, with clashes of profoundly divergent conceptual idiom and *syntax,* every major term and discursive move is potentially implicated in the problematic itself, and, thereby, open to radical questioning and liable to charges of question-begging.

The aim of the present essay is twofold: first, to suggest the more general interest and significance, beyond the fields in which they are being developed, of these emerging reconceptions of belief; and, second, to frame that suggestion in an account which, since it cannot escape the rhetorical difficulties just mentioned, foregrounds them. A number of related themes—notably, symmetry, circularity, reciprocality, and ambivalence—recur throughout and, at various points, are drawn together in accord with the account itself.

Beliefs in Collision

In the confrontation between belief and evidence, belief, as we know, is no pushover. And yet beliefs do change, evidently in response to, among other things, contrary evidence. Taken together, these two observations are not controversial. The urging of one in opposition to the other, however, together with different ways of explaining each, marks a perennial debate pursued in our era as constructivist-interactionist accounts of knowledge versus more or less traditional (rationalist, realist, and so on) epistemologies.[2] The former stress the *participation* of prior belief in the perception of present evidence—that is, the hermeneutic circle. The latter insist on the possibility of the *correction* of prior belief by present

2. The pedigree of the debate is as ancient as Plato's (supposed) exposure of Protagoras's self-refutation. Most intellectual historians date its sharpening in our own era to the publication of Thomas S. Kuhn, *The Structure of Scientific Revolutions* (Chicago, 1962). Since shifting labels and diversely characterized positions contribute to the difficulties here, a caveat is in order: what is meant by "constructivist-interactionist accounts" is indicated by explicit description, exemplification, and other specific usage *in this essay;* the term is not intended to name any otherwise specifically determined position, school, or movement.

Barbara Herrnstein Smith is Braxton Craven Professor of Comparative Literature and English at Duke University and director of its Center for Interdisciplinary Studies in Science and Cultural Theory. The author of, among other works, *Contingencies of Value: Alternative Perspectives for Critical Theory* (1988), she is currently completing a study of contemporary theoretical controversy.

evidence—that is, the possible rupture of the hermeneutic circle by what is posited as autonomous, observer-independent reality—and also on its normative occurrence, as in (genuine) science.

The divergences here are not just matters of emphasis: the two views, at least in the terms just outlined, are mutually incompatible. Efforts at mediation, reconciliation, and transcendence have, however, been made: attempts to narrow and bridge the differences, to modulate what are seen as extreme formulations, and/or to combine what is seen as the best of each side.[3] Two points central to the present account may be noted here. One is that the intellectual success of any such mediating position is just as liable to diverse assessment as the conflicting positions themselves: that is, there is no obvious way to adjudicate objectively (in the classic sense) among them, no evidence that would demonstrate conclusively the correctness of just one of them, no logical analysis that would expose, once and for all, the flaws, failures, or fallacies at the heart of each of the others. It does not follow, however, that these efforts are futile or that the conflicting sides must always remain constituted and divided exactly as before. For—and this is the second point to be noted—at the level both of individual cognitive activity and general intellectual history, the mutual abrasions of mutually resistant beliefs, in interaction with other contingently emerging conditions, may produce significant and stable modifications of each and, thereby, significant and stable *new* cognitive configurations and intellectual alignments. This possibility implies, among other things, that we may speak of conflicting beliefs (theories, accounts, interpretations, and so on) as crucially and (from some perspectives) profitably *affecting* each other without having to maintain that one (and only one) of them must/could be, in the classic sense, correct.

Begging the Question, or the Microdynamics of Incommensurability

The idea of "incommensurability" (implicitly evoked above) figures centrally in these debates—less as an issue actually engaged, however,

3. Thus Hilary Putnam, positing a choice between (supposedly) self-refuting conventionalism and metaphysical realism, asks, "Is there no middle way?" (Hilary Putnam, *Realism with a Human Face*, ed. James Conant [Cambridge, Mass., 1990], p. 26). In addition to Putnam's own proposed alternative ("internal realism"), recent mediating and transcending efforts include Ian Hacking, *Representing and Intervening: Introductory Topics in the Philosophy of Natural Science* (Cambridge, 1983); Richard J. Bernstein, *Beyond Objectivism and Relativism: Science, Hermeneutics, and Praxis* (Philadelphia, 1983); Arthur Fine, "The Natural Ontological Attitude," in *Scientific Realism*, ed. Jarrett Leplin (Berkeley, 1984); and Michael A. Arbib and Mary B. Hesse, *The Construction of Reality* (Cambridge, 1986). Some of these efforts are, from the present perspective, more congenial, evocative, and serviceable than others.

than as an emblem of that profound divergence of conceptual idiom, the possibility of which defines the idea itself. Indeed, the pattern of perplexities routinely displayed in these (non)engagements—matched charges of circularity and self-refutation, stubborn credos and *eccos,* and equally stubborn skepticisms and denials—may be seen to reflect and, perhaps, to illuminate the general cognitive dynamics at issue. A brief consideration of the phenomenon—simultaneously logical, rhetorical, and psychological—of "question-begging" will introduce the broader issues here. That it *is* simultaneously all three, or can be alternatively produced in the diverse conceptual/discursive idioms of each of the disciplines implicated (logic, rhetoric, psychology), is the first point to be noted.

Question-begging, or what is called, in classical logic, *petitio principii,* is not, by its canons, a minor breach of etiquette but a transgression of the first order, nullifying the force of an argument. Similarly, viewed rhetorically, it is not one move among others but a crucial, perhaps definitive, one in these debates. Question-begging could also be seen as a name for the psychological tendency I have elsewhere called epistemic self-privileging:[4] that is, "assuming"—here in the psychological rather than logical sense of the word—the beliefs one is seeking to justify; assuming that what one assumes is not an assumption but an established fact or necessary presupposition; assuming that one's terms are transparent and that the senses in which one uses them are nonproblematic; and assuming that no alternative conceptualizations or formulations are possible, or at least no "adequate," "coherent," or "meaningful" ones. Question-begging also appears to be another name for going around the hermeneutic circle. Indeed, all of these—question-begging, hermeneutic circularity, and epistemic self-privileging—could be seen as names for a single but double-valued (some times/ways advantageous, some times/ways disadvantageous) human tendency, the complex dynamics and variable operation of which yield the confoundments that concern us here. I shall refer to the tendency as "cognitive conservatism," reserving further discussion of it, per se, for a later section.

Contrary to the claims of classical logic, question-begging does not render an argument null and void—not, at least, in the rhetorical sense of ineffective or unpersuasive. Evidence for this counterclaim includes the remarkable effectiveness and persuasiveness, at least in some domains, of what is called (following Kant) "transcendental analysis," which could be described as a method for proving things, independent of empirical appeals, by demonstrating that they are self-evidently presupposed by what is (supposedly) self-evident, or, alternately, as a method for begging the question on a grand scale. Its operation is illustrated in the following passages from an essay by Karl-Otto Apel, who is here defending a classic

---

4. See Barbara Herrnstein Smith, *Contingencies of Value: Alternative Perspectives for Critical Theory* (Cambridge, Mass., 1988), pp. 54–84.

conception of reason, via what he calls "transcendental foundationalism," against skeptics, whom he calls "irrationalists":

> The "vital element" of philosophical arguments is a transcendental language game in which, along with some rules of logic and the existence of a real world, something like . . . the norms of ideal communication are presupposed. . . . Any choice that could be understood as meaningful already presupposes the transcendental language game as its condition of possibility. . . . [It follows that reason] can always confirm its own legitimation through reflection on the fact that it presupposes its own self-understanding of the very rules it opts for. . . . The defense of irrationalism actually refutes [itself] through the accompanying performative act. . . . The point of philosophical foundations lies, then, in the . . . argument that one can . . . decide neither for nor against the rules of the transcendental language game without those rules being presupposed.[5]

These passages suggest the rhetorical power, logical coherence, and psychological effectiveness of transcendental argumentation. Apel observes, claims, and presumably believes that "reason" (as he conceives it and, it seems, assumes is the only way it could be conceived) is necessarily presupposed by all choice "that could be understood as meaningful." Since, for Apel, to decide (that is, to choose meaningfully) *against* (this conception of) reason is, ipso facto, to presuppose it, it follows that the skeptic refutes his own denial of (this conception of) reason in the very act of asserting it. Moreover, being thus "performatively" affirmed by the only one who would otherwise deny it, reason (as Apel conceives it) is universally (and thus, for Apel, objectively) confirmed. Q.E.D.

As here, however, so, often enough, elsewhere: the charge of self-refutation is a mirror and sign of absolute epistemic self-privileging. As Apel's citations indicate, what he means by "the defense of irrationalism" is, among other things, constructivist accounts of knowledge that reject the conceptual idiom that he believes is uniquely proper (what he calls "the 'vital element' of philosophical arguments").[6] From the perspective

5. Karl-Otto Apel, "The Problem of Philosophical Foundations in Light of a Transcendental Pragmatics of Language," in *After Philosophy: End or Transformation?* ed. Kenneth Baynes, James Bohman, and Thomas McCarthy (Cambridge, Mass., 1987), pp. 280–83; hereafter abbreviated "PPF." Some qualifying clauses and elaborations have been omitted here, but the definitive logical moves have, I think, been preserved.

6. Apel cites as his antagonists here "constructivism" and "followers of Kuhn, particularly Feyerabend," remarking of the latter that their views lead "to a relativism of language games. . . , which Popper has correctly characterized as 'the myth of the frameworks' " ("PPF," p. 286 n. 36). He supports the last point as follows: "Not only are there 'language games,' but also . . . *the* transcendental language game" ("PPF," p. 290 n. 70; emphasis added).

of those accounts, however, the question (here crucially begged by Apel) is whether *any* conceptual idiom is uniquely proper. Moreover, in relation to their own alternative conceptions of "reason," "choice," "language game," and so on, constructivist accounts of all these (and rejections of classic conceptions of them) are not self-refuting but self-exemplifying.[7] In other words (precisely—that is, in another conceptual idiom), the irrationalist's alleged self-refutation is an artifact of the rationalist's absolute self-privileging—or, more generally, the Skeptic's annihilation is *required, produced,* and *guaranteed* by the Believer's belief.[8]

Classically posed, the question regarding question-begging is (a) whether its circularity is vicious and (b) if so, whether it is escapable. If "vicious" is understood in the rhetorical sense of making an argument unpersuasive, then the answer to the first part of the question seems to be, *it depends:* specifically, the extent to which a circular argument is persuasive *for some audience* seems to depend on, among other things, the extent to which the concepts and conceptual syntax that the argument "begs"—that is, employs and takes for granted—are also taken for granted by that particular audience. Thus, transcendental demonstrations prove things most readily to those already inclined to believe them. This does not, however, make such demonstrations pointless; on the contrary, in a world where destabilizing skepticism—internal and external—always threatens, the (re)stabilization of belief (the "confirm[ation of] its own legitimation," in Apel's terms) is a continuously required activity. Accordingly, the answer to the second part of the question is that, while total escape from circularity may not be possible, it may also not be, under all conditions and from all perspectives, either necessary or desirable.

---

7. The sociology of knowledge avoids self-refutation (only) by becoming reflexive, that is, by acknowledging that the same general kind of (sociological) account that it proposes to give of all other knowledge could be given of those accounts themselves. For a nice analysis of reflexivity (and a witty enactment of its implications), see Malcolm Ashmore, *The Reflexive Thesis: Wrighting Sociology of Scientific Knowledge* (Chicago, 1989). For a related discussion, see Peter Barker, "The Reflexivity Problem in the Psychology of Science," in *Psychology of Science: Contributions to a Metascience,* ed. Barry Gholson et al. (Cambridge, 1989), pp. 92–115.

8. The self-refutation argument has recently been given its perhaps ultimate turn by Jürgen Habermas, who charges, in connection with his own transcendental demonstration of the necessary presuppositions of communication, that even a spitefully mute skeptic refutes himself "as long as he is . . . alive *at all.*" For, Habermas argues, such a skeptic "cannot, even indirectly, deny . . . that he reproduces his life in [a] web [of communicative action]" and "remains bound" to its "presuppositions"—all as specifically (but clearly not, for Habermas, questionably) derived and described in the transcendental demonstration itself (Jürgen Habermas, *Moral Consciousness and Communicative Action,* trans. Christian Lenhardt and Shierry Weber Nicholsen [Cambridge, Mass., 1990], pp. 100–101).

A Symmetrical Reflection[9]

The preceding discussion is (relatively) evenhanded, but the author's views on these issues are not altogether neutral. On the whole, she finds that constructivist-interactionist accounts of knowledge and belief (along the lines indicated in this essay) offer more conceptually congenial, evocative, and serviceable ways for her to think about matters such as "reason" and "reality" than do traditional realist or rationalist epistemologies. At the same time (and with no apparent undermining of her own relative cognitive stability), she believes that she "believes" those accounts (in the sense of "belief" outlined below), in the same way—that is, for the same general sorts of reasons and by way of the same general cognitive dynamics—as anyone, including the believer in traditional epistemology, believes anything.[10]

Macrodynamics of Belief

The dynamics of belief can be described with respect both to individual subjects during their personal lifetimes and to populations of subjects over larger time scales. The latter (macrodynamics) will be considered here first, and illustrated (reflexively) by changing beliefs about belief.

Classic beliefs (in the sense of prevailing theories) about belief (in the sense of cognitive production/s) seem to be changing in the ways and for the reasons that all beliefs change.[11] Specifically, more or less new beliefs, experienced as more conceptually congenial, evocative, and/or otherwise

9. This essay glances, here and elsewhere, at the "symmetry" postulate proposed by Barry Barnes and David Bloor, in accord with which sociologists of knowledge undertake to give *the same general account* of the knowledge their community accepts as true as they give of the beliefs it rejects as false. See Barry Barnes and David Bloor, "Relativism, Rationalism and the Sociology of Knowledge," in *Rationality and Relativism,* ed. Martin Hollis and Steven Lukes (Cambridge, Mass., 1982), pp. 25–26. *Symmetry* should not be identified with *equality,* and the postulate should not be confused with the objectivist's self-inverting (and, as such, self-refuting) "relativism," a position (probably held by no one) that would assign *equal objective epistemological status* to all beliefs. For further discussion of the phantom heresy of "relativism" and its companion, the Egalitarian Fallacy, see Smith, *Contingencies of Value,* pp. 98–101, 150–56.

10. This reflection, which makes explicit the type of self-exemplification described above (nn. 7, 9), anticipates a charge of self-refutation. As the preceding discussion indicates, however, and as prior experience confirms (see David L. Roochnik, "Can the Relativist Avoid Refuting Herself?" *Philosophy and Literature* 14 [Apr. 1990]: 92–98), to anticipate it is not to forestall it.

11. The observations that follow in this section draw on studies in the philosophy, history, and sociology of science (constructivist and otherwise), including the following: Paul K. Feyerabend, *Against Method: Outline of an Anarchistic Theory of Knowledge* (London, 1975); Bloor, *Knowledge and Social Imagery* (London, 1976); Barnes, *Interests and the Growth of Knowledge* (London, 1977); M. J. Mulkay, *Science and the Sociology of Knowledge* (London, 1979); K. Knorr-Cetina, *The Manufacture of Knowledge: An Essay on the Constructivist and*

serviceable than those they are replacing, are being articulated and appropriated by, and disseminated among, various groups of people. These relatively new beliefs are experienced by those people as more serviceable in relation to a broad array of projects—personal and professional, technological and conceptual—from the explanation of differing literary interpretations to the diagnosis of neurological disorders, and from critiques of classic epistemology to the articulation of alternative accounts of knowledge. Among the people involved in these developments are some with institutional authority and influence in the relevant domains and disciplines: neurologists, literary theorists, philosophers, sociologists of science, and so forth. It appears that the processes described here are at a point where relatively new beliefs about belief have become fairly stable among a considerable portion of the populations mentioned and figure more and more extensively in their various projects.

This description does not speak of enlightenment or progress. It speaks of reasons (plural and heterogeneous) but not of Reason, and, emphasizing specific domains and disciplines and the ongoing pursuits of selected populations, it does not speak of science or human knowledge in the abstract. It may appear that the preference for one belief over another is being regarded here as ("merely") a matter of taste. That is correct. The "merely" disappears, however, for taste, in the present account, would not be distinguished from and opposed to (the operation of) Reason(s) but would be, rather, a way of reconceptualizing the latter.[12]

Another symmetry becomes significant at this point. The reasons (as described above) why (some) people prefer new beliefs about belief are the same *general sorts* that people have had in the past for developing and appropriating beliefs (about belief or anything else) that turned out to be conceptually congenial, imaginatively evocative, and highly serviceable under a broad range of different conditions—or, in one sense of the term, *true*. But they are also the same general sorts of reasons that people have had in the past for entertaining beliefs that turned out (some very quickly,

---

Contextual Nature of Science (Oxford, 1981); Andrew Pickering, *Constructing Quarks: A Sociological History of Particle Physics* (Chicago, 1984); Bruno Latour, *Science in Action: How to Follow Scientists and Engineers through Society* (Cambridge, Mass., 1987); and Latour, *The Pasteurization of France,* trans. Allan Sheridan and John Law (Cambridge, Mass., 1988).

12. Putnam, observing that the " 'cut between the observer and the system' " implied by the Copenhagen Interpretation of quantum physics "would have been as distasteful to Kant as it was to be . . . to Einstein," acknowledges the same taste in himself even as he confers (very dubious) universal status on it: "There is a part of all of us which sides with Einstein—which wants to see the God's-Eye View restored in all its splendor" (Putnam, *Realism with a Human Face,* p. 18). For the relation of taste to cognitive judgments, see Smith, *Contingencies of Value,* pp. 72–77, 104–7. For a pertinent analysis of "mere," see Pickering, "Knowledge, Practice and Mere Construction," *Social Studies of Science* 20 (Nov. 1990): 682–729.

others after quite a long time) to be highly unserviceable and inapplicable under many important conditions—or, in one sense of the term, *false.*

It may be thought that what makes the difference here is, precisely, evidence: the winnowing process of "experimentation," "falsification," "trial and error," "the test of time," and so forth. And, in a way, it does. For all these can be seen as names for our *continuous, more or less (in)formal or (un)controlled playing out of our beliefs under a variety of conditions and evaluating them accordingly.* Nevertheless, the resistances offered by experience and experiment—or, in that sense, contrary evidence—are not seen here as separating the (objectively) true beliefs from the (objectively) false ones. For what is displayed in that process of playing-out-and-evaluating is not, in this account, the truth or falseness that was always there in our beliefs but, rather, their truth/value under, and in relation to, those particular conditions—which is to say, their contingent truth. The distinctions here parallel those between naive and Darwinian understandings of biological "fitness," which is not the intrinsic superiority of certain traits as proved by the survival of the organisms that have them, but the very fact—seen post hoc—that the traits certain organisms happened to have permitted them to thrive under the conditions that happened to occur.

It is instructive to recall here that the "we" who do the testing of "our" beliefs under new conditions will always be more or less different from the population(s) who developed and preferred those beliefs to begin with. The difference is most obvious in the case of socially and institutionally transmitted beliefs, such as those of established science, where the two populations may be physically discrete and separated by considerable expanses of time.[13] It is not, however, restricted to such cases; for "we" are also different from *ourselves* over the course of our individual life-histories, and we continue to play out and evaluate our beliefs under conditions other than those in/from which they first emerged.

The implications of these differences—obscured by allusions to "human progress" or "the advances of Western science"—are substantial. For they mean that not only will the *conditions* (material, cultural, institutional, and so on) under which "our" beliefs operate alter and be extended, but so also will the *considerations* (projects, values, interests, and so on) in relation to which they are preferred. Moreover, *other* skills and knowledge (for example, new instruments, more highly elaborated theories) will be developed along the way in response both to those altered conditions and also to those new explorations and evaluations themselves, all of which will yield significant investments (cognitive as well as material) that future generations (or versions) of "us" will have an interest in protecting. One may think here of how different are the conditions in which Copernican astronomical models are now tested from those in which they

13. See H. M. Collins, *Changing Order: Replication and Induction in Scientific Practice* (London, 1985).

were initially developed, or, at the level of the individual believer, how a born-again Christian's embrace of his faith *itself* transforms the values and projects in relation to which he evaluates that faith.

It would follow that the notion of intellectual enlightenment or scientific progress makes sense only when measured over limited spans of time and in relation to precisely specified populations and particular projects. It would also follow that the judgment of an institutionally transmitted belief (established theory, standard literary interpretation, canonical aesthetic evaluation, and so on) as "true" could only be post hoc and contingent, and that the process of producing true beliefs could no more be normatively methodized than the process of producing fit organisms.

A Historical Reflection

In a recent narrative account, Stephen Jay Gould remarks that "the central principle of all history [is]—contingency."[14] Gould is concerned here primarily with geological time and biological history, but also with human time and intellectual history. It may be surmised that Gould's strictly nonteleological conception of historical change seems right to him, given everything else he believes or thinks he knows. And, on the same basis, he may be persuaded that this conception—as variously formulated and elaborated—will turn out to be cognitively congenial and otherwise serviceable, over a broad range of conditions, for many other people who deal with such ideas. Neither Gould nor anyone else, however, can know in advance what specific conditions—or, for that matter, cognitive tastes—will actually turn up. Under his own account, then, the future history of "the central principle of all history is contingency" is centrally contingent. That, however, could be considered a liability only by someone—unlike Gould, one surmises—who believed that a contingently good belief was not good enough.

Transforming Belief

We return here to microdynamics, specifically to how beliefs can be seen to develop and change over the course of the life of the individual believer.

Beliefs are traditionally conceived as sets of either discrete true/false mental propositions about the world or discrete correct/incorrect interior representations of it. Beliefs may be reconceived, however, as *configurations* of *linked perceptual/behavioral tendencies* of varying *degrees of strength.* That is, rather than sentences about, or pictures of, an *outside*

14. Stephen Jay Gould, *Wonderful Life: The Burgess Shale and the Nature of History* (New York, 1989), p. 283.

world located *inside* the organism's brain or body and motivating its actions accordingly, what we call beliefs could be seen as the *entire* organism's complexly linked—and continuously shifting, growing, weakening, and recombining—tendencies to perceive-and-act-in the world in certain ways. In such a reconception, the configurations of perceptual/ behavioral tendencies that constitute our beliefs would be understood as always only *relatively* stable and coherent for the individual. It would also be supposed, however, that certain of those configurations are, for one reason or another, especially susceptible to verbal articulation and/or especially available to self-perception; and these latter possibilities would be seen as producing and sustaining traditional conceptions of beliefs as sets of logically linked credos and/or as maps of an autonomous exterior reality.

Various features of this alternative conception of belief are relevant to current epistemological controversies. Not all of them can be spelled out here, but three especially significant ones may be indicated.

1. Beliefs are *modified* in the same ways, through the same general mechanisms, as they are *maintained*. Specifically, our individual tendencies to respond in certain ways to certain perceived cues are strengthened, weakened, or reconfigured by the *differential consequences* of our actions. That is, depending on the consequences (harmful/beneficial, as-predicted/contrary-to-prediction, and so on) of the actions that we perform by virtue of the beliefs that we have, certain of our beliefs (tendencies to perceive and behave in certain ways) will be strengthened, others will be weakened, and various sets of them will be reconfigured. I alluded, above, to the idea of beliefs being "winnowed" by experience, experiment, trial and error, and so forth. That quasi-adjudicative action would be seen here (as above, but now in relation to the individual's lifetime) not as a separating-out of beliefs in accord with their putatively objective truth or falseness, but as a continuous process of strengthening, weakening, and reconfiguring of beliefs (perceptual/behavioral tendencies) in response to the variable consequences of their being acted on under the particular contingent conditions encountered.[15]

It is often charged that hermeneutic or constructivist accounts of knowledge make it impossible to explain how beliefs change.[16] Given the

---

15. See Gerald M. Edelman, *Neural Darwinism* (New York, 1987), and Israel Rosenfield, *The Invention of Memory: A New View of the Brain* (New York, 1988). On the relation between the differentially selective (or "winnowing") mechanisms of individual learning and those of natural selection, see also B. F. Skinner, "Selection by Consequences," *Science,* 31 July 1981, pp. 501–4. For a valuable synthesis of relevant research in a number of fields, see George Lakoff, *Women, Fire, and Dangerous Things: What Categories Reveal about the Mind* (Chicago, 1987).

16. Stanley Fish, frequently the target of such charges (see, for example, Norris, *What's Wrong with Postmodernism*), exposes the dubious assumptions that produce them in his recent book, *Doing What Comes Naturally: Change, Rhetoric, and the Practice of Theory in*

general cognitive dynamics described here, however, no special account of how beliefs change is required; for there would be no reason to think they would *not* be changing more or less continuously. To explain why any given set of beliefs—practical, philosophical, religious, political, and so on—was maintained or modified by some individual, what would be required is a specification of the *particular* factors operating in his or her history. For example, to understand why, all other (general social, historical, cultural, and so on) conditions being more or less the same, some of us remain traditional epistemologists rather than becoming constructivists (or vice versa), we would have to examine quite subtle details of our individual life-histories (educational, social, professional, and so on) as played out in relation to our more or less diverse cognitive temperaments.

2. The second feature concerns the limits of human knowledge or of cognition more generally. Our interactions with our environments are a function of our individual structures *and* how they operate. It is not merely that a creature's structure defines what it can *detect* about the world, but that the world it *occupies*—the world it acts *on* and is acted on *by*—is a particular perceptual and behavioral niche. Thus, what we speak of as "*the* environment" of some creature (for example, a bat, a paramecium, or a human being) is unique to that creature insofar as its own structure is unique. The classic epistemological question is whether it is possible for any creature, and specifically a human being, to cognize *the* universe around the corner, so to speak, of the niche that it occupies, and also whether creatures in different niches can come to share the same— thus universal, thus objective—cognitions. The answer to both questions, so posed, would be negative here, but, in terms of the present account, that is not lamentable since it does not destroy or prevent anything (for example, communication, community, science, or the justification of political action) that might be thought to depend on a positive answer.[17]

3. The third and most significant feature of this reconception of belief follows from the two just described and returns us to the hermeneutic circle. The *specific* characteristics of a creature's global (organic) structure at any given time are the joint product of two histories: the evolutionary history of that creature's genetic makeup and its life-history in a particular environment. The fact that our species evolved in a physically particular universe means that whatever specific, innate perceptual/ behavioral tendencies we have must permit our minimal individual survi-

---

Literary and Legal Studies (Durham, N. C., 1989), esp. pp. 141–60; however, he does not, in my view, develop an altogether satisfactory alternative account of the dynamics of belief.

17. The point cannot be adequately (that is, persuasively) developed here. For related discussion, see Smith, *Contingencies of Value*, esp. pp. 85–124, 150–83, and Smith, "The Unquiet Judge: Activism without Objectivism in Law and Politics," in "Rethinking Objectivity," special issue of *Annals of Scholarship*, ed. Allan Megill (forthcoming).

val in such a universe.[18] Neither our individual structures, however, nor the ways they will develop are fixed at birth. On the contrary, throughout our lives we interact with our environments in ways that continuously modify our structures *and* the ways they operate, and these structural/ functional modifications affect our subsequent interactions with our environments, both *what we perceive* and *how we behave*.[19] This continuous *mutual*—and, in that sense, "circular"—process of environmental interaction and organic modification is what we commonly refer to as "cognition" and "learning."[20] The structural/behavioral modifications themselves, when relatively stable and available to both self-perception and verbal articulation, are what we commonly speak of as (acquired) "knowledge" and (changed) "belief."

The process just described may appear quite close to what informal epistemology describes as the resistance offered to our beliefs (scientific theories, historical accounts, literary interpretations, and so on) by facts, rocks, bricks, texts-themselves, and those other (supposedly) intractable objects alluded to at the beginning of this essay. In regard to the key issues, however, its operations are decisively different. For, in the present account, we can never become pure spectators of the universe, observing, cognizing, and representing an altogether exterior, altogether autonomous, reality.[21] Nor—commonly seen as the correlate of that denial—are we forever locked out of the universe, prisoners of our own beliefs and idioms. Rather, ourselves always changing, we are inextricably *interlocked with* our always changing worlds. Our relation to the universe—and the latter includes, of course, other people and what they have produced, including their articulated beliefs (for example, essays such as this)—is both dynamic and reciprocal: our interactions with *it* continuously change *us* and, thereby, the nature of our subsequent interactions with *it*. The hermeneutic circle does not permit access or escape

---

18. Contrary to what is sometimes supposed, this does not mean (or at least not self-evidently) that our "natural," "normal," "ordinary" perceptions (along with? more than? the perceptions of all other extant organisms) must deliver *objectively veridical representations* of the universe. For a supposition along such lines, see Ulric Neisser, "Without Perception, There Is No Knowledge: Implications for Artificial Intelligence" in *Minds: Natural and Artificial*, ed. R. G. Burton (forthcoming). Neisser's central point in the article, namely, that what we call "knowledge" presupposes "motion"—or, in effect, differentially consequential interactions with the environment—is, per se, in accord with the views outlined here. My thanks to David Rubin for the reference.

19. See Susan Oyama, *The Ontogeny of Information: Developmental Systems and Evolution* (Cambridge, Mass., 1985).

20. See Humberto R. Maturana and Francisco J. Varela, *Autopoiesis and Cognition* (Boston, 1980), and *The Tree of Knowledge: The Biological Roots of Human Understanding*, trans. J. Z. Young (Boston, 1988).

21. This conception and ideal of knowledge is the target of Richard Rorty's intellectually abrasive (and, thereby, transformative and productive) critique in *Philosophy and the Mirror of Nature* (Princeton, N. J., 1979).

to an uninterpreted reality; but we do not keep going around in the same path.[22]

The Ambivalent Operations of Belief

Recent studies in the fields of economic psychology and decision science suggest that certain cognitive dispositions and related biases—from the miscalculation of particular forms of probability to the systematic forgetting of disconfirming evidence—are endemic, that is, species-wide.[23] Human fallibility is no news, of course, but of special interest here is the further suggestion that, although such tendencies are clearly disadvantageous under many conditions, they may nevertheless have (had) advantages for the species as a whole or for the individual under a wide range of conditions, or they may be the by-products of structures and mechanisms that have (had) such advantages. Among these double-valued (some times/ways advantageous, some times/ways not) dispositions is, I would suggest, the complex of tendencies explored briefly above as "cognitive conservatism"—or what could also be described as the resistance of belief to resistance. *Plasticity* of belief (in the sense of configurations of perceptual/behavioral tendencies) is obviously advantageous and indeed necessary for any creature that survives, as human beings do, by learning.[24] It does not follow, however, that the more plastic our beliefs, the better off we are. On the contrary, the countertendency—that is, mechanisms that foster the *stability and persistence* of beliefs—would, under a broad range of conditions, *also* be advantageous. We are, it seems, congenitally both docile and stubborn.

Human history indicates that people will maintain their beliefs not only in the face of apparently contrary evidence but even when those beliefs have severely disagreeable and disadvantageous consequences for them—not to mention for many other people. Millenarianism survives

22. Various metaphors for this complex reciprocality have been proposed; especially apt is the evocation by Arbib and Hesse—commenting here on the relations among perception, observation language, and theory—of "a spiraling set of nested feedback systems" (Arbib and Hesse, *The Construction of Reality*, p. 8).

23. See *Judgment under Uncertainty: Heuristics and Biases*, ed. Daniel Kahneman, Paul Slovic, and Amos Tversky (Cambridge, Mass., 1982). The normativity implied by "bias" here is located in other, more formally controlled, types of calculations, for example, mathematical ones. The normative veridicality of mathematics, however, is itself at issue in these controversies. For a constructivist account, see Bloor, *Wittgenstein: A Social Theory of Knowledge* (New York, 1983), pp. 83–111.

24. See H. Ronald Pulliam and Christopher Dunford, *Programmed to Learn: An Essay on the Evolution of Culture* (New York, 1980), and Robert Brandon, "Phenotypic Plasticity, Cultural Transmission, and Human Sociobiology," in *Sociobiology and Epistemology*, ed. James H. Fetzer (Boston, 1985), pp. 57–73. Both are critiques of crucial assumptions of standard sociobiology.

each nonapocalyptic millennium; the dream of flight survives the fall, many times over, of Icarus. Moreover, while the specific (acquired) beliefs of a cat whose beliefs are fatal to her will (usually) die with the cat, those of a human being very often do not. For better and for worse, the cultural and institutional transmission of belief complicates the dynamics of cognition and amplifies the operations of both its plasticity and conservatism.

Biology, like history, is one discourse—one institutional discipline, one conceptual idiom—among others: the evidences of each are subject to multiple, diverse interpretation, the interpretations of each to multiple, diverse appropriation. I invoke biology here and history (and sociology) above as evidence for the constructivist-interactionist views I am proposing. Like history, however, biology is appropriated by other writers to ground traditional epistemologies and to refute constructivism.[25] The arguments thereby generated are, in my view, exceedingly dubious, but this is not the place to examine them. I shall instead appropriate the very existence of such arguments as evidence for a final, symmetrical reflection.

Invocations of evolutionary biology as support for traditional realist or rationalist epistemologies illustrate the energy and resourcefulness of cognitive conservatism, which is not merely the tendency and ability to *hold fast* to one's beliefs, but to *incorporate* into them whatever comes along—and, often enough, to the amazement of skeptics and exasperation of adversaries, to turn what might otherwise be seen as evidence *against* one's beliefs into evidence *for* them. In operating this way, however, cognitive conservatism is also, on both the micro (individual) and macro (sociohistorical) scales, a creative and productive mechanism. For, as intellectual history (and biography) also indicates, it is, often enough, through the intense, obsessive effort to maintain coherence between present evidence and prior belief that our most innovative beliefs—and what sometimes turn out, in the long run, to be most radically transformative ones—are generated.[26]

25. Examples include Ruth Millikan, *Language, Thought, and Other Biological Categories: New Foundations for Realism* (Cambridge, Mass., 1984), and *Evolutionary Epistemology, Rationality, and the Sociology of Knowledge,* ed. Gerard Radnitsky and W. W. Bartley III (La Salle, Ill., 1987). See also Neisser, "Without Perception, There Is No Knowledge."

26. For a piquant example, see Latour, "A Relativistic Account of Einstein's Relativity," *Social Studies of Science* 18 (Feb. 1988): 3–44.

Resistance to Constructed Belief

Robert J. Richards

"That theory will be most generally believed," argued William James, *"which, besides offering us objects able to account satisfactorily for our sensible experience, also offers those which are most interesting, those which appeal most urgently to our aesthetic, emotional, and active needs."*[1] The theories of constructivism, with whose fortunes Barbara Herrnstein Smith allies herself, certainly have captured the interest of historians and philosophers of science, undoubtedly appealing to their aesthetic, emotional, and active needs. When sliding to the extreme, however, these theories fail to retain the Jamesian balance, since they abandon solid historical experience. Yet for many people of "institutional authority and influence," as Smith describes them, such theories have seemed "more conceptually congenial, evocative, and/or otherwise serviceable than those they are replacing" ("Belief and Resistance: A Symmetrical Account," pp. 146, 145–46).

The older rational-realist epistemologies, now scheduled for replacement, stressed that evidence could correct faulty belief, that reason, especially as gone pedantic in science, could arbitrate between beliefs in the cool light of such traditional kinds of evidence as logical coherence, observation, and experiment. These epistemologies, at least as formulated during this century, never claimed that finite rational beings could achieve infallibly true ideas, only corrigible and constantly improved ones. Smith, who at the end of her essay ventures into foreign territory, does from that vantage reasonably observe that webs of belief display patterns derived from our genetic heritage, as well as from our individual histories. The older epistemologies, mindful of the constraints of biology and personal history, nonetheless claimed those webs of belief could capture

1. William James, *The Principles of Psychology*, 2 vols. (New York, 1890), 2:312.

fleeting aspects of nature when, that is, reliable methods were used in their construction. Science, for these epistemologies, constituted that cultural tradition in which such methods were developed, tested, and refined. The history of science seemed to confirm all of this: Ptolemy formulated wonderfully accurate geometrical theories of the planetary system; Copernicus changed some central assumptions, while retaining much of the Ptolemaic technique and data, and set a course leading to modern science; Galen's theories of heart and blood movement were transformed by Harvey, who got it basically right, and that Englishman's physiological discovery has remained virtually intact for almost four hundred years. The history of science displayed the power of logical thinking, empirical observation, and designed experiment—the hard sources of evidence for the progressive development of stable and warranted belief, that is, of knowledge. At the beginning of this century was launched the movement of logical positivism, which attempted to codify those epistemological standards that seemed to lie at the root of science's success. Just after mid-century, however, logical positivism struck a submerged intellectual iceberg, Kuhn's *Structure of Scientific Revolutions*. Constructivists still cling to the melting fragments of that great work.

Constructivism gestated in the mid-1970s among the sociologists and historians of science at Edinburgh and then slid down to Cambridge, London, and the west counties during the 1980s. Kuhn served as the reluctant godfather, but British Marxism and anthropology also stood at the christening. After migrating to the United States in this last decade, it had frequent couplings with the deconstructivists on the literary side and neopragmatists on the philosophical. The blood lines exposed in the footnotes of Smith's essay tell of this genealogy.

Constructivist theories generally come in two varieties, moderate and extreme, labels that reveal, I'm afraid, some tendentiousness on my part. The moderates hold fast to the strong beams of the rational-realist conception of science. Yet struck by some forceful insights and splendid historiographic moments of those whom I have just called extremists, the moderates do recognize that scientists make knowledge claims for a multitude of reasons: logical coherence, observation, and experiment, to be sure; but as well as for high advancement, low politics, and middling institutional favor. The moderates agree with the constructivist tenet that

Robert J. Richards is professor of history and philosophy of science at the University of Chicago. He is the author of *Darwin and the Emergence of Evolutionary Theories of Mind and Behavior* (1987) and *The Meaning of Evolution: The Morphological Construction and Ideological Reconstruction of Darwin's Theory* (1992). Currently he is working on a book tentatively entitled *Romantic Biology in the Nineteenth Century*.

Smith makes central to her own defense, namely, that appeals to evidence will depend on belief—for any evidence attains its significance only when nestled within a web of belief. For Smith the implication of belief in evidence creates, in her terms, a hermeneutic circle. Once the circle is closed, to use a favorite model of the extremists, a language game begins; and no one game can be truer, or more reasonable, or more probable than another.

The moderates, however, seem to be spoilsports. For they will insist on the point of Dewey's remark, as he shucked off his own earlier Hegelian convictions, namely, that a system of belief could be entirely coherent, a hermeneutically sealed language game that goes spiralling toward the empyrean—but still be crazy. Thus the moderates make a critical distinction. Evidence for a scientific theory does depend on belief, but usually not on belief in the theory being tested, rather on more hard cast, perceptual beliefs, ultimately. There is no necessary hermeneutic circle as assumed by those holding the extreme views. The harder, ultimately biologically based beliefs upon which theory will finally rest are constituted by more immediate perceptions and reason, both of which have been measured up, as William James argued, by that great reality principle, natural selection.[2] Those protomen, after all, who perceived the saber-toothed tiger lurking in their path as a large cabbage—well, they have left long lines of extinct descendants. Evolution, as Smith suggests, does weave a web of belief; but the (Stoiclike) *hegimonikon* at the center of that web, so the moderates argue, can feel the thrashings of the natural creatures caught in the web and form reasonable estimates of the prize. Any other assumption makes dark the accomplishments of science, rather, cannot even regard them as accomplishments.[3] Now, moderate historians and philosophers of science are not surprised to find some past scientific theories fitted more to the seductive forms of social interests and ideology than to the elusive shape of nature herself. They maintain, however, that such discoveries should be empirical conclusions, not a priori assumptions of the sort the extreme constructivists make.

2. *"The conceived system, to pass for true, must at least include the reality of the sensible objects in it, by explaining them as effects on us, if nothing more. The system which includes the most of them, and definitely explains or pretends to explain the most of them, will, ceteris paribus, prevail"* (James, *The Principles of Psychology*, 2:312). See also my discussion of the role of Darwinian theory in James's thought in Robert J. Richards, *Darwin and the Emergence of Evolutionary Theories of Mind and Behavior* (Chicago, 1987), pp. 409–50. Smith actually considers as appropriate a natural selection model of belief acquisition, but what seems to appeal to her about this model is that beliefs would be construed as merely locally fit, suited only for a particular environment. The model, in her view, will not justify ascription of truth to such beliefs, only convenience. See her *Contingencies of Value: Alternative Perspectives for Critical Theory* (Cambridge, Mass., 1988), p. 163.

3. In *Darwin and the Emergence of Evolutionary Theories of Mind and Behavior*, pp. 579–93, I, like Smith (see previous note), argue for a Darwinian model of belief selection but one with rather different epistemological implications.

The extreme constructivists forestall empirical historical investigation into past science. They assume at the start that only social causes can mold scientific theories and that scientific method should be regarded—to quote Steven Shapin and Simon Schaffer, two quick-witted and unduly persuasive constructivists—"as crystallizing forms of social organization and as a means of regulating social interaction within the scientific community."[4] The rational-realist historian depicted scientific theory as usually about nature; the extreme constructivist knows ahead of time that, for instance, when Thomas Hobbes construed space as a plenum, this was really, to quote Shapin and Schaffer again, Hobbes's "contribution to the avoidance of civil war," not primarily a belief about the nature of space (*L*, p. 108). It is simply taken by the extreme constructivists as an a priori rule of method, as for instance Bruno Latour does in his book *Science in Action*, that nature must be eliminated as a possible cause in the formation of scientific beliefs.[5] Now, an a priori metaphysics of this sort, which simply supposes social causes to be real and natural causes to be impotent, would normally be sent down for sheer arbitrariness.[6] It is obvious, though, such a metaphysics has its own charms and presumably satisfies, in James's terms, certain "aesthetic, emotional, and active needs." A measure of this latter is the very spirited and interesting defense that Smith constructs.

In addition to the main positive argument concerning the hermeneutic circle, Smith serves up disabling interpretations of the two methods, logical analysis and empirical observation, that are utilized by the rational-realist epistemologies, by science itself, and, as James and Dewey claimed, by common sense. In her first effort, Smith dismisses the principal logical objection to extreme constructivism, namely, the charge of epistemological inconsistency. That charge made by rational-realists runs like this: The constructivists claim to explain what science is really like, that its presumed rational arguments are locally caused by social or political ideology, not by nature; but this claim itself wishes to be taken as other

4. Steven Shapin and Simon Schaffer, *Leviathan and the Air-Pump: Hobbes, Boyle, and the Experimental Life* (Princeton, N.J., 1985), p. 14; hereafter abbreviated *L*. See also David Bloor, *Knowledge and Social Imagery*, 2d ed. (Chicago, 1991), pp. 51–52: "When we think about the nature of knowledge, what we are doing is indirectly reflecting on the principles according to which society is organised."

5. See Bruno Latour, *Science in Action: How to Follow Scientists and Engineers through Society* (Cambridge, Mass., 1987), p. 99: "Our *third rule of method* will read: since the settlement of a controversy is *the cause* of Nature's representation not the consequence, we can never use the outcome—Nature—to explain how and why a controversy has been settled."

6. Latour likes to distinguish his epistemological position from those who, like the Edinburgh sociologists, appeal more directly to political ideology as the ultimate coagulant of scientific ideas. Yet he argues that evidence in scientific disputes finally rests on such socially evocative matters as bulk of citations in a work, number of allies gathered to the cause, impressiveness of machines employed, quantity of grants, and level of institutional position—all falling decently under the rubric of social causation. Cogency of argument and revealing experiment are not listed among the sources of evidence for him.

than a local observation, other than a bit of social or political ideology. After all, if the extreme constructivists must describe science in dour terms, we, who have not been infected by the Calvinist gloom hanging over Edinburgh and now spreading across the Atlantic, *need not* accept their descriptions. Even by their own lights, we *will not* accept their account of science, since we are bathed in the grittier reality of Chicago's environs. Finally, though, if the extreme constructivists are right, then we *should not* accept their account of science, since it is merely their own social background that makes them say those terrible things. As Kant remarked precisely on this question: "Certainly a man cannot dispute with anyone regarding that which depends merely on the mode in which he is himself organized."[7] Smith, however, considers this sort of *tu-quoque* argument as "an artifact of the rationalist's absolute self-privileging." Such demonstrations, she says, "prove things most readily to those already inclined to believe them" (p. 144). Well, yes. But can anyone seriously not believe in the potency of the argument from inconsistency? I must confess, though, some of my own students display a Whitmanesque insouciance about this argument—they don't think it terribly compelling. But shouldn't they? Shouldn't we all?

Smith seems to hold that since the constructivists have abandoned such rational-realist values as logical consistency, they cannot be caught up in any self-refuting proposition; for if asserting contrary properties of the same thing at the same time doesn't cause one to flinch, then the rational-realists cannot induce any epistemological embarrassment. The constructivists, in Smith's terms, have other meanings for *reason* and *truth* and associated traits like logical consistency and objectivity. These new meanings, as she names them in her article, are the *"congenial, evocative, and serviceable ways . . . to think"* (p. 145). Thus constructivists can reflexively apply their theories of socially constructed belief to those very same theories without fear of self-refutation because with the abandonment of logical consistency there can be no self-refuting inconsistency.

A moment's reflection will indicate, however, that without logical consistency there can also be no meaningful interchange of ideas. Moreover, logical incoherence, certainly in science, can hardly be congenial or serviceable; and it will usually evoke only a derisive smile. Finally, the simple point must be made that Smith's proposed new meanings for truth and reason cannot even be intelligibly applied, except under the assumption of the older, rational-realist meanings.

The most interesting (though I do not think true) claim that Smith makes about evidence concerns large-scale changes in belief. Historians of science used to explain scientific revolutions as the result of new facts coming to light that, when embraced by newly available concepts, pro-

---

7. Immanuel Kant, *Critique of Pure Reason*, trans. Norman Kemp Smith (London, 1964), p. 175.

duced evidence for theories smoldering in powerfully charged brains. Historians of biology, for instance, took Darwin seriously when, in his private *Journal,* he wrote concerning South American fossils and Galapagos species that "these facts origin (especially latter) of all my views."[8] But if Darwin's views were highly constrained initially by his social and political milieu, if what was to count as evidence were already determined by that milieu, then it is difficult to understand how his views could change at all. And supposing by some historically inexplicable cause they did change, it would seem impossible, on the premise of extreme constructivism, that Darwin's argument in the *Origin of Species* could have convinced his scientific community, which was socially and thus cognitively indisposed to believe the theory. Yet by the time Darwin died in 1882, virtually no naturalist in England, America, or Germany could be found who wasn't an evolutionist. The greatly different political and social structures of these countries cannot account for the same result, that is, conversion to evolutionism, nor can one appeal to any large-scale changes within these countries that might have coerced their respective scientific communities to accept evolution. The common cause, which undoubtedly worked in concert with a vast array of other causes, was precisely Darwin's argument and the evidence he displayed in the *Origin.* If, however, antecedent belief hermeneutically sealed off its own evidence, keeping the various regnant scientific communities playing their own language games, then the revolutionary acceptance of evolution becomes simply a historical mystery.

Now, everyone loves a mystery, as long as some resolution is eventually provided. Smith's own resolution brings us part of the way; but after turning the last page, we still don't know who or what did it. She says that no special account of such large-scale changes in beliefs, such as the conversion to evolutionism by virtually the whole scientific establishment, is required, since "there would be no reason to think [beliefs] would *not* be changing more or less continuously" (p. 150). But this remark simply doesn't speak to the historian's problem of accounting for large-scale patterns of change. The historian is charged with fixing not only the parameters of such changes—their extent, their depth, their duration— but also, most especially, the *causes* of the changes. Smith does maintain that in any such changes we should look to the particular circumstances of the cognitive histories of the individuals in question. This is part of the resolution, and it is exactly what a responsible history would recommend. If she went further and agreed that common to all of these individual histories of English divines, German zoologists, and American social thinkers were certain coercive facts—that is, having read the *Origin,* considered the rational force of its arguments, weighed its evidence, and hav-

8. Charles Darwin, "Darwin's Journal," ed. Gavin de Beer, *Bulletin of the British Museum (Natural History)* 2, no. 1 (1959): 7.

ing come to understand a bit more accurately the way nature is—then the mystery would seem resolved, at least as unambiguously as one would get, say, in a John le Carré novel. But this agreement would carry implications that move against the grain of the extreme constructivists, whose views Smith endorses. For this resolution supposes that nature and reason have the power to break down even craftily composed systems of belief, to demolish old beliefs and erect new ones on the foundations of logical consistency with the evidence.

In drawing this conclusion, I've been employing a kind of historical transcendental argument: history of science displays certain patterns. What, then, are the conditions of their possibility? Generally, what kinds of causes can plausibly give an account of these patterns and what kinds seem incapable? Again, consider the set of causes proposed by moderate constructivists as opposed to those of the extreme persuasion.

The moderates maintain that evidence provided by rational analysis, observation, and controlled experiment have functioned since the period of Greek science. These methods have allowed belief to track nature, though through a glass darkly. Yet there is no other way, the moderates argue, seriously to understand both the evolving traditions of scientific belief or account for their contemporary spread into every culture. Shapin and Schaffer yet claim, for instance, that in the seventeenth century "there was nothing self-evident or inevitable about the series of historical judgments in that context which yielded a natural philosophical consensus in favour of the experimental programme" (*L*, p. 13).[9] By reason of their assumptions, this is indeed a position they should take; like Smith they suppose that very local contingencies determine the fate

---

9. The passage reads as follows:

Hobbes's views found little support in the English natural philosophical community. Yet we want to show that there was nothing self-evident or inevitable about the series of historical judgments in that context which yielded a natural philosophical consensus in favour of the experimental programme. Given other circumstances bearing upon that philosophical community, Hobbes's views might well have found a different reception. They were not widely credited or believed—but they were *believable*; they were not counted to be correct—but there was nothing inherent in them that prevented a different evaluation. [*L*, p. 13]

Besides the difficulty mentioned in the text above, this historiographic contention about the primacy of local determinations of belief suffers from two other terminal infections. First, Hobbes, as well as Boyle, believed that all knowledge about nature came from the senses; and like Boyle (and most English scientists), Hobbes also thought nature could be manipulated to yield her secrets. His beliefs about experiment, in short, really did not differ from his contemporaries. Shapin and Schaffer's interpretation of Hobbes's views on experiment thus stems from lack of appreciation of his natural philosophy. The second difficulty arises from a lack of awareness of the long, thin traditions of experiment in natural science beginning with Galen and Ptolemy, passing with some augmentation into the Middle Ages, and achieving dramatic success with Harvey's demonstration of blood circulation—an achievement that both Hobbes and Boyle celebrated.

of belief systems, making contingent even acceptance of experiment as a method of science in the seventeenth century. But if the extreme constructivists were correct—a reflexive judgment they themselves could not make—then we ought to see in the present day several large pockets of radically different scientific systems of belief established in the culture, since contingency rules when nature is not tracked. But even in once-traditional societies, whose beliefs differ in so many other areas, the methods of rational analysis, empirical observation, and controlled experiment have largely defeated all others. In Japan, for instance, a very Western science and technology have displaced older systems and have become powerful instruments of success in competition with the nations of their origin. Drive a Honda, and you will intuitively understand how beliefs can be made to track nature.

The history of science is littered with the corpses of theories that yet in their incorruptible innocence still retain their evocative character, certainly their interest, congeniality, and even a faded beauty. In their own time they were serviceable, and as a historian I still find them so. They died, not because of the sort of virtues that Smith recommends for the new epistemology; rather, those virtues propped them up even after their hearts fluttered their last. The older theories in science succumbed to evidence and logical argument. They did not track nature, at least not as well as their successors. This, I believe, is the most serviceable, congenial, and, in the end, the most beautiful view of the matter.

Circling Around, Knocking Over, Playing Out

Barbara Herrnstein Smith

Robert Richards is surely the winner in the skillful bout of shadowboxing enacted here ("Resistance to Constructed Belief," pp. 154–61). He has not only resisted every challenge to his convictions presented by his constructivist rivals, flesh or straw, but has also eluded, without scratch or scrape, virtually the entire text—title, topic, aims, arguments, and punchlines—of my paper. Accordingly, I shall briefly reintroduce "Belief and Resistance" and attempt to give more substance to this exchange.

Contrary to Richards's report of it, "Belief and Resistance," though constructivist in its way, is not a defense of constructivism. It is, rather, the outline of an account of the dynamics of belief—an account, that is, of how beliefs, both those of individuals during their personal lifetimes and those of larger populations over longer periods, are formed, stabilized, and transformed. Central to the account is the idea that each of these sets of beliefs may be seen not, as traditionally, as discrete (accurate or inaccurate) mental representations of, or discrete (true or false) interior propositions about, an autonomous reality, but, rather, as more or less continuously changing configurations of linked perceptual and behavioral tendencies that are strengthened, weakened, or reconfigured through our ongoing interactions with our environments.

This idea is somewhat complex. The terms in which it is discussed in "Belief and Resistance" draw on conceptual idioms that are, in some ways, evidently alien to Richards. The discussion reflects theoretical perspectives that are, by his own declaration, inconceivable to him. These and other incongruities of cognitive taste and conceptual style help explain, I think, his elusive engagement with the paper. Indeed, his selective focusings, filterings, and reconfigurings illustrate with some vividness what I refer to in the paper as "cognitive conservatism" and describe there as the apparently endemic tendency of our cognitive processes (perceptions, classifications, memories, verbal articulations, and so forth) to operate so as to conserve the stability of our prior beliefs (p. 142).

Richards refers to some of these observations as my "ventures into foreign territory"(p. 154). Perhaps. (It may depend on how territories are defined.) He also compliments some of them as "reasonable" (p. 154), though I am not sure which ones because he does not quote me directly, his paraphrases are inaccurate in crucial details, and I find many of his own views on these matters dubious. I find especially dubious the idea that genuine, scientific theories (as distinct from the "crazy" ones [p. 156]) "finally rest" on "the harder, fundamental, ultimately biologically based beliefs . . . constituted by more immediate perceptions and reason" and guaranteed valid by "that great reality principle, natural selection"—a principle that Richards illustrates in the figure of a saber-toothed tiger purging the species of those individuals whose perceptions are askew (p. 156).

In "Belief and Resistance," I distinguish my own sense of the epistemological implications of evolutionary theory from ideas such as these. Indeed, I specifically reject the idea that the survival of our species in a particular universe means that our "natural," "immediate" perceptions must deliver objectively veridical representations of an autonomous reality. I shall not detail here my counterposition (and forbear raising questions as to the epistemological status of the immediate perceptions of beetles, bats, and goldfish), but its major point is simple enough: While our individual perceptual and behavioral tendencies are certainly shaped by, among other things, the history of the species's more or less effective interactions with its environment, the *reciprocal* of this *also* obtains. That is, the features of the environment with which we and past members of the species *could* interact—saber-toothed tigers included—have never been independent of our own particular structures and how we were already operating as perceiving and behaving organisms. In short, the way we have evolved has depended at every point on what we already were—as well as vice versa.

The type of reciprocal determination just mentioned is a recurrent theme in the account of belief offered in "Belief and Resistance." *Reciprocal determination* is also a crucial—indeed, defining—feature of the her-

---

Barbara Herrnstein Smith is Braxton Craven Professor of Comparative Literature and English at Duke University and director of its Center for Interdisciplinary Studies in Science and Cultural Theory. The author of, among other works, *Contingencies of Value: Alternative Perspectives for Critical Theory* (1988), she is currently completing a study of contemporary theoretical controversy.

meneutic circle, which the processes of biological evolution neither evade nor shatter but (in accord with the point just made) sustain and reproduce. Contrary to Richards's ill-informed version of the idea, the dynamics of the hermeneutic circle do not imply that we are *locked out* of the universe—prisoners of fixed beliefs or players of inconsequential language games—but, rather (as I observe explicitly and stress heavily in the paper), that we and our universe, each continuously evolving and changing together, are *reciprocally interlocked.*

Conceptualizations such as the one just outlined are significantly at odds with the sort of evolutionary epistemology that Richards pursues in his commentary here and in his related book.[1] Thus, I agree that beliefs evolve, but only in the sense that they *undergo responsive transformation,* not in the sense that they *go* anywhere in particular. Or, again, I agree that the processes by which beliefs evolve are related to those that Darwin spoke of as natural selection, but I do not believe that the latter principle supports a realist ontology, a rationalist understanding of truth or knowledge, a Whiggish understanding of intellectual history, or a normative epistemology of any kind.

The idea of natural selection is, to my mind, a signal achievement, not least because it opens up a theoretically powerful way to understand the general dynamics of history and to reconceive conventional but problematic notions of causality. Of particular significance in this respect is Darwin's suggestion that all biological phenomena, including the array of highly differentiated species and the exquisitely adapted functioning ("fitness") of organic forms, could be understood not, as then commonly supposed, as evidence of an originating agency and global telos but, instead, as *the continuously emergent products of complex interactions among myriad contingent events.* What I suggest in "Belief and Resistance" is that the microdynamics of our individual cognitive histories, that is, our beliefs as they develop over our personal lifetimes, and also the macrodynamics of intellectual history generally, including those beliefs we call scientific knowledge, can be understood on the same model. Like the evolving forms and diverse species of biology, each of these sets of beliefs can be seen as the continuously emergent products of complex interactions among contingent events—without specific causal agencies, without inherent hierarchy, and without global directionality.

Two implications of this extension of Darwin's thought are especially relevant here. One is that the idea of a noncontingently (or, in that sense, "objectively") true belief would make no more sense than the idea of a noncontingently or "inherently" fit organism. For, of course, given the Darwinian model, the truth of beliefs, like the fitness of organisms, would

1. See Robert J. Richards, *Darwin and the Emergence of Evolutionary Theories of Mind and Behavior* (Chicago, 1987). He acknowledges the disagreement, as such; see his note 3.

be understood as historically contingent and locally specific (or, in biological terms, niche specific).[2] The other implication is that we could no more devise a method for producing absolutely or even just "increasingly" (absolutely) true beliefs than we could devise a method for producing inherently or even just "increasingly" (inherently) fit organisms. Indeed, when assessed in relation to Darwin's views of historical dynamics, normative epistemology along the lines indicated by these supposed possibilities (that is, the effort to devise methods for generating or certifying objectively true beliefs) could be seen as theoretically regressive.

Richards maintains that I leave unsolved the mystery of large-scale changes of belief. "After turning the last page," he remarks, "we still don't know who or what did it" (p. 159). The expectation of a solution to that mystery in terms of a specific causal agent—"who or what did it"—is somewhat surprising from a scholar of evolutionary theory, but notions of singular causal agency (whether God, Nature, or History) die hard, even in the laboratories and archives of biology. If my explicit and relatively extensive account of the macrodynamics of belief slipped right past Richards, it is probably because I frame it in neither the simple causal terms he would himself produce—that is, talk of "coercive" facts yielding universal "conversions"—nor the equally simplistic terms he evidently expects from and projects as "extreme constructivism"—that is, talk of "social causes," "social interests," "social and political milieu," and "political ideology" (pp. 157, 159, 157).[3]

Specifically, what I do suggest in "Belief and Resistance" is that the beliefs of groups of people change over historically measured periods of time (as do the beliefs of individuals during their lifetimes) *in and through the very process of being played out—tried, assessed, and adjusted—under and in response to varying conditions.* In contrast, however, to traditional views of

---

2. Contrary to Richards's odd charge (see his note 2), this is not equivalent to identifying (or "replacing") truth with "convenience."

3. Richards supports this aspect of his projection primarily through citations (misleading, in my view) of works by Steven Shapin and Simon Schaffer, and Bruno Latour. In other of his allusions and allegations, he suggests that the particular version of "extreme constructivism" offered in "Belief and Resistance" (and, he adds, in my book, *Contingencies of Value: Alternative Perspectives for Critical Theory* [Cambridge, Mass., 1988]) would replace hard evidence, controlled experiment, and cogent logic with soft, trivial, and superficial criteria for belief, such as fleeting emotional and aesthetic appeal and convenience. He has, however, read very carelessly the passages he cites as evidence of these supposed views. The reasons I do indicate as likely to be involved in the credibility and communal appropriation of one theory in preference to another are (a) its greater congruence with prior, relatively more stable beliefs, (b) its greater fertility in calling forth new elaborations of familiar ideas and new connections to previously peripheral ones, and (c) its greater effectiveness in solving conceptual puzzles and/or advancing a broad array of practical projects (technological, pedagogic, political, therapeutic, and so forth), both individual and communal. The phrase in which I sum these up in "Belief and Resistance" is "more conceptually congenial, evocative, and/or otherwise serviceable" (pp. 131–32).

the decisively educative ("enlightening") and adjudicative ("winnowing") effects of experience and experiment, I emphasize that the trials in question, no matter how rigorously controlled, cannot "select" or separate out *objectively* true beliefs from *objectively* false ones—at least not if *objective* is understood as immutable and independent of human perspectives, interests, and purposes. For the conditions under which we test and evaluate beliefs, the worlds *in* which we play them out and *to* which we match, measure, adjust, and adapt them (or, in evolutionary terms, make them "fit") include *our changing selves:* not only our evolving structures and operations as perceiving, behaving organisms, but also our heterogeneous, evolving interests and projects, and all the products (also heterogeneous and evolving) of our existence as cultural creatures.

The environment of all human beings ("nature," in that sense) always includes ourselves and our fellow human beings, our and their practices, and what we and they have produced ("culture," in that sense): conceptual systems, verbal idioms, theories, texts, pieces of equipment, technical skills, routines of training, and the institutions that conserve and transmit all of these. The beliefs of human beings cannot be formed or transformed *independent of* such practices and products because our beliefs are formed and transformed, in part, *in response to* them. Contemporary studies of the dynamics of cognition emphasize the significance of just that responsiveness and dependence in the formation and transformation of all beliefs, including those we speak of as "rational truths," "logical inferences," "empirical facts," and "scientific knowledge." That emphasis, along with related efforts to explore the epistemic operations of the cultural practices, products, and institutions in question, is what Richards has reconstructed here, via careless allegation and tendentious description, as "extreme constructivism."[4]

Some brief attention may be given to what Richards sees as "the principal logical objection to extreme constructivism," namely, its supposed self-contradiction. "Can anyone," he asks rhetorically, "seriously not believe in the potency of the argument from inconsistency?" The answer is yes. One can seriously not believe in its potency after one has observed that the charge of self-contradiction is, often as not, hollow and that the

---

4. The ubiquitous, complex, and subtly reciprocal operations of culture (as defined above) in the actual playing out of what Richards calls "our genetic heritage" typically elude standard sociobiology as well as most so-called evolutionary epistemology (p. 154). The resulting oversimplifications of both are, unfortunately, often taken to exhaust the relevance (and, by the same token, to demonstrate the irrelevance) of evolutionary biology for contemporary accounts of human cognition and science. For significantly different approaches and contributions, see the works cited in "Belief and Resistance," notes 15, 19, and 20, and Gonzalo Munevar, "Science as Part of Nature," in *Issues in Evolutionary Epistemology*, ed. Kai Huhlweg and C. A. Hooker (Albany, N.Y., 1989), pp. 475–87.

supposed argument from inconsistency (in the contexts and formulations relevant here) is routinely self-affirming, question begging, and circular.[5]

The charge is certainly hollow when directed against constructivist accounts that are (like "Belief and Resistance" itself) symmetrical and self-exemplifying: accounts, that is, that explain the dynamics of all beliefs, including the particular ones the authors favor, in the same general terms, and that offer themselves—those very accounts—as examples of the ideas proposed. This includes the idea, which constructivists characteristically do not see as scandalous or self-disabling, that the interest and value of all claims and theories, including that very claim and theory, are contingent. As commonly discovered by schoolyard debaters, there's no point repeating *tu quoque*—And you, too, so *there!*—to someone who keeps saying, And me, too, so *what?* Chanting *tu quoque*, however, is evidently not pointless to those who continue to be knocked over by the potency of the charge of self-contradiction here. They are knocked over because, in accord with an ancient and still powerful conception of knowledge, they are convinced that calling the interest or value of a theory *contingent* must be the same as calling the theory *worthless*. Since that conception of knowledge is precisely what is at issue in these debates, to appeal to it in the argument is to beg the question.[6] I point this out in "Belief and Resistance" but, as I anticipate there and for the reason I discuss there, many of those to whom it is pointed out continue to find the argument compelling. The reason is a common tendency—honed to a fine art in transcendental logic—to believe not only that what one believes is true but that it is *necessarily* true and that no other belief is "seriously" conceivable. It is just this tendency (and, as deployed in full-fledged transcendental analysis, artistry) that I refer to in "Belief and Resistance" as "absolute epistemic self-privileging" (p. 143).[7] Like much else in the paper that he missed, Richards missed the precise form of the point as well as its relevant force.

A final word on those naturally selective saber-toothed tigers. Although cognitive conservatism appears to be an evolved (and thus biologically transmitted) tendency, its operations, as I remark at the end of my paper, are significantly amplified and complicated by *cultural* transmis-

---

5. For extended discussion of these points, see my "Unloading the Self-Refutation Charge," *Common Knowledge* 2 (Fall 1993): 81–95.

6. To reject the traditional equation between contingency and worthlessness is not, of course, to "abandon" logical consistency. Richards's strenuously self-affirming charge here just begs the question in a different way—or, one might say, returns him to the same circular argument from a different point of entry.

7. See my discussion, pp. 142–44, of Karl-Otto Apel's demonstration of the rational necessity of (a rationalist conception of) reason.

sion. Thus, while people who still see saber-toothed tigers after they are presumed extinct may be thought "crazy" and, accordingly, socially ostracized and reproductively disabled, they may also be honored by segments of their communities as visionaries and defenders of the old truths and old ways—and, accordingly, may live long, rich, potent lives as priests, poets, and full professors, successfully perpetuating, through cultural *and* biological transmission, both their visions and their visionary powers.

Reasonable Evidence of Reasonableness

Mark Kelman

1

Questions of how we claim to know the things that we know and whose claims to knowledge are treated as authoritative are inescapable in reaching legal judgments. I want to illustrate this generalization by referring to a pair of hypothetical self-defense cases that, I argue, require fact finders to judge both how "accurately" each defendant understood the situation in which he found himself and how accurately policymakers can assess the consequences of alternative legal rules.

The first case I will deal with is one in which the defendant shoots and kills her sleeping husband. The husband had physically abused her over a long period. While the defendant will of course acknowledge that she was in no immediate danger at the moment she killed the man, her preliminary claim (we will explore variations as well) is that she needed to act self-defensively at that moment for fear that she subsequently would be incapable of defending herself against life-threatening attacks that she was convinced would inevitably be made.[1]

The second case is one in which a white defendant shoots and kills a black teenager who has confronted him on the subway, in a situation in which the teenager's "threats" were ambiguous. The shooting victim had

---

1. For a lucid summary discussion of battered-wives self-defense cases, see Donald Creach, "Partially Determined Imperfect Self-Defense: The Battered Wife Kills and Tells Why," *Stanford Law Review* 34 (1982): 615.

This essay originally appeared in *Critical Inquiry* 17 (Summer 1991).

brandished no weapon and made no physical contact with the defendant, but he had "asked" the defendant for money and, in the defendant's mind, displayed a generally threatening demeanor. I will presuppose that this defendant—unlike Bernhard Goetz, the defendant in the notorious New York subway vigilante case on which I partly base this hypothetical model—overtly acknowledges that the race of the victim played a substantial role in his assessment of the danger of the situation. (It is important to note as well that the defendant in my model shoots the victim only once and does not shoot while his victim is retreating from the scene, as Goetz almost surely did.)[2]

While juries seem sympathetic to both classes of defendants, politicized law students rarely see that the cases raise even remotely similar concerns. The handful of self-identified conservative students that I teach show tremendous sympathy for the subway killer and decry the abuse victim's vigilantism; mainstream leftist students invariably not only believe that it is obvious that the wife should be exonerated and the racist subway killer convicted, but they see the subway killer and the abusive husband, not the respective defendants, as the clearly parallel characters in the scenarios.

It is vital to note, though, that the formal legal structure we typically would use in analyzing the cases is essentially identical. Moreover, the deeper factual and normative claims each defendant ultimately is making will, I think, look much the same in broad structural terms as well. If, then, we react differently to the claims, it must be because we believe that the defendant we favor has produced differentially convincing *evidence* to bolster a claim with the same general form. The need to differentiate the claims on the basis of evidence will, I claim, prove particularly problematic for the typical leftist student because, at some more general and theoretical level, he or she is prone to be committed to extreme skepticism about both naive positivist propositions and the possibility of resolving normative disputes on the basis of potentially shared understandings rather than through assertions of power.

2. For a fuller description of the Goetz case, see George Fletcher, *A Crime of Self-Defense: Bernhard Goetz and the Law on Trial* (New York, 1988).

Mark Kelman, professor of law at Stanford University, is the author of *A Guide to Critical Legal Studies* (1987) as well as a number of articles on law and economics, taxation, criminal law, and legal theory.

2

In order to make a successful self-defense claim, a defendant must persuade the fact finder that when he used deadly force against the victim, he both subjectively and reasonably believed that if he had not used such force, he would have been killed or grievously wounded. For purposes of this discussion, I will assume that the fact finder in each case believes the defendant subjectively believed he needed to use force; the tricky question is whether that belief is "reasonable." At first blush, the inquiry is centered on a simple "factual" question: How probable was it that the defendant would have been grievously wounded or killed had he not used deadly force to defend himself? I will argue (in section 8 below) that although the stated norm in self-defense cases makes reference only to the reasonableness of the defendant's factual perceptions, we in fact also expect the jury to judge the reasonableness of his decision to use deadly force, and that two defendants facing an equal chance of grievous bodily harm or death may not and should not always be judged to be acting equally reasonably in doing so. I will also argue (in section 9) that answering questions about the "probability" of a future event poses even more than typically difficult epistemological problems compared, for instance, to questions about whether a particular event in the past occurred. As difficult as it may be to discover whether X killed Y, the question of whether X reasonably feared Y when he killed him—a question requiring probabilistic assessment—is even harder to answer, even if we assume that a judgment of reasonableness hinges solely on the "positive" question of the risk of grievous harm.

We will assume, though, for the time being, that the defendant in each case simply wants to argue that he reasonably believed that there was a "high" probability that he would be grievously injured unless he killed first. What is at issue is not *how* high the level of probability must be to justify the use of force for the particular defendant, but the narrower question of whether the defendant was at "significant" risk.

Both the battered wife and the subway killer will make structurally parallel claims in arguing that they reasonably believed that they were in danger. The preliminary, and most commonplace, claim is that this belief is a "typical" belief, one shared by most people. In operational terms, the defendant simply asks the jurors to ask themselves whether they would have used deadly force if placed in the situation in which the defendant found himself.

The "typical" person may be considered reasonable in two quite distinct ways. First, he might be assumed to be *accurate* in his judgments. Though typical beliefs remain hypothetically falsifiable, we presume that they are true unless we have reason to doubt them. To the degree that the defendant is claiming he was accurate, he is arguing that his conduct was *justified,* not *excused.* A person who claims his conduct is justified argues, in essence, that although the action he took is ordinarily illegal (for example, killing someone, or running a red light), it is affirmatively desirable in the particular situation in which he found himself (in perceived factual danger of being killed unless killing first, or rushing a heart attack victim to a hospital).

Alternatively, the typical person might be deemed "reasonable" not on the supposition that his beliefs are accurate but on the supposition that they are not blameworthy. Thus, for instance, the ultimate victim may have "wielded" a foil gum wrapper that looked just like a gun in the peculiar light; the defendant (and the juror projecting himself into the defendant's position) was *wrong* to believe he was endangered. The defendant in such a case does not claim that he is justified—killing in the particular situation is still something that causes a good deal more unwarranted harm than it prevents. Rather, he claims to be excused, to have done nothing to differentiate himself from typical people. The implicit norm is that blame is reserved for the (statistically) deviant; we are blamed only for those actions and errors in judgment that others would have avoided.

In most battered-wife self-defense cases, the defendant's dominant argument is that she was reasonable in the sense that the juror would have felt just as endangered as she did and would have felt the same imminent need to act.[3] When we hear, though, that battered wives who kill their abusers demand to be allowed to present expert testimony about women's responses to long-term battering by an intimate, we are dealing with a second-level claim. Now we have a situation in which the defendant recognizes that the fact finder believes that the defendant genuinely, subjectively believed she was endangered, but that, from the fact finder's vantage point, the belief was both *mistaken* and atypical. At the formal level, battered wives in such cases acknowledge that they are mistaken if the jurors think they are: they concede (at least for argument's sake) that the jurors' judgment is an accurate assessment of risk. Thus, she seemingly gives up the claim that she is justified. She also gives up the simplest, most straightforward version of the excuse claim (that she is not statistically deviant) in favor of a more sophisticated variant. The argument is that the juror must not simply imagine what he would have done, exercis-

---

3. It is worth noting, though not central to the issues I discuss, that legal doctrine had to change to accommodate one particular feature of the battered wife's situation that rarely arose in "traditional" self-defense cases. Courts have traditionally ordered the fact finder to focus on whether the defendant faced imminent grievous bodily harm or death. See, for example, *State v. Stewart*, 763 P.2d 572 (1988). Some courts today ask instead for the fact finder to determine whether the defendant needed to *act imminently* to prevent grievous harm, even if the harm would not have occurred until much later. Thus, if the juror believes the victim would have followed and harmed the defendant even if she fled the house where he slept, the juror may find that the defendant had to act when she did— that is, considerably before any harm would have befallen her. See, for example, *State v. Norman*, 89 N.C. App. 384 (366 S.E.2d 586 [1986]).

ing his own reflective judgment, had he found himself in the defendant's position on the immediate occasion when the fatality occurred, but he must imagine what sort of judgment he would have made if he had been in the defendant's position over the years. In this view, wrong judgments about risk are excused so long as most people who had lived the life the defendant lived would have reached the same wrong conclusions. The defendant may be hypersensitive and paranoid, and may, through "learned helplessness," underestimate her capacity to escape the situation without using deadly force. But so long as "typical" people exposed to ongoing abuse would develop the same hypersensitivity and sense of help-lessness, the defendant should be excused.[4] There is an implicit wedge between our contingent character—the character we have developed liv-ing the actual life we have lived—and some hypothesized "true" character that ought to be the basis for moral and legal judgment. So long as the juror believes that he too would have developed the same misperceptions the defendant did if exposed to the same external forces, he cannot judge her harshly, for nothing of the defendant's "true" character, the character freed from the influence of unjust pressures, has been revealed. In terms of traditional legal doctrine, the defendant asks that her judgments be compared not to those of all people, but to people in her narrower situa-tion as battering victim; she is reasonable so long as she believes what typi-cal people in her situation believe.

My strong sense is that although lawyers for battered women who have killed their abusers have most carefully developed "excuse" defenses that emphasize the extrinsic forces that created a concededly mistaken judgment, most strong ideological defenders of the battered wife (my left-ist students) actually believe the killings are justified,[5] though they think the typical juror (particularly the typical male juror) will not share the defendant's perception of risk. (I have no idea on what basis they come to believe that there is a radical difference between their perceptions and jury perceptions; jury acquittals of battered wives being tried for murder are common, but whether they are common *enough* for the tastes of my students is harder to say.) There are two interestingly distinct ways of justifying the conduct once one has reached this "third stage" of the controversy.

First, one might embrace traditional doctrinal norms but believe that

4. The development of the sophisticated "excuse" view can be traced especially to Dr. Lenore Walker in, for example, her *Battered Woman* (New York, 1979). For a favorable view of this defense, see Victoria Mather, "The Skeleton in the Closet: The Battered Woman Syndrome, Self-Defense and Expert Testimony," *Mercer Law Review* 39 (1988): 545. An unfavorable view is found in David L. Faigman, "The Battered Woman Syndrome and Self-Defense: A Legal and Empirical Dissent," *Virginia Law Review* 72 (1986): 619.

5. For a good exposition of this view, see Elizabeth M. Schneider, "Describing and Changing: Women's Self-Defense Work and the Problem of Expert Testimony on Batter-ing," *Women's Rights Law Reporter* 9 (1986): 195.

the typical person unreasonably underestimates the danger of death or serious bodily harm the woman faced. In one view, jurors are simply inexperienced or naive compared to the defendant, who knows far more about her particular situation as a result of her bitter experience. It might also be the case, additionally or alternatively, that jurors are ideologically predisposed to underestimate male violence or to overestimate the active complicity of victims.

Alternatively, one might believe the battered wives are justified if one believes that the justificatory principles embodied in traditional self-defense rules were unduly circumscribed and hence normatively unappealing. In this sense, the problem is not that the jury misassesses one risk—the risk of grievous bodily harm—but that the law demands they ignore other sorts of harms that may occur unless she kills her abuser. While death and serious bodily harm are indeed well worth averting, even, perhaps, at the cost of another's life, women who are abused frequently are psychically crushed and demeaned in ways that are at least as horrible as having their bones broken. If a woman needs to kill her dominator to escape the confines of sadistic oppression because she cannot otherwise be rid of him, she should be allowed to, just as she would if he would otherwise seriously injure her. (Rarely discussed in anything but the most covert ways is what to make of cases in which the woman arguably needs to kill to reassert her agency, not because she can escape the ego-destructive relationship if the abusive man is either dead and gone or just plain gone, but because killing itself is the only adequately empowering act she can take. Such a defense, if articulated directly, would obviously be of no avail in our legal system.) It may also be the case that the battered women's ideological defenders believe that traditional justification norms are incomplete because they fail to deal with the possibility that the abuser's conduct was so reprehensible that he is justifiably shorn of the protection of criminal law. While he may not deserve to die, particularly as a state-imposed punishment, neither does he merit protection from private violence, perhaps because those who have done what he has deserve the *risk* of death simply because they do not merit an affirmative response if they suffer.

For my purposes the critical point is that the subway killer is making precisely parallel formal claims. First he claims that the typical person, the juror projecting himself into the situation, would also have killed. Once more, the claim is either that he is justified (it is affirmatively better that the defendant kill the initial aggressor than that the defendant be seriously injured or killed, despite our general norms against intentional killing) or excused (while the victim would not actually have harmed the defendant, typical people would have made the same mistaken judgment and would have performed the same self-defensive acts, and typical people are not blameworthy). His second-line claim also parallels the battered woman's: he claims that what are concededly mistaken judgments as to risk are products of circumstances that would have led the juror into error as well (he was a hypersensitive multiple-mugging victim and/or a product of a particularly racist subculture that led him to overestimate the risk of violence by young black males). Once more, although he may plead to be excused for developing atypical wrong judgments, he and his ideological defenders almost surely believe that he is actually justified, that he is "right" and the jurors are not. Again, this third-level claim, that his actions were justified, may be based on two different claims. First, he believes that jurors simply underestimate the risk of grievous harm or death the defendant really faced; unaccustomed to judging the subtle signals of danger that "experienced" mugging victims are aware of, they irrationally focus on the presence of overt verbal threats or brandished weapons. If willing to acknowledge his racial animus, he may even claim that jurors unself-consciously underestimate the danger he faced in order to protect their "egalitarian" and "color-blind" self-images, just as battered women claim jurors protect an idealized vision of social life by failing to recognize the nature and extent of male violence. Alternatively, just like the battered women, he may believe that the conventional normative scheme is unduly circumscribed, that citizens *ought* to be entitled to use deadly force to be free from robbery—whether or not the robber, unless resisted, would be likely to use deadly force[6]—and/or "terroristic" abuse and the correlative feeling of futile powerlessness, a loose analog to the sort of lack of agency that dominated women feel.[7]

3

What each defendant contests most powerfully, then, is the accuracy of the typical person's judgment of the riskiness of the situation he was in and/or the "moral persuasiveness" of the mainstream justification principles, which seemingly demand that we convict a defendant unless he was averting death or grievous bodily harm. To a lesser extent, each defendant claims that if he is indeed mistaken in his calculation of risk, his "group" of defendants alone is excused, because they alone are a product of circumstances that make it impermissible to judge them harshly for not living up to the standards most of us would be able to reach.

To differentiate the cases, therefore, requires that we assess each defendant's ultimate claim that he knows more about the risks he faced

6. Goetz himself was tried in New York, a jurisdiction in which, quite atypically, people are permitted to use deadly force to avert *any* robbery, even if there is no imminent threat of grievous bodily harm or death. See New York Penal Code, sect. 35.15(2).

7. A neighbor of Goetz's analogized Goetz's reaction to his 1981 mugging to the reaction of a female rape victim, focussing especially on his feelings of vulnerability and fragility. See Robert McFadden, "Bernhard Goetz: A Contrast in Portraits," *Los Angeles Daily Journal,* 8 Jan. 1985, p. 4.

than jurors do; that we judge the relative acceptability of the implicit claims each defendant makes to supplement traditional self-defense law; that we decide that one but not both defendants is excused for developing wrong beliefs; and/or that we focus less on ascertaining precisely what risk each defendant faced and more on the reasonableness of his conduct in an inevitably factually uncertain situation.

Most of my leftist students are quite confident that we have adequate evidence to decide that the wife is indeed at greater risk than the subway killer. The most plausible justification for that claim, in my view, is that the wife's judgment is to be accepted because she has particular knowledge of the person she killed, while the subway killer acts on the basis of generalizations, perhaps stereotypes, that are inherently less trustworthy. While I am fairly sympathetic to this claim, which I discuss in section 7, I will argue that it is neither normatively appealing to accept only particularistic risk assessment by defendants nor possible to identify which defendants are perceiving particulars and which are acting on the basis of generalizations. Somewhat surprisingly, perhaps, my students more typically support the battered wife's claims to both accurate factual perception (of the risks) and appealing normative judgment (about proper grounds for the use of deadly force) by reference to two distinct forms of multiculturalist epistemology. In one decidedly nonskeptical variant, the battered wife's beliefs are judged to be more reasonable because oppressed people generally have particular access to objective truth: the interpreter's pedigree is the central bit of information that we need to know in order to judge the evidence that she proffers. I will discuss problems with this claim in section 5. Alternatively, and in my view somewhat more convincingly, one may (at least claim to) believe that there are ultimately no "true" propositions about either "external facts" (like risk probability rates) or values, but believe that existing institutions will unduly discount the beliefs of oppressed people unless we self-consciously alter their natural tendencies. We must deliberately tilt existing institutions to take outsiders' perspectives into account. I will discuss problems with this claim in section 4. Finally, some may retreat to a naive positivism that most disclaim when asked to state their general epistemological views: in this view, "acontextual" scientific inquiry would reveal the wife to be at greater risk of death or serious bodily harm than the subway killer. I will ultimately criticize this naive positivist position in section 9. I will also very briefly argue, in section 6, that efforts to imply that battered women are excused for developing atypical perceptions, while the subway killer is not, have failed, at least as currently developed.

I will argue in section 8 that ultimately it is most persuasive to focus less on the accuracy of defendants' factual judgments and more on the consequences of their actions in situations in which both they, and we, must inevitably be factually uncertain. What ultimately best differentiates the cases in my view is that the subway killer's errors are more clearly unacceptable, not that he is more clearly in error. I will argue that killing in situations in which people who are perceived to pose great and imminent danger but in fact are utterly innocent is markedly less acceptable than killing those who certainly were not innocent, and it is even more reprehensible to kill when the victims are selected on the basis of their membership in a historically subordinated racial group.

4

If asked to state their general, theoretical position on epistemological issues, leftist law students almost invariably enunciate a hyperskeptical multiculturalist position. In this view, there are no transcendent claims to truth at all. The test of the "veracity" of a proposition is simply its capacity to convince *any* audience that can be identified as forming what might be seen as a subculture.

This epistemological predisposition was developed in a particular context, though, for leftist lawyers. Although it may resonate, weakly, in overheard debates among anthropologists about the cultural imperialism of nonrelativistic observers of non-Western cultures, it gained the sort of political currency lawyers are most prone to care about as a particularly impregnable position to take in politicized battles over university hiring and tenure decisions. Traditional scholars argue that work can be "objectively" distinguished, that some scholars either advance propositions that are objectively "true" or mount evidence in ways that advance decontextualized truth-*seeking*, and others do not. Multiculturalists press the idea that particular canons of verification are nothing but the particular local practices of one of many potential academic subcultures.

Whatever strengths or weaknesses hyperskepticism has in that context, though, it is quite difficult to sustain in the context of the self-defense cases, for the hyperskeptical multiculturalist seems, at first blush, to have no choice but to renounce his capacity to judge each defendant's claim. There are subcultures in which the battered woman's descriptive visions and normative pleas resonate and subcultures in which the subway killer's do. The position is ultimately never sustained in its strong form, largely because it appears incompatible with taking a *critical* stance toward *any* subculture's received understanding, including the racist killer's. One wonders whether the hyperskeptical view in its strong form is ultimately compatible with legal judgment of anything but a defendant's "good faith" in believing that he acted properly. (I will set aside the difficult but hardly unrelated question of whether we would have any access to what the defendant genuinely, subjectively believed that was not at least partly mediated by our judgments about what it is "reasonable" to believe.)

At this point, the relevant *political* question is how to resolve controversies when there is, by hypothesis, no ground on which to resolve them.

It might seem that the default position is that the community as a whole renounces its judgmental force and its capacity to deny the propriety of any genuinely held belief. But there is surely no reason for a multi-culturalist to condemn communities that refuse to renounce judgment; since we have plenty of experience with communities that are anything but shy about making judgments of subcultural norms and, by hypothesis, no vantage point from which to criticize such communities, it is far from lucid that there *is* a default position.

A more attractive alternative is to argue that the essential political task is to insure that each subculture's voice is adequately heard. Thus, in the context of legislatures, we might see multiculturalists demand corporatist, proportional representation schemes. In the context of jury trials, the context we are most concerned with here, the notion would presumably be that the subway killer will get an adequately sympathetic hearing without the aid of expert testimony or cautionary jury instructions, while the battered woman's claims will be unduly discounted and marginalized unless we make special efforts to bolster them. There may be no ultimately objective view of risk determined by evidence; given, though, that a political body (the jury) exists with the power to validate certain views, it must be manipulated to treat each inevitably partial subcultural understanding as equally weighty.

This focus on *procedural* rectification—rather than substantive judgment—appears to allow us to maintain hyperskeptical multiculturalist views while still in some sense favoring the battered woman. But it leaves important questions unanswered. First and most obviously, there is no attempt to account for why we as observers actually favor one claim rather than the other. Second, while the claim seems plausible that jurors are more likely to share racist presuppositions than the fear of long-term abusers, it would appear to be the sort of claim that itself required some substantiation; if it, too, is treated as a claim that is substantiated simply because it resonates for those speakers who utter it, we have not escaped our initial bind.

Finally, and perhaps most subtly, one wonders why hyperskeptics demand a subcultural rather than a wholly solipsistic validation of beliefs. To the degree that one relies on simple factual skepticism, conviction of any individual on the supposition that his factual judgment is wrong is impermissible. Even assuming, quite heroically in my view, that battered wives, either on their own or representing women more generally, form something we would call a community and/or that crime-obsessed racists do not, it is not at all clear why this should matter. Even if we believe oppressed communities deserve more political power, multiculturalists must enunciate a much clearer theory of the relationship between community empowerment and the decriminalization of representative community conduct than they have done. It might ultimately be helpful to analogize these cases to straightforward "mistake of law" cases in which defendants convince juries they are either unaware of or are conscientious objectors to a criminal norm. Traditionally, mistakes about governing norms are nonexculpatory. From the vantage point of certain moralistic individualists, however, this result is troublesome since it allows punishment of those who are unaware that they are choosing to act wrongly. The multiculturalist position on mistakes of law would presumably allow individuals who are unaware of norms to continue to be convicted unless they were unaware of the dominant norm because they held the norm of an alternative cultural entity. The concern, then, is not so much fairness to individuals as maintenance of alternative groups.

But the analogy falters unless we believe that the maintenance of particular beliefs is significant to the survival of the group as a cultural entity. The strongest variant of the multiculturalist view, in my opinion, is that women are, in important ways, that cultural entity with a particularly acute sensitivity to and high estimate of the level of male domination and violence and that "devalidation" of their local understanding of male violence hampers the formation of a vital group life.

5

I have real doubts, though, that even what I view as the most sophisticated procedure-focussed variant of multiculturalist skepticism would comfort my leftist students unless they believed that the women were, in some sense, *right* in their judgments of male violence; shared delusions generally go by the name "false consciousness" in critical circles. Thus, leftist students frequently move, in a partial and tentative fashion, towards an intensely nonskeptical epistemology. Oppressed people, in this view, have privileged access to both moral truths (like the "proper" resolution of the question of what sorts of potential suffering ought to justify the use of deadly force) and the facts of social life (for example, how dangerous and persistent abusive men "really" are). The position in its purest form is almost invariably ambivalent about whether we as observers learn the truth by listening to speakers with oppressed *status* or whether our (separately) derived knowledge of truth enables us to identify the oppressed (those people who are members of oppressed groups who share our vision of the truth). It is surely the case, for instance, that a black subway killer who gunned down other blacks need not be assumed to have privileged insight that the white subway killer lacks: typically, leftists embracing positions like these simply assume that such a black introjected white racist ideology.[8]

The belief that oppression yields knowledge thus proves difficult to

8. See Patricia Williams, "Spirit-Murdering the Messenger: The Discourse of Finger-Pointing as the Law's Response to Racism," *Miami Law Review* 42 (1987):127, esp. n. 6.

sustain. This is dominantly the case because members of oppressed groups often clash with one another in their vision of moral and factual truths. If one's knowledge of the world is driven solely by a (political) need to affirm each utterance that the most oppressed person makes or an (epistemological) belief that we can assess a speaker's veracity solely by reference to her status, ultimately one must either arrange all groups in some hierarchy of oppression and give exclusive credence to the more downtrodden in any controversy, or recognize that we have a more transcendent perspective on truth, even while knowing that our ultimate beliefs will be heavily influenced by our initial predispositions.

The clash has been particularly visible in criminal law because defendants asserting subcultural defenses—discerning a "truth" that the dominant culture decries—have most typically been men claiming that what the dominant culture discerns as criminal is a permissible form of male prerogative in their subculture: for example, what a Hmong defendant would call a ritual of "capture," the complainant would call rape;[9] unless one believes the Hmong defendant misdescribes his culture or (more plausibly in my view) that his culture is anything but unified in its understanding of the contested event, one is forced simply to "choose" between one oppressed group, women, and another, the Hmong refugees.

I think one sees a more interesting variant of this problem in what are now commonplace intraleftist debates on the issue of essentialism. Here is a typical argument: black women cannot simply be subsumed in some essential category of women because their experiences are distinct. Even in relationship to the issue most generally perceived to unite women— opposition to sexual expropriation—black women have a distinct viewpoint because they are aware that black men have been unjustly accused of rape, and that white women have been complicit in these racist accusations.[10] If one tries to unpack this argument, I think one ultimately sees that there must be something like an implicit assumption of the purity and wisdom of the oppressed. A "moderate"—both in political terms and in terms of his attitudes towards verification—presumably believes that

9. For a discussion of the subcultural defense in the context of just such a rape trial, see Spencer Sherman, "When Cultures Collide," *California Lawyer* 6 (1986): 32, and Julia P. Sams, "The Availability of the 'Cultural Defense' as an Excuse for Criminal Behavior," *Georgia Journal of International and Comparative Law* 16 (1986): 335.

10. For a good discussion of the anti-essentialist position, see Angela P. Harris, "Race and Essentialism in Feminist Legal Theory," *Stanford Law Review* 42 (1990): 581, esp. pp. 598–601. My claim is that the essentialism Harris attacks could be understood as demanding that all actors in a category have *identical* beliefs given only an epistemology that centralizes viewpoint as the ultimate validator. If Harris is read to suggest only that one can always construct increasingly accurate demographic subgroups to predict, probabilistically, how the subgroup's respondent will tend to view a social event, I find nothing the least bit problematic in her claim. If this were her claim, though, I see no reason why she wouldn't test *all* the sociological predictors of "attitude" (religious belief, income, party affiliations, and so on) in deconstructing the needlessly large category, "women."

women *infrequently* fabricate rape charges and that our legal culture, dominated by men, historically has adopted rules based on substantial overestimates of the rate of false accusation. However, he would never rule out the possibility that a particular woman has fabricated a charge, whether as a result of racism, personal pathology, influence by men, or other factors; it remains an issue to be decided in particular cases on bases *separate* from and transcending the identity of the contesting witnesses whether the woman is truthful, though the issue would be resolved with a different Bayesian prior and a different presupposition about the general probability of lying than it would for male traditionalists. If that were one's attitude about verification, the black woman would not feel that she must adopt a "separate" identity to question racist rape accusations. Only in a world where the denial of a particular woman's allegations is a badge of group betrayal (at the political level) or the denial of the supposition that we can assess veracity simply by identifying the status of the speaker (at the epistemological level) must we imagine a group chasm. "Women" in this world are seen as that group which identifies itself as an oppressed group that treats all women's claims as unassailable, and "blacks" are seen as that group which treats all black claims of racial oppression likewise. In such a world, it is indeed epistemologically *impossible* to be a black woman in a way that it is not if black women are seen simply to have a different set of preconceptions about the possibility of racist rape accusations than white women typically do.

Because "privileged" groups will often clash in ways that preclude the possibility of resolving disputes simply by adopting the position of the oppressed, leftists may partly abandon this technique of evidence evaluation without ever assessing the underlying plausibility of the claim that oppression yields moral and factual clarity, that, for instance, women are more prone to have access to truth than white men. Obviously, there are a variety of arguments too complex to detail here that suggest why the oppressed might have particular access to moral truth. For instance, Georg Lukács argued that the proletariat could discern political truth because its self-interest was in fact universalistic;[11] Derrick Bell, in the legal academy, makes an argument quite parallel to that for blacks;[12] and certain legal feminists have argued that women are *biologically* morally distinct, in seemingly quite attractive ways, from men.[13]

I tentatively believe that my leftist students are ultimately persuaded by two propositions. First, the notion that suffering is intrinsically both (morally) ennobling and (cognitively) clarifying—a notion vaguely de-

---

11. See Georg Lukács, "Reification and the Consciousness of the Proletariat," *History and Class Consciousness,* trans. Rodney Livingstone (Cambridge, Mass., 1971).

12. See Derrick A. Bell, *And We Are Not Saved* (New York, 1987), esp. chap. 10.

13. See, for example, Robin West, "Jurisprudence and Gender," *University of Chicago Law Review* 55 (1988): 1.

rivative of liberation theology—seems appealing to many. Second, privileging the insights of the oppressed may seem an appealing reaction formation to what is seen as smug, elitist dismissals of their competence. Neither argument, though, is likely to speak clearly to the nonconverted. Suffering is surely as compatible with paranoia as insight, bitterness as well as compassion, self-centeredness as well as altruism. And it certainly seems most plausible to imagine that oppressed people, like everybody else, know more about the details of their own lives than outsiders do, though perhaps no more or less about the structural roots of their condition. Like everybody else, they probably are unduly prone to accept structural accounts in which their suffering is undeserved and their virtues inadequately rewarded. As a legislative policymaker, I might well trust a welfare mother's account of how she both survives and suffers given existing benefit levels better than I trust either an economist's or a home economist's budget projections, yet I am much less prone to believe that she is an absolutely trustworthy predictor of responses to shifts in eligibility rules or tax incentives. The battered wife knows how the police responded to her first call and how the shelter she went to treated her; she does not necessarily know more than a white male sociologist about how police respond more generally or how shelters work[14]—both sorts of questions may be relevant in her trial (the second, in fact, is more relevant if she's claiming justification rather than excuse).

6

The argument that membership in a historically oppressed group gives the actor the sort of clarity of vision that compels us to ratify even those deeds that at first blush look most unreasonable to us is mirrored by an argument that the oppressed subgroup member alone is to be *excused* for his mistakes. In essence, then, there are two descriptive rhetorical moves and each proves useful to reach the same outcome—acquittal—through quite distinct legal methods.

One move invokes images of people "freed" by oppression to develop special insight. In this view, only the oppressed are truly agents in viewing the world. The battered woman really "knows" whereas oppressors' "knowledge" is a veil of self-interested misperception determined by the imperatives of self-aggrandizement, not developed by any "free" self.

The other invokes images of total victimization: oppressed people are

---

14. One of the most attractive statements of the position contrary to the one stated here disparages the possibility of any "transcendent" technocratic knowledge. See Lisa D. Delpit, "The Silenced Dialogue: Power and Pedagogy in Educating Other People's Children," *Harvard Educational Review* 58 (1988): 280.

utterly without agency, unable to think counterhegemonic thoughts or to do anything not explicitly or implicitly demanded of them. As such, they are not responsible for anything, even their own errors. The battered woman's misconstruction of her situation is not of her making, for *nothing* is of her making.[15] We suppress in large part the inevitable discomfort that her act—killing a perceived oppressor—could hardly be seen as the introjection of the oppressor's desires; an account emphasizing her agency is surely available to us. At the same time, the subway killer is seen for the purposes of legal judgment to have developed his paranoid and racist worldview on his own; we invoke the idea that only oppressors are intentioned subjects, not determined objects, suppressing the awareness that a determinist account of the subway killer is readily constructed, and that leftists frequently construct just such accounts outside the trial context in theorizing about unconscious or institutional racism.

7

It is surely most compatible with mainstream legal argument to differentiate the cases on the basis of the *method* by which each claimant reached the particular conclusion to which he came. In this view, the battered wife's claim appears, at least initially, "particularistic" whereas the subway killer's appears unacceptably "statistical." She kills someone she has observed, in detail, for a great deal of time; he relies on generalizations about the criminal predilections of black teenagers since he has never even met these particular people. In the legal academy nowadays, leftists often argue that particular knowledge—of the sort grounded in narrative rather than aggregate data—is the special province of historically marginalized groups,[16] a claim that seems particularly implausible in the legal world given the attraction that ultraconservative victims' rights groups and prosecutors seeking the death penalty have long felt for detailed narrative.

It is surely the case, though, that our legal system shows a strong preference for "local narrative" fact finding, at least in the adjudication context, a preference that obviously antedates left-wing attacks on "hard science." Take an example made famous in the legal academic community

15. Catharine A. MacKinnon wrestles frequently with the problem of ascribing political insight and agency to women who have been deprived, in her view, of all real possibility of developing genuine agency. See her *Feminism Unmodified: Discourses on Life and Law* (Cambridge, Mass., 1987) and *Toward a Feminist Theory of the State* (Cambridge, Mass., 1989); for particular application to the self-defense context, see MacKinnon's review of *Women Who Kill*, by Ann Jones, *Stanford Law Review* 34 (1982): 703.

16. See, for example, Richard Delgado, "Storytelling for Oppositionists and Others: A Plea for Narrative," *Michigan Law Review* 87 (1989): 2411, and West, "Economic Man and Literary Woman: One Contrast," *Mercer Law Review* 39 (1988): 867.

by Laurence Tribe's article attacking "trial by mathematics."[17] A plaintiff who had been run over by a bus could certainly not win a suit against a bus company by showing that the defendant company operated the majority of the buses on the route where he was injured, but he could conceivably win if he brought in a relatively unreliable witness who thought he saw the company's name on the bus as it drove from the accident scene. This appears to be the case even if we believe that the "objective" probability that the named defendant was the tort-feasor was higher in the first than in the second case—that is, we did not believe, for instance, that the failure to adduce *additional* evidence of the culpability of the statistically dominant company was a function of its factual innocence.

I have deep normative doubts about this tradition.[18] Imagine (to follow a hypothetical model offered by Judith Thomson defending particularistic fact finding)[19] that X had shot ninety-nine bullets at V while Y shot only one: statistical, general facts. Imagine, too, that the bullet found in V's body is identified as coming from Y's gun (this is a piece of internal or narrative evidence). However, if we recognize that ballistics tests are themselves inherently inaccurate (for example, imagine that there is a five percent chance that the bullet is falsely identified as coming from Y's gun), the idea that we should be wedded to the "internal" evidence that Y, not X, is the killer, strikes me as mistaking an intelligent rule of thumb (internal evidence will often be more dependable than statistical generalizations) for a principle.

Given the tradition, justified or not, of overweighing particular facts in adjudication, we might believe, by vague analogy, that not just judicial judgment but all human judgment is to be preferred to the degree that it appears inductive and particular, not derivative.

Even if that were so, it is surely the case that the subway killer claims a great deal of particular knowledge. Of course, he does not know the particular people he shoots, but he claims to interpret perfectly particular gestures: he has been mugged before and he has been with people who have not mugged him; he has spoken to people who have been mugged and asked them what happened, and he has observed many interactions where people are not mugged. Moreover, the battered woman almost surely subjectively relies in part on statistical generalizations (the police don't take domestic violence seriously, protective court orders don't work, men who hit make up and then hit harder), just as much as the subway

17. See Laurence Tribe, "Trial by Mathematics: Precision and Ritual in the Legal Process," *Harvard Law Review* 84 (1971): 1329, esp. pp. 1340–41.

18. See Mark Kelman, "The Necessary Myth of Objective Causation Judgments in Liberal Political Theory," *Chicago-Kent Law Review* 63 (1987): 579, esp. pp. 591–93. For an equally skeptical view, see Daniel N. Shaviro, "Statistical-Probability Evidence and the Appearance of Justice," *Harvard Law Review* 103 (1989): 530.

19. See Judith Jarvis Thomson, "Remarks on Causation and Liability," *Philosophy and Public Affairs* 13 (1984): 101, esp. pp. 127–33.

killer did (black teenagers don't often engage in social chitchat with older white businessmen on the subway, and given the high rate of robbery by black teens, those who talk about getting money from people may well take it).[20] Even if the battered woman is *subjectively* a complete localist who does not conceive of herself in terms of the socially available categories that make generalization possible (like "battered wife"), her lawyer, attempting to persuade the jury that they too would have been scared in her situation, will *surely* make use of general evidence and will believe that statistical information about the ineffectiveness of police intervention in domestic violence cases or general information about the escalation of violence in the "battering cycle" is germane. It is, in fact, the subway killer's lawyer who will almost inevitably avoid generalizations in a real case because they are sure to be at least partly race based and hence impolitic.

If we are to make a convincing claim that "local" knowledge of a particular person (the battered wife) is to be systematically preferred to "local" knowledge of subway etiquette (quite broadly defined), we must be implicitly adopting a theory that the sole reasonable basis for prediction is something like inertia. We can, in this view, be confident only that people will do what they have done before. I doubt this epistemological supposition is sound: I suspect, for instance, that I would do much better predicting that a stranger is about to have an affair with someone, on the basis of observed flirting, than I could predict whether my wife were, on the basis of habit. Even if it were sound, we must recognize that many battered women kill in situations where they claim to know that their spouse is about to do something different, something *more* violent than he has ever done to her before.

20. It is not at all obvious what sorts of crime frequency levels would justify making even preliminary group-based judgments of the perception of risk since, whatever else is ambiguous, it is clear that it is always very *unlikely* that anyone is about to commit a crime judged simply on the basis of general facts known about him. Williams feels it helpful to point out, though, that whites dramatically overestimate the proportion of crime committed by blacks, as if differences in global frequencies *would* matter (see Williams, "Spirit-Murdering," nn. 76, 82). But if one focusses on violent crime, and armed robbery in particular, her views of victim misperception seem quite problematic: blacks, who constitute roughly twelve percent of the population, are arrested for sixty-two percent of the armed robberies; thus, the *rate* of robbery arrests among blacks is roughly twelve times the rate of nonblacks (that is, it would be twelve times more probable that a particular black person is a robber than a nonblack, if one had to make a purely race-based estimate). Assuming, quite correctly in my view, that racism leads to overestimates of black robbery even in victimization studies (for example, victims treat more behavior by blacks as threatening, and they identify too many dark-skinned robbers as blacks) *and* assuming that arrests are even more biased than victim reports of the rates of offense, it is nonetheless implausible that actual rates of robbery by race are even close. See also Ronald B. Flowers, *Demographics and Criminality* (New York, 1989), esp. pp. 93–95.

8

It is most persuasive to me that we reject the subway killer's proffered evidence not because he "inaccurately" assessed risks (though he might well have), but because the consequences of acting as he did, given his perception of risk, is so horrible. This would be true even if his judgment were not in part race based; it is even more dramatically true given the fact that it is.

Assume, perhaps counterfactually, that the battered woman was in no greater danger of death or serious bodily harm than the subway killer was. Assume that we could be assured that of twenty subway killers we must judge, one was correct in asserting that he would have died or been grievously wounded unless he used deadly force, and of twenty abused women who kill, the same one in twenty needed to use force to prevent the same dire consequences. The nineteen mistaken subway killers have executed some combination of absolute innocents, taunters, and relatively nonviolent robbers, while the battered wives killed nineteen established assaulters.

Within the *stated* norm, each is equally reasonable, each has equal "evidence" for his or her claim, for the stated norm appears focussed solely on the reasonableness of an individual's fear. But the judgment each exercises has consequences that demonstrate the need to make fuller social assessments of the consequences of error. We may overtly recognize that we are judging a defendant's reasonableness more generally, and that a reasonable person simply has to wait, even at some risk to himself, before harming possible innocents. More typically, though, I suspect we silently imbed this fuller assessment of reasonableness in *our* judgment of the "veracity" of the proffered evidence on risk, though it is not in any obvious way a positivist judgment of veracity.

The subway killer's error is even more unacceptable because the relative innocents he will harm are selected on the basis of their race. Let's hypothesize for the moment that we are dealing not with someone who shoots people he fears, but excludes them: for example, a store owner who uses a buzzer system to exclude people he feels are suspicious.[21] Assume, too, that the storekeeper's judgments are significantly race based. Employers may not, in the hiring context, engage in even economically rational "statistical discrimination" (that is, assuming that each protected group member has traits that are in fact typical of protected group members).[22] Employers must use alternative, more individualized screening

21. See Williams, "Spirit-Murdering," for a chilling description of such buzzer systems.

22. Assume, for instance, that a job requires upper-body strength and men, typically but not invariably, have more than women. An economically rational employer might disqualify all women so long as it costs more to give strength tests to applicants than the employer would gain by expanding the pool of available employees. Still, the employer would clearly be required to give the more individualized test.

tests. The costs of such screening are viewed as acceptably low given that individualized assessment is both fairer to individual applicants and leads to more equitable group participation in social life. In essence, we ask those who make at least partly race-based judgments of a person's violent intentions to use "alternative screening devices" as well; basically, we ask them to wait until an actor makes his violent intentions clearer. In waiting, obviously, there is some risk for the person who wants to defend himself successfully, and some risk for the shopkeeper in letting the "suspicious" person enter, just as there is some cost to the employer in using more individualized screening. But not waiting imposes serious costs as well: young black men are stigmatized, excluded from participation in generally available activities (shopping, riding the subway in anything but a withdrawn fashion), subjected to the demeaning supposition that others know a lot about them when who they truly are as individuals is wholly misassessed.

At the point at which we assess the "error costs" each defendant imposes, we seemingly demand new "evidence," not so much from the particular defendants but from policymakers. How do we judge claims about the impact of crime terrorism, the impact of constant race-based suspicion of black males, or the horror of abusive relationships that don't result in death or grievous bodily harm? If we fear that acquitting the subway killer increases violence towards ambiguously threatening, or simply nonmainstream or boisterous black male teens by implicitly legally privileging it, must we show that the frequency of such incidents is actually sensitive to acquittals? If we hope that acquitting the battered women will deter domestic violence, even though few battered women actually employ counterviolence, must we demonstrate that this is the case?

9

Ultimately, there are epistemological problems implicit in these cases clearly beyond the ken of legal resolution and conceivably beyond the ken of true resolution in any sphere. We must inevitably *categorize* the situation in order to assess the risks, and epistemological questions about how to establish generalizations or categories are obviously no less present here than they would be in historical research. This is apparent whenever we adopt formal categories, and it is perhaps most transparent when the formal categories are of recent, conscious invention (like "battered women"). But it is surely also the case when we generalize based on gestures or speech: does it *really* help us in assessing the risk faced by the subway killer to know whether his victim said, "Give me five dollars" or, say,

"Can you spare some money?" if we know how frequently muggers and nonmuggers each uttered the respective phrases?[23]

The generalizations or categories are certainly not natural or preexisting; they quite clearly seem to respond to a particular community's interests. They may well have a categorical life independent of the particular subject of inquiry, though; battered women were not initially conceived of as a group in order to facilitate the calculation of death or serious bodily harm risk rates for particular persons; they were conceived of as a category in order to serve other social purposes (for example, to attend to issues of needed support systems, like shelters and hotlines, or to help diminish self-blame among people who may have thought they suffered unique harms that they ought to have been able to control personally). Once created, though, the utility of categories as filters of experience is subject to ongoing interrogation; they can indeed die out if they generate falsifiable, and false, predictions. A claim, for instance, that ten percent of women injured by a spouse seriously enough to see a doctor will be, in the next five years, injured seriously enough to be hospitalized would constitute such a falsifiable claim about risk, though the initial focus of the claim—women injured by sexual intimates—was hardly a "natural" category.

Generally, of course, hypothetically falsifiable claims will neither be uncontroversially verified nor falsified; thus, judgments of the plausibility of claims will continue to reflect distinct social understandings that are doubtless as much about aspirations as interpretations. There is a wide range of plausible risk estimates for any particular battered wife who kills her husband while he is passive, just as there is for how often the subway killer, faced with a large sample of "like incidents," would be seriously mugged. We may ultimately trust our normative judgments of error costs more than we trust our capacity to pick a reasonable number, but we are still likely to claim, with unbending support from political allies, that we are assessing factual judgment, objective clarity of vision. We are all, in that sense, closet positivists.

23. Of course, while trials in the Anglo-American system are ostensibly exclusively focussed on individual guilt and on ascertaining facts about a particular situation, it is undeniably sociologically true that some are in large part *not* dominantly about the particular participants at all. Thus, the "real" subject of the trial of *a* battered woman might not be whether *she* was at risk, but whether a socially constructed group ("battered women") is indeed at risk. In that case, the fact that it might be problematic to claim to know the risks the particular defendant faced because we choose to treat her as belonging to one of a series of the possible statistical "groups" she is a "member" of is beside the point. The fact that there might be some profile of past assault victims—of either gender—that better predicts violence or its absence than membership in the battered women group and that shows that the particular defendant was at low risk would then be largely irrelevant.

On Finding Facts

Cass R. Sunstein

Mark Kelman's fine paper ("Reasonable Evidence of Reasonableness," pp. 169–88) is organized around the following puzzle. He and his students think that under certain plausible assumptions, a battered wife has a persuasive claim of self-defense in a case in which she kills her husband. But they also think that a white man, faced with a threatening black teenager on the subway, does not have a similar defense. The two cases might well be similar in the apparently crucial sense that the probability that the battered wife will be subject to grievous bodily harm might be the same as the probability of harm to the white subway rider. If the probability is indeed the same, why are the cases different?

1

Let me begin with two general reactions to this puzzle—one methodological, the other substantive. My first general reaction is that when we think about these two cases, it should appear that the apparent success of certain claims about "social construction" does not mean that we are in chaos, or an abyss, or even that we are disabled from using ideas like truth or objectivity. It may be granted that all our categories are socially constructed, in the sense that they are created by human beings with their own inevitable interpretive filters or prisms. For example, the category "air" is socially constructed in the sense that human beings have created and deployed that particular category when they might have used others. They might, for example, have divided "air" into four, or eight, or fifty different things, or treated air as part of a single category along with "water." (This does not mean that air is socially constructed or that there is no air.)

But the human construction of the category is not inconsistent with the claim that air pollution can threaten human life and health, or that there is too much sulfur dioxide in the air in Chicago, or that we ought to reduce greenhouse gases. All these are claims about facts, about values, and about truth. And what can be said for the category "air" can also be said for other humanly constructed categories, including "at risk," "beaten up," "fair treatment," and "sexual harassment." I will return to all this below.

My second, substantive reaction has to do with the legal culture in general, and for this a little background is in order. Sometimes it is asked: If you think that school segregation was constitutionally unacceptable, how can you possibly approve of affirmative action? Or: If you think that the Supreme Court should allow minimum wage laws, how can you possibly think that the Court should invalidate laws restricting abortion? Or: If you think that the work of Robert Mapplethorpe cannot be censored, how can you be sympathetic with the view that the government should regulate materials combining sex with violence against women? These questions, often taken to be rhetorical ones, have been extremely important in the law, helping to drive it in predictable directions—against affirmative action, against the right to choose abortion, against the regulation of violent pornography.

To strangers to the legal culture, these questions might seem anything but rhetorical. One might think instead: These situations have little or nothing to do with one another. If, for example, I think that the right to abortion should be protected, I have not thereby committed myself to any particular view about minimum wage laws. The questions themselves are in this sense an artifact of particular legal (and more broadly social) ways of setting things up.

More precisely, one might think that all of these cases should be understood by reference to what I will call an anticaste principle, that is, a principle that forbids legal and social arrangements from putting one social group, defined in terms of a morally irrelevant characteristic, systematically below another. Under such a principle, the reason that segregation is unacceptable is that it contributes to a caste system based on race. This very reason argues for, not against, affirmative action. If we are concerned about pornography combining sex with violence against

---

Cass R. Sunstein is the Karl N. Llewellyn Professor of Jurisprudence at the University of Chicago. He is the author of *The Partial Constitution* (1993).

women, it is because such material contributes to a system with castelike features based on sex. This *is* the reason that it is crucial to protect Mapplethorpe and other gay artists from censorship. The very reason that abortion is protected—to ensure against second-class citizenship—[1] is the reason that we might insist on minimum wage laws.

I do not contend that an anticaste principle, described in the abstract, answers particular questions, or necessarily calls for this particular array of controversial conclusions. To support that judgment, an extended argument would be required. But such a principle should at least help inform our inquiry. The same is true for Kelman's puzzle. It might be asked: If we think that the battered wife has a good claim of self-defense, does it not follow that the same is true for the white subway rider? But to this we might respond that the two cases really have little to do with one another. Why does a claim of self-defense for a woman subjected to a steady stream of violence from her husband have any implications for such a claim when offered by a white subway rider who has killed a somewhat threatening black stranger?

More precisely, we might respond that if our sympathies are with the battered wife, it is because she is the victim of a system with castelike features and because those features prominently include disproportionate subjection of women to male violence. One of the defining characteristics of second-class citizenship for women consists precisely in the fact that women are subject to male violence. Men are not similarly subject to female violence. The battered wife issue has everything to do with this problem; it is part of the argument for a presumption in her favor. On the other hand, second-class citizenship for blacks consists precisely in their disproportionate subjection to white violence, public and private, and this very fact argues in favor of skepticism about the white subway rider's claim of self-defense. Hence the very reason that we are reluctant to allow that defense—the social situation of blacks—should make us inclined to allow the same defense for the battered wife.

The words "presumption" and "inclined" are necessary because to decide these cases, we need to know a lot more about the facts. To know who really deserves a legally sufficient defense for killing, much more of course has to be said. We have to find out the details. But I think an anticaste principle helps explain Kelman's intuitions about the two cases. It fits well with his more particular arguments, to which I now turn.

1. The argument is made in Cass R. Sunstein, "Neutrality in Constitutional Law (with Special Reference to Pornography, Abortion, and Surrogacy)," *Columbia Law Review* 92 (Jan. 1992): 1–52.

2

Here are what Kelman sees as some inadequate, tempting solutions:

1. There is no such thing as objective truth and therefore we (a) should not worry about the facts of the matter or, more modestly, (b) should put "truth" to one side and simply attempt to ensure that subcultures, especially disadvantaged ones, are adequately heard.

2. Members of oppressed groups—the battered wife and emphatically not the white subway rider—have especially accurate knowledge of the social world.

3. Particular, local knowledge, held by the battered wife, is more reliable than the abstract, general, statistical knowledge of the subway rider.

All of these claims are popular in some legal, literary, and philosophical circles. It is especially interesting that Kelman, an influential figure in the critical legal studies movement, thinks that all of them are wrong. Let me summarize and elaborate on what I take to be his reasons.

The view that there is no such thing as truth, or objective truth, seems in this context to be especially unhelpful. If we really thought that, how could we proceed? Is it really irrelevant whether either defendant was actually in danger of being hurt? Suppose that the evidence shows that the battered wife really could have left and been safe after doing so? If we do not care about danger, what would we care about in a world in which notions like truth and objectivity were genuinely unavailable?

I think that such a world would be unintelligible; that we would really not be able to say much of anything about what we think, about the defendants in these cases or about anyone in any case. And if the truth with respect to danger is relevant, how can we avoid assessing whether there was an actual danger? Indeed, the notion that subcultures should be allowed to be heard makes most sense, not on the gangster's incoherently relativist theory that everyone deserves a piece of the action, but instead on the ground that truth cannot emerge unless different people, with different perspectives, are allowed to speak and to be heard. That is what the jury system is supposed to be all about; it also undergirds the system of checks and balances. The basic idea may well point toward efforts to reform existing institutions—but precisely in the name of truth. (The Anita Hill/Clarence Thomas hearings are relevant here.)

We should agree that oppressed people will have especially accurate knowledge of what their lives, subjectively, are like and probably of many other things that nonoppressed people do not see or, if they see, misunderstand. But, as Kelman says, battered women may well lack knowledge of (for example) how shelters work or of what options are available and precisely because of their oppression. More generally: Oppression entails extreme deprivation. Extreme deprivation can distort knowledge and perception or in some ways even eliminate them. That is one of the reasons we think of oppression as wrong.[2] So Kelman thinks there is a big problem with the general view that oppressed people have special cognitive capacities or see things more clearly than others. Thus far the argument seems right.

I do think that Kelman may undervalue a version of this argument of special force in the context of the battered women's defense. But I will return to that shortly.

So long as we believe in knowledge, there is no reason to believe that particular knowledge is always better than abstract, statistical knowledge. A scientist's belief that the moon will not fall into the earth tonight may well be statistical, but it is probably even more accurate than my belief that tonight my daughter will go to sleep before 10:30 (as she always does). Thus some people falling in the class of the white subway rider might well have a better sense of the real facts than some people falling in the class of the battered woman.

We might conclude that disparagement of abstract knowledge in favor of local knowledge is unnecessarily abstract. We need to identify the particular abstract knowledge or the particular local knowledge to see which is true. Kelman thinks that if we are really after knowledge, there is nothing wrong with stereotypes based on knowledge. Stereotypes are everywhere, and they help organize our lives. Here too I agree with Kelman.

3

It is easy to understand the conviction, which Kelman seems to share, that the battered woman probably has a stronger defense than the white subway rider. Kelman thinks that if this is so, it is not because of real-world probabilities—not because she has the facts right—but because we think that the consequences of accepting the subway rider's defense are much more terrible than the consequences of accepting the battered wife's defense. He makes two claims. First, the black teenager will be, in some of the relevant cases, a complete innocent and, in other cases, pretty close to that. But at best the husband is an "established assaulter." We are more willing to allow the (by hypothesis unjustified) killing of an assaulter than of a complete innocent.

Worse, in the subway case the killed innocents will have been chosen on the basis of their race. To be sure, the choice might be reasonable statistical discrimination (reasonable in the sense of structurally parallel, in terms of statistical probability, to all sorts of statistical judgments that

2. Some of these issues are discussed in Sunstein, *The Partial Constitution* (Cambridge, Mass., 1993).

we make every day). But statistical discrimination on the basis of race is generally unacceptable in (for example) employment and education; an employer cannot defend against a claim of racial discrimination by show-ing that on some important, relevant variable, blacks really tend to do worse, statistically, than whites. Statistical discrimination in choosing who will die seems far worse than that. Thus Kelman concludes that even if the probabilities in the two cases are the same, different outcomes might be justified because the consequences of error are truly horrifying in the subway case and merely bad in the battered wife case.

These seem to be solid arguments. They show that our assessments of the two cases might turn, not on the facts, but on the consequences of getting them wrong. We can actually extend Kelman's remarks. The black teenager may well have been—it is plausible to say, based on nonin-vidious statistical evidence—subject to a range of social disabilities that make it especially unacceptable if he is killed without really having threat-ened anyone's life. He is in an important sense a social victim, and this helps organize our judgments about the case. The point reveals a larger one. Frequently disagreements about "the facts" are really disagreements about the social world that would be created if we treated the facts one way rather than another. (This will be recognized as a conventional prag-matic claim, suggesting—the pragmatic cliche—that factual inquiries are designed to serve our purposes rather than to map onto anything.) The point bears on evidence very generally, certainly within the law and per-haps outside of it. When we say X is true, we are sometimes saying that we should treat X as if it were true because that route will lead to a better social world for reasons quite independent of accurate assessment of the facts.

I have said that Kelman's argument seems to me solid. But there are other possible explanations for treating the two cases differently. Let me give two alternative accounts.

1. I think that the probabilities may be simply different in the two cases. As a matter of brute fact,[3] a wife who has been repeatedly beaten by her husband will, sooner or later, be subject to grievous bodily harm. Her life is genuinely at risk. (I put to one side the admittedly relevant but very complicated question whether her self-defense claim should be rejected because she could and should have left the house.) By contrast, a white man ambiguously threatened by a black teenager in an open place faces no such danger. He might feel humiliated, at risk, or worse; but realistically his life is probably not in danger, and grievous bodily harm is probably unlikely.

3. Of course we should acknowledge that any claim about brute facts itself depends on human interpretive faculties; it does not rely on unmediated prehuman access to the world. But I think that this acknowledgement is essentially irrelevant to the claim I am making. See my opening commentary on "air"; see also below.

If this is so, we can say something about the two cases that really is just about the facts. It is at least plausible to think that a battered wife has more realistic fear than a white man asked for money on the subway by a black teenager. At least this can be approached as a question of fact. It would be good to have a great deal of data, about general cases of this sort and about the particular cases, to help in that assessment. Perhaps the particular cases really are parallel in terms of risk; from what Kelman tells us, we cannot be sure.[4] But it will help to have a lot more information.

2. One response to the two cases is that the real problem has to do with certain systematic biases, ones that develop into heuristics that help organize our attitudes, fears, and experiences.[5] White people in the category of the white subway rider will use race as a proxy for dangerousness, and this may be bad for two reasons. First, it may just be inaccurate; white people as a class probably see black men as a class as more threatening, in any context, than they actually are. The probabilistic judgments are skewed by the heuristic. Second, the probabilistic judgment may be unacceptable even if it is accurate. As noted, statistical discrimination based on race is unacceptable even if the statistics are true. This is because our prohibition on discrimination is designed, not to root out irrationality, but to eliminate a system with castelike features.[6]

Now compare the case of the battered wife. Here the relevant heuristics and biases will probably run in just the opposite direction. She is likely systematically to underestimate the real risk to her; her assailant is after all her husband, someone she (in a sense) probably loves. While she is underestimating the risk to her, the white subway rider is overestimating the risk to him (or should be treated as if he is doing so). If she acted, it

---

4. For what it is worth, I might note here that it seems to me that under certain assumptions, both defendants should have a defense because of a legitimate risk to life or safety and because the victim in both cases is under those assumptions quite blameworthy. On other assumptions, the battered wife should have been under a duty to leave (though one wants to know a lot more about the situation and the situations of battered wives generally).

I might add that many of my conservative colleagues seem to have opposite reactions to those of Kelman and his students. This may well be a result of the omnipresent phenomenon of selective empathy: Some people think of themselves as plausibly in the shoes of the white defendant, but not the battered wife, and of course vice versa. It is an interesting question how selective empathy interacts with assessments of probabilities and of "error costs," and with efforts to assume an impersonal point of view.

5. On heuristics in general, see Daniel Kahneman and Amos Tversky, "Prospect Theory: An Analysis of Decision under Risk," *Econometrica* 47 (Mar. 1979): 263–91.

6. The point shows that affirmative action is analogous to the prohibition on discrimination; these are not, as is often thought, separate ideas. If we ban racial discrimination, we will ban one form of statistically reasonable stereotyping—and thus impose costs on "innocent victims"—in the interest of long-term social justice. Much the same is true for affirmative action. The point is discussed in more detail in David A. Strauss, "The Myth of Color Blindness," *Supreme Court Review* (1986): 99–134, and Sunstein, "Why Markets Don't Stop Discrimination," *Social Philosophy and Policy* 8, no. 2 (1991): 28–29.

is unusually likely she was in danger. If he acted, we cannot draw this conclusion; indeed, it is unusually likely that he was not.

What is true for our defendants may also be true for judges and juries. Juries may well be biased against the battered woman. They may also be biased in favor of the white subway rider. If so, it is important for the legal system to try to err the other way, simply to correct institutional bias. In a world with racism and sexism, whites who kill blacks will receive the benefit of the doubt, and the reverse is true for battered women who kill their husbands. We should design a legal system that counteracts this bias.

The connection between these various points and a system with castelike features should not be obscure. A characteristic of a caste system (as I understand it here) is that second-class citizens do not protect themselves or receive protection against violence, and that the higher caste can engage in acts of violence with relative impunity. The anticaste principle outlined above thus helps explain why the battered wife is likely to underestimate the relevant risks, why the white subway rider is likely to overestimate them, and why we should design rules of evidence with these distortions in mind.

In addition, then, to Kelman's concern about the social consequences of error, we might add that (a) the facts really may systematically favor battered wives in such cases, and (b) it might be best to build rules to treat battered wives better than threatened white subway riders because of the relevant heuristics and biases.

4

Kelman's essay avoids large speculations about evidence and knowledge; he stays at the microlevel. I want to conclude with some general remarks about Kelman's approach. It seems that from his essay we can get three general propositions about evidence and the legal system. I am not entirely sure whether Kelman would agree with any or all of them. But they do seem to me to be some of the lessons of his essay.

1. There really are facts, and truth, and objectivity, at least for purposes of everything we ought to care about. The very notion of bias—not a dispensable notion—makes sense only with some such assumptions. We should therefore distinguish between two quite different things. The first is the critique of metaphysical realism—the view that human beings have unmediated preinterpretive access to the world. It seems clear that we see what we do through our own prisms and filters. But the critique of metaphysical realism, variously set out by (among many others) Wittgenstein, Putnam, James, and Dewey, need not entail a collection of related views, which are sometimes described variously as relativism, or skepticism, or deconstruction, or postmodernism, or perspectivism, or

solipsism.[7] We do perceive the world through our own categories and constructs. But this does not mean that we are in chaos, or in an abyss, or that we cannot make descriptive (or evaluative) statements on the basis of good arguments, or good reasons, rather than bad ones.

The view that the downfall of metaphysical realism has this consequence—pervasive, I think, in both law and literature—betrays an ironic commitment to a metaphysical conception of truth: a belief that without external or transcendental grounds, human beings really have no basis for thinking or saying anything at all. If we thought that this conception was an unnecessary or even a strange one, then we could proceed, after the downfall of metaphysical realism, to talk as we always have. We could continue to use notions like objectivity and truth and do so without the least embarrassment.

2. Sometimes factual claims are not really factual claims but instead claims about what it is best to do or how it is best to act in the face of factual uncertainty. We might say that we ban racial discrimination because white employers who use race as a proxy for undesirable characteristics are acting "irrationally" or "counter to the facts." But we might really mean that using race as such a proxy tends to perpetuate something like a caste system, even if it is fully rational, and even if a plausible response to the facts. We are dealing here with (among other things) what economists call error costs. An assessment of error costs plays a large role in thinking about factual claims and properly so.

The line between this proposition and proposition (1) is not as crisp as it might appear. We characterize facts as facts for good human reasons—a statement that helps explain both categories. It also helps explain a third.

3. Sometimes factual claims are not really factual claims, or even lurking normative ones of the sort described in (2), but instead claims about how a social or legal system works best in the face of social or institutional bias. There is nothing unprincipled about generally liking the jury system but trying to avoid jury trials in civil rights cases in the South when the jury is likely to be entirely white.

I am not an expert on the law of evidence, but I would not be surprised if evidentiary rules were often devices to overcome bias. Many of those rules might purport to be designed simply to get the facts straight, but they are actually about overcoming institutional problems. Often our reactions to factual claims are really about some such bias, at least as much as it is about what I am calling the brute facts.

7. For more elaborate versions of some of the points in this and the following paragraph, see Hilary Putnam, *Renewing Philosophy* (Cambridge, Mass., 1992), and Martha C. Nussbaum, "Sophistry about Conventions," *Love's Knowledge: Essays on Philosophy and Literature* (New York, 1990), pp. 220–29. I know that I am referring to a lot of different views here, with complex features, and that some of them cannot fairly be accused of seeing the downfall of metaphysical realism as having this consequence.

Let us assume that these lessons are indeed appropriate ones to draw from Kelman's paper. If this is so, there may be interesting implications for the study of law and evidence in general. Fact-skepticism and norm-skepticism, in law and perhaps elsewhere, would be undermined and so, too, for recent critiques of rationalism. An encounter with particular cases makes these sorts of attitudes very hard to sustain. (Return, for example, to the Anita Hill/Clarence Thomas hearings.) We would instead talk very particularly about what legal rules serve what purposes and ask what sorts of human purposes we really want them to serve. Here factual inquiries would be exceptionally important, and objectivity would be a continuing aspiration.

But I want to conclude with the most general point. Armed with an anticaste principle, we can see that the very reason our sympathies are with the battered wife's claim of self-defense calls for some skepticism about the claim of self-defense in the subway case.

A Rejoinder to Cass R. Sunstein

Mark Kelman

I have a number of narrow responses to a handful of the many insightful points raised by Cass Sunstein ("On Finding Facts," pp. 189–98), as well as a broader observation about my project.

1) I am by no means suggesting that epistemological skepticism is related in any way to antirealism. Questions about whether we are able to know whether X killed Y seem to me radically separate from questions about whether he actually did.

However, while I am by no means committed to (nor capable of) exploring the "deep" issues of either metaphysics or epistemology raised by the problem of assessing the reasonableness of judgments of danger, I do believe (perhaps naively) that all the familiar problems of knowledge (and "reality") are more insoluble when we are talking about probabilistic assessment of future events, as we are here, than Sunstein acknowledges.

If I am trying to ascertain *whether* X killed Y, I may well believe that I have no more than a probabilistic estimate about what indeed occurred, but, at the same time, I may believe that in reality, the event either happened or did not. If, though, I am trying to answer the question that is relevant in the self-defense context—*will* X kill Y unless Y defends himself?—I believe that my probabilistic estimate of the future event does not reflect an underlying reality but that I can, at best, hope to develop the best available theory for projecting the future. There is simply no event to discern.

Perhaps an analogy would help. When a weather forecaster says that it rained yesterday in a particular location, the statement is either correct or incorrect (realism); at the same time, we may all have some probabilistic guess about how likely it is that the forecaster is correct in discerning it (epistemology). If, instead, the forecaster says there is a 20 percent chance that it will rain *tomorrow,* what we take this to mean is that given the factors measured—for example, barometric pressure, movement of fronts, precipitation patterns in other regions—if the forecaster faces the same conditions 1000 times and tells us, based on the presence of these conditions, that there is a 20 percent chance of rain, it will rain 200 times. We believe the forecaster is at the peak of this particular positivistic epistemological game if there exist no other set of theories and measurements that permits anyone else to precipitate out some class of days in which he or she over- or underpredicts the number that will be rainy, compared to the system that our upstart newcomer employs. However, we may recognize that on the given day the forecaster says there is a 20 percent chance of rain, the day might actually have some as yet unmeasured feature—not barometric pressure, say, but "light density"—and that if one took all days with the features measured plus the newly discovered "light density" measurements, we would find that it rained on 500, not 200, of the days with all the relevant features. That does not mean, though, that the "real" chance of rain is 50 percent, for we might well believe that if we knew enough, we would eventually predict as well as we measured retrospectively; we believe that with adequate knowledge, we would know with certainty whether it would rain or not. However, we still think of someone as doing the best probabilistic work possible so long as no one can improve on the probability estimates for any subset of events to be predicted; thus, until the "better theory" comes along, the "chance" of rain really should be treated as 20 percent.

When we say that there is a 20 percent chance that Bernhard Goetz or a particular battered woman would be assaulted seriously unless he or she took self-defensive measures, we cannot mean more than that our best theory of traits predictive of assaults puts each defendant into an inevitably incomplete grouping in which assaults have occurred in 20 percent of cases. The self-defense cases are *even* more troublesome, though, than the weather cases, since, given insoluble debates over whether human action is as determined as weather, rather than substantially volitional, "freely willed," and open-ended, we may not believe we can ever predict with certainty whether the ultimate victim of our defendant would have attacked, even if we could describe that ultimate victim in more and more predictive detail.

2) If Sunstein is suggesting that his anticaste principle explains the intuitions in the case in a fashion distinct from the one I have employed

---

Mark Kelman, professor of law at Stanford University, is the author of *A Guide to Critical Legal Studies* (1987) as well as a number of articles on law and economics, taxation, criminal law, and legal theory.

in the text, I am quite puzzled. Though our "anticaste" principles may well look different, the "error cost" analysis that is ultimately the central argument I rely on to distinguish the cases is an argument based on the social consequences of allowing battered women and Goetz-like characters, respectively, to kill those who might not kill them. A large part of the argument is indeed based on the status position of the groups. As I thought I'd made quite explicit in the text, Goetz is killing innocents and contributing, through statistical discrimination, to the disadvantage of an already-disadvantaged group (black male teens). The battered women are killing noninnocents, and contributing to the non-acceptance of subordinating violence.

If, instead, Sunstein means the "anticaste" principle to work at a very high level of generality—we should assume that subordinated people are getting an unfair shake from jurors, from unconscious doctrine decisions, and so on, and we should simply reflexively try to improve their chances in the legal disputes they encounter—I find it worse than unhelpful. The fact that there are indeed social hierarchies does not tell us a whole lot about when jurors (who are placed where in the hierarchy?) will make what particular sorts of cognitive errors, nor does it tell us that a particular legal victory (inculpating the shooter of a black teen, exculpating a battered wife) will remedy unjust subordination. At times, Sunstein seems to use the "anticaste" principle like my left-wing students typically do: it simply helps him identify which team he roots for. I don't see this as especially useful.

3) I am wary of making arguments based on "inaccurate" heuristics since it seems to me, as I tried to point out in the text, that there are a host of "distorting" views here. As I noted, the battered women's defenders will likely believe both that the women themselves (out of both convention and "love") will typically act only when risks are *extremely* high and that jurors will be predisposed to underestimate risks to avoid facing the reality of patriarchy, but I am not at all sure why Sunstein dismisses Goetz's defenders' conceptually parallel point that both subway riders and jurors will be unwilling to acknowledge the probative force of mixed class/race/style judgments because they violate principles they feel they must maintain to retain self-respect.

I agree with Sunstein that it might be helpful to find more epidemiological evidence about both subway violence and intrafamily violence. My point, though, is that people have very strong convictions about what the epidemiological evidence would show when they have no such evidence at hand, let alone evidence that they have assessed critically.

4) That brings me to my last point, a point that is not intended to be responsive, directly, to anything that Sunstein wrote. What seems to me most striking not about the issues that I discussed but the *ways in which the issues are discussed* is that strong antipositivism holds sway largely as a

theoretical position on the left, but in ordinary political "cases and contro-versies," theoretically skeptical leftists fall back on the claim that they have got the cold, brute facts correct.

More generally, what is striking to me is the degree to which the ordinary Enlightenment dogma—facts are universal, values particular; we may despair of building consensus on our ends, but we can agree what means attain these divisive ends, can come to consensus over how the world works—is flipped in ordinary political discourse. Traditional philo-sophical liberals (especially in their economistic mode) draw a sharp fact/value divide; multiculturalists on the left (for very different purposes) attack the claims of scientism and positionlessness of mainstream academics.

When push comes to political shove, though, it seems to me we fre-quently feel we reach reasonable consensus on abstract values while main-taining our unshakeable beliefs in frequently unproven and unprovable "facts." We suppress the fact that we really do differ on what our norma-tive conceptions of racial justice are, but we argue furiously about whether police frequently kill black kids without good reason; all sorts of people come to reject with great confidence right-wing theoretical argu-ments for libertarianism, but we find ourselves clashing over the degree to which any actual state can regulate or redistribute in beneficent ways; we refuse to recognize vast theoretical differences in our conceptions of what it means to say women are or are not empowered in this culture to free themselves from webs of violence, and assert, instead, with un-bounded confidence that we alone know the objective risk-rates battered women face.

The Question of Art History

Donald Preziosi

"What a beautiful book could be composed, telling the life and adventures of a word!... Is it not true that most words are dyed with the idea represented by their outward form? Imagine the genius that has made them!... The bringing together of letters, their forms, the figure they give each word, trace precisely, according to the genius of each nation, unknown beings whose memory is in us.... Is there not in the word *vrai* a sort of supernatural rectitude? Is there not in the terse sound it demands a vague image of chaste nudity, of the simplicity of the true in everything?... Does not every word tell the same story? All are stamped with a living power which they derive from the soul and which they pay back to it by the mysteries of action and the marvellous reaction that exists between speech and thought—like, as it were, a lover drawing from the lips of his mistress as much love as he presses into them."

—Honoré de Balzac, *Louis Lambert*

1

Debates on the nature, aims, and methods of art historical practice have in recent years given rise to a variety of new approaches to the study of the visual arts, to the projection of one or another "new art history," and to a sustained engagement with critical and theoretical issues and controversies in other historical disciplines to a degree unimaginable not very long ago. At the heart of many of these debates has been an explicit and widespread concern with the question of what art objects may be evidence for,

This essay originally appeared in *Critical Inquiry* 18 (Winter 1992).

and with the relative merits of various disciplinary methods and protocols for the elucidation of art historical evidence.

Until fairly recently, most of the attention of art historians and others in these debates has been paid to differences among the partisans of various disciplinary methodologies, or to the differential benefits of one or another school of thought or theoretical perspective in other areas of the humanities and social sciences as these might arguably apply to questions of art historical practice.[1] Yet there has also come about among art historians a renewed interest in the historical origins of the academic discipline itself, and in the relationships of its institutionalization in various countries to the professionalizing of other historical and critical disciplines in the latter part of the nineteenth century. These interests have led increasingly to wider discussion by art historians of the particular nature of disciplinary knowledge, the circumstances and protocols of academic practice, and the relations between the various branches of modern discourse on the visual arts: academic art history, art criticism, aesthetic philosophy, the art market, exhibitions, and museology.[2] What follows does not aim to summarize or characterize these developments but is more simply an attempt to delineate some of the principal characteristics of the discipline as an evidentiary institution in the light of the material conditions of academic practice that arose in the latter half of the nineteenth century in relation to the history of museological display. In brief, this essay is concerned with the circumstances of art history's foundations as a systematic and "scientific" practice, and its focus is limited to a single, albeit paradigmatic, American example.

2

In 1895, twenty-one years after the appointment of Charles Eliot Norton as Lecturer on the History of the Fine Arts as Connected with

1. An extended discussion of these issues may be found in Donald Preziosi, *Rethinking Art History: Meditations on a Coy Science* (New Haven, Conn., 1989), pp. 80–121. See also *The New Art History*, ed. A. L. Rees and Frances Borzello (Atlantic Highlands, N. J., 1988).

2. One important sign of these discussions has been a series of "Views and Overviews" of the discipline appearing in *The Art Bulletin* in recent years, of which the most recent has been perhaps the most extensive and comprehensive: Mieke Bal and Norman Bryson, "Semiotics and Art History," *The Art Bulletin* 73 (June 1991): 174–208.

Donald Preziosi is professor of art history at the University of California, Los Angeles. He is the author of *Rethinking Art History: Mediations on a Coy Science* (1989) and of a forthcoming critical history of the modern art museum.

Literature at Harvard, the Fogg Art Museum was founded as the first institution specifically designed to house the entire disciplinary apparatus of art history in one space.[3] The organization of the Fogg established patterns for the formatting of art historical information, teaching, and study that have been canonical in America down to the present, and that have been replicated through various material and technological transformations by scores of academic departments throughout the world.[4]

The institution of the Fogg provided for several distinct kinds of spaces designed to make the historical development of the visual arts clearly legible: lecture classrooms fitted with facilities for the projection of lantern-slide reproductions of works of art; a library of textual materials on the fine arts of various periods and places; an archive of slides and photographs of works of art organized according to historical period and genre; and space for the exhibition of reproductions of works of art—photographs principally, but also a few plaster casts of sculptures and some architectural models. Despite its name, the Fogg initially was not a museum in the common sense of the term, and no provision was made for the display of actual works of art, despite many pressures to form such a collection.[5]

The Fogg Museum was in fact conceived of as a laboratory for study, demonstration, teaching, and for training in the material circumstances of artistic production. It was intended to be a scientific establishment devoted to the comparison and analysis of works of art of (potentially) all periods and places, to the estimation of their relative worth, and to an understanding of their evidential value with respect to the history and progressive evolution of different nations and ethnic groups.

Photographic technology was central to the Fogg Museum's concep-

3. The Fogg Art Museum was founded in memory of William Hayes Fogg of New York by his widow and served as the home of the discipline at Harvard for thirty-two years, until its replacement by the present Fogg Museum in 1927. See George H. Chase, "The Fine Arts, 1874–1929," in *The Development of Harvard University since the Inauguration of President Eliot, 1869–1929,* ed. Samuel Eliot Morison (Cambridge, 1930), pp. 130–45. See also Caroline A. Jones, *Modern Art at Harvard: The Formation of the Nineteenth- and Twentieth-Century Collections of the Harvard University Art Museums* (New York, 1985), esp. pp. 15–30.

4. See Preziosi, *Rethinking Art History,* pp. 72–79. Useful discussions of the art historical tradition in Germany may be found in Heinrich Dilly, *Kunstgeschichte als Institution: Studien zur Geschichte einer Disziplin* (Frankfurt am Main, 1979); see also Michael Podro, *The Critical Historians of Art* (New Haven, Conn., 1982). Extensive discussions of early art historical programs in America will be found in *Early Departments of Art History in the United States,* ed. Craig Hugh-Smyth, Peter Lukehart, and Henry A. Millon (forthcoming). On England, see sect. 4 below.

5. Pressures were very strong from the outset of the planning for the institution. In the first year of its existence, sixteen Greek vases were loaned by an alumnus, and in 1896 two collections of engravings numbering over thirty thousand, already bequeathed to the university, were transferred to the building. By 1913, extensive alterations were made to the building to accommodate what had by then become a very large collection of original works, sacrificing space previously given over to instruction.

tion as a scientific institution, affording a systematic and uniform formatting of objects of study. Artifacts as diverse as buildings and miniature paintings were reproduced at a common scale for analysis and study—in this case, to two complementary formats: lantern slides for projection on walls and printed photographs of standard size.[6] The entire system was extensively cross-indexed and referenced by means of a card catalog for efficient access.

The institution was in effect a factory for the manufacture of historical, social, and, as we shall see, moral and ethical sense: a site for the production of meaning in several dimensions: aesthetic, semantic, historical. Out of its constantly expanding data mass, the researcher could compose a variety of narratives at various analytic scales: at the level of the individual artwork, or through several kinds of "slices" of works—for example, the use of line or color in the works of a single artist or of artists of different times and places. The system made it possible to trace the "evolution" of many different aspects of pictorial representation in a single civilization or across different cultures and historical periods. One could instantaneously chart, for example, the "development" of perspectival rendering of three-dimensional objects through Mesopotamia, Egypt, Greece, and Rome by means of the juxtaposition of images of paintings or drawings, and the student could calibrate the relationships between thematic content in medieval religious paintings and compositional format as these could be shown to change over time and place.

While the opportunity for the fabrication of narratives about items in the archive might seem unlimited, in practice this capacity was limited by the pedagogical curriculum devised by Norton and expanded and augmented by him and his colleagues over the years. By the time of the foundation of the Fogg, Norton's curriculum included the following sequenced elements:

Fine Arts 1: Principles of Delineation, Color, and Chiaroscuro
Fine Arts 2: Principles of Design in Painting, Sculpture, and
 Architecture
Fine Arts 3: Ancient Art
Fine Arts 4: Roman and Mediaeval Art

6. The use of lantern-slide projection for a variety of purposes is of great antiquity. A description of the process may be found in Athanasius Kircher, *Ars magna lucis et umbrae* (Rome, 1646); for an excellent discussion of optical devices in the nineteenth century, see Jonathan Crary, *Techniques of the Observer: On Vision and Modernity in the Nineteenth Century* (Cambridge, Mass., 1990). The Swiss art historian Heinrich Wölfflin is said to have pioneered double slide projection in the 1880s, wherein two images might be juxtaposed for comparison. On Wölfflin see Joan Hart, "Reinterpreting Wölfflin: Neo-Kantianism and Hermeneutics," *The Art Journal* 42 (Winter 1982): 292–300. See also Preziosi, *Rethinking Art History*, pp. 54–72.

Norton himself occasionally taught advanced courses on specialized topics. By the turn of the century, the Fogg curriculum included courses on the history of architecture, landscape design, Greek and Roman archaeology, the history of the printed book, Renaissance art, Florentine painting, Venetian art, and the art of China and Japan. In 1912–13, the Fogg organized the first art history survey course as we now know it, which attempted to cover the entire "history" of the arts of the world in a single year.[7]

Prior to Norton's appointment in 1874 the only instruction in the technical aspects of art making had been offered by Charles Herbert Moore, who was appointed in 1871 as the first instructor in freehand drawing and watercolor at Harvard. He taught exclusively at the Lawrence Scientific School on campus, where such instruction was deemed necessary to the training of students in the physical and natural sciences. Norton engaged Moore's services for his own new curriculum, and made his classes (Fine Arts 1 and 2) prerequisite to any training in the history of art on the principle that any serious understanding of the history of art should be grounded in hands-on experience of the technical processes of artistic production—a principle at the core of what later came to be known as the "Fogg Method" of formalist connoisseurship.[8]

Norton was an immensely popular lecturer, and his perspectives on the social and ethical implications of the visual arts profoundly influenced several generations of American art historians. By training an expert on medieval Italian literature and a Dante scholar, he became a devotee of medieval Italian art during his extensive travels in Europe after his gradu-

---

7. See Chase, "The Fine Arts, 1874–1929." The Fine Arts division was established at Harvard in 1890–91; prior to that, the department had semi-official status. The university catalog for 1874–75 listed two courses: Fine Arts 1—Principles of Design in Painting, Sculpture, and Architecture, taught by Charles Herbert Moore, and Fine Arts 2—The History of the Fine Arts, and their Relations to Literature, taught by Norton. Norton's course became Fine Arts 3 and 4 by the 1890s. See Charles Eliot Norton, "The Educational Value of the History of the Fine Arts," *The Educational Review* 9 (Apr. 1895): 343–48, wherein Norton observed that "it is in the expression of its ideals by means of the arts . . . that the position of a people in the advance of civilization is ultimately determined" (p. 346). On the relationship of instruction in the history of art to departments of classical languages, see Robert J. Goldwater, "The Teaching of Art in the Colleges of the United States," *College Art Journal* 2 (May 1943): 3–31 (supp.).

8. On the Fogg (or Harvard) method, see Denman W. Ross, *A Theory of Pure Design: Harmony, Balance, Rhythm* (Boston, 1907). The method aimed at developing sensitivity to the grammar of an art object and at elaborating a "scientific language" of art intended to "define, classify, and explain the phenomena of Design" without regard to the personality of the artist (p. vi). This was in contrast to the perspectives of Bernard Berenson, a follower of Norton and graduate of the method, who laid greatest stress on the analysis of the structural properties of an image as an expression of personality. The Fogg method strictly avoided the theorizing about the historical contexts of artworks emphasized in contemporary German scholarship. On the history of connoisseurship, see Preziosi, *Rethinking Art History*, pp. 90–95.

ation from Harvard in 1854. An intense anglophile as well, Norton attended John Ruskin's lectures on Italian art at Oxford prior to his appointment at Harvard—an appointment encouraged by Ruskin himself, who became over the years a close personal friend, model, and mentor.[9]

The creation of the Fogg Museum three years before Norton retired in 1898 was the direct embodiment of the theories of art and of the methodologies of historical analysis espoused by his teaching and inspired by Ruskinian ideals regarding the ethical and social import of artistic practice. In a very direct sense, the founding of the Fogg accomplished what Ruskin himself was unable to bring about, institutionally, at Oxford—the pragmatic synthesis of previously disparate components of art historical and critical practice in a common, scientific, "laboratory" environment.[10] The institution was organized according to

> the principle that the history of the fine arts should always be related to the history of civilization; that monuments should be interpreted as expressions of the peculiar genius of the people who produced them; that fundamental principles of design should be emphasized as a basis for aesthetic judgments; and that opportunities for training in drawing and painting should be provided for all serious students of the subject.[11]

3

The overriding business of the Fogg was the collection of evidence for the demonstration of the aforementioned principles, especially the principle that there is an essential relationship between the aesthetic character of a people's works of visual art and that nation's social, moral, and ethical character. Works of art, then, provide documentary evidence for

9. On Ruskin's immense influence on art historical and aesthetic thought in the United States, see Roger B. Stein, *John Ruskin and Aesthetic Thought in America, 1840–1900* (Cambridge, Mass., 1967), and Solomon Fishman, *The Interpretation of Art: Essays on the Art Criticism of John Ruskin, Walter Pater, Clive Bell, Roger Fry, and Herbert Read* (Berkeley, 1963). At the time of his appointment in 1874, Norton wrote to Ruskin outlining his plans to take groups of students to Venice and Athens in order to "show the similarity and the difference in the principles of the two Republics," in order to demonstrate that "there cannot be good poetry, or good painting, or good sculpture or architecture unless men have something to express which is the result of long training of soul and sense in the ways of high living and true thought" (Norton, letter to Ruskin, 10 Feb. 1874, *The Letters of Charles Eliot Norton*, 2 vols. [Boston, 1913], 2:34).

10. See John Summerson, "What Is a Professor of Fine Art?" (Hull, England, 1961), p. 7; hereafter abbreviated "WP."

11. Chase, "The Fine Arts, 1874–1929," p. 133. Moore was appointed director of the institution in 1896 and served until 1908. Chase himself served as dean of Harvard College after succeeding Moore as chairman of the Department of the Fine Arts.

that character, and that evidence is assumed to be homologous to that which may be evinced from that people's other arts—in particular its literature.[12] At the heart of the institution was its central data bank, in principle an indefinitely expandable archive of uniformly formatted slide and photographic print items organized geographically and chronologically and, within those divisions, by known and unknown artist, by style (where that was not coterminous with historical and geographical divisions), and by medium. Further divisions in the collection were made according to major arts (painting, sculpture, architecture) and minor arts (book illumination, luxury domestic and ceremonial objects, jewelry, and so on). The system is still replicated with essentially minor variations in most art historical collections today.

In principle every object in the archive bears the trace of others, and its meaning is a function of the system's juxtapositions and separations as determined by the physical arrangement of the cabinets in which items are stored.[13] Each informational unit is thus in an *anaphoric* position, cueing absent others, suggesting resonances with related objects, referring both metonymically and metaphorically to other portions of the archival mass. In short, the meaning of an item is a function of its place, its "address" in the system.[14]

The system is genealogical at base, and the archive permits the articulation of a variety of kinships among items in the collection, whether formal or morphological, thematic or iconographic. It is equally teleological in that each item is assumed to bear the stamp of its historical locus in an evolutionary development of artistic practice, on several possible levels—those of technique, individual or ethnic or national evolution, and so on: the archive is never not oriented. The Fogg method of formalist connoisseurship, like other techniques of connoisseurship developed in the latter half of the nineteenth century, stressed the ability of the trained art historical eye to assign a specific and unique address to any artwork encountered; at the same time, the method was attached to an ability to assess the aesthetic—and consequently the moral—value of a work. In this regard, the work is seen as having a certain physiognomic or characterological quality or value, an indexical and iconic relationship to mentality.[15]

12. A significant number of instructors in the Harvard art history program were recruited from departments of literature, most notably classics. This was a pattern to be found at a number of other American universities in the late nineteenth century—such as Johns Hopkins, Princeton, Cornell, and Case Western Reserve—as noted by Goldwater, "The Teaching of Art in the Colleges of the United States," p. 26ff.

13. See Preziosi, *Rethinking Art History*, pp. 75–79.

14. A classic example of this practice is Gisela M. A. Richter, *The Sculpture and Sculptors of the Greeks* (New Haven, Conn., 1929). On the modes of reasoning implicit in such analyses and their historical background, see Timothy J. Reiss, *The Discourse of Modernism* (Ithaca, N.Y., 1982), esp. pp. 21–54, 351–85.

15. See Preziosi, *Rethinking Art History*, pp. 21–40, 90–110.

The system is also organized in what may be termed an *anamorphic* manner, such that relationships among units in the archive are visible (that is, legible) only from certain prefabricated stances, positions, or attitudes toward the system. In effect, the user is invariably cued toward certain positions from which portions of the archival mass achieve coherence and sense. These "windows" are various and have changed in the modern history of the discipline. Among the most persistent anamorphic points is that of the period or period style, consisting of the postulation that all the principal or major works of a time and place will exhibit a certain uniform pattern. Normally, this is morphological in character, but may also involve certain consistent uses of materials, compositional methods, routines of production and consumption, perceptual habits, as well as a consistency of attention to certain genres, subject matters, formats of display, and the like.[16]

The pedagogical requirements of the system involve accessing the archival mass in such a way as to fabricate consistent and internally coherent narratives of development, filiation, evolution, descent, progress, regress: in short, a particular "history" of artistic practice *in the light of* that narrative's relationship to others actually and potentially embedded in the archival system. A particular historical narrative (the evolution of Sung painting; the development of Manet's sense of color composition; the history and fate of women painters in Renaissance Italy; the relationship of Anselm Kiefer's oeuvre to contemporary German society; the evolution of naturalism in Greek sculpture, and so on) is in one sense already written within the archive and is a product of its organizational logic. Every slide is, so to speak, a still in a historicist movie:

> New art is observed as history the very moment it is seen to possess the quality of uniqueness (look at the bibliographies on Picasso or Henry Moore) and this gives the impression that art is constantly receding from modern life—is never possessed by it. It is receding, it seems, into a gigantic landscape—the landscape of ART—which we watch as if from the observation car of a train. . . . in a few years [something new] is simply a grotesque or charming incident in the whole—that whole which we see through the window of the observation car, which is so like the *vitrine* of a museum. Art is behind glass— the history glass. ["WP," p. 17]

4

When Sir John Summerson spoke these words on the occasion of his inauguration as the first Ferens Professor of Fine Art in the University of

16. See Michael Baxandall, *Painting and Experience in Fifteenth-Century Italy* (London, 1972).

Hull in 1960, he was in the midst of a double lament. In the first place, he was at pains to inform his audience about the historical circumstances surrounding the tardiness of England in establishing academic university departments of art history in comparison, most notably, with Germany, where the first art history professorship had been established for G. F. Waagen in Berlin in 1844.[17] Indeed, it was not until 1933 that art history became an independent academic institution in England with the founding of the Courtauld Institute at the University of London—itself, at the time, considered by not a few as a fanciful innovation, as Summerson recorded.

Summerson's inaugural lecture at Hull was entitled, significantly, "What Is a Professor of Fine Art?" and he clearly conveyed his regret at a series of missed opportunities for the establishment of the academic discipline in England during the nineteenth century. In the same year that Waagen was appointed at Berlin, the Reverend Richard Greswell of Oxford, founder of the Oxford Museum, published a monograph arguing for the establishment of three professorships in England (at Oxford, Cambridge, and London). Greswell's plan came to fruition only in 1870, with the bequest of collector Felix Slade. None of these led to the development of a department of art history in England, a fact profoundly (and vociferously) regretted by Ruskin and Roger Fry during their incumbencies as Slade Professors at Oxford.[18]

The second and deeper lament running through Summerson's lecture is a regret that we in the modern world have to deal with the history of art at all—a situation that he sees arising from the problematic nature of art in the nineteenth century. He characterizes the origins of art history in a particular "moment" when

> modern painting began to turn its back on the public and to become deliberately and arrogantly incomprehensible (to put it succinctly, Burckhardt and Courbet were of the same generation); and it can be shown that the rise of Art-History and the rise of modern painting are accountable to the same historical pressures. ["WP," p. 15]

He goes on to note that this change had "nothing to do with the social and mechanical revolutions of [that] century; it was an affair entirely of the

17. See "WP," p. 5. Waagen played an influential role in the life of English collector Felix Slade (himself destined to influence the course of art history in England by his bequest of 1870) and is known to have spent time in England with him in the late 1850s.

18. Summerson's lecture conspicuously fails to mention developments in America, where ironically Ruskin's dream for Oxford was realized at Harvard through the agency of Norton, who might be said to have founded English art history on the wrong side of the Atlantic, across from that country he regarded as his true home. See "WP," pp. 7–11. On connections between Ruskin and Eliot, see n. 9 above and a forthcoming essay by Sybil Kantor in *Early Departments of Art History in the United States*.

perspective of the past, of the way history had been explored, mapped and
then generalized" ("WP," p. 16)—which led him to suggest that the scholarly mind came to imagine the presentation of and accounting for a new
"totality" of art: "a social-historical phenomenon co-extensive with the history and geography of man." For the nineteenth-century artist, a new
"brooding immensity of past [artistic] performance" had the effect of forever condemning the modern artist to a struggle toward ever new and
independent relationships with the "overwhelming mass" of past art
("WP," p. 16).[19] The result, Summerson says, was that "Art has been a
'problem' ever since":

> It is this feeling for art as a 'problem' which not only ties so much of
> modern art to art of the remoter past and detaches it at the same time
> from the currency of modern life but which links it with *an activity
> which is its opposite*—the analytic processes of the art-historian. Thus,
> modern art and Art-History are the inevitable outcome of the same
> cumulative pressure exerted by the toppling achievements of the cen-
> turies. ["WP," pp. 16–17; emphasis added]

Because art has come to be "behind glass—the history glass," it therefore
"has to be peered at, distinguished, demonstrated. And so we have Professors of Fine Art" ("WP," p. 17).

Summerson's thesis regarding the motivations for the rise of the discipline of art history in the nineteenth century rests on the historical con-
vergence he discerns between the withdrawal of modern painting from
more public life, the awareness of the "overwhelming mass" and "brooding immensity" of past artistic achievement, and the rise of what he terms
in his lecture as "totalitarian" art history ("WP," p. 16).[20] At the same time,
he argues that the rise of modern art and of art history were the result of a
new conception of history in the nineteenth century, which he suggests
owed nothing to the "social and mechanical" revolutions of that century.
The new discipline of art history was made possible by a new conception of
art as a universal human phenomenon, a "social-historical phenomenon
co-extensive with" human history and geography, whose emblem was the
new "totalitarian" museum—the museum whose mission was to collect,
classify, and systematically display a universal history of art.

While Summerson's history is rather sweepingly impressionistic, and
if the factors he adduces for the historical rise of art history were for the
most part already in play a century earlier, his scenario nonetheless is a
telling one in that it sketches the outlines of a certain commonplace wis-

19. On crises in the representation of history in the nineteenth century, see Richard
Terdiman, "Deconstructing Memory: On Representing the Past and Theorizing Culture in
France since the Revolution," *Diacritics* 15 (Winter 1985): 13–36.

20. Summerson refers to Jacob Burckhardt's mentor Franz Kugler as the first "'totalitarian' art-historian" in that he dealt equally with "painting, sculpture and architecture
over all time" ("WP," p. 16).

dom in the discipline of art history with regard to the field's origins, missions, and motivations—factors already inscribed in the protocols of modern disciplinary practice.[21] In his assertion that art history is the *opposite* of art making, that it comprises an analytic activity of "peering, distinguishing, and demonstrating," we can see the outlines of the kind of laboratory technologies orchestrated and formalized by the Fogg Museum and other art historical institutions in the late nineteenth and early twentieth centuries in America and Europe. For Summerson, the museum's vitrine—"the history glass" so like the window of the railway observation car moving away from the past—is directly analogous to the microscope slide of the scientist in the laboratory and to its locus in an increasingly expanding and refined taxonomic order of specimens.

As the laboratory scientist dissects, analyzes, and "peers at" specimens, breaking them into their component parts and distinctive features, so too would Summerson's art historian endeavor to read in the specimens the signs and indices of time, place, ethnicity, biography, mentality, or national or individual morality—in short, to read in artworks evidence of their historicity: their position within an ever-expanding mass of work "coextensive with the history and geography of man."

5

As an evidentiary institution, the modern discipline of art history has taken the problem of causality as its particular concern. While in this regard art history has been identical to other areas of disciplinary knowledge, certain aspects of its most common perspectives on evidence and causality distinguish it from other critical and historical fields. The present section examines features by and large shared by art history and other disciplines; features peculiar to the discipline are discussed subsequently.

Within art history's domain of analytic attention, the object or image invariably has been held to be evidential in nature such that the artwork and its parts are seen as effect, trace, result, medium, or sign. Art historical practice has been principally devoted to the restoration of the circumstances that surrounded (and therefore are presumed to have led in some however extended and indirect sense to) the work's production. An important justification for disciplinary practice—as may be adduced from Summerson's lecture no less than from the institution of the Fogg Museum and its progeny—has been that a historical accounting for the circumstantial factors in the production of an object renders the visual artifact more cogently legible to a wider audience. In this regard, art

---

21. See also Hayden White, "The Fictions of Factual Representation," *Tropics of Discourse: Essays in Cultural Criticism* (Baltimore, 1978), pp. 121–34, regarding the modern discipline of history.

historical practice is typically exegetical and cryptographic, and the art historian and the public are led to understand that one may discern *in* works the traces of their particular origins, the unique and specifiable positions in a universal developmental history or evolution of art. In short, the artwork is construed invariably as being reflective of its origins in some determinate and determinable fashion, and the discipline has been organized, throughout its century and a half of academic professionalization, to respond to the *question* of what it is that works of art might be evidence of and for.

The discipline of art history has evolved a number of often quite disparate perspectives on what might constitute a proper or adequate accounting for the origins or "truth" of works of art, including a family of methodologies responding to different notions of explanatory adequacy. At the same time, the discipline has been heir to an immense philosophical tradition of speculation on the nature, functions, and qualities of art, some of it of considerable antiquity, and most of it fairly remote from modern disciplinary practice and institutional organization.[22] Although all art historians would likely agree that a fully adequate explanation of a work's origins requires an accounting of as many conceivable factors as might be adduced for a given product, in actual practice (evidence invariably being fragmentary at best) this remains an ideal explanatory horizon.

It has been the case throughout the history of the discipline that certain modes of explanation are privileged over others, and certain forms of evidence have been deployed as dominant or determinant. For some art historians an adequate explanation of the origins of a work is to be located in the internal or individual conditions of production: the mentality, so to speak, of an artist or studio. For others, external or contextual conditions of production are given primary weight. These latter may be as disparate as the generic mentality, spirit, or aesthetic climate of an age, place, or race; the political, economic, cultural, social, religious, or philosophical environments in which the work appears (its synchronic milieux); or in the sometimes more, sometimes less inexorable systemic logic of the temporal evolution of forms and genres (its diachronic milieux).[23] Art historical and critical attention has been devoted to the articulation of all of these causal factors for several centuries, and most if not all remain in play in contemporary practice.[24] It has been the partisan debate on the adequacy of one

22. See Preziosi, *Rethinking Art History*, pp. 81–121.

23. See ibid., pp. 159–68 on the "social history" of art. On "form" and its "laws" of dispersal over time, see David Summers, "'Form,' Nineteenth-Century Metaphysics, and the Problem of Art Historical Description," *Critical Inquiry* 15 (Winter 1989): 372–406; and compare Walter Benjamin's critique of Wölfflin in his "Rigorous Study of Art," trans. Thomas Y. Levin, *October*, no. 47 (Winter 1988): 84–90.

24. See Preziosi, *Rethinking Art History*, pp. 159–68 for an assessment of the recent "methodological" controversies in the discipline, and also *The New Art History* for British perspectives on recent debates.

or another of these explanatory horizons that has constituted the greater bulk of theoretical and methodological writing in the discipline in modern times.[25]

Characteristic most generally of the disciplinary discursive field in modern times has been an investment shared by most art historians in fixing and locating the particular and unique truth about an artwork. In situating the object in a specifiable relationship to aspects of its original material and/or mental environment, that environment may then be seen to exist in a causal relationship to the object-as-product. In such a framework, the object has evidential status with respect to other factors in a nexus of causal relationships: in the dynamic processes of artistic expression and communication.

The most common theory of the art object in the academic discipline has undoubtedly been the conception of the artwork as a *medium* of communication and/or expression;[26] a *vehicle* by means of which the intentions, values, attitudes, messages, emotions, or agendas of a maker (or, by extension, of his or her time and place) are conveyed (by design or chance) to (targetted or circumstantial) beholders or observers. A correlative supposition is that synchronic or diachronic changes in form will signal changes in what the form conveys to its observers. This supposition is commonly connected to an assumption that changes in form exist so as to produce or effect changes in an audience's understanding of what was formerly conveyed prior to such changes. That is, changes in an artistic practice or tradition are assumed to be an index of variations in an evolving system of thought, belief, or political or social attitudes. In this regard, the object or image, or indeed potentially any detail of the material culture of a people, is treated as evidence of variations in a milieu.[27]

The object of art historical analysis is thus in an important sense a specimen of data insofar as it can be situated in an *interrogative field,* in an environment already predisposed to consider data pertinent only to the

25. An exemplary instance may be found in *The Politics of Interpretation,* ed. W. J. T. Mitchell (Chicago, 1983), pp. 203–48, where T. J. Clark and Michael Fried stage a critical exchange on the subject of modernism in art history (to little profit). See also the Discussions in Contemporary Culture series sponsored by the Dia Art Foundation, in particular *Vision and Visuality,* ed. Hal Foster (Seattle, 1988), and *Remaking History,* ed. Barbara Kruger and Phil Mariani (Seattle, 1989).

26. See Preziosi, *Rethinking Art History,* pp. 44–53, 95–121, regarding the logocentric bias of art historical discourse in modern times, and Jacques Derrida, *The Truth in Painting,* trans. Geoff Bennington and Ian MacLeod (Chicago, 1987), esp. parts 1–3 of "Parergon," pp. 15–82.

27. A useful discussion of the metaphorical foundations of these processes may be found in Baxandall, "The Language of Art History," *New Literary History* 10 (Spring 1979): 453–65. See also Wölfflin, *Principles of Art History: The Problem of the Development of Style in Later Art,* trans. M. D. Hottinger (New York, 1932). A paradigmatic articulation of these processes is that of Hippolyte Taine, whose 1867 essay "De l'ideal dans l'art," *Philosophie de l'art,* 2d ed., 2 vols. (Paris, 1880) developed the concept of *valeur* characteristic of a given

extent that they can be shown to be relevant to a particular family of questions. What determines the "art historicity" of an artifact might be said to be its pertinence to a given field of questions, themselves determined by certain assumptions about the significance or pertinence of material objects.

Such interrogative fields have been various in the history of art history. In sections 2 and 3 above we considered one such field central to the institutionalization of the discipline in America and distinguished early modern art history in this country from developments elsewhere—that is, the organization of the discursive field and its anamorphic archive in quite specific response to Norton's Ruskinian notions regarding the work of art as inescapably evidential with respect to the moral, ethical, and social character of an individual or a people. In Norton's view, the most essential and most deeply enduring characteristics of a people were to be found in its visual art and literature; other, more "material" phenomena of a society—its economic or political institutions—were secondary or marginal to its morality.[28]

In this regard, the institution of the Fogg Museum was a scientific laboratory. Entities, in short, became facts or data in the Fogg system insofar as they could be correlated with (and thereby become *evidence* for and answers to) an underlying *question*. For the Fogg, and for all the interrelated activities that it housed, the generic question would have been: in what way is this monument an expression of the peculiar genius of the people who produced it? The inflection of the question particular to the Fogg and its method concerned the ethical dimension of that peculiar genius.

Underlying the entire evidentiary system of the discipline and its object-domain are three fundamental assumptions: first, that everything about the artwork is significant in *some* way; second, that not everything about the artwork is significant in the *same* way; and third, that not everything about the artwork can be significant in *every* way.

The first of these specifies that there will be no semantically or semiotically null, empty, or insignificant components of a work; that every-

---

epoch in the history of art, intrinsically and systematically connected to all facets of an evolving cultural system; see also Hans Aarsleff, *From Locke to Saussure: Essays on the Study of Language and Intellectual History* (Minneapolis, 1982), pp. 360–61; Preziosi, *Rethinking Art History*, pp. 87–90; and White, "Historicism, History, and the Figurative Imagination," *Tropics of Discourse*, pp. 101–20.

28. Norton was especially deprecatory of German scholarship in the history of art, which he regarded as so abstractly removed from the actual artwork as to be largely useless for systematic and scientific understanding of artistic practice. By contrast, the development of art history at Princeton University in the latter years of the nineteenth century took contemporary German scholarship as its model. On Norton's attitude toward German art history, see Kantor's forthcoming article in *Early Departments of Art History in the United States*.

thing in its finest detail will contribute to the overall meaningfulness and value of the object. The second specifies that the contributions of the parts of a work to the whole—line, color, texture, materials, compositional framework, contextual siting and situation, and so on—are varied and disparate; each detail of the work contributes differentially to the work's overall organization and meaning. The third assumption specifies that the signification of a work is determinate and not arbitrary or subject to promiscuous reading. In other words, parts of an object cannot mean anything or everything but exist where and how they do as the result of some determined intelligence: everything should be understood as having a reason for being there, which the professional practitioner will have become adept at articulating.

These conditions and assumptions articulate a certain determinacy with respect to the analytic domain of art history, criticism, and museology, working to define their disciplinarity as systematic, "scientific" fields of inquiry and exegesis. Form is assumed to have discoverable "laws," which may exist on individual, local, geographic, temporal, and universal levels.[29]

In this regard, art history might be seen as fundamentally similar in its pursuit of scientificity as certain other modern academic disciplines institutionalized in the nineteenth century—for example, literary studies and history.[30] Yet in a number of respects, there are aspects of the evidentiary nature of art historical practice as it has evolved over the past century and a half that find no easy parallel with other fields.

6

In the first place, the art historical object of study has what may be termed a compound existential status. It is simultaneously material and simulacral, tactile and photographic, unique and reproducible. It may appear at first glance that it is inescapably material, and yet the individual, unique, palpable artifacts made, collected, and displayed constitute the

29. See "WP" on the problem of form; on the problem of "style," the fundamental text remains Meyer Schapiro, "Style," in *Anthropology Today*, ed. A. L. Kroeber (Chicago, 1953), pp. 287–312; see also the important recent volume *The Uses of Style in Archaeology*, ed. Margaret W. Conkey and Christine A. Hastorf (Cambridge, 1990), esp. Conkey, "Experimenting with Style in Archaeology: Some Historical and Theoretical Issues" (pp. 5–17) and Ian Hodder, "Style as Historical Quality," (pp. 44–51).

30. The best discussions of these issues with regard to the discipline of history are White, "Historicism, History, and the Figurative Imagination," pp. 101–20, and *Metahistory: The Historical Imagination in Nineteenth-Century Europe* (Baltimore, 1973); Maurice Mandelbaum, *History, Man and Reason: Study in Nineteenth-Century Thought* (Baltimore, 1971), esp. p. 42ff.; and R. G. Collingwood, *The Idea of History* (Oxford, 1946). See also Reiss, *The Discourse of Modernism*, pp. 351–85.

occasion for art historical practice rather than, strictly speaking, the subject matter of art history, which is in fact history itself: that is, the history and development of individuals, groups, and societies.

Nor does the material art object exist simply as data for the art historian, as raw material out of which histories are fabricated. There is an important sense in which the art object exists *as* art only insofar as it may be simulated, replicated, modelled, or represented in historical and critical narratives: that is, insofar as it may be adduced as evidence in the writing of social history.

A certain disciplinary parallel may be drawn here between the study of art and the study of literature. In both cases, professional concern with the original object is ancillary to the business of the discipline, which is historical, theoretical, and critical in nature, concerned with the construction of narrative texts of an exegetical nature in the light of their importance to the understanding of sociohistorical developments in a broad sense. In this regard, the disciplinarity of art history is fundamentally bound up with a *dialogic* concern with the human past; works of art are of interest to the discipline insofar as their quiddity can be argued as having evidential value with respect to particular questions about the past's relation to the present. One of the primary functions of art history, from the time of its founding as an academic discipline, has been that of the restoration of the past into the present so that the past can itself function and do work in and on the present; so that the present may be framed as itself the product of the past; and so that the past may be seen as that from which, for one particular reason or another, we are descended and thereby accounted for.[31]

Art history is thus a mode of writing addressed to the present; addressed, one might say, to the fabrication and maintenance of modernity. As a social and epistemological technology for framing modernity, the discipline has served as one of modernity's central and definitive institutions and instances. Its goals have been fundamentally historicist— which is to say teleological.

Yet at the same time that the art object may bear a relationship to art history homologous to the relationship of an original manuscript to literary history and theory, there is an important sense in which they differ, for the material artwork has a status within the discourse on art as a whole that has no parallel. For one thing, artworks participate in an immensely articulated network of material relationships complementary to and partly intersecting with the evidentiary elements in art historical practice. In other words, art history has existed in tandem with another institution whose subject matter would seem to be artworks: the museum.

31. See White, *The Content of the Form: Narrative Discourse and Historical Representation* (Baltimore, 1987), esp. pp. 104–41.

7

Since their origins in familiar form some two centuries ago, museums of art have functioned as evidentiary institutions in a manner similar to art history itself. In the most general sense, the museology of art has been devoted to the judicious assemblage of objects and images deemed particularly evocative of time, place, personality, mentality, and the artisanry or genius of individuals, groups, races, and nations.[32] At the same time that the museum is a repository of evidence for the seemingly inexhaustible variety of human artistic expression, it has also functioned in the modern world as an institution for the staging of historical and aesthetic development and evolution—that is, for the simulation of historical change and transformation of and through artwork, or, more generally, material culture. In this respect, the museum of art has had distinctly dramaturgical functions in modern life, circulating individuals through spaces articulated and punctuated by sequential arrangements of historical relics. Objects and images are choreographed together with the (motile) bodies of beholders.

Museological space is thereby *correlative* to art historical space and its anamorphic archival stagecraft. A museological tableau is for all intents and purposes intensely *geomantic* in that its proper and judicious siting (sighting)—the mise-en-sequence of objects—works to guarantee the preservation of the spirit of the departed or absent person or group. What is guaranteed above all is the spirit of artisanry and of human creativity as such, the existence of such a phenomenon as art beneath what are staged as its myriad manifestations or exemplars. In spatially formatting examples of characteristic forms of expression of an artist, movement, nation, or period, the visitor or user of the museum is afforded the opportunity to *see* for himself the evidence of what is quintessentially and properly human in all its variety. The absences of the past are peopled with palpably material relics, synechdochal reminders that the present is the product of a certain historical evolution of values, tastes, and manners—or a certain moral sensibility—summarized by and inscribed in museological space.

32. Substantial bibliographies pertaining to the origins and development of museums of art may be found in *The Origins of Museums: The Cabinet of Curiosities in Sixteenth- and Seventeenth-Century Europe*, ed. Oliver Impey and Arthur MacGregor (Oxford, 1985), pp. 281–312, and in Adalgisa Lugli, *Naturalia et mirabilia: Il collezionismo enciclopedico nelle Wunderkammern d'Europa* (Milan, 1983), pp. 243–58. See also Louis Marin, "Fragments d'histoires de musées," *Cahiers du Musée national d'art moderne* 17–18 (1986): 17–36; Hubert Damisch, "The Museum Device: Notes on Institutional Changes," *Lotus International*, no. 35 (1982): 4–11; Stephen Bann, *The Clothing of Clio: A Study of the Representation of History in Nineteenth-Century Britain and France* (Cambridge, 1984), pp. 76–92; and Paul Holdengräber, "'A Visible History of Art': The Forms and Preoccupations of the Early Museum," *Studies in Eighteenth Century Culture*, no. 17 (1987): 107–17.

And yet while the apparatus of art history and the dramaturgy of the museum are similar to the extent that they both are addressed to the task of fabricating and sustaining the present as the product of the past, there is a dimension of museological stagecraft only inferentially present in art history, namely, its address to the self as an object of ethical attention and inward work through the heightened confrontation of beholder and the museological "man-and/as-his work."[33] More about this shortly.

Since the late eighteenth century and the beginning of the transformation of the old curio closets of early collectors into what Summerson termed "totalitarian" museums devoted to the encyclopedic "histories" of art, two principal paradigms for the organization of museological space have dominated the practice of the modern museum.[34] The first of these involved the decoration of a given space—a room, gallery, or ensemble of rooms—in such a way as to simulate the period ambience of a work or works by the inclusion of objects from the historical contexts in which such works would have been originally seen, displayed, or used. Variations on this theme include the exact replication of an artist's studio, or of a space in which such works were originally displayed, suggestive arrangements of period pieces around objects or images, or arrays of relics and mementos of the artist in question. The format may be as minimally articulated as in the case of the Museum of Modern Art in New York, where the modernity of the architecture itself provides a fitting complement to the artistic modernism of twentieth-century artworks deployed therein, or as maximal as the replication of an entire Roman villa for the display of ancient Greek and Roman art in the J. Paul Getty Museum in Malibu. This model has obvious parallels with the familar panoramas of museums of natural history and ethnography, wherein plants, animals, or human effigies may be set up within typically "natural" settings.[35]

The second paradigm of museological display common to museums of art involves the delimitation of designed or appropriated space according to time periods, styles, or schools of art (or of a particular artist). Typically such spaces are more or less coterminous with centuries, the span of political regimes, or national, ethnic, or religious groupings. This mode of museological stagecraft is correlative to the archival space of art historical practice, as well as to the format of the art historical survey text wherein

33. See Preziosi, *Rethinking Art History,* pp. 21–33.

34. See Carol Duncan and Alan Wallach, "The Universal Survey Museum," *Art History* 3 (Dec. 1980): 447–69, and Ignasi de Solà-Morales, "Toward a Modern Museum: From Riegl to Giedion," *Oppositions* 25 (Fall 1982): 68–77.

35. See Bann, *The Clothing of Clio,* pp. 77–85. This model corresponds to that of Alexandre du Sommerard's Musée de Cluny; see also Ann Reynolds, "Reproducing Nature: The Museum of Natural History as Nonsite," *October,* no. 45 (Summer 1988): 109–27, and Ivan Karp and Corinne Kratz, "The Fate of Tipoo's Tiger: A Critical Account of Ethnographic Display," typescript.

portions of the archive or text correspond to episodes in the historical and genealogical development of styles, genres, schools, or artistic careers.[36]

Both dramaturgical devices are addressed to the display of evidence for the "truth" of artworks. The first model affords the possibility that the significance of a work will be construed as a complex function of the multiple relationships among all elements of its contextual environment, of the specificities of the object's history and moment. The second model foregrounds the work's significance on a diachronic axis, and the work is staged as one of a linked series of "solutions" to some aesthetic or iconographic "problem"—for example, the problem of naturalistic rendering of the human form in two dimensions as might be staged by the sequential array of black- and red-figure Greek vases in a gallery, or the problems facing modern designers of furniture, teapots, or political broadsheets.

While it might appear that these two modes of museological stagecraft correspond specifically to art historical paradigms of explanation—the first, that is, similar to modes of sociohistorical explanation in art historical argumentation, with the second paralleling more formalistic argumentation—in fact in both modes of practice the significance, truth, or pertinence of a work is formatted as a function of contextual relationships: in the first case more or less synchronic; in the second instance diachronic.

In the first or panoramic mode of evidentiary display, the object purports to be in some way a distinct and fitting product of its time and place, a "reflection" (in a variety of senses) of a wider milieu of production and consumption. Underlying this mode of stagecraft is the assumption of a certain homogeneity in that original environment, a certain uniformity of style, mentality, or moral or aesthetic sensibility. The inference is that the observer may find traces or symptoms of that specificity in many or all of the material products of that spatiotemporal frame.

In the second mode, the artwork's pertinence or truth is staged incrementally or differentially as a moment in the evolution (commonly staged as progressive) of a tradition, style, school, genre, or problem in morphology or iconography, or of an individual career (Monet at Giverny, Monet in old age, or Picasso after Guernica, for example).

Common to both is the establishment of *predicative* or *interrogative frameworks* for the viewer: enframings of works whose material topologies simulate or perform the associations needed to fix and localize meaning. The institution of the museum functions in a manner not unlike that of the visual, diagrammatic logic of scientific demonstration wherein the actual deployment of evidence—like so many charts, tables, lists, and

---

36. See Bann, *The Clothing of Clio*, pp. 77–85; the second model corresponds to that of Alexandre Lenoir's installations in the Convent of the Petits-Augustins in Paris in the first decades of the nineteenth century. Lenoir distributed objects according to centuries over several rooms of the museum.

diagrams—itself constructs and legitimizes the "truth" of what is intended: conclusions regarding origins, descent, influence, affiliation, progress, historical direction, or the makeup of the mentalities and morals of an age or place. In this regard, museological and art historical practice may be seen as correlative: the object's position in the archival and mnemonic system acquires its cogency in response to (more or less) explicit questions: What time is this place?

Art history and museums of art consequently establish certain conditions of *reading* objects and images in such a way as to foreground the rhetorical economies of metaphorical and metonymic relationships.[37] Both situate their users (operators) in anamorphic positions from which the "history" of art may be seen as unfolding, almost magically, before their eyes. Regardless of the fragmentary or partial nature of a particular museum collection or of a given art historical archive or curriculum, both function as exemplary or emblematic instances of an imaginary, ideal plenitude. Objects known and unknown will have their "place," their proper and fixed locus in that encyclopedic and universal history of art projected onto the horizon of the future. Both art historical and museological practice, to paraphrase Walter Benjamin, deal in allegorical figures that express a certain "will to symbolic totality" and that continually stare out at us as incomplete and imperfect.[38] At the same time, the narrative stagings of these two mechanisms of our modernity, in their evidential and implicational palpabilities, hold out the promise that all will eventually make *sense*. In short, art history and museology constitute the promise that whatever might occur could one day be made meaningful. As evidentiary institutions, both have been grounded in that irony so poignantly articulated by Lacan:

> What is realized in [my] history is not the past definite of what was, since it is no more, or even the present perfect of what has been in what I am, but the future anterior of what I shall have been for what I am in the process of becoming.[39]

Since Hegel and Winckelmann, this irony has deeply informed what art history has taken on itself to afford.

---

37. In Bann's suggestive analysis of the museums of du Sommerard and Lenoir, the former relies on relationships of synechdoche in the associations of objects, the latter on metonymy. A critique of Bann's analyses will be found in Preziosi, "Art History, Museology, and the Staging of Modernity," *Parallel Visions*, ed. Chris Keledjian (forthcoming). See also White, "Foucault's Discourse: The Historiography of Anti-Humanism," *The Content of the Form*, pp. 124–25, and Reiss, *The Discourse of Modernism*, pp. 9–54. The fundamental text is Roman Jakobson, "Closing Statement: Linguistics and Poetics," in *Style in Language*, ed. Thomas A. Sebeok (Cambridge, Mass., 1960), pp. 350–77.

38. Benjamin, *The Origin of the German Tragic Drama*, trans. John Osborne (London, 1977), p. 186.

39. Jacques Lacan, *Écrits* (Paris, 1966), p. 300; my translation.

8

Art history and museology both work to legitimize their truths as original, preconceived, and only recovered from the past. Both have aimed at the dissolution of troubling ambiguities about the past by fixing meaning, locating its source in the artist, the historical moment, the mentality or morality of an age, place, people, race, gender, or class, and by arranging or formatting the past into rationalized genealogy: a clearly ramified ancestry for the present, for the *presence* that constitutes our modernity. The narrative duration of the "history of art" becomes at the same time the representation of and explanation for history. This *reality effect* has constituted the historicist agenda on which art history as a mode of writing addressed to the present has been erected and to which museological theatre alludes.[40]

Both are practices of power wherein the desire for constructing the present is displaced and staged as a desire for knowledge of the past such that the present itself may come to be pictured as ordered and oriented as the effect and product of progressive and inevitable forces. It is clearly the case, for example, that the discourse on art has been deeply concerned, implicitly and explicitly, with the promotion and validation of the idea of the modern nation-state as an entity ideally distinct and homogeneous on ethnic, racial, linguistic, and cultural grounds. Museums of art in particular have served, since their origins in the late eighteenth century, to legitimize the nation-state or the *Volk* as having a distinct, unique, and self-identical persona, style, and aesthetic sensibility. At the same time, art history and the museum have worked to promote the idea of the historical period as itself unified and homogeneous, or dominated by a singular family of values and attitudes.[41]

It will be clear that the underlying and controlling metaphor in this historicist labor is a certain vision of an ideal human selfhood—a persona with a style of its own, and with an exterior directly expressive of an inner spirit or essence. In this regard the labors of art history and museology have traditionally been carried forward along the lines of personification and characterization: what *stamps* Netherlandish art of a certain age or of all ages will ideally be reflected in the painting of a seventeenth-century master as well as in the design of contemporary *bateaux-mouches* plying the canals of Amsterdam in the twentieth century; and the stamp of Picasso's

40. See White, "The Fictions of Factual Representation," *Tropics of Discourse,* pp. 121–34, in connection with the "reality effect" of historical narration.

41. See Preziosi, *Rethinking Art History,* pp. 11–16, and Fredric Jameson, *The Political Unconscious: Narrative as a Socially Symbolic Act* (Ithaca, N.Y., 1981), p. 27, on the question of periodicity. A series of essays on the subject by art historians may be found in *New Literary History* 1 (Winter 1970): 113–44, with discussions by Schapiro, Ernst Gombrich, H. W. Janson, and George Kubler.

persona will be adduced as much from his signature as from his ceramics, glasswork, and painting.

It may not be hyperbolic to suggest that art history and museology have been conventionally guided by a more deeply set metaphor—namely, that in some sense art is to man (and it is necessary to stress the markedness of this gendering) as the world is to God—that human creativity in all of its variety is itself a shadow of divine creativity, its mortal echo. It is in this respect that the confrontation of viewer and artwork in the landscape of the museum embodies one aspect of art historical practice that finds no easy parallel in other historical and critical disciplines. This has to do less with the unique and palpable quiddity of the original artwork as such, and more to do with its compound *siting* in that landscape as an evidential specimen.

The function of the museological specimen as an evidentiary artifact as sketched out above—wherein museological and art historical practice can be seen as correlative—in fact exists in a multiple epistemological space. Insofar as the museum and art history frame the artwork or its photographic simulacrum in an archival mass such as that pioneered by the Fogg, or in teleologically motivated tableaux in space, the object or image acquires evidential status when construed metonymically, synecdochally, or indexically. A certain mode of *reading* the object is specified and afforded by the art historical archive or by museological dramaturgy wherein the object's significance is historical, genealogical, or differential.

At the same time, however, the museological artifact is staged as an object of contemplation paradoxically both inside and outside of "history": as an *occasion* for the imaginative reconstitution of a world, a person, or an age, or of a universe of (aesthetic and/or ethical) sensibility with which the viewed object is materially *congruent* in all of its finest details. In short, the artwork is an occasion for individual meditation and for the alignment of the individual viewing subject with that which appears to be cued by the viewed object. According to David Finn,

> there is no right or wrong way to visit a museum. The most important rule you should keep in mind as you go through the front door is to follow your own instincts. Be prepared to find what excites you, to enjoy what delights your heart and mind, perhaps to have esthetic experiences you will never forget. You have a feast in store for you and you should make the most of it. Stay as long or as short a time as you will, but do your best at all times to let the work of art speak directly to you with a minimum of interference or distraction.[42]

42. David Finn, *How to Visit a Museum* (New York, 1985), p. 10. On the fiction of the work "speaking" to the beholder, see Douglas Crimp, "On the Museum's Ruins," *October*, no. 13 (Summer 1980): 41–58.

It may be argued that the massive art historical and museological attention to the concrete specificity and uniqueness of the work of art, to its particularity and unreplicative materiality, to its auratic quiddity, represents not only a dimension of disciplinarity peculiar to art history and museology, but in one sense more interestingly the perpetuation of a particular mode of epistemological practice antecedent to the historicist scientism, the "analytico-referentiality" characteristic of modern disciplinary practice.[43]

Two modes of knowing might thus be seen to be embodied in the work of the museum, two kinds of propositional or interrogative frameworks: one which relies on a metonymic encoding of phenomena, and one deeply imbued with a metaphoric orientation on the things of this world, grounded in analogical reasoning. With the former, facticity and evidence are formatted syntactically, metonymically, differentially; and the order of the system constructs and legitimizes questions that might be put to sympathetic data. With the latter, form and content are construed as being deeply and essentially congruent, and the form of the work is the *figure* of its truth.[44]

It is here that we may begin to understand the foundational dilemma that would have confronted the formation of a discipline such as art history: how to fabricate a science of objects simultaneously construed as unique and irreducible and as specimens of a class of like phenomena. The solution to this dilemma has been the modern discourse on art, a field of dispersion wherein a series of intersecting institutions—academic art history, art criticism, museology, the art market, connoisseurship—maintain in play contrasting systems of evidence and proof, demonstration and explication, analysis and contemplation, with respect to objects both semantically complete and differential.

In modern disciplinary practice, there are seldom entirely pure examples of these contrastive epistemological technologies, suggesting that art history is no simple science, no uniform mode of cultural practice, but an evidentiary institution housing multiple orientations on an object of study at once semiotic and eucharistic.[45] If the Fogg Museum appears as a paradigmatic instance of scientific labor in the establishment of a histori-

43. See Reiss, *The Discourse of Modernism*, pp. 9–54, and Preziosi, *Rethinking Art History*, pp. 55–56.

44. In effect, this double epistemological framework for the art of art history and of museology corresponds to the contrastive domains of knowledge examined by Michel Foucault, *The Order of Things: An Archeology of the Human Sciences*, trans. pub. (New York, 1970). The suggestion here is that art history and museology preserve, in their object of study, an older analogic order of the same within the play of difference and change.

45. On the subject of a "eucharistic" semiology, see Preziosi, *Rethinking Art History*, pp. 102–6; Marin, *Le Portrait du roi* (Paris, 1981); and Milad Doueihi, review of *Le Portrait du roi*, by Marin, and *Money, Language, and Thought*, by Marc Shell, *Diacritics* 14 (Spring 1984): 66–77.

cal discipline modelled on the protocols of historical and literary inquiry, that labor at the same time was, as Norton and his associates made abundantly clear, in the service of the demonstration of an *ethical practice of the self and its works.*[46] The articulation of a "history of art" was not intended to be an end in itself but was rather antecedent to the formation of moral character on the part of those who would submit to its discipline. Norton's museums, then, bore a more direct relationship to the memory theatre of Giulio Camillo of the Renaissance,[47] or to the ethical cosmos of his beloved Dante, than to the "totalitarian" museums so exasperating to John Summerson.

46. For a suggestive parallel, see David Saunders and Ian Hunter, "Lessons from the 'Literatory': How to Historicise Authorship," *Critical Inquiry* 17 (Spring 1991): 479–509, in connection with the rise of the modern novel, seen as comprising the occasion for the modern practice of the self.

47. See Frances A. Yates, *The Art of Memory* (Chicago, 1966), pp.

A Response to Donald Preziosi

Joel Synder

Donald Preziosi has given us a paper whose breadth and reach are considerable ("The Question of Art History," pp. 203–26). For me, however, its level of abstraction is so high that I find it difficult to specify his views about the way evidence functions in the historical study of visual art, and since this is a book addressing the question of evidence, I want to try to use Preziosi's essay as a means of getting at the topic, if only by way of some sidewise motions. In making these curious steps, it may seem that I am defending conservative art historical practice, which would be uncharacteristic of me. My remarks are not a defense of art history (as it was practiced, say, prior to the advent of post-structuralism) but rather an attempt to suggest that Preziosi's essay, in my judgment, fails to provide us with an adequate analysis of the many different practices that, taken together, have constituted the discipline.

The sweep of Preziosi's essay is at once its achievement and its greatest frustration. Art history, he says, is a "social and epistemological technology for framing modernity" (p. 218). Preziosi intends "technology," not as τέχνη in, say, Plato's sense, but as something like a machinery for cranking out answers to predetermined questions. This view of studying, exhibiting, and criticizing visual art is so broad that it fails, finally, to specify those features distinguishing art history from any other humanistic discipline. We are, I imagine, in complete agreement about the peculiar absence of a self-critical attitude that until rather recently characterized the work of many art historians. And I suppose, further, that each of us has been bored to tears by mindless applications of mechanical step-and-repeat procedures for the amassing of details about the dating or attribution of paintings, or by the endless number of monographs about "great" male artists that do, in fact, trade entirely in origins and influences. But this is only to say that like other humanistic disciplines, art history in America has worked in terms of a trade association model—in which most apprentices earn their authority by learning a few moves and performing variations on them to roomfuls of master and apprentice art historians at regional and national meetings. And I don't think that the change we are now witnessing in the study of art history has put a dent in this tendency towards trade associationism, that is, to the ritual performances of variations on master themes. At the 1992 national convocation of the College Art Association, I went only to a few sessions but heard the expressions "social construction" and "the gaze" invoked countless times in "explanation" of everything needing elucidation.

There is a curious wobbling in Preziosi's essay between a major tendency to lump and a lesser one to split. There is a sweeping architectonic conception of art history as a systematic and monolithic enterprise or a would-be scientific discourse (*scientific* being qualified in some unspecified way by use of quotation marks); a conception of art history as a determinate space with specifiable assumptions about significance; serially arranged artifacts, or reproductions of artifacts together with data correlated to them; characteristic interrogatives predetermining the form and perhaps even the content of their answers; and all this finally in service of establishing the meaning and value of the present as underwritten by a fabricated relation to a fabricated past. In short, when viewed this way, art history is a discipline because its practitioners share assumptions (or since art historians are by and large un–self-critical, perhaps *habits* would be a better term) and practices about the means and ends of discourse. In a particularly sweeping characterization of art historical practice, Preziosi says it is "typically exegetical and cryptographic, and [we] are led to understand that one may discern *in* works the traces of their particular origins, the unique and specifiable positions in a universal developmental history or evolution of art." And then he adds, "the artwork is construed *invariably* [my emphasis] as being reflective of its origins in some determinate and determinable fashion, and the discipline has been organized, throughout its century and a half of academic professionalization, to respond to *the* [my emphasis] *question* of what it is that works of art might be evidence of and for" (p. 214).

Immediately after saying this, Preziosi begins splitting: "The discipline of art history," he writes, "has evolved a number of often quite disparate perspectives on what might constitute a proper or adequate

---

Joel Snyder is professor of art at the University of Chicago and a coeditor of *Critical Inquiry.* He is editor of *American Frontiers: The Photographs of Timothy H. O'Sullivan, 1867–1874* (1981) and coeditor of *The Art of Fixing a Shadow: One Hundred and Fifty Years of Photography* (1989).

accounting for the origins or 'truth' of works of art, including a family of methodologies responding to different notions of explanatory adequacy" (p. 214). Juxtaposed against the large claims about the institutional character of art history, this is a startling statement, for it seems to suggest that art historical technology is not nearly as homogeneous as Preziosi suggests it is. The idea that "different notions of explanatory adequacy" can coexist within the same discursive machinery suggests to me that the notion of a homogeneous discourse is misleading. What constitutes explanatory adequacy is a function of the aims of explanation, and competing conceptions of such adequacy call into question Preziosi's use of "family" as an appropriate grouping label here. This is a family in name only. Let me try getting at this in another way. If art history has room for disparate methodologies with different notions of explanatory adequacy, and if, as I believe, differences in how explanation is conceived entail differences in what counts as evidence, it is simply incorrect to claim that art history has a uniform set of evidentiary practices. So, even if we do agree that the goals of art history are "fundamentally historicist" (p. 218), and even if we could agree that there is a single monolithic enterprise that could be coherently defined as "modernity"—as this term functions in Preziosi's claim that "art history . . . is a mode of writing addressed to . . . the fabrication and maintenance of modernity" (p. 218)—all this would still fail to convince me that very much is clarified by conceiving of art history as underwritten by what Preziosi calls "*the* evidentiary system of the discipline" (p. 216; my emphasis). At least I would like to know how the definite article found its way into this phrase.

In the fifth section of his essay, Preziosi says this: "Underlying the entire evidentiary system of the discipline and its object-domain are three fundamental assumptions: first, that everything about the artwork is significant in *some* way; second, that not everything about the artwork is significant in the *same* way; and third, that not everything about the artwork can be significant in *every* way" (p. 216). And then he adds that these assumptions about significance are fundamentally similar to those of literary studies and history. I am not certain I understand what follows from this claim, and I am likewise uncertain about how these "assumptions" provide a foundation for art history's "object-domain" and evidentiary practices. These "assumptions" strike me as being general requirements for the specification of what it means to function at all as an object in a discourse, that is, for the isolation of a thing, irrespective of field or discipline. These principles might best be construed as stipulating something like this: a discipline has to address its objects as discriminable units. Principles like these are treated by Aristotle in the *Organon* and are employed without discussion in the individual works on the sciences (whether theoretical, practical, or productive) because they are presupposed by discourse as such. Likewise, Foucault's discussion of the rules of object formation appears in the early sections of *The Archaeology of Knowledge* and is intended to characterize, in formal terms, the manner in which objects are secured a place in a discursive formation, again irrespective of field.

There is another assumption here that does need examination: the "classical" postulate that to be an artwork, an object must be more than identifiable; it must also be a unified subject, or to put this in other terms, it must have its own "character." Wölfflin and Norton, among many others, seem never to have questioned the assumption that the extension of the term "art" ranges only across objects having an "internal principle of unity." The impression one often has of the self-fulfilling and self-serving character of art historical studies is tied tightly to the circularity revealed by analyses showing how any particular work subjected to art historical analysis achieves its unified character. Since the object in question enters the discourse on the assumption that it is unified, no evidence whatever could count as showing it is not, since if it were not, it would not be a subject of study. One thing this suggests is that we need to look much harder at how works come to be subject to art historical study. My guess is that it will not be as easy as it might first appear to find regularities or rules governing this process—any easier, say, than determining the supposed rules governing annual changes in "high fashion" clothing.

I do not raise these concerns about Preziosi's treatment of art history's "object-domain" merely to be quarrelsome. It seems to me that calling the objects of an art historian's attention artworks suggests that they enter discourse already formulated; in fact, most make their first appearance having already been *qualified* in some way as being appropriate for art historical study, but they generally enter discourse in an attributed though relatively unformulated state and are, in any case, open to constant reformulation. The objects of art historical attention are constantly reconstituted as subjects of discourse. In other words, it is mistaken to conceive of an object-domain as constituting the subject matter of art historical research. It seems clear to me that the practice of describing objects depends upon the marshaling of evidence and that the identification of an object in some particular way constitutes the delimitation of a subject that is consequently open to certain questions and closed to others. For example, as far as certain Marxist art historians are concerned, nothing whatever will count as supporting evidence for claims about the role played by a *kunstwollen* in the formulation of a particular work of art; claims, say, about the autonomy, or internality, of artistic development make no sense to some art historians.

When Michael Fried describes Thomas Eakins's painting *The Gross Clinic* (1875) in *Realism, Writing, Disfiguration*, he does so in opposition to the descriptions of earlier art historians, and his initial goal is to show that describing the work as an "exact transcription" of an original surgical scene is based upon a failure to note certain facts about the painting—facts he uses as evidence to support an entirely different description of the work. Fried's project is to nullify the "normalizing discourse" underwriting earlier descriptions of the Eakins painting, so that an entirely different set of questions can be asked of it. To claim, as he does, that *The Gross Clinic* allegorizes and embodies the relationship between writing and painting is to insist, at the same time, that his subject, the facts establishing it, and the leads or clues it suggests are simply not available from previous descriptions of the painting.[1]

Similarly, in an essay written in 1934 attempting to certify the identification of the subjects in a double portrait by Jan van Eyck, known as the Arnolfini portrait, Erwin Panofsky notes that the sentence "Johannes de Eyck fuit hic," which appears prominently above the convex mirror in the painting, had recently been incorrectly translated by a Belgian art historian. He uses this putative mistranslation as evidence that the identity of the painting remains open to question. Panofsky then takes the same Latin inscription, in, he says, its grammatically correct translation, as one piece of evidence in an argument showing that the double portrait "had the same importance and implied the same legal consequences as an 'affidavit' deposed by a witness at a modern registrar's office."[2] This identification of the portrait's subject provides Panofsky with a warrant for viewing the painting as both realistic and allegorical.[3] And, in turn, this allows him to address the painting in terms of the facts about its symbology. The iconographic values attributed to objects in the painting achieve factual status in light of the identification of the painting as something like a marriage document. Absent that claimed identification, these are not facts at all. I'm not sure it's useful to generalize here, but it seems worthwhile to think of procedures like Panofsky's as being divisible, at least analytically, into two steps. The first step is the marshaling of evidence in support of a claim that the work is a certain *kind* of, say, picture. And, in turn, this description suggests a field of potential questions and a range of evidential considerations that needs to be addressed in providing answers to them. What I want to caution against is jumping to the conclusion that description forces certain questions and determines certain answers. Panofsky wasn't forced by his identification of the Arnolfini

---

1. Michael Fried, *Realism, Writing, Disfiguration: On Thomas Eakins and Stephen Crane* (Chicago, 1987), pp. 11, 10.

2. Erwin Panofsky, "Jan van Eyck's *Arnolfini* Portrait," *Burlington Magazine* 64 (Mar. 1934): 124.

3. I am not arguing here for the adequacy of Panofsky's account of the painting or of the evidence he brings to bear on questions about the painting. For a remarkable and convincing dismantling of Panofsky's argument and an alternative reading of the painting, see Linda Seidel, "Jan van Eyck's Arnolfini Portrait': Business as Usual?" *Critical Inquiry* 16 (Autumn 1989): 55–86.

portrait as something like a marriage document to posit the presence of a systematic iconography.

I do not pretend to be breaking any new ground in my insistence that object matter and subject matter do not amount to the same thing, but I offer the Fried and Panofsky examples as a way of showing that Preziosi's division of the discipline's evidentiary system from its object-domain is itself problematic. It is, I think, useful to ask if evidentiary practices are not themselves constitutive of a discipline's subject matter.

I want now to turn briefly to two other considerations. The first concerns Preziosi's history or, more accurately, what strikes me as his equivocal relationship to historicism. As I read his essay, he seems committed to telling a story about the past in order to "explain" the present—a procedure that is itself unabashedly genetic. Recall the description of the "evolution" of disparate art historical methodologies. And recall too that Charles Eliot Norton's institutionalization of the machinery of art historical research at the Fogg Museum is identified by Preziosi as the originary moment in which art history, as we know it, was conceived. This account of the origins of art history in the United States is itself an example of a certain kind of reasoning typifying one strand of art historical scholarship, since, as it turns out, the moment of genesis can itself be referred backward to the influence exercised on Norton by Ruskin. So the origin of art historical technology is determinable and indeterminate at the same time; that is, the course of events leading to the modern discipline of art history begins and yet doesn't really originate with Norton at Harvard, since Norton himself is linked causally, by way of influence, to Ruskin. And, of course, Ruskin himself was subject to influence and the pressures of history. This history is teleological and unitary—the unity being achieved subjectively, to give the exercise a Foucauldian spin.

Preziosi writes, "Art history and museology both work to legitimize their truths as original, preconceived, and *only* recovered from the past" (p. 223; my emphasis). Is he addressing the substance of the discipline or the rhetoric of some of its practitioners? Preziosi claims that what art historians really do is fabricate the past. But "fabricate" as opposed to what? Tell the truth? Is fabrication inconsistent with getting at the truth? Don't we routinely fabricate facts? It is worthwhile here to recall that *fact*, *factory*, and *factitious* share a common heritage. *Fabricate* is not synonymous with *concoct*. He also says art history is a practice "of power wherein the desire for constructing the present is displaced and staged as a desire for knowledge of the past such that the present may itself come to be pictured as ordered and oriented as the effect and product of progressive and inevitable forces" (p. 223). Leave out the "progressive" and let us then ask Preziosi how his account of art history's history escapes this characterization. Is his history not "a practice of power"?

Preziosi concludes with a discussion of museums, and I shall likewise end with some questions about museums. It is remarkable that he addresses museums as conservators and representers of the past but overlooks entirely their role in the present—as showplaces for new work, some of which will presumably engage future generations of art historians. Here my questions are really quite simple. Is there any evidentiary *system* at work in the process of organizing exhibits of new work? Is there a *systematic* means for selecting work to place on exhibition? I am not asking if museums know how to co-opt work, say, are capable of mounting the works of artists like Barbara Kruger and Sherry Levine that are supposed to defy what are said to be some of the fundamental assumptions of museum practice. Curators of modern art know better than just about anyone how to hold up their fingers to determine the direction of prevailing winds. I am asking if art historical discourse *determines* curatorial practice in regard to new work. Part of what I want to know is this: does the curatorial practice of selecting new work for display rely on a conceiving of new work as being causally related to the work of the immediate and distant past?

Panofsky's view of the question of new work harmonizes with the tone of Preziosi's remarks. For him, the problem of an art historian or museum curator interested in the work of the present is "to see the present in a perspective picture undistorted by personal or institutional *parti pris*."[4] In dealing with the work of the present moment, there is, he claims, "no room for objective discussion" or historical analysis, no way of addressing new work while honoring the requirements of "historical method and concern for meticulous documentation." Accordingly, for Panofsky, contemporary work cannot be discussed intelligently until "'historical distance'" is achieved ("we normally require from sixty to eighty years," he says).[5]

So, new work must be converted into historical work before it becomes subject to art historical analysis and museum exhibition. Panofsky's concerns here are genuinely epistemological. They outline the conditions for gaining knowledge about putative works of art; the demand for disinterested, unemotional observers; the need for carefully researched documentation; and, presumably, the need to form a judgment about the context of production.

Panofsky's views, however, are not representative of contemporary art historical and museum practice. New work *is* exhibited, analyzed, and discussed without much apparent concern about objectivity or historical

4. Panofsky, "Three Decades of Art History in the United States: Impressions of a Transplanted European," *Meaning in the Visual Arts* (1955; Chicago, 1982), p. 328.
5. Ibid., pp. 328–29. In a bit of uncharacteristic prestidigitation, Panofsky argues that art historians in America got around this problem vis-à-vis European art by replacing temporal distance with the geographic variety; they achieved an undistorted perspective through the disinterest coming with literal distance.

distance. To the contrary, an art historian/critic like Michael Fried champions particular artists very much in terms of his own individualized responses to their work—and glories in the challenge of "universalizing" his own judgment. There has been a profound shift in the way new work finds its way into museums. Quite apart from self-serving gallery promotion, new work is criticized from numerous perspectives and no single voice, no single pressure group, has the final say in its institutionalization. In this respect, Leo Steinberg's attack on Greenbergian formalism and his plea for "other criteria" as means of avoiding the dead hand of past art-critical practice is a direct challenge to Panofsky as well.[6] Steinberg's view assumes that there may or may not be important continuities between difficult new work and canonized work of the recent and distant past. It is always possible, in Steinberg's view, that new work cannot be understood in terms of the past—that it can only be addressed in terms of a critic's sympathetic response to present conditions, which may themselves be inexplicable by reference to our conceptions of the past.

Preziosi argues that "one of the primary functions of art history . . . has been that of the restoration of the past into the present so that the past can itself function and do work in and on the present" (p. 218). But how are we to understand his formulation of the function of art history, criticism, and museology in regard to the art of the present? If we use the past to explain or enforce the present, what do we do in the present with the art of the present? What do art-technological imperatives tell us about the present from the vantage point of the present?

---

6. See Leo Steinberg, "Other Criteria," *Other Criteria: Confrontations with Twentieth-Century Art* (New York, 1978), pp. 55–91.

A Rejoinder to Joel Snyder

Donald Preziosi

Joel Snyder's self-described sidewise approach to my essay ("A Response to Donald Preziosi," pp. 227–34) brings to my mind the image of a plane crabbing into an airport. In turn it makes me feel like the United Airlines terminal at O'Hare. If you were to land there a half-dozen times over the course of a year, you might be able to construct an amusing set of hypotheses to account for the changes at that facility over time. The linked series of observations would not, however, constitute a history of the facility that might be recognizable to the airport authority, nor would they (except by improbable coincidence) correspond to the reasons and motivations for the changes periodically recorded.

In a similar fashion, Snyder's landings at various points in the course of my paper constitute a poignant lesson in critical bricolage, and his sorties fail to add up to a coherent account of my argument, missing entirely both the substance and the thrust of the text. I begin to suspect that he landed at another terminal. Perhaps if he had disembarked at the same gate each time, with a consistent set of assumptions packed away in his critical baggage, I would not have to resort to this tediously extended metaphor, and we could all get down to business much sooner. As things stand, Snyder consistently misses the point of the paper, and his reply seems to be grounded in presuppositions that I suspect, to gather from his other writings, he might very well disavow in the light of day. Such anomalies, however, seem endemic to not a small amount of critical writing in our field, given art history's rather extraordinary and in a number of significant respects unique character as a modern disciplinary enterprise—a field that, when all is said and done, appears at times to be almost perversely designed to deflect the critical understanding of many of the field's most astute observers, of whom Joel Snyder is surely one.

Snyder saw in my text what he termed a "curious wobbling" between, as he put it, "a major tendency to lump and a lesser one to split," between, that is, a conception of art history as a monolithic or epistemologically homogeneous enterprise and a view of the field as a heterogeneous assemblage of disparate perspectives on explanatory adequacy.

It was in fact an explicit and reiterated point of the essay that as a disciplinary project, art history comprised a heterogeneous discursive space of disjoint and contradictory orientations on evidence and explanatory adequacy. I argued that this was not simply a property of a contemporary fragmented and contentious academic discipline, nor simply a result of increasing division into methodological and theoretical schools (despite the current common wisdom), but that such heterogeneity had been a property of the discourse on the visual arts well before its academic professionalization in the middle of the nineteenth century in Europe. I argued, in fact, that what came to be designated professionally as art history a century and a half ago was a disciplined enterprise concerned on a variety of material and rhetorical fronts with the formatting of the visual arts of the past and present as evidentiary phenomena of direct pertinence to the identities and needs of the expanding bourgeoisie of emergent modern nation-states. The epistemological character and evidentiary logic of the discipline of art history were themselves instruments of a massive disciplining of modern populations with respect to the fabrication and maintenance of modernity.

The art historical component of that enterprise was cobbled together around a number of deep contradictions regarding the evidentiary status of works of art—around what it was artworks could be construed as evidence *of*. Moreover, the specifically disciplinary character of art history devolved upon attempts to reconcile opposed conceptions of the work of art as either a unique, irreducible, nonreplicatable product of individual creative effort, exhibiting internal principles of thematic and morphological unity, *or* as a social and cultural artifact that, as a member of a class of like objects, could be shown to obey certain historical laws of formal appearance, evolution, and transformation that transcended or underlay individual consciousness or intentionality. The history of the academic discipline over the past century and a half is in very large part the history of invariably transitory reconciliations of this and other contradictions by means of the rhetorical dominance of one epistemological orthodoxy

---

Donald Preziosi is professor of art history at the University of California, Los Angeles. He is the author of *Rethinking Art History: Meditations on a Coy Science* (1989) and of a forthcoming critical history of the modern art museum.

over marginalized yet always coexistent others—reconciliations that to this day have never been permanent or long lasting.

Very nearly without exception, the traditional historiography of the discipline has comprised one or another bible of begetting, charting the progress of key aesthetic and historical notions and their progenitors. It is a lamentably idealist and historicist enterprise centered until recently upon the intellectual careers of Kantian or Hegelian progeny and, until recently, oblivious to the complex historical circumstances of a wide variety of institutions and discursive practices emerging, coexisting, and interacting mutually over the past two centuries in Europe and America.

Snyder would appear to concur with the importance of understanding how it was that certain objects came to be "subject to art historical study" as he puts it, and he goes on to note that "it will not be as easy as it might first appear to find regularities or rules governing this process—any easier, say, than determining the supposed rules governing annual changes in 'high fashion' clothing" (p. 230). While he rightly observes that to a certain extent there has been a kind of analytic circularity with respect to how particular works came to "qualify" for art historical attention because of certain alleged "internal principles of unity" (what some would have termed in the past aesthetic worth, value, or quality), it seems that Snyder misses an important point of my argument, which was not concerned with fashioning uniform or singular "rules" governing the inclusion of objects in disciplinary discursive space. In point of fact, there are and have always been multiple criteria for securing places for objects in the discursive formation and diverse motivations for such criteria, all of which have been grounded in quite distinct assumptions about the evidentiary value or function of artworks, all of which have coexisted throughout the history of the art historical enterprise since the latter part of the eighteenth century.

The institution of Charles Eliot Norton's Fogg Museum at Harvard was devoted to the explication of the ways in which any given artwork might be shown to be illustrative of the moral and ethical character of the individual, ethnic group, or nation that produced it, measured against an allegedly universal standard of aesthetic value, itself grounded in certain (again, presumably universal) design features of which the criterion of internal unity was held to be primary. In this respect, the Harvard project was consonant with historical principles concurrently articulated during the last quarter of the nineteenth century by Hippolyte Taine in France, as I've discussed at length in a recent work.[1] But the Harvard program's explicit and overriding agenda equally allowed for the incorporation of any cultural artifact in its analytic practices that could demonstrably be relevant to the construction of an ethical profile of an artist, a school, a

1. See Donald Preziosi, *Rethinking Art History: Meditations on a Coy Science* (New Haven, Conn., 1989).

city, a nation, or a race. In this regard, Norton's Ruskinian enterprise bore fundamental similarities to the agendas and motivations of the post-Revolutionary Louvre a century earlier.

Historically, the formal and academic disciplining of the history of the visual arts arose in relationship to collections of a public, civic, and national character that had been assembled on a vast scale in every European country since the eighteenth century. These collections, by the beginning of the nineteenth century, consisted of hundreds of thousands of objects on public display, which had come to be staged how and where they were in order to *demonstrate* diverse series of propositions of a historical, social, cultural, ethical, aesthetic, and pedagogical nature. Some objects served, for their exhibitors, single evidentiary functions, while others more commonly served multiple functions. At the same time, evidence we do have suggests that, for their viewers, such objects also served a variety of functions and not necessarily the same as those apparently intended. It is also the case that the evidentiary weight or value of certain objects changed over time and place. It has certainly been a major preoccupation of professional art historians to chart and account for such changes in the reception and construal of artworks over time and in different venues.

There are two points being made here. The first concerns the spatio-temporal heterogeneity of the evidentiary status of works in the disciplinary discursive formation (and, by implication, the heterogeneity of criteria of explanatory adequacy in art historical methods). The second concerns the character of the discursive formation itself.

It should be apparent in my remarks here, but equally from my original essay, that a critically adequate and historically grounded account of the modern enterprise of art history must concern itself not only with an appreciation of the hybrid epistemological character of academic discourse but also and equally with an appreciation of the embeddedness of that discourse in a variety of interlinked yet from time to time institutionally and professionally disjoint series of practices in and on the visual and plastic "arts." In other words, the modern enterprise of art history has been and remains—in contrast to nearly every other modern academic discipline—diffused across several institutional and professional spaces (or, if one prefers a Foucauldian metaphor, surfaces). It has always been a hybrid and multifaceted enterprise, which fact alone makes conventional historiography framed by the intellectual career of texts on artistic theory or aesthetics not only parochially reductive but grossly fictive. If art history could be called any one thing, it is that nexus of interactive and coimplicative practices with multiple material sites of performance—academic practice, museology, art criticism, connoisseurship, the commodity marketplace, and various permutations of the modern heritage industry devoted to the stabilization and maintenance of modern bourgeois identity and class distinction.

The history of art history is not a simple or direct analogue to the history of other academic disciplines despite the fact that at one time or another art historians meant practices such as these to work as emulatory paradigms for the discipline itself, particularly during the latter half of the nineteenth century and the first half of the twentieth (recall that Charles Eliot Norton, the first university professor of art history in America, had as his official job description and title Instructor in the History of the Fine Arts as Connected with Literature).

Snyder raises a pertinent issue when he observes that it would be "mistaken to conceive of an object-domain as constituting the subject matter of art historical research" (p. 230). Since this is a fundamental point of my essay, it is odd that he concludes that I have concluded otherwise; the point was made in a number of ways throughout my argument. It should have been quite clear that the chief thrust of my paper was that the *subject matter* of art history en bloc was the fabrication of the present(ness) or modernity of the modern nation-state by means of the construction of a universal history or genealogy of the relics of the past— works of art that thereby constitute the *object-domain* of the enterprise. In other words, my point was that the subject matter of art historical practice has been the character of the *present,* presumed to be specifiable as the determinate product of historical forces, the evidence for which was the mass of genealogically (that is, teleologically) formatted objects of material culture seen to be in one way or another directly reflective of those forces, as products, effects, or traces of those forces—in short, as historical documents.

As noted in my essay, that evidentiary "one way or another" comprises the (multidimensional) system of the discipline, whose systematicity was grounded in a singularity of mission and orientation rather than in a homogeneity of criteria of admission to the discursive formation on the basis of the formal or aesthetic properties of objects.

It seems evident that, at certain points, my essay proved an annoyance to some of Snyder's own critical assumptions. He asks if I am "addressing the substance of the discipline or the rhetoric of some of its practitioners" (p. 232). I would have to ask in turn how or where he would fix the distinction and what he would understand by rhetoric, particularly given my explicit orientation upon what might be termed rhetoric in connection with the heterogeneous discursive spaces of art history. He also seems somewhat annoyed by my observations concerning the art historical enterprise as practices of power given his complaint, "Is [my] history not 'a practice of power?'" (p. 232). I must necessarily respond, of course, asking in turn, What is *not?* And, finally, he devotes the entire final section of his reply to suggesting that I seem to be overlooking the role of museums in the present, focussing upon museological preservation and the curatorship of past monuments. I would have to reply to this by noting that, once again, Snyder misses the thrust of my arguments about the museological component of art historical practice. I remain to be convinced (a) that there is any notable difference between the museological treatment of past and current works and (b) that museological stagecraft and dramaturgy are in any way substantially different today than they were at the beginning of the nineteenth century, when (as today) the same basic orientations upon the formatting of objects as evidentiary documents may be observed, the so-called new museology (or the so-called new art history) notwithstanding. I should say finally that Snyder's bringing up the examples of Erwin Panofsky and Michael Fried as "a way of showing that [my] division of the discipline's evidentiary system from its object-domain is itself problematic," followed immediately by a comment that it would be "useful to ask if evidentiary practices are not themselves constitutive of the discipline's subject matter"—are all points already addressed here and in my paper (p. 232).

It should be quite clear that we have different assumptions and perspectives on the question of what constitutes art in the first place, leading necessarily to disjoint notions of what the subject and object of study should be. This difference might be noted in shorthand by saying that for Snyder, *art* is a noun whereas for me it is an adverb and rather more in line with what in ancient Greek would have been termed (one facet of) *techne* (or in Latin *ars*). My paper was concerned at base with the epistemological and institutional consequences of the reformatting of *art* in a nominative fashion as an object, as a *kind* of thing, with a history of its own, as a facet of the epistemic, disciplinary, and institutional revolutions of the Enlightenment.

The modern oscillation between the nominative and adverbial construals of the term, in which the former has, for the past two centuries, been in dominance, constitutes the trompe l'oeil discursive (and theatrical) space of the modern enterprise of art history—a fact that makes our attempts to appreciate and account for that enterprise all the more difficult. The nominative understanding of art has been historically coterminous with the enterprise of modernity; it is a historical and ideological artifact of a particular period in the growth of the modern nation-state. To be able to see before, behind, and after that would constitute a beginning to our understanding of just what the question of art history in fact was.

I am grateful for the opportunity here to rearticulate my arguments in what I hope has been an even stronger fashion. In point of fact, such dialogic opportunities rarely arise within the discursive spaces of the modern discipline of art history, for reasons which I trust my essay and these remarks have made abundantly clear.

HISTORY AND THE
USES OF INQUIRY

Marvelous Facts and Miraculous Evidence in Early Modern Europe

Lorraine Daston

Introduction: *Facts versus Evidence*

According to a commonplace view, facts are evidence *in potentia:* mustered in an argument, deduced from a theory, or simply arranged in a pattern, they shed their proverbial obstinacy and help with the work of proof and disproof. However, in modern usage facts and evidence are nonetheless distinct categories, and crucially so. On their own, facts are notoriously inert—"angular," "stubborn," or even "nasty" in their resistance to interpretation and inference. They are robust in their existence and opaque in their meaning. Only when enlisted in the service of a claim or a conjecture do they become evidence, or facts with significance. Evidence might be described as facts hammered into signposts, which point beyond themselves and their sheer, brute thingness to states of affairs to which we have no direct access: the clues pertaining to a crime committed without witnesses, the observations testing a theory about the true configuration of the solar system or the workings of the mind, the ruins of a civilization that vanished millennia ago, the indices that predict the future.

On this view, facts owe no permanent allegiance to any of the schemes into which they are impressed as evidence. They are the mercenary soldiers of argument, ready to enlist in yours or mine, wherever the evidentiary fit is best. It is exactly this fickle independence that makes

I am grateful to William Clark, Klaus Hentschel, and Katharine Park for their comments on an earlier version of this essay. Part of the research was done with the support of National Science Foundation Grant Dir—89 11169.

This essay originally appeared in *Critical Inquiry* 18 (Autumn 1991).

them so valuable to a certain view of rationality, one that insists upon the neutrality of facts and staunchly denies that they are "theory-laden." Were facts to be frozen into any one evidentiary scheme, fixed signposts forever pointing in the direction of a single conjecture, they would lose their power to arbitrate between rival arguments or theories.

Implicit in this conventional distinction between facts and evidence is that in order for facts to qualify as credible evidence, they must appear innocent of human intention. Facts fabricated as evidence, that is, to make a particular point, are thereby disqualified as evidence. Nature's facts are above suspicion, because presumed free of any intention, but many man-made facts also qualify: the blood-stained weapon found at the scene of a murder counts as incriminating evidence as long as it was not planted there with the intention of incriminating; the unaffected simplicity of the witness adds weight to testimony as long as it was not feigned with the intention of persuading. Similarly, many methodological precautions in contemporary science, such as the double-blind clinical trial and the fixing of statistical significance levels before the experiment, were instituted to thwart the intention, however unconscious, to confirm a pet hypothesis. Note that the planted weapon, the affected testimony, the skewed empirical results lose neither their status as facts nor their potential to serve as evidence for conjectures *other* than those intended: so long as they do not point in the intended direction, these fabricated facts can be made to point somewhere else with no loss of evidentiary force. It is the distinction between facts and evidence that is at issue, not the reality of the facts per se, nor their quality as evidence in general.

I have sketched the well-known distinction between facts and evidence not to defend or attack it (as does a vast literature in the history and philosophy of science), but rather as a preface to a key episode in the history of the conceptual categories of fact and evidence. My question is neither, "Do neutral facts exist?" nor "How does evidence prove or disprove?" but rather, "How did our current conceptions of neutral facts and enlisted evidence, and the distinction between them, come to be?" How did evidence come to be incompatible with intention, and is it possible to imagine a kind of evidence that is intention-laden?

It is my claim that partial answers to these questions lie buried in the sixteenth- and seventeenth-century literature on prodigies and miracles. I shall argue that during this period prodigies briefly became the proto-

---

Lorraine Daston is professor of history and history of science at the University of Chicago. She is author of *Classical Probability in the Enlightenment* (1988) and is currently at work on a history of scientific objectivity.

type for a new kind of scientific fact, and that miracles briefly exemplified a form of evidence patent to the senses and crucially dependent on intention. Both conceptions diverge sharply not only from current notions of facts and evidence, but also from medieval views on the nature of prodigies and miracles. Prodigies were originally closely akin to portents, divine signs revealing God's will and things to come; miracles were more intimately associated with the private experience of grace than with the public evidence of the senses. Prodigies were transformed from signs into nonsignifying facts, and miracles into compelling evidence, as part of more sweeping changes in natural philosophy and theology in the mid-seventeenth century.

My account of both transformations and the context in which they occurred is divided into five parts. I first outline the patristic and medieval distinctions between marvels and miracles, and the related distinctions between natural, preternatural, and supernatural causation. Part 2 traces the gradual naturalization of the preternatural in the early modern period. I then examine in part 3 how prodigies and portents became the first neutral facts in the reformed natural philosophy of the mid-seventeenth century, losing all status as signs. In part 4, I turn to controversies over the definition and meaning of miracles both in Protestant England and Catholic France in the latter half of the seventeenth century, arguing that for some theologians, miracles briefly became "pure" evidence, requiring neither interpretation nor further corroboration. In the fifth, concluding part, I show how the debate over the evidence *of* miracles became a debate over the evidence *for* miracles in the early eighteenth century.

1. Natural, Preternatural, and Supernatural

In the early sixteenth century the received views on miracles, marvels, and their relationship to the natural order still derived principally from the teachings of Augustine, and, especially, from those of Thomas Aquinas. These authorities were sometimes difficult to square with one another. Augustine praised all of nature as a miracle, and complained that familiarity with such marvels as the individuality of each and every human being had unduly blunted our sense of wonder. Since nature was simply the will of God realized, it made no sense to speak of miracles as *contra naturam:* "For how can anything done by the will of God be contrary to nature, when the will of so great a creator constitutes the nature of each created thing?"[1] Marvels shaded into miracles without a sharp break for Augustine, for both testified to how far the power of God exceeded that of

1. Augustine, *De civitate Dei,* trans. W. M. Green, 7 vols. (Cambridge, Mass., 1972), 7:51.

human understanding. This is why Augustine parried the objections of pagan philosophers to Christian miracles like the resurrection by listing natural wonders—the wood of a certain Egyptian fig tree that sinks rather than floats, the Persian stone that waxes and wanes with the moon, the incorruptible flesh of the dead peacock—that also defied explanation: "Now let those unbelievers who refuse to accept the divine writings give an explanation of these marvels, if they can."[2] However, certain events deserved to be singled out from the perpetual wonder of nature as true miracles because of the message they bore. The miracles of the early Christian church were of this sort, consolidating faith and unity by a wave of conversions, and, at least in later life, Augustine was also willing to credit miraculous cures performed by saintly relics and also those performed on behalf of his side of the Donatist controversy as serving the same special ends.[3]

Aquinas treated miracles within an Aristotelian framework that made nature considerably more orderly and autonomous than Augustine's profusion of marvels, ordinary and extraordinary, had allowed. Dividing causes into a higher and lower order, Aquinas contended that God's miracles transgressed only those of the lower order, which exist by God's will, not by necessity.[4] Miracles are of three kinds, and each kind admits of degrees, depending on how far the ordinary powers of nature are surpassed: miracles of substance [miracula quoad substantiam] overcome an absolute impossibility in nature (for example, two bodies in the same place at the same time); miracles of subject [miracula quoad subjectum] accomplish what nature can do, but not in that body (for example, speech in a cat); miracles of mode [miracula quoad modum] accomplish what nature can do in that subject, but not by those means (for example, a sudden cure effected by a holy relic).[5]

Yet according to Aquinas we recognize miracles by their subjective effect on us rather than by their objective causes:

> The word miracle is derived from admiration, which arises when an effect is manifest, whereas its cause is hidden. . . . Now the cause of a manifest effect may be known to one, but unknown to others. . . . : as an eclipse is to a rustic, but not to an astronomer. Now a miracle is so called as being full of wonder; as having a cause absolutely hidden from all: and this cause is God. Wherefore those things which God does outside those causes which we know, are called miracles.[6]

2. Ibid., 7:29.
3. See Peter Brown, *Augustine of Hippo: A Biography* (Berkeley, 1967), pp. 413–18.
4. See Thomas Aquinas, *Summa theologica*, trans. Fathers of the English Dominican Province, 3 vols. (New York, 1947), 1: 520.
5. See Aquinas, *Summa contra gentiles*, trans. English Dominican Fathers, 4 vols. (London, 1928), vol. 3, pt. 2, pp. 60–61.
6. Aquinas, *Summa theologica*, 1:520.

God performs miracles for an audience, which credits them in proportion to the wonder they excite, which wonder in turn measures the magnitude of the audience's ignorance. Miracles convert and convince by their psychological effects; they are God's oratory.

Like Augustine, Aquinas often blurred the boundary between the marvelous and the miraculous, albeit for different reasons. For Augustine, especially in his earlier writings, there existed in principle no sharp distinction between the marvelous and the miraculous (and for that matter, the natural as well), for all sprang directly from God. Augustine was largely unconcerned with how God brings about these effects, much less with orders of causation.

Aquinas, in contrast, drew a principled distinction between the truly supernatural (God's unmediated actions) on the one hand, and the natural (what happens always or most of the time) and the preternatural (what happens rarely, but nonetheless by the agency of created beings), on the other. Marvels belong, properly speaking, to the realm of the preternatural:

> For the order imposed on things by God is in keeping with that which is wont to occur in things for the most part, but it is not everywhere in keeping with what always occurs: because many natural causes produce their effects in the same way usually, but not always; since sometimes, though seldom, it happens otherwise, whether on account of a defect in the power of an agent, or through the indisposition of the matter, or by reason of a stronger agency: as when nature produces a sixth finger in a man.[7]

Not only unaided nature, but created spirits such as angels and demons can produce preternatural effects, although these fall short of true miracles on ontological grounds: spirits must work "through the local movement of a body," for God alone can "induce any form into corporeal matter, as though matter were in this obedient thereto." However, we humans are hard put to separate the supernatural wheat from the preternatural chaff, for both excite wonder when we are ignorant of the causes, and wonder is the hallmark of the miraculous.[8]

As one might expect in a body of beliefs discussed and elaborated over a millennium, medieval views on the relationships between the natural, preternatural, and supernatural were by no means monolithic, and it is possible to find many variants on and exceptions to both the Augustinian and Thomist views, not to mention tensions between the two. The medieval Christian doctrine of miracles was further complicated by the heterogeneity of the category: not only scriptural miracles, but also the

7. Aquinas, *Summa contra gentiles*, vol. 3, pt. 2, p. 57.
8. Ibid., vol. 3, pt. 2, pp. 65–66.

miracles of saints and their shrines and relics, the miracles of the sacraments, the miracles of judicial ordeals (at least until their abolition by the fourth Lateran Council in 1215), the historical miracles recounted by the chronicles, and the "jocular" miracles inserted in sermons all had to be subsumed therein, and the conceptual integrity of the category suffered accordingly.[9]

Nonetheless, the general outlines of the doctrine as it crystallized in the thirteenth and fourteenth centuries can be discerned with some clarity. First, there was a tendency, always present among theologians and increasingly pronounced after the Aristotelian synthesis of the thirteenth century, to segregate the natural and the preternatural from the supernatural, having recourse to the latter only as a last resort. Second, although theologians followed Aquinas in principle by defining miracles by the abrogation of the lower order of causes, they also followed him in practice by making universal wonderment the actual criterion. Third, despite the ensuing practical difficulties of distinguishing between the preternatural marvel and the supernatural miracle, theologians nonetheless continued to insist on the theoretical distinction between the two.

This distinction was fortified in the sixteenth century, when the preternatural came to be ever more closely associated with the dubious and possibly demonic activities of magic and divination.[10] Because of these demonic associations some historians have assumed that medieval theologians deemed theurgy to be supernatural, but this does not do justice to the nicety of the conceptual distinctions that reserved the supernatural for God alone. Although demons, astral intelligences, and other spirits might manipulate natural causes with superhuman dexterity and thereby work marvels, as mere creatures they could never transcend from the preternatural to the supernatural and work genuine miracles. Well into the seventeenth century and beyond, sober thinkers warned against the counterfeit miracles of Satan, who "being a natural Magician ... may perform many acts in ways above our knowledge, though not transcending our natural power."[11]

---

9. On shrines and relics, see Jonathan Sumption, *Pilgrimage: An Image of Mediaeval Religion* (London, 1975), pp. 22–44. On the trial by ordeal, see Robert Bartlett, *Trial by Fire and Water: The Medieval Judicial Ordeal* (Oxford, 1986). On sacramental and jocular miracles, see Benedicta Ward, *Miracles and the Medieval Mind: Theory, Records, and Event, 1000–1215* (Philadelphia, 1982), pp. 13, 213. For a general survey of theological views on miracles, see Bernhard Bron, *Das Wunder: Das theologische Wunderverständnis im Horizont des neuzeitlichen Natur und Geschichtsbegriffs* (Göttingen, 1975).

10. See Jean Céard, *La Nature et les prodiges: L'Insolite au XVIᵉ siècle, en France* (Geneva, 1977), pp. 111–15.

11. Thomas Browne, *Pseudodoxia Epidemica*, in *The Works of Sir Thomas Browne*, ed. Charles Sayle, 3 vols. (Edinburgh, 1912), 1:188. See William Fleetwood, *An Essay upon Miracles*, 2d ed. (London, 1702), p. 108; hereafter abbreviated *EM;* and Joseph Glanvill, *Sadducismus Triumphatus: Or, A full and plain Evidence, Concerning Witches and Apparitions* (London, 1682), p. 52; hereafter abbreviated *ST.*

Theology cemented the barrier between the preternatural and the supernatural; scholastic natural philosophy erected a similar barrier between the preternatural and the natural. The natural order itself was a matter of nature's habitual custom rather than of nature's inviolable law, what usually rather than what infallibly happened.[12] Although *scientia* properly so called dealt in demonstration and therefore in what must be the case, it did not pretend to be comprehensive. There were pockets of experience that defied necessity, and therefore scientific treatment. Magnetism, the virtue of coral to ward off lightning, the antipathy between elephant and dragon—few doubted the existence of such phenomena, but because their occult (that is, "hidden") causes were inaccessible to sense and reason, they formed no part of natural philosophy.[13]

Indeed, particulars and a fortiori singularities of all kinds, whether ascribed to occult causes or to chance, were not readily susceptible to scientific explanation, which trafficked in universals and regularities: Aquinas thought the study of singulars in ethics, alchemy, and medicine might at best approximate but never attain scientific certitude.[14] Thus even strange or singular phenomena without the slightest whiff of the demonic were effectively excluded from the natural, by dint of being excluded from natural philosophy. Although preternatural phenomena were in theory difficult to distinguish from natural events (since they belonged to the same, lower order of causation), and in practice difficult to distinguish from supernatural events (since they evoked the same astonishment and wonder), they nonetheless constituted a third ontological domain until the late seventeenth century.

It might be argued that the inherent conceptual instability of the category of preternatural phenomena predestined it for collapse into the sturdier categories of the natural and supernatural. However, the preternatural was very long in meeting its doom, not only resisting attempts to absorb it into the natural and into the supernatural, but also expanding in extent and intellectual importance throughout the sixteenth century. Fifty years before its demise around the turn of the eighteenth century, the preternatural preoccupied theologians and natural philosophers more urgently than ever before.

The early modern vogue for the preternatural arose from a confluence of circumstances: Marsilio Ficino's revival of magic, both natural and demonic, imbued scholarly Neoplatonism with a strong affinity for the

---

12. On the medieval notion of "natural," see Bert Hansen, *Nicole Oresme and the Marvels of Nature: The "De causis mirabilium"* (Toronto, 1985), p. 64.

13. On occult causes, see Keith Hutchison, "What Happened to Occult Qualities in the Scientific Revolution?" *Isis* 73 (June 1982): 233–53.

14. See Eileen Serene, "Demonstrative Science," in *The Cambridge History of Later Medieval Philosophy: From the Rediscovery of Aristotle to the Disintegration of Scholasticism, 1100–1600*, ed. Norman Kretzmann, Anthony Kenny, and Jan Pinborg (Cambridge, 1982), p. 506n.

occult;[15] the new printing centers north and south of the Alps spewed out edition after edition of books of secrets retailing household recipes, virtues of herbs and stones, tricks of the trades, and "natural magic";[16] the witchcraft trials concentrated theological and legal attention on the precise nature of demonic meddling in human affairs;[17] the voyages of exploration brought back tales and trophies of creatures and landscapes more marvelous than anything in Pliny or Mandeville;[18] the religious and political upheavals set in motion by the Reformation also triggered an avalanche of crude broadsides and learned Latin treatises that anxiously interpreted comets, monstrous births, rains of blood, and any number of other strange phenomena as portents.[19] Although portents were the very prototype of signifying events, spectacular and unsettling messages sent by God to herald triumph or catastrophe, it was this last category of portents and prodigies that ultimately supplied reforming natural philosophers of the seventeenth century with a new kind of fact that signified nothing at all.

2. The Naturalization of the Preternatural

Not all preternatural events qualified as portents or prodigies. Medieval chroniclers enlivened their accounts with comets, earthquakes, monstrous births, and the like, and often, but not always, speculated on their significance. For example, Gerald of Wales in his *Topographia hibernia* (ca. 1185) allows that some strange events may be portents, such as a large fish with three gold teeth caught two years before the arrival of the English, which might "prefigure the imminent conquest of the country," but he records many others—a ship-swallowing whirlpool, a Limerick woman with a beard and a mane—without interpretation.[20]

The difficulty in interpreting preternatural events as divine signs was twofold: first, their ambiguous status between natural and supernatural;

15. See D. P. Walker, *Spiritual and Demonic Magic: From Ficino to Campanella* (Notre Dame, Ind., 1975).

16. See William Eamon, "Arcana Disclosed: The Advent of Printing, the Books of Secrets Tradition and the Development of Experimental Science in the Sixteenth Century," *History of Science* 22 (June 1984): 111–50.

17. See Stuart Clark, "The Scientific Status of Demonology," in *Occult and Scientific Mentalities in the Renaissance,* ed. Brian Vickers (Cambridge, 1984), pp. 351–74.

18. See Mary B. Campbell, *The Witness and the Other World: Exotic European Travel Writing, 400–1600* (Ithaca, N. Y., 1988).

19. See Katharine Park and Lorraine Daston, "Unnatural Conceptions: The Study of Monsters in Sixteenth- and Seventeenth-Century France and England," *Past and Present* 92 (Aug. 1981): 20–54.

20. Gerald of Wales, *The History and Topography of Ireland,* trans. John J. O'Meara (Harmondsworth, 1982), p. 65. On Gerald's treatment of marvels and miracles, see Bartlett, *Gerald of Wales, 1146–1223* (Oxford, 1982).

and second, theological distrust of divination as most likely demonic. Although *bona fide* miracles were always missives from God—signs of divine power, intent, approval or disapproval—establishing their *bona fides* was in practice a delicate matter of balancing theological context against admittedly incomplete natural knowledge. This balancing act became increasingly precarious in the early modern period, when heterodox sects, reformed natural philosophy, and fear of demonic deception forced a reexamination of the definition and function of miracles.

Both context and the possibility[21] of a natural explanation determined which preternatural events counted as signs: in a time of plague, war, or religious schism, the two-headed cat or shooting star that might have otherwise aroused only mild interest as a wonder provoked anxious interpretations as a portent. The interpretations of portents also teetered dangerously close to divination, which (except for predictions based on natural signs—for example, a red sky in the morning presages a storm at sea) was regularly and emphatically condemned from the twelfth century on by the Catholic church as a usurpation of God's perogative to foretell the future. Prodigies were in principle exempt from the ban on divination, as were visitations from God, angels, or saints in dreams, but in practice the distinction was difficult to maintain.[22]

In the latter half of the sixteenth century religious and political turmoil combined with an intense intellectual interest in the preternatural, first, to magnify the portentous associations of strange events and, second, to provoke ever more concerted attempts to distinguish genuine (that is, divine) portents from demonic counterfeits and superstitious divination. (That portents never fully merged with miracles can be seen by the lively interest that Protestant theologians took in their interpretation, however firmly they insisted that miracles per se had ceased after the early Church.)[23] In general, the former trend was fed by the popular press,

21. It is possibility in principle, not the actual availability of a natural explanation that counted here. Nicole Oresme's attempts to "show the causes of some effects which seem to be marvels and to show that the effects occur naturally" (Hansen, *Nicole Oresme and the Marvels of Nature*, p. 137) almost never provide a specific explanation of an individual case; indeed, Oresme despaired of ever being able to provide such explanations: see, for example, his denial that monstrous births are portents (p. 247); also see p. 227 concerning explanations of individual cases. This kind of promissory naturalism, based more on metaphysical faith than scientific competence, remained typical of attempts to naturalize marvels and miracles well into the eighteenth century. See, for example, [John Toland], *Hodegus; proving the pillar of fire, that guided the Israelites in the wilderness, not miraculous, but ambulatory beacons* (London, 1753), and Conyers Middleton, *A Vindication of the Free inquiry into the miraculous powers, which are supposed to have subsisted in the Christian church & c. from the objections of Dr. Dodwell and Dr. Church* (London, 1751).

22. On the importance of signs and divination in sixteenth-century learned culture, see Céard, *La Nature et les prodiges*.

23. See, for example, Calvin's cautious declaration that "cependant je ne nie pas, lors que Dieu veut estendre sa main pour faire quelque jugement digne de memoire au monde,

broadsides, and vernacular tracts, and the latter was sustained by more scholarly writings, although there was some crossover.[24] This distinction in audiences was to play an important role in late seventeenth-century attempts to discredit the ominous significance of portents, and, ultimately, to belittle the importance of miracles.

In the late sixteenth century, however, scholars like Jean Bodin, hack writers like Pierre Boaistuau, and the composers of broadside ballads saw eye-to-eye on the proliferation and meaning of portents in general, even if they differed in their interpretations of specific cases. Bodin took Aristotle to task for claiming that nothing was truly unnatural: "For as to monsters and signs, which occur out of the order of nature [outre l'ordre de nature], one cannot deny that they carry some signification of the wrath of God, which he gives to men to make them repent and convert to Him."[25] Boaistuau and the several other authors of the enormously popular Histoires prodigieuses (1567) argued that God sometimes sent "signs and prodigies, which are most often the heralds, trumpets, and advance couriers of justice."[26] Stephen Batman advertised his 1581 compendium of "the strange Prodigies hapned in the Worlde" with the promise to reveal "divers secrete figures of Revelations tending to mannes stayed conversion towardes God";[27] countless broadsides preached, in the words of a 1619 broadside printed in Augsburg on the occasion of a comet, that: "War and blood are in the door/Hunger and rising prices draw near/ Pestilence hovers in the air/This we have earned by great sin and our godless living."[28] Strange events—monstrous births, oddly shaped fish and animals, apparitions of armies in the clouds, rains of iron and blood, bleeding grape vines, comets, flood tides, swarms of insects and vermin— all became grist for the interpreter's mill, and were as often as not pressed

---

qu'il ne nous advertisse quelquefois par les cometes: mais cela ne sert de rien, pour attacher les hommes et leur condition à une influence perpetuelle du ciel" ["however, I do not deny that when God wants to extend his hand to make some judgment worthy of the memory of the world, that he sometimes advertises (it) to us by comets: but that in no way serves to attach men and their condition to a perpetual influence of the heavens"](quoted in ibid., p. 130).

24. See Park and Daston, "Unnatural Conceptions," concerning mutual learned/ popular borrowing.

25. Jean Bodin, De la démonomanie des sorciers (1580; Hildesheim, 1988), fol. 48, r/v.

26. Pierre Boaistuau, Histoires prodigieuses (Paris, 1567), p. 5. For a full account of the various volumes of the Histoires prodigieuses and their publishing history, see Céard, La Nature et les prodiges, chap. 13.

27. Stephen Batman, The Doome warning all men to the Judgemente. Wherein are contayned for the most parte all the straunge Prodigies hapned in the Worlde, with divers secrete figures of Revelations tending to mannes stayed conversion towardes God (London, 1581).

28. Wahrhafte Neue Zeitung von dem neuen Cometstern . . . welcher zu Augspurg und in vilen Landen ist gesehen worden (Augsburg, 1619).

FIG. 1.—German broadside printed in Frankfurt, 1627, of a celestial apparition, portending, *inter alia*, a Turkish invasion, plague, and hailstorms. Courtesy of the Bayerische Staatsbibliothek, Munich.

into service as propaganda on one or another side of the raging religious controversies of the day.[29]

However, the printed collections of prodigies, learned and lay alike, did not saddle every prodigy they reported with a portentous interpretation. Some might be signs either of impending events (an invasion of Turks, an outbreak of plague, the coming of the Messiah), or religious heresy, or more generally of God's wrath and power—but not all. Bodin believed only comets and monsters to be true portents, and took care to distinguish these from superstitious and impious divination.[30] Boaistuau and his coauthors blithely related prodigies that testified to "the excellence of man" (a man who slept for thirty years, another who washed his face and hands with molten lead, women who had borne litters of children, a prodigiously obese man) and to the fecundity of nature (stones that could render brackish water sweet, nereids and tritons, volcanoes), rather than to divine judgements and messages. Even the German broadsides, generally the gloomiest of a gloom-and-doom genre, sometimes published simple descriptions, without interpretations.

29. See Park and Daston, "Unnatural Conceptions," pp. 27–34.
30. See Bodin, *De la Démonomanie des sorciers*, fol. 49 r/v.

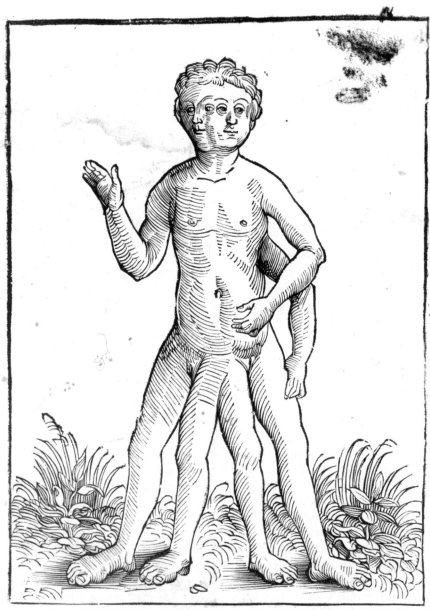

FIG. 2.—German broadside illustrating a monstrous birth in Spalt, 1511. Although described as "a wondrous and terrifying thing," no interpretation is offered. Courtesy of the Bayerische Staatsbibliothek, Munich.

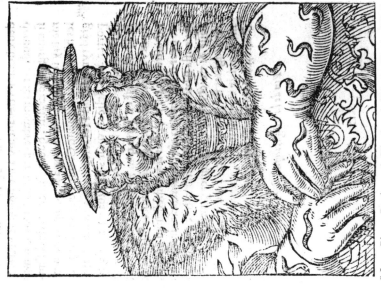

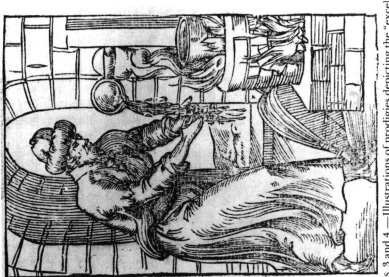

Figs. 3 and 4.— Illustrations of prodigies depicting the "excellence of man" from Pierre Boaistuau's *Histoire prodigieuses* (Paris, 1576). Figure 3 shows a "man of our times, who washed his face and hands in molten lead"; figure 4 is of the astonishingly obese Denis Heracleot, who had to resort to leeches to extract the fat. Both figures reproduced by courtesy of the Niedersächsische Staats- und Universitätsbibliothek Göttingen.

In these collections of strange events, popular and learned, the genuinely intermediate character of the preternatural, that twilight zone between the natural and supernatural, stubbornly asserted itself, whatever the declared orientation of the author. Avowedly naturalist accounts could not expunge the numinous association that clung to Siamese twins or an aurora borealis; avowedly supernaturalist accounts were equally unable to resist the temptation to include patently unportentous natural wonders such as hot springs and petrified forests. The cabinets of curiosities, those museums of the preternatural, contained a great many objects, secular as well as religious, that can only be described as relics—for example, the Ashmolean Museum in Oxford had among its holdings St. Augustine's pastoral crook.[31]

Analogously, churches had long displayed curiosities of no particular religious significance, such as a giant's bones, ostrich eggs, and unicorn horns, alongside splinters of the true cross and other more conventional objects of devotion.[32] Pious authors heaven-bent on assembling instances of divine providences padded their account of remarkable deliverances at sea and blasphemers struck down by lightning in mid-oath with tales of a man who had voided a serpent seven ells long and kidney stones in the shape of "divers sorts of Animals." No pretense was made of drawing religious lessons from these latter "prodigious and astonishing" things.[33] Until the late seventeenth century the category of the preternatural retained a certain phenomenological homogeneity—wondrous objects and events not unambiguously miraculous in the strict sense—that defied tidy attempts to divide it in half down the line of natural versus supernatural causes. Preternatural events always qualified as wonders, but only sometimes as signs.

Sixteenth-century demonology briefly reinforced this phenomenological homogeneity with a causal unity of sorts. Increasingly, preternatural events were attributed not just to any remarkable conjunction of natural causes, but to conjunctions of natural causes cunningly wrought by demons. The effect of such demonic attributions was to weaken ties not only with purely natural explanations but also with purely supernatural ones. Indeed, the latter tendency was the more pronounced, for the religious peril of becoming a dupe to a counterfeit miracle, staged by the

31. See R. F. Ovenell, *The Ashmolean Museum, 1683–1894* (Oxford, 1986), p. 37. On the composition of the cabinets, see *The Origins of Museums: The Cabinet of Curiosities in Sixteenth- and Seventeenth-Century Europe,* ed. Oliver Impey and Arthur MacGregor (Oxford, 1985).

32. See Julius von Schlosser, *Die Kunst- und Wunderkammern der Spätrenaissance: Ein Beitrag zur Geschichte des Sammelwesens* (1908; Braunschweig, 1978), and David Murray, *Museums: Their History and Their Use* (Glasgow, 1904).

33. Increase Mather, *An Essay for the Recording of Illustrious Providences* (1684; New York, 1977), chap. 9. On the background to collections of providences, see Keith Thomas, *Religion and the Decline of Magic* (New York, 1971), chap. 4.

devil to trap the unwary, loomed large in an imagination haunted by the terrors of heresy, demonic magic, and witchcraft.[34] Alert to this peril, writers on the demonic preternatural actually tended to emphasize the natural character of preternatural events, in order to steal the devil's thunder. Thus Sir Thomas Browne accused Satan of "distorting the order and theory of causes perpendicular to their effects," deluding the credulous into taking stars and meteors as portents: "Thus hath he [Satan] also made the ignorant sort believe that natural effects immediately and commonly proceed from supernatural powers."[35] William Fleetwood, recalling St. Paul's warning about the "lying wonders of Satan" (2 Thess. 2:9), denied demons the power of working true miracles, although he did "not deny but that Spirits may foresee many Events that lye hid in their Natural Causes, which are concealed from *Us* but not from *Them;* because I do not know the extent of their intellectual Powers" (*EM*, p. 108).

Nor were these worries about how to distinguish preternatural, demonic wonders from supernatural, divine miracles confined to English Protestants: a Sieur de Sainte-Foy (possibly the pseudonym for the Jesuit Père Annat) insinuated that the Port-Royal miracle of the Sacred Thorn was a false miracle, the work of demons manipulating subtle natural causes in order to mislead good Catholics into the Jansenist heresy.[36] French Catholic writers on demonic imposture, however, did tend to concentrate more on superstitions like divination than on portents, possibly because they were saddled with the additional task of keeping sacramental as well as revelatory miracles pure from the taint of demonic imposture.[37]

The proximate impact of these warnings was to discredit preternatural phenomena as true signs from on high; they were rather to be rejected as forgeries from below. The ultimate impact was to naturalize almost all of them, even when natural explanations for specific cases were wanting, as was the rule rather than the exception. The writings of the demonologists show that it was not sufficient simply to posit natural causes for preternatural phenomena in order to naturalize them fully; it was also necessary to rid nature of demonic agency. To simplify the historical sequence somewhat: first, preternatural phenomena were demonized and thereby incidentally naturalized; then the demons were deleted, leaving only the natural causes. This two-step process should not be insisted on too adamantly: there were plenty of respectable theologians, both Protestant and Catholic, who invoked demonic plots well into the eighteenth

34. See Jean Delumeau, *La Peur en Occident, XIVe–XVIIIe siècles, une cité assiégée* (Paris, 1978). See also Walker, *Spiritual and Demonic Magic*, and Clark, "The Scientific Status of Demonology," on the growing fear of demons in the sixteenth century.

35. Browne, *Pseudodoxia Epidemica*, 1:193.

36. See Tetsuya Shiokawa, *Pascal et les miracles* (Paris, 1977), p. 112.

37. See, for example, Jean-Baptiste Thiers, *Traité des superstitions qui regardent les sacrements*, 4th ed., 4 vols. (Paris, 1741), and Pierre Le Brun, *Histoire critique des pratiques superstitieuses* (Paris, 1702).

century. In general, however, the activities and autonomy of the devil declined steadily in the last quarter of the seventeenth century, for reasons I shall discuss in part 5. The overall thrust of attempts to demonize preternatural phenomena was to discredit them as true signs. Counterfeit portents and false miracles pretended to a status they did not deserve, namely, that of the "signs and wonders" (Heb. 2:4) that truly announce God's will and doctrine.

While miracles became ever more closely associated with evidence, especially in the writings of late seventeenth-century Protestant theologians, preternatural phenomena became ever less so. The English Hebraist John Spencer, writing in 1665, condemned the belief that prodigies were portents as "a very Vulgar and Pernicious Error," endangering philosophy by inhibiting the search for natural causes, corrupting divinity by allowing "a liberty for men to bring into it what Divine signs they please without warrant from Scripture or reason," and undermining the state by giving "every pitiful Prodigy-monger . . . credit enough with the People" to gainsay authority "by telling them that heaven frowns upon the laws, and that God writes his displeasure against them in black and visible Characters when some sad accident befals the complyers with them." Spencer did blame the devil for fobbing off prodigies as miracles in an attempt to deceive the gullible, but he was at least as concerned about the human manipulation of such alleged signs for nefarious purposes.[38] Meric Casaubon was willing to allow for sincere (though mistaken) claims to the power of divination, suggesting that "many natural things before they come to that passe, as to be generally known or visible, have some kind of obscure beginnings, by which they be known by some long before." People or animals with unusually acute senses may indeed foretell coming events by these "natural foregoing signes."[39] Although these indicators were in Casaubon's view genuine signs, they were neither supernatural nor preternatural, but prosaically natural—for example, the throbbing bunions that precede a storm.[40]

3. From Signs to Facts

Thus did preternatural phenomena lose their religious meaning as signs. But they did not cease to be of interest for learned as well as for lay audiences. Not only did vernacular collections of prodigies, now frankly advertised as "pregnant with pleasure and delight," continue to spill forth

38. See John Spencer, preface, *A Discourse concerning Prodigies*, 2d ed. (London, 1665); see also pp. 59–60; hereafter abbreviated *DCP*.

39. Meric Casaubon, *A Treatise Concerning Enthusiasme, As it is an Effect of Nature: but is mistaken by many for either Divine Inspiration, or Diabolical Possession* (London, 1655), p. 42.

40. On natural divination, see also Céard, *La Nature et les prodiges*, pp. 115ff., and Thiers, *Traité des superstitions qui regardent les sacrements*, pp. 294–95.

from the presses in multiple editions; the annals of the fledgling scientific academies and other journals serving the Republic of Letters also devoted many pages to monstrous births, celestial apparitions, cyclones, diamonds that glowed in the dark, and other strange phenomena. These entries in the *Philosophical Transactions of the Royal Society of London,* the *Journal des Savants,* the *Histoires et Mémoires de l'Académie Royale des Science,* and other new journals concerned primarily with natural philosophy testify to a new status for preternatural phenomena. Long marginal to scholastic natural philosophy, and now stripped of their religious significance, they had become the first scientific facts. The very traits that had previously unfitted them for use in natural philosophy, and which had then disqualified them from use in theology, made this new role possible.

I have shown elsewhere in detail how this transformation came about in mid-seventeenth-century natural philosophy;[41] here, I shall very briefly rehearse the main lines of this argument, as it relates to early modern views about the meaning of preternatural phenomena. As we have seen, preternatural phenomena, even when free of many portentous associations, had been in principle excluded from scholastic natural philosophy: *scientia,* properly speaking, was the corpus of demonstrated, universal truths, and preternatural phenomena were by definition exceptions to "that which is always or of that which is for the most part."[42] Neither Aristotle nor his medieval followers denied the existence of such oddities, but they did deny that anomalies resulting from chance and variability could form the subject matter of true science, for "there can be no demonstrative knowledge of the fortuitous."[43] Nicole Oresme's *De causis mirabilium* (ca. 1370) shows how it was possible for Scholastic philosophers to simultaneously maintain that individual prodigies were wholly natural but nonetheless not susceptible to scientific explanation: "Therefore these things are not known point by point, except by God alone, who knows unlimited things. And why does a black hair appear on the head right next to a white one? Who can know so small a difference in cause?"[44] Well into the seventeenth century, natural philosophy continued to restrict its investigations to common experience.[45]

41. See Daston, "Baconian Facts, Academic Civility, and the Prehistory of Objectivity," *Annals of Scholarship* (forthcoming), and "The Factual Sensibility," review of *The Origins of Museums,* ed. Impey and MacGregor, *Tradescant's Rarities: Essays on the Foundation of the Ashmolean Museum, 1683,* ed. MacGregor, and *The Ashmolean Museum, 1683–1894,* by Ovenell, *Isis* 79 (Sept. 1988): 452–67.

42. Aristotle, *Metaphysics,* 1027a20–27.

43. Aristotle, *Posterior Analytics,* 87b19–20.

44. Hansen, *Nicole Oresme and the Marvels of Nature,* p. 279.

45. See Peter Dear, "*Totius in verba:* Rhetoric and Authority in the Early Royal Society," *Isis* 76 (June 1985): 145–61, and "Jesuit Mathematical Science and the Reconstitution of Experience in the Early Seventeenth Century," *Studies in History and Philosophy of Science* 18 (June 1987): 133–75, on the transformation of the scholastic conception of experience.

Aristotelian natural philosophy shunned not only singular events, but all particulars, however commonplace, unless these led to generalizations and the discovery of causes.[46] The proper domain of particulars, of facts, as they came to be called, was history, not philosophy: "The register of *Knowledge of Fact* is called *History*. Whereof there be two sorts: one called *Naturall History;* which is the History of such Facts, or Effects of Nature. . . . The other is *Civill History;* which is the History of the Voluntary Actions of men in Common-wealths."[47] History could contribute the raw materials and illustrations to natural philosophy—thus Aristotle's *History of Animals* was to prepare the way for a philosophical zoology—but by itself it was an inferior sort of knowledge, subordinated to the study of universals in philosophy or poetry.[48] Jurisprudence, like history, also relied predominantly on facts and inferences from them, rather than on universals and demonstrations about them. However, this was simply proof positive of the inferiority of legal reasoning, even in the view of the jurists themselves.[49]

This does not mean that Aristotelian philosophy was not empirical, only that its empiricism was not of facts, in the sense of deracinated particulars untethered to any theory or explanation. Examples drawn from daily experience pepper the pages of Aristotelian treatises in natural philosophy, but they are just that—examples, and mundane ones at that. Examples illuminate or illustrate a general claim or theory; counter-examples contradict these claims only when an alternative universal lies ready at hand. Examples do not float free of an argumentative context;[50] they are, in our parlance, evidence rather than facts. To have served up particulars, even prosaic ones, without an explanatory sauce would have thereby demoted natural philosophy to natural history. To have served up preternatural particulars would have added insult to injury in the view not only of orthodox Aristotelians but also of innovators who, like Galileo or Descartes, still upheld the demonstrative ideal of science.[51]

Only a reformer intent on destroying this ideal, as well as specific claims of Aristotelian natural philosophy, would have been able to embrace preternatural particulars with open arms, and such was Francis Bacon. Impatient with Scholastic logic and scornful of the syllogism as an instrument for the investigation of nature, Bacon also challenged the validity of the axioms on which Aristotelian demonstrations were

46. See Aristotle, *Parts of Animals*, 639a13–640a10.
47. Thomas Hobbes, *Leviathan*, ed. C. B. Macpherson (1651; Harmondsworth, 1981), p. 148.
48. See Aristotle, *Poetics*, 1451b1–7.
49. See, for example, Jean Domat, *Les Loix civiles dans leur ordre naturel*, 2d ed., 3 vols. (Paris, 1696–97), 2:346–47.
50. I owe this view of scholastic empiricism to a paper by Joan Cadden on Albertus Magnus, to my knowledge never published.
51. See Daston, "Baconian Facts, Academic Civility, and the Prehistory of Objectivity."

grounded. Human nature being what it is, we rashly generalize our axioms from an experience too scanty to reveal the true rules and species of nature.[52] Bacon prescribed a cautionary dose of natural history to correct these prematurely formed axioms. Nor would ordinary natural history of what happens always or most of the time ("nature in course") suffice, for common experience does not probe nature deeply enough. Natural philosophers must also collect "*Deviating* instances, such as the errors of nature, or strange and monstrous objects, in which nature deviates and turns from her ordinary course" (*NO,* 14:138/ii. 29). In short, natural philosophy would have to take not only particulars, but preternatural particulars seriously.

Bacon's grounds for studying the preternatural were metaphysical as well as epistemological. Although he still spoke the language of "nature in course" and "nature erring," he also initiated a unified and thoroughgoing determinism. Dissolving the ontological barriers between natural and artificial, and between natural and preternatural, Bacon insisted that natural philosophy explain all such phenomena, and all by appeal to the same kind of causes. In particular, marvels and prodigies were no longer exempted from scientific explanation: "Nor should we desist from inquiry, until the properties and qualities of those things, which may be deemed miracles, as it were, of nature, be reduced to, and comprehended in, some form or certain law; so that all irregularity or singularity may be found to depend on some common form" (*NO,* 14:137/ii. 29). A due attention to preternatural phenomena would also act as an epistemological brake to over-hasty axioms and, Bacon further believed, offer privileged insights into the essential but often hidden workings of nature; they would "reveal common forms" as well as "rectify the understanding in opposition to common habit" (*NO,* 14:138/ii. 29).

Baconian facts were new not because they were particulars, nor even because they were preternatural. Particulars were the stuff of history, natural and civil, and expressly preternatural particulars had been a staple of both sorts of history since Herodotus and Pliny.[53] They were new because they now belonged to natural philosophy, expanding its realm beyond the universal and the commonplace. Within natural philosophy they supplemented the empiricism of examples used to confirm and instruct with a collection of counterexamples that were a standing reproach to all extant theories. Indeed, Baconian facts were handpicked for their recalcitrance, anomalies that undermined superficial classifications and exceptions that broke glib rules. This is why the first scientific facts retailed in the annals

52. See Francis Bacon, *Novum organum,* in *The Works of Francis Bacon,* ed. Basil Montagu, 17 vols. (1620; London, 1825–34), 14:34/i. 28, 73–74/i. 104; hereafter abbreviated *NO.*

53. See Charles William Fornara, *The Nature of History in Ancient Greece and Rome* (Berkeley, 1983), pp. 96–97.

of the Royal Society of London and the Paris Académie des Sciences were often such strange ones, for natural philosophy required the shock of repeated contact with the bizarre, the heteroclite, and the singular in order to sunder the age-old link between "a datum of experience" and "the conclusions that may be based on it"; in other words, to sunder facts from evidence.

Thus in the course of the sixteenth and seventeenth centuries preternatural phenomena swung from the almost-supernatural extreme of portents to the almost-natural extreme of Baconian facts. They began as signs par excellence and ended as stubbornly insignificant. The crucial step in this astonishing transformation was the naturalization of preternatural phenomena. However, it would be a mistake to conclude that Spencer, Casaubon, and others who attacked the portentous interpretation of prodigies were always or even usually asserting the autonomy and inviolability of natural laws, à la David Hume. First, these so-called naturalizers countenanced the most unnatural of natural causes in their attempts to debunk false miracles. Pietro Pomponazzi's *De naturalium effectuum causis; sive, De incantationibus* (1556) explained putative miraculous cures and apparitions by causes almost as wondrous: occult virtues of animals, plants, and humans; astral influences; the power of the imagination on animate and inanimate bodies.[54] Bacon was equally willing to grasp at the imagination as a natural alternative to a supernatural explanation. Reviewing stories about corpses bleeding anew in the presence of their murderers, he commented: "It may be, that this participateth of a miracle, by God's just judgment, who usually bringeth murders to light: but if it be natural, it must be referred to imagination."[55]

Second, the structure of natural causes was not always mechanical or even deterministic. Spencer, for example, invoked the metaphor of natural law, but so literally that nature, like human legislators, was granted considerable freedom to make exceptions: "the more private and common Laws of Motion" only hold until superseded by "some more catholick and indispensable Laws . . . as the Statutes and Customs of private Corporations take place, till their power be suspended by some more catholick and inforcing Law of State" (*DCP*, p. 5). Similarly, when he likened nature to clockwork, it was a mechanism whose "blind and decaying Powers must be managed and perpetually woond up by an Hand of Power and Counsel, or they will either stand still, or perform their motions without time and method" (*DCP*, p. 136).

Thirdly, a natural explanation did not always preclude a preternatural or supernatural one. The cause of a monstrous birth might be both

54. See Pietro Pomponazzi, *De naturalium effectuum causis; sive, De incantationibus* (1556; Hildesheim, 1970).

55. Bacon, *Sylva Sylvarum: or, A Natural History in Ten Centuries* [1627], in *The Works of Francis Bacon*, 4:516–17.

the bestiality of the parents *and* divine displeasure at such sinful acts.[56] The doctrine of providence was based on the assumption that primary and secondary causes sometimes worked in tandem to "bring about striking accidents or coincidences."[57] Natural philosophers from Jean Buridan through John Evelyn believed that comets were due to natural causes *and* foretold the death of kings. Since God controlled the natural and moral orders, there was no reason for him not to synchronize them.[58] Thus sixteenth- and seventeenth-century naturalism was synonymous neither with strict mechanical materialism nor with ironclad determinism nor with the autonomy of secondary causes. The impulses that eventually made it so were as much political and theological as philosophical, as the debate over the evidence of miracles reveals.

4. The Pure Evidence of Miracles

The idealized miracle of the seventeenth-century theologians takes place in the pages of Bacon's unfinished utopia, *The New Atlantis*. The governor of the island of Bensalem explains to his shipwrecked guests how the islanders were converted to Christianity by "a great pillar of light," topped by a still-brighter cross at sea, which one of the wise men of Solomon's House certified as a genuine heavenly sign with the following prayer:

> "Lord God of heaven and earth, thou hast vouchsafed of thy grace, to those of our order, to know thy works of creation, and the secrets of them; and to discern, as far as appertaineth to the generations of men, between divine miracles, works of nature, works of art, and impostures and illusions of all sorts. I do here acknowledge and testify before this people, that the thing which we now see before our eyes, is thy finger, and a true miracle; and forasmuch as we learn in our books, that thou never workest miracles, but to a divine and excellent end, for the laws of nature are thine own laws, and thou exceedest them not but upon great cause, we most humbly beseech thee to prosper this great sign, and to give us the interpretation and use of it in mercy; which thou dost in some part secretly promise by sending it unto us."[59]

This fictional (and atypical, since unrelated to healing) miracle includes almost all of the elements that preoccupied seventeenth-century writers on miracles. First, the miracle is a public rather than a private sign, on display for all the people of Bensalem to inspect and wonder at. Tradi-

---

56. See Ambroise Paré, *Des monstres et prodiges*, ed. Céard (1573; Geneva, 1971), p. 4.
57. Thomas, *Religion and the Decline of Magic*, p. 80.
58. Ibid., p. 91.
59. Bacon, *New Atlantis* [1627], in *The Works of Francis Bacon*, 2:336.

tionally, private revelations, particularly sudden conversions, had counted as miracles, and many biblical miracles were directed at select persons or groups.[60] However, many seventeenth-century theologians, particularly Protestant theologians intent on discrediting sacramental miracles, insisted on "a public and visible demonstration."[61] Second, experts (here the members of the House of Solomon) are needed to distinguish the supernatural from the preternatural, natural, and artifical, and to guard against fraud. Since the members of the House of Solomon actually experiment with "all manner of feats of juggling, false apparitions, impostures, and illusions" that might be disguised "to make them seem more miraculous,"[62] we may assume that Bacon himself was primarily concerned with human fraud. His contemporaries, however, also warned against demonic fraud, though still achieved by manipulation of natural causes. Third, God ideally delivers the proper interpretation of the miracle on the spot, in the form of revealed doctrine (the Bensalemites receive a box containing the Old and New Testaments, plus an explanatory letter from St. Bartholomew), which forestalls conjecture and dispute. These three elements—publicity, inspection for fraud, and interpretation in light of doctrine—defined the seventeenth-century concept of the miracle as evidence. I shall discuss each in turn, showing how all three tended to shift the focus of seventeenth-century debate from the evidence *of* miracles to the evidence *for* miracles.

It is striking that those seventeenth-century writers most exercised by the topic of miracles were those who insisted that miracles had long ago ceased. Protestants challenged by Catholics to produce miracles in attestation of their reformed faith retorted that there was no need for God to confirm the revelations of Christianity anew, for the Protestants meant to reinforce, not break with the teachings of the Bible.[63] Although there was some internecine wrangling as to exactly when miracles had ceased,[64] that they had done so many centuries ago was above dispute for Protestant authors. Edward Stillingfleet inquired rhetorically, "What imaginable necessity or pretext can there be contrived for a power of miracles, especially among such as already own the *Divine revelation* of the *Scriptures?*" It would be otiose for God to heap miracle on miracle in order to re-prove

60. See Romano Guardini, "Das Wunder als Zeichen," in *Studien und Berichte der Katholischen Akademie in Bayern*, Heft 17, *Wunder und Magie* (Würzburg, 1962), pp. 75–93.

61. See John Tillotson, "Jesus the Son of God Proved by His Resurrection," *Tillotson's Sermons*, ed. G. W. Weldon (London, 1886), p. 372.

62. Bacon, *New Atlantis*, 2:375.

63. Although this view had Augustinian antecedents, it was vigorously revived by Calvin during the reformation: see Jean Calvin, "Epistre," *Institution de la religion chrestienne* (n. p., 1541).

64. See, for example, William Whiston, *Account of the exact time when miraculous gifts ceas'd in the church* (London, 1749).

the proven, "meerly for satisfaction of mens *vain curiosities*."[65] John Tillotson had a similarly parsimonious interpretation of God's miracle-working: "when the end is obtained, the means cease; and the wise God, who is never wanting in what is necessary, does not use to be lavish in that which is superfluous."[66]

Yet their very preoccupation with explaining why miracles could no longer be expected drove Protestant theologians to develop a new view of miracles as evidence: if miracles were proofs, how and what did they prove? Many medieval miracles were probative, certifying the sanctity of persons and the authenticity of relics.[67] Many others, however, presupposed and confirmed faith rather than compelling it.[68] Biblical miracles sometimes converted the skeptical as well as confirmed the faithful, but their evidence was not irresistible, for some remained unconvinced or at least unresolved—not all who witnessed Christ's miracles and those of the martyrs became Christians, and even Christ's disciples deserted him at his trial and execution. What I shall call the evidentiary school of seventeenth-century Protestant theology narrowed the function of miracles to that of providing irrefragable evidence for the truth of Christian revelation.[69] Some argued that miracles were only part of the evidence for the truth of Christianity,[70] but the general tendency was to concentrate ever more exclusively on the evidence of miracles, if only because "*an extraordinary message to the world, in the name of, and by commission of God*" demanded "more then ordinary *evidence* of such *authority*" (*OS*, p. 142). At the same time that preternatural events were losing all their evidentiary associations, supernatural events were strengthening theirs.

Not just any kind of evidence would do: a miracle was a "supernatural Effect evident and wonderful to Sense" (*WJT*, 2:495). Tillotson offered this definition with an eye toward excluding the sacramental miracles of the Catholics; later writers such as Stillingfleet also used it to exclude the private revelation of the fanatic or enthusiast: "this *inward sense* can be no *ground* to another person to *believe* his *doctrine divine*, because ... it is impossible to another person to distinguish the *actings* of the *divine Spirit* from strong *impressions* of *fancy* by the *force* and *energy* of them" (*OS*, p.

65. Edward Stillingfleet, *Origines sacrae, or a Rational Account of the Grounds of Christian Faith, as to the Truth and Divine Authority of the Scriptures, And the matters therein contained* (London, 1663), pp. 140, 147; hereafter abbreviated *OS*.

66. Tillotson, "The General and Effectual Publication of the Gospel by the Apostles," *Tillotson's Sermons*, p. 236.

67. See Sumption, *Pilgrimage*, pp. 39, 70.

68. See Campbell, *The Witness and the Other World*, pp. 31–33.

69. For a full account of the evidentiary school of British theology as background to the later debate over the existence of miracles, see R. M. Burns, *The Great Debate on Miracles: From Joseph Glanvill to David Hume* (Lewisburg, Pa., 1981).

70. See Tillotson, *The Works of the Most Reverend Dr. John Tillotson*, 3d ed., 2 vols. (London, 1722), 2:501; hereafter abbreviated *WJT*; and Casaubon, *Of Credulity and Incredulity in Things Divine and Spiritual* (London, 1670), p. 116.

143). Thus sudden conversions and other inward visitations of grace ceased to be miraculous by the new evidentiary criteria. John Toland went so far as to brand all such secret miracles as false.[71]

However, the evidence of miracles was more than a spectacular appeal to the senses. Ideally, it was pure evidence, unequivocal in its interpretation, and irresistible in its persuasive power. The evidence of miracles straddled the distinction between the "internal" evidence of things and the "external" evidence of testimony, a distinction that was to dominate later debates over the evidence for miracles in the late seventeenth and early eighteenth centuries.[72] The evidence of miracles was internal, insofar as it was a thing or event. Moreover, its internal evidence, read off from the very nature of the event, was of a special sort, pointing unmistakably to supernatural agency, just as fingerprints point to a certain hand. At the same time, the evidence of miracles was external, a form of testimony from God that the miracle-worker's message was an authentic revelation. In both cases, the evidence of miracles was saturated with intention, God's intention to suspend the natural order to certify his messenger, and God's intention to establish certain doctrines. Because miracles accompanied doctrine, their meaning was clear; because God was the author of miracles, they proved beyond a shadow of a doubt.

However, the faith in pure evidence was short lived. The evidentiary theologians soon became preoccupied with the question, "What distinguished a true miracle from a false one?" Definitions of miracles proliferated in the late seventeenth century, as theologians and natural philosophers groped for some clear-cut criterion. The very number and diversity of these definitions testifies to their failure to find such. Almost every imaginable position found a supporter; a few examples from major writers suffice to suggest the breadth of opinion and the lack of agreement.

Tillotson asserted a miracle must be a "supernatural Effect," but admitted that since angels and demons can "exceed any natural Power known to us," their works would often be indistinguishable from those of God (*WJT*, 2:496). Casaubon eluded the problem of distinguishing supernatural and natural effects by reasserting the Augustinian position that there was nothing so ordinary "but, if looked into Philosophically, did

71. See Toland, *Christianity Not Mysterious* (1696; Stuttgart-Bad Canstatt, 1964), p. 155. On Toland's ambiguous position on miracles, see Robert E. Sullivan, *John Toland and the Deist Controversy: A Study in Adaptations* (Cambridge, Mass., 1982), pp. 128, 223.

72. The *locus classicus* of the distinction is Antoine Arnauld and Pierre Nicole, *La Logique, ou l'art de penser*, ed. Pierre Clair and Francois Girbal (1662; Paris; 1965), p. 340. On the significance of the distinction for seventeenth-century conceptions of evidence, see Ian Hacking, *The Emergence of Probability: A Philosophical Study of Early Ideas about Probability, Induction and Statistical Reference* (Cambridge, 1975), chaps. 1–5. On its role in the later debate over miracles, see Daston, *Classical Probability in the Enlightenment* (Princeton, N. J., 1988), chap. 6, sect. 3.

afford me a miracle," in the sense of being inexplicable.[73] Joseph Glanvill confronted the difficulty head-on, and pronounced it irresoluble,

> for we are ignorant of the *Extent* and *Bounds* of *Natures Sphere,* and possibilities; and if this were the *Character* and *essential Mark* of a Miracle, we could not know what was *so;* except we could determine the *Extent* of Natural causalities, and fix their *Bounds,* and be able to say to *Nature, Hitherto canst thou go, and no farther.*

Hence Glanvill required that putative miracles not only exceed the known powers of nature but also be performed by "Persons of Simplicity, Truth, and Holiness, void of Ambition, and all *secular Designs*" (*ST,* p. 52). Fleetwood thought it was enough that miracles violated the "setled Laws of Nature," these latter being observationally defined as "Operations that are constant, certain, and expected" (*EM,* p. 2). Samuel Clarke was more cautious than Fleetwood in qualifying "the Course of Nature" as the "perfectly *Arbitrary*" workings of divine will, "as easie to be *altered* at any time, as to be *preserved,*" but also opted for a rarity criterion: "'tis only *usualness* or *unusualness* that makes the distinction."[74] John Locke faced these epistemological difficulties squarely, and retreated to the subjective appreciation of the miracle, defined as a "sensible operation, which, being above the comprehension of the spectator, and in his opinion contrary to the established course of nature, is taken by him to be divine."[75]

These definitions were always convoluted and often circular or self-contradictory to boot. Only the intensity of the desire for such a hard-and-fast criterion can explain the willingness to wrestle with definitions that could not command internal consistency, much less consensus. What drove these writers into the definitional quagmire was the threat of false miracles; what altered in the course of the debate was not the fear of being deceived, but rather the identity of the suspected deceiver.

Increasingly in the last quarter of the seventeenth century, the enemy was the enthusiast rather than the devil. In the middle decades of the seventeenth century, the devil was still a force to reckon with: Browne contended that Satan counterfeited miracles to spread idolatry and superstition;[76] Pascal was deeply disquieted by the Jesuit insinuation that the Port-Royal miracle of the Sacred Thorn was a demonic imposture;[77]

---

73. Casaubon, *Of Credulity and Incredulity in Things Divine and Spiritual,* p. 107.

74. Samuel Clarke, *A Discourse Concerning the Being and Attributes of God, the Obligations of Natural Religion, and the Truth and Certainty of the Christian Revelation* [Boyle lectures of 1705], 8th ed. (London, 1732), pp. 377, 375; hereafter abbreviated *D.*

75. John Locke, *A Discourse of Miracles,* in *The Works of John Locke,* 10 vols. (London, 1823), 9:256.

76. See Browne, *Pseudodoxia Epidemica,* chaps. 10–11.

77. See Blaise Pascal, "Le Miracle de la Sainte Épine," in *Oeuvres complètes,* ed. Fortunat Strowski, 3 vols. (Paris, 1923–31), 2:434–50.

Glanvill warned that witches and evil spirits could simulate miracles with "wonderful Combinations of *natural Causes*" (*ST*, p. 52). But already in the 1660s the devil had yielded the title of Great Deceiver to enthusiasts, both sincere and feigned. Long before Shaftesbury called on a witness in favor of a "new Prophesying Sect" and its purported miracles to prove himself "wholly free of melancholy, and . . . incapable of all Enthusiasm besides,"[78] portents and miracles had become associated among the learned with "all the common causes of deceit, *Superstition, Melancholy, natural weakness of sight, softness of imagination*" and other flaws of body and soul (*DCP*, p. 183). To judge from Clarke's 1705 Boyle lectures, even Christ was in some circles suspected of baneful enthusiasm (see *D*, p. 373).

The deep-seated anxiety about imposture, both diabolical and human, was simply the obverse of the emphasis on miracles as evidence. For the evidentiary theologians, the truth of Christian revelation was chiefly supported "by the many infallible *Signs and Miracles*, which the Author of it worked publickly as the Evidence of his Divine Commission" (*D*, p. 372).[79] Miracles were God's signature, "the greatest testimony of *Divine authority* and *revelation*" (*OS*, p. 139). However, in contrast to most testimonial evidence, what must be proved is not the trustworthiness but rather the identity of the witness, for once God's identity was established, absolute trustworthiness followed necessarily for seventeenth-century theologians.[80] Since belief in revelation and, conversely, rejection of heresy was in their view the gravest of human duties, no pain should be spared in distinguishing divine signatures from forgeries. Fleetwood went so far as to make the miracle itself subsidiary to the signature, advising his readers that "you are under no obligation of Necessity, to believe all that a Man shall say, who works Miracles, without declaring he is sent of God, and telling you, that God has given him that miraculous Power, in order to obtain Credit with you" (*EM*, p. 117). Confident that God always provides "sufficient marks" for the "impartial Enquirers after Truth" to distinguish true from false miracles (*WJT*, 2:499), the theologians sought the signs that would validate the "Signs and Wonders." The claim that miracles were irrefutable evidence thus led willy-nilly to the demand for still further evidence that the miracles in question were genuine.

The clinching evidence for the authenticity of an ambiguous miracle was doctrinal. As we have seen, both the objective criterion of supernatural causation and the subjective criterion of wonder dissolved under the scrutiny of seventeenth-century theologians: too little was known of nature to locate the boundary between natural and supernatural causes,

---

78. [Shaftesbury], *A Letter Concerning Enthusiasm, to My Lord* ***** (London, 1708), pp. 68–69.

79. See also *WJT*, 2:498, and *OS*, pp. 138–39.

80. Sometimes, however, theologians entertained the possibility that God might allow false prophecies to be fulfilled to "try the People's Faith and Constancy" (*EM*, p. 57).

an uncertainty exacerbated rather than mitigated by the discoveries of the new natural philosophy; too much was known of the uncritical human tendency to wonder at the wrong objects to lodge much confidence in admiration and astonishment. Their solution was to let doctrine certify the miracle, just as miracles certified the doctrine: "For it is my Opinion, that the Doctrine, in general at least, should always be first laid down, and then the Miracle be wrought to give the Messenger Authority and Credit to establish it in People's Minds; which would prevent all manner of Abuses of any Accidental Miracles" (*EM,* p. 63).[81]

The evidentialists were well aware of the potential circularity of this criterion, but insisted that the tautology was only apparent. Pascal summed up the problem in a laconic "Règle": "One must judge doctrine by miracles, and one must judge miracles by doctrine. All of this is true, but not contradictory. For it is necessary to distinguish the times [*distinguer les temps*]."[82] The English evidentialists wriggled out of the difficulty by arguing that it was only the *kind* of doctrine which had to pass muster, not the specifics of its content. The doctrine must be inaccessible to human reason, for otherwise it need not be vouchsafed as revelation; moreover, it must not tend to promote idolatry and other impieties: "*If* the Doctrine attested by Miracles, be in it self *impious,* or manifestly *tending to promote Vice;* then without all question the Miracles, how great soever they may appear to Us, are neither worked by God himself, nor by his Commission" (*D,* p. 382). However, the elasticity of the term *impious,* which could be stretched to encompass all that contradicted a particular orthodoxy, blurred the boundary between kind and content of miracles that the evidentialists had hoped would protect them from tautology.

In cases of contested doctrine, the evidentiary import of the miracle, even one universally acknowledged to be genuine, was effectively neutralized by competing interpretations. When for example Pascal's niece was cured of a lachrymal fistula by contact with a thorn from the crown of Jesus on 24 March 1656, even the most bitter opponents of the Port-Royal Jansenists submitted to the official decision certifying the miracle as authentic. But whereas Pascal and his allies took the miracle as a divine vindication, their Jesuit critics argued that it was a divine warning to forsake their heresy.[83] The miracle remained a divine sign, but an inscrutable one.

The end result of the doctrinal criterion was to weaken dramatically the evidentiary force of miracles. Miracles alone, no matter how public and palpable to the senses, no longer sufficed to prove a doctrine or messenger heaven-sent. Further proof, in the form of harmony with preexist-

---

81. See *D,* p. 387; *WJT,* 2:498; and Casaubon, *Of Credulity and Incredulity in Things Divine and Spiritual,* p. 120.

82. Quoted in Shiokawa, *Pascal et les miracles,* p. 162.

83. See ibid., pp. 128–29, 136–37.

ing doctrine, was required to establish divine credentials. If the doctrine was disputed, miracles could no longer settle the issue, for they then became signs without clear signification. A miracle unannounced by doctrine was no miracle at all, even if not under suspicion of fraud. Glanvill quoted with approval the Reverend Doctor R. Dean's opinion that the cures performed by Greatrakes, the "Irish Stroker," were " 'more than *ordinary*' " but " 'not miraculous' ": for not only did Greatrakes's patients occasionally suffer relapses, "He pretends not to give *Testimony* to any *Doctrine*" (*ST*, p. 53). Although Locke shook his head over the credulity of the ancients, who accepted their religion without any evidence—that is, without miracles—he was quick to rule out any mission inconsistent with "natural religion and the rules of morality," however wondrous its works.[84] In seventeenth-century evidentiary theology, miracles began as "the principal external Proof and Confirmation of the Divinity of a Doctrine"; they ended as themselves requiring "Proof and Confirmation" from doctrine.

Conclusion: Naturalization and the Reassertion of Authority

Even after miracles had lost their peculiar evidentiary power to compel belief unambiguously and automatically in early eighteenth-century theology, they did not immediately wither away. It took some forty years before the likes of Hume and Voltaire could discuss the problem of miracles as if it were one of the evidence *for* miracles, as opposed to the evidence *of* miracles.[85] However, evidentialist theologians did unintentionally prepare the way for this shift. First, by depriving miracles of evidentiary autonomy, they also deprived them of their ostensive function. If miracles require the evidence of doctrine, who needs the evidence of miracles? Among orthodox British theologians, not to speak of Deists like Toland and Anthony Collins, portents and miracles played an ever more modest role in Christian apologetics. Although none of them would have thought of denying their existence or importance in the early Church, late seventeenth-century theologians assumed an ever more condescending tone toward their predecessors for requiring such a vulgar sort of proof. Whereas Christ had been forced by his motley audience to address "the lower faculties of the Soul, phancy and imagination" with showy miracles, nowadays "all things are to be managed in a more sedate, cool, and silent manner," by invoking "steady and calm arguments" (*DCP*, p. 27–28). Just because miracles were "such sensible Demonstrations," they penetrated

---

84. Locke, *A Discourse of Miracles*, 9:261.
85. See Voltaire, "Miracles," *Dictionnaire philosophique*, in *Oeuvres complètes* (1764; Paris, 1783), 42:88–113, and David Hume, "On Miracles," *Essays Moral, Political and Literary* (1741–42; London, 1963).

even "the *weakest* Judgments and *strongest* Imaginations," but the enlightened had no need of them (*D*, p. 403).[86]

This lofty manner points to the second unintentional contribution evidentialist theology made to the frontal attack on the very existence of miracles. By associating miracles with the bumptious and unlettered, they anticipated Hume's guilt-by-association argument that wonders proliferated most among the ignorant and barbarous. Thus Casaubon thought it necessary to apologize for St. Augustine's credulity in matters marvelous as unbecoming an educated man: "It may be, *St. Augustine* may be thought by some, to have been somewhat more credulous in this point of strange relations, then became so wise, so Learned, and judicious a man, as certainly he was: neither do I think my self bound to believe all things in this kind, which he may be thought by his words to have believed."[87] More dangerously, miracles had come to be linked with rabble-rousing enthusiasts, who sincerely or maliciously pretended to a divine mission in order to undermine the powers-that-be. This was one of Stillingfleet's most telling arguments for the cessation of miracles, for otherwise public order would be at the mercy of "an innumerable company of *croaking Enthusiasts* [who] would be continually pretending *commissions* from heaven" (*OS*, p. 109).

Although Catholic theologians in principle did not subscribe to the doctrine of the cessation of miracles, nor to the claim that miracles must be palpable to the senses, they were in practice as concerned about the destabilizing effects, theological and political, of alleged miracles as their Protestant colleagues. The Council of Trent stiffened the evidentiary requirements for miracles, and placed the responsibility for a thorough investigation in the hands of the local bishop, with the intent of reining in the deviations of popular religion.[88] Both the reasoning behind and the execution of the new regulations closely paralleled Protestant developments. Catholic reformers emphasized the need to distinguish between true religion and superstition, and since they further contended that superstitions were the work of the devil, the problem boiled down to distinguishing genuine miracles from demonic counterfeits. So rigorous were the diocesan investigations that the number of certified miracles in France declined precipitously in the second half of the seventeenth century.[89] Those that did pass through the fine sieve of official scrutiny were backed by so much legal and medical evidence that historian Jean de Viguerie has argued that they are among the best-documented historical

---

86. See also Casaubon, *Of Credulity and Incredulity in Things Divine and Spiritual*, p. 10.

87. Ibid., p. 116.

88. See Delumeau, *Un Chemin d'histoire: Chrétienté et christianisation* (Paris, 1981), p. 194.

89. See Jean de Viguerie, "Le Miracle dans la France du XVIIe siècle," *XVIIe siècle* 35 (July–Sept. 1983): 313–31.

facts of the early modern period.[90] However, as for Protestants, doctrine steered Catholic deliberations over evidence, no matter how solid and copious the latter. Hume noted that the healing miracles performed in the Parisian parish of Saint-Médard in 1731 were immeasurably better confirmed than those of Christ and his disciples,[91] but after a meticulous investigation the Archbishop Vintimille condemned the Saint-Médard cures for fostering Jansensism and "subvert[ing] the natural, established order of the Church."[92] De facto if not de jure, the Catholic church also subscribed to the doctrine of the cessation of miracles, and for much the same reasons that John Calvin had, namely, that miracles "could disturb and arouse doubts in a mind that would otherwise be tranquil [*en repos*]."[93]

The reaffirmation of political and religious authority reflected in the official dismissal of unsettling portents and miracles on both sides of the Channel had its theological analogue in the centralization of divine power, especially in Protestant writings. Both the natural and, particularly, the preternatural domains lost territory as a result. Robert Boyle attacked natural philosophers who granted nature an unseemly amount of autonomy by endowing it with plastic powers and capricious deviations; nature was simply brute, passive matter set in motion and sustained by God.[94] Neither mechanistic nor Newtonian natural philosophy necessarily promoted nature's independence and the inviolability of natural law. As Clarke put it in his Boyle lectures of 1705, "what Men commonly call the *Course of Nature*, or the *Power of Nature*" is simply the "*Will of God*" which "is as easie to be *altered* at any time, as to be *preserved*" (*D,* p. 377).

The preternatural had depended crucially on insubordination to divine decree, both nature's and the devil's, and therefore virtually disappeared as a result of God's new, tightened regime. Although few went so far as to deny the devil's existence, he was, like nature, put on a very short leash. Clarke thought God could at least partially restrain evil spirits (see *D,* p. 391), and Fleetwood essentially demoted the devil to God's lieutenant, "for his Power or Impotence, it depends entirely on God, how far he will restrain or limit him" (*EM,* p. 50). By granting God a monopoly on agency in the universe, late seventeenth-century Protestant theologians, at least English ones, radically simplified ontology as well. Spinoza's pantheistic critique of miracles was a scandal because it merged God with nature, but the simplifying ontological tendencies of the *Tractatus theologico-politicus* (1670), as well as the contempt for the low understanding of the "masses," were echoed in numerous, more orthodox works.

90. Ibid., p. 316.

91. See Hume, "On Miracles."

92. B. Robert Kreiser, *Miracles, Convulsions, and Ecclesiastical Politics in Early Eighteenth-Century Paris* (Princeton, N. J., 1978), p. 370.

93. Calvin, "Epistre."

94. Robert Boyle, "A Free Inquiry into the Vulgarly Received Notion of Nature," in *Works of the Honourable Robert Boyle,* ed. Thomas Birch, 5 vols. (1685; London, 1744), 4:398.

There were early eighteenth-century voices, most famously Leibniz's, that called for a more aloof relationship between God and his creation, insisting on the integrity of the "laws of nature, and the beautiful pre-established order."[95] Were it not for Newton's equally famous objection to Leibniz, it would be tempting to ascribe this vision of a determined, immutable nature wholly to the successes of late seventeenth-century natural philosophy, most notably to those of Newton himself. However, the impulse for naturalization had other sources besides natural philosophy, or even metaphysics.[96] The motives behind excluding miracles in principle, as Leibniz and many eighteenth-century philosophes did, and excluding them in practice, as many devout Protestant and Catholic theologians did, sometimes converged in a form of naturalization. Pierre Bayle, ridiculing portentous interpretations of the comet of 1682, argued that the ordinary laws of nature were sufficient to show the will and benevolence of God, whereas natural phenomena cried up as portents merely misled the people into superstition and idolatry.[97] In addition to the usual naturalizing maxims that, in Thomas Burnet's words, to shift explanations from God's ordinary to his extraordinary providence was "but, as the Proverb says, to rob *Peter* to pay *Paul*,"[98] Bayle contended that a naturalized religion was also a sounder religion.

In view of the often subversive uses to which portents and miracles were often put, it is not surprising to find more candid arguments that a naturalized religion was a safer, more pleasant one as well. Spencer complained that a religion rife with portents was incompatible with "the peace and tranquility of common life," for *"how can a man, as he is councelled,* eat his bread with joy, and drink his wine with a chearful heart (Eccles. 9.7); *if every strange accident must perswade him that there is some sword of vengeance hanging over his head"* (*DCP*, fig. A4v). Stillingfleet ruled out the possibility of new revelations, supported by new miracles, on grounds of inconvenience: "For if *God* may still make new *articles of faith*, or constitute new *duties* by fresh *miracles,* I must go and enquire what *miracles* are wrought in every *place,* to see that I miss nothing that may be *necessary* for me, in order to my happiness in another world" (*OS*, pp. 147–48). A hankering for peace and quiet was by no means the only reason for promoting the naturalization of marvels and miracles, but it was a powerful one. A great deal of the rhapsodizing over law-abiding, commonplace nature that filled

95. *The Leibniz-Clarke Correspondence*, ed. H. G. Alexander (1717; Manchester, 1970), p. 12.

96. The metaphysical grounds were most powerfully argued in Benedict Spinoza, *A Theological-Political Treatise* [*Tractatus theologico-politicus*], in *The Chief Works of Benedict de Spinoza*, trans. R. H. M. Elwes, 2 vols. (New York, 1951), 1:84.

97. See Pierre Bayle, *Pensées diverses, écrites à un docteur de Sorbonne, à l'occasion de la comète qui parut au mois de décembre 1680* (Rotterdam, 1683), pp. 256–57, 700–708.

98. Thomas Burnet, *The Sacred Theory of the Earth* (1691; London, 1965), p. 221.

the writings of the natural theologians appealed to the desire for a calm religious life, free from nasty surprises and inspired upstarts.

Scientific facts also became more regular and more commonplace, although the transition from bizarre singularities to mundane universals was a gradual and uneven one.[99] However, even after scientific facts had been domesticated, the distinction between facts and evidence remained part of the conceptual framework of natural science, often contested (starting with Descartes and continuing to the present day) but never completely extirpated. Long after scientific facts ceased to be the anomalies and exceptions Bacon used to destroy Aristotelian axioms and natural kinds, they retained their reputation for orneriness. The portentous-sign-turned-scientific-fact left deeply etched traces in our way of thinking about evidence. In contrast, the contributions of the evidentiary miracle were not so long lived. Before worries first over demonic counterfeits and later over human enthusiasm reduced miracles to rubber-stamping extant doctrine, miracles seemed the purest form of evidence: their meaning was patent to all who had eyes to see, and they compelled belief as irresistibly as a mathematical demonstration—indeed, more so, since they required neither the training nor the concentration of a mathematician. Miracles were God's privy seal and letters patent, certifying a doctrine as divine and thereby convincing onlookers of its truth. Ideally, miracles were transparent, requiring no interpretation, and were as satisfying to the senses and to the imagination as to reason.

This dream of pure evidence evaporated with the division of evidence into the internal evidence of things and the external evidence of testimony, which division structured the debate over the evidence *for* miracles.[100] The pure evidence of miracles, at least as conceived in the mid-seventeenth century, straddled the line between internal and external evidence: as sensible events miracles belonged to the realm of things, but as supernatural events they also bore witness. They were the last form of evidence compatible with intention, in this case divine intention, and it is ironic that suspicions of human intention—that is, the intent to feign miracles in order to usurp political and religious authority—ultimately deprived them of evidentiary value.

99. On this transition, see Daston, "The Cold Light of Facts and the Facts of Cold Light: Luminescence and the Transformation of the Scientific Fact 1600–1750," paper presented to the workshop on "The Technologies of Objectivity," University of California, Los Angeles, February 1990.

100. On the early eighteenth-century debate in general, see Burns, *The Great Debate on Miracles*. On the role played by the distinction between internal and external evidence, see Daston, *Classical Probability in the Enlightenment*, pp. 323–30.

Proving a History of Evidence

James Chandler

Lorraine Daston's "Marvelous Facts and Miraculous Evidence in Early Modern Europe" (pp. 243–74) recounts a key episode in the development of Western evidentiary practices. The essay's frame of reference is the now-commonplace distinction between neutral facts and enlisted evidence. She suggests, plausibly enough, that in the view of many modern inquirers this conceptual relationship makes intelligible the work of "proof." To put the matter in terms only slightly different from her own, *proof*, in our usage, can connote either the testing or the demonstration of theories. Without neutral facts, theories could not be tested; without enlisted evidence, they could not be demonstrated. Where the facts are skewed by an intention to prove a theory, they cease to count as evidence for that theory, though that obviously does not rule out their counting as evidence for something else.

Daston concedes that this conceptual picture is a controversial one, but for reasons unstated she declines to offer a view of its value or validity. She means instead to historicize it. Her questions, she says, are not of the sort, "'Do neutral facts exist?'" but rather of the sort, How did the commonplace distinction "'come to be?'" (p. 244). And it is to answer just this kind of question that she turns to the sixteenth- and seventeenth-century literature on prodigies and miracles. For her, these texts document part of a history; they themselves provide evidence for a "key episode" (p. 244) in a narrative of conceptual change. In ways that are clear enough in the essay, and clearer still in her book on eighteenth-century theories of probability, this narrative eventually issues in a reconceptualization of historical evidence in such Enlightenment texts as David Hume's essay "Of Miracles" (first sketched out in 1748) and Richard Price's 1767 response to it, "On the Importance of Christianity, the Nature of Historical Evidence, and Miracles."[1] Daston's project thus has a curiously reflexive dimension. She enlists her early modern texts as evidence in a history of historical evidence.

In pursuing the questions of its distinctively genetic inquiry, the essay invariably raises others, and my aim here is to formulate some of them. Among these, I will focus on several questions that have to do with the historical particulars of the account; but others, of a more general kind, should not get lost in the shuffle. What, for example, is at stake in the sort of conceptual history that Daston is writing here? Can the empirical component of this kind of history be specified? How might one locate this sort of project in respect to the traditional history of ideas? As for this particular conceptual history, how is its own peculiar course of change to be located; that is, just where might this history be said to take place? Precisely what bearing might it be said to have on the current contestation of the fact-evidence distinction? What bearing might a position on that distinction have on contemporary *Wissenschaften?*

The story Daston actually tells, marvelously well, has a bifurcated plot involving two parallel transformations. One follows the development of the concept of the neutral fact out of the debates on prodigies. The other follows the development of the notion of pure evidence (at once patent to the senses and crucially intentional) out of the debates on miracles. Both involve the unstable concept of the preternatural, which mediated the categories of natural and supernatural in late medieval thought. The twofold utility of the concept of the preternatural to theology and natural philosophy—that is, in relation to the natural and the supernatural—kept it in play long enough for it to be temporarily fortified under those early modern conditions that also made possible the very archive from which Daston cites evidence for her conceptual genesis of the neutral fact. Marsilio Ficino and his active circle begin to introduce elements of magic into the vogue for Neoplatonism and disseminate illustrations of their views; numerous witchcraft trials begin to be prosecuted and recorded; voyages of exploration lead to reports of what Stephen Greenblatt calls "marvelous possessions."[2] Most noteworthy among the new developments, for Daston's purposes, are the Reformation upheav-

---

1. See Lorraine Daston, *Classical Probability in the Enlightenment* (Princeton, N.J., 1988), pp. 296–369.

2. For Greenblatt's mediation of the way marvels were mediated in the writings of the conquistadors, see his discussion of Bernal Díaz as "the go-between" in Stephen Greenblatt, *Marvelous Possessions: The Wonder of the New World* (Chicago, 1991), pp. 119–94.

James Chandler, professor of English at the University of Chicago, is the author of *Wordsworth's Second Nature* (1984). He is currently completing *England in 1819,* studies in and of romantic case history.

als that, from the new publishing centers, generated a flood of printed texts, prodigious in itself, that frequently construed various prodigies and monstrosities as portents and signs of divine praise or blame. These texts, with their remarkable illustrations, comprise the heart of Daston's archive, and she uses them to show how the portentous prodigies represented in these texts, "the very prototype of signifying events," supplied antischolastic philosophers of the school of Francis Bacon with "a new kind of fact that signified nothing at all" (p. 250).

My questions about this part of the argument largely pertain to the issue of explanation, particularly to the levels and character of the causal claims Daston ventures for the conceptual transformation she is tracking. On the one hand, there are obviously linkages to be made between the various cultural developments themselves (the witchcraft trials and the Reformation rivalries, for example). On the other, there are lower levels of specificity in which connections might be made between particular local conditions and particular evidentiary practices; as it is, the whole of "Early Modern Europe" seems to remain the vast field of inquiry here. How then do these explanatory conditions sort with each other? How might they be more precisely identified and correlated with specific discourses? My other questions about this section pertain to evidence, but I will return to them in a different context below.

The line I have just been tracing in Daston's bifurcated narrative concerns the conceptual history of fact. The other concerns a parallel history of the concept of evidence and therefore involves debates over the issue of what, and how, miracles can be said to prove. More specifically, it charts the stages by which the problem of the evidence *of* miracles becomes the problem of the evidence *for* miracles, as that problem will appear, say, in Hume. Daston is particularly interested in the way in which, for what she calls the "evidentiary school of seventeenth-century Protestant theology," miracles momentarily achieved the status of "pure evidence, unequivocal in its interpretation, and irresistible in its persuasive power" (pp. 265, 266). Pure evidence, so conceived, defies the eighteenth-century distinction between internal and external evidence—an opposition that in turn, I would suggest, becomes the basis for the nineteenth-century distinction between "remains" and "sources" for such theorists of historical method as Johann Gustav Droysen.[3] Taken as a thing or an event, the miracle (in Daston's history) once offered compelling internal evidence, the kind of sign that Peirce called an index, a fingerprint of the hand of God, a perfectly preserved relic. Taken as God's testimony, on the other hand, it amounted to compelling external evidence that authenticated the miracle worker's message, an impeccable source.

Of course, this paradigm survived only as long as one did not trouble

---

3. Johann Gustav Droysen, *Outline of the Principles of History* [Grundriss Der Historik], trans. E. Benjamin Andrews (Boston, 1897), pp. 18–21.

to pose and press the metaquestion of what distinguishes true from false miracles. As soon as the evidentialists began to acknowledge that metaquestion, and to propose that doctrine does as much to certify miracles as miracles do to certify doctrine, they prepared the way for the Enlightenment inquiry into the evidence *for* miracles. Daston's narrativization of these intellectual issues by way of the unasked metaquestions is eye-opening, though it raises what might be called a meta-metaquestion: How is it that the questioning of that crucial distinction between true and false miracles, the questioning that seems irrepressible to us now, managed to be suspended at all?

The important last stage of Daston's narrative proper is introduced with a characteristically lucid transition. If what led the evidentialists into definitional confusion was the threat of false miracles, she says, "what altered the course of the debate was not the fear of being deceived, but rather the identity of the suspected deceiver"; as we move toward the end of the century, the enemy becomes "the enthusiast rather than the devil" (p. 267). Since I find this section of the argument immensely suggestive but a bit sketchy as it stands, I want to urge some elaboration. For example, although Daston claims that the devil yielded the title of Great Deceiver to the enthusiasts within a very short span in the mid-seventeenth century, she offers for this no explanation of the sort she supplies for arguably less puzzling changes in the sixteenth century. She mentions that much of the conceptual change is already accomplished in the evidentialist discourse of the 1660s, but although most of her texts here are English, not much reference is made to the English Revolution of 1640–60 or to the Restoration of 1660. She refers to the perception of the enthusiasts as dangerous rabble-rousers, but I want to ask if there is not something peculiar to English social changes in the seventeenth century that inflects the term *enthusiasm* with its new function in the debates. This issue returns us to the problem of local and general explanations in the essay. In this instance, the question could be restated: Is the relation of English and European development sufficiently uneven by the mid-seventeenth century to make the field of early modern Europe something less than fully intelligible as an explanatory domain for these purposes?

Second, more might be said to distinguish calculated deception from self-deception in the narrative according to which enthusiasm displaces the demonic as the evidentialists' enemy. Daston's focus is on the humanization of the *external* (once demonic) deceiver in the evidentialists' accounts. But the credulity that is a condition of being so deceived sometimes amounts to serious participation in the process. Hume, it should be recalled, actually concludes his discussion of miracles with the ironic observation that

the *Christian Religion* not only was at first attended with miracles, but even at this day cannot be believed by any reasonable person without one. Mere reason is insufficient to convince us of its veracity: And whoever is moved by *Faith* to assent to it, is conscious of a continued miracle in his own person, which subverts all the principles of his understanding, and gives him a determination to believe what is most contrary to custom and experience.[4]

Hume's tone is notoriously labile, and the irony of this passage especially cuts both ways; enthusiastic self-deception figures here as a kind of second order miracle, the continued miracle in one's own person of one's susceptibility to believe miracles. This susceptibility is at once a stubborn fact of Western history *and* an evidence of a trait that runs deeper than reason itself in what Hume called human nature. We know, of course, that Hume is perfectly willing to see enthusiasts as deliberate deceivers; he is as trenchant about monkish cynicism as he is about "monkish superstition," as is clear, say, in his account of St. Dunstan's forging of miracles for political purposes early on in *The History of England*.[5] Yet Hume seems less interested in the cynical manipulation of enthusiasm than in the enthusiastic credulity that makes it possible. Indeed, this credulity seems more than a matter of interest to him; it seems to inspire Hume's own reluctant sense of wonder.[6]

My last set of questions pertain to a piece of text unmentioned by Daston but, I think, relevant to her historical account. I adduce it here to call attention to her own evidentiary procedures in this conceptual history of evidence; that is, to see what she herself does with a potentially anomalous fact, how it might become evidence for or against the narrative account she proposes. The passage is by an author Daston cites, the Earl of Shaftesbury, but from *Advice to an Author* (1710), the third treatise collected in his *Characteristicks of Men, Manners, Opinions, Times,* rather than the first, *Letter Concerning Enthusiasm* (1708). It is the discussion of reading, late in the third treatise, and it explicitly addresses the literature of the marvelous and its deleterious effects on contemporary taste: "Our Relish or *Taste* must of necessity grow barbarous, whilst *Barbarian* Customs, *Savage* Manners, *Indian* Wars and Wonders of the *Terra Incognita,* employ our leisure Hours, and are the chief Materials to furnish out a

---

4. David Hume, "Of Miracles," *An Enquiry Concerning Human Understanding,* in *Enquiries Concerning Human Understanding and Concerning the Principles of Morals,* ed. P. H. Nidditch (1777; Oxford, 1975), p. 131.

5. See Hume, *The History of England from the Invasion of Julius Caesar to the Revolution in 1688,* 6 vols. (Indianapolis, 1983), 1:104–5.

6. While on the subject of the *History,* we might also ask what is to be made of Hume's own implicit history of evidence, embedded in his discussion of the evidentiary procedures of the Anglo-Saxon system. See the heading "Rules of Proof" in the first historical appendix, *The History of England,* 1:179–82. Are such passages to be classed as conceptual history? The course Hume charts for the history of evidence is through legal rather than theological discourse. Need its terms be squared with the terms of the present account?

Library."[7] Part of the relevance of Shaftesbury's text to the present discussion is that, like Hume, he employs the language of miracle and wonder to discuss the very belief in miracles:

> THESE [travel tales] are in our present Days, what *Books of Chivalry* were in those of our Forefathers. I know not what *Faith* valiant Ancestors may have in the Storys of their Giants, their Dragons, and St. George's. But for our *Faith* indeed, as well as our *Taste*, in this other way of reading; I must confess I can't consider it, without Astonishment. [*AA*, 1:344]

Where Hume speaks of the sense of the miraculous occasioned by the very credulity in miracles, Shaftesbury expresses astonishment at the very fact of astonishment.

One of the problems posed to Daston's account by Shaftesbury's text is that it does not much respect the distinctions between miracle and marvel, supernatural and preternatural; the miraculous and the monstrous, as they appear in the travel writings Shaftesbury contemns, seem to have roughly the same status. Perhaps this can be explained by its late appearance in the history Daston traces. But Shaftesbury's text is more (to reinvoke Droysen's distinction) than a relic of a late episode in this history; it is also a source for it. That is, it proposes, in the terms of an emergent discourse on taste, its own account of seventeenth-century developments in the literature of marvels. What Daston describes as the "avalanche" (p. 250) of printed marvels in early modern Europe appears (though with emphasis on the travel literature) not so much to be supplying anti-scholastic philosophy with "a new kind of fact" as to be conditioning, culturally, a new kind of sensibility, one that Shaftesbury regards as unfortunate, degenerate, even as itself somehow monstrous.[8]

Shaftesbury has his own evidence to offer: Shakespeare no less. He wittily adduces the courtship scene from *Othello*—the Moor's seduction of Desdemona with tales of wonder—as itself a marvelous sign of things to come:

> THIS Humour [the one that gives rise to the passion for marvelous tales] our old *Tragick Poet* seems to have discover'd. He hit our *Taste* in giving us a *Moorish* Hero, full fraught with Prodigy; a wondrous *Story-Teller!* But for the attentive Part, the Poet chose to give it to Woman-kind. What passionate Reader of *Travels*, or student in the

7. Anthony Ashley Cooper, Third Earl of Shaftesbury, *Soliloquy: Or, Advice to an Author,* in *Characteristicks of Men, Manners, Opinions, Times*, 3 vols. (1711; London, 1737), 1:344; hereafter abbreviated *AA*.

8. This notion of an intellectual monstrosity that develops as a concomitant of the study of monsters becomes clearer elsewhere in *Characteristicks* when Shaftesbury describes the figure of the scholarly "virtuoso." See "Miscellaneous Reflections," *Characteristicks of Men, Manners, Opinions, Times*, 3:156–62.

prodigious Sciences, can refuse to pity that fair Lady, who fell in Love with the *miraculous* MOOR. [*AA*, 1:347]

While the supernatural-preternatural distinction is blurred in Shaftesbury's account, other categories are introduced. Specifically, Shaftesbury credits Shakespeare's text as having portended, under what he calls "this dark *Type*," that the categories of race and gender will be crucial in grasping the state of English readership and literary taste at the turn of the eighteenth century; "that about a hundred Years after his Time, the Fair Sex of this Island shou'd, by other monstrous *Tales*, be so seduc'd, as to turn their Favour chiefly on the Persons of the Tale-tellers" (*AA*, 1:348); that a "thousand DESDEMONA'S" would be "ready to present themselves, and wou'd frankly resign Fathers, Relations, Country-men, and Country it-self, to follow the Fortunes of a *Hero* of the black Tribe" of exotic author-adventurers (*AA*, 1:349).

Race and gender do not appear in Daston's history, and to be honest, such is the power of her own narrative, I did not miss them until I remembered once teaching this passage from the *Characteristicks*. It is hard to tell if these categories are being used metaphorically or literally here. Are Shaftesbury's "thousand Desdemonas" a reference to a newly developing female readership, forerunner of the later readership for the novel, a group often mocked by commentators very much in Shaftesbury's vein? Are the "go-betweens" who composed these travel narratives supposed, by virtue of their production of these tales, to have "gone native"? Or, finally, to add a final question to an already long barrage: Is Shaftesbury's strange tale of the seventeenth century, taken more generally either as evidentiary relic or evidentiary source, a document compatible with the story Daston tells, somehow at odds with it, or simply for her purposes beside the point?

Historical Epistemology

Lorraine Daston

First and foremost, I would like to thank James Chandler most heartily for his thoughtful and thought-provoking commentary and also for drawing our attention to the splendid Shaftesbury extract from *Advice to an Author* in *Characteristicks of Men, Manners, Opinions, Times* (1710). I don't think the space allotted here is long enough by half to address all the points he raises, so I shall restrict myself to what seem to me to be his three principal queries. First, what is the larger historical project of which my essay is a part, and how does it bear on the validity of the current fact/evidence distinction? Second, to what extent must this story about marvelous facts and miraculous evidence be embedded in contexts more local than "'Early Modern Europe'" (p. 277)? And third, what about Shaftesbury?

What Kind of History Is This?

Chandler asks to which genre my "conceptual history" (p. 276) of facts and evidence belongs, how that genre might relate to better-known genres such as the history of ideas and, albeit implicitly (he is too polite to pose the question aloud), what good is such a new genre, if new it be? I think the best label for what I attempted in this essay is "historical epistemology," which I understand to be the history of the categories that structure our thought, pattern our arguments and proofs, and certify our standards for explanation. Historical epistemology can be (indeed, must be) instantiated by the history of ideas, but it poses a different kind of question: not the history of this or that particular use of, say, infinitesimals in the mathematical demonstrations of the sixteenth and seventeenth centuries, but the history of the changing forms and standards of mathematical demonstration during this period; not the history of the establishment of this or that empirical fact in, say, the physiology of the mid-nineteenth century, but rather the history of the competing forms of facticity—statistical, experimental, and other—in the physiological institutes and laboratories circa 1870; not the historical judgment as to whether this or that discipline has attained objectivity, and if so, when and how, but rather a historical investigation into the multiple meanings and scientific manifestations of objectivity.

I lay no claim whatsoever to originality in the genre of historical epistemology; not even the name is mine. (I confess I am not sure as to the provenance of the name, though it has a resonantly Hacking-esque ring.) To my mind, the most able practitioners of historical epistemology these days are philosophers rather than historians—I think of the remarkable recent work of Ian Hacking and Arnold Davidson—[1] although I think they, intellectual historians, and historians of science might well make common cause in such a venture. Historical epistemology not only transcends the history of ideas, by asking the Kantian question about the preconditions that make thinking this or that idea possible; it also drastically curtails the chronological scope of the history of ideas as traditionally conceived, for it radically challenges the assumption of resemblance between ideas advanced by thinkers working within different conceptual categories. The vast arcs traced from classical antiquity to the present through various instantiations of the "same" idea lose much of their continuity if the trajectories must span contrasting conceptual categories of argument, explanation, and rationality. In any given case such continuity may be possible, but as a general premise it loses much of its a priori plausibility.

Chandler will not allow me to take refuge from current controversies over the fact/evidence distinction by historicizing them and quite properly asks how knowing more about the origins of our categories of fact and evidence bears on still-raging debates. Posed more generally, the question is, What good is historical epistemology? A ready answer springs quickly, too quickly, to mind: this is an intellectual equivalent of psychoanalysis, releasing us from our bondage to the past by hauling that past

---

1. See, for example, Arnold I. Davidson, "The Horror of Monsters," in *The Boundaries of Humanity: Humans, Animals, Machines*, ed. James J. Sheehan and Morton Sosna (Berkeley, 1991), pp. 36–67, and Ian Hacking, "'Style' for Historians and Philosophers," *Studies in History and Philosophy of Science* 23 (Mar. 1992): 1–20.

Lorraine Daston is professor of history and history of science at the University of Chicago. She is author of *Classical Probability in the Enlightenment* (1988) and is currently at work on a history of scientific objectivity.

into conscious view. Alas, historical truth alone will not set us free, and that for two reasons. First, it is not enough to reveal the contingent and accidental character of our current conceptual categories in order to abandon them. We must also have something better to put in their place, and both the "something" and the "better" tax the mightiest imaginations. Second, the plain historical fact that a form of argument or standard of explanation or ideal of objectivity is of contingent origins does not thereby render it invalid. To claim it did would be to commit the genetic fallacy. It might, for example, be an extraordinary stroke of luck or genius or both that forged an insight about how to think from the tangle of historical accidents we call fifth-century Athens or seventeenth-century England. That is, historicizing is not identical to relativizing, much less to debunking.

But there is no denying that, at least for those who yearn for absolute certainties and unshakeable foundations, such historical revelations about the origins of our categories of fact or evidence provoke a certain intellectual vertigo. They are thereby driven to a kind of philosophical existentialism, in which they must simultaneously renounce all hopes for a transcendental justification of what they believe, but nonetheless stand Gibraltar-firm in word and deed behind those evanescent beliefs. So just as it is possible for existentialists to embrace a code of ethics while abandoning its religious roots, so it is possible to admit the historicity of our conceptual categories without flinching in our allegiance to them. As in the case of existentialist ethics, this stance requires a kind of bleak, defiant courage familiar to the readers of Camus novels. I do not recommend this *courage de méfiance* in all cases, but it is not an unthinkable stance.

In the particular and controversial case of allegedly neutral facts, historical epistemology cannot decide the issue of whether they are (a) possible and (b) desirable. But it can open up conceptual windows that may significantly transform the debate. Given the rarity of creative metaphysicians in any age, all conceptual alternatives to how we currently think are a welcome enrichment to our constrained philosophical imaginations. First, historical epistemology teaches us that the "facts" in question are protean creatures, amalgamated of several historical layers, like an archeological site. We must be scrupulous in specifying which kinds of facts we are discussing, for the salient properties of, say, statistical and anomalous facts differ crucially. Second, historical epistemology shows us that there exists a spectrum of theory ladenness, from the relatively innocuous selection of topic, in the sense of Max Weber, to the sinister extreme of ideology, in the sense of Karl Marx, with almost all points in between. Neutrality and contamination are matters of degree. Third, and most important, historical epistemology challenges the language of "neutrality" and "contamination" by exposing the soteriological epistemology that underpins both compliment and insult. This is the epistemology of grace, in which knowledge is given freely (the literal sense of *data* as the "givens"), without work, artifice, construction, and all the other postlaps-arian curses. As in the beatitudes, grace descends preferentially upon the simple and pure of heart—and even the blank of mind. Not only do scientific biographies since the eighteenth century almost invariably por-tray their subjects as humble, unworldly, and secluded; scientists them-selves repeatedly conflate innocence with ignorance, sometimes to the point of preferring the testimony of the uneducated to the expert in deli-cate empirical matters, fearing the preconceptions of the sophisticated more than the errors of the naive. Instead of asking whether facts are constructed, historical epistemology may prompt us to ask why we regard construction as a cardinal sin, incompatible with truth and intellectual honesty.

2. Should Historical Context Be Local or Global?

Chandler worries about the texture of description and explana-tion in my essay, suggesting that a more finely woven version of both might tether the episodes I discuss in more local circumstances; for ex-ample, particularizing generalizations about the late seventeenth- and early eighteenth-century shift in early modern European views on the evidence of miracles to reactions of latitudinarian divines in Restoration England. I quite agree that more minute attention to local circumstances would no doubt reveal more local variation—the more specific and local the cause, the more specific and local the effect. Moreover, I think such a comparative study along national and/or confessional lines would be most interesting. Why, for example, does German, alone among the ma-jor European languages, make no distinction between "marvel" and "miracle," subsuming both under the single rubric *Wunder?* Why, where, and how do the forms, objects, and respectability of the emotion of won-der vary so widely during this period—shifting its affective associations from reverential awe to probing, even prying philosophical curiosity; shifting its objects from rarities like the aurora borealis or a bearded grape cluster to commonplaces like the anatomy of an insect; shifting its status from the mark of the philosopher to that of the unlettered, gaping rube? These transitions take place at very different paces (if they take place at all) at the center and periphery of eighteenth-century culture; for example, by the 1730s Parisian academicians are positively hostile towards the wonder-mongering so characteristic of natural philosophy a generation before, whereas the annals of the Royal Society of London, the local academies of Halle, Dresden, and other German principalities as well as those of Dijon and Bordeaux still bristle with reports of monstrous births, strange weather, and other marvels well into the 1780s.

Nonetheless, I persist in thinking that there is also something to be gained by hovering at a level of greater geographic, cultural, and conceptual generality. In the case Chandler takes up—namely, the fear of deception (including self-deception) by the false miracles of enthusiasts rather than by those of the devil—a distinctive field of meanings is certainly attached to the term *enthusiasm* in post-1660 England. However, the shifted perception of the threat from diabolical to human agency, and more particularly to human agency inspired or simply inflamed by intensely emotional, strongly collective forms of heterodox piety, is far more general, crossing confessional and national lines. As Jesuit responses to the Port-Royal miracle of the Holy Thorn of 1656 and Archbishop Vintimille's response to the massively documented Jansenist miracles at Saint-Médard in 1731 show, official skepticism and defensiveness was hardly a Protestant, English monopoly. It could not be such because the tactics of religious insubordination, almost always linked to political and social subordination, crossed confessional and national boundaries. Charismatic sects also partook of the debate over the evidence of miracles insofar as they exploited that evidence as their most powerful, and often only, weapon against orthodoxy.

Moreover, the existence of a more global, or at least European, context in the case of evidentiary miracles did not depend on such structural considerations alone. There were both preconditions for and engines of universalization. Preconditions included a shared biblical tradition, larded with generation upon generation of theological commentary and sermon homilies and made concrete by pilgrimages to shrines and the cult of saintly relics, about the possible kinds and meanings of miracles that permeated almost every corner of Latin Christendom. As David Sabean's study of early modern German popular culture reveals, even miracles reported by illiterate Swabian peasants were thickly encrusted with biblical and liturgical associations; it is hard to imagine bleeding grape vines speaking so powerfully to a non-Christian culture.[2] Among the engines of universalization, the printing press figures most prominently in early modern Europe, reaching downward with the illustrated broadside ballad or upward with the learned Latin treatise, but in any case outward with an unprecedented radius and density of coverage.

The point I wish to make is that the breadth of the context suitable for analysis is very much dependent on the breadth of the question posed and that universalization of intellectual-cum-cultural phenomena deserves at least as much historical attention as the narrowly local contexts in which such phenomena originally emerge. This is a tension all too familiar to historians of science, who have recently been struggling to unite a decade's worth of exquisitely detailed microstudies of "science in context" with the spread of conceptual and technical innovations to cul-

---

2. See David Warren Sabean, *Power in the Blood: Popular Culture and Village Discourse in Early Modern Germany* (Cambridge, 1984), pp. 61–93.

tures that share few or none of the assumptions and values that seemed necessary to make the novelty possible and plausible. As yet, we understand very little about the phenomenon of universalization, but it is not a phenomenon we can afford to ignore.

3. Is Shaftesbury an Exception?

One of the several attitudes that diffuses very rapidly and widely among European intellectuals at the end of the seventeenth century is not only that false miracles are the products of human rather than diabolic deception but that this deception on the part of humans is often unwitting. Enthusiasts, Jansenists, and other heterodox sects are perfectly sincere, so ran the story, but nonetheless victimized by their own extravagant imaginations. In the extreme case, not only their minds but also their bodies are duped—duped into curing paralysis, tumors, cataracts, and the other ailments that figure so prominently in accounts of healing miracles. Wonder-working is not debunked but rather naturalized, albeit by a most unnaturally amplified force of imagination, hardly less wondrous in its effects than the wonders it is meant to explain away.

Shaftesbury's *Letter Concerning Enthusiasm* (1708) is perhaps the best-known and best-tempered statement of this view, recommending that the "new Venders of Prophesy and Miracles" first ascertain that they are "sedate, cool, and impartial; free of every byassing Passion, every giddy Vapor, or melancholy fume."[3] In the 1710 excerpt to which Chandler has drawn our attention (see p. 280), Shaftesbury is more concerned with marvels than miracles, but he is also here preoccupied with the kind of sensibility—once again a pathological sensibility—capable of such outlandish tastes and such misplaced credulity. It is a sensibility that Shaftesbury locates in two quite distinct groups: on the one hand, those "Virtuoso's" who will scruple at a Christian miracle but gobble up "the monstrous Accounts of Monstrous Men, and Manners" (*L*, p. 345) and, on the other, "the silliest Woman or merest Boy" (*L*, p. 350) or, more generally, the "vulgar." I may note in passing that in my reading, Shaftesbury implicitly relies on the distinction between marvel and miracle: for example, his contrast of "Christian miracles" and "prodigy of Moorish and Pagan Countrys" (*L*, p. 345) depends on it, and exemplifies a familiar genre of early eighteenth-century apologetics, which accused the more skeptical virtuosi of applying standards of evidence and argument to Christian doctrines that their own natural philosophy or even mathemat-

3. [Anthony Ashley Cooper, Third Earl of Shaftesbury], *A Letter Concerning Enthusiasm, to My Lord ****** (London, 1708), p. 83; hereafter abbreviated *L*.

ics would not survive.[4] Even Hume tacitly observes this distinction between marvels and miracles in his essay "Of Miracles,"[5] when he distinguishes between the merely marvelous darkness of several days' duration (which we might credit) and the alleged miracle of Queen Elizabeth's resurrection (which we may on no account believe). Whether or not my reading here is correct, Shaftesbury's essay in fact deals almost exclusively with marvels, including the now highly suspect category of portents.

I interpret his ridicule for marvel-mongers as part of the literary attack (Swift, Shadwell, Dryden, Butler, and Pope also enlisted) on the virtuosi, a genre that has been thoroughly investigated by Walter Houghton, Marjorie Hope Nicolson, and other literary historians.[6] Although the charges are familiar—an unseemly obsession with the trivial and even the disgusting, a voracious appetite for marvels and exotica, credulity in all matters but faith—Shaftesbury gives them an original twist by linking them to Desdemona and to superstition. In my reading, both connections are intended to shame the virtuosi out of their marvel-mongering in much the same way Hume attempted to shame his audience out of their belief in miracles, namely, by the strategy of guilt by association. Moreover, the associations are in both cases the same: the vulgar, women, and children. They are the most susceptible to the pathological sensibility that craves marvels and exotica. (It is somewhat anachronistic to apply the categories of gender and race without further nuance here; the "vulgar" scorned by early modern literati has a different extension and penumbra of associations than either taken singly or both together.)

Here the play on Desdemona's name is most revealing. Shaftesbury's translation of it as "superstition" is rather loose; the Greek *desmos* signifies a bond or fetter, and, metaphorically, a spell or enchantment. For Shaftesbury, such spells or enchantments approximate superstitions, first, by being illusions ungrounded in reality and, second, by betokening a willfully fearful temperament, which reads "Fate, Destiny, or the Anger of Heaven" into every "unusual Sight or Hearing" (*L,* p. 349). Shaftesbury has fully accomplished the transition, so characteristic of early Enlightenment thought, from superstition as a corruption of religion because it worships false gods that are nonetheless real entities (that is, demons) to superstition as belief in unreal entities. Both forms of superstition were closely associated with the vulgar, that "most deceptable part of Man-

4. Compare George Berkeley, *The Analyst; Or a Discourse Addressed to an Infidel Mathematician* (London, 1734).

5. See David Hume, "Of Miracles," *Philosophical Essays Concerning Human Understanding,* 2d rev. ed. (1748; London, 1750), pp. 173–207.

6. See Walter E. Houghton, Jr., "The English Virtuoso in the Seventeenth Century," pts. 1 and 2, *Journal of the History of Ideas* 3 (Jan. and Apr. 1942): 51–73, 190–219, and Marjorie Hope Nicolson, "Virtuoso," *Dictionary of the History of Ideas,* ed. Philip P. Wiener, 5 vols. (New York, 1973), 4:486–90.

kind," as Sir Thomas Browne called them,[7] but the deception practiced on the vulgar in the two cases is strikingly different. The deception has become internalized, a matter of a perverse psychology and a false ontology rather than demonic fraud. The vulgar, and women and children of all classes, remain the victims, but they are now victims of themselves. Those who "love the marvellous"—which in Shaftesbury's day had only recently become an insult—had become marvels themselves, possessors of (or more accurately, possessed by) an imagination that rivalled the power of demons in its force and ingenuity.

7. Thomas Browne, *Pseudodoxia Epidemica; Or, Enquiries into Very Many Received Tenets and Commonly Presumed Truths* (1646), in *The Works of Sir Thomas Browne*, ed. Charles Sayle, 3 vols. (Edinburgh, 1912), 1:132.

Checking the Evidence: The Judge and the Historian

Carlo Ginzburg

1

Evidence, like *clue* or *proof,* is a crucial word for the historian and the judge. This affinity implies convergences, and divergences as well, which have been recognized for a long time. Some recent developments in the historian's work shed new light on this old topic.[1]

In the last 2500 years, since the beginnings in ancient Greece of the literary genre we call "history," the relationship between history and law has been very close. True, the Greek word *historia* is derived from medical language, but the argumentative ability it implied was related to the judicial sphere. History, as Arnaldo Momigliano emphasized some years ago, emerged as an independent intellectual activity at the intersection of med-

---

1. I have dealt with some of the issues mentioned in this paper in my following works: "Clues: Roots of an Evidential Paradigm" and "The Inquisitor as Anthropologist," *Clues, Myths, and the Historical Method,* trans. John and Anne C. Tedeschi (Baltimore, 1989), pp. 96–125, 156–64; introduction to Peter Burke, *Cultura popolare nell'Europa moderna,* trans. Federico Canobbio-Codelli (Milan, 1980), pp. xiv–xv; "Proofs and Possibilities: In the Margins of Natalie Zemon Davis' *The Return of Martin Guerre,*" trans. Anthony Guneratne, *Yearbook of Comparative and General Literature,* no. 37 (1988): 114–27, esp. p. 116 n. 7; "Montrer et citer: La Vérité de l'histoire," *Le Débat* 56 (Sept.–Oct. 1989): 43–54; and "Just One Witness," in *Probing the Limits of Representation: Nazism and the Final Solution,* ed. Saul Friedlander (Cambridge, Mass., forthcoming). This paper is based partly on passages taken from my book, *Il giudice e lo storico: Considerazioni in margine al processo Sofri* (Torino, 1991).

This essay originally appeared in *Critical Inquiry* 18 (Autumn 1991).

icine and rhetoric. Following the example of the former, the historian analyzed specific cases and situations looking for their natural causes; following the prescriptions of the latter—a technique, or an art, born in tribunals—he communicated the results of his inquiry.[2]

Within the classical tradition, historical writing (and poetry as well) had to display a feature the Greeks called *enargheia*, and the Romans, *evidentia in narratione:* the ability to convey a vivid representation of characters and situations. The historian, like the lawyer, was expected to make a convincing argument by communicating the illusion of reality, not by exhibiting proofs collected either by himself or by others.[3] Collecting proofs was, until the mid-eighteenth century, an activity practiced by antiquarians and erudites, not by historians.[4] When, in his *Traité des différentes sortes de preuves qui servent à établir la vérité de l'histoire* (1769), the erudite Jesuit Henri Griffet compared the historian to a judge who carefully evaluates proofs and witnesses, he was expressing a still-unaddressed intellectual need. Only a few years later Edward Gibbon published his *Decline and Fall of the Roman Empire,* the first work that effectively combined historical narrative with an antiquarian approach.[5]

The comparison between the historian and the judge has had a lasting life. In his famous motto (first pronounced by Schiller) *Die Weltgeschichte ist das Weltgericht,* Hegel expressed, through the double meaning of *Weltgericht* ["world's court of justice" as well as "final judgement"], the core of his own philosophy of history: the secularization of the Christian view of world history [*Weltgeschichte*].[6] The motto, with all its

2. See Arnaldo Momigliano, "History between Medicine and Rhetoric," *Ottavo contributo alla storia degli studi classici e del mondo antico,* trans. Riccardo Di Donato (Rome, 1987), pp. 14–25.

3. See Ginzburg, "Montrer et citer."

4. See Momigliano, "Ancient History and the Antiquarian," *Contributo alla storia degli studi classici* (Rome, 1955), pp. 67–106.

5. See Henri Griffet, *Traité des différentes sortes de preuves qui servent à établir la vérité de l'histoire,* 2d ed. (Liège, 1770). Allen Johnson, in his *Historian and Historical Evidence* (New York, 1926), speaks of the *Traité* as "the most significant book on method after Mabillon's *De re diplomatica*" (p. 114). See also Momigliano, "Ancient History and the Antiquarian," p. 81, and Ginzburg, "Just One Witness." On Gibbon, see Momigliano, *Sesto contributo alla storia degli studi classici e del mondo antico* (Rome, 1980), pp. 231–84.

6. Compare Karl Löwith, *Meaning in History* (Chicago, 1949), p. 12: "the history of the world is the world's court of justice." In this English translation the motto's religious implications, emphasized by Löwith (p. 58), disappear. As it has been pointed out to me by Alberto Gajano, Hegel quotes the motto at least three times: compare "Heidelberger

Carlo Ginzburg is Franklin D. Murphy Professor of Italian Renaissance Studies at the University of California, Los Angeles. His two most recent books are *Ecstacies: Deciphering the Witches' Sabbath* (1991) and *Il giudice e lo storico* (1991).

ambiguity, emphasizes the judge's sentence. Griffet, on the contrary, had focused on the previous stage, in which the judge (and the historian as well) proceeds to a fair evaluation of proofs and witnesses. Towards the end of the century Lord Acton, in his opening lecture as Regius Professor of Modern History at Cambridge (1895), stressed the relevance of both stages: historiography, insofar as it is based on evidence, can overcome feuds and tensions by becoming "an accepted tribunal, and the same for all."[7] These words reflected a widespread tendency of thought, reinforced by the prevailing positivist atmosphere. From the end of the nineteenth century and through the first decades of the twentieth, much historiography—above all, political historiography and, in a most special way, the historiography on the French Revolution—developed in a courtlike atmosphere.[8] But here a split emerged. A historian like Hippolyte Taine, who regarded himself as a "moral zoologist," elicited reserved reactions from those historians who attempted to combine political engagement and scientific neutrality. Alphonse Aulard, for instance, compared Taine's attitude towards the Revolution to that of a "superior, detached judge." Both Aulard and his opponent, Albert Mathiez, preferred to take the role either of state prosecutors or of lawyers in order to prove, on the basis of detailed files, Robespierre's guilt or Danton's corruption. This tradition, based on moral and political court-speeches, followed by condemnations or acquittals, has gone on for a long time: Un Jury pour la Révolution, by Jacques Godechot, the well-known historian of the French Revolution, was published in 1974.[9]

This judicial model, by emphasizing already existing tendencies, has had a double impact on historiography. On one hand, it urges historians

---

Enziklopädie," §448, Vorlesungen über die Philosophie der Geschichte, vol. 12 of Werke in zwanzig Bänden, ed. Eva Moldenhauer and Karl Markus Michel (Frankfurt am Main, 1970), p. 559; Enzyklopädie der philosophischen Wissenschaften im Grundrisse, §548, vol. 10 of Werke in zwanzig Bänden, p. 347; and Grundlinien der Philosophie des Rechts, §340, vol. 7 of Werke in zwanzig Bänden, p. 503. From a general point of view, compare Reinhart Koselleck, Futures Past: On the Semantics of Historical Time, trans. Keith Tribe (Cambridge, Mass., 1985), pp. 34, 106, 253.

7. Lord Acton, "Inaugural Lecture on the Study of History," Lectures on Modern History, ed. John Neville Figgis and Reginald Vere Laurence (London, 1906), p. 17.

8. On "judicial historiography," see the insightful remarks by Luigi Ferrajoli, Il manifesto, 23–24 Feb. 1983.

9. See Jacques Godechot, Un Jury pour la Révolution (Paris, 1974). See also L'albero della Rivoluzione: Le interpretazioni della Rivoluzione Francese, ed. Bruno Bongiovanni and Luciano Guerci (Torino, 1989), which I found very helpful, in particular the entries "Alphonse Aulard" and "Albert Mathiez," by Michel Vovelle, and "Hippolyte Taine," by Regina Pozzi. Alphonse Aulard, Taine: Historien de la Révolution française (Paris, 1907), contains this characteristic remark: "Je crois donc être sûr, je ne dis pas de paraître impartial, mais d'être impartial" (p. vii). See also Sitzungsberichte der Akademie der Wissenschaften, Eine Jury für Jacques Roux: Dem Wirken Walter Markovs gewidmet, ed. Manfred Kossok (Berlin, 1981).

to focus on events (political, military, diplomatic) that could be easily ascribed to specific actions performed by one or more individuals; on the other, it disregards those phenomena (like social life, *mentalités,* and so on) that resist an approach based on this explanatory framework. As in a photographic negative, we recognize the reversed catchwords of the *Annales d'histoire économique et sociale,* the journal started by Marc Bloch and Lucien Febvre in 1929: the rejection of the so-called *histoire événementielle* as well as the emphasis on less evident, but more deeply significant historical phenomena. Not surprisingly, in Bloch's unfinished book on historical method we find the following ironical utterance: "Robespierrists! Anti-Robespierrists! For pity's sake, simply tell us what Robespierre was." Being confronted with the dilemma "Judging or Understanding," Bloch chose unhesitatingly the latter.[10]

Retrospectively, it seems obvious that this necessarily had to have been the victorious alternative. To make this point, two examples taken from the historiography on the French revolution will suffice. Mathiez's attempt to explain Danton's politics through his friends' and his own corruption looks clearly inadequate today; on the contrary, the reconstruction of the Great Fear of 1789 provided by Georges Lefebvre is now considered to be a classic of contemporary historiography.[11] Strictly speaking, Lefebvre was not a member of the *Annales* group, but his *Grande Peur de 1789* would have never been written without *Les Rois thaumaturges,* published by Bloch in 1924, when he was still a colleague of Lefebvre at the University of Strasbourg.[12] Both books deal with nonexistent entities: the power to heal scrofula ascribed to French and English kings and the attacks launched by phantomlike bandits in order to support an alleged "aristocratic conspiracy." The historical relevance of such events, which never took place, is based on their symbolic effectiveness: that is, on the way in which they were perceived by a multitude of anonymous individuals. We are clearly very far from the moralistic historiography inspired by a judicial model.

The diminished prestige of this kind of historiography must be hailed, I believe, as a positive phenomenon. But although twenty years ago it was possible to subscribe without any qualification to the clear-cut dis-

10. Marc Bloch, *The Historian's Craft,* trans. Peter Putnam (New York, 1953), p. 140.

11. See Albert Mathiez, *La Corruption parlementaire sous la Terreur,* 2d ed. (Paris, 1927), and Georges Lefebvre, *La Grande Peur de 1789* (Paris, 1932). The antithesis between these two books is merely symbolic; for example, it is does not account for Mathiez's *Vie chère et le mouvement social sous la Terreur* (Paris, 1927). On Mathiez, see François Furet and Mona Ozouf, *Dictionnaire critique de la Révolution française* (Paris, 1988), s.v. "Histoire universitaire de la Révolution," pp. 990–91. On Lefebvre, see Jacques Revel's introduction to Lefebvre, *La Grande Peur de 1789.*

12. See Bloch, *Les Rois thaumaturges: Études sur la caractère surnaturel attribué à la puissance royale, particulièrement en France et en Angleterre* (Strasbourg, 1924). Compare Guerci, "Georges Lefebvre," in *L'albero della Rivoluzione.*

junction between judge and historian suggested by Bloch, today things seem more complicated. More and more, we grow impatient not only with a historiography inspired by a judicial model but also with the element that had suggested to Griffet his analogy between the historian and the judge: the notion of proof.

2

In the last twenty-five years words like *proof,* or even *truth* (connected to the former by a strong, albeit historical, nexus), have acquired in the social sciences an unfashionable ring, evoking positivist implications. This indiscriminate reaction implies, I think, a confusion, which needs to be clarified. There is an element in positivism that must be unequivocally rejected: the tendency to simplify the relationship between evidence and reality. In a positivist perspective, the evidence is analyzed only in order to ascertain if, and when, it implies a distortion, either intentional or unintentional. The historian is thus confronted with various possibilities: a document can be a fake; a document can be authentic, but unreliable, insofar as the information it provides can be either lies or mistakes; or a document can be authentic and reliable. In the first two cases the evidence is dismissed; in the latter, it is accepted, but only as evidence of something *else.* In other words, the evidence is not regarded as a historical document in itself, but as a transparent medium—as an open window that gives us direct access to reality.

These assumptions, still shared by many contemporary historians (including some fierce critics of positivism), are undoubtedly wrong and intellectually unfruitful. But the skeptical approach that has become so pervasive in the social sciences goes much beyond the just rejection of these premises by falling into what I would call the opposite trap. Instead of dealing with the evidence as an open window, contemporary skeptics regard it as a wall, which by definition precludes any access to reality. This extreme antipositivistic attitude, which considers all referential assumptions as a theoretical naiveté, turns out to be a sort of inverted positivism.[13] Theoretical naiveté and theoretical sophistication share a common, rather simplistic assumption: they both take for granted the relationship between evidence and reality.

Yet such a relationship must be regarded as highly problematic. Many years ago, in his pioneering *Arnaldo da Brescia nelle fonti del secolo XII*

13. Marcel Mauss's attitude was largely different: see his "Rapports réels et pratiques de la psychologie et de la sociologie," *Sociologie et anthropologie* (Paris, 1960), pp. 281–310; trans. Ben Brewster, under the title *Sociology and Psychology: Essays* (Boston, 1979). See especially page 287, where he rejects the tendency to separate "la conscience du groupe de tout son substrat matériel et concret. Dans la société, il y a autre chose que des représentations collectives, si importantes ou si dominantes qu'elles soient."

(1954), Arsenio Frugoni effectively denounced the widespread erudite fallacy by which different pieces of evidence, written from various (sometimes even conflicting) perspectives, are combined in order to build up a smooth, homogeneous narrative.[14] Frugoni's conclusions, based on the analysis of a group of literary texts, have a more general value. It must be stressed that historians—whether they deal with distant, recent, or even ongoing phenomena—never take a direct approach to reality. Their work is necessarily inferential. A piece of historical evidence can be either involuntary (a skull, a footprint, a food relic) or voluntary (a chronicle, a notarial act, a fork). But in both cases a specific interpretive framework is needed, which must be related (in the latter case) to the specific code according to which the evidence has been constructed.[15] Evidence of both kinds could be compared to a distorted glass. Without a thorough analysis of its inherent distortions (the codes according to which it has been constructed and/or it must be perceived), a sound historical reconstruction is impossible. But this statement should be read also the other way around: a purely internal reading of the evidence, without any reference to its referential dimension, is impossible as well. The ultimate failure of *Le Miroir d'Hérodote*, François Hartog's brilliant but flawed book, is instructive. To reconstruct Herodotus's representation of the Other (the Scythians) exclusively on the basis of Herodotus's text has proved to be an unattainable goal.[16] The fashionable injunction to study reality as a text should be supplemented by the awareness that no text can be understood without a reference to extratextual realities.

Even if we reject positivism, therefore, we must still confront ourselves with notions like "reality," "proof," and "truth." This does not mean, of course, that nonexistent phenomena or false documents are historically less relevant to the historian. Seventy years ago, Bloch and Lefebvre taught the opposite. But the analysis of social representations cannot disregard the principle of reality. The scare of French peasants in the summer of 1789 has deeper, more revealing, more significant implications insofar as it is possible to demonstrate that the phenomenon that triggered it—those much-feared wandering bandits—never existed. We can conclude, therefore, that the tasks of both the historian and the judge imply the ability to demonstrate, according to specific rules, that x did y, where x can designate the main actor, albeit unnamed, of a historical event

14. See Arsenio Frugoni, *Arnaldo da Brescia nelle fonti del secolo XII* (1954; Torino, 1989), with an introduction by Giuseppe Sergi, "Arsenio Frugoni e la storiografia del restauro." See also Ginzburg, "Proofs and Possibilities," pp. 123–24.

15. I would like to thank Immanuel Wallerstein with whom three years ago I had a long conversation on this topic, involving many fruitful disagreements.

16. See François Hartog, *Le Miroir d'Hérodote: Essai sur la représentation de l'autre* (Paris, 1980); trans. Janet Lloyd, under the title *The Mirror of Herodotus: The Representation of the Other in the Writing of History* (Berkeley, 1988). See also Ginzburg, "Proofs and Possibilities," pp. 121–22.

or of a legal act, and *y* designates any sort of action.[17] But sometimes cases a judge would dismiss as juridically nonexistent turn out to be fruitful to a historian's eye.

3

In fact, historians and judges traditionally have had widely divergent aims. For a long time historians dealt exclusively with political and military events: with states, not with individuals. Now states, contrary to individuals, cannot be brought to court. From Thucydides to Machiavelli, to Hegel and beyond, this undeniable fact has inspired deep, sometimes tragic reflections on the amorality of power, on the state as instrument of a superior form of morality, and so on.

There is, however, a somewhat borderline genre, which deals with individual lives: biography. Even this kind of intellectual activity has been transmitted to us by the ancient Greeks. In his Harvard lectures, *The Development of Greek Biography*, Momigliano emphasized the lasting difference between history and biography as literary genres.[18] Droysen, the great nineteenth-century historian, wrote that it was possible to write the biography of Alcibiades, Cesare Borgia, and Mirabeau—but not of Caesar or Frederick the Great. As Momigliano glossed, "the adventurer, the failure, the marginal figure, were the subjects for biography."[19] The lives, however, of "world-historical individuals," as Hegel labelled them, were supposed to be identified with universal history.

But the nineteenth century was not only Napoleon's century. It was also the century of the bourgeoisie's full access to power, of the transformation of the European countryside, of the wild growth of the cities, of the first workers' struggles, and of the beginnings of women's emancipation. For a historical analysis of these phenomena new theoretical categories, new research methods, and new stylistic devices were needed. But social history, the intellectual successor of the eighteenth-century *histoire des moeurs*, developed slowly. An early example of history written from the bottom up, Augustin Thierry's well-known *Essai sur l'histoire de la formation et du progrès du Tiers Etat* (1850), took the form of an "imaginary biography." In a short essay called "Histoire véritable de Jacques Bonhomme, d'après les documens authentiques" (1820), Thierry traced the biography of Jacques, the prototypical French peasant—a biography lasting twenty centuries, from the Roman invasion to the present. This was obviously meant to be "a joke," *une plaisanterie*, but a bitter one. By

17. On the judicial notion of proof, see Ferrajoli, *Diritto e ragione: Teoria del garantismo penale* (Rome, 1989), p. 108.

18. See Momigliano, *The Development of Greek Biography* (Cambridge, Mass., 1971).

19. Ibid., pp. 2–3.

focusing on a single character Thierry emphasized that in the long run the masters were different (Romans, Franks, Absolute Monarchy, Republic, Empire, Constitutional Monarchy), the forms of power had changed, but the domination over the peasants went on and on, one generation after another.[20] The same narrative device was used by Michelet in the first section of his *La Sorcière* (1862): the transformations, as well as the hidden continuity of medieval witchcraft, were expressed by a woman, the Witch, acting through a series of events that in fact had lasted for centuries. It seems obvious that Michelet took his inspiration from Thierry. In both cases a symbolic character pointed to a multitude of lives downtrodden by misery and oppression: the lives of those individuals who, as Baudelaire's unforgettable line reads, "n'ont jamais vécu!"[21] In this way historians answered the challenge coming from a novelist like Balzac.[22] The mixture of imaginary biography and *documents authentiques* allowed historians the opportunity to overcome a triple obstacle: the irrelevance of the topic (peasants, witches) according to the traditional criteria; the scarcity of evidence; and the absence of stylistic models. Something similar had already happened after the triumph of Christianity, when the emergence of new human types—bishops, male and female saints—had inspired attempts to reshape old biographical models, as well as to create new ones.[23]

Virginia Woolf's *Orlando* (1928) can be considered as a converging, albeit nonidentical, experiment, insofar as it is based more on literary invention than on historical reconstruction. In this case the hero, who proudly walks across the centuries, is more marginal than ever: an androgyne. This work seems to be a further proof that the narrative device I am describing, far from having purely technical implications, was a conscious attempt to suggest a hidden, or at least scarcely visible, historical dimension. Eternal characters constructed on a more-than-human

20. This short essay first appeared in *Le Censeur européen*, 12 May 1820; rept. in Augustin Thierry, *Dix ans d'études historiques* (Paris, 1835), pp. 308–17. I have used the 1842 Milan edition. See also Lionel Gossman, *Augustin Thierry and Liberal Historiography*, suppl. to *History and Theory*, no. 15 (1976): 1–83; Pozzi, introduction to Thierry, *Scritti storici* (Torino, 1983); and Marcel Gauchet, "Les *Lettres sur l'histoire de France* d'Augustin Thierry," in *Les Lieux de mémoire*, ed. Pierre Nora, 2 vols. (Paris, 1986), vol. 2, pt. 1, pp. 247–316.

21. "Encore la plupart n'ont-ils jamais connu / La douceur du foyer et n'ont jamais vécu!" (Charles Baudelaire, "Le Crépuscule du soir," 11. 38–39, *Les Fleur du mal*, in *Oeuvres complètes*, ed. Y.-G. le Dantec (Paris, 1961), p. 91.

22. See Ginzburg, "Proofs and Possibilities," p. 120. In remarking that *L'Histoire véritable de Jacques Bonhomme* was immediately followed in *Le Censeur européen* by an enthusiastic review, also by Thierry, of Walter Scott's *Ivanhoe*, Gauchet comments: "Ce que les sources suggèrent, le roman historique révèle que la technique existe qui permet l'explorer" (Gauchet, "Les *Lettres sur l'histoire de France* d'Augustin Thierry," p. 274).

23. See Momigliano, "Marcel Mauss e il problema della persona nella biografia greca" and "The Life of St. Macrina by Gregory of Nyssa," in *Ottavo contributo alla storia degli studi classici e del mondo antico*, pp. 179–90, 333–47.

scale, like Jacques Bonhomme or the Witch, were conceived as symbolic projections of a multitude of forgotten lives, doomed to complete irrelevance.[24]

4

To mention in this context a historical (not to say judicial) notion of evidence would be obviously meaningless. After all, none among the books I just mentioned can be regarded as a typical example of historical writing. Even *La Sorcière* was dismissed as a sort of novel at the time of its publication in an atmosphere already impregnated with positivism.[25] But things have changed since then. Today Michelet's book is widely regarded as one of the masterworks of nineteenth-century historiography. This shift in appreciation is related to a larger one, which (as the examples I am going to analyze will show) has brought that peripheral, blurred area between history and fiction close to the center of contemporary historiographical debate.

Let's start with Eileen Power's *Medieval People* (1924). Power was responsible, with Sir John Clapham, for the project of *The Cambridge Economic History of Europe;* for many years, until her premature death in 1941, she taught economic history at the London School of Economics.[26] *Medieval People* is a brilliant book, based on first-hand research but addressed to a general audience. It provides an image of medieval society based on a series of portraits of "quite ordinary people and unknown to fame, with the exception of Marco Polo." Power remarks in her introduction that "there is often as much material for reconstructing the life of some quite ordinary person as there is for writing a history of Robert of Normandy or of Philippa of Hainault."[27] This challenging statement is probably exaggerated. Notwithstanding her unusual ability in combining erudition and imagination, Power fails to fully demonstrate her thesis. Significantly, Madame Eglentyne and the Ménagier's wife, the only two women in the series, are taken from two widely different literary texts, both written by males: Chaucer and the so-called Ménagier de Paris, the

24. I wonder whether the central idea of Virginia Woolf's *Orlando: A Biography* (New York, 1928) was inspired by *She, a History of Adventure* (London, 1887), the successful Victorian novel by Henry Rider Haggard.

25. See the preface by Paul Viallaneix to Jules Michelet, *La Sorcière* (Paris, 1966), p. 20.

26. See M. M. Postan's preface to *Economic Organization and Policies in the Middle Ages,* vol. 3 of *The Cambridge Economic History of Europe*, ed. Postan, E. E. Rich, and Edward Miller (Cambridge, 1965), p. v, and J. H. Clapham's preface to this work's first edition, ed. Clapham and Eileen Power (Cambridge, 1941), pp. v–viii. On Power, as seen as a feminine counterpart to Bloch, see Natalie Zemon Davis, "History's Two Bodies," *American Historical Review* 93 (Feb. 1988): 1–30, esp. p. 18.

27. Power, *Medieval People* (Boston, 1924), pp. viii, vii; hereafter abbreviated *MP.*

author of a book of instructions to his wife, written between 1392 and 1394. Even more significant is the fact that the hero of Power's first chapter, Bodo the peasant, is little more than a name inscribed in an estate book compiled during the reign of Charlemagne by Irminon, abbot of Saint-Germain-des-Prés. From this document we learn that Bodo had a wife, Ermentrude, and three sons, Wido, Gerbert, and Hildegard; we also gather some information on the lands he used to toil. In order to add some concreteness to these bare data, Power delineates the social environment in which Bodo lived. She explains the organization of the work on the abbey's lands, the relationship between the seigneurial and tributary manses, and the amount of labor demanded of the tenants. Then she goes on: "Let us try and imagine a day in his life. On a fine spring morning towards the end of Charlemagne's reign Bodo gets up early" (*MP*, p. 7). The description that follows includes an attempt to reconstruct Bodo's beliefs and superstitions: "If you had followed behind Bodo when he broke his first furrow you would have probably seen him take out of his jerkin a little cake, baked for him by Ermentrude out of different kinds of meal, and you would have seen him stoop and lay it under the furrow and sing: "Earth, Earth, Earth! O Earth, our mother!" (Here a text of an Anglo-Saxon charm follows; *MP*, p. 12).

There is no need to stress the differences between the life of Jacques Bonhomme sketched in a few strokes by Thierry in 1820 and the detailed description of the life of Bodo provided by Power one century later. In the former, the evidence, focusing on a symbolic hero, is spread across twenty centuries; in the latter, it is concentrated around a real individual, within a homogeneous time. In both cases, however, scanty, fragmented evidence has been supplemented with elements taken from the context (diachronic in the former case, synchronic in the latter). But Power, who starts from a realistic, not symbolic premise, uses the notion of context in a rather flexible way. For instance, it is unlikely that Bodo, a dweller of the Île-de-France, ever sang an Anglo-Saxon charm. Moreover, when we read that "Bodo would certainly take a holiday and go to the fair" (*MP*, p. 21),[28] we immediately understand that this is a conjecture. But only a naive reader, in reading a nonconjectural sentence like "Bodo goes whistling off in the cold" (*MP*, p. 7), could ask whether it is based on some evidence. The former integration, like many others in Power's book, relies on a specific historical compatibility, the latter, on a vague, general plausibility (today's peasants whistle; they certainly whistled even in Charlemagne's times). But human whistling, being a cultural practice, cannot be automatically projected into a society.

In her preface to *Medieval People*, Power says that "social history lends itself particularly to what may be called a personal treatment" (*MP*, p. vii).

---

28. The word "certainly" here means "presumably," an often-recurring switch in the historian's language.

In this passage "personal" means "typical"—although elsewhere Power expresses some reservations concerning Max Weber's concept of "ideal type."[29] For a long time, in fact, historians have either explicitly or (more often) implicitly dismissed the possibility of reconstructing the lives of underprivileged individuals from a distant past. According to a typical statement made by François Furet in 1963, historians can deal with groups placed at the bottom of the social ladder only in a quantitative, anonymous perspective, based on sociology and historical demography.[30] A few year later, however, some historians started to disprove this exceedingly pessimistic conclusion by trying to reconstruct the lives of individual men and women from the popular classes of the past. Quite significantly, the richest (not to say the only available) evidence for this enterprise has been provided, either directly or indirectly, by court records from distant places and times: fourteenth- or sixteenth-century France, seventeenth-century Italy or China.[31] This new contiguity between the historian and the judge brought again to the forefront, albeit in a different perspective, the aforementioned convergences and divergences between their respective approaches.[32]

Natalie Davis's book *The Return of Martin Guerre* illustrates the contradictory implications of this contiguity. The trial against the man who pretended to be Martin Guerre is apparently lost. Davis was compelled to work on the detailed commentary provided by Jean de Coras, the judge who conducted the trial. Therefore, she says:

> In the absence of the full testimony from the trial (all such records for criminal cases before 1600 are missing from the Parlement of Toulouse), I have worked through the registers of Parlementary sentences to find out more about the affair and about the practice and attitudes of the judges. In pursuit of my rural actors, I have searched through notarial contracts in villages all over the dioceses of Rieux and Lombez. When I could not find my individual man or woman in Hendaye, in Artigat, in Sajas, or in Burgos, then I did my best

29. See Davis, "History's Two Bodies," p. 22, where she quotes Power's critical remarks on Weber in her essay, "On Medieval History as a Social Study," *Economica*, n.s. 1 (Feb. 1934): 20–21.

30. See Furet, "Pour une définition des classes inférieures a l'époque moderne," *Annales: Économies, Sociétés, Civilisations* 18 (May–June 1963): 459–74, esp. p. 459.

31. See Emmanuel Le Roy Ladurie, *Montaillou, village occitan de 1294 à 1314* (Paris, 1975), trans. Barbara Bray, under the title *Montaillou: The Promised Land of Error* (New York, 1978); Davis, *The Return of Martin Guerre* (Cambridge, Mass., 1983); Ginzburg, *I benandanti* (Torino, 1966), trans. Tedeschi and Tedeschi, under the title *The Night Battles: Witchcraft and Agrarian Cults in the Sixteenth and Seventeenth Centuries* (Baltimore, 1983); Ginzburg, *Il formaggio e i vermi: Il cosmo di un mugnaio del 1500* (Torino, 1976), trans. Tedeschi and Tedeschi, under the title *The Cheese and the Worms: The Cosmos of a Sixteenth-Century Miller* (Baltimore, 1980); and Jonathan D. Spence, *The Death of Woman Wang* (New York, 1978).

32. See Ginzburg, "The Inquisitor as Anthropologist."

through other sources from the period and place to discover the world they would have seen and the reactions they might have had.[33]

We are inevitably reminded of Power. In fact, in a recent essay Davis traced a warm, engaging intellectual portrait of her.[34] But Davis is much more careful than Power in distinguishing truths from possibilities. Instead of concealing within the indicative mood the integrations she made in order to fill up documentary gaps, Davis emphasizes them by using either a conditional mood or expressions like "perhaps" and "may have been." We can compare her approach to modern art-restoration techniques, like the so-called *rigatino,* in which the lacunae in the painted surface are emphasized by fine hatches instead of concealed by repainting, as they were in the past.[35] The context, seen as a space of historical possibilities, gives the historian the possibility to integrate the evidence, often consisting only of scattered fragments, about an individual's life. We are obviously very far from a judicial perspective.

The use of court records, therefore, does not imply that historians, disguised as judges, should try to reenact the trials of the past—an aim that would be pointless, if it were not intrinsically impossible. Debates like the one engaged in by Robert Finlay and Natalie Davis on the guilt or innocence of Bertrande de Rols, the wife of Martin Guerre, seem a bit off the mark. Even Davis's remark on the importance of her reconstruction of the context as a mere "additional goal" seems to me marked by a certain theoretical timidity.[36] The specific aim of this kind of historical research should be, I think, the reconstruction of the *relationship* (about which we know so little) between individual lives and the contexts in which they unfold.[37]

Attempts to connect these two poles are often conjectural. But not all conjectures are equally acceptable. Let us take a look at another book based on the literary account of a lost trial: Jonathan Spence's *Death of Woman Wang.* In a bold attempt to reconstruct what Wang, the poor peasant who is the book's main character, was dreaming immediately before her violent death, Spence used a series of fragments from the literary works of P'u Sung-ling, a seventeenth-century Chinese writer who lived in a neighboring region. "By combining some of [his] images in montage form, it seemed to me," Spence wrote, "that we might break out

33. Davis, *The Return of Martin Guerre,* p. 5.

34. See Davis, "History's Two Bodies."

35. See Ginzburg, "Proofs and Possibilities," pp. 122–25. See also A. Lloyd Moote, review of *The Return of Martin Guerre,* by Davis, *American Historical Review* 90 (Oct. 1985): 943.

36. Davis, "On the Lame," *American Historical Review* 93 (June 1988): 573. See Robert Finlay, "The Refashioning of Martin Guerre," *American Historical Review* 93 (June 1988): 553–71.

37. See Giovanni Levi, "Les Usages de la biographie," *Annales: Économies, Sociétés, Civilisations* 44 (Nov.–Dec. 1989): 1325–36.

beyond the other sources from that lost world, and come near to expressing what might have been in the mind of woman Wang as she slept before death."[38] I am not questioning Spence's fairness towards his readers: the dream has been printed in italics. We are therefore in an intermediate zone, pointing to historical possibility ("what might have been") and not hard evidence. But to recreate the dream of a poor peasant woman through the words of a learned essayist and storyteller looks like a somewhat gratuitous exercise.

5

My attitude towards the issues of evidence and proof is deeply indebted to the work of Arnaldo Momigliano. It is not by chance that I have quoted him so often. In an essay published some years before his death, he expressed with characteristic bluntness the "fundamental point" as follows:

> [1] The historian works on evidence. [2] Rhetoric is not his business. [3] The historian has to assume ordinary commonsense criteria for judging his own evidence. [4] He must not allow himself to be persuaded that his criteria of truth are relative, and that what is true for him today will no longer be true for him to-morrow.[39]

(1) has become less and less obvious, both in itself and in its implications. It seems to me absolutely true, but (2) seems to me, on the contrary, impossible to accept, above all if we assume that the historian's language has cognitive and not merely rhetorical implications. (3) looks like a conscious provocation, contradicted by Momigliano's whole work, in which he explored the long and complex history of those alleged "commonsense criteria." I regard the rejection of relativism, so strongly expressed in (4), as particularly important, and basically true. But I would suggest that a distinction should be made between truth, as a regulative principle, and criteria of truth.[40] The examples I analyzed before show that the respective roles of truth and possibility are, in contemporary historical research, a debated and still open issue. It is impossible to foresee if a new scholarly consensus, comparable to the one that

38. Spence, *The Death of Woman Wang*, pp. xiv–xv. See also pp. 128–31, 160–61.

39. Momigliano, "Considerations on History in an Age of Ideologies," *Settimo contributo alla storia degli studi classici e del mondo antico* (Rome, 1984), p. 268; in the passage quoted above, the numbers in square brackets are mine. See also his "Rhetoric of History and the History of Rhetoric: On Hayden White's Tropes," pp. 49–59 of the same volume.

40. On the (Kantian) notion of "regulative ideas," see Amos Funkenstein, *Theology and the Scientific Imagination from the Middle Ages to the Seventeenth Century* (Princeton, N.J., 1986), pp. 18–22.

emerged at the end of the eighteenth century around the relevance of antiquarian methods, will emerge on these issues. But this (to quote Momigliano again) "is not [our] business."

A simple analogy could be suggested in this context. Neither the past and future developments of the language we speak, nor the existence of other languages, affect our commitment to the language we speak or its grip over reality. Translatability and relativism are not synonymous.

Carlo Ginzburg and the Renewal of Historiography

Arnold I. Davidson

> Le strade del giudice e quelle dello storico, coincidenti per un tratto, divergono poi inevitabilmente. Chi tenta di ridurre lo storico a giudice semplifica e impoverisce la conoscenza storiografica; ma chi tenta di ridurre il giudice a storico inquina irrimediabilmente l'esercizio della giustizia.
>
> —CARLO GINZBURG, *Il giudice e lo storico*

1

The epigraph to my essay—"The ways of the judge and those of the historian coinciding for a while then inevitably diverge. Whoever attempts to reduce the historian to a judge simplifies and impoverishes historiographical consciousness; but whoever attempts to reduce the judge to a historian irredeemably pollutes the exercise of justice"—is taken from Carlo Ginzburg's recently published book, *Il giudice e lo storico*.[1] This book provides the most recent extended basis for Ginzburg's reflections on the topic of evidence and related concepts, and the epigraph I have chosen highlights his attempt to chart both the initial convergences and ultimate divergences between the tasks of the judge and the historian, as well as their philosophical underpinnings. Ginzburg's historical work has been so significant and powerful that it is all too easy to overlook the fundamental contribution of his historiographical considerations; these latter considerations, although spread out over a wide range of

All translations, except where cited, are my own.

1. Carlo Ginzburg, *Il giudice e lo storico: Considerazioni in margine al processo Sofri* (Turin, 1991), pp. 109–10.

books and articles, when taken together provide a compelling framework of questions, issues, and theoretical conclusions that ought to inform how our histories—intellectual, cultural, and social—are constructed and written.[2]

2

Ginzburg shows that in the classical tradition both the historian and the lawyer were "expected to make a convincing argument by communicating the illusion of reality, not by exhibiting proofs collected either by himself or by others" (p. 291). Following Arnaldo Momigliano he argues that until the mid-eighteenth century collecting proofs was "an activity practiced by antiquarians and erudites, not by historians" (p. 291). In "Montrer et citer" he traces the historiographical role and fate of the ancient concept of *enargeia*, of the idea that the historian must produce accounts that are clear and palpable, that are living narratives conveying an impression of life that will move and convince their readers.[3] The requirement of *enargeia* was linked to a rhetorical tradition in which the orator made some nonexistent object visible to his audience by "the almost magical force of his words" ("MC," p. 47). *Enargeia* was always associated with the sphere of direct experience, with a witnessing by the historian that allowed him to put an invisible reality before the eyes of his readers. "*Enargeia* was an instrument appropriate to communicating *autopsia*, in other words, a direct view, by the force of style" ("MC," p. 47). And annals were contrasted with history by ancient and medieval writers; history recounted events in which the narrator had taken part, which he had himself viewed, while annals were concerned with a more remote past that was not directly present to the historian and his generation (see "MC," secs. 9–10). Moreover, by the sixteenth century, the dullness of style found in annals and their absence of true narrative structure were

2. Ginzburg's historiographical writings are cited in the first footnote of "Checking the Evidence: The Judge and the Historian," p. 290. I have used all of these sources, as well as others I shall mention shortly, in writing this essay.
3. Ginzburg, "Montrer et citer: La Vérité de l'histoire," *Le Débat,* no. 56 (Sept.–Oct. 1989): 43–54; hereafter abbreviated "MC." See especially secs. 4–7.

Arnold I. Davidson, the executive editor of *Critical Inquiry,* is professor of philosophy and a member of the Committee on the Conceptual Foundations of Science at the University of Chicago. Appointed a fellow at the Wissenschaftskolleg, Berlin for 1994–95, he has recently published a series of essays on the tradition of spiritual exercises in philosophy and is completing a book on the history of horror and wonder.

sometimes praised in comparison with the rhetorically seductive images offered by history, as though the fragmentary and rough features of the former were better sources of evidence than the smooth, almost self-cohering pictures of the latter (see "MC," p. 51).

The ways in which the notion of *enargeia* gave way to the notions of evidence and proof furnish a crucial chapter in the history of the emergence of modern historiography. Treatises such as Henri Griffet's 1769 *Traité des différents sortes de preuves qui servent à établir la vérité de l'histoire* explicitly compared the historian to a judge who tested the reliability of witness and evaluated the claims of proofs.[4] Ginzburg writes that Griffet's work expressed "a still-unaddressed intellectual need" (p. 291), and I understand him to have expressed this need in his own words when he writes that we believe that

> historians must be ready to support their considerations by proofs of one kind or another. Or, if you prefer a descriptive proposition rather than a normative one: we at least believe (the neo-skeptics included, I suppose) that historians (neo-skeptics included) can only produce an "effect of truth" by linking their observations to some sort of proof. Citation (direct or indirect) has supplanted *enargeia*. ["MC," p. 53]

Ginzburg is, of course, fully aware of the fact that the judicial model of historiography has also emphasized the judge's sentence, that it can lead to a "moralistic historiography" based on "moral and political court-speeches, followed by condemnations or acquittals" (pp. 293, 292). And as Ginzburg remarks in his considerations on the Sofri trial, insisting on the ultimate divergences between the tasks of the historian and the judge, "moral certainty does not have the value [*non ha valore*] of proof."[5] A "deleterious model of judicial summations pronounced by an outmoded political historiography" is not the only model available to the historian who is committed to the notion of proof.[6] Moreover, I have not yet even mentioned the more subtle effects, enumerated by Ginzburg, of the judicial model, those seen, for example, in his claim that "on the one hand, it urges historians to focus on events (political, military, diplomatic) that could be easily ascribed to specific actions performed by one or more individuals; on the other, it disregards those phenomena (like social life, *mentalités*, and so on) that resist an approach based on this explanatory framework." Ginzburg acknowledges "the diminished prestige of this

---

4. On Griffet, see also Carlo Ginzburg, "Just One Witness," in *Probing the Limits of Representation: Nazism and the Final Solution*, ed. Saul Friedlander (Cambridge, Mass., 1992), p. 85.

5. Carlo Ginzburg, *Il giudice e lo storico*, p. 110.

6. Carlo Ginzburg, "Proofs and Possibilities: In the Margins of Natalie Zemon Davis' *The Return of Martin Guerre*," trans. Anthony Guneratne, *Yearbook of Comparative and General Literature* 37 (1988): 115.

kind of historiography . . . as a positive phenomenon" (pp. 292–93, 293).[7]
But such an acknowledgment does not require, as some historians appear
to have believed, that we simply dismiss the notion of proof, as if history
without evidence were the royal road to historiographical satisfaction.
Whatever theoretical impatience, or even embarrassment, might today
surround the notion of proof, what is called for is a more detailed investigation of the legitimate roles of proof, evidence, and truth in historical
writing *as opposed to* legal and judicial argumentation and judgment.
There is not some one notion of proof and evidence applicable by both
the judge and the historian to their respective domains. But just as we
must be careful not to pollute the exercise of justice, we must be vigilant
in not simplifying historiographical consciousness. Jettisoning proof, evidence, and truth from our consciousness is an impoverishment hardly
distinguishable from abject poverty.

3

Perhaps the most pervasive underlying distinctions between the
judge and the historian revolve around the different ideals that regulate
their tasks. The judge must render a just sentence: the historian must
provide a truthful account. As John Rawls has precisely and unforgettably
formulated this claim, at the beginning of the first section of *A Theory of
Justice*, "Justice is the first virtue of social institutions, as truth is of systems
of thought. A theory however elegant and economical must be rejected
or revised if it is untrue; likewise laws and institutions no matter how
efficient and well-arranged must be reformed or abolished if they are
unjust."[8] Both judges and historians invoke the notions of evidence and
proof, but their respective regulative ideals of justice and truth decisively
contribute to the understanding of what is to count as a piece of evidence,
what is to count as a proof. Legal evidence and historical evidence may
overlap, but the former is in the service of establishing a just verdict,
while the latter is relevant for securing a truthful account of events,
whether they be individual or social, long or short term. What is evidence
for some purposes may be beside the point for others. Obviously enough,
the *concepts* of justice and truth are compatible with a diversity of conflicting *conceptions* of justice and truth; or, to put it another way, the regulative
ideals of justice and truth are open to divergent interpretations of these
ideals.[9] But the fact that there are substantive disagreements about which
particular conception of justice or truth is most defensible does not imply
that a judge's deliberations should not be shaped by the ideal of justice

7. For what follows, see "Just One Witness," pp. 85–86.
8. John Rawls, *A Theory of Justice* (Cambridge, Mass., 1971), p. 3.
9. On the distinction between concepts and conceptions, see ibid., pp. 5–6. See also
Carlo Ginzburg, "Checking the Evidence," p. 302.

nor that a historian's reconstructions can ignore the demands of truth.[10] Ginzburg recognizes this fact in his use of the phrase "effect of truth" that I have already cited. He says that he has used the phrase "effect of truth" rather than "truth"

> in order to emphasize that different cultures have given different interpretations of the concept of truth. But as far as I know the distinction between false and true statements—and at first sight through their connection to the facts—has always been an essential element of historical knowledge, of whatever kind, everywhere that one has cultivated, up to the present, historical knowledge as a form of social activity. ["MC," p. 53]

In mentioning, even in passing, the regulative ideal of justice with respect to the judge, I cannot forbear invoking, in this context, an extraordinary book by Natalia Ginzburg, which takes up issues of evidence, proof, truth, law, and, ultimately, justice. *Serena Cruz o la vera giustizia* discusses a celebrated Italian case of adoption, of a baby named Serena Cruz, involving claims and counterevidence and finally culminating in a judicial verdict that decided the fate of the young child. At the very end of her discussion, Ginzburg quotes an Italian citation of an American Supreme Court judge, who responded to a lawyer's invocation of justice by saying, "I am not here to render justice [*per fare giustizia*] but to apply the law." [11] Ginzburg writes that she cannot understand these words, that they seem to her "devoid of meaning." She argues that not only should justice and the law be one but that since the laws are made to defend justice, when the two part ways, when the laws are defective, judges should "turn somersaults to apply it [the law] as justly as possible" (*SC*, pp. 95, 96). And the last two lines of her book insist on the regulative role of the ideal of justice in the most unambiguous terms: "Might something exist that is more important than justice in the government of countries, in the relations with human events and aspirations? But nothing exists that is more important than justice" (*SC*, p. 96). In his discussion of the Sofri case Carlo Ginzburg shows, in effect, that if one displaces the principle *in dubio pro re* (according to which the accused can be convicted only if one is absolutely certain of his guilt) from its regulative role in judicial proceedings, one may well be led to misuse completely the notion of proof, sliding tacitly from the plane of mere possibility to that of the assertion of fact.

---

10. For a discussion of some recent philosophical attempts to debunk truth and on the problems with these attempts, see Cora Diamond, "Truth: Defenders, Debunkers, Despisers," in *Commitment in Reflection: Essays in Literature and Moral Philosophy*, ed. Leona Toker (New York, 1994), pp. 195–221.

11. Quoted in Natalia Ginzburg, *Serena Cruz o la vera giustizia* (Turin, 1990), p. 95; hereafter abbreviated *SC*.

By making logical compatibility function as if it were equivalent to actual verification, one could well convict an innocent person. This might be acceptable if one's regulative ideal were *in dubio pro re publica*—for instance, the will of *il Duce*—but reasons of state ought to have no regulative role in the halls of justice.[12] The judge, insofar as he is governed by justice, must make use of specific conceptions of evidence and proof, forged by the ideals to which his role commits him.

Shifting briefly to the regulative ideal of truth in historical inquiry, we can see some of the distortions, the epistemological deficiencies, that result from an attempt to ignore it by looking at Ginzburg's recent debate with Hayden White. I want to insist, first of all, that it is an arduous undertaking for a historian to try to proceed consistently without the concept of truth. Indeed, in many of these debates, a given historian will employ the rhetoric of truth, arguing as though he is doing nothing more than advocating a specific conception of truth different from that of his interlocutors. But a short analysis will show that his specific conception of so-called truth has no philosophical plausibility whatsoever as an interpretation of the concept of truth and that it is only the demands of the regulative ideal of truth, exerting themselves despite attempts to ignore them, that account for the rhetoric employed, a rhetoric that, in this context, wears its emptiness virtually on its surface. It is no accident that some of the starkest instances of these issues can be found in discussions of the "revisionist" interpretation of the Holocaust. Taking up White's objections to Pierre Vidal-Naquet's conclusions about the Robert Faurisson affair, Ginzburg, quoting White, summarizes as follows:

> The Zionist historical interpretation of the Holocaust, White says, is not a *contre-vérité* (as has been suggested by Vidal-Naquet) but a truth: "its truth, as a historical interpretation, consists precisely in its *effectiveness* [Ginzburg's italics] in justifying a wide range of current Israeli political policies that, from the standpoint of those who articulate them, are crucial to the security and indeed the very existence of the Jewish people." In the same way, "the effort of the Palestinian people to mount a politically *effective* [Ginzburg's italics] response to Israeli policies entails the production of a similarly *effective* [Ginzburg's italics] ideology, complete with an interpretation of their history capable of endowing it with a meaning that it has hitherto lacked."

Ginzburg's next sentence conveys his own philosophical stance: "We can conclude that if Faurisson's narrative were ever to prove *effective*, it would be regarded by White as true as well."[13]

Ginzburg's remark is, I think, meant as a kind of *reductio ad absurdum*

---

12. See Carlo Ginzburg, *Il giudice e lo storico*, pp. 110–11.
13. Carlo Ginzburg, "Just One Witness," p. 93.

of the identification of political effectiveness and truth. He implies that an interpretation or conception of truth that makes it equivalent to political effectiveness falls outside of the boundaries, however flexible, of our understanding of the concept of truth. It is to give up the very concept of truth, as shown by the fact that however effective Faurisson's account might be (it is, as Vidal-Naquet has shown, not very effective, and we should even wonder how effective it could be), we would not conclude that it was a true account. I suppose that someone might respond by claiming that White is doing nothing more epistemologically vicious than proposing a pragmatist conception of truth. But I would argue, though I shall not undertake this here, that a survey of the history of philosophy as well as an analysis of philosophical debates about the nature of truth would show that in no way is this even a defensible construal of the pragmatist notion of truth, that the pragmatists wanted to provide an interpretation of truth that did much more than brutely force its identification with political effectiveness.[14]

Someone might, I guess, respond further that whether we call a historical account true or effective is a matter of words, up to us to choose according to our interests. If it serves our purposes to call an account true because it is effective, then nothing forbids us from doing so, nothing compels us to withhold the label "true." But whether someone possesses the concept of truth is not up to us to so decide; it is not a matter of legislative decree, as though possessing a concept were like being granted the right to vote.[15] Neither declaration nor rhetorical convolution is sufficient to show that someone who understands political effectiveness *by that very fact* possesses the concept of truth. And Ginzburg's claim against White is, first, that White's response to Vidal-Naquet forgoes the concept of truth and, second, that this concept regulates the enquiries of the historian. From these claims, it does follow that Faurisson's narrative does not count as history; and this strikes me as precisely the appropriate standpoint to have.

In the preface to the reprinting of his brilliant essay "Un Eichmann de papier," one of the most powerful contributions to the topics of this volume I know, Vidal-Naquet expresses the point of view that is implied by the essential intertwining of history and the regulative ideal of truth. It is a point of view that I believe he shares with Ginzburg, and in both cases it is a consequence of some of their basic historiographical claims, claims that converge around the roles that each ascribes to evidence, proof, and truth:

14. On these issues, see many of the essays in Hilary Putnam, *Realism with a Human Face*, ed. James Conant (Cambridge, Mass., 1990). I note especially the last paragraph of the essay "William James' Ideas."

15. The best discussion of this topic is Stanely Cavell, *The Claim of Reason: Wittgenstein, Skepticism, Morality, and Tragedy* (New York, 1979), pt. 1.

What is at stake here is not feeling but truth. . . . A dialogue between two parties, even if they are adversaries, presupposes a common ground, a common respect—in this case for truth. But with the "revisionists," such ground does not exist. Could one conceive of an astrophysicist entering into dialogue with a "researcher" claiming that the moon is made of Roquefort cheese? Such is the level at which the parties would have to be situated. And, of course, no more than there is an absolute truth is there an absolute lie, even though the "revisionists" have made valiant efforts to attain that ideal. By which I mean that were it to be determined that the passengers of a rocket or a spaceship had left a few grams of Roquefort on the moon, there would be no point in denying their presence. Until now, the contribution of the "revisionists" to our knowledge may be compared to the correction, in a long text, of a few typographical errors. That does not justify a dialogue, since they have above all amplified beyond measure the register of falsehood.[16]

4

After Ginzburg's discussion of White at the conference "Nazism and the 'Final Solution,'" I heard several audience members complain that Ginzburg, in his defense of evidence, truth, and proof, was just a conservative positivist. Passing over the fact that there were left-wing as well as right-wing versions of positivism, I found these murmurings incoherent after thinking about Ginzburg's own historical writings and procedures. As Ginzburg clearly states in "Checking the Evidence," a certain positivistic conception of the relationship between evidence and reality must be "unequivocally rejected." Evidence is not a "transparent medium . . . an open window that gives us direct access to reality." But neither is evidence "a wall, which by definition precludes any access to reality." As Ginzburg correctly diagnoses it, "this extreme antipositivistic attitude . . . turns out to be a sort of inverted positivism" (p. 000).

In examining the history of positivism and antipositivism in twentieth-century history and philosophy of science, Peter Galison has recently argued that in light of their obvious differences, the latter being a reaction against the former, we must be careful not to overlook the fact that these positivisms and antipositivisms are "flip-side versions of one another" and that "in their mirror reflections there is a good deal of similarity." Each has a "privileged vantage point"—whether the observational foundation from which the positivist builds up or the paradigm or conceptual scheme from which the antipositivist looks down—that carries

---

16. Pierre Vidal-Naquet, *Assassins of Memory: Essays on the Denial of the Holocaust*, trans. Jeffrey Mehlman (New York, 1992), p. xxiv.

similar historiographical consequences.[17] A common picture of both scientific unity and periodization can be found running through the issues that divided positivist and antipositivist history and philosophy of science.[18] Indeed, I would add that it is part of the cultural dominance of this common picture that *we* are led to believe that if someone rejects positivist foundationalism and observational transparency, then he or she must be an antipositivist, who considers "all referential assumptions as a theoretical naiveté" since discourse (or theory, or narrative tropes) constitutes the objects that it pretends to describe realistically (p. 294).[19] This structuring of the alternatives—either the direct, virtually unmediated access to reality dreamed of by positivism or the self-sustaining, walled-in antipositivist discourse that precludes access to reality—makes it extraordinarily difficult to see how there could be any other possibility. The common structure of these mirror images threatens to exhaust the space of epistemological options. His detailed historical studies have allowed Galison to propose a conceptualization of the dynamics of scientific theory, experimentation, and instrumentation that stands outside the purview of the common picture, thus also allowing him to throw into relief the historiographical burdens of the traditional positivism/antipositivism debates.[20] If we examine Ginzburg's historical practice, we will see that although not an antipositivist, one who rejects the historiographical legitimacy of notions like evidence and proof, neither is he a positivist, who takes these notions as given, as though they involve an unproblematic relation with truth and reality.

Ginzburg's essay "The Inquisitor as Anthropologist" is one of our clearest and most profound discussions of the problems with positivist interpretations of evidence and truth. Ginzburg recognizes an unsettling analogy between inquisitors, anthropologists, and historians, an analogy that manifests a fundamental epistemological difficulty with certain forms of evidence and especially with those forms of evidence employed by Ginzburg himself in *The Night Battles* and *The Cheese and the Worms*:

> The elusive evidence that inquisitors were trying to elicit from defendants was not so different, after all, from our own objectives; what was different, of course, were their means and ultimate ends. . . . The inquisitors' urge for truth (their own truth, of course) has produced for us extremely rich evidence—deeply distorted, however, by the psychological and physical pressures which played such a powerful role in witchcraft trials. Suggestive questioning was especially appar-

17. Peter Galison, "History, Philosophy, and the Central Metaphor," *Science in Context* 2 (Spring 1988): 207.

18. Ibid., secs. 2–3.

19. See Carlo Ginzburg, "Just One Witness," p. 89.

20. See Galison, "History, Philosophy, and the Central Metaphor," sec. 4. See also Galison, *How Experiments End* (Chicago, 1987).

ent in inquisitors' interrogations related to the witches' sabbat, the very essense of witchcraft, according to demonologists. When this occurred, defendants echoed, more or less spontaneously, the inquisitorial stereotypes which were diffused throughout Europe by preachers, theologians, and jurists. . . . Similarly, the comparison between inquisitorial trials and anthropological field notes could have, from the historian's point of view, a negative implication: the presence of those long-ago anthropologists would be so obtrusive as to prevent us from knowing the beliefs and thoughts of the unhappy natives brought before them.[21]

Rather than drawing a completely pessimistic conclusion from the presence of this epistemological problem (as many antipositivists do), Ginzburg insists on the importance of the fact that historians never have direct access to reality. As he puts it in "Checking the Evidence":

A piece of historical evidence can be either involuntary (a skull, a footprint, a food relic) or voluntary (a chronicle, a notarial act, a fork). But in both cases a specific interpretative framework is needed, which must be related (in the latter case) to the specific code according to which the evidence has been constructed. Evidence of both kinds could be compared to a distorted glass. Without a thorough analysis of its inherent distortions (the codes according to which it has been constructed and/or it must be perceived), a sound historical reconstruction is impossible. [P. 295]

Evidence is mediated by codes, and an adequate historiography must attend to the heterogeneous procedures by which we encode evidence. According to Ginzburg, there are no neutral documents: "even a notarial inventory implies a code, which we must decipher." And the evidence gathered from inquisitorial trials certainly does not "convey to us 'objective' information" ("IA," pp. 161, 160). But these codes are not prisons in which we find ourselves forever confined. We must understand the processes of encoding, of different kinds of evidential distortion, in order to interpret the evidence, to assess its reliability or unreliability, to know what it is evidence *of*. Codes that seemed impenetrable can eventually be deciphered, and new evidence, encoded in new ways, can shed light on old evidence, changing our interpretations of codes we had believed were unambiguous. Ginzburg's remarks about inquisitorial evidence should be applied, mutatis mutandis, to a whole range of historical evidence:

21. Carlo Ginzburg, "The Inquisitor as Anthropologist," *Clues, Myths, and the Historical Method*, trans. John and Anne C. Tedeschi (Baltimore, 1989), pp. 158–59; hereafter abbreviated "IA."

> In order to decipher them [the documents of inquisitors], we must learn to catch, behind the smooth surface of the text, a subtle interplay of threats and fears, of attacks and withdrawals. We must learn to disentangle the different threads which form the textual fabric of these dialogues. ["IA," pp. 160–61]

There is no formalizable set of rules that tells us how to decipher historical evidence (here the analogy with a code is loosened), but there are truly great historical works whose power partly resides in the ability of a historian to read the evidence, to show us how to enter into the codes of evidence in order to see *what* the evidence *is*, what it shows us about the phenomena we are interested in, what the phenomena are.

Let me now briefly turn to Ginzburg's groundbreaking contribution in this area. In the prefaces to the English and Italian editions of his book *The Night Battles,* Ginzburg stresses that the exceptional nature of the documents he used lies in "the gap between the questions of the judges and the confessions of the accused which was gradually reduced only in the course of decades."[22] Many historians had come to believe that all of the confessions of those accused of witchcraft were the consequences of torture and suggestive questioning on the part of the judges, that these confessions possessed no spontaneity or independence and were therefore evidence of the judges' beliefs, providing no access to the practices or beliefs of the witches. Ginzburg's Friulian sources, when critically decoded, allowed him to conclude that "the Friuli diabolical witchcraft grew out of the deformation of a preceding agrarian cult" (*NB*, pp. xx–xxi).[23] That is, Ginzburg's reading of the sources showed a gap, what he called "a clash between different, even conflicting voices," or, following Bakhtin, a dialogue ("IA," p. 160), and it was this subtle but significant gap that made it possible for Ginzburg to reconstruct the process that revealed

> how a cult with such obviously popular characteristics as that of the benandanti gradually was transformed under inquisitorial pressure, ending up with the distinctive features of traditional witchcraft. But this discrepancy, this gap between the image underlying the interrogations of the judges and the actual testimony of the accused, permits us to reach a genuinely popular stratum of beliefs which was later deformed, and then expunged by the superimposition of the schema of the educated classes. Because of this discrepancy, which endured over several decades, the benandanti trials constitute a precious

22. Carlo Ginzburg, *The Night Battles: Witchcraft and Agrarian Cults in the Sixteenth and Seventeenth Centuries,* trans. John and Anne Tedeschi (1966; New York, 1985), p. xiv; hereafter abbreviated *NB*.

23. See also, more generally, Carlo Ginzburg, *Ecstasies: Deciphering the Witches' Sabbath,* trans. Raymond Rosenthal (New York, 1991).

source for the reconstruction of the peasant mentality of this period. [*NB*, p. xviii][24]

Ultimately, the nocturnal gatherings of the *benandanti*, which were intended to induce fertility, were transformed into the devil's sabbat, with the storms and destruction that followed (see *NB*, p. xx). However, the lack of communication between judges and accused allowed "the emergence of a real dialogue—in the Bakhtinian sense of an unresolved clash of conflicting voices" ("IA," p. 164). Ginzburg's readings of these dialogues permitted him (and us) to see the existence of a "deep cultural layer which was totally foreign to the inquisitors." As he notes, "the very word benandante was unknown to them: . . . was it a synonym of "witch" or, on the contrary, 'counterwitch'?" ("IA," p. 164). The meaning of this word was one of the stakes in the struggle between the *benandanti* and inquisitors. Although power settled the semantic dispute in favor of the inquisitors, and *benandanti* became witches, the miscommunications and struggles provided evidence about the *benandanti* not otherwise available (see "IA," p. 160). Ginzburg's historiographical exploitation of these gaps, his extraordinary ability to read the codes, furnishes evidence for a set of phenomena that gives us a *more accurate* characterization of the *benandanti*. Whatever the distortions of the inquisitorial evidence, Ginzburg's procedure of reading the gaps does culminate in genuine evidence about a cultural reality that is no longer inaccessible to us.

In *The Cheese and the Worms*, again using inquisitorial documents, Ginzburg's reconstruction of the cosmology of Domenico Scandella, known as Menocchio, encounters similar problems concerning evidence and proof. Ginzburg's reading of these documents uses the gaps, miscommunications, resistances, and struggles as evidence of the existence of a peasant and oral culture that was "the patrimony not only of Menocchio but also of a vast segment of sixteenth-century society" (*CW*, p. xii). As in the case of the *benandanti*, only such a procedure of deciphering the documents will allow us to come to grips with the inherent distortions of the evidence created by the relationship of unequal power between Menocchio and his inquisitors. It is precisely the discrepancies and divergences in the documents that provide some of the most compelling evidence for Ginzburg's conclusions. But the case of Menocchio has its own particular difficulties:

> Here, too [as in the case of the *benandanti*], the fact that many of Menocchio's utterances cannot be reduced to familiar themes permits us to perceive a previously untapped level of popular beliefs, of obscure peasant mythologies. But what renders Menocchio's case

24. For some of Ginzburg's later doubts about the notion of mentality, see his *The Cheese and the Worms: The Cosmos of a Sixteenth-Century Miller*, trans. John and Anne Tedeschi (New York, 1982), pp. xxiii–xxiv; hereafter abbreviated *CW*.

that much more complicated is the fact that these obscure popular elements are grafted onto an extremely clear and logical complex of ideas, from religious radicalism, to a naturalism tending toward the scientific, to utopian aspirations of social reform. [*CW,* p. xix]

The fact that although Menocchio's ideas seem to be derived from an "ancient oral tradition," they at the same time "recall a series of motifs worked out by humanistically educated heretical groups" should not lead us to exaggerate the importance of educated culture, as though Menocchio's ideas must really be derived from the latter, since ideas "originate *always and only* in educated circles" (*CW,* pp. xxii, 155). Ginzburg's reading of the documents, encoded as they are, exhibits "the gulf between the texts read by Menocchio and the way in which he understood them and reported them to the inquisitors," a gulf that indicates "a filter, a grill that Menocchio interposed unconsciously between himself and the texts" and which itself presupposed the peasant culture of which he was part (*CW,* pp. xxii, xii). The route to this peasant culture is hardly unproblematic, "given the fact that the documentation reflects the relationship of power between the classes of a given society" (*CW,* p. 155). Ginzburg's stunning achievement is to have used positively these distorted reflections in order to provide access to peasant, oral culture. What I have called his procedure of reading the gaps permits him to construct the evidence *more accurately,* so as to conclude that

> even if Menocchio had been in more or less indirect contact with educated circles, his statements in favor of religious tolerance and his desire for a radical renewal of society have an original stamp to them and do not appear to be the result of passively received outside influences. The roots of his utterances and of his aspirations were sunk in an obscure, almost unfathomable, layer of remote peasant traditions. [*CW,* pp. xxii–xxiii]

One of the main aims of *The Cheese and the Worms* was to use the case of Menocchio in order to help demonstrate that "between the culture of the dominant classes and that of the subordinate classes there existed, in preindustrial Europe, a circular relationship composed of reciprocal influences which traveled from low to high as well as from high to low"(*CW,* p. xii). But such a demonstration depends on the possibility of constructing the evidence so that one can have access to peasant culture, of not reducing this culture merely to a shadow of written culture. No "reciprocal movement between the two levels of culture" can be shown if there is no way to distinguish or disentangle the two levels or if it is assumed that there is no independence whatsoever to oral culture, since its ideas must ultimately be traced back to written culture (*CW,* p. xiv). Contrary to Paola Zambelli's interpretation, Ginzburg did not want to establish "'the absolute autonomy of peasant culture,'" which would have defeated his goal of trying to show that "we are in the presence of two cultures, linked, however—and this is the point—by circular (reciprocal) relationships," relationships that, as Ginzburg acknowledges, have "to be analytically demonstrated case by case," as in the case of Menocchio (*CW,* pp. 154–55).[25] But he did need to establish the relative autonomy or independence of peasant culture, the existence of *two* cultures, and, given the distorted nature of the evidence, the fact that "the thoughts, beliefs, and the aspirations of the peasants and artisans of the past reach us (if and when they do) almost always through distorting viewpoints and intermediaries," the existence of these *two* cultures could not be taken for granted (*CW,* p. xv). Ginzburg needed to show how to decode the evidence in order to demonstrate that we were in fact in the presence of two cultures, while showing also that these two cultures were reciprocally linked. As he says, "The fact that a source is not 'objective' . . . does not mean that it is useless" (*CW,* p. xvii). Both *The Cheese and the Worms* and *The Night Battles* provide extraordinary examples of how a nonobjective source can be useful, supply us with concrete lessons in how we might decipher a nonobjective source so that it can be seen to have evidentiary value. Ginzburg's historiographical commitment consists in not rejecting a distorted source outright just because it is distorted. And his historical practice consists in allowing us to see precisely those procedures of reading and interpretation that produce compelling evidence on the basis of nonobjective sources, thereby demonstrating that although the relationship between evidence and reality is problematic, it is not hopeless.

Before concluding, I want to mention a set of examples that comes from the history of psychiatry and psychology and that raises problems of evidence, proof, and reality as acute as those of Ginzburg's inquisitors. In his already-classic paper "Making up People," Ian Hacking describes a philosophical notion that he calls dynamic nominalism, a notion that he applies to his own account of the invention of split personality and to my account of the invention of the homosexual:

> The claim of dynamic nominalism is . . . that a kind of person came into being at the same time as the kind itself was being invented. In some cases, that is, our classifications and our classes conspire to emerge hand in hand, each egging the other on. . . . Dynamic nominalism remains an intriguing doctrine, arguing that numerous kinds of human beings and human acts come into being hand in hand with our own invention of the categories labelling them. It is for me the only intelligible species of nominalism, the only one that can even

---

25. Paolo Zambelli's interpretation can be found in his "Uno, due, tre, mille Menocchio?" *Archivio storico italiano* 137, no. 499 (1979): 51–90.

gesture at an account of how common names and the named could so tidily fit together.[26]

Leaving aside the general epistemological complexities of dynamic nominalism, I want to focus on some questions of evidence that are analogous to those raised by Ginzburg's work on inquisitorial documents. My own account of the history of perversion and perverts has been a heavily top-down account, emphasizing the role of psychiatric concepts and categories in creating the reality of homosexuality, masochism, and sadism. I have argued that we do not have evidence of the homosexual preexisting the concepts and categories of nineteenth-century psychiatry, that this supposed evidence is actually evidence of sodomy, and that it was only retrospectively (mis)interpreted as evidence of homosexuality after the concept of the homosexual was well entrenched in psychiatric theory and practice.[27] Hacking's early work on multiple personality also emphasized the top-down aspects of the creation of the multiple, but his more recent work has also carefully considered another vector, the vector that comes from below, that comes from, so to speak, nonexpert culture.[28] Hacking recognized the existence of these two vectors right from the beginning of his work. He wrote:

> I do not believe there is a general story to be told about making up people. Each category has its own history. If we wish to present a partial framework in which to describe such events, we might think of two vectors. One is the vector of labeling from above, from a community of experts who create a "reality" that some people make their own. Different from this is the vector of the autonomous behavior of the person so labeled, which presses from below, creating a reality every expert must face. ["MP," p. 234]

The evidential problem related to these two vectors stems from the fact that virtually all of the early nineteenth-century evidence we have comes from above, that the case reports encode the evidence in terms of the concepts and categories of psychiatry, and that we have, at best, very

---

26. Ian Hacking, "Making up People," in *Reconstructing Individualism: Autonomy, Individuality, and the Self in Western Thought,* ed. Thomas C. Heller et al. (Stanford, Calif., 1986), pp. 228, 236; hereafter abbreviated "MP."

27. Arnold I. Davidson, "Closing up the Corpses: Diseases of Sexuality and the Emergence of the Psychiatric Style of Reasoning," in *Meaning and Method: Essays in Honor of Hilary Putnam,* ed. George Boolos (Cambridge, 1990) and "Sex and the Emergence of Sexuality," *Critical Inquiry* 14 (Autumn 1987): 16–48.

28. For his earliest work on multiple personality, see Hacking, "The Invention of Split Personalities," *Human Nature and Natural Knowledge: Essays Presented to Marjorie Grene on the Occasion of Her Seventy-Fifth Birthday,* ed. Alan Donagan, Anthony N. Perovich, Jr., and Michael V. Wedin (Dordrecht, 1986), pp. 63–86. For his most recent contribution to this subject, see "Two Souls in One Body," pp. 433–62 of this volume.

marginal access to any vector from below. Perhaps we are faced here with some examples, limited though they are, in which we start with only *one* culture, the culture of medicine, which creates a reality that then becomes relatively autonomous over time. It might well be that beginning with the creation of the homosexual by psychiatry, homosexual culture only gradually evolved a life of its own that exerted greater and greater autonomy with respect to the concepts, categories, and practices that created it. But it might also be the case that, like many historians of witchcraft, we have failed to read the evidence correctly; we have neglected to exploit the gaps, miscommunications, and resistances, and so we have failed to see the existence, from the beginning, of a partially autonomous reality from below. Ginzburg's procedure of reading the gaps in distorted evidence may help us to correct conclusions that have been too hastily drawn from unexamined historiographical assumptions. Without assuming that evidence concerning homosexuality, multiple personality, and other psychiatric disease categories will yield identical conclusions, I want to look at one such piece of evidence, while heeding the lessons of Ginzburg's historical practice.

The piece of evidence I have in mind is reproduced by Hacking in "Making up People" and comes from an 1886 article by Pierre Janet. Hacking adduces it as "one all-too-tidy example of how a new person can be made up" ("MP," p. 224).[29] Janet is speaking to Lucie, who, having the habit of automatic writing, is responding to him in writing, without her normal self's awareness:

Janet.	Do you understand me?
Lucie (writes).	No.
J.	But to reply you must understand me!
L.	Oh yes, absolutely.
J.	Then what are you doing?
L.	Don't know.
J.	It is certain that someone is understanding me.
L.	Yes.
J.	Who is that?
L.	Somebody besides Lucie.
J.	Aha! Another person. Would you like to give her a name?
L.	No.
J.	Yes. It would be far easier that way.
L.	Oh well. If you want: Adrienne.
J.	Then, Adrienne, do you understand me?
L.	Yes.

["MP," pp. 224–25]

29. See Pierre Janet, "Les Actes inconscients et le dédoublement de la personnalité pendant le somnambulisme provoqué," *Revue Philosophique* 22 (Dec. 1886): 577–92.

When I first read this exchange, I, in effect, took it as evidence not only of the dominance of medical culture in making up people but as exhibiting the absence of evidence of any competing or conflicting cultural reality. But after studying Ginzburg's procedures of reading distorted evidence, I wonder whether I was not too quick in my implicit conclusions. For this exchange, brief as it is, is full of gaps, miscommunications, and resistances. Lucie's alternating "yes" and "no," her initial refusal to provide another name, followed by her "Oh well. If you want: Adrienne," show, if not a full-fledged Bakhtinian clash of conflicting voices, at least the existence of a real gap. Janet does not have to exert much force to create Adrienne out of Lucie, but Lucie's resistances could be evidence of another level of reality, one quite foreign to Janet. If we had pages and pages of such dialogue, as Ginzburg had of his inquisitorial dialogues, then it would be easier to read the gaps, to know whether we could exploit them as evidence of a partially autonomous culture from below, a cultural reality that is systematically distorted by an unequal power relationship. That the distortions could be so great as to make the evidence unrecoverable goes without saying. But that even this brief, highly distorted exchange between Janet and Lucie exhibits visible gaps, if only one knows how to look for them, should give us cause for historiographical reflection. We must follow Ginzburg's lead in this area and not let inherent distortion of the evidence pass us by, as it so easily can, without further examination. We must look patiently for dialogic discrepancies, divergences, and misunderstandings, attending detectivelike to the always encoded evidence we do have, learning, as Ginzburg has taught us, "to catch, behind the smooth surface of the text, a subtle interplay of threats and fears, of attacks and withdrawals" ("IA," p. 161).

A Rejoinder to Arnold I. Davidson

Carlo Ginzburg

I am deeply grateful to Arnold Davidson for his perceptive reading of my paper ("Carlo Ginzburg and the Renewal of Historiography," pp. 304–20). The following remarks have been inspired by Davidson's thoughtful analysis of the relationship between positivism and positivism in historiography.

This issue concerns me directly insofar as I have been accused of being a conservative positivist (as Davidson observes). Quoting from my paper as well as from some of my earlier works, Davidson remarks that I have repeatedly argued against the central tenet of positivistic history, that is, the more or less tacit assumption of a transparent relationship between historical evidence and historical reality. The rejection of that assumption was already implicit, I believe, in the decision I made as an apprentice historian to focus more on sixteenth-century witchcraft than on the persecution of it. I learned to read witchcraft trials as texts, which provided direct evidence on the inquisitors and lay judges behind them, as well as some indirect and usually distorted evidence on the defendants. All of my subsequent work has been shaped by this early research experience.

Retrospectively, I think that my antipositivistic record is fairly respectable. But I wonder what *positivism* means in this context. Certainly it means something rather different from *positivism* in the historical sense of the word, as a label referring either to Auguste Comte and his disciples, or—in a broader sense—to the late nineteenth-century intellectual atmosphere in which the works of Claude Bernard and Charles Darwin, of Maupassant and Chekhov, emerged. To this intellectual tradition, or at least to some elements of it, I feel deeply indebted. I do not have in mind those grandiose treatises that claimed to explain everything from amoeba to God; rather, I am thinking of those intellectual enterprises that expressed positivism's double, contradictory heritage: the Enlightenment on the one hand, the romantic movement on the other. The first name to be mentioned in this context is Sigmund Freud's. His attempt to use reason as an instrument to explore the foreign territory of dreams, slips of the tongue, and neurotic symptoms exemplifies the tension I have just mentioned. The same man who wrote a tribute to the Enlightenment tradition (*The Future of an Illusion*) rediscovered in *Beyond the Pleasure Principle* a typical romantic category like the death instinct. This Januslike emphasis on both reason and the irrational seems to me an obvious outcome of Freud's deeply positivistic orientation, which has so often been erased and forgotten. A well-known intellectual historian has recently rejected positivism in allegedly Freudian terms—in this way betraying his lack of familiarity with Freud and positivism as well.

Some years ago I wrote an essay in which I traced the complex genealogy of an intellectual approach based on marginal details, on clues. My account started from three individuals, two of them real, the third fully fictitious: Morelli, the art historian, Freud, and Sherlock Holmes. Retrospectively, I see that all of them shared the apparently divergent point I made in my paper: a strong concern for proof and an awareness that new problems may imply a reformulation of the standards of proof. Morelli devised a new method of connoisseurship based on minor details like nails or ear lobes, rephrasing in seemingly positivistic language the romantic concern for artistic creativity he had absorbed in his youth. Freud, who claimed to have been influenced by Morelli, relied on minor details like slips of the tongue or fragments of dreams in his approach to neuroses. The scientific communities to which Morelli and Freud respectively belonged considered them for some time charlatans or impostors. This dismissive attitude reinforced both Morelli's and Freud's emphasis on proof as a guarantee of the scientific level of their own work. One of Freud's later works—"Constructions in Analysis"—written from a perspective that seems far removed from positivism, is in fact inspired by the worrisome possibility that his own work could be regarded either as unproved or (worse yet) as based on a pseudoscientific notion of proof.

The same obsession with proof was obviously shared by the third character in my triad, Sherlock Holmes—even more so by his creator, Arthur Conan Doyle, who, in a rather extraordinary (and apparently

---

Carlo Ginzburg is Franklin D. Murphy Professor of Italian Renaissance Studies at the University of California, Los Angeles. His two most recent books are *Ecstasies: Deciphering the Witches' Sabbath* (1991) and *Il giudice e lo storico* (1991).

serious) pamphlet, claimed to have captured the final proof of the existence of fairies (who obviously were exact replicas of Peter Pan's companion) with his camera. Such an example looks like a caricature, an exaggerated version of the picture I was evoking before. The attempt to use reason in order to explore irrational (or apparently irrational) phenomena could have widely different outcomes, from metalogic to metaphysics (the latter is used with the meaning I found in the West Los Angeles yellow pages, under "Occult Supplies").

The discovery of new areas of inquiry generates new questions, which often generate new experiments, which sometimes generate new criteria of proof. But this sequence is far from being unilinear. All kinds of constraints can interact, obstructing or accelerating this process. I mentioned elsewhere a text by Cesare Baronio, the Counter-Reformation historian, in which he apologized to the readers of his *Annales Ecclesiastici* because, after much uncertainty, he had finally decided to include quotations from documents (presumably medieval) written in poor Latin. In this way Baronio sacrificed rhetoric for truth. His fight against Protestant historians like the so-called Magdeburg *centuriatores* seemed more important to him. The choice made by Jonathan Spence in reconstructing the last dream of his peasant hero, woman Wang, moves, in a sense, in the opposite direction. By weaving bits and pieces taken from different literary texts into a smooth narrative, historical truth has been sacrificed for a rhetorical effect. The result, as I said in my paper, is not falsehood, insofar as Spence, by printing the reconstructed dream in italics, obliquely suggested what is plainly declared in the corresponding footnote: that is, the lack of any evidence (either hard or soft) for it. Spence's literary skills are remarkable, but the result curiously resembles television docudramas. Let me qualify this. We should be grateful to Oliver Stone for having indirectly succeeded, through his movie *JFK*, in making some files related to Kennedy's assassination available to the public (I think that *JFK* is a bad movie, but this is beside the point here). In this kind of movie, which is based on a historical event, color is traditionally perceived as related to fiction, black and white to reality. Stone's insertion of fictional black-and-white flashbacks baffles the audience's expectations, creating a deliberate confusion among facts, conjectures, and reconstructions in docudrama style. Stone's use of black and white and Spence's italics are generated by the same atmosphere. Scholarly flexibility towards standards of proof seems to me related to a wider attitude, shared by mass culture as well.

The idea that reality is the result of a construction at various levels (perceptual, social, and so forth) is not new. I have never been able to fully explain to myself the mass appeal of this sophisticated idea (especially, but not only, in the U.S.). In order to do that, we should try to develop the unforgettable remarks made by Adorno in the forties when the prerequisites for the phenomenon I am speaking about first emerged.

The reassuring, pervasive experience of the media, particularly television, and its presentation of a totally artificial world, must powerfully reinforce the idea that every reality is basically a construction. Then suddenly something terrible happens. We naively believe that the coded and distorted messages we get through the television set must be related to some reality out there. But this is just a parenthesis. Ordinary life begins again. We are plunged back into advertisements, docudramas, "reality."

Atlantis and the Nations

Pierre Vidal-Naquet

Translated by Janet Lloyd

The story is a strange one. It starts in about 355 B.C., with Plato's *Timaeus* and *Critias*. I say "it starts" advisedly, for, despite all efforts, nobody has been able to prove that this myth was ever told before Plato recounted it. The tale itself is so well known that I need hardly summarize the essentials. Plato presents it as a story, a *muthos* that is told to the Athenian lawgiver and poet Solon, "the wisest of the Seven" wise men,[1] by an old priest of the goddess Neïth at Sais in Egypt. Solon has just been telling what he believes to be the oldest legends of the Greek people, but the priest knows better. "O Solon, Solon, you Greeks are always children: there is not such a thing as an old Greek" (*T,* 22B). The Athenians do not know their own history, recorded in the archives of Egypt. These go back eight thousand years, but as much as nine thousand years before Solon's time (*T,* 23D–E), Athens used to be a model city, that is to say, a city constructed according to Plato's own principles. This Athens was a perfect city, a land-based and consequently hoplite power that came up against an antimodel, Atlantis, a huge island power, "larger than Asia and Libya [Africa] together" (*T,* 24E). Constantly evolving, this kingdom, founded by Poseidon to shelter the children that he fathered by the nymph Clito,

---

The present text was published in French as "L'Atlantide et les nations," in Pierre Vidal-Naquet, *La Démocratie grecque vue d'ailleurs: Essais d'historiographie ancienne et moderne* (Paris, 1990), pp. 139–59, and has many points in common with my article "Hérodote et l'Atlantide: Entre les Grecs et les Juifs; Réflexions sur l'historiographie du siècle des lumières," *Quaderni di storia* 16 (July–Dec. 1982): 3–76.

1. Plato, *Timaeus,* 20D; hereafter abbreviated *T.*

This essay originally appeared in *Critical Inquiry* 18 (Winter 1992).

became at once a sea power and an evil power—two associated, or even twin, concepts in Plato's view.[2] Naturally, Atlantis was an imperial power, and, although situated in the West, it puts one in mind of the Persia of the Persian Wars. Atlantis launched its ships and soldiers against the Mediterranean and clashed with the Athenian army. The Athenians won the day, but thereupon vanquished and victors alike were swallowed up by a great flood. Atlantis disappeared into the ocean that now bears its name. It no longer existed except in the archives and memories of the Egyptians. Athens did survive, reduced however to the mere bones of the ancient city. Thanks to the priest in Sais, Solon carried the heroic story back to Athens, where he passed it on to Critias, then a child, to

2. For more details, see my "Athènes et l'Atlantide: Structure et signification d'un mythe platonicien," *Revue des études grecques* 77 (July–Dec. 1964): 420–44, which also appears in a more complete form in my *Black Hunter: Forms of Thought and Forms of Society in the Greek World,* trans. Andrew Szegedy-Maszak (Baltimore, 1986), pp. 263–84. Parallel and complementary points have also been treated in Luc Brisson, "De la philosophie politique à l'épopée: Le 'Critias' de Platon," *Revue de métaphysique et de morale* 75 (Oct.–Dec. 1970): 402–38, and *Platon, les mots et les mythes* (Paris, 1982); Christopher Gill, "The Origin of the Atlantis Myth," *Trivium* 11 (1976): 1–11, "The Genre of the Atlantis Story," *Classical Philology* 72 (July 1977): 287–304, and *Plato, the Atlantis Story* (Bristol, 1980). These works, together with my own article, "Hérodote et l'Atlantide: Entre les Grecs et les Juifs; Réflexions sur l'historiographie du siècle des lumières," *Quaderni di storia* 16 (July–Dec. 1982): 3–76, provide a very full bibliography. The whole succession of works on this subject, most of them quite mad, may be followed thanks to the Platonic bibliographies published in *Lustrum,* first under the editorship of Harold F. Cherniss and then under Luc Brisson. For an example of the unbelievable seriousness of some of these works, see Barbara Pischel, *Die Atlantische Lehre: Übersetzung und Interpretation der Platon-Texte aus Timaios und Kritias* (Frankfurt am Main, 1982).

Pierre Vidal-Naquet is director of the Centre Louis Gernet de Recherches Comparées sur les Sociétés Anciennes at the École des Hautes Études en Sciences Sociales in Paris. His most recent publications are *Le Trait empoisonné: Réflexions sur l'affaire Jean Moulin* (1993); the second volume of *Les Juifs, la mémoire et le présent* (1991); *La Grèce ancienne 1: Du mythe à la raison,* with Jean-Pierre Vernant (1990); and *La Démocratie grecque vue d'ailleurs* (1990). Among his works to have appeared in English are *Myth and Tragedy in Ancient Greece,* with Jean-Pierre Vernant (1988), and *The Black Hunter: Forms of Thought and Forms of Society in the Greek World* (1986). **Janet Lloyd** is a supervisor for a number of colleges in Cambridge University, where she gives classes in French language and literature. Among her more recent translations are Yves Mény's *Government and Politics in Western Europe: Britain, France, Italy, West Germany* (1990) and Marie-Claire Bergère's *Golden Age of the Chinese Bourgeoisie, 1911–1937* (1989). In progress are translations of works on Shakespeare, Pericles' Athens, and a historical geography of France.

be handed down to his descendants, of whom Plato was one of the best known.

I will not dwell overlong on the "meaning" of this story. But let me make two essential points. Plato tells us this story as though it were true: it is "a tale which, though passing strange, is yet wholly true."[3] Those words were to be translated into every language in the world and used to justify the most realistic fantasies. That is quite understandable, for Plato's story started something new.[4] With a perversity that was to ensure him great success, Plato had laid the foundations for the historical novel, that is to say, the novel set in a particular place and a particular time.[5] We are now quite accustomed to historical novels, and we also know that in every detective story there comes a moment when the detective declares that real life is not much like what happens in detective stories; it is far more complicated. But that was not the case in the fourth century B.C. Plato's words were taken seriously, not by everyone, but by many, down through the centuries. And it is not too hard to see that some people continue to take them seriously today.

As for the "meaning," following others and together with others, I have tried elsewhere to show that essentially it is quite clear: the Athens and Atlantis of ancient lore represent the two faces of Plato's own Athens.[6] The former, the old primordial Athens, is what Plato would have liked the city of which he was a citizen to be; the latter is what Athens was in the age of Pericles and Cleon, an imperialistic power whose very existence constituted a threat to other Greek cities.[7]

That was the starting point. Has there ever been an end to the story? A glance at the newspaper, which Hegel called "the prayer of a realist's morning," shows that there never has. As recently as September 1984 a Soviet flotilla of submarines gave up the search for Atlantis, offshore from Gibraltar.[8] As we shall see, similar forays in Sweden might have been equally justified. More recently still, an archaeologist from Ghent situated

3. The Greek text reads: "λόγου μάλα μὲν ἀτόπου, παντάπασί γε μὴν ἀληθοῦς" (*T*, 20D).
4. A number of precedents exist: Xenophon's *Cyropaedia*, more or less contemporary with the *Republic* (about 380 B.C.) and, as Sally Humphreys has pointed out to me, in Herodotus, the Persian leaders' discussion on the subject of the best constitution, which the author presents as authentic. See Herodotus, *The Histories*, 3.80 and 6.43.
5. See in particular the works by Brisson mentioned above in note 2, which show how carefully Plato planned the setting for his story.
6. See the works by Vidal-Naquet, Brisson, and Gill mentioned above in note 2.
7. It was the Piedmontese scholar Giuseppe Bartoli, I believe, who first hit on this explanation for the myth. See his *Essai sur l'explication historique que Platon a donnée de sa "Republique" et de son Atlantide et qu'on n'a pas considérée jusqu'à maintenant* (Stockholm, 1779–80).
8. See "Russians Say Site Is Not Atlantis," *International Herald Tribune*, 20 Sept. 1984, p. 7. I am grateful to Jesper Svenbro for telling me that more information is to be found in "Tracked Soviet Mini-submarine," *International Defense Review* 17 (Nov. 1984): 1601.

the capital of Atlantis in the neighborhood of Sens, where he was hoping to find Viking remains. His tactful discovery won him vociferous praise.[9]

However, I shall not explore those avenues, for there are too many of them and they are too overgrown. But when did *scholars*, or at least people considered to be such, cease to look for Atlantis? In 1841 Thomas-Henri Martin, a philosophy professor at Rennes University and a disciple of Victor Cousin, published in Paris a work that has become a classic: *Études sur le Timée de Platon*. It included a long and passionate "Dissertation sur l'Atlantide" in which the author patiently noted all or virtually all the identifications that had been proposed for the continent described by Plato. In Martin's view their very number proved that no single one could definitively outbid the rest. He concluded: "Some people have seen the New World as Atlantis. But no: it belongs to *another world,* one that exists not in the domain of space but in that of thought."[10] Of course 1841 did not mark the end of the quest,[11] or even arrest it momentarily, but for historians of the "real world" it certainly represents a turning point.

The year 1841 is interesting at another level, too. It was some time between 1830 and 1840 that a new form of history, based on archives, came into its own. Archives—that is, the use of archives—became the test of scientificity.[12] Of course, in the quest for origins, the myth did not disappear: this was, after all, the period when, from Finland right across to the Balkans, emerging nations were trying to discover *Iliads* of their own. Where national history was concerned, however, the myth was now beside the point. Up until this time, national archives had been an instrument of the government; now they became the historian's "laboratory."

Martin spoke of "the domain of thought." Today we should speak, rather, of the realm of imaginary representations, a realm that also has a history, fed not by "facts" alone but also by "interpretations."[13] Martin

---

There we learn, for instance, that the Soviet "archeological" explorations were taking place from 1973 to 1984.

9. See the article in *Courrier de Gand,* 22 Feb. 1985: "The huge work of M. Mestdagh, the exemplary discretion and scientific rigor, shows—if it needed to be shown—that there are still natives of Ghent who bring honor both to their own land and to their neighbor's." I am indebted to Yvon Garlan for this press clipping.

10. Thomas-Henri Martin, *Études sur le Timée de Platon* (Paris, 1841), p. 332. The "Dissertation" fills pp. 257–332.

11. This was shown by the identification of Atlantis and Italy just the year before. See note 71 below.

12. See Pierre Nora, "Archives et construction d'une histoire nationale: Le Cas français," in *Les Arabes par leurs archives (XVIᵉ–XXᵉ siècles),* ed. Jacques Berque and Dominique Chevallier (Paris, 1979), pp. 321–32. See also Marcel Gauchet, "Les 'Lettres sur l'histoire de France' d'Augustin Thierry," in *Les Lieux de la mémoire,* ed. Nora, 2 vols. (Paris, 1986), 2:247–316.

13. On this point Alexander von Humboldt, a very eminent scholar in the synoptic vein, was less radical in his critique than Martin, but showed more scholarly imagination

may seem to have established the principles for that kind of history, but he certainly did not begin to practice it. One is bound to be struck by the fact that, in his list, he sees no need to distinguish between identifications of the location of Atlantis, on the one hand, and interpretations of the text on the other. He is content to prove that there never was an Atlantis that could be shown on a map in the way that so many people had tried to show it. He makes no attempt to understand what so many imaginative interpretations had contributed to the idea of Atlantis.[14] Of course, space limitations preclude me from considering the subject exhaustively here, so I shall limit myself to a single theme: what I shall call the "nationalistic" aspect of the story of Atlantis.

Let us therefore leave to one side the intellectual debate that followed the appearance of the *Timaeus* and the *Critias,* a debate that was devoted to the question of whether Plato's description and story should be taken literally. Aristotle and Eratosthenes, for their part, were skeptical. The debate even split the Academy, as we know from the detailed commentary on the *Timaeus* left us by Proclus.

Our point of departure must be a series of events that were completely unforeseeable, however much theologians, followed by historians, have strived to detect a rationality in them. In the second and third centuries A.D., the Mediterranean world began to turn Christian. Particularly for the intellectuals who sought to come to terms with the change, this meant replacing their mythology and history, from the War of the Giants down to the Trojan War, with the mythology and history of the Hebrews and the Jews, from Adam down to the birth of Christ.

Of course, it was not as simple as that. A compromise between Jewish chronology and Greek chronology had already begun to be elaborated as early as the second century B.C., as is evident from the ancient parts of the *Sibylline Oracles.* At that point, it was the Jews who were seeking to be included, and it was up to them to assimilate themselves into the Greek systems. When the Christian church began to seek to dominate and, in the time first of Constantine, then of Theodosius, even acquired the instruments of domination, the Greek intellectuals at work in that world— Clement of Alexandria and Eusebius of Caesarea, for example—were, in

---

regarding the "mythical geography" of the Greeks. See Alexander von Humboldt, *Histoire de la géographie du nouveau continent et des progrès de l'astronomie nautique aux quinzième et seizième siècles,* 5 vols. (Paris, 1836–39), esp. 1:112–15 and 1:167–80.

14. Fairly recent studies on this may be found in the (not altogether reliable) book by Lyon Sprague de Camp, *Lost Continents: The Atlantis Theme in History, Science, and Literature* (New York, 1954), and in *Atlantis, Fact or Fiction?* ed. Edwin S. Ramage (Bloomington, Ind., 1978).

their turn, obliged to elaborate a compromise.[15] They acknowledged the greatness of Plato and the existence of the Trojan War, but it was fundamental that Plato should be a disciple of Moses and that this Jewish lawgiver should antedate the time of Achilles. This "Eusebian compromise" was to have a long and tenacious life, lasting in its essentials right down to the seventeenth century.

How did Atlantis fare in this colossal reorganization? Occasionally, Plato's story is evoked as an exemplum by Jewish or Christian authors,[16] but the only really significant text is to be found in the *Christian Topography* written by Cosmas Indicopleustès, who was probably a monk from the East and who declares that he had travelled in the Orient in the sixth century A.D. The story of Atlantis is presented here as at once Greek fiction and Eastern truth. Moses, followed by the Chaldeans, are said to be its distant authors. The West is said to have been substituted for the East, for instead of Solon receiving instruction from an Egyptian priest, it was Plato to whom an Egyptian, by the strange name of Solomon, addressed the famous exclamation: "You Greeks are always children."[17] We should take good note of this date, for it records the first meeting between Atlantis and the Jews.

I could, at a pinch, now leap over more than nine centuries and come to the event that, on its own, radically altered the situation: the discovery of America. But a few markers at least, over the intervening years, might be helpful.

We Europeans have become accustomed to thinking that our nations began with the collapse of the Roman Empire in the West. For example, the title of Suzanne Teillet's recently published book is *Des Goths à la nation gothique: Les origines de l'idée de nation en Occident du Ve au VIIe siècle.*[18] The nation in question is the "Gothic nation" of Spain, but at least one other European nation, Sweden, was also to discover its "roots" in a Gothic tradition or myth (it is not always easy to choose between those two terms). And it would assuredly be possible to write a similar work on the Franks. I cannot summarize Teillet's book here, but let me make a few points, rather more forcefully perhaps than that scholarly author did.

These emerging "nations," or rather the intellectuals who claimed to speak in their name—their ideologists is really what they should be called—were faced with a choice between two models of sovereignty: the imperial Roman model or the royal Hebrew one. They had to choose

---

15. See, for example, Jean Sirinelli, *Les Vues historiques d'Eusèbe de Césarée durant la période prénicéene* (Dakar, 1961).

16. The references may be found in my "Hérodote et l'Atlantide," p. 50 n. 24.

17. See Cosmas Indicopleustès, *Topographie Chrétienne,* trans. Wanda Wolska-Conus, 3 vols. (Paris, 1968–73), bk. 12, §§ 2-3, 7.

18. See Suzanne Teillet, *Des Goths à la nation gothique: Les Origines de l'idée de nation en Occident du Ve au VIIe siècle* (Paris, 1984).

between Caesar and David. In what was to become France, as in what was to become Spain, the choice—except in the brief Carolingian interval—fell upon Israelite royalty, a fact that is not without relevance to the elaboration of the concept of "magic kings."[19] The Visigoth King Wamba was probably the first Western sovereign, in 672, to receive the royal unction, in accordance with an Israelite model reworked and rethought by Isidore of Seville and Julian of Toledo, whose *Vita Wambae* is modelled on the Book of Kings in the Bible.[20] And when Gregory of Tours speaks of the *gentes* fighting against Clovis, he most explicitly assimilates them to the *goyim*, peoples foreign to Israel.[21]

This produced one essential consequence, namely, a proliferation of "chosen peoples": a spin-off from ancient Israel. Traces of that proliferation still survive today, and from the Renaissance on it played a role of capital importance in the ideological landscape first of Europe, then of America; but it goes right back to the times that followed the collapse of the Roman Empire in the West. However, it was not enough to be a chosen people, or rather, that idea could not simply apply to the entire people. The established aristocracies and royal families had to have their own particular genealogies. In Spain, the Goths—a minority if ever there were one—remained the largely mythical ancestors of the nobility, even when, following the Arab invasion, they had disappeared as a community. The "Gothic Blood," pure blood par excellence, was to be transmitted through the ages. In France, a legend borrowed from the pagan tradition, namely, the legend of Troy, was used to confer prestige on the three successive royal dynasties.[22] France, like Spain—but unlike, for instance, Sweden—was a country where two "races" coexisted. The Trojan legend was used to give one of those races a sense of superiority.

All these elements were present centuries before the Renaissance. But, of course, with the Renaissance and the renewal of the Latin culture, they received a definite boost. Nor was biblical mythology forgotten, nor that strange association that had been established between Greek litera-

19. Here I would refer the reader to Marc Bloch, *Les Rois thaumaturges: Études sur le caractère surnaturel attribué à la puissance royale, particulièrement en France et en Angleterre* (1924; Paris, 1983); trans. J. E. Anderson, under the title *The Royal Touch: Sacred Monarchy and Scrofula in England and France* (London, 1973).

20. See Teillet, *Des Goths à la nation gothique*, pp. 602–11. On Isidore of Seville's ideas on royalty, see Marc Reydellet, *La Royauté dans la littérature latine, de Sidoine Apollinaire à Isidore de Séville* (Rome, 1981), pp. 556–68. Reydellet stresses the mediatory role played by the image of Christ. The fundamental work on the medieval concept of kingship is still Ernst Hartwig Kantorowicz, *The King's Two Bodies: A Study in Medieval Political Theology* (Princeton, N.J., 1957).

21. See Teillet, *Des Goths à la nation gothique*, p. 404.

22. On these questions the basic work is Arno Borst, *Der Turmbau von Babel: Geschichte der Meinungen über Ursprung und Viefalt der Sprachen und Völker*, 4 vols. (Stuttgart, 1957–63). See also Léon Poliakov, *Le Mythe aryen: Essai sur las sources du racisme et du nationalisme* (1971; Brussels, 1987).

ture and the Jewish tradition between the second and the fourth centuries A.D.

During the Renaissance, Noah was a particularly important figure.[23] It was, of course, generally accepted that all men were descended from Noah, but, to adapt George Orwell's expression, some were descended better and more directly than others. Naturally, Ham's descendants were accursed, but various claims to primogeniture could be and indeed were advanced in connection with the descendants of Shem and Japheth.

As an ancestor, Japheth was all the more distinguished in that he enjoyed the immense advantage, made known by the *Sibylline Oracles,* of being both the son of Noah and, at the same time, as Iapetus, the Titan of Greek mythology, the father of Prometheus and Atlas, the latter himself a namesake of Atlantis.[24]

True, the masses took little interest in speculations such as these, but in this period from the late sixth century on, which witnessed a large-scale reappearance of imperialistic policies in the shape of the Italian Wars, ideologists were in a position to play an important role. Here is one remarkable example. At the end of the fifteenth century, in 1498, Giovanni Nanni, better known as Annius of Viterbo, published a whole series of false fragments from famous historians of classical and hellenistic Greece and ancient Rome, figures as widely diverse as Cato, Xenophon and the Chaldean Berosus. Some of these pagans were apparently perfectly familiar with Noah, whom they called Janus, and his sons. Ham remained accursed. An unknown son of Noah, who bore almost the same name as the Tuisto whom Tacitus made the ancestor of the Germans, was Tuyscon, who reigned over the Germanic territories. One of Japheth's sons, Gomer, also known as Gallus, sent his son Samothes from Italy to found the kingdom of France.[25] What language did these distant ances-

---

23. Apart from Borst's book, the essential work on this question is Don Cameron Allen, *The Legend of Noah: Renaissance Rationalism in Art, Science and Letters* (Urbana, Ill., 1949).

24. See the *Sibylline Oracles,* bk. 3, 1. 110.

25. I know of only one recent general work on Annius of Viterbo: Giovanni Baffioni and Paolo Mattiangeli, *Annio da Viterbo: Documenti e ricerche* (Rome, 1981). It is essentially devoted to a critical edition of a new history of Viterbo and iconographical studies, and contains a full bibliography (p. 24). Among the works that I have found useful are: Allen, *The Legend of Noah;* Borst, *Der Turmbau von Babel,* esp. 3: 975–77 and passim; and Eugène Napoleon Tigerstedt, "Iohannes Annius and 'Graecia Mendax,'" in *Classical, Mediaeval and Renaissance Studies in Honor of Berthold Louis Ullman,* ed. Charles Henderson, Jr., 2 vols. (Rome, 1964), 2: 293–310.

Annius of Viterbo's Italian patriotism which was, in truth, an extension of his local patriotism, is marked by the fact that the earliest of his forgeries, attributed to Myrsilius of Lesbos and Cato, are devoted to the "origins" of the Italians and the Etruscans, but his text potentially offered glorious lineages to most nations. He was particularly enthusiastic about Spain, the Spanish ambassador having helped to finance the publication of his book.

tors speak? The classic answer, which had already incurred Dante's criticism, was that it was Hebrew.[26]

The ideologists of the various nations had a natural tendency to claim that their own language was the primordial one. In the sixteenth century, the Florentine Giovanni Battista Gelli similarly tried to prove that, in the course of his travels, Noah-Janus, later buried beneath the Janiculum in Rome, had founded Florence;[27] meanwhile, Annius of Viterbo claimed that the honor of being founded by Noah-Janus went to his own hometown.

As was to be expected, the intellectuals of France soon reacted to these Italian claims. A strange cabalist by the name of Guillaume Postel, one of the fathers of Celtomania, declared that Japheth had been banished from Italy by the ghastly Ham and had come to Gaul to work on his astronomical investigations. As for Noah himself, he had travelled all over the world, including—of course—in Atlantis.[28]

The next step was taken by Postel's disciple Guy Le Fèvre de la Broderie who, in his *Galliade, ou de la Révolution des arts et sciences* (1578), declared that Gaul was the first piece of land to emerge from the Flood. Finally, a century later, Pierre Audigier hit upon the perfect solution: Noah's true name, quite simply, was Gallus.[29] To which it should be added that the kings of France were said to be the descendants of both Japheth and Shem—which made it possible for them to claim cousinship with Jesus and Mary.[30]

Now that that general framework is sketched in, the question is: what happened to Atlantis? The myth had quietly survived throughout the Middle Ages, mainly transmitted by the prologue to the *Timaeus*, made known by Calcidius's translation.[31] Perhaps it can also be detected in the

26. See Maurice Olender, *Les Langues du paradis: Ayrens et Sémites, un couple unprovidentiel* (Paris, 1989), esp. pp. 26, 124–26.

27. Giovanni Battista Gelli's *Delle origini di Firenze* dates from 1542. See Paolo Simoncelli, *La Lingua di Adamo: Guillaume Postel tra accademici e fuoriusciti Fiorentini* (Florence, 1984), p. 18.

28. On Guillaume Postel and Celtomania, see Claude-Gilbert Dubois, *Celtes et Gaulois au XVIe siècle: Le Developpement littéraire d'un mythe nationaliste* (Paris, 1972); on the relationships with Annius of Viterbo, see p. 85. See also the essential work by William James Bouwsma, *Concordi Mundi: The Career and Thought of Guillaume Postel, 1510–1581* (Cambridge, 1957); on the travels of Noah, see pp. 257–58.

29. See Pierre Audigier, *L'Origine des François, et de leur empire*, 2 vols. (Paris, 1676), esp. pp. 214–17.

30. See Joseph R. Strayer, "France: The Holy Land, the Chosen People and the Most Christian King," in *Action and Conviction in Early Modern Europe: Essays in Memory of E. H. Harbison,* ed. Theodore K. Rabb and Jerrold E. Seigel (Princeton, N.J., 1969), pp. 3–16. On similar themes in Germany, see Frank L. Borchardt, *German Antiquity in Renaissance Myth* (Baltimore, 1971). For a comparative study, the essential work is *National Consciousness, History, and Political Culture in Early-Modern Europe,* ed. Orest Ranum (Baltimore, 1975).

31. See Raymond Klibansky, *The Continuity of the Platonic Tradition during the Middle Ages* (London, 1939), which also served as the introduction to the *Corpus Platonicum Medii*

Irish legend of Saint Brendan.[32] Medieval maps speculated on the where-
abouts of plenty of mythical lands, ranging from the earthly paradise to
the land of Gog and Magog and the kingdom of the Priest John, which was
where the antichrist was going to manifest himself. One example was the
1375 *Catalan Atlas,* another the map commissioned from the Venetian
Fra Mauro in 1459, at the time of the discoveries by Alfonso of Portugal.
However, Atlantis was not included among those mythical places. A fortiori, no nation at that time claimed any kind of monopoly over Atlantis. In
1485 the humanist Marsilio Ficino translated Plato's works into Latin,
accompanying his translation of the *Critias* with a commentary. His verdict was that the story was true, but only in the Platonic sense of the word,
which did not make it possible to locate Atlantis on a map. He too connected Plato with the biblical tradition.[33]

Seven years after this translation, however, something happened that
was to change everything: America was discovered. True, it is not known
whether Christopher Columbus himself knew of Plato's story, although it
has sometimes been mentioned in this connection.[34] But Atlantis was soon
to enter into general circulation. As has been pointed out,

> a continent barely touched by man lay exposed to men whose greed
> could no longer be satisfied by their own continent. Everything
> would be called into question by this second sin: God, morality and
> law. In simultaneous yet contradictory fashion, everything would be
> verified in practice and revoked in principle: the Garden of Eden, the
> Golden Age of antiquity, the Fountain of youth, Atlantis, the
> Hesperides, the Islands of the Blessed, would be found to be true; but

---

Aevi, 4 vols. (London, 1951–75); volume 4 is the *Timaeus,* ed. J. H. Waszink, whose commentary shows the extent to which the importance of the Hebrew influence on Plato was
considered to go without saying, but makes no mention of Atlantis.

32. See the introduction by Ian Short and Brian Merrilees to Benedeit, *The Anglo-
Norman Voyage of St. Brendan,* ed. Short and Merrilees (Manchester, 1979).

33. See Raymond Marcel, *Marsile Ficin, 1433–1499* (Paris, 1958), esp. pp. 630–31.

34. In particular by von Humboldt, whose intellectual portrait of Columbus remains
unrivalled, despite the errors in the first two volumes of the *Histoire.* Charles Minguet's
study on this text does not really do him justice. See Charles Minguet, *Alexandre de
Humboldt, historien et géographe de l'Amérique espagnole, 1799–1804* (Paris, 1969), pp. 584–
603. Von Humboldt notes the absence of any mention of Atlantis from Columbus's writings but nevertheless maintains that Columbus "took pleasure in Solon's references to
Atlantis" (von Humboldt, *Histoire de la géographie du nouveau continent,* 1:167). Nor is it true
that Columbus's son, Fernando, in his biography of his father, made any connections, even
in a muddled fashion, between his father's achievements and Plato's myth. Although he
does refer to Atlantis in a polemic directed against Gonzalo Fernández de Oviedo, it is as a
story with which his father was, precisely, unfamiliar. See Fernando Colón, *The Life of the
Admiral Christopher Columbus by His Son, Ferdinand,* trans. Benjamin Keen (New Brunswick,
N.J., 1959), pp. 28–34. The original Spanish text has been lost; all modern editions refer to
the Italian translation.

revelation, salvation, customs and law would be challenged by the spectacle of a purer, happier race of men (who, of course, were not really purer or happier, although a deep-seated remorse made them appear so).[35]

The discovery of America marked the decisive turning point. It was certainly very quickly recognized that this was a "new world," that is to say, a different world.[36] But, as Lévi-Strauss has explained, this "brave new world," to which Shakespeare was to refer in *The Tempest,* could at first be apprehended only by means of the concepts and ideas derived from the twofold tradition that informed the works of the period: the classical culture and the Christian—and hence Jewish—culture, a twofold tradition which, it must be said, was regarded as a single one by most educated people.[37]

In the name of logic, we should recognize that, in the theories that were elaborated after 1492, Atlantis occupied every logical position that might a priori be conceived. In the name of the human mind and to its glory, we should add that, at least by the end of the sixteenth century, skeptics were making themselves heard, particularly Montaigne in France and, in Spain, José de Acosta, the founder of modern anthropology.[38]

What solutions were conceivable? America could either be biblical or Platonic, that is to say, Atlantis. Atlantis itself could be interpreted either through the Bible or in the light of the great new discoveries; and these were all solutions that could easily be combined as well as opposed. The common preoccupation that united them was the now-primary need,

35. Claude Lévi-Strauss, *Tristes Tropiques,* trans. John and Doreen Weightman (New York, 1973), p. 74. Contrary to what is frequently ascribed to him through quoting him incorrectly, Lévi-Strauss nowhere states that the Spaniards went off "to verify old legends," including that of Atlantis. Anyone interested in this little polemic is referred to Jacques Lafaye, *Les Conquistadors* (Paris, 1964), p. 111; Marianne Mahn-Lot, *La Découverte de l'Amérique* (Paris, 1970), p. 90; and Numa Broc, *La Géographie de la Renaissance (1420–1620)* (Paris, 1980), p. 166. All refer to and quote each other without having taken the trouble to check the text by Lévi-Strauss that is is incorrectly cited by Lafaye. Lévi-Strauss himself has provided me with the correct reference.

36. The credit for recognizing this must go in the first place to Pietro Martire d'Anghiera's letter from Barcelona to Cardinal Ascanio; Amerigo Vespucci's intervention came a full ten years later. See W. G. L. Randles, "Le Nouveau Monde, l'autre monde et la pluralité des mondes," *Congresso international história descobrimentos,* vol. 4 (Lisbon, 1961).

37. On Atlantis and the great discoveries, the two essential works are Ida Rodriguez Prampolini, *La Atlantida de Platón en los cronistas del siglo XVI* (Mexico City, 1947), and Giuliano Gliozzi, *Adamo e il nuovo mondo: La nascita dell'antropologia come ideologia coloniale, dalle genealogie bibliche alle teorie razziali (1500–1700)* (Florence, 1977), esp. pp. 177–246. Antonello Gerbi's *Natura delle Indie nove: Da Cristoforo Colombo a Gonzalo Fernandez de Oviedo* (Milan, 1975), although extremely scholarly, manages to make no reference at all to Atlantis except in an insignificant note on p. 379.

38. See Montaigne's famous "On Cannibals," *The Essays of Montaigne,* trans. George B. Ives, 4 vols. (Cambridge, Mass., 1925), bk. 1, chap. 31. See also José de Acosta, *Historia natural y moral de las Indias* (Seville, 1590), bk. 1, chap. 20.

except for the skeptics, to locate Atlantis—a need that was characteristic of the sixteenth century,[39] although it had, in contrast, been quite absent from works such as Ficino's.

In his edition of Plato, Jean de Serres (Serranus) provided a commentary on both the *Timaeus* and the *Critias*. In it he suggested that the Greeks were indeed children, as the Egyptian priest had observed to Solon. If we compare Plato "with the simple truth of history as told by Moses," it becomes evident that the description of Atlantis is quite simply a picture of the world before the Flood, before Noah.[40] That is just one text, but it is one that we should not forget because, in the eighteenth century, many scholars were to refine that solution, "proving" that Atlantis was, quite simply, Palestine.

And what was America supposed to be? For many scholars and ideologists, it was the country where the ten tribes of Israel had found refuge. This myth of the disappearance and reappearance of the ten tribes was a particularly splendid one. And it was not only in connection with America that it was seized on, for in 1944 I was most seriously assured that the tribe of Dan had become Denmark. The origin of these traditions is to be found in a famous passage from the biblical Apocrypha:

> Then you saw him collecting a different company, a peaceful one. They are the ten tribes which were taken off into exile in the time of King Hoshea, whom Shalmaneser king of Assyria took prisoner. He deported them beyond the River, and they were taken away into a strange country. But then they resolved to leave the country populated by the Gentiles and go to a distant land never yet inhabited by man, and there at last to be obedient to their laws, which in their own country they had failed to keep.[41]

In the sixteenth century, echoes from that text resounded widely through the Christian world. But some Jews also accepted it—notably Manasseh ben Israel, a friend of Rembrandt's in Amsterdam, who took it up in his *Esperança de Israel* (1648), illustrating it in a novel, in which, however, he insisted upon the crucial qualification that only a fraction of the Indians—those most remarkable for their beauty—should be identified as Jews.[42]

39. On this point the essential works are Gliozzi, *Adamo e il Nuovo Mondo*, and Broc, *La Géographie de la Renaissance*.

40. Jean de Serres in the commentary to his translation of Plato, *Opera quae extant omnia*, 3 vols. (Geneva, 1578), 3:105.

41. 2 Esd. 13:39–42. The astonishing history of this text has been studied in a vast work entitled *Moïse géographes: Recherches sur les représentations juives et chrétiennes de l'espace*, ed. Alan Desreumaux and Francis Schmidt (Paris, 1988). A basic commentary and bibliography are also to be found in Manasseh ben Joseph ben Israel, *The Hope of Israel*, trans. Moses Wall, ed. Henry Méchoulan and Gérard Nahon (1648; New York, 1987).

42. On this subject see also Marcel Bataillon, "L'Unité du genre humain du P. Acosta au P. Clavigero," *Mélanges à la mémoire de Jean Sarrailh*, 2 vols. (Paris, 1966), 1:75–95; Lee

It was also possible to interpret America without the Bible, using Plato's text on its own,[43] and this was indeed done early on, earlier than is generally believed[44]—in fact by 1527—to take account only of published works: at this date, the illustrious Bartolomé de las Casas was declaring that Christopher Columbus could be reasonably sure that at least part of the continent described by Plato had been unaffected by the disaster.[45] It was logically predictable that the two models, the Atlantic and the biblical, should eventually be combined, as indeed they were by Francis Bacon in his utopia, *New Atlantis,* published posthumously in 1627.[46] Here, Atlantis is an island situated to the west of Peru, in the "southern seas," where Hebrew, Greek, and excellent Spanish are all spoken, for this is a perfect society of scholars. It is a fragment that was detached from the island that Plato described and is Jewish by origin and Christian by conversion, but with a respected Jewish minority. In this particular case, Plato and the Bible complemented one another. In 1655, however, it was just the other way around: in *Pre-Adamitae,* the work of a pro-Jewish Protestant by the name of Isaac de la Peyrère, Adam is regarded as, not the first man, but the first Jew. In this author's view, the traditional biblical chronology was clearly incompatible with the nine thousand years that preceded Solon, whom Plato had credited with the idea of Atlantis. Atlantis must accordingly have been inhabited by men who predated Adam.[47]

But to my mind what is of essential interest is the link that is hence-

---

Eldridge Huddleston, *Origins of the American Indians: European Concepts 1492–1729* (Austin, Tex., 1967); and Lynn Glaser, *Indians or Jews: An Introduction to a Reprint* (Gilroy, Calif., 1973). On the Spanish side to the question, see Méchoulan, *Le Sang de l'autre ou l'honneur de Dieu: Juifs, Indiens et Maures au siècle d'or* (Paris, 1979).

43. In de Acosta, the two major solutions to the mystery of America, both of which he refutes, are (1) the ten tribes and (2) Atlantis. See de Acosta, *Historia natural y moral de las Indias.*

44. The text usually mentioned here is Francisco López de Gómara, *Historia General de las Indias* (Zaragoza, 1553). Gliozzi's *Adamo e il Nuovo Mondo* goes farther back, citing Giralamo Fracastoros, *Syphilidis, sive morbi Gallici* (Verona, 1530), bk. 3, 11. 165–86.

45. See Bartolomé de las Casas, *Historia de las Indias,* ed. Juan Perez de Tudela Bueso (Madrid, 1957), pp. 36–39. The *Historia* was begun in 1520 and completed in 1561, but was not published until 1875–76. I am indebted to Ida Rodriguez Prampolini for referring me to this work.

46. See the commentary by Michèle Le Doeuff and Margaret Llasera in Francis Bacon, *La Nouvelle Atlantide: Voyage dans la pensée baroque,* trans. and ed. Le Doeuff and Llasera (Paris, 1983).

47. See Isaac de la Peyrère, *Prae-adamitae, sive exercitatio super versibus duodecimo, decimotertio, et decimoquarto, capitis quinti epistolae d. Pauli ad Romanos: Quibus inducuntur primi homines ante Adamum conditi* (Amsterdam, 1655), pp. 176–80. This very logical line of argument by la Peyrère has not been noted in the works on him that I have read, not even in the excellent *thèse du troisième cycle* by J.-P. Oddos, *Recherches sur la vie et l'oeuvre d'Isaac de la Peyrère* (Grenoble, 1977). The same applies to Richard H. Popkin's indispensable *Isaac la Peyrère (1596–1676): His Life, Work, and Influence* (New York, 1987).

forth established between the lands of fable, of which Atlantis is probably the most famous, and the nationalistic myths that we have seen sprouting from the ruins of the Roman Empire and being forcefully resuscitated during the Renaissance. If a German jurist could discern in the language of the Indians *"nescio quid Cimbricum, seu priscum Teutonicum"* ["something or other that brings to mind the *Cimbres* and the ancient Teutons"], for example the word "papa," which is "common both to us Europeans and to Americans," we may be sure that he was not alone in doing so.[48]

For obvious reasons, the place par excellence where the fusion between the lands and times of fable and the modernized ideology of the chosen people took place was the Spain of the Conquistadors. It began, as it happened, not with Atlantis but with the ancient garden of the Hesperides. Gonzalo Fernandez de Oviedo, who was appointed official chronicler of the Indies in 1532, produced the first part of his *Historia general y natural de las Indias* in 1535. In it he declared that the Antilles, that is to say the land of the Hesperides, had already long been possessions of the Spanish Crown. Charles V, informed in advance of these investigations and discoveries, on 25 October 1533 expressed his keen satisfaction at learning that "for three thousand and ninety-one years these lands have been among the royal possessions of Spain, so that it is not surprising that, after so many years, God has restored them to their owner."[49]

The next step was taken by a Flemish subject of the King of Spain, Jan van Gorop (Goropius Becanus). According to him, ancient Tartessus, the Tartessus of both the Bible and Herodotus, was the ancestor of modern Spain and the capital of Atlantis, which had been founded by two brothers, Atlas-Tartessus and Ulysses-Hesperus, both grandsons of Japheth. Of the two it was the elder, Atlas-Tartessus, who held the power of primogeniture, and his descendants, the kings of Spain, thus possessed obvious rights over Atlantic Africa and America.[50]

The clearest formulation of what we may now call Atlanto-nationalism was produced in 1572, for the sole profit of Philip II of Spain, by Pedro Sarmiento de Gamboa, in his *Historia general llamada Indica.*[51]

48. Christoph Besold, *De novo orbe, conjectanea,* in *Dissertationes singulares* (Tübingen, 1619), p. 24.

49. Gonzalo Fernández de Oviedo y Valdés, *Historia general y natural de las Indias* (Seville, 1535), pp. 379–80; on the question of the Hesperides, see pp. 365–83; the whole mythico-biblical argument (Tubal-Hercules and so on) is derived from Annius of Viterbo. The essential work on Oviedo is Gerbi, *La natura delle Indie nove.*

50. See Jan Goropius Becanus, *Hispanica,* in *Opera hactenus in lucem non edita* (Antwerp, 1580), pp. 35, 62, 105–58. See also Gliozzi, *Adamo e il nuovo mondo,* pp. 25–27. Having died in 1574, van Gorop's book was published posthumously. His hispanophilia did not prevent him from also discovering a number of connections between the Indian languages and Flemish. The link between Tartessus and Atlantis was to be "rediscovered" in the twentieth century by Adolf Schulten; see his *Tartessos: Ein Beitrag zur ältesten Geschichte des Westen* (Hamburg, 1922), esp. pp. 53–56.

51. Pedro Sarmiento de Gamboa's *Historia general llamada Indica* was not published

On the basis of the Platonic text, which places Atlantis beyond the Pillars of Hercules, Sarmiento claimed that this was a continent that, long ago, had adjoined Spain. America, its distant remains, thus belonged by divine right to the Spanish Crown.[52]

Spain had thus made use of both the Gothic myth and the myth of Atlantis. But here, so far as I know, there was not the slightest connection between the two. That was not to be the case in another country that also used the Gothic myth, namely, Sweden.

Now we must tackle a question of considerable importance: what became of the myth of Atlantis during the Enlightenment, that is to say from about 1670, the beginning of what Paul Hazard has called *la crise de la conscience européenne*, down to the French Revolution? The early years of those extremely troubled times saw the appearance of the work of the man who, following Sarmiento but with infinitely more brilliance, was the real creator of the nationalistic Atlantis myth: Olof Rudbeck.[53]

A few rules of interpretation need to be sketched in at this point. What I shall refer to as the Enlightenment was faced with a huge problem, just the opposite of that which had faced the Greek Fathers of the second to the fourth centuries and which, by and large, had been retackled by the men of the Renaissance. The task of the Fathers was to reconcile Greek historiography and the biblical tradition as best they could. The men of the Enlightenment had, on the contrary, to put paid to using the Jewish people as a vector of universal history, a role in which they had been most splendidly confirmed by Jacques Bénigue Bossuet's *Discours sur l'histoire universelle* as late as 1681. What now needed to be done was to find a new chosen people, even if—provisionally—this meant resuscitating some form of paganism.[54] And of course, the men of the Enlightenment were

until 1902. I am referring to the version that appears in the appendix to Garcilaso de la Vega, *Obras completas del Inca Garcilaso de la Vega,* ed. Carmelo Sáenz de Santa María, 4 vols. (Madrid, 1960), esp. 4:201–5.

52. Carles Miralles, my colleague from Barcelona, has pointed out that the nationalistic Atlantis myth appeared in Catalonia in the late nineteenth century in the form of a Catalan epic by Jacinto Verdaguer, *L'Atlantida* (Barcelona, 1877), and was later set to music by Manuel de Falla. Here again we find a fusion of the legends of the Hesperides and Atlantis, for the last queen of Atlantis, saved by Hercules and installed by him in Spain as his wife, is none other than Hesperus. A French translation by Albert Savine of Verdaguer's text is entitled *L'Atlantide* (Paris, 1883). See also the vast bibliography cited in Carles Miralles, "L'Arbre i la Lira," in *Festschrift Antoni Comas* (Barcelona, 1985), pp. 289–304.

53. For a more detailed account of the Atlantis myth in the Enlightenment, see my "Hérodote et l'Atlantide."

54. The literature on this subject is, of course, extensive. Outstanding for their clarity are Peter Gay, *The Enlightenment: An Interpretation,* 2 vols. (New York, 1966–69), and Frank E. Manuel, *The Eighteenth Century Confronts the Gods* (1959; New York, 1967). See also Jean

not alone. There were rivals to be contended with, who knew how to turn the tables. In the eighteenth century, one was just as likely to discover a Jewish prophet behind Plato or Homer as to find a pagan god behind the sacred figure of Jesus Christ. The Enlightenment was—it need hardly be said—not a conscious movement at all levels nor where all its participants were concerned. Many helped in practice to "crush the beast," quite unaware that they were collaborating in that endeavor.

At the time of the Enlightenment, Atlantis was a kind of substitute for the Jewish people in the economy of universal history. But what I should like to discuss, more specifically, is Atlantis used as a *national* substitute. The people who once constituted Atlantis were a chosen people and, as such, deserved the primacy that every imperial power believes itself to possess.

Admittedly, Atlantis as a national substitute was not the only function of the myth in the Enlightenment. Quite apart from any particular national ancestry, Atlantis could be considered as the origin of all the nations, or as a golden age, which is indeed how the astronomer Jean Sylvain Bailly regarded it. Beyond humanity and above it, Atlantis, for Nicolas Boulanger, was a cosmic episode, one particular moment in the universal floods that, he believed, punctuate history.[55] But Atlantis also always functioned as a substitute.

Olof Rudbeck (1630–1702) was rector of Uppsala University. In his immense work *Atlantica (Atland eller Manheim)*, he set out to show that Atlantis, the cradle of human civilization, was none other than Sweden, with its capital at Uppsala.[56]

Starobinski, "Le Mythe au XVIIIe siècle," review of *The Rise of Modern Mythology, 1680–1860,* by Burton Feldman and Robert D. Richardson, *Critique* 33 (Nov. 1977): 975–97.

55. These points are developed fully in my "Hérodote et l'Atlantide."

56. See Olof Rudbeck, *Atlantica,* 3 vols. (Uppsala, 1679–1702); see the more modern edition, *Atland eller Manheim,* ed. Axel Nelson, 4 vols. (Uppsala, 1937–50); volume 4 contains a very useful collection of *testimonia* on the reception of the work (pp. 205–65). There is a vast bibliography on Rudbeck and Gothically inclined ideology, most of it in Swedish. I will cite only a handful here: Erika Simon, *Reveil national et culture populaire en Scandinavie: La Genèse de la Højskole nordique, 1844–1878* (Paris, 1960); Ernst Ekman, "Gothic Patriotism and Olof Rudbeck," *Journal of Modern History* 34 (Mar. 1962): 52–63; Josef Gusten Algot Svennung, *Zur Geschichte des Goticismus* (Stockholm, 1967); of capital importance with a large bibliography is Jesper Svenbro, "L'Idéologie 'gothisante' et l'*Atlantica* d'Olof Rudbeck: Le Mythe platonicien de l'Atlantide au service de l'Empire suédois du XVIIe siècle," *Quaderni di storia* 11 (Jan.–June 1980): 121–56; Gunnar Eriksson, "Gestalter i Svensk lärdomshistoria I: Olof Rudbeck D. Ä.," *Lychnos* (1984): 77–119; English summary: "Swedes in the History of Science and Learning I: Olaus Rudbecksen," pp. 116–18; thanks to Svenbro for this reference. I would like to express my warmest thanks to Nils and Renée Andersson for showing me, in Uppsala, the places and images connected with the Rudbeck saga. I notice, in the articles cited above in note 8, however, that when the Soviet submarines "visited" the Stockholm archipelago in October 1982, no mention was made of the identification of Atlantis and Sweden, nor of Atlantis's capital with Uppsala.

I must confess that ever since I first came across Rudbeck's oeuvre, over a quarter of a century ago, the man and his work have always fascinated me. He was a scholar of considerable stature, a great anatomist who discovered the network of lymph ducts, and was also responsible for the construction of an amphitheatre that still stands today in Uppsala. But he was not only a doctor and a biologist. He knew everything there was to be known about language and history, and he used it all in *Atlantica,* the work to which he devoted his maturity and old age. There is no truth in the idea that there were two Rudbecks, one a doctor, the other a historian,[57] any more than in the notion that there were two Descartes, one responsible for the *Cogito,* the other the author of reflections on the circulation of the blood that today seem totally risible.

Throughout his work, Rudbeck remained faithful to an empiricism inherited from Francis Bacon. Yet some of his contemporaries, Pierre Bayle in particular,[58] realized that that empiricism bordered on paranoia. Unquestionably, he was well aware of the dangers of his project—as we all should be when it comes to speculations of our own. In his first volume, Rudbeck presents a discussion on the subject of the Indies, presided over by Apollo, in which the participants are a number of august scholars and one humble gardener, Hortulanus. Apollo and the eminent doctors have much to say on this rich subject, but the little gardener does not agree with them, dismissing all that he has heard as *chimerae atque deliramenta,* "fantasies and nonsense." He tells his interlocutors: "Assuredly, *et nos homines:* we too are men";[59] but so, equally, are the great doctors: *et vos homines.* On the frontispiece of his atlas (fig. 1), Rudbeck, the great scholar par excellence, had that maxim repeated—ET NOS HOMINES—thereby feigning to cast himself in the role of a little gardener, possibly sensing that he had laid himself open to the attacks of any other little gardener who happened along.

As the scholar who devoted the greater part of his life to the mystery of Atlantis, Rudbeck managed to create a national myth comprising two separate elements: the quest for Noah and his heirs, with which we are well familiar, and the Gothic myth, one of whose early manifestations we have noted in Visigoth Spain.[60] I will not embark here on the history of

57. Only Rudbeck the doctor is mentioned in *Petit Larousse* (Paris, 1973). However, Rudbeck's unity as a baroque scholar is strongly underlined in Eriksson, "Gestalter i Svensk lärdomhistoria I," n. 61.

58. See Pierre Bayle, "Olavi Rudbeckii *Atlantica* sive *Manheim,*" *Nouvelles de la république de lettres* 3 (Jan. and Feb. 1685): 49–69 and 119–36.

59. See Rudbeck, *Atlantica,* 1:890.

60. But we should not forget that as early as the sixth century, Cassiodorus's *History of the Goths,* which survives only in an abridgement by Jordanes, created the myth of the Goths as a Nordic people. See Teillet, *Des Goths à la nation gothique,* pp. 305–34; and, on the specifically mythical aspect, see Gilbert Dagron and Marin, "Discours utopique et récit des origines," *Annales: Économies, Sociétés, Civilisations* 26 (Mar.–Apr. 1971): 290–327.

Fig. 1.—Olof Rudbeck, anatomist and geographer: Atlantis-Sweden revealed. Frontispiece to the atlas of Rudbeck's *Atlantica*. Photo: Bibliothèque Nationale.

that myth from its distant origins in the sixth century A.D. down to the point at which it was solemnly revived at the Council of Basel in 1434, when the bishop Nicholas Ragvaldi forcefully claimed that the kingdom of Sweden was older, more powerful, and more noble than any other. Far from having been conquered by the monarchs of Rome, it had forced the Romans themselves to become its allies.

It was mainly in the seventeenth century, in the period of history when Sweden was known as a great power, namely, the reign of Gustavus Adolphus (1611–32), that the primacy of the Goths became the national myth of the Swedish people.

To show how the quest for Noah was fused with the Gothic ideology of Sweden, let us limit ourselves to the study of two documents. The first is the frontispiece of volume 1 of the *Atlantica* (fig. 2). Originating in Noah, seated somewhere in the vicinity of Mount Ararat, three lines of descent branch out. One, that of Ham, is soon lost in the sands of Africa. The other two, those of Shem and Japheth, are closely intertwined, as in the French monarchical tradition. Shem's family tree is a vine, the top of which is watered by the blood of Jesus (Rudbeck definitely remained Christian). The other tree, which is thicker, belongs to Japheth only up to the point where it is taken over by his son Atlas, a figure from Greek mythology. Atlas's tree grows in Sweden. It is an apple tree and is accordingly assimilated to the tree of the Garden of Eden, whose apples thud to the ground, symbolizing all the different nations. These include the Turks, the Trojans, the Goths of Spain, the Moors, and the Gauls. The Greeks are absent from this symbolism. Atlas is directly succeeded by Boreas, who in turn is directly succeeded by kings who bear Swedish names: Eric, Gustavus, and so forth. The tree of power thus interweaves its branches with those of the tree of religion, still present at this point. One day, it was to disappear.

The second document shows Rudbeck himself, very much the great scholar, portrayed as a geographer and an anatomist (see fig. 1).[61] He is the central figure in this picture, the anatomist and archaeologist who is to discover Atlantis right under the skin of Sweden. He is surrounded by eleven other figures, bringing the number in this group up to that of the apostles (the only biblical reference in the picture). The first of these figures, on Rudbeck's right and recognized by his scythe, is Time (Chronos); then, ringing the globe, come the rest, all but one of them named: Hesiod, Plato, Aristotle, Apollodorus, Tacitus, Ulysses, Ptolemy, Plutarch, the anonymous one, and Orpheus. The anonymous figure really does not need to be named, for blind as he is and crowned with a laurel wreath, he is clearly Homer. One great figure is conspicuous by his absence:

61. I owe much to the commentary by Allan Ellenius, "Olaus Rudbecks Atlantiska Anatomi," *Lychnos* (1959): 40–54; English summary: "Olaus Rudbeck's Atlantic Anatomy," pp. 53–54.

FIG. 2.—The tree of Shem and that of Atlas: religion and power. Frontispiece of the first volume of Rudbeck's *Atlantica*. Photo: François Demerliac.

Herodotus, who was guilty of having failed to mention the peoples with Germanic languages. Those who are present, however, are the most eminent representatives of classical culture and learning, and they are gathered here to proclaim the primacy of Sweden, the land of Origins par excellence.

Confronted with this totalitarian proclamation, it was Bayle, exiled in Rotterdam, who assumed the role of the little gardener.[62] He quite simply pointed out that there were many nations in the world and that each one could lay claim to primacy with equally good arguments. In 1676, after all, Pierre Audigier, a Frenchman, had similarly announced the primacy of Gaul.[63]

Giambattista Vico was a citizen in a country that was still no more than "a geographical expression," but the Lombards provided it with an equivalent to the Goths and furthermore could draw on the Etruscans, whose claims to be hailed as the princes of Origins were very serious indeed. In his first major work, *De antiquissima Italorum sapientia* (1710), Vico was momentarily tempted by an argument resembling Rudbeck's, which he had read but then rejected, rallying to the view that, in the eyes of God and in the Cycle of History, all nations are equal.[64] Elsewhere, notably in France and Germany, Rudbeck's discourse on Origins was turned around and restored to the Christian faith. Atlantis was indeed the place of Origins, but that place was none other than Palestine.[65]

Rudbeck's nationalistic Atlantism, like the Gothic myth, was a typical product of the period of great powers. In 1779, seven years after King Gustavus III had seized power to set on the ruins of party oppositions a typical enlightened despotism, the political climate was very different. It was then that a Piedmontese scholar, Giuseppe Bartoli, published and commented on the inaugural speech that the king of Sweden had delivered to the Riksdag in 1778. The Gothic-inspired ideology had collapsed, following the failure of the latest venture of Swedish nationalism led by Charles XII (king from 1697 to 1718). When Bartoli successfully argued that Atlantis was an image of imperialistic Athens, he was in truth referring to Sweden, but to a Sweden now disabused of its illusions.[66]

Meanwhile, what Bayle had foreseen and predicted came to pass. The

---

62. See Bayle, "Olavi Rudbeckii *Atlantica* sive *Manheim*."

63. See Audigier, *L'Origine des François*.

64. See Gustavo Costa, *Le Antichità germaniche nella cultura italiana de Machiavelli a Vico* (Naples, 1977).

65. My "Hérodote et l'Atlantide," pp. 25–28, provides all the necessary references.

66. On Bartoli and Sweden, see my "Hérodote et l'Atlantide," pp. 43–46, and, more recently, Franco Venturi, *Il patriotismo repubblicano e gli imperi dell'Est*, vol. 4, bk. 2 of *Settecento Riformatore* (Turin, 1984), p. 899.

ideologists of other countries also saw themselves as heirs to Atlantis; and they must be mentioned here, if only to note a certain degeneration from the level of myth to that of the novel, to speak in the manner of Georges Dumézil and Lévi-Strauss.[67]

France, however, was not affected by this particular malady; and the explanation is simple enough. What with her confidence in her own great king,[68] her status as a great nation, and her own great emperor, she was sufficient unto herself and, insofar as she indulged in talk of Origins, the Gauls, the Romans, and the Franks provided quite enough material to satisfy any ideologist. Atlantis was, it is true, a favorite topic of the intelligentsia, but it was a prenational Atlantis (a golden age), a cosmic or Christian Atlantis (Palestine), or a geographical Atlantis (the Canary Islands or America), not a national Atlantis. There was one exception that proved the rule. In 1808 a native of Avignon by the name of Fortia d'Urban published a thesis designed to show that a primitive people composed of Celts and Iberians had brought the civilization of Atlantis from Spain to France.[69] But this Atlanto-Occitanism had very little impact.

Italy, for its part, did have a problem with Origins, and during the Enlightenment there were numerous candidates for the position of primacy, with the Italics, the Etruscans, the Germans, and the Greeks all to the fore. The nationalistic-Atlantic theme did also manage to slip in its own little say, however. Its first spokesman was Count Gianrinaldo Carli (1720–95), an interesting reformist figure.[70] Carli produced what was, a priori, an unpredictable merge between the American theme of Atlantis and the thesis of Italian primacy at the origins of civilization. At the time of Atlantis, according to him, Italy was the link between America and the eastern Mediterranean. After Janus, the indigenous king, Saturn came from Atlantis to Italy, and it was Italy that then transmitted to Greece all the arts and virtues of Atlantis.

Much later, in 1840, Angelo Mazzoldi explained that Italy actually *had been* Atlantis and, as such, had civilized the entire eastern Mediterra-

67. See Georges Dumézil, *Du mythe au roman: La Saga de Hadingus et autres essais* (Paris, 1970), and Lévi-Strauss, *Anthropologie Structurale (Deux)* (Paris, 1973), pp. 312–15.

68. On French historiography and Louis XIV, see the fundamental work by Ranum, *Artisans of Glory, Writers and Historical Thought in Seventeenth-Century France* (Chapel Hill, N.C., 1980), and, more recently, Blandine Barret-Kriegel, *Les Historiens et la monarchie*, 4 vols. (Paris, 1988).

69. See Fortia d'Urban, *Antiquités et monumens du département de Vaucluse*, 2 vols. (Paris, 1808), 2:408–79.

70. See the article on Gianrinaldo Carli (also known as Giovanni Rinaldo Carli in some bibliographies) in *Illuministi italiani: Riformatori Lombardi, Piemontesi e Toscani*, ed. Venturi, vol. 46, bk. 3 of *La letteratura italiana: Storia e testi*, ed. Raffaele Mattioli, Pietro Pancrazi, and Alfredo Schiaffini (Milan, 1958), pp. 419–79; on the subject with which we are concerned here, the essential work by Carli is *Lettere americane (1770–1781)*, in *Opere* (Milan, 1779); trans. Jean Baptiste Lefebvre de Villebrune, under the title *Lettres americaines*, 2 vols. (Paris, 1788). For more information, see my "Hérodote et l'Atlantide."

nean.[71] What he was doing—and he was not the first to do so—was turning upside down the tradition of Greece as the ancient origin of civilization. At this late date, his book was received with respect.

England poses a different problem. So far as I know, there was no nationalistic-Atlantism there, neither in the seventeenth century nor in the Enlightenment. James Harrington's *Commonwealth of Oceana* (1656) was dedicated to Oliver Cromwell, who was later to send the author to prison. As John Toland pointed out in his biographical essay, when the work could finally be published at the beginning of the eighteenth century, it was "written after the manner of a Romance, in imitation of Plato's *Atlantic Story*," but except as a literary genre, this apologia for a Republican and merchant England had nothing at all in common with Plato.[72]

The two nationalistic versions of Atlantis that I have found in England belong to the occultist and preromantic tradition rather than to the tradition of the Enlightenment proper. It is accordingly more rewarding to compare them to works such as that of Fabre d'Olivet than to Rudbeck's.

They are worth mentioning, however. William Blake (1757–1827) produced a strange combination of Celtic, Jewish, and Atlantic lore. According to him, Atlas was another name for the Breton patriarch Albion; Abraham and Noah were both druids; and the vanished continent was a link between England and the new America that Blake exalted in so many of his poems. The underlying principle here is that "the antiquities of every Nation under Heaven, is no less sacred than that of the Jews,"[73] but the consequences that Blake drew from that fundamental principle of modern nationalist messianism made for fusion rather than for distinction. England was the land of the twelve tribes of Israel.[74]

One of Blake's contemporaries, Captain F. Wilford, an Indianist, with great originality discovered in the *Puranas* some faraway white islands in the West. Combining these texts with a number of others culled from Greek sources, he concluded that these white isles (the *S'weta-dwípa*) were at once Great Britain and also Atlantis, going on to observe forthrightly, "admitting my position to be right, I am conscious that *Britain* cannot

71. See Angelo Mazzoldi, *Delle origini italiche e della diffusione dell'incivilmento italiano alla Fenicia, alla Grecia e a tutte le nazioni asiatiche poste sul Mediterraneo* (Milan, 1840), pp. 44, 172–87. On the respectful reception given to the book, see Benedetto Croce, *Storia della storiografica italiana nel secolo decimonono*, vol. 15 of *Scritti di storia letteraria e politica* (Bari, 1921), p. 56.

72. John Toland, "The Life of James Harrington," in *The Oceana of James Harrington and His Other Works*, ed. Toland (London, 1700), p. 2.

73. William Blake, "A Descriptive Catalogue," *The Complete Writings of William Blake*, ed. Geoffrey Keynes (London, 1966), p. 578.

74. See Blake, "Jerusalem," *The Complete Writings of William Blake*, pp. 635–36. For more details and a bibliography, see my "Hérodote et l'Atlantide," p. 24.

receive any additional lustre from it."[75] The myth was, in fact, to pass from England to Ireland, where it was extremely popular in the nineteenth century.[76]

At this point, having covered the chronological ground that I set out to, I could well come to a halt. But I cannot refrain from mentioning two other nationalistic versions of Atlantis that belong to times much closer to our own. It was Plato's bitter patriotism that gave birth to the myth of Atlantis, the antithetical model to that of an Athens which was itself imaginary. The most popular modern identification of Plato's continent assimilates the destruction of Atlantis to the explosion that partially destroyed the island of Santorini around the middle of the second millennium B.C. This theory, which is as absurd as all the others, owes much to the patriotism of the Greek archaeologist Spyridon Marinatos and his disciples,[77] and it has continued to be exploited for patriotic ends.[78] As an irony of history would have it, however, the name of the Greek ship sent to collect the unfortunate Yasir Arafat from Beirut in 1982 happened to be *Atlantis* too. In a more optimistic vein, it is perhaps worth noting that Atlantis was also the name given to one of the American space shuttles of the late 1980s.

The Atlantis of German National Socialism was an idea that had much more far-reaching consequences, the repercussions of which still have not died out. The last disciples of Rudbeck were to be found among Hitler's National Socialists even before they came to power. Alfred Rosenberg's *Myth of the Twentieth Century* explained that the people of Atlantis, the ancestors of the Germanic peoples, had spread all over the world, including Palestine, a fact that made it very likely, indeed certain, that Jesus, a Galilean and accordingly a foreigner, was not a Jew.[79] After the Nazis came to power, the same thesis was advanced in a book written by a geographer, Albert Herrmann (a professor at the University of Berlin but also the *Führer* of the German press).[80] This was a remarkable example of imperialism in which North Africa, for example, was represented as part of the Atlanto-Germanic heritage and the Roman amphitheatre of El

75. F. Wilford, "An Essay on the Sacred Isles in the West," *Asiatic Researches* 8 (1808): 246.

76. The best illustration is provided by Henry O'Brien's novel, *The Round Towers of Ireland; or, The History of the Tuath-de-Danaans for the First Time Unveiled* (London, 1834), recently reprinted under the title *Atlantis in Ireland* (Blauvelt, N.Y., 1976).

77. Marinatos published this theory in an article well before his own excavations revealed the splendors of Minoan Santorini. See Spyridon Nikolaou Marinatos, "On the Atlantis Legend" (in Greek), *Kretika Chronika* 4 (1950): 195–213; trans. under the title *Some Words about the Legend of Atlantis* (Athens, 1969). For a general account of the thesis, see John Victor Luce, *Lost Atlantis: New Light on an Old Legend* (New York, 1969).

78. See James W. Mavor, Jr., *Voyage to Atlantis* (New York, 1969).

79. See Alfred Rosenberg, *Der Mythus des 20. Jahrhunderts: Eine Wertung der Seelischgeistigen Gestaltenkämpfe Unserer Zeit* (Munich, 1930), pp. 43–48.

80. See Albert Herrmann, *Unsere Ahnen und Atlantis: Nordische Seeherrschaft von Skandinavien bis nach Nordafrika* (Berlin, 1934).

Djem in Tunisia, was also claimed as the work of the Atlantic race. Similar ideas were diffused in occupied Europe, particularly in France.[81] This was no isolated phenomenon. In the notorious Ahnenerbe Institut [National Heritage Institute], the agency set up to foster SS ideology, Atlantis was a frequently mentioned subject and one in which the Reichsführer-SS Heinrich Himmler himself took a personal interest.[82] It was within this institution that the name for the island of Helgoland (*das heilige Land,* sacred or holy land) was first proposed.[83] The purpose here was clearly to find German names for German origins, so that these could display a superiority that owed nothing to Abraham. After the war, similar ideas were repeated by Jürgen Spanuth, a Nazi pastor who pretended that it was he who had discovered the identity of Atlantis and Helgoland and for a while enjoyed a certain success in Germany.[84] It seems hardly necessary to point out that such ideas are still not dead.

The time has come to bring this inquiry to a close. The successive nationalistic versions of Atlantis that we have examined represent but one aspect of a widespread ideological phenomenon: the quest for Origins, which is to be found among proud and humiliated peoples alike. It draws on monuments, ancient texts, unknown or little-known peoples, and even, as in the case of Atlantis, imaginary peoples. Seven Greek cities all claimed the honor of being the birthplace of Homer. But where was Troy? One theory, which has recently enjoyed considerable success in Yugoslavia, is that Homer's Troy was situated not at Hissarlik, in Turkey, but between Split and Dubrovnik, at the mouth of the Neretva.[85] This theory has not crossed the Albanian border; but in Albania, which passionately claims descent from the ancient Illyrians,[86] serious consideration has apparently been given to the idea that, during the Trojan War, the Illyrians played a

81. See Pascal Ory, *Le Petit Nazi illustré; Une Pédagogie hitlérienne en culture française: "Le Téméraire" (1943– 1944),* ed. Ory (Paris, 1979), pp. 53–57. My colleague Axel Seeberg of the University of Oslo, tells me that a similar pedagogical cartoon strip was published at the same time in occupied Norway, presumably on orders from Berlin.

82. See the fundamental work by Michael H. Kater, *Das "Ahnenerbe" der SS 1935–1945: Ein Beitrag zur Kulturpolitik des Dritten Reiches* (Stuttgart, 1974), esp. pp. 51, 71, 372 (Himmler's intervention), 378.

83. Ibid., p. 378 n. 109. Herrmann, who was a correspondent for the Institute, interpreted Atlantis as *Adland,* the *noble* land (p. 51).

84. See Jürgen Spanuth, *Das Enträtselte Atlantis* (Stuttgart, 1953); trans. Henri Daussy, under the title *L'Atlantide retrouvée* (Paris, 1954); and Spanuth, *Atlantis, Heimat, Reich und Schicksal der Germanen* (Tübingen, 1965). The latter was published by Grabert Verlag, an openly Nazi publisher.

85. See Roberto Salinas Price, *Homer's Blind Audience: An Essay on the "Iliad"'s Geographical Prerequisites for the Site of Ilias* (San Antonio, Tex., 1984).

86. See *Les Illyriens,* ed. S. Islami (Tirana, 1985). Although this book is not free of retrospective nationalism, it is a worthy work of serious scholarship.

role of crucial importance.[87] As for the Etruscans, is it not obvious that they were Turks?[88] That is one way of settling a few old scores with the Greeks.

Faced with so many fantasies, what is to be done with Atlantis? In the first place, we should study its history as a history of human imaginary representations, and that, indeed, is what I have briefly attempted to do here. But also—why not?—we can make pictures of it, setting down on paper drawings of the geometric colony precisely imagined by Plato (fig. 3).[89] Perhaps that is the best use to which Atlantis can be put in this day and age.

87. See Engjëll Sedaj, "Les Tribus illyriennes dans les chansons homériques," *Studia Albanica* 23 (1986): 157–72.

88. See Adile Ayda, *Les Étrusques étaient des Turcs* (Ankara, 1985). Other examples from the Middle East may be found in my "Flavius Josèphe et les prophètes," *Cahiers du Centre d'études du Proche-Orient ancien* (Geneva, 1989): 11–31.

89. See the splendid collection made by the architect H. R. Stahel, *Atlantis Illustrated* (New York, 1982). I am most grateful to Alain Schnapp for bringing this work to my attention, and I have borrowed figure 3 from it. Unfortunately, in his preface to Stahel's book, Isaac Asimov echoes Marinatos's theory on Santorini, as does Kater in his *Das "Ahnenerbe" der SS 1935–1945*, p. 372 n. 119. Jean-Pierre Adam (in his *Passé recomposé: Chroniques d'archéologie fantasque* [Paris, 1988], esp. pp. 38–64) certainly puts a number of mad theories in their place but only to replace them with a hypothesis that is neither new nor convincing. But then, clearly, one can't expect everything.

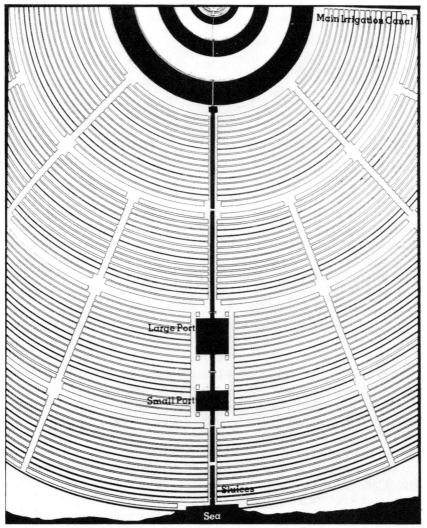

FIG. 3.—Putting Atlantis to good use: the Platonic city and its system of canals at the center of the sea, according to H. R. Stahel, *Atlantis Illustrated* (New York, 1982), p. 91.

Using and Abusing Fiction

Elizabeth Helsinger

"The story is a strange one." I repeat the opening sentence of Pierre Vidal-Naquet's essay, which can serve to introduce these remarks as well. The story Vidal-Naquet tells is not Plato's original narrative of the lost island-state of Atlantis, recounted in the *Timaeus* and *Critias*. "Atlantis and the Nations" (pp. 325–51) shifts the object of historical inquiry to the afterlife of this originating text, itself in all likelihood Plato's monitory, fictional representation of fifth-century Athens and its imperial ambitions. Vidal-Naquet's subject, then, is a history of "imaginary representations" (p. 328) that are themselves interpretations of a work of historical fiction, an invented myth. The article focuses on one period (late seventeenth through early nineteenth centuries) and one genre of such imaginary representations, texts which appropriate the story of Atlantis and reinterpret it to serve as a foundational narrative for one or another of the emerging European nations. These imaginative appropriations of a historical fiction are of particular interest to Vidal-Naquet and to us because they are offered by serious scholars as history.

What counts as evidence for these Enlightenment scholars who reclaim Plato's account of Atlantis as national history? How do we explain the relegation of such attempts to the margins of what is considered serious historical scholarship in the nineteenth and twentieth centuries? And what is the status of Vidal-Naquet's own strange story: what makes it count, as it undoubtedly does, as history, and what does it tell us about shifts in our understanding of the long and troubled relations between history and fiction, in which questions of evidence may be deployed to police changing boundaries? Vidal-Naquet's essay suggests answers to the first two of these questions: why these fictions were once taken as serious history, and why they are now so thoroughly discounted. I would like to address the last question, what Vidal-Naquet's essay can tell us about the relations between history and fiction, by exploring the links between his story and two other works of the same moment. Like his essay, these works review critically the uses of historical fictions in the construction of national identities. Both these works, however, are themselves presented not as histories of the human imaginary, but as instances of it. They are offered as fictions about the relation of myth to history. I will be referring to the German (formerly East German) novelist Christa Wolf's *Cassandra* and her four essays, "Conditions of a Narrative" (in this country published together with the novella in a single volume); and to the African-American writer Toni Morrison's novel, *Song of Solomon*.[1]

As Vidal-Naquet points out, the nationalist appropriations of Atlantis he examines participate in a skeptical Enlightenment project; they can be read as efforts to secularize the story of human civilization, displacing the Judeo-Christian account of the Jews as originary, chosen people, to which all other stories of origins were assimilated by medieval and Renaissance Christian historians. Substituting Swedes or Italians or British for the biblical people, these eighteenth-century scholars constructed elaborate genealogies (and geographies) that connected the modern, historical nations with both the lost Atlantis (and its supposed founder, Atlas) and the survivors of the biblical flood, the sons of Noah, as the foundation for a secular history. As evidence these accounts sometimes invoked linguistic phenomena (Hebrew names reportedly in use in the New World, one traditional site for Atlantis). But more often they seem to have relied on the ingeniousness and the inclusiveness of their explanatory accounts (their ability to bring together into a single narrative as many ancient and classical names and stories as possible), underwritten by the reputation for learning of the authors—and, of course, emergent national pride.

By the mid-nineteenth century, a demand for corroborating textual or archaeological evidence makes the purely hermeneutic achievements of Enlightenment scholars no longer count as respectable history. Between 1830 and 1840, Vidal-Naquet notes, archives become "the historian's 'laboratory'" (p. 328). And Heinrich Schliemann's spectacular discoveries at Troy and Mycenae fifty years later open a whole new direction for those in pursuit of historicity, sending Atlantis-hunters off on improb-

---

1. See Christa Wolf, *Cassandra: A Novel and Four Essays*, trans. Jan van Heurck (1983; New York, 1984), hereafter abbreviated *C*; and Toni Morrison, *Song of Solomon* (1977; New York, 1978), hereafter abbreviated *SS*.

Elizabeth Helsinger is professor of English and General Studies in the Humanities at the University of Chicago and a coeditor of *Critical Inquiry*. She is author of *Ruskin and the Art of the Beholder* (1982). Her book in progress is *Rural Scenes and National Representation*.

able ventures on the ocean floor for the next hundred years. (Vidal-Naquet cites a Soviet submarine search for the buried city off the coast of Spain, abandoned as recently as 1984.) Already in 1841, the French historian Thomas-Henri Martin, reviewing Enlightenment efforts to locate Atlantis in space and time, can conclude that such attempts are simply misguided: "'[Atlantis] belongs to *another world,* one that exists not in the domain of space but in that of thought'" (p. 328). Contemporary historians are inclined to concur.

Except, of course, insofar as that other world, the domain of thought, has its own history, one which must be understood to participate in more properly historical narratives. Here Vidal-Naquet's earlier work on Plato's Atlantis story anticipates the kind of history he offers in "Athens and the Nations."[2] Both essays take texts once offered as true accounts but now viewed as fictions and give them historical place and meaning, not just with reference to a history of ideas or texts, but also as intimate actors in political history as that has been understood since the nineteenth century, that is, as national history. Both essays set aside the question of the historicity of Atlantis for the—to us more interesting, or at least more properly historical—question of the history and historicity of the retellings of that original story within a particular national context.

Vidal-Naquet's project, then, can be read as both historical and critical. On the one hand, he too works as a historian, in a sense that would be recognizable at least since the mid-nineteenth century. One might properly invoke questions of evidence to test both the status as artifact of the Enlightenment texts he cites and the explanatory narrative he constructs around them. On the other hand, this particular history functions as critical commentary on the kind of history practiced not only by his eighteenth-century scholars but also by many of their nineteenth- and twentieth-century critics: nationalist history. The need to secure a national past (or to critique a national present), Vidal-Naquet's account suggests, may conflict with questions of evidence invoked to maintain the distinctions between history and myth, or history and fiction.

It is here that Vidal-Naquet's "Atlantis and the Nations," the longer, French version of which was published in 1982, intersects with Toni Morrison's 1977 *Song of Solomon* and Christa Wolf's 1983 *Cassandra.*[3] All three were written at a moment—no longer ours—when nationalism appeared to be largely a thing of the past. From that perspective, nationalism's role

2. See Pierre Vidal-Naquet, "Athènes et l'Atlantide: Structure et signification d'un mythe Platonicien," *Revue des études grecques* 77 (July–Dec. 1964): 420–44; trans. Andrew Szegedy-Maszak, under the title "Athens and Atlantis: Structure and Meaning of a Platonic Myth," *The Black Hunter: Forms of Thought and Forms of Society in the Greek World* (Baltimore, 1986), pp. 263–84.

3. See Vidal-Naquet, "Hérodote et l'Atlantide—entre les Grecs et les Juifs: Réflexions sur l'historiographie du siècle des lumières," *Quaderni di storia,* no. 16 (July–Dec. 1982): 3–76.

in determining or undermining distinctions between fiction, myth, and history could itself become a subject for historians and novelists.

Taking Aeschylus's Cassandra as her starting point, Wolf used fiction, she wrote, to "retrace the path out of the myth, into its (supposed) social and historical coordinates": to reclaim Cassandra and Troy for history (*C*, p. 256). But not the "history" inherited from the nineteenth century. Her project is intended to be critical and transformative; the turn to fiction is necessary to bypass the "linear narrative" of nationalist history (*C*, p. 262). Aeschylus's trilogy, dramatizing the institution of a state system of justice as a foundational moment in the history of Athens, helps to put such a linear narrative into place. This "history as the story of heroes" Wolf explicitly rejects as "a custom which no longer meets the needs of our time" (*C*, p. 262). So her Cassandra, already alienated from a Troy that increasingly resembles the new Greek city-states that defeat it, refuses to leave with Aeneas, who will of course become the hero of another foundational epic of empire. Against the ultimately destructive appropriation of myth to the service of states seeking to construct a past for the sake of dominating a future, Wolf sets her story of an alternative sociality arising outside the walls of Troy and the camps of the Greeks, a community that keeps alive memories of other modes of collectivity in its oppositional present practice, but with no expectation of any future.

Wolf's fictional reconstruction of Cassandra's history—not linear but a "narrative network" linking "social and historical coordinates"— undoes the erasure almost effected by Aeschylus's story of Athens's transformation into a modern city-state (*C*, pp. 262, 256). Cassandra's function is less to foresee than to remember. To remember not only Troy and the nameless community that is its other but also, against the resistance of the elders of ancient Mycenae and the citizens of modern Athens, to remember past injustices that both the hero's story and the state's ask us to forget. "For what meaning," Wolf asks, "would there be in the victims, in the thousands of the homeless, the gnawing pain of exile that went on for decades, for a people without a memory? Storytelling is the assignment of meaning" (*C*, p. 174).

Toni Morrison also resists a dominant national history by reclaiming in fiction this historical function for narrative, that is, to give meaning to loss by reconstructing memory. Names, in Morrison's *Song of Solomon*, both conceal and preserve memories for African-Americans who have been denied history and even genealogy, the power to perpetuate family lineage and pass on family names. Macon Dead (whose own name was the mistake of a drunken white clerk filling out his father's freedman's registration form) longs for "a name that was real. A name given to him at birth with love and seriousness. A name that was not a joke, nor a disguise, nor a brand name" (*SS*, p. 17). His son Milkman takes up the quest for an ancestor who can give him a "real" name, despite his father's insistence that that "lithe young man with onyx skin and legs as straight as cane stalks . . . would never be known. No. Nor his name" (*SS*, pp. 17–18). Macon compensates for the irretrievable loss of a past that might have conferred a present identity by acquiring property. His sister respects names as talismans of a past even when they are not "real names" and seem to have no meaning. Like the storyteller Morrison herself, Milkman chooses his aunt's talismanic names as the better route to recovering a history. Beneath the corrupted names preserved in a children's song ("O Sugarman done fly away"), he finds the traces of a mythical lost ancestor (Solomon, Suleyman, or Shalimar). He also comes to value names that seem to offer no continuous past, no genealogical link with a mythical founding father, but constitute another kind of history, neither linear nor heroic. "He closed his eyes and thought of the black men in Shalimar, Roanoke, Petersburg, . . . in the pool halls, the barbershops. Their names. Names they got from yearnings, gestures, flaws, events, mistakes, weaknesses. Names that bore witness" (*SS*, p. 333). These names, redeemed into meaning by the storyteller, give back to Milkman and Macon the past that history denies them. Like Wolf, however, Morrison refuses to construct a story of origins that will authorize the fantasy of a national future. "Sugarman done fly away"—in a gesture that signals, for his children's children, his triumph over white history, while it also marks his departure from theirs.

The novelists, like the historian, draw our attention to transgressions of the boundaries between history and myth or fiction. And like Plato, whose "true account" of Atlantis can serve, as Vidal-Naquet observes, as a point of origin for a history of such deliberate transgressions, they turn to fiction in order to criticize what counts as history—for Wolf, Morrison, and Vidal-Naquet, writing circa 1980, nationalist histories that raise questions both of evidence and of justice.

But what then? What happens once these shifting relations are made visible? How does the novelist or the historian resettle the boundaries between history and fiction without which "history" would cease to be a meaningful category? Wolf accompanies her novella with four essays that situate her fictional narrative in the place and time that produced it. Historicizing her fictional text, she urges its capacity to "assign meaning" to a present that, for Europeans living with the imminent threat of nuclear war, might have no future if nationalist priorities are pursued. Her essays assert the desire for a "history without heroes" or the nations that require them, a history toward which her fictions might point the way. Morrison returns in her later novel, *Beloved,* to problematize even the storyteller's alternative histories. "This is not a story to pass on," she concludes—yet it is a story that cannot be forgotten.[4] Vidal-Naquet is more confident, in 1982, than Wolf or Morrison that excursions into a history of the imaginary will confirm the existence of a history that is not fictive. He ends his

4. Morrison, *Beloved* (New York, 1987), p. 275.

account of national appropriations of Atlantis with the counterexample of Giuseppe Bartoli, who even in the eighteenth century preferred, as did Vidal-Naquet in 1964, to historicize Plato's fictional text rather than to construct national history out of Plato's fictions. "Il fallait donc qu'après l'étude des écarts soit aussi tentée celle de la vérité," Vidal-Naquet concludes ["After the study of errors one must also attempt that of truth"].[5] Five years later, in *Les Assassins de la memoire*, Vidal-Naquet condemned the crimes of a revisionist history against the necessary memory of the Holocaust.[6]

His 1991 essay, however, ends more tentatively. To the question, "Faced with so many fantasies, what is to be done with Atlantis?" the historian replies that once we have studied his "history of human imaginary representations" of Atlantis, "why not . . . make pictures of it, setting down on paper drawings of the geometric colony precisely imagined by Plato[?] Perhaps that is the best use to which Atlantis can be put in this day and age" (p. 350). Nationalist fictions disarmed as art? I too admire that fine geometric imagination, but Atlantis is, as Vidal-Naquet has himself argued, not a utopian but a critical image. Those pictures of Plato's Atlantis will surely send us back, once again, to ponder the uses and abuses of fiction by history. The novelists would argue that fiction can be a tool to criticize the impulse toward nationalist history, and even that, in some circumstances, fiction can restore a necessary memory that history threatens to obliterate. But perhaps this has become, in the 1990s, a more dangerous argument than it appeared to be in 1980—especially for a historian.

---

5. Vidal-Naquet, "Hérodote et l'Atlantide," p. 46.
6. See Vidal-Naquet, *Les Assassins de la memoire: "Un Eichmann de papier" et autres essais sur le révisionnisme* (Paris, 1987); trans. Jeffrey Mehlman, under the title *Assassins of Memory: Essays on the Denial of the Holocaust* (New York, 1992).

How to Get beyond Myth?

Pierre Vidal-Naquet

Translated by Ann Hobart and Arnold I. Davidson

In "Using and Abusing Fiction" (pp. 352–57), Elizabeth Helsinger has put her finger on what seems to me the essential problem in the modern history of Atlantis. In referring to the works of Christa Wolf and Toni Morrison, she provides a very useful counterpoint to my observations. I would simply like to add a few comments.

First, what makes the business of Atlantis exciting is that in the beginning there is a fiction that was taken as a true story [*histoire*]. There are precedents, certainly, beginning with the *Odyssey* of Homer, but in Homer's time there was no history as constituted knowledge. This is no more true in the time of Plato. The true adversaries of Plato are the historians Herodotus and Thucydides. In the Platonic republic, the historian was at best the king of the shadows in the cave. But the narrative of Plato, which on the literary plane gave birth to the historical novel—and all Greek novels were presented, in their way, as historical narratives—was taken very seriously as a narrative that was all the more authentic because it was so remote.

Second, the modern history of the myth begins with the Enlightenment, more specifically with what Paul Hazard in a classic book called the crisis of European consciousness [*conscience*].[1] Atlantis, since the major work of Olof Rudbeck, functions as a substitute for Judeo-Christian myth. It testifies by its very existence to the extraordinary difficulty of passing

---

1. See Paul Hazard, *La Crise de la conscience européenne, 1680–1715*, 2 vols. (1935; Paris, 1968); trans. J. Lewis May, under the title *The European Mind, The Critical Years, 1680–1715* (New Haven, Conn., 1953).

from myth to reason, an operation that formerly was considered very simple. As Helsinger well understands, this history functions as a critique of all nationalist historiographies. It is striking, for example, that an analogous legend, about which I said a few words in my text, was widespread in Yugoslavia before the breakup of that country. The official news agency Tanjug, we recall, edited a book that explained that the Troy of Homer must have been located between Split and Dubrovnik, at the mouth of the Neretva. This place is today in Croatia. Are we to witness the conflict between Serbs and Croats in order to know who is in possession of the traces of Troy?

Third, Helsinger alludes to my book, *Assassins of Memory*. I will add to her remarks one detail: in the ideology known as the New Right, of which the representatives are not all enrolled, indeed far from it, in the camp of the "negationists," an important place is accorded to the Indo-European myth. For a certain number of these intellectuals, it is a great satisfaction to realize that they descend not from Abraham but from those who several millennia ago created the ideology of trifunctionalism. Thus reasons, for example, Jean-Louis Tristani, one of the intellectuals who was convinced by the "arguments" of Arthur Butz and Robert Faurisson.[2] Georges Dumézil, the inventor of this ideology, was accused of ideological sympathy with Nazism. It seems to me that this accusation has been re-

2. See Pierre Vidal-Naquet, *Assassins of Memory: Essays on the Denial of the Holocaust*, trans. Jeffrey Mehlman (New York, 1992), p. 166 n. 27.

Pierre Vidal-Naquet is director of the Centre Louis Gernet de Recherches Comparées sur les Sociétés Anciennes at the École des Hautes Études en Sciences Sociales in Paris. His most recent publications are *Le Trait empoisonné: Réflexions sur l'affaire Jean Moulin* (1993); the second volume of *Les Juifs, la mémoire et le présent* (1991); *La Grèce ancienne 1: Du mythe à la raison*, with Jean-Pierre Vernant (1990); and *La Démocratie grecque vue d'ailleurs* (1990). Among his works to have appeared in English are *Myth and Tragedy in Ancient Greece*, with Jean-Pierre Vernant (1988), and *The Black Hunter: Forms of Thought and Forms of Society in the Greek World* (1986). **Ann Hobart** is manuscript editor of *Critical Inquiry* and a freelance translator. She has published several essays on nineteenth-century British fiction and social criticism, most recently in *Victorian Studies*. **Arnold I. Davidson,** the executive editor of *Critical Inquiry*, is professor of philosophy and a member of the Committee on the Conceptual Foundations of Science at the University of Chicago. Appointed a fellow at Wissenschaftskolleg, Berlin for 1994–95, he has recently published a series of essays on the tradition of spiritual exercises in philosophy and is completing a book on the history of horror and wonder.

futed.[3] But that is not the important point. Those who seized upon Dumézil, whose enterprise claimed to be scientific—and was to a very large extent—simply wanted to substitute one myth for another.

Fourth, I will give a last example, that of Martin Bernal's *Black Athena*.[4] That it is a book with scientific aspects is beyond doubt. The historiographic part, particularly that devoted to the formation of Greek myth, especially in the German-speaking world of the nineteenth century, is very enriching. Unfortunately, when Bernal wants to provide a reconstruction, he is satisfied with repeating, in scholarly form, what Herodotus said, and this on the basis of etymological hypotheses that few qualified philologists are ready to take up on their own account. His *Black Athena* thus functions exactly as do the Atlanto-nationalist myths that I analyzed in my essay.

That such phenomena occur in the twentieth century shows that, in this domain as well, the notion of progress must be called into question.

3. See Didier Eribon, *Faut-il brûler Dumézil? Mythologie, science et politique* (Paris, 1992). This book was the object of sharp criticisms, but they have not changed my mind on the main issue.

4. See Martin Bernal, *Black Athena: The Afroasiatic Roots of Classical Civilization*, 2 vols. (New Brunswick, N.J., 1987–91).

EXPERIENCE AND THE
DISCIPLINES OF PROOF

The Evidence of Experience

Joan W. Scott

Becoming Visible

There is a section in Samuel Delany's magnificent autobiographical meditation, *The Motion of Light in Water,* that dramatically raises the problem of writing the history of difference, the history, that is, of the designation of "other," of the attribution of characteristics that distinguish categories of people from some presumed (and usually unstated) norm.[1]

I am grateful to Tom Keenan for inviting me to the conference ("History Today—and Tonight," Rutgers and Princeton Universities, March 1990) where I tried out some of these ideas, and to the many people there whose questions and comments led to a first round of revisions and reformulations. The students in my graduate seminar at Rutgers in the spring of 1990 helped immeasurably in the clarification of my ideas about "experience" and about what it means to historicize. Criticism from members of the "History" seminar during 1990–91 in the School of Social Science at the Institute for Advanced Study helped give this paper its final—and, I think, much improved—form. As usual, Elizabeth Weed provided the crucial suggestions for the conceptualization of this paper. I also appreciate the important contributions of Judith Butler, Christina Crosby, Nicholas Dirks, Christopher Fynsk, Clifford Geertz, Donna Haraway, Susan Harding, Gyan Prakash, Donald Scott, and William Sewell, Jr. Karen Swann's astute comments led me to rethink and rewrite the final section of this paper. I learned a great deal from her and from that exercise. In a letter he wrote in July 1987, Reginald Zelnick challenged me to articulate a definition of "experience" that might work for historians. Although I'm not sure he will find this essay the answer he was looking for, I'm indebted to him for that early provocation.

1. For an important discussion of the "dilemma of difference," see Martha Minow. "Justice Engendered," foreword to "The Supreme Court, 1986 Term," *Harvard Law Review* 101 (Nov. 1987): 10–95.

This essay originally appeared in *Critical Inquiry* 17 (Summer 1991).

Delany (a gay man, a black man, a writer of science fiction) recounts his reaction to his first visit to the St. Marks bathhouse in 1963. He remembers standing on the threshold of a "gym-sized room" dimly lit by blue bulbs. The room was full of people, some standing, the rest

> an undulating mass of naked, male bodies, spread wall to wall.
> My first response was a kind of heart-thudding astonishment, very close to fear.
> I have written of a space at certain libidinal saturation before. That was not what frightened me. It was rather that the saturation was not only kinesthetic but visible.[2]

Watching the scene establishes for Delany a "fact that flew in the face" of the prevailing representation of homosexuals in the 1950s as "isolated perverts," as subjects "gone awry." The "apprehension of massed bodies" gave him (as it does, he argues, anyone, "male, female, working or middle class") a "sense of political power":

> what *this* experience said was that there was a population—not of individual homosexuals . . . not of hundreds, not of thousands, but rather of millions of gay men, and that history had, actively and already, created for us whole galleries of institutions, good and bad, to accommodate our sex. [*M*, p. 174]

The sense of political possibility is frightening and exhilarating for Delany. He emphasizes not the discovery of an identity, but a sense of participation in a movement; indeed, it is the extent (as well as the existence) of these sexual practices that matters most in his account. Numbers— massed bodies—constitute a movement and this, even if subterranean, belies enforced silences about the range and diversity of human sexual practices. Making the movement visible breaks the silence about it, challenges prevailing notions, and opens new possibilities for everyone. Delany imagines, even from the vantage of 1988, a future utopian moment of genuine sexual revolution, "once the AIDS crisis is brought

2. Samuel R. Delany, *The Motion of Light in Water: Sex and Science Fiction Writing in the East Village, 1957–1965* (New York, 1988), p. 173; hereafter abbreviated *M*.

Joan W. Scott is professor of social science at the Institute for Advanced Study in Princeton, New Jersey. She is the author, most recently, of *Gender and the Politics of History* (1988) and is currently at work on a history of feminist claims for political rights in France during the period 1789–1945 as a way of exploring arguments about equality and difference.

under control":

> That revolution will come precisely because of the infiltration of clear
> and articulate language into the marginal areas of human sexual
> exploration, such as this book from time to time describes, and of
> which it is only the most modest example. Now that a significant
> range of people have begun to get a clearer idea of what has been pos-
> sible among the varieties of human pleasure in the recent past, heter-
> osexuals and homosexuals, females and males will insist on exploring
> them even further. [*M*, p. 175]

By writing about the bathhouse Delany seeks not, he says, "to romanticize that time into some cornucopia of sexual plenty," but rather to break
an "absolutely sanctioned public silence" on questions of sexual practice,
to reveal something that existed but that had been suppressed.

> Only the coyest and the most indirect articulations could occasionally
> indicate the boundaries of a phenomenon whose centers could not be
> spoken or written of, even figuratively: and that coyness was medical
> and legal as well as literary; and, as Foucault has told us, it was, in its
> coyness, a huge and pervasive discourse. But what that coyness means
> is that there is no way to gain from it a clear, accurate, and extensive
> picture of extant public sexual institutions. That discourse only
> touched on highly select margins when they transgressed the legal
> and/or medical standards of a populace that firmly wished to main-
> tain that no such institutions existed. [*M*, pp. 175–76]

The point of Delany's description, indeed of his entire book, is to document the existence of those institutions in all their variety and multiplicity,
to write about and thus to render historical what has hitherto been hidden
from history.

As I read it, a metaphor of visibility as literal transparency is crucial to
his project. The blue lights illuminate a scene he has participated in before
(in darkened trucks parked along the docks under the West Side Highway,
in men's rooms in subway stations), but understood only in a fragmented
way. "No one ever got *to see* its whole" (*M*, p. 174; emphasis added). He
attributes the impact of the bathhouse scene to its visibility: "You could *see*
what was going on throughout the dorm" (*M*, p. 173; emphasis added).
Seeing enables him to comprehend the relationship between his personal
activities and politics: "the first direct sense of political power comes from
the apprehension of massed bodies." Recounting that moment also allows
him to explain the aim of his book: to provide a "clear, accurate, and
extensive *picture* of extant public sexual institutions" so that others may
learn about and explore them (*M*, pp. 174, 176; emphasis added). Knowledge is gained through vision; vision is a direct apprehension of a world of
transparent objects. In this conceptualization, the visible is privileged;

writing is then put at its service.[3] Seeing is the origin of knowing. Writing is reproduction, transmission—the communication of knowledge gained through (visual, visceral) experience.

This kind of communication has long been the mission of historians documenting the lives of those omitted or overlooked in accounts of the past. It has produced a wealth of new evidence previously ignored about these others and has drawn attention to dimensions of human life and activity usually deemed unworthy of mention in conventional histories. It has also occasioned a crisis for orthodox history by multiplying not only stories but subjects, and by insisting that histories are written from fundamentally different—indeed irreconcilable—perspectives or standpoints, none of which is complete or completely "true." Like Delany's memoir, these histories have provided evidence for a world of alternative values and practices whose existence gives the lie to hegemonic constructions of social worlds, whether these constructions vaunt the political superiority of white men, the coherence and unity of selves, the naturalness of heterosexual monogamy, or the inevitability of scientific progress and economic development. The challenge to normative history has been described, in terms of conventional historical understandings of evidence, as an enlargement of the picture, a correction to oversights resulting from inaccurate or incomplete vision, and it has rested its claim to legitimacy on the authority of experience, the direct experience of others, as well as of the historian who learns to see and illuminate the lives of those others in his or her texts.

Documenting the experience of others in this way has been at once a highly successful and limiting strategy for historians of difference. It has been successful because it remains so comfortably within the disciplinary framework of history, working according to rules that permit calling old narratives into question when new evidence is discovered. The status of evidence is, of course, ambiguous for historians. On the one hand, they acknowledge that "evidence only counts as evidence and is only recognized as such in relation to a potential narrative, so that the narrative can be said to determine the evidence as much as the evidence determines the narrative."[4] On the other hand, historians' rhetorical treatment of evidence and their use of it to falsify prevailing interpretations, depends on a referential notion of evidence which denies that it is anything but a reflection of the real.[5] Michel de Certeau's description is apt. Historical

3. On the distinction between seeing and writing in formulations of identity, see Homi K. Bhabha, "Interrogating Identity," in *Identity: The Real Me*, ed. Lisa Appignanesi (London, 1987), pp. 5–11.

4. Lionel Gossman, *Towards a Rational Historiography*, Transactions of the American Philosophical Society, n.s. 79, pt. 3 (Philadelphia, 1989), p. 26.

5. On the "documentary" or "objectivist" model used by historians, see Dominick LaCapra, "Rhetoric and History," *History and Criticism* (Ithaca, N.Y., 1985), pp. 15–44.

discourse, he writes,

> gives itself credibility in the name of the reality which it is supposed to represent, but this authorized appearance of the "real" serves precisely to camouflage the practice which in fact determines it. Representation thus disguises the praxis that organizes it.[6]

When the evidence offered is the evidence of "experience," the claim for referentiality is further buttressed—what could be truer, after all, than a subject's own account of what he or she has lived through? It is precisely this kind of appeal to experience as uncontestable evidence and as an originary point of explanation—as a foundation on which analysis is based—that weakens the critical thrust of histories of difference. By remaining within the epistemological frame of orthodox history, these studies lose the possibility of examining those assumptions and practices that excluded considerations of difference in the first place. They take as self-evident the identities of those whose experience is being documented and thus naturalize their difference. They locate resistance outside its discursive construction and reify agency as an inherent attribute of individuals, thus decontextualizing it. When experience is taken as the origin of knowledge, the vision of the individual subject (the person who had the experience or the historian who recounts it) becomes the bedrock of evidence on which explanation is built. Questions about the constructed nature of experience, about how subjects are constituted as different in the first place, about how one's vision is structured—about language (or discourse) and history—are left aside. The evidence of experience then becomes evidence for the fact of difference, rather than a way of exploring how difference is established, how it operates, how and in what ways it constitutes subjects who see and act in the world.[7]

6. Michel de Certeau, "History: Science and Fiction," in *Heterologies: Discourse on the Other*, trans. Brian Massumi (Minneapolis, 1986), p. 203; hereafter abbreviated "H."

7. Vision, as Donna Haraway points out, is not passive reflection. "All eyes, including our own organic ones, are active perceptual systems, building in translations and specific *ways* of seeing—that is, ways of life" (Donna Haraway, "Situated Knowledges: The Science Question in Feminism and the Privilege of Partial Perspective," *Feminist Studies* 14 [Fall 1988]: 583). In another essay she pushes the optical metaphor further: "The rays from my optical device diffract rather than reflect. These diffracting rays compose *interference* patterns, not reflecting images.... A diffraction pattern does not map where differences appear, but rather where the *effects* of differences appear" (Haraway, "The Promises of Monsters: Reproductive Politics for Inappropriate/d Others," typescript). In this connection, see also Minnie Bruce Pratt's discussion of her eye that "has only let in what I have been taught to see," in her "Identity: Skin   Blood   Heart," in Elly Bulkin, Pratt, and Barbara Smith, *Yours in Struggle: Three Feminist Perspectives on Anti-Semitism and Racism* (Brooklyn, N.Y., 1984), and the analysis of Pratt's autobiographical essay by Biddy Martin and Chandra Talpade Mohanty, "Feminist Politics: What's Home Got to Do with It?" in *Feminist Studies/Critical Studies*, ed. Teresa de Lauretis (Bloomington, Ind., 1986), pp. 191–212.

To put it another way, the evidence of experience, whether conceived through a metaphor of visibility or in any other way that takes meaning as transparent, reproduces rather than contests given ideological systems—those that assume that the facts of history speak for themselves and those that rest on notions of a natural or established opposition between, say, sexual practices and social conventions, or between homosexuality and heterosexuality. Histories that document the "hidden" world of homosexuality, for example, show the impact of silence and repression on the lives of those affected by it and bring to light the history of their suppression and exploitation. But the project of making experience visible precludes critical examination of the workings of the ideological system itself, its categories of representation (homosexual/heterosexual, man/woman, black/white as fixed immutable identities), its premises about what these categories mean and how they operate, and of its notions of subjects, origin, and cause. Homosexual practices are seen as the result of desire, conceived as a natural force operating outside or in opposition to social regulation. In these stories homosexuality is presented as a repressed desire (experience denied), made to seem invisible, abnormal, and silenced by a "society" that legislates heterosexuality as the only normal practice.[8] Because this kind of (homosexual) desire cannot ultimately be repressed—because experience is there—it invents institutions to accommodate itself. These institutions are unacknowledged but not invisible; indeed, it is the possibility that they can be seen that threatens order and ultimately overcomes repression. Resistance and agency are presented as driven by uncontainable desire; emancipation is a teleological story in which desire ultimately overcomes social control and becomes visible. History is a chronology that makes experience visible, but in which categories appear as nonetheless ahistorical: desire, homosexuality, heterosexuality, femininity, masculinity, sex, and even sexual practices become so many fixed entities being played out over time, but not themselves historicized. Presenting the story in this way excludes, or at least understates, the historically variable interrelationship between the meanings "homosexual" and "heterosexual," the constitutive force each has for the other, and the contested and changing nature of the terrain that they simultaneously occupy. "The importance—an importance—of the category 'homosexual,'" writes Eve Kosofsky Sedgwick,

> comes not necessarily from its regulatory relation to a nascent or already-constituted minority of homosexual people or desires, but from its potential for giving whoever wields it a structuring defini-

---

8. On the disruptive, antisocial nature of desire, see Leo Bersani, *A Future for Astyanax: Character and Desire in Literature* (Boston, 1976).

tional leverage over the whole range of male bonds that shape the social constitution.[9]

Not only does homosexuality define heterosexuality by specifying its negative limits, and not only is the boundary between the two a shifting one, but both operate within the structures of the same "phallic economy"—an economy whose workings are not taken into account by studies that seek simply to make homosexual experience visible. One way to describe this economy is to say that desire is defined through the pursuit of the phallus—that veiled and evasive signifier which is at once fully present but unattainable, and which gains its power through the promise it holds out but never entirely fulfills.[10] Theorized this way, homosexuality and heterosexuality work according to the same economy, their social institutions mirroring one another. The social institutions through which gay sex is practiced may invert those associated with dominant heterosexual behavior (promiscuous versus restrained, public versus private, anonymous versus known, and so on), but they both operate within a system structured according to presence and lack.[11] To the extent that this system constructs desiring subjects (those who are legitimate as well as those who are not), it simultaneously establishes them and itself as given and outside of time, as the way things work, the way they inevitably are.

The project of making experience visible precludes analysis of the workings of this system and of its historicity; instead, it reproduces its terms. We come to appreciate the consequences of the closeting of homosexuals and we understand repression as an interested act of power or domination; alternative behaviors and institutions also become available to us. What we don't have is a way of placing those alternatives within the framework of (historically contingent) dominant patterns of sexuality and the ideology that supports them. We know they exist, but not how they have been constructed; we know their existence offers a critique of normative practices, but not the extent of the critique. Making visible the experience of a different group exposes the existence of repressive mechanisms, but not their inner workings or logics; we know that difference exists, but we don't understand it as relationally constituted. For that we need to attend to the historical processes that, through discourse, position subjects and produce their experiences. It is not individuals who have experience, but subjects who are constituted through experience. Experience in this

9. Eve Kosofsky Sedgwick, *Between Men: English Literature and Male Homosocial Desire* (New York, 1985), p. 86.

10. See Jane Gallop, *The Daughter's Seduction: Feminism and Psychoanalysis* (Ithaca, N.Y., 1982); de Lauretis, *Alice Doesn't: Feminism, Semiotics, Cinema* (Bloomington, Ind., 1984), esp. chap. 5, "Desire in Narrative," pp. 103–57; Sedgwick, *Between Men;* and Jacques Lacan, "The Signification of the Phallus," *Écrits: A Selection*, trans. Alan Sheridan (New York, 1977), pp. 281–91.

11. Discussions with Elizabeth Weed on this point were helpful.

definition then becomes not the origin of our explanation, not the authoritative (because seen or felt) evidence that grounds what is known, but rather that which we seek to explain, that about which knowledge is produced. To think about experience in this way is to historicize it as well as to historicize the identities it produces. This kind of historicizing represents a reply to the many contemporary historians who have argued that an unproblematized "experience" is the foundation of their practice; it is a historicizing that implies critical scrutiny of all explanatory categories usually taken for granted, including the category of "experience."

The Authority of Experience

History has been largely a foundationalist discourse. By this I mean that its explanations seem to be unthinkable if they do not take for granted some primary premises, categories, or presumptions. These foundations (however varied, whatever they are at a particular moment) are unquestioned and unquestionable; they are considered permanent and transcendent. As such they create a common ground for historians and their objects of study in the past and so authorize and legitimize analysis; indeed, analysis seems not to be able to proceed without them.[12] In the minds of some foundationalists, in fact, nihilism, anarchy, and moral confusion are the sure alternatives to these givens, which have the status (if not the philosophical definition) of eternal truths.

Historians have had recourse to many kinds of foundations, some more obviously empiricist than others. What is most striking these days is the determined embrace, the strident defense, of some reified, transcendent category of explanation by historians who have used insights drawn from the sociology of knowledge, structural linguistics, feminist theory, or cultural anthropology to develop sharp critiques of empiricism. This turn to foundations even by antifoundationalists appears, in Fredric Jameson's characterization, as "some extreme form of the return of the repressed."[13]

"Experience" is one of the foundations that has been reintroduced into historical writing in the wake of the critique of empiricism; unlike "brute fact" or "simple reality," its connotations are more varied and elusive. It has recently emerged as a critical term in debates among historians about the limits of interpretation and especially about the uses and limits of post-structuralist theory for history. In these debates those most open to interpretive innovation—those who have insisted on the study of collective mentalities, of economic, social, or cultural determinations of individual behavior, and even of the influences of unconscious motives on

12. I am grateful to Judith Butler for discussions on this point.
13. Fredric Jameson, "Immanence and Nominalism in Postmodern Theory," *Postmodernism, or, the Cultural Logic of Late Capitalism* (Durham, N.C., 1991), p. 199.

thought and action—are among the most ardent defenders of the need to attend to "experience." Feminist historians critical of biases in "male-stream" histories and seeking to install women as viable subjects, social historians insisting on the materialist basis of the discipline on the one hand and on the "agency" of individuals or groups on the other, and cultural historians who have brought symbolic analysis to the study of behavior, have joined political historians whose stories privilege the purposive actions of rational actors and intellectual historians who maintain that thought originates in the minds of individuals. All seem to have converged on the argument that experience is an "irreducible" ground for history.

The evolution of "experience" appears to solve a problem of explanation for professed anti-empiricists even as it reinstates a foundational ground. For this reason it is interesting to examine the uses of "experience" by historians. Such an examination allows us to ask whether history can exist without foundations and what it might look like if it did.

In *Keywords* Raymond Williams sketches the alternative senses in which the term *experience* has been employed in the Anglo-American tradition. These he summarizes as "(i) knowledge gathered from past events, whether by conscious observation or by consideration and reflection; and (ii) a particular kind of consciousness, which can in some contexts be distinguished from 'reason' or 'knowledge.'"[14] Until the early eighteenth century, he says, experience and experiment were closely connected terms, designating how knowledge was arrived at through testing and observation (here the visual metaphor is important). In the eighteenth century, experience still contained this notion of consideration or reflection on observed events, of lessons gained from the past, but it also referred to a particular kind of consciousness. This consciousness, in the twentieth century, has come to mean a "full and active 'awareness,'" including feeling as well as thought (*K*, p. 127). The notion of experience as subjective witness, writes Williams, is "offered not only as truth, but as the most authentic kind of truth," as "the ground for all (subsequent) reasoning and analysis" (*K*, p. 128). According to Williams, experience has acquired another connotation in the twentieth century different from these notions of subjective testimony as immediate, true, and authentic. In this usage it refers to influences external to individuals—social conditions, institutions, forms of belief or perception—"real" things outside them that they react to, and does not include their thought or consideration.[15]

14. Raymond Williams, *Keywords: A Vocabulary of Culture and Society*, rev. ed. (New York, 1985), p. 126; hereafter abbreviated *K*.

15. On the ways knowledge is conceived "as an assemblage of accurate representations," see Richard Rorty, *Philosophy and the Mirror of Nature* (Princeton, N.J., 1979), esp. p. 163.

In the various usages described by Williams, "experience," whether conceived as internal or external, subjective or objective, establishes the prior existence of individuals. When it is defined as internal, it is an expression of an individual's being or consciousness; when external, it is the material on which consciousness then acts. Talking about experience in these ways leads us to take the existence of individuals for granted (experience is something people have) rather than to ask how conceptions of selves (of subjects and their identities) are produced.[16] It operates within an ideological construction that not only makes individuals the starting point of knowledge, but that also naturalizes categories such as man, woman, black, white, heterosexual, and homosexual by treating them as given characteristics of individuals.

Teresa de Lauretis's redefinition of experience exposes the workings of this ideology. "Experience," she writes, is the

> process by which, for all social beings, subjectivity is constructed. Through that process one places oneself or is placed in social re- ality, and so perceives and comprehends as subjective (referring to, originating in, oneself) those relations—material, economic, and interpersonal—which are in fact social and, in a larger perspective, historical.[17]

The process that de Lauretis describes operates crucially through differ- entiation; its effect is to constitute subjects as fixed and autonomous, and who are considered reliable sources of a knowledge that comes from access to the real by means of their experience.[18] When talking about his- torians and other students of the human sciences it is important to note that this subject is both the object of inquiry—the person one studies in the present or the past—and the investigator him- or herself—the histo- rian who produces knowledge of the past based on "experience" in the

---

16. Bhabha puts it this way: "*To see* a missing person, or *to look* at Invisibleness, is to emphasize the subject's *transitive* demand for a *direct* object of self-reflection; a point of presence which would maintain its privileged enunciatory position *qua subject*" (Bhabha, "Interrogating Identity," p. 5).

17. De Lauretis, *Alice Doesn't*, p. 159.

18. Gayatri Chakravorty Spivak describes this as "positing a metalepsis":

A subject-effect can be briefly plotted as follows: that which seems to operate as a sub- ject may be part of an immense discontinuous network . . . of strands that may be termed politics, ideology, economics, history, sexuality, language, and so on. . . . Dif- ferent knottings and configurations of these strands, determined by heterogeneous determinations which are themselves dependent upon myriad circumstances, produce the effect of an operating subject. Yet the continuist and homogenist deliberative con- sciousness symptomatically requires a continuous and homogeneous cause for this effect and thus posits a sovereign and determining subject. This latter is, then, the effect of an effect, and its positing a metalepsis, or the substitution of an effect for a cause. [Gayatri Chakravorty Spivak, *In Other Worlds: Essays in Cultural Politics* (New York, 1987), p. 204]

archives or the anthropologist who produces knowledge of other cultures based on "experience" as a participant observer.

The concepts of experience described by Williams preclude inquiry into processes of subject-construction; and they avoid examining the relationships between discourse, cognition, and reality, the relevance of the position or situatedness of subjects to the knowledge they produce, and the effects of difference on knowledge. Questions are not raised about, for example, whether it matters for the history they write that historians are men, women, white, black, straight, or gay; instead, as de Certeau writes, "the authority of the 'subject of knowledge' [is measured] by the elimination of everything concerning the speaker" ("H," p. 218). His knowledge, reflecting as it does something apart from him, is legitimated and presented as universal, accessible to all. There is no power or politics in these notions of knowledge and experience.

An example of the way "experience" establishes the authority of an historian can be found in R. G. Collingwood's *Idea of History,* the 1946 classic that has been required reading in historiography courses for several generations. For Collingwood, the ability of the historian to reenact past experience is tied to his autonomy, "where by autonomy I mean the condition of being one's own authority, making statements or taking action on one's own initiative and not because those statements or actions are authorized or prescribed by anyone else."[19] The question of where the historian is situated—who he is, how he is defined in relation to others, what the political effects of his history may be—never enters the discussion. Indeed, being free of these matters seems to be tied to Collingwood's definition of autonomy, an issue so critical for him that he launches into an uncharacteristic tirade about it. In his quest for certainty, the historian must not let others make up his mind for him, Collingwood insists, because to do that means

> giving up his autonomy as an historian and allowing someone else to do for him what, if he is a scientific thinker, he can only do for himself. There is no need for me to offer the reader any proof of this statement. If he knows anything of historical work, he already knows of his own experience that it is true. If he does not already know that it is true, he does not know enough about history to read this essay with any profit, and the best thing he can do is to stop here and now.[20]

For Collingwood it is axiomatic that experience is a reliable source of knowledge because it rests on direct contact between the historian's perception and reality (even if the passage of time makes it necessary for the historian to imaginatively reenact events of the past). Thinking on his own

19. R. G. Collingwood, *The Idea of History* (Oxford, 1946), pp. 274–75.
20. Ibid., p. 256.

means owning his own thoughts, and this proprietary relationship guarantees an individual's independence, his ability to read the past correctly, and the authority of the knowledge he produces. The claim is not only for the historian's autonomy, but also for his originality. Here "experience" grounds the identity of the researcher as an historian.

Another, very different use of "experience" can be found in E. P. Thompson's *Making of the English Working Class,* the book that revolutionized social and labor history. Thompson specifically set out to free the concept of "class" from the ossified categories of Marxist structuralism. For this project "experience" was a key concept. "We explored," Thompson writes of himself and his fellow New Left historians, "both in theory and in practice, those junction-concepts (such as 'need', 'class', and 'determine') by which, through the missing term, 'experience', structure is transmuted into process, and the subject re-enters into history."[21]

Thompson's notion of experience joined ideas of external influence and subjective feeling, the structural and the psychological. This gave him a mediating influence between social structure and social consciousness. For him experience meant "social being"—the lived realities of social life, especially the affective domains of family and religion and the symbolic dimensions of expression. This definition separated the affective and the symbolic from the economic and the rational. "People do not only experience their own experience as ideas, within thought and its procedures," he maintained, "they also experience their own experience as *feeling*" ("PT," p. 171). This statement grants importance to the psychological dimension of experience, and it allows Thompson to account for agency. Feeling, Thompson insists, is "handled" culturally as "norms, familial and kinship obligations and reciprocities, as values or (through more elaborated forms) within art and religious beliefs" ("PT," p. 171). At the same time it somehow precedes these forms of expression and so provides an escape from a strong structural determination: "For any living generation, in any 'now,'" Thompson asserts, "the ways in which they 'handle' experience defies prediction and escapes from any narrow definition of determination" ("PT," p. 171).[22]

And yet in his use of it, experience, because it is ultimately shaped by relations of production, is a unifying phenomenon, overriding other kinds of diversity. Since these relations of production are common to workers of different ethnicities, religions, regions, and trades they necessarily provide a common denominator and emerge as a more salient determinant of

21. E. P. Thompson, "The Poverty of Theory or an Orrery of Errors," *The Poverty of Theory and Other Essays* (New York, 1978), p. 170; hereafter abbreviated "PT."

22. Williams's discussion of "structures of feeling" takes on some of these same issues in a more extended way. See Williams, *The Long Revolution* (New York, 1961), and the interview about it in his *Politics and Letters: Interviews with New Left Review* (1979; London, 1981), pp. 133–74. I am grateful to Chun Lin for directing me to these texts.

"experience" than anything else. In Thompson's use of the term, experience is the start of a process that culminates in the realization and articulation of social consciousness, in this case a common identity of class. It serves an integrating function, joining the individual and the structural, and bringing together diverse people into that coherent (totalizing) whole which is a distinctive sense of class.[23] "'Experience' (we have found) has, in the last instance, been generated in 'material life', has been structured in class ways, and hence 'social being' has determined 'social consciousness'" ("PT," p. 171). In this way unequivocal and uniform identity is produced through objective circumstances and there is no reason to ask how this identity achieved predominance—it had to.

The unifying aspect of experience excludes whole realms of human activity by simply not counting them as experience, at least not with any consequences for social organization or politics. When class becomes an overriding identity, other subject-positions are subsumed by it, those of gender, for example (or, in other instances of this kind, of history, race, ethnicity, and sexuality). The positions of men and women and their different relationships to politics are taken as reflections of material and social arrangements rather than as products of class politics itself; they are part of the "experience" of capitalism. Instead of asking how some experiences become more salient than others, how what matters to Thompson is defined as experience, and how differences are dissolved, experience becomes itself cumulative and homogenizing, providing the common denominator on which class consciousness is built.

Thompson's own role in determining the salience of certain things and not others is never addressed. Although his author's voice intervenes powerfully with moral and ethical judgments about the situations he is recounting, the presentation of the experiences themselves is meant to secure their objective status. We forget that Thompson's history, like the accounts offered by political organizers in the nineteenth century of what mattered in workers' lives, is an interpretation, a selective ordering of information that through its use of originary categories and teleological accounts legitimizes a particular kind of politics (it becomes the only possible politics) and a particular way of doing history (as a reflection of what happened, the description of which is little influenced by the historian if, in this case, he only has the requisite moral vision that permits identification with the experiences of workers in the past).

In Thompson's account class is finally an identity rooted in structural relations that preexist politics. What this obscures is the contradictory and contested process by which class itself was conceptualized and by which diverse kinds of subject-positions were assigned, felt, contested, or embraced. As a result, Thompson's brilliant history of the English work-

---

23. On the integrative functions of "experience," see Judith Butler, *Gender Trouble: Feminism and the Subversion of Identity* (New York, 1990), pp. 22–25.

ing class, which set out to historicize the category of class, ends up essentializing it. The ground may seem to be displaced from structure to agency by insisting on the subjectively felt nature of experience, but the problem Thompson sought to address isn't really solved. Working-class "experience" is now the ontological foundation of working-class identity, politics, and history.[24]

This kind of use of experience has the same foundational status if we substitute "women's" or "black" or "lesbian" or "homosexual" for "working-class" in the previous sentence. Among feminist historians, for example, "experience" has helped to legitimize a critique of the false claims to objectivity of traditional historical accounts. Part of the project of some feminist history has been to unmask all claims to objectivity as an ideological cover for masculine bias by pointing out the shortcomings, incompleteness, and exclusiveness of mainstream history. This has been achieved by providing documentation about women in the past that calls into question existing interpretations made without consideration of gender. But how do we authorize the new knowledge if the possibility of all historical objectivity has been questioned? By appealing to experience, which in this usage connotes both reality and its subjective apprehension—the experience of women in the past and of women historians who can recognize something of themselves in their foremothers.

Judith Newton, a literary historian writing about the neglect of feminism by contemporary critical theorists, argues that women, too, arrived at the critique of objectivity usually associated with deconstruction or the new historicism. This feminist critique came "straight out of reflection on our own, that is, women's experience, out of the contradictions we felt between the different ways we were represented even to ourselves, out of the inequities we had long experienced in our situations."[25] Newton's appeal to experience seems to bypass the issue of objectivity (by not raising the question of whether feminist work can be objective) but it rests firmly on a foundational ground (experience). In her work the relationship between thought and experience is represented as transparent (the visual metaphor combines with the visceral) and so is directly accessible, as it is in historian Christine Stansell's insistence that "social practices," in all their "immediacy and entirety," constitute a domain of "sensuous experience" (a prediscursive reality directly felt, seen, and known) that cannot be subsumed by "language."[26] The effect of these kinds of statements, which

24. For a different reading of Thompson on experience, see William H. Sewell, Jr., "How Classes Are Made: Critical Reflections on E. P. Thompson's Theory of Working-class Formation," in *E. P. Thompson: Critical Debates*, ed. Harvey J. Kay and Keith McClelland (Philadelphia, 1990), pp. 50–77. I also have benefitted from Sylvia Schafer's "Writing about 'Experience': Workers and Historians Tormented by Industrialization," typescript.

25. Judith Newton, "History as Usual? Feminism and the 'New Historicism,'" *Cultural Critique* 9 (Spring 1988): 93.

26. Christine Stansell, "A Response to Joan Scott," *International Labor and Working-*

attribute an indisputable authenticity to women's experience, is to establish incontrovertibly women's identity as people with agency. It is also to universalize the identity of women and thus to ground claims for the legitimacy of women's history in the shared experience of historians of women and those women whose stories they tell. In addition, it literally equates the personal with the political, for the lived experience of women is seen as leading directly to resistance to oppression, that is, to feminism.[27] Indeed, the possibility of politics is said to rest on, to follow from, a preexisting women's experience.

"Because of its drive towards a political massing together of women," writes Denise Riley, "feminism can never wholeheartedly dismantle 'women's experience,' however much this category conflates the attributed, the imposed, and the lived, and then sanctifies the resulting mélange." The kind of argument for a women's history (and for a feminist politics) that Riley criticizes closes down inquiry into the ways in which female subjectivity is produced, the ways in which agency is made possible, the ways in which race and sexuality intersect with gender, the ways in which politics organize and interpret experience—in sum, the ways in which identity is a contested terrain, the site of multiple and conflicting claims. In Riley's words, "it masks the likelihood that ... [experiences] have accrued to women not by virtue of their womanhood alone, but as traces of domination, whether natural or political."[28] I would add that it masks the necessarily discursive character of these experiences as well.

But it is precisely the discursive character of experience that is at issue for some historians because attributing experience to discourse seems somehow to deny its status as an unquestionable ground of explanation. This seems to be the case for John Toews, who wrote a long article in the *American Historical Review* in 1987 called "Intellectual History after the Linguistic Turn: The Autonomy of Meaning and the Irreducibility of Experience." The term *linguistic turn* is a comprehensive one used by Toews to refer to approaches to the study of meaning that draw on a num-

---

Class History, no. 31 (Spring 1987): 28. Often this kind of invocation of experience leads back to the biological or physical "experience" of the body. See, for example, the arguments about rape and violence offered by Mary E. Hawkesworth, "Knowers, Knowing, Known: Feminist Theory and Claims of Truth," *Signs* 14 (Spring 1989): 533–57.

27. This is one of the meanings of the slogan "the personal is the political." Personal knowledge, that is, the experience of oppression is the source of resistance to it. This is what Mohanty calls "the feminist osmosis thesis: females are feminists by association and identification with the experiences which constitute us as female" (Mohanty, "Feminist Encounters: Locating the Politics of Experience," *Copyright* 1 [Fall 1987]: 32). See also an important article by Katie King, "The Situation of Lesbianism as Feminism's Magical Sign: Contests for Meaning and the U.S. Women's Movement, 1968–1972," *Communication* 9 (1986): 65–91.

28. Denise Riley, *"Am I That Name?" Feminism and the Category of Women in History* (Minneapolis, 1988), pp. 100, 99.

ber of disciplines, but especially on theories of language "since the primary medium of meaning was obviously language."[29] The question for Toews is how far linguistic analysis has gone and should go, especially in view of the post-structuralist challenge to foundationalism. Reviewing a number of books that take on questions of meaning and its analysis, Toews concludes that

> the predominant tendency [among intellectual historians] is to adapt traditional historical concerns for extralinguistic origins and reference to the semiological challenge, to reaffirm in new ways that, in spite of the relative autonomy of cultural meanings, human subjects still make and remake the worlds of meaning in which they are suspended, and to insist that these worlds are not creations *ex nihilo* but responses to, and shapings of, changing worlds of experience ultimately irreducible to the linguistic forms in which they appear. ["IH," p. 882]

By definition, he argues, history is concerned with explanation; it is not a radical hermeneutics, but an attempt to account for the origin, persistence, and disappearance of certain meanings "at particular times and in specific sociocultural situations" ("IH," p. 882). For him explanation requires a separation of experience and meaning: experience is that reality which demands meaningful response. "Experience," in Toews's usage, is taken to be so self-evident that he never defines the term. This is telling in an article that insists on establishing the importance and independence, the irreducibility of "experience." The absence of definition allows experience to resonate in many ways, but it also allows it to function as a universally understood category—the undefined word creates a sense of consensus by attributing to it an assumed, stable, and shared meaning.

Experience, for Toews, is a foundational concept. While recognizing that meanings differ and that the historian's task is to analyze the different meanings produced in societies and over time, Toews protects "experience" from this kind of relativism. In doing so he establishes the possibility for objective knowledge and for communication among historians, however diverse their positions and views. This has the effect (among others) of removing historians from critical scrutiny as active producers of knowledge.

The insistence on the separation of meaning and experience is crucial for Toews, not only because it seems the only way to account for change, but also because it protects the world from "the hubris of wordmakers who claim to be makers of reality" ("IH," p. 906). Even if Toews here uses "wordmakers" metaphorically to refer to those who produce texts, those who engage in signification, his opposition between "words" and "reality"

---

29. John E. Toews, "Intellectual History after the Linguistic Turn: The Autonomy of Meaning and the Irreducibility of Experience," *American Historical Review* 92 (Oct. 1987): 881; hereafter abbreviated "IH."

echoes the distinction he makes earlier in the article between language (or meaning) and experience. This opposition guarantees both an independent status for human agents and the common ground on which they can communicate and act. It produces a possibility for "intersubjective communication" among individuals despite differences between them, and also reaffirms their existence as thinking beings outside the discursive practices they devise and employ.

Toews is critical of J. G. A. Pocock's vision of "intersubjective communication" based on rational consensus in a community of free individuals, all of whom are equally masters of their own wills. "Pocock's theories," he writes, "often seem like theoretical reflections of familiar practices because the world they assume is also the world in which many contemporary Anglo-American historians live or think they live" ("IH," p. 893). Yet the separation of meaning and experience that Toews offers does not really provide an alternative. A more diverse community can be posited, of course, with different meanings given to experience. Since the phenomenon of experience itself can be analyzed outside the meanings given to it, the subjective position of historians then can seem to have nothing to do with the knowledge they produce.[30] In this way experience authorizes historians and it enables them to counter the radical historicist stance that, Toews says, "undermines the traditional historians' quest for unity, continuity, and purpose by robbing them of any standpoint from which a relationship between past, present, and future could be objectively reconstructed" ("IH," p. 902). Here he establishes as self-evident (and unproblematic) the reflective nature of historical representation, and he assumes that it will override whatever diversity there is in the background, culture, and outlook of historians. Attention to experience, he concludes, "is essential for our self-understanding, and thus also for fulfilling the historian's task of connecting memory with hope" ("IH," p. 907).[31]

30. De Certeau puts it this way:

That the particularity of the place where discourse is produced is relevant will be naturally more apparent where historiographical discourse treats matters that put the subject-producer of knowledge into question: the history of women, of blacks, of Jews, of cultural minorities, etc. In these fields one can, of course, either maintain that the personal status of the author is a matter of indifference (in relation to the objectivity of his or her work) or that he or she alone authorizes or invalidates the discourse (according to whether he or she is "of it" or not). But this debate requires what has been concealed by an epistemology, namely, the impact of subject-to-subject relationships (men and women, blacks and whites, etc.) on the use of apparently "neutral" techniques and in the organization of discourses that are, perhaps, equally scientific. For example, from the fact of the differentiation of the sexes, must one conclude that a woman produces a different historiography from that of a man? Of course, I do not answer this question, but I do assert that this interrogation puts the place of the subject in question and requires a treatment of it unlike the epistemology that constructed the "truth" of the work on the foundation of the speaker's irrelevance. ["H," pp. 217–18]

31. Here we have an example of what Foucault characterized as "continuous history": "the indispensable correlative of the founding function of the subject: the guarantee that

Toews's "experience" thus provides an object for historians that can be known apart from their own role as meaning makers and it then guarantees not only the objectivity of their knowledge, but their ability to persuade others of its importance. Whatever diversity and conflict may exist among them, Toews's community of historians is rendered homogeneous by its shared object (experience). But as Ellen Rooney has so effectively pointed out, using the field of literary theory as her example, this kind of homogeneity can exist only because of the exclusion of the possibility that "historically irreducible interests divide and define reading communities."[32] Inclusiveness is achieved by denying that exclusion is inevitable, that difference is established through exclusion, and that the fundamental differences that accompany inequalities of power and position cannot be overcome by persuasion. In Toews's article no disagreement about the meaning of the term *experience* can be entertained, since experience itself lies somehow outside its signification. For that reason, perhaps, Toews never defines it.

Even among those historians who do not share all of Toews's ideas about the objectivity or continuous quality of history writing, the defense of "experience" works in much the same way: it establishes a realm of reality outside of discourse and it authorizes the historian who has access to it. The evidence of experience works as a foundation providing both a starting point and a conclusive kind of explanation, beyond which few questions can or need to be asked. And yet it is precisely the questions precluded—questions about discourse, difference, and subjectivity, as well as about what counts as experience and who gets to make that determination—that would enable us to historicize experience, and to reflect critically on the history we write about it, rather than to premise our history on it.

Historicizing "Experience"

Gayatri Chakravorty Spivak begins an essay addressed to the Subaltern Studies collective with a contrast between the work of historians and literary scholars:

> A historian confronts a text of counterinsurgency or gendering where the subaltern has been represented. He unravels the text to assign a new subject-position to the subaltern, gendered or otherwise.

---

everything that has eluded him may be restored to him; the certainty that time will disperse nothing without restoring it in reconstituted unity" (Michel Foucault, *The Archaeology of Knowledge*, trans. A. M. Sheridan Smith [New York, 1972], p. 12).

32. Ellen Rooney, *Seductive Reasoning: Pluralism as the Problematic of Contemporary Theory* (Ithaca, N.Y., 1989), p. 6.

A teacher of literature confronts a sympathetic text where the gendered subaltern has been represented. She unravels the text to make visible the assignment of subject-positions. . . .

The performance of these tasks, of the historian and the teacher of literature, must critically "interrupt" each other, bring each other to crisis, in order to serve their constituencies; especially when each seems to claim all for its own.[33]

Spivak's argument here seems to be that there is a difference between history and literature that is both methodological and political. History provides categories that enable us to understand the social and structural positions of people (as workers, subalterns, and so on) in new terms, and these terms define a collective identity with potential political (maybe even revolutionary, but certainly subversive) effects. Literature relativizes the categories history assigns, and exposes the processes that construct and position subjects. In Spivak's discussion, both are critical operations, although she clearly favors the deconstructive task of literature.[34] Although her essay has to be read in the context of a specific debate within Indian historiography, its general points must also be considered. In effect, her statements raise the question of whether historians can do other than construct subjects by describing their experience in terms of an essentialized identity.

Spivak's characterization of the Subaltern Studies historians' reliance on a notion of consciousness as a "*strategic* use of positivist essentialism" doesn't really solve the problem of writing history either, since whether it's strategic or not, essentialism appeals to the idea that there are fixed identities, visible to us as social or natural facts.[35] A refusal of essentialism seems particularly important once again these days within the field of history, as disciplinary pressure builds to defend the unitary subject in the name of his or her "experience." Neither does Spivak's invocation of the special political status of the subaltern justify a history aimed at producing subjects without interrogating and relativizing the means of their production. In the case of colonial and postcolonial peoples, but also of various others in the West, it has been precisely the imposition of a categorical (and universal) subject-status (*the* worker, *the* peasant, *the* woman, *the*

33. Spivak, "A Literary Representation of the Subaltern: A Woman's Text from the Third World," *In Other Worlds*, p. 241.

34. Her argument is based on a set of oppositions between history and literature, male and female, identity and difference, practical politics and theory, and she repeatedly privileges the second set of terms. These polarities speak to the specifics of the debate she is engaged in with the (largely male) Subaltern Studies collective, historians working within a Marxist, especially Gramscian, frame.

35. Spivak, "Subaltern Studies: Deconstructing Historiography," *In Other Worlds*, p. 205. See also Spivak (with Rooney), "In a Word. *Interview*," *differences* 1 (Summer 1989): 124–54, esp. p. 128. On essentialism, see Diana Fuss, *Essentially Speaking: Feminism, Nature and Difference* (New York, 1989).

black) that has masked the operations of difference in the organization of social life. Each category taken as fixed works to solidify the ideological process of subject-construction, making the process less rather than more apparent, naturalizing rather than analyzing it.

It ought to be possible for historians (as for the teachers of literature Spivak so dazzlingly exemplifies) to "make visible the assignment of subject-positions," not in the sense of capturing the reality of the objects seen, but of trying to understand the operations of the complex and changing discursive processes by which identities are ascribed, resisted, or embraced, and which processes themselves are unremarked and indeed achieve their effect because they are not noticed. To do this a change of object seems to be required, one that takes the emergence of concepts and identities as historical events in need of explanation. This does not mean that one dismisses the *effects* of such concepts and identities, nor that one does not explain behavior in terms of their operations. It does mean assuming that the appearance of a new identity is not inevitable or determined, not something that was always there simply waiting to be expressed, not something that will always exist in the form it was given in a particular political movement or at a particular historical moment. Stuart Hall writes:

> The fact is 'black' has never been just there either. It has always been an unstable identity, psychically, culturally and politically. It, too, is a narrative, a story, a history. Something constructed, told, spoken, not simply found. People now speak of the society I come from in totally unrecognizable ways. Of course Jamaica is a black society, they say. In reality it is a society of black and brown people who lived for three or four hundred years without ever being able to speak of themselves as 'black'. Black is an identity which had to be learned and could only be learned in a certain moment. In Jamaica that moment is the 1970s.[36]

To take the history of Jamaican black identity as an object of inquiry in these terms is necessarily to analyze subject-positioning, at least in part, as the effect of discourses that placed Jamaica in a late twentieth-century international racist political economy; it is to historicize the "experience" of blackness.[37]

Treating the emergence of a new identity as a discursive event is not

36. Stuart Hall, "Minimal Selves," in *Identity: The Real Me*, p. 45. See also Barbara J. Fields, "Ideology and Race in American History," in *Region, Race and Reconstruction: Essays in Honor of C. Vann Woodward*, ed. J. Morgan Kousser and James M. McPherson (New York, 1982), pp. 143–77. Fields's article is notable for its contradictions: the way, for example, that it historicizes race, naturalizes class, and refuses to talk at all about gender.

37. An excellent example of the historicizing of black women's "experience" is Hazel Carby's *Reconstructing Womanhood: The Emergence of the Afro-American Woman Novelist* (New York, 1987).

to introduce a new form of linguistic determinism, nor to deprive subjects of agency. It is to refuse a separation between "experience" and language and to insist instead on the productive quality of discourse. Subjects are constituted discursively, but there are conflicts among discursive systems, contradictions within any one of them, multiple meanings possible for the concepts they deploy.[38] And subjects do have agency. They are not unified, autonomous individuals exercising free will, but rather subjects whose agency is created through situations and statuses conferred on them. Being a subject means being "subject to definite conditions of existence, conditions of endowment of agents and conditions of exercise."[39] These conditions enable choices, although they are not unlimited. Subjects are constituted discursively and experience is a linguistic event (it doesn't happen outside established meanings), but neither is it confined to a fixed order of meaning. Since discourse is by definition shared, experience is collective as well as individual. Experience can both confirm what is already known (we see what we have learned to see) and upset what has been taken for granted (when different meanings are in conflict we readjust our vision to take account of the conflict or to resolve it—that is what is meant by "learning from experience," though not everyone learns the same lesson or learns it at the same time or in the same way). Experience is a subject's history. Language is the site of history's enactment. Historical explanation cannot, therefore, separate the two.

The question then becomes how to analyze language, and here historians often (though not always and not necessarily) confront the limits of a discipline that has typically constructed itself in opposition to literature. (These are not the same limits Spivak points to; her contrast is about the different kinds of knowledge produced by history and literature, mine is about different ways of reading and the different understandings of the relationship between words and things implicit in those readings. In neither case are the limits obligatory for historians; indeed, recognition of them makes it possible for us to get beyond them.) The kind of reading I have in mind would not assume a direct correspondence between words and things, nor confine itself to single meanings, nor aim for the resolution of contradiction. It would not render process as linear, nor rest explanation on simple correlations or single variables. Rather it would grant to

38. For discussions of how change operates within and across discourses, see James J. Bono, "Science, Discourse, and Literature: The Role/Rule of Metaphor in Science," in *Literature and Science: Theory and Practice,* ed. Stuart Peterfreund (Boston, 1990), pp. 59–89. See also, Mary Poovey, *Uneven Developments: The Ideological Work of Gender in Mid-Victorian England* (Chicago, 1988), pp. 1–23.

39. Parveen Adams and Jeff Minson, "The 'Subject' of Feminism," *m/f,* no. 2 (1978), p. 52. On the constitution of the subject, see Foucault, *The Archaeology of Knowledge,* pp. 95–96; Felicity A. Nussbaum, *The Autobiographical Subject: Gender and Ideology in Eighteenth-Century England* (Baltimore, 1989); and Peter de Bolla, *The Discourse of the Sublime: Readings in History, Aesthetics, and the Subject* (New York, 1989).

"the literary" an integral, even irreducible, status of its own. To grant such status is not to make "the literary" foundational, but to open new possibilities for analyzing discursive productions of social and political reality as complex, contradictory processes.

The reading I offered of Delany at the beginning of this essay is an example of the kind of reading I want to avoid. I would like now to present another reading—one suggested to me by literary critic Karen Swann—as a way of indicating what might be involved in historicizing the notion of experience. It is also a way of agreeing with and appreciating Swann's argument about "the importance of 'the literary' to the historical project."[40]

For Delany, witnessing the scene at the bathhouse (an "undulating mass of naked male bodies" seen under a dim blue light) was an event. It marked what in one kind of reading we would call a coming to consciousness of himself, a recognition of his authentic identity, one he had always shared, would always share with others like himself. Another kind of reading, closer to Delany's preoccupation with memory and the self in this autobiography, sees this event not as the discovery of truth (conceived as the reflection of a prediscursive reality), but as the substitution of one interpretation for another. Delany presents this substitution as a conversion experience, a clarifying moment, after which he sees (that is, understands) differently. But there is all the difference between subjective perceptual clarity and transparent vision; one does not necessarily follow from the other even if the subjective state is metaphorically presented as a visual experience. Moreover, as Swann has pointed out, "the properties of the medium through which the visible appears—here, the dim blue light, whose distorting, refracting qualities produce a wavering of the visible"— make any claim to unmediated transparency impossible. Instead, the wavering light permits a vision beyond the visible, a vision that contains the fantastic projections ("millions of gay men" for whom "history had, actively and already, created . . . whole galleries of institutions") that are the basis for political identification. "In this version of the story," Swann notes, "political consciousness and power originate, not in a presumedly unmediated experience of presumedly real gay identities, but out of an apprehension of the moving, differencing properties of the representational medium—the motion of light in water."

The question of representation is central to Delany's memoir. It is a question of social categories, personal understanding, and language, all of which are connected, none of which are or can be a direct reflection of the others. What does it mean to be black, gay, a writer, he asks, and is there a realm of personal identity possible apart from social constraint? The

40. Karen Swann's comments on this paper were presented at the Little Three Faculty Colloquium on "The Social and Political Construction of Reality" at Wesleyan University in January 1991. The comments exist only in typescript.

answer is that the social and the personal are imbricated in one another and that both are historically variable. The meanings of the categories of identity change and with them the possibilities for thinking the self:

> At that time, the words "black" and "gay"—for openers—didn't exist with their current meanings, usage, history. 1961 had still been, really, part of the fifties. The political consciousness that was to form by the end of the sixties had not been part of my world. There were only Negroes and homosexuals, both of whom—along with artists— were hugely devalued in the social hierarchy. It's even hard to speak of that world. [*M*, p. 242]

But the available social categories aren't sufficient for Delany's story. It is difficult, if not impossible to use a single narrative to account for his experience. Instead he makes entries in a notebook, at the front about material things, at the back about sexual desire. These are "parallel narratives, in parallel columns" (*M*, p. 29). Although one seems to be about society, the public, and the political, and the other about the individual, the private, and the psychological, in fact both narratives are inescapably historical; they are discursive productions of knowledge of the self, not reflections either of external or internal truth. "That the two columns must be the Marxist and the Freudian—the material column and the column of desire—is only a modernist prejudice. The autonomy of each is subverted by the same excesses, just as severely" (*M*, p. 212). The two columns are constitutive of one another, yet the relationship between them is difficult to specify. Does the social and economic determine the subjective? Is the private entirely separate from or completely integral to the public? Delany voices the desire to resolve the problem: "Certainly one must be the lie that is illuminated by the other's truth" (*M*, p. 212). And then he denies that resolution is possible since answers to these questions do not exist apart from the discourses that produce them:

> If it *is* the split—the space between the two columns (one resplendent and lucid with the writings of legitimacy, the other dark and hollow with the voices of the illegitimate)—that constitutes the subject, it is only after the Romantic inflation of the private into the subjective that such a split can even be located. That locus, that margin, that split itself first allows, then demands the appropriation of language— now spoken, now written—in both directions, over the gap. [*M*, pp. 29–30]

It is finally by tracking "the appropriation of language . . . in both directions, over the gap," and by situating and contextualizing that language that one historicizes the terms by which experience is represented, and so historicizes "experience" itself.

Conclusion

Reading for "the literary" does not seem at all inappropriate for those whose discipline is devoted to the study of change. It is not the only kind of reading I am advocating, although more documents than those written by literary figures are susceptible to such readings. Rather it is a way of changing the focus and the philosophy of our history, from one bent on naturalizing "experience" through a belief in the unmediated relationship between words and things, to one that takes all categories of analysis as contextual, contested, and contingent. How have categories of representation and analysis—such as class, race, gender, relations of production, biology, identity, subjectivity, agency, experience, even culture—achieved their foundational status? What have been the effects of their articulations? What does it mean for historians to study the past in terms of these categories and for individuals to think of themselves in these terms? What is the relationship between the salience of such categories in our own time and their existence in the past? Questions such as these open consideration of what Dominick LaCapra has referred to as the "transferential" relationship between the historian and the past, that is, of the relationship between the power of the historian's analytic frame and the events that are the object of his or her study.[41] And they historicize both sides of that relationship by denying the fixity and transcendence of anything that appears to operate as a foundation, turning attention instead to the history of foundationalist concepts themselves. The history of these concepts (understood to be contested and contradictory) then becomes the evidence by which "experience" can be grasped and by which the historian's relationship to the past he or she writes about can be articulated. This is what Foucault meant by genealogy:

> If interpretation were the slow exposure of the meaning hidden in an origin, then only metaphysics could interpret the development of humanity. But if interpretation is the violent or surreptitious appropriation of a system of rules, which in itself has no essential meaning, in order to impose a direction, to bend it to a new will, to force its participation in a different game, and to subject it to secondary rules, then the development of humanity is a series of interpretations. The role of genealogy is to record its history: the history of morals, ideals, and metaphysical concepts, the history of the concept of liberty or of the ascetic life; as they stand for the emergence of different interpretations, they must be made to appear as events on the stage of historical process.[42]

41. See LaCapra, "Is Everyone a *Mentalité* Case? Transference and the 'Culture' Concept," *History and Criticism*, pp. 71–94.

42. Foucault, "Nietzsche, Genealogy, History," *Language, Counter-Memory, Practice: Selected Essays and Interviews*, trans. Donald F. Bouchard and Sherry Simon, ed. Bouchard (Ithaca, N.Y., 1977), pp. 151–52.

Experience is not a word we can do without, although, given its usage to essentialize identity and reify the subject, it is tempting to abandon it altogether. But *experience* is so much a part of everyday language, so imbricated in our narratives that it seems futile to argue for its expulsion. It serves as a way of talking about what happened, of establishing difference and similarity, of claiming knowledge that is "unassailable."[43] Given the ubiquity of the term, it seems to me more useful to work with it, to analyze its operations and to redefine its meaning. This entails focussing on processes of identity production, insisting on the discursive nature of "experience" and on the politics of its construction. Experience is at once always already an interpretation *and* something that needs to be interpreted. What counts as experience is neither self-evident nor straightforward; it is always contested, and always therefore political. The study of experience, therefore, must call into question its originary status in historical explanation. This will happen when historians take as their project *not* the reproduction and transmission of knowledge said to be arrived at through experience, but the analysis of the production of that knowledge itself. Such an analysis would constitute a genuinely nonfoundational history, one which retains its explanatory power and its interest in change but does not stand on or reproduce naturalized categories.[44] It also cannot guarantee the historian's neutrality, for deciding which categories to historicize is inevitably political, necessarily tied to the historian's recognition of his or her stake in the production of knowledge. Experience is, in this approach, not the origin of our explanation, but that which we want to explain. This kind of approach does not undercut politics by denying the existence of subjects; it instead interrogates the processes of their creation and, in so doing, refigures history and the role of the historian and opens new ways for thinking about change.[45]

43. Ruth Roach Pierson, "Experience, Difference, and Dominance in the Writings of Women's History," typescript.

44. Conversations with Christopher Fynsk helped clarify these points for me.

45. For an important attempt to describe a post-structuralist history, see de Bolla, "Disfiguring History," *Diacritics* 16 (Winter 1986): 49–58.

Experience and the Politics
of Intellectual Inquiry

Thomas C. Holt

Joan W. Scott's essay ("The Evidence of Experience," pp. 363–87) is a forceful and stimulating reflection on the multiple interrelations among identity, experience, and historical explanation. Addressing issues both of history writing (scholarship) and history making (politics), she argues that the effective pursuit of either must decenter the putative authenticity of social identity, recognize that "experience" is dependent on discursive regimes and practices, and understand that history is fashioned within an indeterminate space between hegemony and agency, which are themselves historically contingent. "Subjects are constituted discursively," she writes, "and experience is a linguistic event (it doesn't happen outside established meanings), but neither is it confined to a fixed order of meaning." Moreover, she continues, "experience is a subject's history. Language is the site of history's enactment. Historical explanation cannot, therefore, separate the two" (p. 383). As a necessary consequence, understanding any given identity requires negotiating the space between the social and the personal, which are "imbricated in one another" and connected through the media of discourse (p. 385). Both the social and personal appear somehow also to be situated in the media of history: that is, "the meanings of the categories of identity change and with them the possibilities for thinking the self" (p. 385). Although Scott is not always as clear as one might wish about exactly what history is, she is fairly clear about what it is *not*. It is not some neutral space from which unmediated, transparent experience can be simply extracted or recovered. This argument alone has significant implications for both history writing and its politics.

Scott's main targets are those insurgent challengers to conventional history who, having defined their task as one of recovering experiences previously ignored or not seen, have inadvertently trapped themselves and their subjects within the paradigms of those they challenge—thereby blunting both the challenge and its political potential. Agreeing with Michel de Certeau, Scott argues that in conventional historical discourse, History (I will capitalize the institutionalized enterprise of explanation as distinct from its object) is assumed to reflect or represent a transparent reality, without realizing that reality must first be discursively constituted to become part of any historical narrative. Despite the temptation to take the historically disfranchised subject's own account as authoritative, therefore, one must recognize that their experience is not self-evident either. Indeed, the experience of the socially "different," when taken as a given, tends to naturalize that difference rather than interrogate it. That interrogation requires more than simply exposing the mechanisms of repression that victimize; it requires exploring "their inner workings or logics" (p. 369) and understanding that any identity can only be constituted (that is, made meaningful) in relation to some other identity (for example, heterosexual vis-à-vis homosexual, white vis-à-vis black, and so on).

So far so good. There is much valuable and stimulating material to reflect on in Scott's analysis of how we think about identity, experience, and history and how we practice our craft. But much more is at stake here: first, the relative values of and relations between discourse analysis and other forms remain unnecessarily vague and likely to produce mischief; moreover, there are important political consequences involved in destabilizing the connection between experience and knowledge that are not adequately addressed.

Structuring the essay as a deconstruction of any possible claim for a foundational status for experience involves not only a challenge to how History is done but how the community of historians is imagined to be constituted. Having overturned conventional notions of objectivity and empiricist methodology in their pursuit of a more inclusive historical record, she argues, radical historians and others have tended to substitute experience as the integrative object of historical inquiry. It is both the arbitrator of competing truth-claims among diverse intellectual standpoints and the ostensible basis for shared intellectual values that might permit communication among historians of different agendas and genders and diverse racial origins. In short, a shared belief in transparent

---

Thomas C. Holt is James Westfall Thompson Professor of History at the University of Chicago. He is the author of *The Problem of Freedom: Race, Labor, and Politics in Jamaica and Britain, 1832–1938* (1992) and is currently working on a biography of W. E. B. Du Bois and on the problem of race in American history.

reality, epistemological reliability, and the irreducibility of experience form an ostensible basis for redrawing the boundaries of the profession as well as its subject matter—of the "we" and of the "it."

The weight of Scott's critique is that this is an illusory grounding for radically reconstituting the "old" history; one that stops short of a thorough critique of our concepts and terms of reference; one inadequate to the necessary politics of intellectual inquiry. What is required, she urges, is that we undertake "to historicize experience, and to reflect critically on the history we write about it, rather than premise our history on it" (p. 380). And for this larger task, she insists, "we need to attend to the historical processes that, through discourse, position subjects and produce their experiences. It is not individuals who have experience, but subjects who are constituted through experience" (p. 369).

These last statements appear to embody two related but quite different claims: Historical processes have a reality separate from discourse, but they work through discursive media to identify ("locate") subjects and express ("produce") their experience; and, second, subjects are the sum of their experiences, that is, of their histories. Thus experience is history, and History is a temporally ordered string of collective experiences. But History is also explanation—both the recounting of and accounting for experience—which is by definition a discursive process. The danger of circularity can be avoided here, therefore, only by rigorously distinguishing the different meanings of *history*. Some distinction must be made between history as a process—meaning the interactions among humans and of humans with their physical environment—and History as the summary, analytic narrative of those processes. Failing that, no grounding for historical inquiry—foundational or otherwise—may be possible.

A careless reading of this essay might convey the impression that discourse is all. But Scott takes care—entering numerous caveats and disclaimers—not to identify with any such notion. What she wants is that we resist "a belief in the unmediated relationship between words and things," recognize "all categories of analysis as contextual, contested, and contingent," and thus realize that a rigorous discursive analysis is essential to our craft (p. 386). She never discusses or provides an example of how discursive analysis might work in conjunction with other modes, however, and thus leaves an opening for the (mis?)interpretation that it occupies a kind of conceptual and methodological primacy.

Given this lacuna and ambiguity in her argument, the essay inevitably raises two questions relevant to evaluating experience both as evidence for History and as a source for political mobilization. Can experience-as-such be prediscursive? Can the experience that is *marshalled as historical evidence* be prediscursive? The answer to the latter question is easily no. History (lowercase *h*) is only accessible via an already existing discourse. The very act of recording and recollecting an experience as History entails discursive practices, including the selection of its elements, their arrangement in relation or opposition to some preexisting narrative, the assigning of the actors their respective parts, the necessary exclusion of other actors.

The answer to the first question, however, is more difficult. Unless *discourse* is broadened to include every form of human interaction—and thus become rather meaningless—the interactions denoted by historical processes must be taken as prediscursive. Indeed, they are the material from which discourses are created, what discourse is about. Consequently, if Scott's contention that "language is the site of history's enactment" intends to say that experience-as-such has no meaningful existence except within a given system of discourse, it is either self-evident or says too much. One might well argue that experience must be thought, if not articulated, to be accessible even to the experiencing subject and that the act of thinking (and certainly of speaking or writing) already presumes the existence of a thinking subject, a social being necessarily invested with some form of identity that is itself a discursive product. But by the same token, given that any specific discursive system is itself a product of historical processes, of negotiation and contestation, then is it not also a priori a product of previous human experiences?

Politically speaking, and more to the point, is a counterhegemonic discourse, a discourse of resistance, possible without an experience semi-autonomous from and/or contradictory to dominant discursive constructions? Could slaves, for example, rebel without drawing on an experience independent of that described by the dominant discourse of a slave society? The answer would appear to be yes and no. No, because a revolt against enslavement per se (as opposed to resistance to the excesses of the system) cannot even be thought without there first developing an antislavery discourse among the slaves. Yes, because no such contrary interpretation or discourse is feasible without an experience-to-be-interpreted that contradicts the prevailing discourse of the slaveholders. No, again, because the histories of actual slave revolts demonstrate that the slaves' counterhegemonic discourse most often included not only the ruminations of the soon-to-be rebels on their own lived experience but those of white and black abolitionists and other rebellious slaves as well.[1] Yes, because even those discourses could have had effect only when resonant with the lived experience of the rebels. Thus both the discourse about and the materiality of the slaves' lived experience appear necessary to the political act of rebellion and to the historian's subsequent effort to account for it.

---

1. The seminal text in this regard remains C. L. R. James, *The Black Jacobins: Toussaint L'Ouverture and the San Domingo Revolution*, 2d ed. (New York, 1963). See also Eugene D. Genovese, *From Rebellion to Revolution: Afro-American Slave Revolts in the Making of the Modern*

But what space does Scott's History leave for taking account of material life? Where would such factors as the differences between crop regimes (sugar versus cotton), colonial demographics, and the cutoff of the slave trade fit in her explanation of a slave revolt? Would the discourse of the French Revolution have had the same efficacy in Haiti in the absence of such factors? Can we account for the failure of a similar revolutionary discourse in tidewater Virginia during the same period without recourse to such factors?

Through her explication of Samuel Delany's memoir, Scott argues that one can only historicize experience by first historicizing the language ("the terms") in which it is expressed. This inevitably implies, despite numerous caveats and disclaimers elsewhere, a privileged position for such discursive analyses in any historical inquiry. It is a move exemplified earlier by a recommendation for a "change of object" for historical explanation, wherein "the emergence of concepts and identities" as objects of study be distinguished from their *"effects"* (p. 382). Scott offers as an example of such an approach Stuart Hall's commentary on the emergence of black identity among African-Jamaicans, which he dates in the late twentieth century. Citing this passage approvingly as an example of how the origins of discursive constructions of identity and resistance need to become the subjects of inquiry, she appears to suggest that Hall's position is politically as well as intellectually preferable to Gayatri Spivak's "strategic essentialisms" discussed immediately before. And although African-Jamaicans' material circumstances are noted as important to the story ("a late twentieth-century international racist political economy"), they enter that story in a decidedly secondary role ("the effects of discourses").

As a student of Jamaican history, I have fixed on this passage perhaps because its historicizing appears somewhat out of joint. First of all, this particular discursive construction must be moved back a bit earlier than Hall would have it—say, a hundred years earlier, at least. Second, the distinction between the discursive and material sources of that construction of blackness seems so muddled that the impact of neither one is very clear.

A few days before launching a bloody rebellion at Morant Bay in 1865, African-Jamaican Paul Bogle told his followers "to kill the whites," "cleave to the black," and to claim the island's land and wealth for "blacks." By any measure Bogle's appeal manifested the ability of African-Jamaicans—a full century earlier than Hall would have it—"to speak of themselves as black." Moreover it manifested a rather explicit "politics of identity." Finally, as I have argued elsewhere, the African-Jamaicans' historical experience—enslavement and the oppressive emancipation

---

World (New York, 1981), and Mary Turner, *Slaves and Missionaries: The Disintegration of Jamaican Slave Society, 1787–1834* (Urbana, Ill., 1982).

that followed—determined the meaning of *black* and *white* in Bogle's discourse.[2] During the ensuing rebellion black solidarity sometimes meant taking a terrible vengeance on some blacks while showing surprising mercy to some whites. Thus contrary to the dominant discursive system, which identified blacks as those who worked and whites as those who ruled, the Morant Bay rebels appear generally to have recognized as white those directly implicated in the system of their oppression (planters, magistrates, and their supporters) and as black those who were the victims of that system. In more liminal but protected statuses were those less directly implicated in the system, like white medical doctors, and those almost entirely outside it, like the physically black Maroons who by treaty had secured a separate existence from "the blacks." Of course, this is not to say that their own discursive system for recognizing the enemy bore any better resemblance to reality than did the dominant white discourse. The Maroons were soon organized by "the whites" into a fierce counterinsurgency force to crush the rebellion of "the blacks."

Given this example, what, then, is the status of discourse, identity, experience, and history? First, a discursive/ideological system gave meaning to the experience that white colonial authorities and African-Jamaicans lived and is key to our efforts to retrieve it. But it seems equally clear that there were competing discursive systems within that same historical space. Secular and sacred traditions (together with touchingly naive notions of a benign British Crown) shaped an ideology of justice and economic entitlement that fueled a mighty rebellion and with it a powerful claim to a very different identity. Part of those secular and sacred traditions, and part of what made the rebels' resistance possible, was a very different reading of their recent history, of slavery, of emancipation, and of the historically based, moral sources for their entitlement to the land.

Clearly none of this was autonomous from the dominant discursive regime or from the received history, but historians cannot possibly recover these traditions through that dominant regime alone, notwithstanding the fact that it is often only via that discursive regime—that is, government reports, memoirs, statistics—that the counterdiscourse is accessible at all. Consequently, often the latter discourse (of the dominated) can be recovered only by reading the former (of the dominators) "against the grain." To propose to read against the grain can reference many different strategies and techniques, but one of them certainly is to read *as if* experience were something separate from the discourse through which it is apprehended. As if African-Jamaican participation in specific systems of production, distribution, and consumption determined the conditions of possibility for the discourses both they and their colonial overlords could sustain. As if producing for a world market as

---

2. See Thomas C. Holt, *The Problem of Freedom: Race, Labor, and Politics in Jamaica and Britain, 1832–1938* (Baltimore, 1992), chap. 8.

peasants were different than as slaves. As if freedpeople did exercise choices after emancipation about where and when to expend their labor and how to organize their family life as free workers. As if they were freer to contest control of their religious life and beliefs, and thus worldview, as freedpeople than as slaves. All this is posited against the grain of a dominant discursive regime—seemingly timeless and immutable—that marked "the blacks" as an ahistorical category, which implied in short that none of this variability of experience mattered. All this, by contrast, shows that the experience did matter, that history—the collective and contested experiences of freed slaves, planters, bureaucrats, and abolitionists—was radically shifting the ground beneath their feet and, with it, the political stakes.

Yet I, too, would insist on the importance of recognizing that we are still reading these experiences within some discursive system that gives it meaning. But now it is our own contemporary one, one that conjures with signifiers like classes, peasants, families, rule, resistance, accommodation, and collaboration. All of these terms embody tensions between their possible meanings for the historical subjects we study and a partly obscured teleological significance we ourselves never entirely succeed in shedding. We still bear the burden, then, of sustaining a reflexive awareness that no knowledge is transparent; whatever we do there is ever a perceptual shield between us and the object of our inquiry. The burden of our historical analysis, then, is one involving four interrelated and ultimately reflexive forms of inquiry: (1) an inquiry into the processes by which the subject is constructed; (2) an examination of the relationships among discourse, cognition, and reality; (3) an inquiry into—or at least awareness of—how the standpoint or situatedness of the inquirer shapes her or his answers; and consequent to all of the above (4) an inquiry into "the effects of difference on knowledge."

Scott's essay addresses the first two of these but not the latter, or at least not in as sustained or rigorous a fashion as the former. For example, she never successfully or directly reengages the second set of issues she raises—the necessarily revised basis for claims for diversity of racial and gender representation within the profession once experience is disempowered. The problem, bluntly stated, is that if one accepts that white people can study blacks and that men can study women, then what *intellectual* need is there—as opposed to a moral and political one—for colleges and universities to aggressively recruit black or female historians? Heretofore, many of us have avoided the essentialist, ahistorical (and patently false) trap that only blacks can study blacks and only women can study women by invoking the value brought to intellectual inquiry by the differences in people's experience—something that can be learned as well as lived. Moreover, such diversity is crucial, we have argued, not only because it might provide a different perspective on the history of excluded groups but because such perspectives brought to bear on yet other groups different from themselves can profoundly reshape the interpretation of the collective, general history; that is, blacks should also study whites and women should study men. Absent this claim to the value of a diversity of experience, what authorizes a claim to a diversity of representation? What claim have I to affirmative efforts by the academy to include me in, if not that by virtue of my identification with a previously excluded group I *may* bring something to the common effort that is lacking? I say "may bring" because Scott is absolutely right that nothing in my lived experience is a given or determining—including being black, heterosexual, and a man. Within the cumulative discourse about blacks each of those categories has been, in some measure, contested, often with extraordinary brutality. But the material conditions of the collective black experience—poverty, sharecropping, segregated schools—has also decisively shaped the conditions of possibility of my encounter with that discourse and with the academy. Collapsing those preconditions into the discourse about them—however much they are mutually imbricated—is not a useful or illuminating step.

Although I am in substantial agreement with much that Scott has to say, I believe, however, that there are serious questions still to be addressed or clarified. How in the practical business of history writing are we to negotiate the necessary and symbiotic relationship between discourse analysis and material analysis without privileging one over the other? How in the crucial business of history making, that is, politics, are we to mobilize around politicized identities without naturalizing identity? The contradictions of so-called identity politics—in a world bent on denying me any constructive identity at all—are, it seems to me, *necessary* ones; they demand not an abrupt denial of that form of politics but more reflexivity and sensitivity in its exercise.

And, finally, there is a need to recognize that both my presence in the academy and the character of my work has much to do with *who* I am, with both my personal history and the collective historical legacy of African-Americans, with both my lived experience and what I have learned from that history and experience. True, my education and political experience have contributed a language with which to interpret and give political force to that experience, but then they too are a part of my lived experience. That experience, moreover, is not frozen in the past; it is ongoing. It informs my claim (or rather the claim of someone like me) to be represented in the academy, and, hopefully, it is part of the renewal process that helps keep me honest. By this last step experience becomes part of an ongoing political self-testing rather than—à la Clarence Thomas before the Senate Judiciary Committee—simply a claim to some primordial and timeless authenticity. It is a necessary reminder that neither my identity, my history, nor my experience is autonomous from systems of coercion within a larger history. It is a necessary factor in whatever contribution I might make to my craft and to the academy because they will likely arise precisely from my critical consciousness about my location—a location history has determined—at the institutional boundary between the powerful and their victims. To forget that is not only to risk my effectiveness, but—in the sense that W. E. B. Du Bois invoked the word almost a century ago—my soul.[3]

3. There are two senses of the word in Du Bois's work: the fundamental character and aspirations of a people as shaped by their collective historical experience (what he calls "strivings") and the integrity of one's commitment to human emancipation as a consequence of embracing that identity and aspirations. See W. E. B. Du Bois, *The Souls of Black Folk* (Chicago, 1903). For further elaboration of this point, see Holt, "The Political Uses of Alienation: W. E. B. Du Bois on Politics, Race, and Culture, 1903–1940," *American Quarterly* 42 (June 1990): 100–15.

A Rejoinder to Thomas C. Holt

Joan W. Scott

I appreciate Thomas Holt's intelligent and critical reading ("Experience and the Politics of Intellectual Inquiry," pp. 388–96) of my essay on experience. I think our approaches and concerns converge on most issues; indeed, he offers some historical examples that beautifully illustrate one of my central points—that experience and the group identity it confers is the product of politics, not the prerequisite for it. As he recounts it, the Morant Bay rebellion demonstrates the complex and contradictory nature of identities; black and white were not simply categories that described the color of one's skin but indicators of complex and shifting relationships of power, and those relationships did not correlate completely with race. Thus physically black Maroons, he writes, "were soon organized by 'the whites' into a fierce counterinsurgency force to crush the rebellion of 'the blacks'" (p. 393).

This example suggests that the interrelationship between what Holt at some points distinguishes as "discourse analysis" and "material analysis" in fact precludes any opposition between them (p. 395). Holt well understands that historians are always dealing with a multiplicity of discourses, their own as well as those of the past. I do not think it does any good to attempt to master complexity and multiplicity by simplifying them in the form of binary oppositions between the material and the discursive (which for so many people imply oppositions between such inseparable concepts as reality and language, or experience and ideology). Rather, I would argue that we need to make complexity, and more especially contradiction, the object of our analysis.

I think attention to the contradictory constructions of conceptualizations, categories, linguistic usages, systems (and that includes plantation economies and segregated schools) gives historians an especially useful way of thinking not only about the operations of difference but about how resistance and opposition are constituted within relationships of power. Such attention to contradiction offers a thoroughly historical way of thinking about agency and politics. To take the question of slavery again, I would argue that understanding the experience of slavery has to take account both of blackness and whiteness (race is a relationship, not a separate group identity) and of the context in which it operates. In countries with political and/or religious systems premised on some notion of universal rights or universal humanity, the experience of slavery can be described—and felt and resisted—as a contradiction of those principles and practices that have been racialized by being restricted to whites. The experience that gives rise to or legitimizes protest, in other words, is relational; it is not autonomous, not independent of what Holt calls a "dominant discourse" (p. 391). Rather, we need to think in terms of discursive or ideological fields, which are inherently contradictory and whose contradictions provide space for dissent and opposing points of view. The stability of any ideological system requires the repression of its contradictions; in the United States, slavery is one of these contradictions in a democracy devoted to the universal principle of equality. (Contradictions in religious discourse are also crucial for this history.) The organization of opposition to slavery, by slaves and abolitionists, exposes and builds on the contradiction at the heart of the American republic. Slaves take literally the promise (both political and religious) of equality. They identify slaves as those denied their rights, at once accepting prevailing political and religious language and inverting its meanings. In the contradiction between the universal language of rights and the denial of rights to black people, the resistance to slavery—and the agency of slaves as political resisters—is conceived.

I would make a similar argument—necessarily specifying different contexts and discursive fields—about resistance based in the exposure of the appeal to contradiction for workers, women, gay rights advocates, and so on. The methodological point is technically deconstructive. It understands attempts to demarcate difference in terms of clear binary oppositions (black/white, slave/master, woman/man, working class/bourgeoisie) as inherently contradictory because they try to obscure the interrelationship, the interdependence, of the terms. This leads me to

Joan W. Scott is professor of social science at the Institute for Advanced Study in Princeton, New Jersey. She is the author, most recently, of *Gender and the Politics of History* (1988) and is currently at work on a history of feminist claims for political rights in France during the period 1789–1945 as a way of exploring arguments about equality and difference.

understand political resistance as involving the exposure of interdependence and of contradiction that has been denied or repressed. The terms by which differentials of power are constructed are the terms by which they are also resisted.

This does not mean there is an absolute correlation between one's social position or location and the knowledge one produces. Holt is quite right to point to the need for further exploration of the question of "the effects of difference on knowledge" and to suggest that experience might be one way of answering it (p. 394). My worry is that experience has become a way of avoiding the complexities of the answer. In some circles experience is the ground for an identity politics that understands differences among its constituents to be matters of false consciousness or opportunism. Experience is taken as an accurate description of closed systems of domination and oppression; knowledge is taken to be the simple reflection of that objective experience. That's the version of experience I want to call into question, substituting for it a notion of experience as a theorized reading that is made possible, but not inevitably or singularly, by one's relationship to dominant institutions and discourses.

Still, given the way experience is often used these days to authorize both reductive and closed analyses of power, and homogenizing, essentializing politics, I don't think appeals to it are the best way to make a case for affirmative action and multiculturalism. (It is one thing to track the uses of a concept, to theorize and historicize experience, and quite another to try to use it to do political work.) Neither Holt nor I would argue in the pluralist mode that the simple diversification of experience is what affirmative action is about anyway. Rather, we insist on the presence of fundamentally different political visions, fundamentally different points of view, in order to make visible the fact that knowledge is always complex and contested. We want to include in the academy those who have been previously excluded because they have had, and continue to have, a different relationship to the production of knowledge from those who were routinely granted access because of their color, sex, class, ethnicity, or family affiliation. The presence of those who have a different relationship to the production of knowledge opens questions that those who believe in the sanctity of tradition and the objective character of scholarship would rather were never asked. The presence of those with a different relationship to the production of knowledge makes it necessary to explore the complex problem Holt raises about the effects of difference on knowledge. Once this issue is raised knowledge can no longer be considered finite, nor standards universal. Instead of being banished as obstacles to the pursuits of truth and beauty, power and difference become serious issues of scholarly concern.

Rather than make the case for affirmative action in epistemological terms (people with different experience have different knowledge to share with us), I would make the case for affirmative action in terms of its effect on the process of knowledge production (the presence of different knowledges exposes the contested and contradictory nature of any asser-tion or system that claims to be closed). In this way, we can avoid the trap set by the authority of personal testimony (which takes intellectual or political disagreement as personal insult because it denies the authen-ticity of an individual's experience) and turn instead to the debates about interpretation, theory, and politics that it is the business of universities to encourage.

Figures of Arithmetic, Figures of Speech: The Discourse of Statistics in the 1830s

Mary Poovey

When the British Association for the Advancement of Science was established in 1831, its founders were almost universally agreed that statistics did not belong in their organization because it was not a "science." "Science," as the BAAS institutionalized the concept, was knowledge that was theoretical before it was practical, value-free and objective, and, above all, impervious to political controversy. Astronomy, especially as it had been practiced since Sir Isaac Newton, epitomized this kind of knowledge.[1] Statistics, in stark contrast to astronomy, lacked a theoretical foundation, was thought to be governed by the values of its practitioners, and, most decisively for the BAAS, was already embroiled in the political debate about the "condition of England." When the BAAS bowed to pressure from Charles Babbage in 1833 and established a statistical section, the organization's president, Adam Sedgwick, did everything he could to ensure that the kind of statistics the BAAS admitted would be limited to counting and would be value-free. Sedgwick warned the statisticians that "if they went into provinces not belonging to them, and opened a door of

1. Susan Faye Cannon discusses the authority of astronomy in *Science in Culture: The Early Victorian Period* (New York, 1978), p. 2. The relationship to truth that mathematics was understood to have is especially complex and interesting in this period, although this subject lies beyond the scope of my analysis. See Joan L. Richards, "The Art and the Science of British Algebra: A Study in the Perception of Mathematical Truth," *Historica Mathematica* 7 (1980): 343–65, and *Mathematical Visions: The Pursuit of Geometry in Victorian England* (Boston, 1988), esp. chap. 2.

The essay originally appeared in *Critical Inquiry* 19 (Winter 1993).

communication with the dreary world of politics, that instant would the foul demon of discord find his way into their Eden of philosophy."[2]

A scant two years after the BAAS reluctantly established its statistical section, the respected Irish journalist William Cooke Taylor confidently asserted that statistics *had* acquired the "dignity of a science." This achievement was partly a function of the "tabular form" of statistical representation, which presumably helped create the appearance of scientific objectivity; partly a function of statistical metl ɔd, which followed the "Baconian philosophy" of testing "established principles" so as to discover "new laws of action"; and partly a function of the statistical goal, which was to connect "its facts together by a chain of causation." Despite his unqualified assertion, however, as Taylor elaborated the precise nature of statistics, its status as a "science" seemed less secure as its relation to politics loomed larger:

> It is sometimes said that statistics bears the same relation to economic science as mathematics to pure physics; it would be far more correct to compare their connexion to that between experimental and abstract science, or between astronomical observations and astronomical science. Like every other branch of human knowledge, the political and economic sciences should be based on an induction from facts, and these facts should be accurately observed and copiously supplied. . . .
> ʾThe state of our commerce and manufactures, the results of

---

2. Quoted in Jack Morrell and Arnold Thackray, *Gentlemen of Science: Early Years of the British Association for the Advancement of Science* (New York, 1981), p. 292; see also pp. 246, 260–61, 266, 291–96. Here is the relevant excerpt from Sedgwick's address:

By science, then, *I understand the consideration of all objects, whether of pure or mixed nature, capable of being reduced to measurement and calculation.* All things comprehended under the categories of space, time, and number belong to our investigations, and *all phenomena capable of being brought under the semblance of law are legitimate objects of our inquiry.* . . .
Can then statistical inquiries be made compatible with our subjects, and taken into the bosom of our society? I think they unquestionably may, *so far as they have to do with matters of fact, with mere abstractions, and with numerical results.* Considered in this light they give what may be called the raw material for political economy and political philosophy; and by their help the lasting foundations of these sciences may be perhaps ultimately laid. [quoted in Victor L. Hilts, "*Aliis exterendum,* or, The Origins of the Statistical Society of London," *Isis* 69 (Mar. 1978): 34]

Mary Poovey is professor of English at The Johns Hopkins University. She is the author of *The Proper Lady and the Woman Writer: Ideology as Style in the Works of Mary Wollstonecraft, Mary Shelley, and Jane Austen* (1984) and *Uneven Developments: The Ideological Work of Gender in Mid-Victorian England* (1988). She is currently at work on a study of statistical thinking in the eighteenth and nineteenth centuries.

machinery, the effects of free trade, are mere arithmetical problems, more or less involved, that may be worked out if correct data are obtained. Their solutions thus educed should be as certain and as little open to cavil as a proposition in Euclid, or the determination of an algebraic equation. Do we possess any such certainty? Have we even approached to it? On the contrary, is it not notorious that on all and each of these subjects fierce controversies rage, and every disputant is prepared to support his own views with a formidable array of figures? It is unfortunately too evident, in every debate on these subjects, that pre-conceived opinions usurp the place of facts, and speculations as unsubstantial as "the baseless fabric of a vision" are substituted for correct observation.[3]

In Taylor's description we see the discourse of statistics dwindling from the "dignity of a science" to the ignominious position of serving other sciences, and descending from discovering new laws to disputing frankly politicized figures. This slippage reveals beneath Taylor's assertions another version of the uncertainty with which the gentlemen of the BAAS viewed statistics. Taylor attributes the descent of statistics into politics to a function of the immaturity of the "science"—the fact that insufficient data had yet to be accumulated—but he is finally as unclear about what kind of knowledge statistical representation can produce as was Sedgwick. This uncertainty, which concerned the epistemology of statistics as well as its social authority, marks every effort to define or defend statistics in the 1830s. Even after statistics was institutionalized—in the Board of Trade (1832), the BAAS (1833), the Manchester Statistical Society (1833), and the Statistical Society of London (1834)—proponents and critics of this discourse continued to disagree (with each other and themselves) about what statistics was and what it did.[4] Far from being a sign of disciplinary immaturity or inadequate implementation, these disagreements are traces of the tensions and contradictions inherent in statistical discourse as it was consolidated in Britain in the first decades of the nineteenth century. As a form of representation, statistics was (and remains) a mixed genre; it juxtaposed numerical, often tabular, formulations to discursive, sometimes historical or explanatory, narratives. The knowledge constituted by statistics was also mixed; it purported to record empirical, objective observations about the social system at the same time that it always embodied and often specifically recommended frankly interested

3. William Cooke Taylor, "Objects and Advantages of Statistical Science," review of *Sur l'homme et le developpement de ses facultés, ou essai de physique sociale,* by Adolphe Quételet, *Foreign Quarterly Review* 16 (Oct. 1835): 205–7; hereafter abbreviated "O." Although this article is unsigned, it is attributed to Taylor in the *Wellesley Index to Victorian Periodicals, 1824–1900,* ed. Walter E. Houghton, 5 vols. (Toronto, 1966–89).

4. This uncertainty continued even after statistics was further institutionalized in an international association. See Eric Brian, "Statistique administrative et internationalisme statistique pendant la seconde moitie du XIXᵉ siècle," *Histoire et Mesure* 4 (1989): 201–24.

conclusions about social policy and legislation. The mixed nature of early nineteenth-century statistics in particular was partly a function of the historical circumstances in which it was institutionalized, for early statistics sought both to approach the "norm of truth" epitomized by Newtonian science[5] and to claim some role in defining and formulating policies about the social problems that industrialization and urbanization had exacerbated. The mixed nature of statistics is partly the heritage of the discrepant and even antithetical enterprises from which statistics was descended, and partly a function of the contradiction between the ambitions of the discourse to "map" the world and the peculiar limitations statisticians imposed on this form of representation. Fully explaining the mixed nature of statistics would require a historical analysis more extensive than space permits, but it is possible to delineate the tensions between the claims made for statistics in the 1830s and the limitations its practitioners embraced. Doing so should help clarify the peculiar combination of respect and suspicion that statistical knowledge has elicited since its institutionalization.

Even in the 1830s there was, of course, no single discourse of statistics. Statistics about trade were gathered and used in very different ways from statistics about crime; statistics about geography were demonstrable in a manner very different from statistics about suicide. The texts I take for my analysis should make it clear, however, that despite variations in the modes by which statistics were compiled and the objects that such figures quantified, statistical representation was sufficiently codified by 1830 to constitute a discourse in the Foucauldian sense. To indicate the range of definitional issues associated with statistics in this decade, I include one official statement by a statistical organization, two (additional) apologies for statistics published in two quarterlies of different political persuasions, and two critical analyses of statistics (one analytical, the other satirical). These texts, in order of publication, are J. R. McCulloch's "State and Defects of British Statistics," published in the Whig *Edinburgh Review* in April 1835; William Cooke Taylor's "Objects and Advantages of Statistical Science," which appeared in the nonpartisan *Foreign Quarterly Review* in October of that year; Charles Dickens's 1837 send-up of the BAAS, the "Full Report of the First Meeting of the Mudfog Association for the Advancement of Everything," published in the antipolitical *Bentley's Miscellany;* John Robertson's review of the *Transactions of the Statistical Society of London,* published in the radical *London and Westminster Review* in April 1838; the introduction to the first volume of the *Journal of the Statistical Society of London* and the "Fourth Annual Report of the Council of the Statistical Society," which are part of the volume Robertson reviewed (May 1838); and Herman

5. This is Cannon's phrase; see *Science in Culture,* chap. 1.

Merivale's April 1839 review article, "Moral and Intellectual Statistics of France," also published in the *Edinburgh Review.*[6]

In the course of explaining the importance of statistical knowledge, Taylor referred to an opposition that statistical apologists were increasingly fond of citing. He explains that when the descendant of William Petty and friend of statistics, the Marquis of Lansdowne, "entered public life, not only did the figures of speech reign triumphant over the figures of arithmetic, but a numerical statement was regarded as a kind of conjurer's juggle, to be admired, applauded, and forgotten, to be any thing but examined" ("O," p. 207). Later in his essay, Taylor elaborates this opposition, this time in relation to debates about factory legislation. "The manufacturers answered the charges made against them by an appeal to incontrovertible facts," Taylor notes approvingly, "the tables of mortality, the records of hospitals and police-offices, the registers of parishes and courts of justice; but there are still people in the world, who prefer the figures of speech to the figures of arithmetic, and the rules of Longinus to those of Cocker. Pathetic tales, more than sufficient to supply a whole generation of novelists, prevailed over a dull, dry parade of stupid figures" ("O," p. 216).

The opposition Taylor mobilizes, between "figures of arithmetic" and "figures of speech," is intended to prove the superiority of numerical facts over sheer rhetoric, sublime though figures of speech may be. The report ultimately issued by the factory commissioners, Taylor continues, is a document "in which the exactness of science is for the first time fully proved to be the only guide for enlightened humanity and really useful charity" (ibid.). Yet despite Taylor's explicit endorsement of figures of arithmetic, his own formulation acknowledges that there is something paradoxical about statistics. This is revealed in the two responses that Taylor fears statistics might provoke. On the one hand, he worries that readers may find numerical representation fanciful or even deceitful—"a kind of conjurer's juggle" not worth serious debate. On the other hand, he suggests that a "dull, dry parade of stupid figures" may lull legislators to sleep, especially when the "stupid figures" have to compete with novelistic anecdotes. These two antithetical fantasies point to Taylor's own indecision about statistics: is this discourse too imaginative, in the sense that numbers can conjure any meaning out of scant evidence? or is it so denuded of imagination that it will stupefy, if not remain altogether unreadable? As if to underscore his own uncertainty, Taylor most frequently presents statistical tables when he wants to make conclusive arguments, but he turns to "a few anecdotes" when he wants to "prove" his central polemical point:

6. All attributions are from the *Wellesley Index.*

that future government commissions should investigate not only the number of pupils but also the qualifications of the masters ("O," p. 227).

The charges that numbers can be made to say anything and that they
are boring if not unreadable appear repeatedly in early accounts of statistical representation. Before I turn to their theoretical implications, however, let me follow the logic of the opposition Taylor is trying to maintain.
In the "Fourth Annual Report of the Council of the Statistical Society of
London," Taylor's opposition recurs, this time with a more extensive
explanation: "It is indeed truly said that, the spirit of the present age has
an evident tendency to confront the figures of speech with the figures of
arithmetic; it being impossible not to observe a growing distrust of mere
hypothetical theory and *à priori* assumption, and the appearance of a general conviction that, in the business of social science, principles are valid
for application only inasmuch as they are legitimate inductions from facts,
accurately observed and methodically classified."[7] The "growing distrust"
referred to here echoes Taylor's skepticism about the "pre-conceived
opinions" that "usurp the place of facts." This hostility toward a priori theorizing spilled over into the reluctance, on the part of some statisticians, to
draw conclusions from the data they gathered or to speculate about the
causes of the phenomena they recorded. "It is the business of a statisti-
cian to collect and tabulate facts in order to discover the laws of their
occurrence," Taylor explained; "it is no part of his proper duty to investigate their causes" ("O," p. 213). The organizers of the Statistical Society of
London were even more circumspect in their claims. "Like other sciences,
that of Statistics seeks to deduce from well-established facts certain general principles which interest and affect mankind," they explained in the
first number of the association's journal; "it uses the same instruments of
comparison, calculation, and deduction: but its peculiarity is that it proceeds wholly by the accumulation and comparison of facts, and does not
admit of any kind of speculation; it aims, like other sciences, at truth, and
advances, *pari passu,* with its development."[8] To symbolize their commitment to theoretical caution, the founders of the society adopted as their
seal an engraving of a wheat sheaf wrapped round with the phrase "*aliis
exterendum*"—"to be threshed out by others."[9]

By 1838, the Statistical Society of London's claims had come under
fire from John Robertson, the brash young subeditor of the radical *London and Westminster Review.*[10] Robertson attacked the society not because

7. "Fourth Annual Report of the Council of the Statistical Society of London," *Journal
of the Statistical Society of London* 1 (1839): 8.

8. Introduction to the *Journal of the Statistical Society of London* 1 (1839): 3.

9. See Hilts, "*Aliis exterendum.*"

10. Robertson was a Scotsman who was hired as subeditor by John Stuart Mill in 1837.
Robertson's professed desire as a journalist was to shake up all the learned societies by
directly addressing scientific and social issues.

It should be noted that the Manchester Statistical Society, which was founded in 1833,

the scientific goal of objectivity was undesirable but because the statisticians' method seemed philosophically indefensible. Robertson offers four objections to the society's rule, all of which ultimately rest on his assertion that theory cannot be separated from practice, hypothesis cannot be severed from fact. Here are some of Robertson's attempts to formulate this assertion: "theories themselves are not only facts but the kind of facts about the truth of which most care is taken, and which naturally therefore are oftener true or have more truth in them than details, and particulars about the accuracy of which less pains are taken"; "the whole of science is fact: it is either the facts which prove or the facts which are proved"; "opinion is what is most wanted where truth is the object, it is the parent and precursor of truth"; "the exclusion of opinions is the exclusion of the only guides which can conduct . . . researches to any useful end"; "before you can inquire you must have something that you seek"; "the end is the guide of the means. . . . When men go to seek they know not what, they become puzzled how to set about it, and the most common effect is, that they do nothing"; "facts are valuable only in relation to what they prove—the evidence is important or otherwise according to the proposition to which it relates."[11] Finally, here is Robertson's analysis of the heart of the society's contradictory thinking: "There is an ambiguity in the word facts which enables the council to pass off a most mischievous fallacy: it either means evidences or it means anything which exists. The fact, the thing as it is without any relation to anything else, is a matter of no importance or concern whatever: its relation to what it evinces, the fact viewed as evidence, is alone important" ("E," p. 69).

When Robertson attributes the contradiction in the society's rule to the ambiguity of "facts," he reveals the extent to which a theory of representation is at issue here. Equally important is the observation that Robertson intimates but can't quite formulate—the idea that facts cannot exist in isolation from theories because facts are only identifiable as such by the theories that define them and render them meaningful. Theories are more "true" than facts, according to this argument, not because more care is taken with them but because the latter only acquires any meaning

---

did not so strictly delimit its aims or claim that "opinions" and theory could be separated from the collection of data. See T. S. Ashton, *Economic and Social Investigations in Manchester, 1833–1933; A Centenary History of the Manchester Statistical Society* (London, 1934), chap. 2; David Elesh, "The Manchester Statistical Society : A Case Study of a Discontinuity in the History of Empirical Social Research," *Journal of the History of the Behavioral Sciences* 8 (July–Oct. 1972): 280–301, 407–17; and Lawrence Goldman, "The Origins of British 'Social Science': Political Economy, Natural Science and Statistics, 1830–1835," *The Historical Journal* 26 (Sept. 1983): 587–616.

11. John Robertson, "Exclusion of Opinions," review of vol. 1, pt. 1 of *Transactions of the Statistical Society of London, London and Westminster Review* 31 (Apr. 1838): 48–51, 57; hereafter abbreviated "E."

in relation to theory. Thus theory or "opinion" inevitably guides empirical observation, for without opinion nothing would be recognizable *as* a fact.

One reason that early apologists for statistics sought to ward off criticisms such as this was that, especially as party divisions began to widen after 1828, "opinion" was linked to party politics, which in turn was virtually synonymous with "interest" and therefore with both power and money. But despite the cautionary restrictions issued to the statistical section by the BAAS and the protestations of disinterest published by early statistical societies, charges of political interest greeted almost all statistical publications.[12] This was true partly because of the principle identified by Robertson that data cannot be collected in the absence of a theory about the nature of the object being analyzed. Beyond this abstract point, however, lies the much more obvious fact that most of the subjects investigated by early statisticians were social issues, among which were the most controversial topics of the day. The four types of statistics endorsed by the statistical section of the BAAS signal the controversial subject matter of the science: economical statistics, political statistics, medical statistics, and moral and intellectual statistics. Given the fact that in 1833, when the section was established, no one was certain at what price—or even whether— the factory system would triumph or machinery would transform the labor process, the questions subsumed in these categories inevitably provoked disagreement.

Statisticians' involvement in politics shows up in their nearly universal concern with legislation. In theory, of course, the aim of statistical knowledge was to anchor legislation in incontrovertible "accurate information" so as to obviate the need "to legislate in the dark." As J. R. McCulloch, the well-known popularizer of statistics, confidently claimed, "the accumulation of minute and detailed information from all parts of the country would, at length, enable politicians and legislators to come to a correct conclusion as to many highly interesting practical questions that have hitherto been involved in the greatest doubt and uncertainty."[13] Gathering what Taylor called "the only true foundation of all sound legislation, statistical facts" ("O," p. 206), was ultimately part of a project of measuring and enhancing the "progress" of the nation. By the 1830s, *progress* had replaced *improvement* (and, for radicals like William Godwin, *perfectibility*) as the term most generally considered applicable to the nation's development, a development that the rule of Parliament ensured would be partly a matter of legislation and therefore of politics.

12. One of the central arguments of Michael J. Cullen, *The Statistical Movement in Early Victorian Britain: The Foundations of Empirical Social Research* (New York, 1975) is that all statistical efforts were marked by politics. While I disagree with parts of Cullen's interpretation of this material, I agree with his general thesis.

13. J. R. McCulloch, "State and Defects of British Statistics," *Edinburgh Review* 61 (Apr. 1835): 178; hereafter abbreviated "S."

As McCulloch noted, measuring the progress of a nation is inevitably a comparative activity, involving comparisons of the present and the past as well as between countries. Paradoxically, as apologists for statistics worked out these comparisons, they found their nation to be advancing in nearly every area except one—the science of statistical knowledge. Lamenting that "our observations of the facts on which the social sciences must rest are miserably scanty," Taylor charged that these "facts . . . have been made with imperfect instruments, and they are scandalously inaccurate. . . . In no civilized state are all these evils more glaringly exemplified than in the British empire," Taylor indignantly concludes ("O," p. 206). McCulloch concurs; he calls for the founding of more enterprises like the Statistical Society of London so that "we shall no longer be the only civilized nation in Europe which has made no progress in this highly interesting science" ("S," p. 156). Specifically, to rectify Britain's backwardness, McCulloch recommends establishing an official statistical board in London that could organize the data collected by a professional corps of agents who would reside permanently in various parts of England, Scotland, and Ireland (see "S," pp. 177–81).

The link between numerical representation and government—or, more specifically, centralized government bureaucracy—was forged by the seventeenth-century practice of "political arithmetic."[14] By the mid-1830s, numbers had begun to play a prominent role in producing both a single "imagined community" where various communities had once competed for loyalty and the government apparatus by which this national community could be governed.[15] Inevitably, then, the debate about statistics became embroiled in the debate about whether government was most effectively organized at the local or national levels—a debate that broke generally (although not precisely) along party lines.[16] But even if one sided with the newly ascendant Whigs and endorsed a centralized government, uncertainties remained. For, given that Great Britain was divided into united but separate kingdoms, representing the nation numerically necessarily involved addressing the problem of internal difference—or, more precisely in the period in question, the problem of Ireland.

One facet of the dilemma presented by Ireland in the 1830s emerges in McCulloch's discussion of the defects of contemporary statistical knowl-

14. See Peter Buck, "Seventeenth-Century Political Arithmetic: Civil Strife and Vital Statistics," *Isis* 68 (Mar. 1977): 67–84, and A. M. Endres, "The Functions of Numerical Data in the Writings of Graunt, Petty, and Davenant," *History of Political Economy* 17 (Summer 1985): 245–64.

15. The phrase "imagined community" comes from Benedict Anderson, *Imagined Communities: Reflections on the Origin and Spread of Nationalism* (London, 1983). See also Gerald Newman, *The Rise of English Nationalism: A Cultural History, 1740–1830* (New York, 1987).

16. See Peter Mandler, *Aristocratic Government in the Age of Reform: Whigs and Liberals, 1830–1852* (Oxford, 1990), esp. chaps. 1, 4, 5.

edge. He notes with approval that trade restrictions between England and Ireland on all commodities except corn were removed in 1825. While this measure closed the conceptual gulf between "these two grand divisions of the empire," making them conform more nearly to the union established in 1801, the erasure of trade restrictions also obliterated a line of demarcation that McCulloch thinks important: "The want of any accounts of the articles they reciprocally import and export, has been, in a statistical point of view, very pernicious; and has led to many unfounded inferences and conclusions" ("S," p. 173). This "pernicious" statistical amalgamation was exacerbated in 1830, when Westminster, "in a miserable attempt to save the salaries of some four or five clerks," stopped providing separate economic accounts for England, Scotland, and Ireland and reported instead only the average. McCulloch's disapproval of this measure was unqualified. "Nothing so absurd was ever imagined," he declared. "It not only, by mixing such discordant elements together in one mass, rendered the accounts unworthy of attention, but it rendered it impossible to compare the revenue, foreign trade, shipping, &c. of England, Scotland, or Ireland, at any time posterior to 1830, with their state at any antecedent period!" ("S," pp. 174–75). Recognizing the shortcomings of their cost-cutting measure, McCulloch notes with approval, the new ministry soon abandoned this mode of representation and returned to differential accounting.

McCulloch's primary objections to the representational amalgamation of the three parts of Great Britain seem to be that it undermines historical analysis and that it obscures the specific details of international trade. This last impression is strengthened by the inclusion of a tabular account of "Foreign Trade of the United Kingdom in 1832, 1833, and 1834" that does not discriminate among the three parts of the empire ("S," p. 173). Both of these records would have been considered important to an assessment of Great Britain's "progress." But while McCulloch's specific complaints focus on historical and international accounting, his commentary also reveals both that Scotland's place in Great Britain (not to mention that of Wales, which the writer does not even bother to name) is not at issue and that Ireland's place—relative to the other parts of the empire—is. "The condition and circumstances of Ireland are, in very many respects, altogether different from those of Great Britain," he explains, thereby excluding Ireland from the rhetorical unit constituted by its other parts; "and, however it may be explained, the fact is certain, that the one part of the empire has rapidly advanced, while the other has remained stationary, or nearly so" ("S," pp. 173–74). "Accurate knowledge of the quantity or value of the articles passing between" the two parts, McCulloch continues, would provide the means for "the best and most unerring tests by which to measure the progress and to appreciate the state of each" ("S," p. 174).

McCulloch explicitly declines to speculate on the reasons for

Ireland's backwardness, but many of his contemporaries were not so reserved. In fact, the question of whether Ireland's difference was a consequence of race or of such legislatable matters as education was a subject of intense debate in the 1830s.[17] One line this argument could take is set out by the classical scholar Herman Merivale in his 1839 review of French population statistics. Merivale's specific subject concerns the various groups that inhabit France, but his passing suggestion that application of the "ethnographical sciences" should be made to "other countries also, in which we have an interest above that of mere curiosity" suggests that countries geographically closer to hand are on his mind.[18] Merivale argues that statistics that measure economic or physical changes in a population over time cannot adequately explain—or even describe—something crucial about that population. According to Merivale, "national character, that bundle of tendencies and habits which make up the mind of a people, whether of a country or province,—is far more determined by causes which we cannot trace, and far less influenced by those which we can trace, than statistical philosophers readily allow. There is a strength in hereditary vices and virtues which seems proof, at least through many generations, against the influence which changes of external circumstances may produce" ("M," pp. 60–61). As Merivale continues, it becomes clear that the hereditary features he has in mind are a function of what he calls race, although his juxtaposition of brain size with dialect shows how far his notion of race is from ours. These "racial" characteristics, according to Merivale, tend naturally to grow stronger, if not disturbed: "The peculiarities which mark different races of men (whether physical, such as the supposed cerebral conformation of different races, or merely arising from habit and education, such as differences of dialect), have a tendency to grow stronger instead of weaker in periods of peace and orderly habits" ("M," p. 61). Not surprisingly, Merivale's argument about racial difference is really an argument about racial "purity" (read "superiority"). He tells us that even if a black person marries a white, subsequent union with white will make "the blood . . . run clear in four generations. . . . This effect is produced much sooner," Merivale continues,

---

17. The transitional nature of the term *race* in the 1830s led writers to conflate biological with cultural or ethnic characteristics. See George W. Stocking, Jr., *Victorian Anthropology* (New York, 1987), esp. p. 64.

18. Herman Merivale, "Moral and Intellectual Statistics of France," review of *Essai sur la statistique de la population française, considérée sous quelques uns de ses rapports physiques et moraux,* by A. d'Angeville, *Edinburgh Review* 69 (Apr. 1839): 73; hereafter abbreviated "M." References to the racial differences within France or between the French and the English often served as displacements of an explicit discussion of the race or class differences within Great Britain. See Mary Poovey, "Domesticity and Class Formation: Chadwick's 1842 *Sanitary Report*," in *Subject to History: Ideology, Class, Gender,* ed. David Simpson (Ithaca, N.Y., 1991), pp. 65–83.

"where the admixture is of the less degrading blood of the Indians" ("M,"
p. 62).

The idea that blood could "run itself clear" through generations of
marriage obviously had implications for ideas about how the two parts
that were widely considered to house two distinct races could be fused into
one nation. In addition to the discussion about how to unify Great Britain,
Merivale's essay also belongs to another debate that concerned British
legislators in the 1830s, the debate over whether—or to what extent—
human beings were governed by forces beyond their control or capable of
governing themselves. The cluster of issues implicit in this debate is set
out by Merivale early in his review when he tries to account for the distrust with which many people viewed statistical representation:

> habituated as we are to consider the movements and actions of human
> beings as the result of their own free agency—regarding every indi-
> vidual as a microcosm, a creature of impulses and habits, partly,
> indeed, determined by circumstances, but still mainly his own, and
> from whose conduct, under given conditions, it appears almost
> impossible to conclude with any high degree of moral probability as
> to the conduct of another—many are apt to regard as a mere chi-
> mera, the notion of arriving by numerical calculations, at results suf-
> ficiently regular, to afford data for reasoning on the conduct of
> thousands and of millions. And yet the more we examine the subject,
> the more certainly do we discover that the same rule prevails in moral
> as in physical phenomena—that we can fix the probability of a partic-
> ular event, in one case, from investigating a number of similar past
> events. To take an example familiar to every understanding. If we
> had no materials for comparing the value of different lives—in other
> words, if the statistics of life were unknown to us—it would be obvi-
> ously impossible to form any calculation whatever of the probable
> length of an individual life. But by examining the particulars of a
> great many cases, we arrive at conclusions sufficiently accurate to
> influence our conduct, and are enabled to subject what is roughly
> called accident, or destiny, to general rules of calculation. The life of
> one man is liable to a thousand contingencies which mock our powers
> of divination. Compare a thousand more lives similarly circum-
> stanced, and the influence of contingencies seems to disappear before
> that of general laws. The case is precisely the same with those effects
> of which the proximate cause is the free will of man. Nothing at first
> sight seems more arbitrary or uncertain than the course which any
> one man will pursue, where circumstances, so far as they are known
> to us, do not seem to act with any compulsory force on his judgment.
> Take ten—one hundred—or one thousand men, whose choice is
> made under similar circumstances; and the greater the number of
> individuals compared, the more does the slightest pressure of exter-
> nal influence—the mere balance of motives—seem to amount to an
> irresistible force, effacing all varieties of human choice or caprice.

The results of an individual will seem to disappear, it has been well said, before the mean results of innumerable wills: in other words, under the weight of the vast machinery of moral causes; and differences of temper and disposition sink into mere modifications of general laws, subject to calculation equally with those laws themselves. ["M," pp. 50–51]

Merivale's central observation brings together two related issues, the first being the issue of free agency versus general laws. If the former reigns supreme, then presumably social change can be facilitated through moral education, which will discipline every individual's "impulses and habits." If the latter really governs human behavior, social change can still be engineered, but not through educating individuals; instead, meticulous investigations must be undertaken into the exact conditions under which crimes are committed so that legislative measures can alter those conditions. Notice that Merivale's definition of race as encompassing traits acquired from "habit and education" as well as heredity renders even race potentially amenable to environmental influence. The environmentalism common to early statistical thinking also appears in Taylor's essay. Referring to Adolphe Quételet's concept of the average man, Taylor reminds his reader that "the average man of one country in duration of life, enjoyment of comfort, mental development and countless other important particulars, may and does differ materially from the average man of another. Nay more, these representative abstractions will differ in localities at no great distance from each other, in an agricultural and manufacturing county, in town and country; in a city and its suburbs" ("O," p. 215).

Merivale and Taylor both link the theory of general laws to a second issue, that of probability. If the behaviors of different individuals can be seen to obey general laws rather than to express will or caprice, then "we can fix the probability of a particular event . . . from investigating a number of similar past events" ("M," p. 51). The fact that aggregated behaviors conform to mathematical laws, according to Taylor, could have immediate, practical application. If, for example, statistics prove that "in France, the proportion of suicides to homicides is nearly as 5 to 3, consequently, if a dead body be found in France, without any evidence appearing for the cause of death, there is a much greater probability of the deceased having fallen by self-violence than by the hand of an assassin. If it appear that the deceased has died by suffocation or strangulation, the probabilities for suicide are so greatly increased as, in the absence of some other evidence, to justify a verdict" ("O," pp. 214–15). Taylor contrasts the certainty of such mathematical logic with the obscurity of what he calls "frightful empiricism" ("O," p. 222).

The theory of probability has a complex history, which I will not be able to recount here.[19] For present purposes, it is enough to note that the application of mathematical probability to human behavior requires a conceptual move from the empirically observable individual to an abstracted concept like Quételet's average man or William Farr's "human aggregate." Taylor calls this abstraction human nature: "To know human nature is to know the general laws of human action, to ascertain the general course of man's physical and moral faculties" ("O," p. 212). The abstractions "human nature," "average man," and "human aggregate" are inextricably tied not only to the notion that general laws operate in nature but also to the idea that these "physical and moral laws of nature . . . are ascertainable only by observing, collecting, and registering the positive facts of experience."[20] Herein lies the double paradox of statistical thinking: "frightful empiricism" is the only means by which general laws can be deduced; the individual, who is undeniably as capable of not conforming to general laws as the reverse, is the unit on which the average is based. And further, the individual human being, who gathers statistical data, forms the basis of statistical representation, and presumably constitutes the beneficiary of statistical knowledge, is obliterated by the numerical average or aggregate that replaces him: "The results of an individual will seem to disappear, it has been well said, before the mean results of innumerable wills" ("M," p. 51).

Mean, indeed, were the effects of such representation, according to Charles Dickens. In his satirical report on the annual meeting of the BAAS in 1837, Dickens caricatures a session of the statistical section (presided over by Mr. Woodensconse, Mr. Ledbrain, and Mr. Timbered). Among other papers, the participants are treated to "a very ingenious communication" that counts and commodifies legs where some other observers might have seen people and measured poverty. "It appeared that the total number of legs belonging to the manufacturing population of one great town in Yorkshire was, in round numbers, forty thousand, while the total number of chair and stool legs in their houses was only thirty thousand, which, upon the very favourable average of three legs to a seat, yielded only ten thousand seats in all. From this calculation it would appear,—not taking wooden or cork legs into the account, but allowing two legs to every person,—that ten thousand individuals (one-half of the whole population) were either destitute of any rest from their legs at all, or passed the whole of their leisure time in sitting upon boxes."[21]

19. Important studies of probability in the seventeenth through the early nineteenth centuries include Ian Hacking, *The Emergence of Probability: A Philosophical Study of Early Ideas about Probability, Induction and Statistical Inference* (Cambridge, 1975); Barbara J. Shapiro, *Probability and Certainty in Seventeenth-Century England: A Study of the Relationships between Natural Science, Religion, History, Law, and Literature* (Princeton, N.J., 1983); and Lorraine Daston, *Classical Probability in the Enlightenment* (Princeton, N.J., 1988).

20. "Fourth Annual Report of the Council of the Statistical Society of London," p. 8.

21. Charles Dickens, "Full Report of the First Meeting of the Mudfog Association

Dickens is obviously mocking the absurdity of the objects some statisticians counted as well as the intense labor used to generate self-evident conclusions, but he is also highlighting the sheer irrelevance of their conclusions to the problems at hand. Less concerned with the general laws that statistics were said to reveal than with the dehumanization inherent in the process of aggregation, Dickens is also scathing about the sanctimonious moralization with which statisticians lard their deadening numbers. This criticism emerges most clearly in Dickens's satirical portrait of Mr. Slug's report of "the state of infant education among the middle classes of London." Slug tabulates the number of children's books in circulation by title, then openly deplores the results: "He found that the proportion of Robinson Crusoes to Philip Quarlls was as four and a half to one; and that the preponderance of Valentine and Orsons over Goody Two Shoeses was as three and an eighth of the former to half a one of the latter: a comparison of Seven Champions with Simple Simons gave the same result. The ignorance that prevailed was lamentable. One child, on being asked whether he would rather be Saint George of England or a respectable tallow-chandler, instantly replied, 'Taint George of Ingling'" ("F," p. 409). One of the members of the association joins Slug in his general condemnation of the offending books, but begs to exempt Jack and Jill "inasmuch as the hero and heroine, in the very outset of the tale, were depicted as going *up* a hill to fetch a pail of water, which was a laborious and useful occupation,—supposing the family linen was being washed." Slug's response is unequivocal: "the whole work had this one great fault, *it was not true*" ("F," p. 410).

Dickens's claim that the professed objectivity of statisticians was often undermined by the passion with which they advocated certain moralistic principles is obviously related to Robertson's point about the necessary relationship between facts and the theories by which they are identified as such, but it also points to another problem of early statistical representation. The environmentalism associated with the concept of general laws and theoretically bolstered by statisticians' tendency to gather and tabulate data by geographical areas was often undercut in the presentation of statistical results by a kind of moralism that harkened back to the individualistic thinking that the concept of the average man was intended to transcend. The paradox inherent in this problem appears most starkly in the kind of educational reports that Dickens mocks. Its pretensions, as well as its contradictory claims, are explored by John Robertson in his discussion of G. R. Porter's study of crime and education.

Porter's paper, which appeared in the first volume of the *Journal of the Statistical Society of London*, was intended to combat the scandalous

for the Advancement of Everything," *Bentley's Miscellany* 2 (1837): 411; hereafter abbreviated "F."

effects of the Frenchman André Michel Guerry's *Essay on the Moral Statistics of France*. In this study, Guerry had concluded that education tends to increase rather than decrease the incidence of crime. Porter's statistical survey purports to demonstrate conclusively that just the opposite is true. Robertson summarizes Porter's argument at great length, quoting both tables and commentary extensively. Then, equally extensively, he ridicules Porter's conclusions:

> Mr Porter as we have said, must either intend to prove that the teaching of reading and writing acts against crime, or that the moral education to which he every now and then alludes, has a moral tendency. To prove that moral education has a moral effect is uncalled for, since no one denies it, and trivial, since it would merely be showing by tables and figures, that making men moral *is* making men moral. But the object is to show that education in reading and writing acts restrainingly on crime: that teaching to read is giving men honest habits, and instructing them in calligraphy schooling their passions. Now, to those uninstructed in the mystic revelations of statistics, it does appear that, though you enable a man to write so well that he could copy Mr Porter's paper in the space covered by a sixpence, and surround it with a forest of "ornamental penmanship," you would not, by continuing the discipline of his eyes and fingers until doomsday, communicate either a principle or a habit of refraining from his neighbour's goods. Reading is the act of connecting certain sounds and significations with certain symbols. . . . Honesty and self-restraint, which are the virtues opposed to fraud and violence, are habits of character, formed in the mind by the presence and power of moral, religious and sympathetic considerations. . . . The expectation of those who expect from reading, which is not a moral operation, a moral result, who think that exercising the faculty of association upon symbols and sounds, is forming habits of morality in character, assuredly is an expectation of figs from thorns. . . .
>
> The argument of Mr Porter is, that in proportion to the degree of education in any class of society is the degree of crime . . . . His object is to prove that the one is the cause of the other; he assumes that he does so when he shows that they co-exist in the same classes. Oats and wheat grow on the same estate, therefore the oats have a tendency to produce the wheat. But there are many causes of a *moral* nature which adequately account for fewer crimes being among those who can read and write well than among those who cannot. . . . The parents who are most virtuous are most certain never to neglect mere elementary tuition, whatever their rank in life. Honour, opinion, enlightened views of interest, fewer temptations in consequence of superior advantages,—the lessons of pure-hearted mothers, the persuasions and warnings of religion, the stirring memories of good and heroic deeds and men—the heaven-sent blessings of family affections—all these influences, though not confined to any classes, are best in degree and greatest in power among the instructed classes,

where, in many a favoured spot, they make ideas of duty sweet and grand to young hearts, and throw around many characters, in the course of formation, an atmosphere which makes goodness sink into their natures as infallibly as the sunshine imbues the flowers of the fields with the colours of beauty. . . . There is not a word of all this in Mr Porter's paper, and its figures and facts are adduced to show that morality, religion, affection, duty, virtue and benevolence do not produce, but are produced by reading and spelling, penmanship and small-text. ["E," pp. 66–67]

Robertson's criticism first ridicules statisticians' claims that quantification and correlation uncover chains of causation, then lambastes this form of representation for what it cannot depict. How can numbers record "the lessons of pure-hearted mothers," the "heaven-sent blessings of family affections"? As Robertson's prose shifts into its most ornamental mode at the end of this passage, he demonstrates what numbers leave untold—numbers cannot record moral influences because they do not yield to quantification, and they cannot capture the aestheticizing rhetoric that gives such virtues life in the texts that Porter (and Dickens) would teach children to read.

At issue in the Guerry-Porter debate about education and crime and, more importantly for my purposes, in the controversy over what kind of knowledge statistics constitutes are the complex questions about determination I have already alluded to in the debate about environmentalism and free will. What turns individuals to crime? these writers ask—poor education or general laws? What form of representation can depict, so as to explain, such deviance—moralizing celebrations of pure-hearted mothers or numerical tables of crimes? And what, if any, form of representation can counteract crime—the imaginatively engaging narratives of heroic deeds that both Robertson and Dickens champion or the kind of facts and figures that Porter presents? If statistical tables are, in some sense, unreadable, as J. R. McCulloch admitted in 1837, then how can they persuade readers accustomed to anecdotes, sentimental rhetoric, and pathetic tales?

The vexing question of how various forms of causation and representation relate to or can be made to coexist with each other lies behind some of the paradoxes apparent in these early statistical apologies. A writer's tendency to juxtapose environmental paradigms with moralistic explanations is one symptom of the uncertainty about causation and representation. Another is the use of the ambiguous concept of "sympathy," which, in one section of Taylor's essay, functions both to signal the limitations of the idea that general laws cause crime and to bridge the gulf between such a counterintuitive mode of explanation and the more readily imaginable paradigm of imitation. Sympathy could both signal uncertainty and link environmentalism and individualism because it was itself an indeterminant concept: *sympathy* belonged both to a physiological vocabulary, in which it described the involuntary response of nerves, and to what we would call a psychological vocabulary, in which it referred to acts of imaginative identification that were neither simply voluntary nor involuntary. Note that in the two examples Taylor cites to prove the presence of sympathy, the relation between involuntary and voluntary models of response becomes increasingly unclear. Note also how vexed are Taylor's presentation of the theoretical notion of causation and his treatment of representational issues:

> It is the business of the statistician to collect and tabulate facts in order to discover the laws of their occurrence; it is no part of his proper duty to investigate their causes. But in the present instance there are other authenticated facts, that seem at least to illustrate a general principle connected with this table [of murders in France], which deserve to be noticed. There is no better attested, nor more astonishing, record in history, than the sudden appearance of a disposition to commit some certain crime in a definite manner spreading like a contagious disease, reaching a fearful height in defiance of every effort to repress it, and then gradually sinking into oblivion. The madness of witch-finding in our country and in New England, the crime of poisoning in France when the *Chambres Ardentes* were established, the rick-burning in England within our own memory, are familiar examples. Does not this seem to prove that we might reckon a certain sympathy or principle of imitation among the leading incentives to crime? ["O," p. 213]

Taylor proceeds to give two examples of this phenomenon. The first is the coincidence of suicides, especially among soldiers. The second example concerns something that is apparently too terrible to be named. This phenomenon, Taylor begins, "is of too grave importance to be passed over lightly":

> A clergyman, the master of a very large and popular school, the locality of which, for reasons that will presently appear, we must not specify, recently informed one of his friends, that he had discovered a new pupil in the act of practising a disgraceful vice. "Send him home to his parents and say nothing about it," was the friend's judicious recommendation. The schoolmaster however, placed great confidence in his own eloquence and the corrective powers of birch; he assembled his boys, made an excellent harangue on the guilt of the delinquent, and gave him a sound flogging. The example of crime proved more influential than the example of punishment, and the vice spread so rapidly that the whole school was broken up in consequence. These and countless similar facts lead us to question the propriety of

describing vice at all, in the moral tales designed for young persons, even though the consequent punishment be ever so strongly depicted. ["O," p. 214]

This second example seems at first to have nothing to do with statistics. No tabular or numerical representations are provided to measure this "disgraceful vice"—indeed, the "similar facts" are said to be "countless," presumably meaning beyond enumeration. Nor is it clear that this constitutes an example of the general laws that statistics supposedly uncover. As more than an extension of the metaphor of contagious disease with which this one-page "deviation" is introduced, the example of the spreading vice seems to shift the emphasis of the term *sympathy* away from involuntary nervous response and toward at least quasi-voluntary imitation or even desire. That is, one lesson of the vice story seems to run counter to the statistical principle that general laws work through individuals, suggesting instead that human beings respond imaginatively to each other's pleasure, regardless of threatened pain.

But another lesson concerns representation. Once more, it is unclear exactly what Taylor has in mind. From one perspective this seems to be a cautionary tale about narrative descriptions, presumably in favor of some less stimulating form of representation—like numbers, perhaps. Maybe if the vice had been recorded numerically, those in the know—the parents and schoolmasters—would have been appropriately alerted, while those who were still innocent—the boys—would have been spared the incitement of description. But Taylor has told us that his examples of such vice are "countless." Thus, from another perspective, what Taylor calls a deviation from his own apology for statistics can be read as a story about statistics—or, more precisely, about the relationship between statistics as a self-consciously limited form of representation and the sublime, as that which is in excess of, or lies beyond, figuration.

Taylor never specifies the nature of the "disgraceful vice," although the setting of the story and the imitation it occasions would have identified it for virtually any middle-class reader. Taylor's imprecision, however, is not incidental to the story; it is, in a sense, the point of the story, for it is an attempt not to duplicate the pattern that the overconfident schoolmaster inaugurated when *he* described the vice in his "harangue." In attempting to convey to his readers both that this vice exists and that it must not be represented, Taylor *produces* whatever the word *vice* suggests as excess, as beyond or outside of representation. The word *masturbation* could be written, in other words, but when Taylor refuses to do so he provokes fantasies that the words he does use cannot contain. This, according to Taylor, is a safer, more disciplined way to go about administering his "grave" lesson, but given the fact that this "deviation" marks the undecidability of Taylor's own argument—his uncertainty about whether human actions follow general laws or each other—it is not so clear that Taylor's strategy is less disruptive than the schoolmaster's.

The implicit lesson of this "deviation" is that statistical representation is like Taylor's euphemistic story in that it too both limits what it will depict and necessarily produces an uncontrollable excess. The self-imposed limitations of statistics are obvious—even if the writers I have been examining disagree about what they should be. According to various accounts, statistics limits itself to recording observable facts, rejecting theories, opinions, and politics; it limits itself to a static description of the present, scorning historical and comparative narratives; it limits itself to what can be counted, shunning the immeasurable influence of "pure-hearted mothers"; it limits itself to recording effects, leaving others to "thresh out" chains of causation and legislation. Even this self-consciously limited discourse, however, both depends on and produces that which lies beyond representation. Statistics *depends* on the unfigured in the sense that its characteristic tables always include the uncounted; the figures imply, if they do not in fact record, not exact counts but *estimates*. The pretense of statistical representation to coverage—to record a totality—is always a pretense, in other words. No census-taker ever counts every individual in his or her district; no social scientist ever records every suicide; no schoolmaster ever knows about every boy who masturbates. The very idea of an aggregate implies generalization, but it also reflects or records generalization. Indeed, many critics charge that, especially after the initial enthusiasm waned, even members of statistical societies no longer actually collected data about the subjects they studied; instead, they increasingly relied on data already collected and on estimates generated from a few examples.[22]

Statistics *produces* excess in two senses. First, as the "raw material" for other "sciences," statistics enables others to generate theories and legislation that are figured nowhere in the numbers themselves. Secondly, as a discourse that *claims* a transparent relation to the objects it represents, statistical representation masks the meanings it does produce at the same time that it puts these meanings into play. Largely though not exclusively an effect of the categories by which statistical representation organizes materials, these meanings are being constructed before the statistics are compiled; they then radiate from the starkest tables. It is partly because such signification characterizes statistical representation—even if it is nowhere acknowledged—that theory and legislation *can* be generated from numbers. If statistics are made up of one kind of generalization, in other words, they produce another—and all in the guise of recording only what exists.

The sublime effects of statistical representation, along with statistics's simultaneous scorn for and gravitation toward that which lies beyond rep-

---

22. See Elesh, "The Manchester Statistical Society," pp. 280, 413.

resentation, helps explain some of the discourse's most characteristic paradoxes: the distrust of theory that seems always to embody and generate theory; the scorn for politics in a discourse devoted to legislative action; the manipulation of difference so as to form a homogenized nation or to mask that nation's internal unevenness; the oscillation between environmentalism and moralism; the alternating celebration of general laws and imitation. As a discourse self-consciously placed in opposition to fiction, the figures of arithmetic were always open to the claim that they, too, were merely figures of speech. Or, as John Robertson charges, "statistics has in the experience of many thoughtful men realized an effect which has a tinge of the marvellous in it, by making them doubt demonstration and disbelieve arithmetic. Built seemingly on a foundation which partakes of the certainty of numerical computation, it has nevertheless presented such fallacies and errors to the public, that to minds scrupulous in matters of belief it has successfully evinced the claims of numerical figures to a rivalry with the figures of speech in powers of fiction" ("E," p. 47).

A Response to Mary Poovey

Harry Harootunian

Mary Poovey's "Figures of Arithmetic, Figures of Speech: The Discourse of Statistics in the 1830s" (pp. 401–21) makes the important observation that the inaugural moment of statistics as an organized disciplinary practice in nineteenth-century England was marked by a controversy over its validity as science. In fact, there seems to have been a significant separation between the practice itself and the formation of a discourse that continued to air and discuss the various aporias of statistics. It shows that, at the time of its own establishment in 1831, the British Association for the Advancement of Science (BAAS), the professional custodian of science in England, rejected statistical representation as unscientific because it had failed to correspond to its "institutionalized . . . concept" (p. 401) of a knowledge that was at once practical, objective, and value-neutral. This conception sought to institutionalize in scientific practice, and thereby maintain, the separation of science from politics, knowledge from power, and understanding from daily life—a relationship apparently best exemplified by the astronomy of Sir Issac Newton. Yet it is important to recognize that early on statistics was seen as a departure from this paradigmatic relationship principally because it "lacked a theoretical foundation" (p. 401) and, worse, because its practitioners seemed incapable of removing their personal values from the practice. Poovey tells us that by 1831 statistics was already deeply implicated in a growing political controversy concerning the "'condition of England'" (p. 401). Indeed, when the BAAS finally agreed to establish a statistical section two years after its founding, the association's president put statisticians on warning to remain free from the "'dreary world of politics'" (p. 402).

From the beginning, then, social discourse concentrating on statistics became the sign of an uneasy relationship between statistics's seemingly uncontrollable propensity for political and ideological involvement and its status as an institutionalized science that sought to uphold transcendent claims of objectivity and neutrality. Science also tried to maintain capitalism's separation of spheres and structures as a principal condition of its own autonomy. The discourse on statistics revealed the constant conflict between knowledge (science) and power (the described world of politics), which the new, official scientific organization wished to discount as definitively as artists pursued an art for art's sake. One of the interesting ironies of Poovey's account is that the BAAS sought to promote independence from politics as a natural vocation of science from a site of institutionalized political power; the BAAS thus offered its critique of statistics's erring affiliation with politics from what seems to have been an entrenched political base. But Poovey's analysis neither examines this crucial aporia nor considers the broader historical problem of how class society was implicated in the attempt to expunge politics from science or art in order to create a bourgeois social formation comprised of semiautonomous domains of activity. Yet this historical context, any consideration of which is absent from Poovey's analysis, reveals its force as a principal determinant of both the discourse and discord concerning statistics.

The controversy over the scientific claims of statistics signifies something about a historical context that only obliquely manages to wedge itself into the nineteenth-century discussion but remains outside of Poovey's own portrayal. Although Poovey's paper provides a wonderfully informative and analytic account of the controversy between official science and statistics, it does so largely in terms of the formal constraints of the discourse itself; the discourse still needs to be read as a sign of a history. Such a reading might go some way toward explaining both the intensity of critical combat and the insistence of its defenders and institutional custodians that science, to be science, must be free of politics and ideology. Science, according to the institutional argument, must avoid any arrangement in which the personal values of practitioners or the views of a larger social group become implicated in the scientific practice itself. The discourse of statistics that Poovey narrates signified a history that had already problematized the relationship of science and politics in which an institution promoted scientific inquiry—the production of new knowledge—unfettered by political and social considerations. After all,

Harry Harootunian, a coeditor of *Critical Inquiry* and Max Palevsky Professor of History and East Asian Languages and Civilizations at the University of Chicago, is the author of *Things Seen and Unseen: Discourse and Ideology in Tokugawa* (1988) and editor, with Masao Miyoshi, of *Postmodernism and Japan* (1989) and *Japan in the World* (1993).

science was constituted within the BAAS, an institutional site that risked betraying its own interests; its content remained inscribed within the space of this ideological site.[1]

Poovey tells us that, in these early days, defenders explained statistics's descent into politics by claiming that it was still immature as a science or that it had not yet accumulated sufficient data. Other, perhaps less sympathetic, observers were simply unclear about what statistical representation was supposed to do. But she is convinced that from the very beginning, far from being either immature or unclear in its purpose, statistical practice was marked by a number of contradictions and by a generic blurring that constantly mixed numerical and tabular formulations with discursive, historical, and explanatory narratives. Moreover, its identification of evidential knowledge also resulted in a further mingling of presumably unmediated observational data derived from the social formation, considerations of social policy, and ideas for possible legislation.

According to Poovey, these ceaseless border crossings of genre account for producing the particular tensions, contradictions, and identities in the practice of a statistical discipline. The numerous paradoxes reveal a representational order that necessarily had to rely on the unrepresented and the unfigured. By making this move, statistics invariably ended up affirming what it had denied. Its distrust of theory was theoretical; its "scorn for politics" in practice aimed to satisfy social policy and legislative action (p. 421). Though devoted to the real, statistics promoted an imaginary: a homogeneous national community that suppressed social differences and unevenness. It swung breathlessly from moral to environmental explanations and oscillated between "general laws" and "imitation" as accounts of behavior (p. 417). But I wonder if these paradoxes or contradictions could not be explained by proposing that, unlike earlier sciences such as astronomy or physics, the particular contest that was being played out derived its form from a particular historical and social conjuncture that they functioned to efface. This is not to say that history at an earlier time did not enter into the production of other sciences but only that the growth of industrial society in the nineteenth century was the enabling condition of statistics and that statistics was the form that signified or marked this particular historical moment. Its development and subsequent implementation would have been inconceivable without the existence of the metropolitan, industrial site. Yet if we accept this observation, we are also obliged to interrogate the conditions of historicity that accompany the development of statistics as a scientific practice. It is entirely possible that the mixing of representational forms by statisticians announced an early rejection of capitalistic social abstraction. Only by carefully eliminating narrative modes could statistics be legiti-

1. See Jacques Rancière, "Theory of Ideology—Althusser's Politics," in *A Radical Philosophy Reader,* ed. Roy Edgley and Richard Osborne (London, 1985), pp. 116–17.

mated as a science by the BAAS. While Poovey is undoubtedly right to sort out the internal contestations of discourse and to show the limits of discussion, there is still an outside to discourse, an exteriority that leaves its watermark on the inside—the utterances—that needs to be accounted for (though I am not suggesting that she merely reduce the instance of thought to material conditions as if the former obediently reflected the latter).

This observation leads to a consideration of how statistics became complicit in affirming a conception of social order even as it sought only to gather evidence about it. Poovey's article shows that statistics, because of its desire to break away from politics, constructed a method that declared its neutrality as a condition of acting politically to affirm the present. It is another irony of her narrative that by appealing to its scientific veracity statistics became an even more effective support of the received social order than the BAAS, which sought to save science from politics but probably feared the politicizing of science more. Hence, critics were seen calling into question the presumed relationship between the image of a national community and representation, between quantification and correlation, and the consequences for causal explanation. They also ridiculed the way numbers fell short of recording the "'lessons of pure-hearted mothers'" or the "'heaven-sent blessings of family affections'" in examining the bond linking statistical probability to the possibility of predictability (p. 417).

Poovey shows how deeply involved statistics was in constructing imaginaries through the assertion of causal explanations. She reminds us that this move was made precisely at the moment when the advocates of statistics were appealing to the authority of "scientific" operations devoted to accumulating aggregate data from observation. What this recognition demonstrates, persuasively I think, is how statistics was early constituted as a social science of industrializing society or the industrial city—an archetype almost in its privileging of quantification over qualitative narrative, abstraction over the concreteness of factual experience, and for its willingness to become what Loren Baritz described years ago as a "servant of power." [2] Observation and the accumulation of data were supposed to sanction the construction of a social imaginary. Poovey argues that statistics, in this connection, based its conception of representation on a sublime, an unrepresented, a surplus that always escaped representation itself, and that it was this surplus that made representation possible. But why use *sublime* to describe an absent something, or nothing? It seems just as accurate to say that what was being represented was something that simply did not exist and that data were being marshalled to give substance to an image of the social that existed prior to

2. See Loren Baritz, *The Servants of Power: A History of the Use of Social Science in American Industry* (Middletown, Conn., 1960).

the actual accumulation of evidence, even though it was made to appear as its effect. The whole move toward establishing an average, for example, was not simply a construction but part of an overwhelming effort to install a conception of normativity, with all of its implications for political ordering and social control, as the principle binding society together. The identification of social consensus with social reality opened the way for a science of society devoted precisely to "recording observable facts" (p. 420) (that is, constituting facticity) and rejecting theories, opinions, and politics—a static view of an unchanging present, no longer in need of historicizing or narrativizing, constrained only by what could be counted.

What this science excluded was not so much the unfigured, in the sense of the uncounted or the deferred, but rather what might already exist as a serious problem to be investigated or as a challenge to the authority of a constructed imaginary. Here, Poovey proposes that statistics produced a surplus in two ways: (1) as "'raw material'" for other "'sciences'" to generate theories and legislation nowhere "figured" in "the numbers themselves" (p. 420); and (2) as a discourse that claimed a transparent relationship to the objects it purported to reflect in representation while it sought to mask the meanings it was producing. But statistics, regardless of its claim to transparency or its avowed status as raw material, was filled from the beginning with meaning that it worked to put into play under the authority of objectivity and neutrality. In this sense, statistics, as the archetypal social science, was inescapably linked to affirming a constructed conception of social and political order as a condition for suppressing the possibility of an alternative and historically grounded existing formation from which it withheld figuration and representation.

Finally, statistics, in Poovey's reading, seems to operate very much like the narratives and historical explanations it came to eschew. It employed the same strategy of referentiality by which the referent—the social system or social reality that representation was supposed to transparently reflect—was made to appear outside of representation. But all of this was no more than a managed effect of the language of generalization that produced the categories that authorized the accumulation and organization of data or evidence. The constructed categories, undoubtedly derived from a prior conception of the social, authorized the collection of evidence. Even so, the categories existed within representation, not outside of it, and were a product of it, in spite of appealing to an outside referent. Hence, the vaunted referent of a positive science was a fiction, or certainly acted like one, and was smuggled in only after the categories had been constituted by and in language. Nowhere does this seem more evident in Poovey's essay than in those criticisms calling into question the kind of knowledge statistics was supposed to make available, its proper form of representation, and the putative reliance on "general laws," what William Cooke Taylor called "'frightful empiricism'" (p. 413), which managed to produce only moralizing, or categories constructed to justify research for social engineering, and invidious comparisons of national character, the staple of a good deal of later social science that unfortunately still echoes in contemporary practices.

Grand Narrative or Historical Overdetermination?

Mary Poovey

Harry Harootunian's comments ("A Response to Mary Poovey," pp. 422–27) are very much in keeping with the spirit of the inquiry I have undertaken in the name of statistics, and I want to thank him for some very helpful formulations of this problematic. In particular, I appreciate Harootunian's illumination of the account that statistical representation forecloses. "Statistics," Harootunian writes, "as the archetypal social science, was inescapably linked to affirming a constructed conception of social and political order as a condition for suppressing the possibility of an alternative and historically grounded existing formation from which it withheld figuration and representation" (p. 426). The alternative formation (formulation?) to which he alludes I take to be a *narrative* account that would describe the historical constitution of just that "constructed conception of [the] social and political order" the reality of which statisticians claimed to represent. As a form of representation, according to this argument, statistics vied with and eventually (if unevenly) displaced other forms of representation, which would have told other stories and differently.

But perhaps I am wrong. Perhaps Harootunian did not mean to write *formulation* when he wrote *formation*. Perhaps his point is not that statistics was one form of representation among others but that statisticians created one version of reality instead of describing a "historically grounded . . . formation" that really did exist. The difference between these two statements—that statistics was one form of representation among others and that statistics ostentatiously refused to represent something that cried out for figuration—resonates throughout Harootunian's comment. In so doing, it directs our attention to a set of problems about how to describe—and explain—the relationship between representation and its referent, what we call reality.

At one point, Harootunian chides me for attributing the paradoxes I identify in statistical representation to the logic of the discourse itself instead of to the "conditions of historicity that accompany the development of statistics as a scientific practice" (p. 424). I think what is really at issue here is the mode of analysis in this essay and my decision (which Harootunian could not have known) to begin the book of which this is the first chapter with a *description* of the characteristic tensions within statistics before moving to a historical account that would also *explain* these tensions. Leaving aside for a moment my (perhaps misguided) analytic strategy, let's look at Harootunian's argument. When I chart "internal contestations" particular to this discourse, he writes, I fail to illuminate something else. "There is still an outside to discourse," Harootunian reminds us, "an exteriority that leaves its watermark on the inside" (p. 425).

Harootunian immediately assures us that he is not suggesting some pre-Foucauldian opposition between representation and reality, and, leaving aside the undecidability of formation/formulation, he offers a fairly consistent account of the constitutive (rather than mimetic) nature of statistical representation. "It seems just as accurate to say that what was being represented was something that simply did not exist," Harootunian explains, "and that data were being marshalled to give substance to an image of the social that existed prior to the actual accumulation of evidence" (pp. 425–26). I couldn't agree more with this last statement, and in my discussion of Adam Smith I show how this "image of the social," which preceded information gathering, was developed in the mid-eighteenth century. Even though Harootunian and I might agree that theory precedes and informs what statisticians identified as relevant data, however, I suspect that we would still (politely) disagree both about the nature of that "outside" that leaves its indelible stain on discourse and about what, for want of a better word, I will call the intentionality of statistics.

"The whole move toward establishing an average," Harootunian writes, "was not simply a construction but part of an overwhelming effort

Mary Poovey is professor of English at The Johns Hopkins University. She is the author of *The Proper Lady and the Woman Writer: Ideology as Style in the Works of Mary Wollstonecraft, Mary Shelley, and Jane Austen* (1984) and *Uneven Developments: The Ideological Work of Gender in Mid-Victorian England* (1988). She is currently at work on a study of statistical thinking in the eighteenth and nineteenth centuries.

to install a conception of normativity" (p. 426). And who was making this effort? "Class society," he explains, "was implicated in the attempt to expunge politics from science [and] art in order to create a bourgeois social formation comprised of semiautonomous domains of activity" (p. 423). Now, my question is this: What kind of an agent is "class society" such that it can make this "overwhelming effort"? Or, better still, what kind of narrative is Harootunian writing such that something like "class society" constitutes the "formation" that the formulation of statistical representation simultaneously normalizes and dehistoricizes?

I (respectfully) submit that the narrative that Harootunian offers as a corrective to my formalist description of statistics is the familiar story of the "rise of capitalism" told with a post-structuralist twist. In this story, statistical representation is the "servant of power" and power is wielded by "class society"—or, somewhat more precisely, by the "bourgeois social formation" that both spun off and now parades as a society comprised of classes in conflict. While I agree with Harootunian that statistical representation has something to do with power, I wonder if casting the explanation as the narrative of capital logic doesn't blind us to some important features of the way that statistical representation worked—and failed to work—as a servant or handmaid of power. Let me briefly offer another account, which differs in emphasis rather than substance from Harootunian's story. Perhaps this will also hint at the explanation that I offer in the rest of the book of which this is a part.

I suggest that it is important to describe the constitutive tensions of statistical representation at the moment it was institutionalized because these tensions constitute traces of the historical contests in which the discursive strains eventually consolidated *as* statistics were involved. This formulation has several implications. First, it suggests that what eventually became statistical representation did not serve a single agenda. Indeed, the various projects for which early predictive/descriptive systems of quantification were used ranged from the legitimation of a powerful, all-knowing, sovereign state to the description of the economy as a realm so regular and ramified that it could not be known even to the sovereign. Now, both William Petty's political arithmetic and Adam Smith's political economy (whose programs I have just described) can be *assimilated* to the "rise of capitalism" or the "formation of class society," but to do so obscures the differences between these two heuristic paradigms. It seems to me that what links political arithmetic to political economy to statistics is not the interest they served or even the effect to which they contributed but the common, if differently conceptualized, problem these discourses were all developed to address. As I understand it, this problem involved imagining the kind of government that could simultaneously guarantee the prosperity of a specific group of people (understood as the country's security, which came to be assimilated to its national identity) and provide for the well-being of the individuals in that group. Because of the particular solutions theorists devised to the specific problems they confronted, certain themes dominated the representational modes they developed. Among these themes were the identification and mastery of some (racial or national) other, the equation of individual health with national prosperity, and the constitution of "value" in quantifiable (that is, monetary) terms. These themes did not always work in the same way, however; they were not consistently articulated in the same terms or directed toward the same ends. Some of the tensions we see in the 1830s are signs that these divergent articulations were carried over into statistics *as* inconsistencies. The *explanation* for the paradoxes I describe, then, is not ultimately formal but historical. I read formal incoherence as the sign of historical overdetermination.

The second implication of my analysis follows from this. If statistical representation is conceptualized not as the "servant" of some more or less coherent "formation" struggling to achieve being-as-such but as a heterogeneous motley of solutions to historical problems that subsequently disappeared or took new forms, then we can better understand why statistical representation elicited such contradictory responses and why even its apologists were uncertain about how reliable an instrument it was. On the one hand, in 1830 as now, statistical representation was treated as if it were absolutely authoritative—"scientific" in just the sense Harootunian describes. On the other hand, however, statistical representation was treated even by its supporters as a discourse so malleable that it could be made to say anything. Equally suggestive, to my mind, is the fact that even those individuals most committed to statistics as a mode of knowledge, like James Phillips Kay, a founder of the Manchester Statistical Society, repeatedly supplemented his statistical tables with anecdotes, because the former could not achieve what the latter could do so well— move its readers to tears or to action.

My point is that even if statistical representation was in some sense "complicit" in producing a normative representation of social relations, a narrative that casts it as the "servant of power" cannot account for effects that must be unintended according to this story (or whose "reason" must be supplied retrospectively). Among these effects are (on what I would call the positive side) the creation of a Board of Public Health in England in 1848 and the laying of hundreds of miles of sewage lines to improve the well-being of the urban poor and (on what I would call the negative side) the exclusion of women's waged labor from calculations of the "value" of a nation's resources.

In highlighting the differences between the narrative Harootunian suggests and the reading of formal tensions as signs of overdetermination and therefore as producers of multiple, often contradictory effects, I am not arguing that a "logic" or even an agenda cannot retrospectively be written into history. I am suggesting that to do so too singlemindedly may make it difficult both to see the incoherence that characterizes the vehicles by which certain (interested) interpretations were advanced and to appreciate the multiplicity of the effects such vehicles generated. Of course, my formulation does not address the question of why some interested interpretations triumphed (more or less) over others. Perhaps we need an entire book to answer a question like that.

Two Souls in One Body

Ian Hacking

Bernice R. broke down so badly, when she turned nineteen, and behaved so much like a retarded child that she was committed to the Ohio State Bureau of Juvenile Research. Its director, Henry Herbert Goddard, a psychologist of some distinction, recognized that she suffered from multiple personality disorder. She underwent a course of treatment lasting nearly five years, after which "the dissociation seems to be overcome and replaced by a complete synthesis. [She] is working regularly a half day and seems reasonably happy in her reactions to her environment."[1] Therapy enabled her core personality and her main alter to make contact with each other, and for her to understand her past and, to some extent, why she had split.

Her story prompts questions about evidence, objectivity, historical truth, psychological reality, self-knowledge, and the soul. It involves that

1. Henry Herbert Goddard, "A Case of Dual Personality," *Journal of Abnormal and Social Psychology* 21 (July 1926): 191; hereafter abbreviated "CDP." The "[She]" replaces "Norma," Goddard's pseudonym for his patient in her "normal" state. The present paper replaces Goddard's pseudonyms for family members with their actual first names. Miss R.'s birth certificate and some records of the family are known to the author, but confidentiality should still be preserved. See also Goddard, *Two Souls in One Body? A Case of Dual Personality. A Study of a Remarkable Case: Its Significance for Education and for the Mental Hygiene of Childhood* (New York, 1927); hereafter abbreviated *TS*. Unpublished letters quoted in this essay are from the H. H. Goddard collection, M 331, Archives of the History of Psychology, University of Akron, Akron, Ohio; hereafter abbreviated HHG. I would like to thank the librarians for their assistance.

This essay originally appeared in *Critical Inquiry* 17 (Summer 1991).

powerful intersection of morality and metaphysics: why is it of value to have a self-understanding founded on true beliefs about ourselves and our past, or at any rate on memories that are not strictly false? To what extent is such self-knowledge based on evidence? To what extent is it knowledge at all?

What follows has three levels: versions of the events; evidence for those versions; and reflections on the different kinds of evidence brought into play. The more I know what really happened, the more I wonder if there is a "what really happened." Everything about this puzzle generalizes, but only in its dense detail and turnings in upon itself do we begin to face up to the question of truth—and partly because so much of the evidence is so plain in its style: clinical reports, letters and archives, and so forth, the veritable carriers of truth. Here are four specific questions that bear on the case of Bernice, each followed in parentheses by an all-too-immediate generalization.

"Medical": Is multiple personality an objective state or condition of some disturbed or unhappy people? (What is it for an abnormal mental condition to be a "real" state of a person, especially when there is no plausible physiological or organic abnormality?)

Diagnostic: If there is such a state as multiple personality, did Bernice suffer from it? (What are grounds for diagnosis, especially when some respected experts deny there is any such ailment?)

An "outsider's" question: We rely, or begin by relying, on Goddard's two reports of his case. Was he trustworthy? Not, as it happens, entirely so. (Therapies, especially abreactive therapies, involve a relation between patient and therapist; what are we to make of the case reports when we know that the reporter is not a passive witness but an active agent in the case?)

An "insider's" question: Bernice's conception of who she was, of her nature, her soul, was in part a product of memories achieved by synthesis and cure. Yet she could have emerged well-cured, by a strikingly similar method of therapy, but with an importantly different set of memories—or so I shall argue. Probably her actual memories were false. If she was well, went on to live a decent life, and was at almost no risk of having her memories undone, so what? (It is undoubtedly important that our self-conception should be founded on recollections of our own past that are not strictly false. Why?)

Ian Hacking, a philosopher, is a University Professor at the University of Toronto and the author of *Taming Chance* (1990). He is completing a book called *Multiple Personality and the Politics of Memory* (forthcoming).

Does Multiple Personality Exist?

Multiple personality has had its ups and downs. The idea of a double or split self arises simultaneously in the stories and novels and plays of the romantic period and in occasional cases such as the now-celebrated Mary Reynolds of Pennsylvania, briefly described in 1816, or a case reported at greater length in Scotland in 1822.[2] There continued to be scattered reports in America and Europe, but "double personality" became a medical concept for the first time in France in 1875.[3] It was picked up in the United States by William James and Morton Prince, but multiples faded away. Bernice was one of the last two cases of the first American wave of multiples.

In 1968 the American Psychiatric Association published a taxonomy of mental illness, *Diagnostic and Statistical Manual–II.*[4] It contained no description of multiple personality, which was subsumed under hysterical neurosis. There had been a number of multiples recorded as curiosities from 1927 to 1973, of whom by far the most famous was "Eve."[5] But the revival of multiples as a clear medical concept can be put at 1973, when Cornelia Wilbur's case of "Sybil" was published, again as a popular book.[6] Wilbur describes herself as a maverick psychoanalyst. She thought her work important because it was the first psychoanalysis of a multiple personality. But its effect was different. Being a psychoanalyst, she elicited repressed childhood trauma. During the decade of the analysis, child abuse had, quite independently, become an almost obsessive concern of the American public.[7] A new doctrine emerged in the practice of a persuasive few: multiple personality was a reaction to childhood trauma, child abuse, and particularly sexual abuse. From that point on a small group of psychiatrists fostered what we may call a multiple personality movement,

2. For a remarkable account of Mary Reynolds, including the successive medical reports and selections from her own letters, see Michael G. Kenny, *The Passion of Ansel Bourne: Multiple Personality in American Culture* (Washington, D. C., 1986), chap. 1. Goddard's "two souls" metaphor was used of an American lady who dissociated in 1802: "She appeared as a person might be supposed to do, who had two souls, each occasionally dormant, and occasionally active, and utterly ignorant of what the other is doing" (Benjamin W. Dwight, "Facts Illustrative of the Powers and Operations of the Human Mind," *American Journal of Science* 1 [1818]: 433).

3. For an account of these successive waves and a theory about their occurrence, see Ian Hacking, "Multiple Personality Disorder and Its Hosts," *History of the Human Sciences* 4 (June 1992).

4. See The Committee on Nomenclature and Statistics of the American Psychiatric Association, *Diagnostic and Statistical Manual of Mental Disorders*, 2d ed. (Washington, D. C., 1968); widely referred to by the acronym *DSM–II.*

5. See Corbett H. Thigpen and Hervey M. Cleckley, *The Three Faces of Eve* (New York, 1957).

6. See Flora R. Schreiber, *Sybil* (Chicago, 1973).

7. One account of this is in Hacking, "The Making and Molding of Child Abuse," *Critical Inquiry* 17 (Winter 1991): 253–88.

whose success was flagged in 1982 with an essay about the "epidemic" of multiples.[8] *Diagnostic and Statistical Manual–III* of 1980 placed multiple personality disorder in its taxonomy and provided clear criteria.[9] It said that the disorder was rare; this qualification is modified in the revised manual, *DSM–III* of 1989.

Students of the disorder began to recognize themselves as specialists in the late 1970s, with teach-in seminars at the meetings of the American Psychiatric Association. They established a newsletter, "Speaking for Ourselves." They had their first International Conference in 1984.[10] They acquired a niche in the National Institute of Mental Health, with a Dissociative Disorders Unit. They founded their technical journal *Dissociation* in 1988. The standard textbook was published in 1989.[11] Hardly anyone says "multiple personality disorder" any more. MPD suffices, proof positive that there is such a thing.

There are, nevertheless, complete skeptics. They say there is no such disorder, and that pulp publicity in the media conspires with psychiatrists in the multiple personality movement to create the symptoms. In the United States opposition is muted. The most vigorous American denial comes, strikingly, from the two psychiatrists who treated "Eve." In 1984 they inveighed against the proliferation of multiples, which they held to be real but very rare.[12] A distinguished Canadian psychiatrist has gone through the entire "canon" of multiples, rediagnosing each one as suffering from a less florid complaint.[13] Ottawa psychologists have shown how

8. See Myron Boor, "The Multiple Personality Epidemic: Additional Cases and Inferences Regarding Diagnosis, Etiology, Dynamics and Treatment," *Journal of Nervous and Mental Disease* 170 (May 1982): 302–4.

9. See American Psychiatric Association, *Diagnostic and Statistical Manual of Mental Disorders*, 3d ed. (Washington, D. C., 1980); hereafter abbreviated *DSM–III*.

10. "International" is a sign of empire building. Multiple personality is strictly American with Canadian branch plants. For proceedings see the March 1984 issue of *Psychiatric Clinics of North America*. The year saw this and three other major journals publishing entire issues on multiple personality, featuring central members of the movement: Ralph B. Allison, Eugene L. Bliss, Bennett G. Braun, Philip M. Coons, Richard P. Kluft, Frank W. Putnam, Jr., and Cornelia B. Wilbur. See *American Journal of Clinical Hypnosis* (Oct. 1983), *Psychiatric Annals* (Jan. 1984), and *International Journal of Clinical and Experimental Hypnosis* (Apr. 1984).

11. See Frank W. Putnam, *Diagnosis and Treatment of Multiple Personality Disorder* (New York, 1989).

12. See Thigpen and Cleckley, "On the Incidence of Multiple Personality Disorder: A Brief Communication," *International Journal of Clinical and Experimental Hypnosis* 32 (Apr. 1984): 63–66. Their treatment differed from that of the post-1973 multiple-movement in two ways. First, they elicited three personalities instead of many. Secondly, they do not link multiple personality to child abuse. Chris Costner Sizemore, the original of Eve, broke long ago with her doctors. She developed twenty-two subsequent personalities and took to the lecture circuit. See Chris Costner Sizemore and Elen Sain Pittillo, *I'm Eve!* (Garden City, N. Y., 1977).

13. See Harold M. Merskey, "The Manufacture of Personalities: The Production of Multiple Personality Disorder," *British Journal of Psychiatry* (forthcoming).

students with minimum coaching "spontaneously" produce the symptoms.[14] A British book is subtitled "An Exercise in Deception."[15] Physicians and psychologists have to be cautious in suggesting that the existence of the phenomena has more to do with their colleagues than with the psyche. In print, at any rate, it is left to Karl Miller, professor of literature, editor of the *London Review of Books,* and author of a stunning survey of manifestations of doubleness in the romantic period, to say of the first modern multiple, Sybil, what many say less artfully in private:

> As for the umpteen selves exposed in the Book of Sybil, it is safe to conclude that they are a manner of speaking, and of conjuring—that they are produced out of a hat in the manner of some strange fiction of duality, and by a trio of conjurors. Every life is made up, put on, imagined—including, *hypocrite lecteur,* yours. Sybil's life was made up by Sybil, by her doctor, when she became a case, and again, when she became a book, by her author. Sixteen selves were imagined. But it is not even entirely certain that there were as many as two.[16]

Note how the "diagnostic" question runs into the "medical" question. Miller is doubting that the first paradigm modern multiple, Sybil, had even two personalities: by implication, there is no such "disease." But we can usefully separate the two doubts, and can also sort out several questions portmanteau'd into "does multiple personality exist?" Some have clear answers. Different kinds of evidence bear on each. In general, there is less a question about evidence than about questions, although of course the positivist equation is right: the meaning of a sentence is its method of verification. You can't grasp one without the other. Becoming clearer about evidence and becoming clearer about meanings are one of a piece. Here it suffices to distinguish three versions of "does multiple personality exist?" They concern state, criteria, and therapy.

a) *State:* Is multiple personality a real, objective state of some people, perhaps connected with some, we hope, identifiable neurological, biochemical, or physiological abnormality?

b) *Criteria:* Is there a set of core behavioral criteria, applicable at least across a substantial part of Western culture, and such that these criteria are satisfied in sufficiently many different times and places to suppose that

14. See Nicholas P. Spanos, John R. Weekes, and Lorne D. Bertrand, "Multiple Personality: A Social Psychological Perspective," *Journal of Abnormal Psychology* 94 (Aug. 1984): 362–76. See also Spanos et al., "Hypnotic Interview and Age Regression Procedures in the Elicitation of Multiple Personality Symptoms: A Simulation Study," *Psychiatry* 49 (Nov. 1986): 298–311.

15. See Ray Aldridge-Morris, *Multiple Personality: An Exercise in Deception* (London, 1989).

16. Karl Miller, *Doubles: Studies in Literary History* (Oxford, 1985), p. 348.

they single out one possible kind of behavior?[17] A positive answer might be noncommittal or even negative about the disorder being a "state" in any clearly understood neurological sense. It might hold that multiple personality is a response to the constraints of the militant forms of Protestantism that emerged in the course of industrialization.[18]

c) *Therapy:* However we answer the two preceding questions, is it the case that there is a substantial number of troubled people who can be helped by treating their multiplicity as a real part of their character, and whose therapy actively involved working with their alter personalities?

I shall discuss these questions in reverse order. The third can be left to eclectic therapy. There are good reasons for a cautious "yes" to (b). There are none for answering (a) in the affirmative—except that if, according to (b), some people behave as multiples, then it is a sensible research program to try to identify some features of these people over and above their overt behavior.

Therapy: Question (c) is a matter for the judgement of practitioners, and I shall leave it to them. Note that an eclectic could hold that there is *no* state; that the present rash of multiples is cultural aberration, an anomic response to industrial Protestantism, or whatever; nevertheless, in the present state of things it helps to treat some patients as multiples. Some disturbed people have seen multiples on TV, read pulp magazines, heard of sensational trials, have friends who say they are multiples. Even physicians who hate the present fad for multiplicity (as they might call it) could find it expedient to treat a patient along the lines laid down in a multiple personality textbook—and find that it works just fine. They might even attribute this to media conditioning of the patient.

Criteria: DSM–III has a set of well-defined criteria for multiple per-

---

17. I say "Western" rather than human because the idea of the integrated and unique self is primarily Western, and a splitting of the self has a clear place only in "our" culture. In addition to the three questions above, about the "existence" of multiple personality, one can distinguish several others, for example, about the extent to which it is a purely "cultural" phenomenon, as suggested in the final chapter of Kenny's *Ansel Bourne,* and Aldridge-Morris's *Multiple Personality.* I extend this list of "kinds of existence" in "Multiple Personality Disorder and Its Hosts."

18. In *Ansel Bourne* Kenny argues that American nineteenth- and early twentieth-century multiplicity was a response to American Protestantism. But his eponymous born-again (a triple pun) preacher Ansel Bourne, hero of William James, was not a multiple in the sense of this paper. He had a "fugue." It may seem odd for me to add "industrial" to Kenny's "Protestant" when, for example, the famous Mary Reynolds, the first American multiple, grew up in "the wilds of Pennsylvania." But her parents had left England more for political than for religious reasons, insofar as those can be separated, and in immediate response to the industrial riots of Manchester in 1796. All well-documented multiples are instance of the detritus of industrialization. The French paradigm, Félida X, was a piecework seamstress, the trade adopted by her mother when her father, first mate on a merchant vessel, was drowned at sea. Our Bernice grew up in a small town south of booming Youngstown, Ohio; the father of her tubercular, diphtheria-ridden family was a petty accountant and the mother a telephone operator.

sonality disorder. A growing number of practitioners encounter more and more patients who satisfy the criteria. That does not impress the skeptics, who believe that "multipliers" train their patients. One might even note, sardonically, that one of the symptoms of multiplicity is that the patient has been diagnosed as suffering from a wide range of other ailments! Skeptics observe that industrial societies such as France, outside the sphere of influence of the American Psychiatric Association, never see a multiple. That puts anyone in a bind who critically asks whether *DSM–III* criteria are "really" satisfied by anyone untouched by the media or by the movement. What is one left with? History. For me the most powerful piece of evidence has been the discovery of a whole tradition of multiples entirely outside the "canon" published in the literature of the movement.[19] The reporters were not part of any movement, and had no interest in multiplying multiples. The cases so well fit the criteria that I say, "Yes, this is a way to be crazy, at least in an industrial/romantic, Protestant society." In that modest sense, I assert, *there is such a thing as multiple personality.* In just that sense I can go on to ask, "Was Bernice another individual suffering from multiple personality disorder?" This is perfectly consistent with admitting that every single case might be diagnosed as suffering from some other complaint, and in particular admitting that she could also fit under another set of criteria for some other malady. I shall give ample evidence that she was a multiple, but such is the nature of this evidence that its role is to characterize her in such a way, not to settle her nature eternally.

State: If there is such a thing as multiple personality, there is good reason to look for something over and above a set of behaviors. The one fixed point in the modern movement is etiology: multiplicity is caused by childhood trauma, chiefly child sexual abuse. Hardly any abused children become multiples, so that does not take us very far in defining a "state." Every generation of multipliers has produced speculations about the physical condition of persons suffering from multiple personality disorder. These are, uniformly, a pastiche on some current science. Goddard is typical:

> If we turn our attention to the neurological aspect once more, we know that the brain neurons are storehouses of energy, that a minute stimulus such as the finest particles of matter that impinge upon the nerves in the mucous membrane of the nose may start an immense amount of nerve action. We may even have what is called by Cajal, avalanche conduction. . . . Now suppose that these cell bodies which are the supposed storehouses of energy are, as a result of physical dis-

19. In "Multiple Personality Disorder and Its Hosts" I mention some hitherto unnoticed medical descriptions of the mid-nineteenth century, which with awesome accuracy conform to the criteria set forth in *DSM–III*.

ease or weakness, possessed not of their full quota of energy, but barely enough, let us say, to start the next neuron into activity. Not enough to flood it but barely enough to set it going. Moreover, it in its turn can barely stimulate the next one. And wherever the axon of one nerve cell is in contact with two or three dendrites, instead of having sufficient energy to arouse them all at once, it will arouse only one, and that will be the one where the synaptic resistance is least. ["CDP," p. 189][20]

Got it? After a bit more about the neurokyme and so on, we get two neurologically disconnected bodies of memories. The same kind of writing occurs today, but now we have quarks and gluons cropping up in the multiple personality literature.[21] The double cerebellum hypothesis has been going the rounds since 1844—two souls, because of two disconnected brains.[22] Commisurotomy gave a recent boost to that old idea. There has been rubbish about alpha-rhythms (one characteristic rhythm for each personality).[23] It has been said that myopic multiples change their requisite eyeglass correction as they switch from state to state. Most leading advocates of multiple personality now stay clear of all that.

Bernice Was a Multiple Personality

There are three kinds of evidence for this, each taken from Goddard's own description of the case. The three kinds of evidence are:

DSM–III criteria: Bernice exemplified almost everything *DSM–III* says about multiple personality disorder.[24]

Additional current criteria: She confirmed many beliefs about multiples that have been cherished by the multiple personality movement of the 1980s.

20. Phony science is usually a vehicle for moral interpretation as well. Bernice had "a nervous system deficient in energy" ("CDP," p. 191). Protestant, or in Goddard's case Quaker, values have been foisted upon neurology: Bernice does not have that cardinal vice, lack of energy, but her nervous system does.

21. No kidding. See Bennett G. Braun, "Toward a Theory of Multiple Personality and Other Dissociative Phenomena," *Psychiatric Clinics of North America* 7 (Mar. 1984): 171–93, with the message in a footnote, "The implication of this is that as we are constructed of subatomic particles, we must follow the basic rules of physics" (p. 177).

22. See Arthur Ladbroke Wigan, *A New View of Insanity: The duality of the mind proved by the structure, functions, and diseases of the brain, and by the phenomena of mental derangement, and shown to be essential to moral responsibility* (London, 1844).

23. If anything, nonmultiples vary more than multiples in their rhythms. See Philip M. Coons, Victor Milstein, and Carma Marley, "EEG Studies of Two Multiple Personalities and a Control," *Archives of General Psychiatry* 39 (July 1982): 823–25.

24. I use *DSM–III* rather than the revised version of 1989. The latter differs chiefly in making it *easier* to satisfy the main criteria, in increasing the possible number of alters to 100, and in allowing that the disorder is less rare than suggested by *DSM–III*.

Relative innocence: On present evidence the case of Bernice cannot be successfully criticized along any of the lines used by skeptics about multiple personality.

Relative Innocence

Skeptics worry about patients imitating and thereby faking symptoms, and about doctors training patients. Nothing in multiple personality is proof against doubts, but the Goddard-Bernice case is as clean as any 1920s case of multiplicity could possibly be. Bernice was an avid reader of newspapers and loved going to the movies. But Goddard was pretty careful about faking, and has a serious discussion of the one incident that he found suspect, quite late in his treatment (see *TS*, pp. 153–54). Bernice was sent to Goddard's bureau because from 10 September she had gone into a trance and repeatedly waked as a four-year-old named "Polly." She had been visiting a family that had adopted her baby sister. The family became so desperate that they had Bernice committed, and she was sent by a court order to Goddard's bureau, which specialized in adolescents with mental or criminal problems. Until she arrived, no one in the bureau had the slightest interest in multiples. This is not a case of a clinic finding patients that suit it.

Skeptics worry that the doctors who treat multiple personality are in the grip of a theory. They make suggestions, often using hypnosis, to encourage new personalities or to revive lost memories. Goddard had the opposite vice, a certain grim positivism: "When a child is naturally timid or has acquired an unreasonable fear, the method is not to argue with him persistently but as far as possible to ignore it. In other words, *to help him to forget it,* because, as we have already seen, what is forgotten has no effect upon the personality" (*TS*, p. 208). Goddard was trained at Clark University by G. Stanley Hall, the man who made American psychology a science of measurement. His own contribution was the measurement of intelligence. He brought Alfred Binet's tests to America, sponsoring the translation of Binet's work.[25] It was he who, with Lewis Terman, legitimated intelligence testing by the tests designed for the American draft in World War I. After the war, when Goddard took a job at the Ohio Bureau of Juvenile Research, he was preoccupied by tests to administer to juvenile delinquents.

25. Under Goddard's sponsorship his assistant at the Vineland Training School, New Jersey, Elizabeth S. Kite translated all of the work of Binet and Théodore Simon on intelligence and the feebleminded—a total of 664 pages: *The Development of Intelligence in Children* (Baltimore, 1916), and *The Intelligence of the Feeble-Minded* (Baltimore, 1916). He had cultivated, even hero-worshiped, Binet during a visit to France in 1908. Now Binet had been much interested in multiple personality—see his *Les Altérations de la personnalité* (Paris, 1892)—but there is no indication that Goddard's interests, in 1908, went beyond intelligence.

Spiritism played a major role in American multiple personality, starting with William James. It was guessed that alternate personalities might be good mediums, excellent at extrasensory perception, or even reincarnations of the dead.[26] Goddard was dead against ghosts, and repeatedly emphasized in his book and newspaper interviews that "Polly" had nothing to do with the supernatural.

There is only one ground for suspecting that Goddard was a closet multiplier. He was an associate editor of Morton Prince's *Journal of Abnormal Psychology*. The editorial board was pretty eclectic—William McDougall was also on it and Ernest Jones had only just quit in a huff. Prince was indeed the prince of the old American multiple movement, which had fallen on sad times for lack of multiples. Prince did strongly encourage Goddard to write up the case for the *Journal*.[27] He used the tricks of Prince and his French predecessors—lots of hypnotism. But there is no reason to think that he suggested personalities that had not emerged spontaneously. Nor is there any reason to think he much adapted his story to please Prince.

This is not to say he did not use Bernice when she arrived in September 1921. He was badly in need of good press to divert attention from problems at the Bureau. It had gone through a bad patch earlier in the year, with half the staff quitting, and "rumors and reports in daily papers concerning the conditions existing at present in the Department of the Juvenile Research." The legislature cut Goddard's salary from $7,500 to $4,000.[28] The publicity attaching to "Polly" was surely a godsend.

The chief message of Goddard's book was completely unconnected with duality. He wanted more child welfare, and more care for parents to ensure healthy children. He concludes quoting a celebrated tirade by Dr. J. N. Hurty of Indiana on the indifference of that state to children and mothers: a heavy-handed parable about how funds are always available for sick hogs, but not for sick mothers and children. "'*MORAL:* Be a hog and be worth saving'" (*TS*, p. 197). Goddard wanted state support for families, and, immediately, for the Bureau of Juvenile Research.

In short: Goddard was a very ordinary professional person with a

26. Although this was primarily an American interest, it began in France where Charles Richet "borrowed" a famous multiple of Paul Janet's and used her in the first randomized experiments of parapsychology in 1885. See Hacking, "Telepathy: Origins of Randomization in Experimental Design," *Isis* 79 (Sept. 1988): 427–51.

27. Goddard, letter to William H. Pritchard, 29 Jan. 1927, HHG: "Some four years ago I reported the case at the meeting of the Psychological Association. Dr. Prince was present and asked me for an article on the subject; which I promised him. I never got to the point where I felt ready to write it. But the managing editor kept writing me until finally I hastily prepared the article to get rid of him."

28. This was a highly unedifying fight, to some extent caused by Goddard, with subordinates accusing each other, for example, of "postmenopausal insanity" (HHG). The quotation is from the *Ohio State House Journal*, 29 Apr. 1921, p. 817. The salary cut was after the 20 May appropriations sessions.

commonplace bundle of virtues, vices, abilities, and blind spots. I shall later show that he lied in his article about Bernice, but that fact does not show that the entire case is an artifact. The lies are humdrum ones, claims to greater success and competence than were warranted. My story is banal, the actors dull, Goddard bland, Bernice pathetic. But it is not a story in which the patient has fabricated her disease or the doctor cultivated it; we are unlikely to find a much more innocent story in the annals of multiple personality.

DSM–III *Criteria*

DSM-III defined multiple personality disorder as "the existence within the individual of two or more distinct personalities, each of which is dominant at a particular time" (*DSM–III*, p. 257). Moreover "the personality that is dominant at any particular time determines the individual's behavior" (*DSM–III*, p. 259). Goddard said of Bernice and her four-year-old alter Polly that each was "complex and integrated with its own unique behavior patterns and social relationships" (*DSM–III*, p. 259). We can pair off Goddard's report and the words of *DSM–III* as follows.

"The individual personalities are nearly always quite discrepant and frequently seem to be opposites"—"a quiet, retiring spinster" and "flamboyant, promiscuous bar habitué" being given as instances (*DSM–III*, p. 257). "The contrast of the two personalities was most marked" ("CDP," p. 173). In general Polly was "loud, coarse, wilful, emotional, changeable, disobedient, selfish, egotistical, excitable and unreasonable" ("CDP," p. 174). Adjectives applied to Bernice include: attractive, modest, almost diffident, very neat, of excellent intelligence, generous almost to a fault, unselfish, absolutely truthful, good taste in clothing, polite, well mannered, quick and accurate at work.

"Transition from one personality to another is sudden" (*DSM–III*, p. 257). The transition was usually via an intervening and very troubled sleep or trance. Polly's "going to sleep during the daytime generally was literally a fall. If she was standing she would fall to the floor as though suddenly struck dead" ("CDP," pp. 175–76).

"Usually the original personality has no knowledge or awareness of the existence of any of the other personalities" (*DSM–III*, p. 257). At the beginning of treatment, Bernice "had absolutely no memory of anything that had occurred while she was Polly" ("CDP," p. 170).

"The original personality and all of the subpersonalities are aware of lost periods of time" (*DSM–III*, p. 257). Bernice "found it hard to understand the lapse of time when she had been Polly for several days" ("CDP," p. 175). However Polly, who was four, did not have this problem, just picking up the thread of her life where she had left it, consistent, some would say, with a four-year-old's sensibility to time.

When we turn to *DSM–III*'s "associated features" we find that alters may be of different age, sex, or race. Goddard reports only age. "Each subpersonality . . . displays behaviors characteristic of its stated age, which is usually younger than the actual age" (*DSM–III*, p. 257). That was true of Polly: "asked her age, she said 'four years'. And her behavior was consistent" ("CDP," p. 170). The same was true of a less-developed alter, Louise, aged fifteen or sixteen. "One or more of the personalities may . . . report having talked with or engaged in activities with one or more of the other personalities" (*DSM–III*, p. 258). Polly said Bernice was " 'a friend of mine who is coming to see me'" (*TS*, p. 69). Five days after she entered the Bureau, Goddard tried to use automatic writing. He had Polly write a letter, which begins "Bernice is coming down to see me."[29]

"Psychosocial stress most often precipitates the transition from one personality to another" (*DSM–III*, p. 258). That was true enough in Bernice's story, as we shall see. "Hypnosis may also effect this change" (*DSM-III*, p. 258). To get his patient out of the most annoying versions of Polly, Goddard would hypnotize her and bring her back as Bernice. Likewise with the second alter, the fifteen-year-old Louise whom "we could bring back by hypnotic suggestion" ("CDP," p. 181).

DSM–III also notes somatoform disorders are common in individuals with multiple personality. In fact Polly behaved more like a traditional hysteric. She was usually almost completely anaesthetic. "Pinching, pricking with needles, tickling, etc., produced not even reflex muscular twitching. A needle thrust under the thumb nail to the root of the nail elicited no response of any kind" ("CDP," p. 175). She also experienced loss of various types of motor control, and a brief inability to see or hear. Goddard interestingly comments on the lack of those symptoms of hysteria that *DSM–III* calls somatoform. Persistent indigestion "seems more likely to have been a real disturbance." The peculiar thing is not Bernice's somatoform problems "but that there were not more of them during such a long period. This may possibly be accounted for by the youth of the patient and consequent poverty of ideas and perhaps also to the fact that we were also extremely careful not to suggest things to her" ("CDP," p. 185).

In short Bernice was a classic multiple personality. This does not mean that the diagnosis is uncontroversial. It is possible to rediagnose every historical multiple personality, arguing that there is no such disorder. I am observing only that there are a set of criteria that Bernice satisfies.

---

29. The letter, dated "New York, Sept. 10, 1921," is printed in *TS*, facing page 19. It is the only time the name "Bernice" (as opposed to the pseudonym Norma) can be found in Goddard's publications. The letter was written on 28 September. Goddard does not draw attention to the fact that 10 September 1921, the date of the letter, is the day that Bernice fell into a trance, after eating some candy, and awoke for the first time as a clearly defined Polly. Polly was rather obsessed with candy. Goddard does not note that 10 September 1919 is the probable date that Bernice learned of her mother's death.

1980s Expectations about Multiples

There is a wide consensus among multiple personality practitioners that *DSM–III* underemphasized or omitted important features. "An absolute essential criterion for the diagnosis of multiple personality is the presence of amnesia. Usually the original personality is amnesic for the other secondary personalities."[30] When she entered treatment Bernice "had absolutely no memory of anything that occurred while she was Polly" ("CDP," p. 170).

Virtually all recent multiples are highly hypnotizable, and it is conjectured that all lie in the upper quartile for hypnotizability on the Stanford Hypnotic Susceptibility Scale. Hypnotizability has been proposed as a necessary condition of multiple personality. Bernice was eminently hypnotizable. Then there is the matter of sleep. "Sleep disturbance is a commonly noted feature of MPD . . . with recurrent nightmares and terrifying hypnogenic and hypnopompic phenomena."[31] Bernice's troubled sleep is uncomfortable even to read about (see "CDP," pp. 175–77). Previous to evincing multiple personality she had severe sleep disorders, was hospitalized around age eighteen, and would sleep for two or three days at a time. She recalled problematic sleepwalking from the age of six.

It is now held by many dedicated workers that it is a necessary condition of being a multiple that there should be more than two personalities —that dual personality or double consciousness itself would be a freak. *DSM–III* allows that there may be up to 100 multiples, although most workers agree that there will be at most 10 or so readily on call at any time. The mean number of alters in a recent study of adolescent multiples is 24.1.[32] Old historical cases, it is argued, are merely "double consciousness" because one was not on the lookout for further alters and certainly they were not allowed to develop. Bernice had at least a third alter: "Much to our surprise just before Christmas," 1921, an alter of about sixteen presented herself after sleep. That was Bernice's age just before she had to quit school because of illness. Goddard thought she might "be the true person rather than" Bernice ("CDP," p. 181). But he decided that this was simply amnesia, a part of her that had forgotten what had passed in the last three years. Hence "we ceased to encourage it, and after a period of perhaps a couple of weeks this personality never appeared again" ("CDP," p. 182). Louise is not named in the 1926 article, and only appears in a couple of paragraphs. In the 1927 book she obtains two chapters, or 48 pages of a 215-page text.

30. Coons, "The Differential Diagnosis of Multiple Personality," *Psychiatric Clinics of North America* 7 (Mar. 1984): 53.

31. Putnam, *Diagnosis and Treatment of Multiple Personality Disorder*, p. 59.

32. See Paul F. Dell and James W. Eisenhower, "Adolescent Multiple Personality Disorder: A Preliminary Study of Eleven Cases," *Journal of the American Academy of Child and Adolescent Psychiatry* 29 (May 1990): 359–66.

Today's multiple therapist might criticize Goddard for not developing Louise, but she does confirm the doctrine of "more-than-two." On the
other hand Bernice was mercifully free of persecuting alters, which are
nowadays found in the majority of multiple personality patients. In the
recent survey of adolescents, "all patients had angry protector alters,
depressed alters, scared alters, and child alters."[33] They "appear to have
become alter at a mean age of about three years." I shall discuss this later
when contemplating a fictitious Bernice in 1990.

I have already stated the most firmly entrenched item of 1980s theory of multiplicity: the disorder is caused by childhood trauma. There is
no strong evidence that Bernice was cruelly treated or viciously neglected
in early life, but she had a ghastly childhood for all that. Siblings dropped
dead like flies. She had an identical twin Beatrice. They were the oldest of
ten children. She had an identity problem from the start; the parents
could not tell the twins apart and her mother would force Beatrice's medicine on Bernice by mistake. Or was this neglect, anger, or punishment, as
we might hear from many a child abuse investigator today? More charita-
bly, we should think about a tubercular mother looking after a tubercular
father and a raft of sick children. The twins became deathly ill of diph-
theria at age ten. Beatrice died. Bernice "seems to have had a fairly happy
early childhood, though always frail; her first grief came at ten when her
twin sister died" ("CDP," p. 182).

Bernice's menarche was at thirteen years, three months; she "was
greatly frightened at her first experience" ("CDP," p. 182). Tuberculosis
was rampant in the family, killing two other siblings; the father went to a
sanitarium when she was fifteen and died in a year. Her mother too had
TB during that time, leaving Bernice with a lot of responsibility for sick
and dying children; Betty Jane, the youngest, would have been one year
old at the time. The family was broken up when mother also went to the
sanitarium; she died when Bernice was seventeen. She worked as a house-
cleaner in a rotting old home where she was scared of intruders; in an
attempt to conquer this fear her employer repeatedly mocked, tricked,
and terrified her. At eighteen the girl had a breakdown whose chief manifestation was sleep. After hospitalization the ever-decent if ailing Bernice
was sent to a charity home "which deals mainly with girls who have fallen
morally" ("CDP," p. 186). There was no shortage of trauma, and we suspect Goddard of insensitivity when he suggests all went well before she
was ten, just because she could not recall earlier unhappiness.

In addition to abuse or neglect, it is now standardly expected that a
multiple will have experienced severe caretaker sexual abuse, typically
from a trusted person. Goddard thought not, but most readers will infer
from his account that Bernice was sexually molested and quite probably
raped by her father when she was fourteen. If Goddard were to deliver his

33. Ibid., p. 359.

paper as a lecture today, he would be hooted off the podium by militants in the audience.

Hallucinosis Incestus Patris

In addition to these [minor hysterical symptoms], there were other manifestations, such as one expects to find in a psychogenic case. For example, we had a marked case of transference, which finally ended as abruptly as it began. The vita sexualis was manifested through a hallucinosis incestus patris. This was somewhat unusual in its persistence and in the fact that it was concurred in by all the personalities and in hypnosis. She had told this in the home where she was staying before she came to us and it was reported to me by them as one of her unfortunate experiences. She told it to me on the second day [on the first day she had been four-year-old Polly] and was evidently living through the imaginary experience in the restless sleep which we have described. There were many things to make one believe that it was a genuine experience and not an hallucination. But the fact that we were dealing with a phase of hysteria where, as someone has put it, when we do not find this particular hallucination it is the exception rather than the rule, this coupled with her statement that this occurred when she was fourteen years old, but had never been mentioned to anyone until she was nineteen and a half, compelled me to hold fast to the hallucination possibility, even in the face of the constant reiteration by all the personalities, as already stated. ["CDP," p. 185]

I am not aware of any more explicit case of professional "denial" of incest. Every detail makes it probable (to us in 1991) that Bernice was telling the simple truth. The girl's silence is to be expected and is not evidence for later hallucination. During hypnotic sleep she not only talked about the incident but acted it out. There was no need for any elicited abreaction to bring the event to consciousness; quite the contrary. She had already told her "home," and it is practically the first thing that she told the Bureau of Juvenile Research. She and her alters valiantly resisted his overt skepticism.

One becomes increasingly uncomfortable in reading Goddard. The "vita sexualis" is kept for the professional journal, and then the unspeakable sin is named only in Latin. The subsequent book omits this altogether. There we find something unnerving, absent from the paper. Polly began by giving female names to everyone in the Bureau, "Sarah" to Goddard. But in due course she came to call Goddard "Daddy," and later Bernice then did so, too (*TS*, p. 153). The one incident of possible fakery (mentioned above) discussed by Goddard involved Louise calling Goddard "Daddy" and then apologizing, "O! I forgot, excuse me." Today a psychiatrist with a patient who clearly and distinctly asserts she was raped by her father at fourteen would not treat this transference so lightly. Nor would he so unreflectively quote Bernice saying to him, "Daddy, I am going to do as you want me to" (*TS*, p. 161). Here is a dream of 2–3 October 1921, reported without comment in Appendix C to the book; she is in the Hotel Statler in Cleveland planning to go to the theater. "Mr. B. was her daddy"—mentioning the name of her baby sister's adoptive father. She is shot in the back by "a man dressed like an old-fashioned guard" (*TS*, p. 238).

Today a therapist would do a lot of work on the incest. Goddard thought of Polly's fascination with candy as just part of child's play. But maybe it is not so benign. Bernice did her first well-reported switch on 10 September 1921—eating candy. Rewards with candy occur so often in reports of childhood fondling and early abuse that this theme in the life of the patient would certainly be explored.

At any rate we can be rather confident that the remembered incest would, today, be reinforced in Bernice's mind as a permanent part of her life history. Goddard's procedure was exactly the opposite. Rather than encourage the memory of the parental assault, he turned it into self-conscious fantasy. "It was of course important to get at the truth in this case because if this were not an hallucination, it could be taken as an important element in causing the trouble, whereas if it were an hallucination, it was a result and not a cause. I was led to adopt the procedure which, I think, finally elicited the facts" ("CDP," p. 186).

Why was Goddard so skeptical? He thought that her acting out during her sleep was "incomplete," to the extent that although at first he "was fearful that other observers would discover the truth" ("CDP," p. 186), her acting and talking were not specific enough unless one was first told that this was all about incest. He next found that her vagueness and indefiniteness were "not due . . . so much to the delicacy of the subject as to her own defective picture."

He proceeded as follows. He avoided all "leading questions" and

the appearance of making much of the matter. I hit upon the plan of asking her one question at a time, days apart, until I was finally satisfied that I had gotten from her the complete story as it existed in her mind.

The story thus obtained was so clearly the imagining of one totally ignorant even of the human anatomy that any idea that it could have been a real experience was absurd. When I later explained this to her, putting it on the basis of a dream, she admitted that it might be. ["CDP," p. 186]

What was the origin of the "fantasy"? A year before coming to Goddard she had a partial breakdown and was hospitalized. She would sometimes sleep for two or three days at a time. When she recovered she went to a semipublic charity "which deals mainly with girls who have fallen morally, but who are being helped back to a normal life." She said she knew nothing of "such things" and was ridiculed by the other girls.

Vague references were continually made both by the girls and by their caretakers. No real information about the truth of such matters was given [so Goddard inanely hypothesizes]. This seems to be a perfect way to develop fears and fancies, to arouse abnormal cravings with no real knowledge or explanation to keep the balance. In her weakened state physically, it is probably only natural that she should dream that something had happened to her. ["CDP," p. 187]

Polly's Origin

Goddard thought he knew where Polly came from. When Bernice was in the abominable charity home for wayward girls, she visited her baby sister Betty Jane, then aged four, who had been placed in a happy family, in contrast to Bernice. It was "an ideal home where she was cared for and loved and favored, where she had everything that a child could want" ("CDP," p. 189). Bernice was visiting there at the time her duality began. She "doubtless many times wished that she were in the place of her little sister, dreamed by day and by night that she was in that position" ("CDP," p. 189). She had another sister named Pauline who died at age eleven, and "Polly" is some sort of wish amalgam of the two.

This is by no means implausible. Goddard could have added to his report the observation that Betty Jane had been adopted, and so the four-year-old herself had changed her name. Today a standard strategy would be quite different. One might guess that the Polly character was an "imaginary playmate," namely, a Peter Pannery person of age four who had never grown up. Current lore has it that the childhood alters of age n are either stages of the patient at age n—perhaps self-fantasies at age n. Or else they are imaginary playmates or companions of the child, usually contemporary, that is, of age about n. Imaginary playmates are usually benign—children with them are happier than the less imaginative who don't have them.[34] Nevertheless it is argued that given excessive trauma a playmate can become more and more real until it becomes a fixed role for the child to take on, and at least a latent alter.

Goddard's Therapy

Abreaction—working through—was plainly not a major focus of Goddard's work with Bernice, but it was there all the time as he kept on

---

34. See Maya Pines, "Invisible Playmates," *Psychology Today* 12 (Sept. 1978): 38–42, 106.

probing into the past. The attempt to restore memory by talk and by hypnosis is a standard feature of all the models available for Goddard to follow, including those of Prince, Binet, and Pierre Janet. He also had, like them, a clear conception of what a cure would be: it would consist in "bringing the two personalities together in a normal form" ("CDP," p. 180). His model was integration, not exorcism, despite his belief, quoted above, that events forgotten had no effect on the personality.

He tried three types of cure. First of all he tried to "age" Polly, in the expectation that when she became nineteen she would merge with the normal Bernice. This was done by hypnotic suggestion when Polly was asleep. Age regression in hypnosis is as old as hypnosis, and is also what encouraged the idea of abreaction, bringing childhood or adolescent incidents to light. Age progression didn't help much, and Polly usually declined to get up to Bernice's real age. "At different times in her history she has been eight and ten in fact almost any age for short periods. Generally, however, she was fifteen" ("CDP," p. 174). Goddard took her session by session up by half-year notches until Polly made a slip; while writing the ages of her brothers and sisters she gave her twin as nineteen, and accepted a deductive argument that therefore she too was nineteen. Henceforth she glossed over this. (This may suggest to our skeptical side that Polly was just playing along.) She now stayed fifteen-or-nineteen for some weeks (scoring fifteen on the Binet scale, whereas when four years old she was below four on the scale of "mental age"). This older Polly was thoroughly not the docile Bernice, but just like the four-year-old, "loud, coarse, wilful, emotional, changeable, disobedient, selfish, egotistical, excitable and unreasonable." In short, a pain. Then she woke up as Bernice, and mostly stayed that way for a while, but there was no suggestion that the two figures had been synthesized.

The second method was to hypnotize Polly every time she did appear, and telling her to wake up as Bernice. So she did, but Polly would keep on coming back. Moreover Polly disliked the whole business, objecting to going to sleep, for fear she would miss something.

Finally Goddard stopped trying to trick Polly and instead tried to get her to collaborate. She was, he told her, "well" only when she was Bernice. Polly demanded to know more about her older self, and so Goddard agreed to introduce them when Polly was asleep. When she was hypnotized, he told her she would know all about Bernice and remember it on waking. She did. Goddard then did the same in reverse. Bernice and Polly were made, in today's jargon, "co-conscious."

Various things then happened. When the patient awoke in the mornings she would be "herself," but she would assume more and more Polly traits as the day went on and she became tired. There was also the emergence of the new Louise mentioned above, who according to Goddard's article was not allowed to develop, but seems to have had quite a life in his book. Polly and Bernice collaborated almost spontaneously once they knew each other, and there is a general fuzzing over of their distinctiveness. Polly gradually agreed to disappear, and at the time of the report in 1926, that was how it was, despite the tantalizing observation that "there were, it is true, a number of interesting episodes which we cannot take time to narrate here" ("CDP," p. 182). There are more incidents in Goddard's book, especially involving Louise, but it is by no means clear what Goddard meant.

Therapy in the 1980s

Multiple personality therapists come from a good many distinct psychiatric backgrounds, but their practice is less different than their training. Integration, synthesis, and fusion are the watchwords of modern therapy. Child abuse has increasingly dominated the diagnosis, etiology, and treatment of multiples. Hence abreaction of the early traumatic incidents has become more and more central regardless of the therapeutic orientation of the physician.

No one today would try Goddard's first technique, of age progression for Polly. A few practitioners might try a slightly more sophisticated version of hypnotically "training" Polly not to appear. Goddard's third technique, in contrast, anticipates modern practice. Work with the alters. Try to make them co-conscious. When this is impossible, "talk through" one to the other, on the assumption that the other is "listening in." Make contracts with one or another about what role it will play in the immediate future life, and how it will not interfere with the life of another alter. Modern multiples usually come with one or more vicious alters. Suicide— understood as internal homicide, one alter murdering the body to kill another alter—is regarded as a real threat. Initial contracts are precise agreements with each alter not to hurt anyone. Then encourage mutual caring relationships among alters, so that in the end synthesis will be voluntary on the part of every alter, and no one will be eliminated, "killed." Some workers think that eliminating an alter, rather than having it join in the resultant soul, is a kind of murder.

The metaphors of killing and murder may seem too strong, but they were very present in Goddard's day. He went public with the case, giving the story to newspaper reporters on 1 December 1921. A front-page story in the *Columbus Citizen* has the subheadline, "Columbus Scientist Is 'Killing' Child Soul." It continues, "Science is slowly but surely killing Polly R. at the State Bureau of Juvenile Research here. But offsetting this, science is surely saving the life of Bernice R., 19."[35] The more sensational organ,

35. C. C. Lyons, "Young Woman Is in Turn a Girl of 19 and a Baby of 4," *Columbus Citizen,* 1 Dec. 1921. The paper gave regular reports from the front: "Girl, 4 Monday, Is 'Grown Up' Today," 6 Dec. 1921; "Polly Fights Game Battle," 14 Dec. 1921; "How Bernice Feels When She's Polly," 16 Dec. 1921; "Double Personality Girl Is Well Again," 12 Jan.

the *Ohio State Journal,* reported complete success on 13 January 1922, under the heading "Polly R. is Dead: Bernice Again Normal":

> Died—At the Ohio bureau of juvenile research Polly R., aged 4. There will be no funeral services, for Polly never had a body. She was the strange second personality which tried for months to steal the body of Bernice R., of Cleveland, and there is no one to mourn her passing.[36]

The Resultant Soul

There are two predictable ways in which a cured 1980s Bernice would be different from the 1920s Bernice. First she would have undergone a treatment in which a goodly number of multiples would have been activated and developed. With many therapists one can be almost sure that an internal helper and a persecutor would have been found. It is true that after fusion some former multiples forget a lot of what went on during therapy, so the remarkable alters fade away. It appears, however, that most products of fusions do remember at least five or ten persistent, recurring alters. This is no great feat because the alters are typically stock characters with bizarre but completely unimaginative character traits, each one a stereotype or one might say TV-type who readily contrasts with all the other characters. Persona-switching now happens much more suddenly and instantaneously than in the past. There is no need for a trance or sleep period between alters. The model is "zapping," of switching channels on television. One has little doubt that Bernice in the 1980s would be very much like this, and would, indeed, be an avid TV-watcher—I've noted above her repeated requests to go to the "show," that is, the movies, and dreaming of going to the theater in an evening gown. A cured 1980s Bernice would have memories of

---

1922. The story was also carried on the wires and appeared across the nation; at the end of *TS* Goddard quotes letters he has received from newspaper readers in Bloomfield, New Jersey; Pueblo, Colorado; Portland, Oregon; Chattanooga, Tennessee, as well as Phoenix, San Francisco, Chicago, and Bernice's home state.

36. "Polly R. Is Dead; Bernice Again Normal," *Ohio State Journal,* 13 Jan. 1922, p. 13. I owe the newspaper references to Ben Harshman, who conjectures on the basis of other stories that Goddard wanted favorable publicity over Bernice to obtain more funds for the Bureau of Juvenile Research, and, more widely, more funds for the care and education of the feebleminded. Or, as the *Citizen* reported more graphically in its lead story of 9 Dec. 1921, "Imbecile Menace in Ohio Grows as Politicians Quarrel over Spending Taxpayers' Relief Fund." Lyons, who was following the Polly story above, wrote on 12 Dec. 1921, under "Imbecile Peril and the Cure," about how 1800 feebleminded prisoners in the Ohio jails confirmed "the claim of Dr. H. H. Goddard . . . that every feeble-minded person is a potential criminal."

a bunch of stock characters, each associated with an original trauma, usually from early life.

1980s Bernice would also have abreacted her paternal incest in detail, and would almost certainly have recovered some earlier sexual molestation by her father or another relative or caretaker. We would not be surprised to find her remembering that she had been bribed by candies when being fondled at about age four. And there would be a good deal of attention to nonsexual trauma of which there was plenty in her family. In short, 1980s Bernice today, in 1991, would have a different soul from the one that 1920s Bernice had in 1930. Memories of matters fundamental to who she is would be substantially different, both in the variety of alters that she would recall from her therapy, and in the memories of incidents in her own past.

Historical Reality: Incest

Whose memories are true, those of the 1930 Bernice or the 1991 Bernice? "We will never know!" On the contrary, I think that we can know that some memories are true, some false, and that a great many others are neither true nor false.

Let's start with incest. 1991 Bernice knows that she was molested by her father and has worked through the vivid and painful events in great detail, grieving and making peace, as best she can, with her past. 1930 Bernice pretty well believes that the incest was a fantasy, and she understands where it came from. But what actually happened? Jeffrey Masson famously threw a monkey wrench into psychoanalytic complacency when he argued that Freud just fooled himself, or worse, when he retracted his claim that his patients had endured real childhood incest.[37] I do not share the loathing for Freud that has become fashionable of late. I am sure that *fin-de-siècle* Vienna was full of family sex that was painful to children.[38] We know that in recent decades there has been a great deal of sexual molestation of infants and youngsters by older family members, starting with siblings—possibly the most frequent perpetrators—and proceeding through parents, grandparents, and various collaterals. And I am sure that small-town Ohio in the early years of this century was no better than Vienna or Ohio today. One telling sentence is Goddard's, quoted earlier: "We were dealing with a phase of hysteria where, as someone put it, when we do not find this particular hallucination it is the exception rather than the rule." That is a stunning assertion. Goddard's fraternity of doctors and psychologists were finding that aside from some exceptional cases

37. See Jeffrey Mousaieff Masson, *The Assault on Truth: Freud's Suppression of the Seduction Theory* (New York, 1984).

38. Some facts and many speculations are recounted by Larry Wolff, *Postcards from the End of the World: Child Abuse in Freud's Vienna* (New York, 1988).

every single hysteric patient (or only females?) during a certain phase was claiming paternal incest. And it was an hallucination.

These women almost uniformly believed they had been incestuously assaulted. That is not something they could have readily picked up from magazines or the general vision of the age. Today it is commonplace, and one must be on guard against imagined events, but that guard was less needed in 1921. Spontaneously, it appears, and without collusion, all these patients said they had been assaulted. There are only two explanations. Most of them were in fact victims of incest—or there is some powerful psychic drive to fabricate such fantasies when one is in a certain state. Freud had a theory in which such a drive has a plausible place. Goddard had no theory. He faced two opposite poles: either the stories are true, or there is a completely mysterious and inexplicable drive in the minds of sick women to imagine they have been raped by their fathers. His fraternity resolutely denied what the patients said. In my unpopular opinion it was intelligible for Freudians to make the denial—but for the likes of Prince and Goddard it was downright dishonest.

Thus I assert that with high probability Bernice's assertion of father's incest was historically correct. But nothing is simple. The age-old relatively innocent conception of father-daughter incest is of consummated sexual intercourse. Since the mid-1970s incest has increasingly been used to cover many kinds of sexual abuse perpetrated by parents. Consummated intercourse is relatively rare compared to various types of "bad touching." The psychoanalyst who founded the multiple movement, Cornelia Wilbur, goes further: "chronic exposure to sexual displays and sexual acts during infancy and early childhood is abusive. This occurs when parents insist that a child sleep in the parents' bedroom until 8 or 9 years of age."[39] Some of Bernice's siblings and perhaps Bernice herself will have slept with the parents. Where else do enormous poor families sleep? But of course that's not what Bernice was talking about, but what she was talking about may not be clearly defined. Nevertheless, why should we not believe her? Because her account of intercourse does not tally with Goddard's idea of how one has sex? Under Goddard's tutelage, Bernice came to believe that her memory of it was an hallucination. After she had been cured, she had what I think were false beliefs about items of fundamental importance in her own past. Her soul had false consciousness, untrue memories—at least if Goddard's therapy worked as well as he thought it did.

39. Cornelia B. Wilbur, "Multiple Personality and Child Abuse: An Overview," *Psychiatric Clinics of North America* 7 (Mar. 1984): 3.

Historical Reality: Alters

We suppose that in 1930 Bernice had a memory of a Polly with whom she had made peace. In 1990 she would typically have a memory of a large number of alters, each connected with something experienced as dreadful, often early in life. In 1990 that would be part of her personality structure. Let us suppose that exactly such an array of alters could have been elicited from Bernice in the 1920s. Does the historical Bernice have false consciousness because she does not know of these alters, and knows only of Polly?

I think not, but yet another distinction must be made. Skeptics have always proposed that alters are a product of the interaction between patient and therapist. It takes two to multiply. But three distinct propositions must be noticed:

a) Every alter is iatrogenic.

b) Many or most, but not all, of the panoply of alters, up to 100 in number, are a product of the therapy.

c) The entire array of alters is a real part of the patient's structure of personalities.

Skeptics maintain (a). Most members of the community of multiple-doctors favor (c). You can see why. Members of the movement think (b) is a threat. If some multiples are products of the doctor-patient duet, the next thing you'll hear is (a). Skeptics are equally scared of (b). They fear that if they grant (b), anything goes. Yet (b) I propose is eminently plausible.

The multiple-movement readily grants that patients don't walk in the door with a host of alters. They are painstakingly ferreted out. In no way need we suppose that suggestion is the norm. We need only imagine that after a while it becomes almost routine to invoke a new alter to deal with a new problem that is in the course of being abreacted. It is curiously said that the characters of the alters are so vivid that only a great actor could sustain them. I do not suggest that the patient is acting. But the argument is fallacious. Stock characters are easy to act. They are roles that a patient can grow into rather than adopt. It is plain that the therapist moves in with the suggestion that a lot of alters are a good thing. "How many of there are you?"—that is a starting point. "I want you all to be listening now while I talk to the Terminator, even those of you who have not declared yourselves yet."

My remarks are not skeptical about initial alters like Polly. I have made plain my position—Bernice entered the Bureau of Juvenile Research a multiple. Nor are these remarks skeptical about the modern practice of multiplying multiples. It may be a valuable device for quickly abreacting a complex series of traumas. I am quite happy to agree with one of the leaders of the movement, Richard P. Kluft, that most alters are spontaneously produced by the patient in the course of therapy, and are in that sense not iatrogenic.[40] On the other hand, had the patient not gone into this kind of therapy, she would never become conscious of so many specific alters.

What's the difference? It requires a very philosophical statement. It is not either true or false that when Bernice entered therapy in 1921 she had a personality structure with more than one or two alters. It is true that she had at least one alter in September 1921, namely, Polly. It is also true that if she had undergone a 1980s course of treatment, she would have evinced a number of alters. If you like, multiples like Bernice have a soul that has the potentiality to evolve in that way, suitably reinforced. But there is no "actuality" in Bernice except this potentiality, which she shares with any other multiple. I believe that if Polly had met Jesus in the year 32 she would have jumped into the soul of a Gadarene pig and run to drown in the Sea of Galilee, but this too is no "actuality" in Bernice. It is a certain type of suggestibility. Hence, I say, in 1930 Bernice was not suffering from false consciousness because she knew of only one developed alter in her past, namely, Polly. There was no important actuality, in this respect, that was hidden from her by false consciousness. There was no psychological reality that was concealed from her. "Know thyself" may be a moral imperative, but "Know thyselves" is not.

Of course there is a quite different point. It might be the case that for a multiple, the easiest way to abreact repressed trauma is through the procedure of alters, eliciting one alter per significant trauma. So as a point of expediency, the great panoply of alters may be wanted, but not because they, as opposed to their potentiality, are an intrinsic part of Bernice. It is because without them it is unlikely that she will bring to consciousness things that are of deep importance to her.

In short: Some of Bernice's profoundly important memories in 1930 were false. Moreover she did not recall events in her past that a 1980s treatment would strive for. But her ignorance of a personality structure that would have been elicited in a 1980s-style treatment was not ignorance of any significant matter of fact about herself.

False Consciousness

What's wrong with false consciousness? Suppose Bernice's father had not died when she was seventeen and Betty Jane was an infant. Many would bet their bottom dollar that father would be after Betty Jane in a while. If so, Goddard would have achieved an evil consequence. Bernice, who might have given the alarm, is now silenced. She no longer remembers what once she knew. But the false consciousness is not what is wrong.

40. Richard P. Kluft, "Iatrogenic Creation of New Alter Personalities," *Dissociation* 2 (June 1989): 83–91.

It is the fact that Bernice was deprived of a crucial piece of information that matters to young Betty Jane.

False beliefs about one's past can have less dramatic bad consequences. Most of us find it embarrassing to be contradicted, even in matters of no significance. But in the story as told, there were no survivors to contradict Bernice. Sister Pauline had died at age eleven. It would be different had the treatment occurred in the 1960s. Bernice would be about fifty, and she would have a mid-life crisis indeed, for she could hardly ignore or hide from herself the news that incest is rampant, and all her old terror might be restored.

In the historical case, however, Betty Jane is safe (we hope) in her adoptive home and almost everyone else is dead. It is 1991; given Bernice's health record, I expect that she died before incest made the front page news. There was no occasion for any cognitive dissonance. One may feel there is the terrible danger that the whole incest thing would have erupted in her mind all over again. I think we have no right to think this more or less probable than that a 1991 cure will relapse. A great many do.

There may be no utilitarian argument to show that Bernice's false consciousness in 1991 is a bad thing. She violates the ancient injunction, "Know thyself." So what? Bernice has a coherent soul. It works, or so we are told. What better truth for her is needed? The therapist will say, perhaps, none. He is glad to get Bernice back to an almost natural life.[41] The pragmatist will say there is no need for some "historical" truth: Bernice's soul worked.

There are serious grounds for caution. Bernice and indeed Polly and Louise had a deep-seated belief about their father that was removed by another father figure whom they called "Daddy" for a while. Even if the belief was a fantasy, the destruction of that horrible belief about the father by a "father," leaving her no sense of self-trust, no confidence about her own inner springs of self-knowledge, would, in the opinion of many therapists today, have left all sorts of hidden scars on her soul.

That is a practical reason for doubting that Bernice's soul did in fact "work." But something additional is nagging me. We do have another vision of the soul and self-knowledge. What is its basis? It surely comes from deeply rooted convictions and sensibilities about what it is to be a

---

41. There's a slight dissonance. Goddard's article ends by saying that Bernice is quite happy working half-days, but in the book we learn "it will take time to bring her back to the point where she will be strong enough to earn her own living" (p. 170). In the light of the correspondence reported below, we see that is quite an understatement. Up to this point in the essay, I have been discussing a hypothetical Bernice as if Goddard's report were in the main factually accurate. Harshman has established that in May 1922 Bernice was working as a clerk in Goddard's bureau for pay. Goddard moved to a chair at Ohio State University in the fall of 1922, and Bernice soon followed him; from December 1922 she was for several months working in the University Hospital for room and board.

fully developed human being. We inherit an Aristotelian tradition of teleology, of the ends for which a person exists, to grow into that complete
person. We inherit a nominalist tradition, according to which personal
identity is constituted by memory. Any type of amnesia results in something being stolen from oneself; how much worse if it is replaced by false
memories, a nonself.

There is also a further consideration, connected with the kind of
material that is and is not in the false consciousness of Bernice. She has
been built into the male-dominated world of Professor Goddard, in which
fathers never molest their daughters. She is a tidy and polite half-day
clerk. Any possible autonomy of this already much-weakened woman has
been effectively annihilated. Things are not so great in 1991 either. But at
least with the consciousness that she would acquire now, and some serious
sisterly support, there would be some possibility that she would find a self
to which it would be worth her while to be true. But beware of cant: One
has no confidence that 1991 Bernice is going to lead a happier or even
better life in the rough and tumble of fuller knowledge. A truer consciousness may be a bed of thistles compared to which her historical false
consciousness was thorny, but a rose garden.[42]

Waiting for Goddard

When we examine psychological material, we tend not to scrutinize
the therapist, except in the rare case of a giant like Freud. Goddard is
ordinary. In photographs taken at the prime of life, Henry Herbert
Goddard (1866–1957) is severe, intense, fully bald. Later he was more
relaxed, with a full head of distinguished hair. Brought up as a Quaker at
home and at Haverford, he had a firm conviction of righteousness. He

42. I am well aware that I have scarcely touched on deep issues, of the sort addressed in
Donald P. Spence, *Narrative Truth and Historical Truth: Meaning and Interpretation in Psychoanalysis* (New York, 1982). For discussions of the realities of abreactive and analytic recollection, one can go back to Sigmund Freud, *Screen Memories, The Standard Edition of the
Complete Psychological Works of Sigmund Freud*, trans. and ed. James Strachey, 24 vols. (London, 1953–74), 3: 304–22. And on for example to John Forrester, *The Seductions of Psychoanalysis: Freud, Lacan, and Derrida* (Cambridge, 1990), starting at, say, pp. 205–6. We should
note, however, that recollections by multiple personalities are now in a state of crisis. From
1975 it was taken for granted that any recollection of almost any kind of child abuse by any
alter was an historical memory, the abusive event having caused the alter personality to
develop. But as the satanic or ritual abuse scare mounts, so do alters who remember some
very remarkable things. One frantic physician in Smyrna, Georgia, reports that half the
patients in his clinic, like most similar clinics in North America, "are reporting vividly
detailed memories of cannibalistic revels, and extensive experiences such as being used by
cults during adolescence as serial baby breeders for ritual sacrifices" (quoted in George K.
Ganaway, "Historical Versus Narrative Truth: Clarifying the Role of Exogenous Trauma in
the Etiology of Multiple Personality Disorder and Its Variants," *Dissociation* 2 [Dec. 1989]:
205–20).

invented the technical word *moron* for those who, on Binet's scale, had a "mental age" of between eight and twelve. He was capable of self-amusement, expressing delight when a porter on a Pullman car called him—a moron. He was the man who brought football to California when in 1887 he was an instructor at the newly founded and ambitiously named University of Southern California. Now that's a claim to fame: the first coach of the future Trojans. He avidly climbed the mountains of Europe, Colorado, and British Columbia. He had more than a passing interest in nudism and suffered from chronic constipation. He was fascinated by Egypt, the Dionne quintuplets, and wanted to go to the North Pole. He retired to Santa Barbara, after putting up a dogged fight against the retirement policies of Ohio State University. At the age of eighty-two he published a book about children of the atomic age. In 1953, when eighty-seven years of age, he and his second wife made the grand tour of Alaska, and he walked most of the way up Mount Rainier on the way back. He died peacefully at ninety.[43]

A good life, but: He had a strong influence on a piece of American history of which no one now is proud. His most famous book is the 1912 *Kallikak Family*, which developed from observations on a girl at the Vineland Training School, New Jersey, whose mother was of normal intelligence but whose father was stupid.[44] "Kallikak" is an invented name for the union of good and bad (Greek *kalos* and *kakos*). Goddard proved that for six generations back the paternal family consisted of imbeciles and idiots, and took this to establish that intelligence and the lack of it is strongly inherited. Worse, feeblemindedness is dominant, for when an imbecile breeds with a normal person, the resulting line is damned.

Goddard became an ardent eugenicist, possibly with more effect than his Quaker predecessor Francis Galton, founder of the English eugenics movement. He did favor sterilization of those of low measured IQ, but selective training was his motto.[45] He did research at Ellis Island on immigrants who travelled third class or steerage on the steamers. "One can hardly escape the conviction that the intelligence of the average 'third class' immigrant is low, perhaps of moron grade."[46] He did not think this

---

43. These personal matters are culled from the unsorted residual material in HHG labelled "depot."

44. See Goddard, *The Kallikak Family: A Study in the Heredity of Feeble-Mindedness* (New York, 1912).

45. See Goddard, *Feeble-Mindedness: Its Causes and Consequences* (New York, 1914).

46. Goddard, "Mental Tests and the Immigrant," *Journal of Delinquency* 2 (Sept. 1917): 243. His sample did not include those whom the inspectors at Ellis Island had already recognized as feebleminded—despite the fact that this had increased by 350 percent in 1913 and 570 percent in 1914 over the annual total five years earlier. Even so 40 percent tested feebleminded, of "mental age" between four and eight. The statistics for Hungarians, Italians, Jews, and Russians were indistinguishable. His most "intelligent" subject was a tailor who spoke four languages and ran a small business, with a mental age of twelve.

necessarily bad, so long as immigrants could be trained for work that Americans did not want. He became the darling of those who sought to control the racial stock of immigrants, and provided testimony to Congress.

His "methodology" in the Kallikak story has long been criticized, but not until someone took pains to find out who the Kallikaks were did it transpire that Goddard's genealogy and description of family members was as defective as he alleged the family itself to be. He presumed a lot of facts that are refuted even as soon as one turns to census returns, let alone family research.[47] These snippets of biography don't bear directly on Bernice. She was all right, scoring well on "the scale," one of us, not them. The facts do, however, suggest we tread warily. Goddard seems willing to have tempered his reports and investigations to what he expected to find.

The rather benign picture of cure—in terms of which I posed the possibility of a 1990 Bernice having a soul different from the real 1930 Bernice—is based on Goddard's reports. Are they honest? In the 1920s Dr. William H. Pritchard (1867–1936) was superintendent of the Columbus State Hospital (for the insane). At year's end, 1926, he angrily wrote Goddard about Bernice's time at the University Hospital before being transferred to his institution on 30 August:

> You will doubtless recall that during the latter part of the period, during which she was a patient at the University Hospital, her behavior had become very bad; that the "Polly" personality had been in the ascendancy almost continually; that her conduct had been such that she was regarded by the committing physicians, Dr. Wagenhals and Dr. McCampbell, as one suffering from an attack of Acute Mania; that she was brought to the State Hospital "bound hand and foot to a stretcher, and was held down by a canvas restraining sheet; and that she was boisterous and noisy with much loud childish talk and swearing." The article referred to states (Page 182), referring presumably to the period prior to her entering the State Hospital, that: "Gradually the Bernice personality became established and Polly rarely appeared." This statement is hardly consistent with the condition in which she was brought to the State hospital.

Pritchard continues by noting that "the hypnosis and other psychological methods to which she had been subjected" do not seem to have helped much; on the contrary, she got better in hospital after as little as twenty-four hours. "It would seem that the friendly routine disciplinary measures of the hospital, the absence of suggestions due to freedom from newspa-

---

47. See J. David Smith, *Minds Made Feeble: The Myth and Legacy of the Kallikaks* (Rockville, Md., 1985).

per publicity, and the common sense medical attention given this girl by Dr. Bradley should be given some of the credit for her improvement."[48]

We possess two replies by Goddard, a defensive one of three pages, marked "Not sent," and a conciliatory one of a page promising to make amends in the book. Neither rebuts Pritchard's version of the facts. Amends in the book are meagre.[49] We are told that during the summer of 1922 Bernice was in the country, stayed there until October, returned and was hospitalized at the University Hospital. It was crowded, and moreover she was used in teaching clinics where "hysterical symptoms were pointed out" (in the relatively cured Bernice!). She "began to have Polly episodes again," although she was fine much of the time.

> Finally, it seemed best to transfer her to the Columbus State Hospital where there was more opportunity for quiet and rest. The transfer was made on the 30th of August, 1923. Although she had been a very violent Polly for some days before the transfer, possibly induced by the thought of a change, as soon as she was received at the hospital, she woke up as [Bernice] and now for three years has been perfectly normal with the exception of two short periods when something disturbed her and the Polly personality appeared for a very brief period. [*TS*, p. 169]

In fact Bernice's fate was decided the previous day in Probate Court, with the laconic conclusion: "Case 45068—Benuice R.: lunacy."[50] The newspapers were anything but laconic. A Columbus paper reported that "a Mr. Hyde spirit won superiority over a Dr. Jekyll body yesterday when Miss Bernice R., 22, was committed. . . . So real did the assumed personality become to the young woman that she insisted she really was possessed of two souls in the same human body. The younger personality, she told the doctors, was named 'Polly.'"[51]

Goddard saved perhaps the choicest newspaper story for himself, the

48. William H. Pritchard, letter to Goddard, 30 Dec. 1926, HHG.

49. In the preface, after thanking various advisors and the doctor who took some X-rays, and another who performed a tonsillectomy, Goddard writes, "I wish also to express my appreciation of the excellent care and treatment [Bernice] has received at the Columbus State Hospital through the interest and skill of Dr. Pritchard and Dr. Bradley of that institution" (*TS*, p. ix).

50. *Daily Reporter,* Columbus, Ohio ("Daily Law Journal and Daily Legal News"), 30 Aug. 1923. The name "Bernice" was misspelled.

51. *Ohio State Journal,* 30 Aug. 1923, p. 1. The *OSJ* had been developing the theme since 2 Dec. 1921, under the headline "Jekyll-Hyde Parallel Is Found in Cleveland Girl." At that date Goddard had been optimistic: "Soon the two personalities which have fought for mastery of the same body will be merged into one and what is perhaps the strangest case which has ever confronted Ohio psychologists will be closed." Once again, thanks to Ben Harshman for locating the newspaper stories.

only clipping that he kept together in his files with his correspondence with Pritchard:

> Science lost ground to psychic abnormality today in one of the strangest battles ever waged. The center of the long fight is Miss Bernice R. For nearly three years master psychologists have been puzzled by two distinct personalities struggling to rule her slender body. . . . At one time about a year ago psychologists believed the girl's "baby self" completely "killed out." Recently the personality changes have become more frequent again. Today efforts of science to banish "Polly" came to an end. Attendants of Ohio State University Hospital where Miss R. has been a patient since December, prepared for her removal to the State Hospital for the Insane. . . . According to Dr. Paul Charlton, house physician at the University Hospital, Miss R.'s health is declining rapidly. She will be given good care, but it is not likely that the corrective work can be continued at the hospital.[52]

---

52. From an unidentified clipping loose in the HHG file, with the dateline "Columbus, O., Aug. 30."

Aristotle Re-membered

Jean Comaroff

The principle of division, splitting, or psychic disintegration was not restricted to psychopathology [in the nineteenth century]. Psychiatric institutions may be viewed as a social theatre whose significations were provided by their location within a wider cultural arena . . . Jung comments on the recurrent problem in Goethe of the "two souls," a problem taken up by many other German romantics. . . . The theme of split man . . . emphasizes the recurrent motif of the "double existence" and the *doppleganger* [as] a recurrent motif in nineteenth-century literature.[1]

"Even when silenced and excluded, madness has value as a language," says Michel Foucault; "one must regard [the] various aspects of mental illness as ontological forms."[2] Ian Hacking's paper ("Two Souls in One Body," pp. 433–62) presents an intriguing set of reflections on the story of Bernice R., who entered the Ohio State Bureau of Juvenile Research in 1921 at the age of nineteen. Here the director, a distinguished psychologist named Henry Herbert Goddard, "recognized" that she suffered from multiple personality disorder (p. 433). And during a course of treatment lasting nearly five years, he employed what were then conventional forms of therapy—talk and hypnosis—to try to "restore memory" and bring her "'two personalities together in a normal form'" (p. 450). Hacking pursues the creation of Bernice as psychological persona, working from Goddard's texts and practices, and from a welter of sensationalist

1. Robert J. Barrett, "Schizophrenia and Personhood," paper presented in the Department of Anthropology, University of Chicago, 9 Feb. 1987.
2. Michel Foucault, *Mental Illness and Psychology*, trans. Alan Sheridan (1976; Berkeley, 1987), pp. 80, 84–85.

reportage. Clearly Bernice was, as Lévi-Strauss might have put it, unusually good to think with. Hacking contrasts the treatment of this Bernice of the 1920s with that of her hypothetical double in the 1980s, showing that in effect, history makes multiples of us all. He suggests that in the 1920s, therapists tended to assume that sufferers were inhabited by two strongly contrasting personalities; they were also apt to treat reports of incest as fantasy. Between then and the late 1970s, the syndrome fell into disrepute. Recently, however, it has undergone a partial revival.[3] In the clinic of the inflationary 1980s, Bernice would be expected to play host to a much larger array of alters, stereotyped characters who would come and go like images on a TV screen. And she would probably be encouraged to "remember" her early history as one of "real" physical abuse by a close relative or caretaker. She might, indeed, be possessed of "a different soul" from that of her predecessor.

To his credit, Hacking seeks the source of Bernice's tale in its very banality. The perplexing interplay of these dull doctors and pathetic patients was grounded more in the brute realities of poverty, child abuse, and sexist discourse than in exotic conspiracy. But for him the case raises a dazzling array of larger questions, both philosophical and historical— "questions about evidence, objectivity, historical truth, psychological reality, self-knowledge, and the soul" (p. 433). "Why is it of value," he asks, "to have a self-understanding founded on true beliefs about ourselves and our past, or at any rate on memories that are not strictly false? To what extent is such self-knowledge based on evidence?" (p. 434).

Now this is no small agenda to address in one short paper, and it is hardly surprising that many of Hacking's questions remain suggestively rhetorical. As an anthropologist, I am trained in a somewhat different style of argument, one based on other kinds of evidence. I would read questions about the value of self-understanding, memory, and evidence as being issues of cultural ontology: Why has it been important to particular people in particular times and places to define and secure themselves in terms of certain notions of selfhood and certain sorts of corroborating practices? In a telling remark about the case of Bernice, Hacking says: "The more I know what really happened, the more I wonder if there is

3. See Milton Rosenbaum and Glenn M. Weaver, "Dissociated State: Status of a Case after Thirty-Eight Years," *The Journal of Nervous and Mental Disease* 168 (Oct. 1980): 597–603.

Jean Comaroff is professor of anthropology at the University of Chicago. She is the author of *Body of Power, Spirit of Resistance* (1985). With John Comaroff, she has published *Of Revelation and Revolution* (1991), *Ethnography and the Historical Imagination* (1992), and *Modernity and Its Malcontents* (1993). She is currently writing on childhood, "commoditization," and nightmares of the "new world order."

a 'what really happened'" (p. 434). I suspect that for many historically minded readers, this is less a matter of speculation than certainty. Note that I do not use *history* here to mean what happened in some objective, unmediated sense; I imply rather that what happened is inseparable from the conventions of meaning and power that shape the horizon of happening. In such a view, our sense of "truth" is always provisional, our evidence contextual.

The compelling case of Bernice, then, would prompt me to mount an argument more sociological than logical. By this I mean that I would be less concerned with exploring propositions about the "facticity" of Bernice's condition and its evidential basis—whether or not she and her doctor could be said to have fabricated her disease, for instance; or whether or not she was the victim of "real" incest. To me these are less significant issues than what Foucault would call the truth effects of the whole discourse. The first question I would ask would be why the language of multiple personality seemed meaningful to the early twentieth-century imagination. Why, moreover, has it come to seem thinkable again, as our century reaches its close? Multiple personality, from this perspective, would be no less fascinating or consequential a "social fact" if it could be "proved," in retrospect, to have been largely a matter of lies and conspiracy. In its time and place, many people have found it plausible; and even though its status as etiology has never been quite secure (a fact that warrants explanation in itself) it has been a viable enough narrative to configure lives and create evidence. It has resonated, if largely in the inverse, with contemporary notions of selfhood, sentience, sex, sickness, and science. My first concern, then, would be with how the syndrome achieved such verisimilitude—how it went on to incite the popular and artistic imagination. How, and with what consequences for whom?

Now it is true that Hacking's argument does lead him in this general direction, if by a rather different route. He concludes that, despite recent historical shifts in the discourse about multiples, the earlier Bernice cannot be held to have been denied some fundamental psychological reality by false consciousness; the multiple personality syndrome, he seems to be saying, was as viable an idiom as any for "knowing herself" in her world. But Hacking remains rightly uneasy with such extreme relativism: how effective *was* this discourse in making the patient whole? How coherent was the soul of "Bernice the multiple," and how might such coherence have imposed on her the values of a male-dominated world? Here Hacking calls upon an ally who seems to stand outside the shifting sands of the immediate past and the present; he reminds us that we have "another vision of the soul and self-knowledge . . . that comes from deeply rooted convictions and sensibilities about what it is to be a fully developed human being" (pp. 457–58). This vision, he implies, is our hallowed classical legacy—a teleological notion of the person that vests identity in recollection and sees false memory as a form of nonself. This Aristotelian alibi seems to stand erect amidst the sea of half-truths churned up by changing clinical practice; Hacking implies that it could serve as a referent, making it possible for us to raise certain questions about the falsity of Bernice's consciousness, old and new.

I am not entirely happy with this final move: I am less sanguine than Hacking that this Aristotelian vision is itself relatively free of the ravages of history and power; that it might present us (and Bernice) with a transcendent image of selfhood that is not enmeshed in the structures of industrial Protestant society—the very society that Hacking suggests was the breeding ground for the multiple personality disorder in the first place (see p. 439).

I would proceed, instead, by assuming that both these visions of the self—the Aristotelian and the dissociated—stand equally inside of history; that while they have held different positions within our universe of discourse and practice, they reciprocally entail each other. Neither is beyond the workings of power or the processes that reproduce what we today see as inequities of gender, class, race, or age. And both are tangible in our explicit philosophies, as well as in the mundane, technical aspects of our world—clinical or quotidian. Take the matter of psychiatric evidence, for instance. Hacking notes the paradox of such evidence: "clinical reports, letters and archives, and so forth" seem such plainclothes "carriers of truth" (p. 434). He sets about destabilizing them by showing their internal discontinuities, revealing, for example, how Goddard rewrote Bernice's memories and gave misleading accounts of the efficacy of his treatment. I would go further; I would stress that, irrespective of its content, psychiatric discourse itself constructs certain kinds of subjects—its medium is its message. As Bourdieu has said of biography, such forms of inscription create a particular kind of person—one whose ancestry may be classical but whose full realization as a discrete, rational, self-producing agent has been peculiar to the modern, bourgeois West .[4] Such a model of the self is constitutive both in the honor and the breach. It has remained an ideal against which countless categories of others—the mad, the indigent, women, children, blacks, the Irish, and a score of other colonized subjects at home and abroad—have fallen more or less short. Modern bureaucratic media (like case histories) are models of such developmental being. They imply a telos of becoming through a narrative that is by its very nature progressive and integrative. And such techniques, whether in the hands of doctors, teachers, clergymen, or whomever, produce both selves and counterselves: what is not singular is multiple, what is not concerted is "dissociative," and so on.

The logic "discovered" in the multiple personality syndrome, in short, is prefigured (if often in the inverse) in a plethora of practices,

---

4. See Pierre Bourdieu, "The Biographical Illusion," *Center for Psychosocial Studies Working Paper,* no. 14 (1987).

routines, and representations that have made and monitored the "modern" subject. For despite its dominant stereotype, this subject has never been all-pervasive or unambiguous. In fact, nineteenth-century social and psychiatric thought seemed to pivot on a tension between two concepts of personhood—the ego unified and indivisible, and the ego fractured and divided. Both multiple personality syndrome and schizophrenia were to embody this conflict, and in this regard, both were cut from the same cultural cloth. Indeed, the two have often not been clearly separable in psychiatric theory and practice, a fact that highlights the shifting, contextual nature of the categories themselves.[5] Milton Rosenbaum argues, for instance, that between the early twentieth century and the 1980s (the time between Bernice the First and the Second) multiples were all but subsumed under the sign of schizophrenia.[6] They have emerged again only recently in a postmodern climate where the reality of fractured selfhood has imposed itself even upon those in the mainstream.

In fact, it is instructive to consider the interplay between psychiatric discourses and the wider nineteenth-century arena. It was an arena in which romantic thought, no less than Durkheimian sociology, addressed the paradoxical coexistence of individual being and "homo duplex."[7] Complex links existed between such discourse and the world of everyday experience, a world rent by differences of class, gender, and regional culture; but a host of manifestations from spirit mediumship to hysteria suggest an intense preoccupation with the unitary yet partible self. The fascination with hypnotism and polypsychism also expressed the plausibility of split consciousness;[8] and spiritism, directly linked to the phenomenon of multiple personality by the likes of William James (see p. 442), played upon antimonist notions of mysticism. All this implies that multiple personality was not as distinctive a category in its time as Hacking's account sometimes implies; divided individuality was a major theme in nineteenth-century thought.[9] Such themes, and the experiences they represented, anticipated and structured categories like multiple personality and schizophrenia, as well as a range of other variations on the theme of splitting (like dissociative psychosis or *dementia sejunctiva*) produced by a rising tide of psychiatric professionals. All of these and more were ways to be crazy in an industrial, Protestant society (see p. 439)—at least at that moment. For it was a world still resisting the forces that

5. See Barrett, "Schizophrenia and Personhood."

6. See Rosenbaum, "The Role of Schizophrenia in the Decline of Diagnoses of Multiple Personality," *Archives of General Psychiatry* 37 (Dec. 1980): 1383–85.

7. See Barrett, "Schizophrenia and Personhood."

8. See Richard Noll, review of "Unity and Multiplicity in Hypnosis, Commissurotomy, and Multiple Personality Disorder," by D. G. Benner and C. S. Evans, *The Journal of Mind and Behavior* 5 (1984): 422–32, and "Multiple Personality, Possession Trance, and the Psychic Unit of Mankind," by E. Bourguignon, in *Die Wilde Seele*, ed. H. P. Duerr, *Transcultural Psychiatric Research Review* 22, no. 4 (1985): 237–40.

9. See Barrett, "Schizophrenia and Personhood."

formed monism and materialism, where spirit still intruded, even in bourgeois bodies; where bourgeois minds found meaning in parables like *The Strange Case of Dr. Jekyll and Mr. Hyde*. Indeed, the very fact that multiple personality was realized more in writing than in patients, standing at the intersection of case history, autobiography, and literary fiction, suggests its significance as archetype of modern selfhood.[10] If it makes palpable the fission that threatened the logocentric being of high modernism, the multiple personality syndrome may indeed appear apt as a sign of our current times.

One last thought: it is this status as archetypal antiself that might suggest a link between multiple personality and incest—at least, in our collective imagination. I limit myself to the latter in light of the problematic status, in our society, of the "reality" of childhood sexual abuse, an issue to which Hacking is very sensitive himself. In current debate about the nature of and evidence for such abuse, opinion ranges from the conviction that serious domestic violence remains rampant (if widely undetectable), to the suspicion that the zealous search for abusers has become a kind of witch-hunt.[11] Incest does figure frequently in reports of multiple personality, though at least some observers suggest its incidence might have been exaggerated;[12] obviously, the vast proportion of children diagnosed as abused do not become multiples. However, there remains a close association between incest and "split personality" in psychiatric and popular discourse.[13] Such fission is commonly described as an act of self-protection against the pain of abuse, a telling connection in a society that has sought the origins of selfhood in the oedipal myth and that has sought the birth of human culture in the incest taboo.[14]

Anthropologists have long stressed that notions of incest differ widely in time and space; in some unilineal African societies, for instance, it typically refers to sexual intercourse between people who share common descent stretching back as far as six generations.[15] As "standardized nightmare," such incest beliefs reveal the organizing principles and deepseated tensions in the worlds that produce them. Incest in Africa is often held to disrupt not only the physical and moral capacities of offenders but the integrity of the social corpus to which they belong. In our own society, the child—born and unborn—has become the focus of increasing deep-seated anxiety and debate; the child is the pristine but endangered

10. See ibid.

11. See the heated debate sparked by Carol Tavris, "Beware the Incest-Survivor Machine," *New York Times Book Review*, 3 Jan. 1993, pp. 1, 16–17, in the letters section of *New York Times Book Review*, 14 Feb. 1993, pp. 3, 27.

12. See Rosenbaum and Weaver, "Dissociated State," p. 602.

13. See Daniel Goleman, "Probing the Enigma of Multiple Personality," *New York Times*, 28 June 1988, pp. C1, C13.

14. See Claude Lévi-Strauss, *The Elementary Structures of Kinship*, trans. James Harle Bell and John Richard von Sturmer, ed. Rodney Needham (1949; London, 1969).

15. See E. E. Evans-Pritchard, *Kinship and Marriage among the Nuer* (Oxford, 1951).

citizen of a new world order, threatened by aborting mothers, abusive fathers, perverted child-minders, postmodern families, and the "liberal" forces of society itself. Incest, increasingly more generally defined as child abuse, is the epitome of that concern, linked directly to fears about the reproduction of an orderly world, one peopled by whole, rational, self-producing subjects. Is it to be wondered, then, that we find so intimate a link between incest and the deconstruction of the viable self; that incest is the paradigmatic act that splits the atom of coherent, modern personhood? Are incest and multiple personality not two predictable tropes in a narrative of counterbeing in the late twentieth-century world?

Aristotle Meets Incest—and Innocence

Ian Hacking

I wrote about two people, Bernice R. and Henry Herbert Goddard, because, as Jean Comaroff says ("Aristotle Re-membered," pp. 463–69), they were good to think with. We should be wary when using lives. It makes us forget people and their pain. It is too easy to invent grandiose intellectual schemes portraying the Malaise of Our Times, the Question of the Family, the Loss of American Innocence, and so forth. As we engage in the free sport of the mind, let us not forget the main event. There are people out there at least as troubled as Bernice, some being helped and some being betrayed by their doctors and therapists. I myself, in using Bernice to think with, ignored a part of her life. She was a twin whose twin sister died. Some would say that this had more to do with the form her illness took than anything addressed by Goddard, or by me.[1] Bernice, wherever you are, I apologize.

Comaroff has used Bernice to add some remarkable thoughts of her own. Just for a moment you can see each of us as a caricature, I as dod-

1. In a personal letter dated 7 March 1991, Denis Donovan, coauthor (with Deborah McIntyre) of *Healing the Hurt Child: A Developmental-Contextual Approach* (New York, 1990), wrote:

> Seeing Bernice as Bernice, a person with a history and a present, is very different from seeing her as a potential multiple. There is one very good and very simple reason that Bernice may have had but one alter, and you touch upon it on page 851. Among other powerful experiences that can demand of children extraordinary cognitive and emotional accommodation, Bernice is a *surviving twin*, not just a potential multiple. . . . Bernice is not really of interest to you as a person but as an example, a convenient case to do some cultural-historical comparing. "Is she or isn't she?" is the wrong question, as, in my view, such questions of nosological accuracy usually are. The real, much more interesting question, is: what do Bernice's history and behavior teach us, what sense can we make of them? And then, how can such understanding inform a genuinely helpful therapeutics, a problem solving therapeutics.

dering philosopher, she as obsessed ethnographer. The philosopher invokes Aristotle. The anthropologist ends with incest. My Aristotle seems gratuitous, but incest fits because those who diagnose or work with multiples *know* that childhood trauma is the cause of splitting. The trauma almost always involves familial sexual abuse. That means some sort of sexual interaction with parents, uncles, siblings, grandparents, or other members of today's extended family, such as baby-sitters and people who run day care centers. People tend not to put baby-sitters and day care in the incest box, but they should as soon as they think like ethnographers about what the family is. And "incest beliefs," writes Comaroff, "reveal the organizing principles and deep-seated tensions in the worlds that produce them" (p. 468).

I have one reservation. Incest marks a boundary: acts are prohibited to some people and permitted to others. Oedipus was forbidden to marry his mother, but there was nothing illicit about his father's wedding night. We, however, forbid sex with children to absolutely everyone, including other children. Is child abuse incest, then, or a new kind of incest, or not incest at all because not a boundary concept? Could the dominant aspect of child abuse be not incest but ravaged innocence? Is the primary vice less pollution (incest) than corruption (of innocents)? I shall presently develop that question, hoping to add another element to Comaroff's rich train of thought. But first I pause to emphasize my positivist attitude to questions of evidence.

Comaroff says it is "hardly surprising" that many of my questions remain "suggestively rhetorical" (p. 464). May I protest? "Two Souls in One Body" formally lists more questions than any other contribution to this book. Page 434 poses four specific questions about Bernice, each followed by a generalized question. The general questions are subdivided; the first, for example, is broken down into three questions on pages 437–38. I answered every one of my questions, with varying degrees of confidence and gave reasons and evidence to support each answer.

I did say that sometimes I feel that the more I know the facts of the matter, the less I am sure that there is a fact of the matter. Comaroff says that for many historically minded people, this is less a matter of specula-

---

After quoting a passage in which I compare how Bernice was treated in the 1920s and how she would have been treated in the 1980s, Dr. Donovan concludes, "And that is not what Bernice needed then, nor what she would need, were she alive and suffering today."

Ian Hacking, a philosopher, is a University Professor at the University of Toronto and the author of *Taming Chance* (1990). He is completing a book called *Multiple Personality and the Politics of Memory* (forthcoming).

tion than of conviction. I am less speedy than that. I distinguished a number of facts of the matter: Bernice was sexually assaulted by her father, contrary to what Goddard claimed. Had she been treated in the 1980s by a movement therapist she would have developed a large number of alters. I say on page 456 that ignorance of her potential alters was not ignorance of any significant matter of fact about herself—there was no matter of fact about how many alters she really had. More interestingly, although I am confident of some sort of sexual assault from the father, it is entirely possible that the paternal perceptions were very different from those of the child and that even by the time Bernice was nineteen—let alone seventy years later—there may be no fact of the matter about what happened between them. Thus my doubts as to whether there is a fact of the matter arise from carefully stated distinctions.

As for suggestive questions, Comaroff ends her own exhilarating discussion with the words, "Are incest and multiple personality not two predictable tropes in a narrative of counterbeing in the late twentieth-century world?" (p. 469). I can't answer that. I have no idea what "a trope in a narrative of counterbeing" is. I can answer a more humdrum question, "Are not incest and multiple personality two predictable obsessions of late twentieth-century America?" My answer is a resounding no. I take *predictable* to mean "could have been predicted." In 1970, not a single person did predict, and no one could reasonably have predicted, that tens of thousands of people would be diagnosed with multiple personality twenty years later. Incest is different. In 1970, someone might have hoped that an incest obsession, in the form of raised consciousness about familial sexual child abuse, was about to take off. In private people were beginning to talk that way, although incest did not go public until 1975. So the incest concern may have been predictable. But no one could have predicted that multiple personality disorder would have found child sexual abuse to be such a hospitable host.[2]

I am about to engage in rhetoric or, at any rate, innuendo. So I will not end this comment with the purest positivism. I do go as far down that road as I am able, even in complex psychological and cultural territory. What do I think is going to happen to multiple personality disorder? To answer is foolhardy; but what use is it to invite a positivist to publish in your book if you do not get him to do some predicting? In fact I will put prediction to an additional use—to illustrate how variable, in my opinion, is the phenomenon we are discussing. Comaroff has been very helpful in giving a global vision of multiple personality. I want her panoramic view to be accompanied by my own myopic one.

I predict that multiple personality disorder as we know it will go

---

2. For a discussion between David Spiegel, who chaired this section of the *DSM–IV,* and the Executive Council of the International Society for Multiple Personality and Dissociation, see *International Society for the Study of Multiple Personality Disorder News* 11 (Aug. 1993): 13–16.

away within a decade. This is quite consistent with maintaining the opinion, argued in "Two Souls in One Body," that Bernice suffered from *DSM-III* multiple personality disorder and that this is a real condition that troubles a great many people today—about three times as many people as when I wrote that paper over two years ago. Moreover I do not think that all dissociative symptoms will disappear. The dissociative disorders, of which MPD is an instance, will figure very powerfully in American psychotherapy, but multiplicity will not be the big draw. Dissociation will do its best to encompass terrain from which it is now largely excluded, such as the eating disorders. The dissociative disorders will be the troubles of the middle classes. They will encompass problems that are not routinely paid for by the coming scheme of national health insurance. Public coverage, abetted by the drug companies, will largely restrict its benefits to disorders that respond to, or are made quiescent by, exposure to chemicals. Multiple personality will have a place in the new configuration only through a revised idea of personality fragments. The doctrine of traumatic causation will be firmly in place, but a far greater role will be found for the psychological as opposed to the historical reality of traumatic events.

I have no space to give reasons for my prediction. As this comment goes to press I can record that the prediction is closer to confirmation than when I wrote the previous paragraph. For the very name Multiple Personality Disorder will be replaced in the 1994 edition of the *Diagnostic and Statistical Manual of Mental Disorders (DSM–IV)*. The official diagnosis will become Dissociative Identity Disorder.[3] I can also diagram one line of thought by stating an even more curious conjecture, that multiple personality will track many of the important events that took place a century ago, in the early days of psychoanalysis. I choose that comparison because it will be more familiar to the present audience than the recent ups and downs of MPD.

MPD clinicians encourage an entire personality system of alters, each of whom is a response to a specific trauma. The alters are to be worked on by enabling them to recall the missing trauma that brought them into being. Thus far we have caught up with Breuer and Freud, *Studies in Hysteria* (1893) and "The Aetiology of Hysteria" (1895). This regression to the earliest Freud is all the more remarkable in that Freud was long

---

3. On the idea that multiple personality needs a "host," see my "Multiple Personality Disorder and Its Hosts," *History of the Human Sciences* 4 (June 1992); cited in "Two Souls in One Body," p. 435 n. 3. As for prediction, the best-placed person might have been the late Cornelia Wilbur, the maverick psychoanalyst who treated Sybil (see n. 6 of "Two Souls in One Body"). In the course of a brief conversation on 21 October 1987, I did ask if she had foreseen how multiple personality would develop in pace with the child abuse movement. I understood her to say that she had not realized how successful the child abuse movement would prove to be. I cite this only as a remembered anecdote of which I took a note. The question was too brief, probably not clearly expressed, and she was doubtless too busy to reflect on the matter.

banned from the multiple personality clinic, and for obvious reasons. Mature Freud was, in the 1970s and 1980s, anathema to feminism, and since the multiple movement came to take child sexual abuse more seriously than any other branch of psychiatry or psychology, it wished to place itself close to popular versions of militant feminism. But now early Freud is back, and Breuer's treatment of Anna O. is commended.[4]

How close is the next step, the famous letter to Fliess of 21 September 1897, in which Freud abandoned the universal theory of child seduction as the cause of hysteria? Contrary to what has become a commonplace, Freud did not deny the reality of infant "seduction," but he did deny that it was a universal precursor of hysteria. Will this pulling back occur also with child abuse and MPD? One reason to suspect that it may is that in the 1980s clinicians were very confident of being able to "integrate" a patient or, at least, make her "functional" in no more than six years—a time comparable to psychoanalysis. But now there are relapses. Everyone remembers Freud's letter to Fliess as doubting the universal reality of memories of sexual assault on infants. But also Freud was depressed by the failure to make lasting cures or complete analyses.[5] The comparable threat to MPD is very real, even if it is at present discussed only in the closed corridors of the movement.

And what about the reality of the traumata? Freud was concerned with a handful of patients; in our media-enriched times we play on a bigger screen and we have to meet the public. The False Memory Syndrome Foundation was established in Philadelphia early in February 1992. I mentioned it briefly in May 1992, in my spoken reply to Comaroff. The audience seemed skeptical and amused. As I revise my notes in February 1993, the foundation claims over four thousand paid-up members. At the November 1992 annual meeting of the International

4. Thus in the standard textbook of MPD, Freud is mentioned only in connection with depersonalization and hypnoid states. See Frank W. Putnam, *Diagnosis and Treatment of Multiple Personality Disorder* (New York, 1989), pp. 15–17. A more polemical textbook published in the same year is more blunt: "Freud did to the unconscious mind, with his theories, what New York City does to the ocean with its garbage" (Colin A. Ross, *Multiple Personality Disorder: Diagnosis, Clinical Features, and Treatment* [New York, 1989], p. 181). But things are changing. Putnam has just published a popular article taking Anna O., the origin of "the talking cure," as a paradigm case of MPD. See Putnam, "Altered States: Peeling Away the Layers of a Multiple Personality," *The Sciences* (Nov.-Dec. 1992): 30–37.

5. Freud speaks of "the continual disappointment in my efforts to bring a single analysis to a real conclusion; the running away of people who for a period of time had been most gripped [by analysis]; the absence of the complete successes on which I had counted; the possibility of explaining to myself the partial successes in other ways, in the usual fashion" (Sigmund Freud, *The Complete Letters of Sigmund Freud to Wilhelm Fliess 1887–1904*, trans. and ed. Jeffrey Moussaieff Masson [New York, 1985], p. 264). To emphasize this "first group" of reasons Freud gave for his retraction is not to join the analysts in defending Freud against Masson, *The Assault on Truth: Freud's Suppression of the Seduction Theory* (New York, 1984). In my opinion Marianne Krüll, *Freud and His Father*, trans. Arnold J. Pomerans (New York, 1986) is compelling psychobiography.

Society for the Study of Multiple Personality Disorder and Dissociative States, members of the movement were running scared. There was much public speculation that a Very Rich Man was behind FMS. When he was unmasked the antimovement would fall apart. I do find the FMS Foundation suspect, but no amount of mere unmasking is going to undo its present momentum.

The false memory countermovement thrives on one of the populist wings of the multiple movement: the amazing surge of strange stories about Satanic Ritual Abuse.[6] Many of these bizarre tales seem beyond the bounds of credibility. Some are patently impossible. Movement clinicians, like early Freud, always believed the alters with their tales of terror and trauma. That confidence may now be shattered; like Freud, the movement may conclude that some of the memories are psychogenic. A more conservative tactic is to turn SRA (as it is known in the trade, that is, Satanic Ritual Abuse) into Sadistic Ritual Abuse. That might lead back to safe terrain, good old-fashioned systematic cruelty to children. But I can't tell. The language of SRA (whatever that stands for) is evolving faster than one can keep track of it. The buzzword is *programming*. Victims of SRA are programmed by their Satanic torturers to switch into different alter personalities; our task is to deprogram Satan. The rank and file of the movement will not gladly give up the archfiend for something as wishy-washy as sadism.

I find that I am increasingly local and cultural in my understanding of multiple personality. I attend to how the languages of doubling and multiplying have been in flux ever since they first emerged among the mesmerists two hundred years ago. That does not preclude a cross-cultural analysis, such as the one just presented by Comaroff, but it does invite a complementary set of descriptions. I began by noticing that what we commonly mean by incest is something that is prohibited to one class of people and permitted to others. Child sexual activity is forbidden to all. Now suppose the central metaphor is not incest but innocence. That invokes an entirely different vein of myths. It recalls the innocent Christ dying for our sins and the myth of Victorian Christianity about the innocence of the child.

The experience of trauma recollection, which always occurs in close work with a therapist or clinician, is very much like a Protestant conversion experience. It begins with the watchword *denial*. Peterlike, one thrice denies past abuse. Ever since Augustine, conversion experiences have been accompanied by confession. Here I don't mean the confessional, the place where the believer owns up to the priest. I mean the confession as a retelling of one's own past, giving the true past that one had been denying. Comaroff aptly recalls Bourdieu on the role of biography in scripting

6. For one resumé of this vexing topic, see Hacking, "Multiple Personality and Its Hosts," pp. 17–19.

one's sense of oneself, a modification of the more ancient pattern of confession.

So far, so familiar, therapy as conversion, confession, and the restructuring of remembrances of one's past. Then comes an almighty twist. Accusation. Your confession is not to *your* sins but to your father's sins. We do not have Christ the son taking on the sins of the world. The father takes on the sins that have destroyed your life, for he committed those very sins. We are not concerned with Jesus, the Sacrificial Lamb, but with an old goat, a literal scapegoat, the father, the Sacrificial Ram.

I am not suggesting that accusations against parents or family are unfounded. I am not a closet False Memory Syndrome advocate.[7] Recall that I believed Bernice, not Goddard. I'm on her side and on the side of modern victims. I am following Comaroff, asking if there is a more general symbolic representation of what is going on. I see multiple personality founded less on incest than on a Jewish and Christian vision of guilt, scapegoating, sacrifice, confession, absolution, accusation, and innocence. It is not surprising that Satan the exile is now near the head of the multiple table, for who is better qualified to defile the innocence of babes? Some victims recall Satanic assaults even on the fetus, a feat only He could achieve. It is uncanny how Freud's early adventures are repeated. He laid no stress on innocence, but do you recall how he had to revise all his early conceptions of the aetiology of hysteria, when he "discovered" that the babe is not innocent after all? We call that the discovery of infantile sexuality. Is MPD destined to step into even that Freudian footstep? (God forbid that it should revive the Oedipus complex; that would be too much.)

Comaroff sees our time as one in which the self is put in question and in which multiple personality is the perfect symbol of that doubt. She sees our time as one in which the family is in disarray and thus as one in which the most poignant challenge to the family, namely incest, is highlighted. The two strands join: incest becomes the cause of multiple personality. That is a powerful analysis.

Beside that I would place a more situated, historical, and Western suggestion. The West is not in a state of collapse. Its historic religion is not in tatters. For better or worse (worse, say we Aristotelians) the more vital Christian churches in America have never been stronger. Multiple personality is an essentially Christian complaint, a complaint in which both the Testaments play major roles, as in all fundamentalist Christianity. I'm not saying that multiples necessarily have religious backgrounds but that multiplicity flourishes in certain essentially religious cultures. When, in "Two Souls in One Body," I wanted to think about why memo-

7. For the record, I am a paid-up member of both the False Memory Syndrome Foundation and the International Society for the Study of Multiple Personality Disorder and Dissociation. Both fees are covered by a small research grant from the Social Sciences and Humanities Research Council of Canada, to whom I extend thanks for support in this work.

ries should matter, I wanted a non-Christian place where the current enthusiasm for memory as narrative (read confession) could be traded in for a well–thought-out pagan model of self-knowledge. When I began to ask, why is it important that we should have memories that more or less correspond to what happened in our lives, I turned (just once, and briefly, on page 458) to a more prosaic pagan figure, namely, Aristotle. Aristotle stands for a moral sensibility that is not Christian, not Hebrew, not densely involved in the rhetoric of confession and scapegoat. He had no illusions of lost innocence.

I was name-dropping. Comaroff notes that Aristotle is hardly free of "the ravages of history and power" (p. 466). He has certainly been used as a pillar of the Catholic Church and of other patriarchal establishments. His views about the relations between the sexes have been rightly trashed of late. Doubtless what Comaroff calls a "transcendent image of selfhood" is "enmeshed in the structures of industrial Protestant society" (p. 466). But who introduced transcendence? Not me. Aristotle is *the* philosopher of antitranscendence, of the ordinary. He is precisely not the philosopher of The Subject, The Self, The Person, all those phonies that live in certain high-minded philosophies. And with Aristotle we don't have to waste our energies in the currently popular self-righteous activity of dismembering The Subject. We desperately need Aristotle's awareness that if I misremember my past it matters to my sense of who I am and what I am doing. It matters to how I live and how I feel about my life. We need some such lowbrow pagan talk to pull our wits together in the face of that utopian-Christian rhetoric of lost innocence that forms the early 1990s language of multiple personality disorder.

Facts and the Factitious in Natural Sciences

R. C. Lewontin

The social structure of scholarly work and its rhetorical practices have given rise to the belief, even among the most sophisticated, that there is a fundamental difference between the concept and role of "facts" in science and in history. It is by no means clear that such a fundamental difference exists, and there are serious questions about the evidence on which that belief is based.

The problem that confronts us when we try to compare the structure of discourse and explanation in different domains of knowledge is that no one is an insider in more than one field, and insider information is essential. An observer who is not immersed in the practice of a particular scholarship and who wants to understand it is at the mercy of the practitioners. Yet those practitioners are themselves mystified by a largely unexamined communal myth of how scholarship is carried on. R. G. Collingwood, although primarily a philosopher, was immersed in the community of historians and understood how history is done, so that he has had an immense influence on our ideas about historiography. Every historian knows *The Idea of History*.[1] He was also a metaphysician, yet his influence on scientists' understanding of nature, and of science, has been nil, and it is a rare scientist indeed who has ever heard of Collingwood or read *The Idea of Nature*.[2] Collingwood's views of the structure of science had to be constructed in large part from the elabo-

1. See R. G. Collingwood, *The Idea of History* (Oxford, 1946).
2. See Collingwood, *The Idea of Nature* (Oxford, 1945).

This essay originally appeared in *Critical Inquiry* 18 (Autumn 1991).

rate fictions created by scientists and by an earlier generation of philosophers and historians of science who participated in the Baconian myth of the hypothetical-deductive scheme.

The asymmetry between historians' views of historiography and of science stems only in part from their positions as outsiders. It is the consequence of the depauperate view that *scientists* have of science. There are no equivalents in the literature of natural science of those pluralistic and ambiguous characterizations of history that appear in *The Idea of History*. Historians of science, epistemologists, and, when they are in a contemplative mood, natural scientists picture science as having a single mode and form. While they may differ radically on the question of what that mode is, running the gamut from Hempel to Feyerabend, each has a univocal understanding of the subject. Most natural scientists, and especially biologists, are really positivists. They rely heavily both on confirmation and falsification, and they believe that the gathering of facts, followed by inference rather than the testing of theories, is the primary enterprise of science. At times they speak highly of "strong inference," by which they mean something close to a Popperian falsification criterion, but this is not the modal form of biological work. They are daily reinforced in their view of science by reading and writing the literature of science. A scientific paper, at least one in experimental science, has a standard form, beginning with a brief "Introduction" stating the history and current state of the problem, passing on to the "Materials and Methods," and then to an objective narrative of the outcome of the experiment in the "Results" section. Then follows a "Discussion" in which anomalies are explained and the objective results of the previous section are explicitly related to the state of scientific theory. There is some leeway for speculation in the "Discussion," which is considered somewhat adventitious since, after all, the "Results" speak for themselves. An excessively articulated and discursive "Discussion" will be truncated by the editor in the interests of space. Indeed, a really good experiment would need no "Discussion." Finally, there is a "Conclusion" and "Summary" that state the new scientific truth that has been uncovered. More or less the same sequence is enforced by governmental granting agencies who prescribe a form for grant requests that must be rigidly adhered to if a scientist expects to be funded. So, even

---

R. C. Lewontin is Alexander Agassiz Professor at Harvard University. He is an experimental and theoretical evolutionary geneticist who has also worked extensively on epistemological issues in biology. He is the author of *The Genetic Basis of Evolutionary Change* (1974) and, with Richard Levins, of *The Dialectical Biologist* (1985). His current research concerns the nature of genetic variation among individuals within species.

if one's knowledge of science comes from a close reading of the scientific work, the same picture is reinforced. Science consists, in this view, of the postulation of more or less general assertions about causation and the necessary interconnection between repeatable phenomena. These postulations demand the gathering of facts: observations from nature or from the deliberate perturbations of nature that are called experiments. When the facts are in, they can be compared with the postulated relations to confirm or falsify the hypothetical world.

To be able to look behind the mask of rhetoric requires an understanding of the esoteric language of a science as well as a knowledge of the immense body of phenomenology that is assumed by the current literature of a scientific subject. But, in addition, it requires a quotidian intimacy with the practitioners. That is, we must be essentially one of them. The absence of this intimacy has meant that historians have accepted the scientists' unreflective view of how science operates. The attempt to turn history into a "social science" has thus been the attempt to lay onto history a model of science claimed by scientists and their positivist allies, producing as its ideal outcome a journal paper with the "Results" section written by Ranke and the "Introduction" and "Conclusions" by Ibn Khaldûn.

For their own part, scientists have views of what it is to do history that are uninformed by the discussions of historians and philosophers of history. They see history through the eyes of Karl Popper and share his disdain for the poverty of historicism, and thus are reinforced in their acceptance of the contrast between historical methods and the truly scientific process of conjecture and refutation mediated by objective facts. Consequently, they accept the view that claims history, being only existentially quantified, is not subject to refutation, while science, being a set of universal claims, can always be tested. Of course, the rise of the Kuhnian model of paradigm shifts has somewhat tempered scientists' attitudes toward refutation. They admit that there is a certain leeway for coping with inconvenient facts, but even Popper admitted that a variety of "conservative ploys" were available to scientists to explain away apparent falsifying instances. Whatever the popularity of notions about "normal science" and "paradigm shifts," the ideal of the "critical experiment" and "strong inference" remain the chief epistemological commitments of scientific ideology.

The Diversity of Scientific Modes

Before we can ask about the nature of scientific evidence, we need to look briefly at the modes of scientific statements. If one examines science as it is actually carried out, it becomes immediately clear that the assertion that it consists of universal claims as opposed to merely historical statements is rubbish. The actual body of scientific theory and practice is a heterogeneous collection of modalities, illustrated, for example, by the current state of biology. Putting aside the fact that living organisms are natural objects subject to the general physical constraints of all matter, the most universal claims made by biology are, for example, that all life comes from previously existing life and that, therefore, all life now on earth has evolved from previously existing life, and second that the DNA code that specifies what sequence of DNA will be interpreted as what protein, is universal (the same in all organisms). But the first of these is admitted to be a purely historical statement that could not always have been true because, after all, life originated from nonlife. The real claim is that *present* conditions on earth make it impossible for life to arise from inanimate matter. This assertion is, in practice, both trivially true as a general rule and impervious to refutation in a particular case. For if life could be created in the laboratory, as scientists believe will be possible, it would be precisely in special experimental conditions that would not threaten the generality of the claim because the conditions are "unnatural" in the historical sense. If, on the other hand, it could be shown that in some remote hot spring, rich in nutrients, life was arising from nonlife we would simply say, "Ah, we did not realize that there is a place where the special conditions for the origin of life still exist. What a wonderful opportunity to study what those conditions *used to be.*" The second claim, that of the universality of the DNA code, is in fact false, and several cases of exceptional codes are now known. The response to these discoveries was, again, historicist. Either more than one vestige of the independent origins of the genetic code are still extant or some mutations of the code occurred in one or two ancestral lines a long time ago. Nothing important is at stake. The code is still (almost) universal.

At a somewhat less general level are statements about reproduction, for example, Mendel's laws for sexually reproducing organisms, or even more contingent, Darwin's mechanism for evolution, natural selection. Many organisms do not reproduce sexually, and some that do fail to observe Mendel's rules for some of their genes. Natural selection is certainly not the only mechanism for evolutionary change, and there is at present a major struggle in evolutionary biology about how commonly natural selection operates.

A great deal of the body of biological research and knowledge consists of narrative statements. The reconstruction of the history of living organisms by paleontologists is a historicist enterprise, and all of systematics (the science of inferring evolutionary relationships among organisms) is an attempt to tell the story of the common ancestry of organisms *wie es eigentlich gewesen*. Evolutionary biology, like historical geology, soil science, and cosmology, is a historical science. It is the purpose of all of these sciences to provide a correct narrative of the sequence of past events and an account of the causal forces and antecedent conditions that led to that sequence. Moreover, all these historical sciences assume the existence of several forces simultaneously operating and include the importance of chance, viewed either ontologically or epistemologically. The actual event is seen as the nexus of these forces and their chance perturbations. The historian may have some difficulty in distinguishing this description of evolutionary theory from, say, the structure of Khaldûn's *Universal History*.[3]

The Role of Fact in the Particular and in the General

In biology, as in history, the distinction to be made in understanding the role of "fact" is between assertions about particular sample paths and general assertions about types of events. Within these two groups of assertions, there is again a dichotomy between narrative statements in a paratactic mode and causal assertions in a hypotactic one. It is important to note that, at least in biology, there may be *general* statements, but there are no universals, and that actual events are the nexus of multiple causal pathways and chance perturbations. As a consequence, in an ironic reversal of the Popperian claim, the least general and most specific statements of science are the least protected against contrary evidence, while the most general can survive numerous apparent factual disagreements.

It was long held that the ornate head-armor of the Ceratopsian dinosaurs had changed progressively from a simple form with no horns or frills to the famous *Triceratops* with three rhinoceros-like facial horns and a larger bony spiked head-shield. It was at one time supposed that these were successively better adaptations to protect against carnivorous predators. Then, fossils of the most ornately armored forms were found to be contemporaneous with the simplest one so the entire narrative collapsed and with it a classical example of progressive evolutionary adaptation. As a contrasting case, we may consider the generally observed trend in the evolution of mammalian groups toward an increase in size. This trend can be attributed to the greater energetic efficiency of large animals who have a correspondingly smaller surface to volume ratio and so find it easier to maintain their body temperature. Some lines of descent, as for example some rodents and insectivores, have not increased their body size and would seem to be quite inefficiently built. But this is not regarded as invalidating the general (not universal) "law" of increasing body size nor its causal explanation. The theoretical claim is that body size *tends* to increase but that other causal mechanisms may produce countervailing tendencies. So, insectivores may remain small in order to live off small, widely spaced

---

3. The *Kitâb al-'Ibar* [*Universal History*] of Ibn Khaldûn begins with a volume on general historical theory (the *Muqaddimah*) and then provides a specific narrative history of the Arabs and the Berbers in later volumes. See Ibn Khaldûn, *The Muqaddimah*, trans. Franz Rosenthal (New York, 1958).

insect prey, and they may "solve" their heat regulation problem by staying under ground as moles do. So no counterexample to the general trend is critical or even disquieting. It might be thought that these contrary observations could be, in fact, taken as evidence for the correctness of the causal assertion, namely, that energy conservation is the driving force in the evolution of these mammals however that may be accomplished. But that cannot be universally true because the smallest of all insectivorous mammals, the shrews, spend their time *above* ground and must eat constantly to maintain their body temperature. Undaunted, the evolutionist maintains that there is yet another causal pathway, as yet unknown, that will provide the explanation. In a curious reversal of the role of observation and theory, the fact that shrews exist, coupled with the unquestioned theory that heat regulation is a critical issue for the evolution of mammals is taken as compelling evidence for the existence of an undiscovered fact about shrews.

The robustness of causal claims against contrary evidence when systems have complex interacting causes leads to the possibility that very general causal theories about large domains of phenomena may become totally impervious to evidence. The consequence is that, although observations may abound, *evidence* ceases to exist as theories become dogma. That is the situation in which both particle physics and evolutionary biology find themselves. Particle physics inherits from the chemistry of the nineteenth century the belief that all matter is made up of some ultimate, indivisible units. A hundred and fifty years of the reduction of matter from molecules to atoms, from atoms to nuclei, from nuclei to nuclear particles, from particles to quarks has failed to produce the ultimate unit, although each historical stage claimed to have found it. The belief in a world made up of ultimate, discrete units is an aspect of the ideology of individualism against which no observation of yet further atomization can be taken as evidence. Taking into account the accepted wave-particle nature of matter, it is hard to imagine what could constitute such evidence. There used to be a man who appeared yearly at the American Physical Society meetings to give a paper on "The Latest Value for the Prout." The Prout was his ultimate physical unit of which all values of physical constants were simple multiples. Of course, he had to recalculate the Prout each year as new values for physical units were announced.

Optimal adaptation is the Prout of evolutionary biology. There is a powerful strain in evolutionary theory exemplified by sociobiology that seeks to explain every aspect of the anatomy, physiology, behavior, and cellular mechanics of all organisms as the consequence of optimal adaptation by natural selection. The technical literature of evolutionary genetics provides many alternatives to this view. For example, chance events in the reproduction of a population, the lack of the appropriate genetic variations, the fact that genes have multiple developmental effects, the phenomenon of nonproportional scaling of body parts, all suggest that many

evolutionary changes may not produce optimal adaptation.[4] But no observation can disprove or even seriously call into question optimal adaptation
as an explanation because of the complexity of the relations between
organisms and the world they create and inhabit. On the contrary, all
observations can be claimed as support. "The Heavens declare the glory
of God, and the firmament showeth his handiwork." A case in illustration
is the "central place forager."[5] Some animals, notably nesting birds, go out
to find food but carry it back to a central spot before consuming it.
Clearly, it would not pay an animal to take the first bit of food, irrespective
of size, and carry it back because its consumption might not repay the
energy of the round trip. Nor would it be useful to take only extremely
large food items since the time spent in search for such items might again
consume more energy than they are worth. An optimal forager will
restrict its search to food of an intermediate size, which we may calculate
from a knowledge of the distribution of available food particles. When
birds are observed, they do, indeed, skew their search toward larger than
random sizes, but not enough to correspond to the calculated optimum. Is
this evidence against the theory of optimal foraging? No, because, it is
claimed, the optimal use of energy is not the only problem a bird must
solve. It must also not stay away from the nest too long, or else its young
will be unprotected from predators. Indeed, the bird's failure to be an
optimal forager is taken as evidence *for* its optimum behavior as a parent.
Optimal adaptation is a Panglossian ideology that determines the evidentiary valency of observations.

It should not be supposed that the ad hoc appropriation of evidence
occurs only when there is a single unquestioned paradigm of explanation.
The loose relation between observation and theory in systems of complex
causation can also allow opposite theories to consume the same evidentiary nutrition. In population genetics, there has been a long-standing
struggle between those who believe that most heritable variation between
organisms is subject to natural selection (the "selectionist" school) and
those who regard purely chance events as determining the variation and,
consequently, a great deal of the evolution of species (the "neutralist"
school).[6] The evidence marshalled by these schools is virtually the same,
for its ambiguity is sufficient to allow both parties to claim it. For example,
in populations of fruit flies living on Pacific archipelagos, the closer the

4. For an extensive discussion of the general causes of evolutionary change, see
Stephen J. Gould and R. C. Lewontin, "The Spandrels of San Marco and the Panglossian
Paradigm: A Critique of the Adaptationist Programme," *Proceedings of the Royal Society of
London* B205 (1979): 581–98.
    5. See Gordon H. Orians and Nolan E. Pearson, "On the Theory of Central Place For-
aging," in *Analysis of Ecological Systems,* ed. David J. Horn, Gordon R. Stairs, and Rodger D.
Mitchell (Columbus, Ohio, 1979), pp. 155–77.
    6. For a general historical discussion of this struggle, see Lewontin, *The Genetic Basis of
Evolutionary Change* (New York, 1974).

islands the more similar the frequencies of certain inherited protein variants. Whereas the neutralist school takes this as evidence that the variants
are not selected but have their frequencies determined solely by migration
patterns between near and distant islands, the selectionists, who made the
observation in the first place, claim that, obviously, the closer that islands
are geographically the more similar are their environments and, thus, the
more similar the conditions of natural selection.

Structuring Facts from Unstructured Nature

In his Trevelyan lectures, E. H. Carr considers the problem of when
an event becomes a historical fact. He gives the example of a gingerbread
vendor who was kicked to death by an angry mob in 1850, an event that
was on its way to becoming part of the body of historical fact by virtue of
its being cited by historians.[7] But to cite it as a fact of history requires that
in the first place it be cut out of the continuum of historical flow as a recognizable and unitary event. This epistemic step is unproblematic for the
historian because our psychic development, social experience, and education create for us a structure of perception that makes some things obviously bounded events. The problem is not so easily solved when we
contemplate nature. What is the "correct" way to describe an organism?
Indeed, for colonial organisms like corals or violets, where does one
organism begin and another end? Facts in science do not present themselves in a preexistent shape. Rather it is the experimental or observational protocol that constructs facts out of an undifferentiated nature.
And if we do not like what we see, we can rearrange the description of
nature to have a more pleasing aspect. So facts make a theory, but it takes a
theory to make facts, and occasionally, but only occasionally, this dialectic
becomes disturbingly clear to the practitioners of science. Again, evolutionary biology provides a clear case.

Systematics is the science of inferring the evolutionary relationships
of organisms, usually extant species. It consists in attempting to draw family trees that link organisms to each other through hypothetical common
ancestors in the remote past. The problem is to reconstruct genealogies
without the actual names or records of ancestors, so the only evidence that
can be used is the set of observed similarities and differences between the
still-living forms. The assumption is that the more similar two species are,
the more closely they are related. But we cannot decide how similar two
organisms are until we have a list of descriptors, which cannot be drawn up
until we answer the question of how to anatomize a natural object, an
organism. Of course, biologists do not come to organisms with an innocent eye. By tradition and experience, each group of organisms has

7. See E. H. Carr, *What Is History?* (New York, 1961).

attached to it a conventional list of ways of describing it, and this list differs from group to group. Obviously, one does not describe plants in the same terms as insects, but even within insects, beetles are characterized along different dimensions of description than, say, ants. Once a preliminary list of attributes is decided on, an evolutionary reconstruction of the possible ancestral tree is made using one form or another of a parsimony rule. A common set of rules is that evolutionary reversals are rare and that the repeated independent origin of new features does not occur. So, if two organisms share a trait that others do not have, it is assumed that they acquired it from a common ancestor. Whenever the process of family tree construction is carried out on more than a few species for more than a few traits, the most parsimonious genealogical tree (or trees—they need not be unique) contains a lot of contradictions. That is, try as he or she may, the systematist cannot create a tree in which there are no reversals or independent origins of traits. One response to this result is to redefine the traits. New ones are introduced and old ones dropped. Systematists argue about whether molecular traits, like DNA and protein sequences, give better results than morphological traits. And if one uses anatomical traits, is it simply lengths and widths, or the ratio or product of these that is appropriate? New facts about the organisms are created in an attempt to find a set of descriptions that minimizes the contradictions. The problem is that there is a noncountable infinity of ways to describe an organism, to make the facts of its existence. One soon grows tired of trying new ways and, anyway, everybody knows that reversals and independent origins of the same trait *do* happen sometimes, so a tree, even the correct one, must have contradictions.

Living and Dead Facts

Carr's example of the gingerbread vendor raises questions not only about the facts of history but about the history of fact. In science, the same observations move in and out of the body of scientific fact. Philosophers and historians of science have dealt with the ways in which scientific theories assimilate contrary facts or are given fatal indigestion by them. They do not consider, however, that observations may be spat out again if they prove unchewable. Every science has its rubbish heap of discarded observations that do not fit anywhere and that are rejected as flukes of chance, or bad experiments, or the products of crackpots, as indeed many or most of them are. But every science also has a repertoire of coherent observations that have neither been refuted nor explained, but simply cannot be related in any way to the current theoretical structure of the science. The consequence is that this coherent body of observation is pushed to the back of the collective scientific consciousness. Sometimes the problematic of the field changes, making it conveniently possible to forget puzzling observations in the intellectual press of new activity and the excitement of new concepts. Sometimes the observations can be explained away as the product of a few eccentrics who are then marginalized so that their results need not be taken into the body of evidence. If they cannot be marginalized because of their unchallengeable status, the scientific community is reduced to head-shaking and muttering that there must be something wrong somewhere. It is important to note that we are not considering here heterodox *theories*, like the theory of continental drift that, despite compelling evidence, was scoffed at by geologists for decades, although it is now the orthodoxy. The issue of the rise of new theories that resolve disturbing contradictions in accepted evidence is the standard problem treated by the various models of scientific development. Rather, we are concerned with the problem of converting observations into evidence when they have not been dreamt of in our philosophy. The history of genetics over the last fifty years has been marked by repeated instances of the phenomenon.

Since the end of the Second World War, the unchallenged truth of genetics has been that genes produce organisms but that there is no reciprocal pathway of causation from organisms to genes. That is, the theory that the developmentally acquired characteristics of organisms could be passed on to their offspring by altering the nature of the biological information contained in fertilized eggs has been totally rejected. Genetics, and biology in general, is totally Weismannian, separating the soma from the germ. During the 1940s and 1950s, a major challenge to this Mendelian-Weismannian picture was thrown up by the Lysenkoist movement in the Soviet Union.[8] T. D. Lysenko and his followers claimed to have compelling evidence for the inheritance of acquired characteristics and rejected totally the internal/external dichotomy of orthodox genetics. When Stalin's government made Lysenkoism the official doctrine and purged geneticists from the scientific institutions, the cold war spread into biology, and Western biologists almost without exception rallied around the flag of Mendelism to defeat the politically inspired, antiscientific charlatanism of Lysenko. What the standard history of these events does not reveal is that genetics itself was by no means consolidated before the Second World War. There was a tradition of research and a body of observation being produced by well-established geneticists in Europe, America, and Japan that seemed to show the inheritance of acquired characteristics. There were, for example, *dauermodifikatie*, effects of temperature on organisms that disappeared only slowly over the course of several genera-

8. The standard history of Lysenkoism is David Joravsky, *The Lysenko Affair* (Cambridge, Mass., 1970). An examination of the state of genetics and Weismannism that was antecedent to the rise of Lysenkoism is given in Richard Levins and Lewontin, "The Problem of Lysenkoism," in *The Radicalisation of Science: Ideology of/in the Natural Sciences*, ed. Hilary Rose and Steven Rose (London, 1976), pp. 32–64.

tions after the treatment. There were graft hybrids in which the offspring of somatically joined plant varieties showed some traits of each graft partner. The effect of the politicization of genetics during the cold war was a consolidation of geneticists on the side of Mendelism-Weismannism and a delegitimation of research on the alternatives. It is not that the observations have been assimilated into accepted theory, nor do they even exist as contradictory evidence challenging and threatening the theory. They have simply disappeared from view. They are not mentioned in the technical literature or in textbooks and courses. They are observations that have ceased to be evidence. They are the decommissioned battleships of a past scientific war. Whether they have only been put into mothballs or have already been cut up for scrap is still unclear.

When observations have been excluded from the body of evidence, they may later enter in the form of prefigurations. During the 1940s and 1950s, two well-known yeast geneticists, Carl and Gertrude Lindegren, produced a mass of observation that did not conform to the ratios of offspring expected in crosses according to Mendel's laws.[9] The Lindegrens, who had previously been regarded as competent and trusted, were quickly marginalized, and their claims became a source of snickering reference in cocktail bars at scientific meetings. Within ten years, quite independent discoveries in molecular genetics led to an expectation of unorthodox results similar to those of the Lindegrens, and a great deal of similar, now assimilable, evidence was produced. The Lindegrens' observations were then incorporated, but as historical relics, prefigurations of evidence, but playing no role in the establishment of new ideas.

It is not always possible to prevent the conversion of observations into disturbing evidence by the marginalization of their producers. For twenty-five years, one of the world's leading geneticists, Barbara McClintock, reported in both oral presentations and published accounts that genes in corn were hopping around from one chromosome to another.[10] No one believed this to be possible, yet McClintock was of such high status (she was one of the very few women members of the National Academy of Sciences), undoubted sanity, and clear competence that her observations could not be rejected. The general reaction among her colleagues was one of bemused puzzlement and grudging admission that something odd was going on but, with the exception of one other corn geneticist, no one tried to fold the observations into their understanding of genetics. Then, in the 1970s, quite separate lines of evidence began to make clear that a simple molecular mechanism would result in the movement of genetic material from one location on the chromosome to another, and that "transposable elements" were not all that rare.

9. See Carl C. Lindegren, *The Yeast Cell, Its Genetics and Cytology* (St. Louis, 1949).
10. See Evelyn Fox Keller, *A Feel for the Organism: The Life and Work of Barbara McClintock* (San Francisco, 1983).

McClintock then reaped great credit as a prophet and her observations became, retroactively, evidence, although no longer of any critical importance.

Canons of Evidence

The demands for rigor of experimental design in theoretical inference vary widely in science from field to field, sometimes between very closely allied domains of research. While there is some clear rationality in the general outlines of these canons of evidence, there are also informal agreements on what constitutes evidence that are of uncertain justification. For example, in establishing the DNA sequence of a gene that has never previously been sequenced, it is obvious for reasons of technical artifact that both strands of the double helix must be independently sequenced, even though, in principle, one strand can be predicted from the other. The informal rule, however, is that, in addition, one of the two complementary strands must have its sequence determined twice. Clearly, the more independent information the better, but why only twice? The rule has simply become a communally agreed-upon standard.

The origins of differences in required rigor are not always easy to discern, but sometimes it is obvious that ideology is a dominant force. Repeatedly, natural scientists have quite willingly adopted standards of evidence that they would ordinarily scorn as belonging to "softer" domains of knowledge, when ideological presumptions and demands for rigor clash. There have been two recent episodes in genetics and evolution that can only be understood as the triumph of ideology over rigor.

The major agony of social and political life in democratic bourgeois societies has been the contradiction between the ideology of equality on the one hand, and the manifest inequalities of status, wealth, and power, together with the passage of social power from parents to children, on the other. The dominant mode of explanation of the divergence between ideal and reality is the claim that there are intrinsic and biologically heritable differences between individuals in temperament and ability that account for their differing social roles and powers. A particular manifestation of this claim is that intelligence, as measured by IQ tests, is biologically inherited and that the upper classes are biologically superior to the *lumpenproletariat.*[11] The evidence offered for this claim comes from statistical comparisons of the IQ test scores of relatives of various degrees, including the comparison of identical twins. The analysis is a special application to human IQ scores of a general methodology for studying the genetics of continuously varying traits, which has a very long history. The

11. For a discussion of the weakening of canons of evidence in this case, see Leon J. Kamin, *The Science and Politics of I. Q.* (Potomac, Md., 1974).

same methodology is used to understand yield in corn and growth rate in swine. At the very basis of the method there is an assumption that the similarity between relatives derives only from their shared biological heredity and not their shared environment. Unless this assumption is met, *no estimate at all of the influence of genes can be made*. For that reason, the canons of evidence in the genetics of agricultural plants and domestic animals include the demand that environmental similarities be rigorously excluded. In humans, with a family and class structure, it is quite impossible to eliminate environmental correlations. Yet, quantitative geneticists who study the heritability of human IQ give the problem scant or no recognition, or give elaborate justification for a priori assumptions about environment. The papers on the subject that appear in the journals of behavior genetics would never pass review for publication in the journals of agronomy and animal breeding. *Quod licet Jove non licet bove.* If the rigorous demands placed on swine breeders were applied to the geneticists of human behavior, no strong claim could be made for the heritability of IQ, and the empirical evidence on which the biological determinist argument is made would disappear.

Accompanying the assertion that there are inherited *differences* between individuals is the theory that there are inherited *universals* of human behavior constituting "human nature." The universals, which are said to include xenophobia, aggression, religiosity, entrepreneurship, and indoctrinability, are supposed to be encoded in the human genome. Their possession makes impossible the creation of any society that is not based on hierarchies of status, wealth, and power. This is the theory that has reached immense currency both in scholarly and public discourse under the name of human sociobiology.[12] There are two lines of observation offered as evidence for the existence of genes for human nature as described. First, many animals, including monkeys and apes, have some of these characteristics (although perhaps they lack genes for religiosity), and, after all, we are descended from nonhuman primates and got our genes from them. Second, if we look around, most people fit the description, so on that ground alone we must assume that genes lie at the basis of our nature.[13] It is hard to know what a swine breeder would make of such an argument, although more than one swine geneticist accepts the statements of human sociobiology. The same people can, of course, demand quite different criteria of evidence for different purposes.

A second feature of the sociobiological argument is that natural selection has established the genes for human nature because such a nature

12. See Edward O. Wilson, *On Human Nature* (Cambridge, Mass., 1978).

13. So, Wilson writes, of the human sexual division of labor: "In hunter-gatherer societies, men hunt and women stay at home. This strong bias persists in most agricultural and industrial societies and, *on that ground alone*, appears to have a genetic origin" (Wilson, "Human Decency Is Animal," *New York Times Magazine*, 12 Oct. 1975, p. 48).

insures the probability of survival and reproduction of its possessors. In evolutionary genetics and demography there is a well-established methodology for estimating the survivorship and fertility of different types and using these measurements to make predictions about natural selection. None of this apparatus is used by human sociobiology. Instead, purely hypothetical plausibility arguments are used to tell "Just So Stories" about the superior fitness of present human nature. The substitution of anecdote for more rigorous canons of evidence is reinforced by the existence of a separate community of sociobiologists with their own journals, societies, and symposia.

What the examples of the genetics of IQ and of sociobiology teach us is not that ideology influences scientific theories, an idea that is obvious to any historian or social theorist (although denied by many scientists).[14] Rather, they warn us that the quality of evidence itself is tailored to fit ideological demands. In this, as in everything else, natural science as a way of understanding the natural world differs rather less from other systems of knowledge than its practitioners would have one believe.

14. As an example, consider the indignation of the famous chemist M. F. Perutz at the claim that Darwin owed his idea for natural selection and the struggle for existence to his reading of the political economy of the nineteenth century and his immersion in nineteenth-century laissez-faire ideology. See M. F. Perutz, "High on Science," *New York Review of Books*, 16 Aug. 1990, pp. 12–15.

Lewontin's Evidence (That There Isn't Any)

William Wimsatt

Let me say at the start that this title is guilty of rhetorical overstatement. Or since I am a philosopher, and never use rhetoric, it would be more honest of me to admit to a deeper failing. I saw in Dick Lewontin's paper many embarrassments for the canonical concept of evidence that philosophers of science used to like so well ("Facts and the Factitious in the Natural Sciences," pp. 478–91). Because we still suffer from the stultifying—indeed mortifying—rigors of the belief that only that which is general is worth knowing, on first reaction, I *took* this as doing away with our concept of evidence. (While the defenders of evidence look in vain for a decontextualized, general, and preferably logical relation, the attackers also accept the same ground rules; they seem to expect that a single or a small number of counterexamples should bring down the house. The first is unattainable, and the second foolish.) But Lewontin is onto something much richer. Nancy Cartwright has said that the laws of physics lie.[1] It would appear that the most general laws of biology (that is, if you thought there were any) do not show any consistent respect for the proper evidential authorities either. Lewontin states,

> At least in biology, there may be *general* statements, but there are no universals, and . . . actual events are the nexus of multiple causal pathways and chance perturbations. As a consequence, in an ironic reversal of the Popperian claim, the least general and most specific statements of science are the least protected against contrary evi-

I wish to thank Dick Lewontin, Stuart Glennan, and Jeff Schank for useful substantive and didactic commentary on these remarks and Dave Raup for continuing discussion (now extending over sixteen years) of the possibilities and effects of large body impacts.
    1. See Nancy Cartwright, *How the Laws of Physics Lie* (New York, 1983).

dence, while the most general can survive numerous apparent factual disagreements. [P. 144]

Lewontin follows with a list of scientists in flagrante delicto providing compromising copy for criticisms of the leveling voice of scientific evidence. The kinds of examples he provides are also found in fields beyond biology, but there is no need (or space, here) to go further afield. Within biology we have plenty of embarrassments for our traditional beliefs about the power and objectivity of evidence. We have inconclusive arguments (for example, the neutralist-selectionist debate over which forces, if any, power evolution) in which both sides bash each other with what appears to be virtually the same evidence. In his earlier discussion of this case, Lewontin falsifies roughly Popper$_1$ through Popper$_{13}$ on his way to a much richer account of the dialectical dynamics of scientific disputes than found in any traditional falsificationist accounts or their descendants.[2] Elsewhere, we have apparently shameless curve fitting and ad hoc-ery (in the service of the adaptationist program and sociobiology— in defense of central place foragers who are supposedly maximizers but who often appear to settle for less than they might). Here the failure of the generalizations to face the facts seems to entail (to their defenders, at least) not that they are false but that yet-undiscovered facts have yet to come to their rescue. Does *anyone* give up their theories in the face of contrary evidence? No one surrenders gracefully—if at all—in today's philosophy of science.

Perhaps most embarrassing are baseless variations in the standard of evidence used by different disciplines working on the same kinds of problems. Is this perhaps a reflection of a caste system in science, with the standards of rigor matching one's position in the hierarchy of the sciences, with the good guys from the higher sciences still trying to educate the teeming unsophisticates, and the basic scientists educating their applied brethren? But not so fast. Look who comes out on top: the genetic speculations of some "pure scientists"—human ethologists and IQ

2. See R. C. Lewontin, *The Genetic Basis of Evolutionary Change* (New York, 1974). Popper's defenders have been in the habit of inventing numerically subscripted versions of that philosopher, with higher numbers indicating more sophisticated versions of his views, all in the service of preventing it from being falsified. The subscripts in the literature, however, have so far gone no higher than 3 or 4.

William Wimsatt, professor of philosophy at the University of Chicago and member of the Committee on Evolutionary Biology and the Committee on the Conceptual Foundations of Science, has written extensively on methodological problems in the study of complex systems. His most recent work is a study of the evolution of generative structures in biology and culture.

researchers—are compared with the quantitative genetics of animal and plant breeders and found wanting. This last is a cruel slap. Those who have most slavishly imitated the positivists in their demands for quantification and operationalism have promised us the largest array of "value free" facts and those who have touted themselves as practitioners of "high science" are shown to be grossly inferior in their methodological practice to a bunch of applied agricultural geneticists. (Of course it helps if the "applied boys" learned their stuff from Sewall Wright.) *Generalizing from these cases, the problem seems to be not that "evidence" is not to be had but that it's to be had too easily by anyone who wants it, and he who supports everything sustains nothing.*

I cannot manage much motivation for defending classical concepts of evidence or for defending every foible of various scientists' (and sciences') use of evidence. Nor am I ready for the anything goes flavor of much of the "postmodernist" relativism of many current sociologists of science. We need to be much less absolutist and much more contingent, contextual, and historicist in our analyses of science. But we must do this by recognizing the real complexities we are increasingly able to study in natural systems whose simplicity we have been taking for granted for decades or centuries. A major fraction of these complexities are not a function of our conceptual schemes, language, or interests, but products of the way the world is. Realism lives! But any wise realist must recognize that the social, cultural, and ideational entities of the "social relativists" are real, too, and embed them with the natural entities we theorize about. We do this via the idealized models we construct and the carpentered, "natural" entities, tools, practices, procedures, and phenomena we experiment with and on. We recognize we are guided, regulated, and maintained by the social structures, languages, and values of science as a part of the appropriate (panrealist) world picture.

1. Is Evidence Impotent or Just Inconstant?

Lewontin's paper must be taken as exemplifying his own thesis. Philosophy of science makes happy methodological bedfellows with history and evolutionary biology in this as in some other respects. All are messy, complex, richly textured subjects that cover an enormous diversity of things with deceptively simple and unitary labels. Lewontin has given "evidence" for a generalization (not a universal) that is immune to counterattack by simply counting counterexamples because the "actual events [of theory construction, discovery, and the marshalling of facts and counterexamples] are the nexus of multiple causal [and inferential] pathways and chance perturbations" (p. 482). In this context, *in principle* arguments now work side by side with empirical evidence—sometimes merely bounding possible solutions, sometimes finding accurate pivot points around which the whole argument must turn—all in the service of simply trying to tie the phenomena down. In this underdetermined context (and we should not assume as philosophers commonly do that all theoretical contexts are significantly underdetermined), what used to be thought of as refuting counterevidence often becomes just a stimulus for new elaborative investigation.

Just? But it is an effective stimulus, and that is not at all bad. At least it is a response, showing that the offering of the evidence was not totally without effect. The response may sometimes be just curve fitting, but more often, I think, it is not. There can be responsible denials of counterexamples and even responsible adoption of them without jumping ship. If the counterexamples are good and deep ones, they should be treasured and closely studied, even if we don't know how to deal with them. But we should not be naive falsificationists. If they are good ones, our generalizations should not be as fragile as all that, and even when they are false, they may be very useful tools nonetheless—a topic I will return to in the next section.

The culprit, if there is one, is the assumption that we must remove any contradictions or tensions in the theory before we proceed any further. (This is traditional advice for beginning philosophers; they justify close conceptual analyses and careful definitions of terms, as if these had to be temporally as well as logically prior to any theory construction or revision, but it is poor counsel for any practicing scientist and, arguably, for philosophers as well.) We need to have some idea of *how* to remove the contradictions. Remove the contradictions we must, and it is important to identify them, if possible to localize them, and to keep them in mind when revising the theory, but often no way of removing them immediately suggests itself as desirable on other grounds, and the further development of the theory in directions guided by other constraints and desiderata will suggest new and natural ways of resolving the problem if we ignore it for the time being. (Indeed, the faith that this will happen represents an often unappreciated commitment to scientific realism. Nature, after all, does not tolerate contradictions.)[3] Contradictions should be treated like holes in the ice that we skate around gingerly. We look for ways to bridge or fix them rather than act as if we have just had a total meltdown and everything has to stop until we fix it.

The thing we worry about most is that ad hoc responses to counter-

---

3. In saying (with deliberate and self-indulgent animism) that nature does not tolerate contradictions, I explicitly do *not* here wish to be denying the importance of the use of contradictions in argument (for example, *reductio* proofs) and of efforts to avoid them in the elaboration of theory, or the importance of conflict among the contradictory theories, or "collisions" between "contradictory" forces, optima, constraints, desiderata, or design requirements in the development of adaptive structures generally—including organisms and

examples could enervate our generalizations, rendering their empirical force so unclear that they are deprived of useful consequences we would stand by, thus making the theory so formless that it is unclear what could *either* confirm *or* compromise it. With this worry, it is useful to contemplate some fact-generated paradigm shifts just to remind ourselves that it can happen. *If evidence were impotent for forcing theory change, how could we account for the occasional keystone facts—apparently isolated facts whose acceptance has far-reaching consequences?* This can happen even in messy complex areas where one would expect more opportunities to take up the slack and resist change. Such a case—the "iridium anomaly," which led to the so-called Alvarez hypothesis that the extinction of the dinosaurs was caused by an asteroid impact—has in the dozen years since its initial publication changed almost everyone's mind except perhaps for some of those most strongly affected by it: the vertebrate paleontologists, keepers of the life histories of the dinosaurs. I think it is now only a matter of time until the last of them cave in.

One of the delightful ironies of this case was that Walter Alvarez started out to do an interesting but quite conservative application of existing science. The measurement of iridium was made on the assumption that its source was a steady rain of meteoric dust at a known slow rate, which could then be used as a "clock" to tell how rapidly the various sedimentary layers were deposited. But the amount of iridium present was so high that sediment would have had to be deposited at an impossibly slow rate—hundreds of times slower than normal—so the assumption of a constant deposition rate had to be given up, an inferential path that led to the hypothesis of a large body impact.

Did the great Cretaceous extinction (sixty-five million years ago) issue from a collision with a comet, asteroid, or large meteor? The resulting debates across and within disciplines made us aware of a variety of other

---

theories as two special cases. Thus, this view is quite consistent with the claim that scientific investigation, problem solving, and theory competition are sometimes (or always) dialectical processes. It raises more problems, I think, for scientific instrumentalism. Once it is accepted that we can and do work, and work well, with theories that contain contradictions, *it is not clear how the instrumentalist can expect, explain, or justify their removal.* There is, to my knowledge, only one form of formal contradiction that we do not generally attempt to remove, though we are forced to justify it and may be pushed to understand its limitations more carefully: the approximations that link together various parts of any quantitative theory of any significant size and moment in the mathematical and natural sciences. For an important start on the analysis (and a catalogue of some of the variety) of these important tools, see Jeffry L. Ramsey, "Beyond Numerical and Causal Accuracy: Expanding the Set of Justificational Criteria," in *PSA: Proceedings of the Biennial Meeting,* ed. Arthur Fine, Micky Forbes, and Linda Wessels, 2 vols. (East Lansing, Mich., 1990), 1:485–99 and "Towards an Expanded Epistemology for Approximations," in *PSA: Proceedings of the Biennial Meeting,* ed. Kathleen Okruhlik, Fine, and Forbes, 2 vols. (East Lansing, Mich., 1992), 1:154–64.

facts and led to conceptual and strategic readjustments producing a variety of new foci for research. A very partial list would include:[4]

a. the search for the smoking gun(s). There is robust evidence of contemporaneous collisions found (only recently) in the form of craters of the appropriate age off Yucatan and in Iowa;

b. searches with increasing success for similar causes (like iridium and for later discovered carbon layers indicating collisions and massive resultant forest fires) of earlier mass extinctions;

c. revised theories and evidence of collision activities on other bodies, particularly the moon and Mars, and new ideas in planetary geology;

d. relations to other theories of mass extinction (volcanic eruptions and ecological collapse, which are not necessarily competitors);

e. periodic extinction theories (and the question of what kinds of causes could be found for very long-period fluctuations in extinction rates);

f. new correlative questions about the meaning of long-range stability as applied to terrestrial processes, leading back to Poincaré and chaotic dynamics in the solar system and to intermediate-range orbital periodicities (Milankovitch cycles of 20, 40, 100, 400 thousand years) whose biotic effects had not been seriously considered before;

g. a new interest in theories of disturbance, their causes and effects: for example, fire ecology, nuclear winter, greenhouse effects, and ice ages;

h. the relation to punctuated equilibrium theories of evolution (a facilitating theoretical change, which made it easier for some biologists to accept Alvarez);

i. and correlative new attention to the duration of mass extinction events;

j. more general consideration of extraterrestrial causes of biotic events (and a recognition that our planetary and galactic surroundings are not in steady-state equilibrium on a time scale appropriate to even intermediate-range evolutionary processes);

k. development and application of stochastic theories regularizing rare events (consider especially frequency versus size distributions of collisions);

l. a changing assessment of the importance of catastrophic/uniformitarian arguments in which the latter—holder of the high ground for the last 130 years—has recently suffered serious inroads, as illustrated by the following set of hypotheses taken from a research news article in *Science:* the suggestion that the earth was kept hot by large body collisions with

---

4. For more details on these, see David M. Raup, *The Nemesis Affair: The Story of the Death of Dinosaurs and the Life of Science* (New York, 1986) and *Extinction: Bad Genes or Bad Luck?* (New York, 1991).

declining frequency until more recently (4.0–3.8 billion years ago) than had heretofore been supposed; that life may have evolved (and been wiped out) several times by collisions with asteroids having diameters in the 200–400 mile range; and that in consequence, life may evolve much more rapidly, and originate much more easily, than we have supposed.

The problem posed by Lewontin's examples and this additional one is not that facts are sometimes efficacious in producing theoretical (and factual) change, and sometimes not. It is that we have no general theory of when they will or when they won't, and furthermore, that they sometimes appear to do so when they shouldn't or fail to do so when they should—epistemologically, morally, and sometimes both. But perhaps this means that we have just been seeking too simple a theory of evidence.

Some of Lewontin's other examples, such as the inconclusive neutralist-selectionist debates, show a similar pattern of territorial contests resulting in often productively elaborated arguments. These debates (heightened in 1966 by Hubby and Lewontin, with their adaptation of gel electrophoresis to discover unanticipated amounts of genetic variation in natural populations)[5] have led to new understandings of macroscopic constraints on the evolution of complex genotypes, and their rates of evolution, the limitations of genetic load arguments, and new tools, ranging from hardware and assay procedure through new statistical techniques and new conceptual insights and models to characterize the new forms of variation. Even if we don't have final answers, the debate has forced clearer formulation of the questions, significant shifts in the grounds of debate, and new attention to the causal factors and mechanisms affecting phenotypic evolution. And that is more important, I submit, than exactly how the investigation comes out in this case.[6]

2. False Models as Means to Truer Theories

There is another practice (one probably affecting some of the cases Lewontin discusses) that can produce apparent waffling over the evi-

5. See J. L. Hubby and Lewontin, "A Molecular Approach to the Study of Genic Heterozygosity in Natural Populations: I. The Number of Alleles at Different Loci in *Drosophila pseudoobscura*," *Genetics* 54 (Aug. 1966): 577–94.

6. This is not quite right. It would make a substantial difference to evolutionary theory if either more than 99.9 percent or less than .1 percent of the variation were adaptive, but these extremes are pretty clearly ruled out, and quite major variations in between these figures (say, 90 percent versus 10 percent) would not matter too much—in part because there is at present enough uncertainty about other important factors that the right scales of difference for distinguishable positions are measured by orders of magnitude rather than by percentages. (These uncertain factors would include questions such as how many distinguishable functional units of the genome there are, how many of them are under selection at any given time, how much of the neutrality we observe among allelic variants is itself a product of selective design elsewhere in the phenotype, and, perhaps most generally, how developmental programs are organized, how they respond to selection, and whether any

dence. We do many more things in science than test theories.[7] And for some of these things it is not important that the model or theory be right—only that we have some good idea of the place or places where it is wrong. *If this is so, then we may misinterpret what is going on when a theory or model is not discarded in the face of apparently damaging counterevidence.* In at least some of these cases, it is not the evidence (or the theory) that is to blame but our view that the only relations between facts and models or theories are evidential. We need to look at another important class of ways of using models or theories in science, which could be called template matching.

We have to recognize that our best theories and models are idealizations—deliberate simplifications, usually made with knowledge that they are false and where (not to say that we therefore know what is true). We can use these falsehoods as heuristic tools, as baselines to organize and productively restructure our perceptions of the data.[8] These idealizations can be used in a variety of ways.

1. We can study the effects of a subset of the causal interactions without the further complications added by including the rest. This can serve several functions: the effects may not be at all obvious; they may not be experimentally isolable in real systems; they may have been experimentally isolated but studied piecemeal under different conditions and never put together before; or this may just be an initial stage that provides a benchmark to understand the effects of added complexities.

2. There are a variety of things that can be accomplished by what might be called residual analysis—where the aim is not to test the model against the data but to detect and analyze the deviations between the model and the real world. This could serve:

a. to estimate and then remove main effects captured by the model that are much larger than the effects you want to study and submerge them;

b. to be able to figure out how to model the causes of those deviations and add these factors to this or to another related model (note: doing this supposes that you have the factors already included in the model roughly right);

---

of the forces causing systematic rearrangement of the genome somatically during development are available for evolutionary modification—and if so, how frequently.)

7. For another activity not considered here—the status of experiments as demonstrations, or paradigm justifying or extending moves—see Douglas Allchin, "How Do You Falsify a Question? Crucial Tests Versus Crucial Demonstrations," in the 1992 *PSA: Proceedings of the Biennial Meeting,* 1:74–88.

8. On heuristics and their biases, see William C. Wimsatt, "Heuristics and the Study of Human Behavior," in *Metatheory in Social Science: Pluralisms and Subjectivities,* ed. Donald W. Fiske and Richard A. Shweder (Chicago, 1986), pp. 293–314. On the effective use of false models, see Wimsatt, "False Models as Means to Truer Theories," in *Neutral Models in Biology,* ed. Matthew H. Nitecki and Antoni Hoffman (New York, 1987), pp. 23–55.

c. to be able to evaluate the magnitude of a deviation, either as a calibration of the model for accuracy of prediction by determining how accurate it is under different circumstances, or as part of a strategy to figure out how detailed a model is needed to predict with reasonable accuracy.

3. We can generate limiting results. These are used sometimes for predictive simplicity, to bound or to bracket a range of outcomes or to provide "conservative" estimates on the magnitude of effects.[9]

a. There may be one-way limiting results, which provide upper or lower bounds for the real case and which can thereby rule out possible causal factors, mechanisms, or theories that would require conditions or values in the "forbidden" region. These one-way bounds may also be important in risk-benefit analysis.

b. We may construct two-way (or multiway) limiting results that "bracket" the real case. It is often true that one can model and solve for idealized limiting cases much more easily and then, with these "spanning" cases, get a better idea of what is going on in the real case. Qualitatively, this was important in conceptualizing the nature of partial linkage in genetics, bounding its nature between pleiotropy or absolute linkage for factors in unbreakable chromosomes, and the independent assortment for factors in different chromosomes, and suggesting its cause as intrachromosomal recombination in chromosomes that break sometimes, and whose factors separate with a frequency roughly proportional to their distance. Later in the same series of successively better models of linkage, this "bracketing" strategy was used even more elegantly by Haldane, who constructed three "limiting" models and then abstracted from them a parameterized metamodel to characterize the nature of interference.[10]

4. Idealizations and isolations in experimental design have basically the same character as constructed simplifications in mathematical models. Both the contrast between the conditions in nature and those found in the laboratory, and the differences between treatment and control con-

9. The history of conservative estimates shows that they often fail to be conservative, particularly when the estimator has an interest in how the results come out—for example, estimates of risk by an industry responsible for adopting safeguards commensurate with the risk. These can also be dangerously flawed because it is hard to estimate the effects of qualitatively different causes that have not been considered. (Witness Kelvin's "robust" estimates that there were not more than 100 million years available for evolution—flawed by his lack of knowledge of thermonuclear processes in the sun and radioactive heating in the earth. See Joe D. Burchfield, *Lord Kelvin and the Age of the Earth* [1975; Chicago, 1990].)

10. See J. B. S. Haldane, "The Combination of Linkage Values, and the Calculation of Distances between the Loci of Linked Factors," *Journal of Genetics* 8 (Sept. 1919): 299–309. For an analysis of this paper, see Wimsatt, "Golden Generalities and Co-opted Anomalies: Haldane Versus Muller and the *Drosophila* Group on the Theory and Practice of Linkage Mapping," in *Fisher, Haldane, Muller, and Wright: Founders of the Modern Mathematical Theory of Evolution*, ed. S. Sarkar (Dordrecht, 1992), pp. 107–66.

ditions[11] (as well as deciding when an outlier is a "rogue" that should be treated differently—and perhaps not even analyzed with the rest of the data)[12] have features very much like those found in modelling.

3. Narrative Accounts and Theory as Montage

> It is the purpose of all these [historical] sciences to provide a correct narrative of the sequence of past events and an account of the causal forces and antecedent conditions that led to that sequence. . . . [They] assume the existence of several forces simultaneously operating and include the importance of chance. . . . The actual event is seen as the nexus of these forces and their chance perturbations. [Pp. 143–44]

Lewontin's account seems right here not only for the obviously historical sciences but, more broadly, for any of those that study complex mechanisms.[13] A mechanism is after all a distributed causal structure designed so that its parts articulate through time to produce desired effects under a possible diversity of controlling inputs; in its operation, it undergoes historical trajectories. And, by extension, the things that we call mechanisms undergo sequences of causal interactions. But aren't causal mechanisms designed to behave regularly and reliably—that is, to minimize the effects of chance perturbations? Perhaps so, but then the designer of such a mechanism must consider the range of possible perturbations, if his or her mechanism is to behave reliably. (Indeed, to design a mechanism to [reliably] behave randomly may be an even harder task—as most computer modellers know.)[14] We need to evaluate how the causes work or would work in a *range* of actual and possible circumstances in part because we often do not know what the actual circumstances were, or will be, and would thus prefer an explanation (or a mechanism) that is not too sensitive to these details. This is also in part to understand how the general purpose tools work in a range of circumstances; so we can tell where else they may be applicable.

11. See J. C. Schank, "The Integrative Role of Model Building and Computer Simulation in Experimental Biology" (Ph.D. diss., The University of Chicago, 1991) and "Levels of Analysis, Control Mechanisms, and a Program Model of Experimental Design," unpub. paper.

12. "Treasure your exceptions" is a homily at least as well attended to by the contextualist generalizer as it is by the naive falsificationist. To the latter it provides grounds to trash the relevant universal. To the former it provides not only grounds to qualify the generalization but also usually information about how to do so.

13. See Stuart S. Glennan, "Mechanisms, Models, and Causation" (Ph.D. diss., The University of Chicago, 1992) for a strikingly different and, to my mind, the best available account of the nature of causation, causal mechanisms, and mechanistic explanation.

14. See William Dembski's elegant, eloquent, and informative essay on the nature of randomness, "Randomness by Design," *Nous* 25 (Mar. 1991): 76–106.

But surely in historical explanations, one might urge, our only concern is with the actual. True, but misleading. Even where the search is not for any level of broader generality but only for historical accuracy in this particular case, the search for how the proposed mechanism would work under various possible circumstances also serves to determine the *robustness* of the proposed explanations. We need this to evaluate the appropriate level of analysis of the causes in question so as not to suffer unduly from the "for want of a nail" syndrome. "For want of a nail" may have been part of the explanation for Napoleon's loss at Waterloo—and such explanations surely increase the sense of drama—but it was far from the whole cause. In fact, one could more plausibly characterize the cause as a structural condition; it was part of Napoleon's failure that he was unable to secure the conditions necessary to make *this* kind of failure improbable. But for a proper account of generalizations in the messy sciences, we do need to see them as tools as well as ends. *Universals* may be commonly viewed as ends in science, but both unqualified and exceptionless *idealizations* and gappy and sloppy *generalizations* are often happier as tools—admittedly general purpose tools for which we have an aesthetics of design and admiration and which we critique to improve their function.

We have a reason to expect gaps in our generalizations if we want to have modularity and near decomposability in our theoretical structures. A theory of everything may seem OK in cosmology where it seems to unify the very large and slow with the very small and quick. (A theory of everything is in effect a fractal theory of the organization of things on the cosmologically intermediate scale driven by a topological theory of ten-dimensional strings that have been unkinking in ways determined by accidents of the very small, fast, and compact in the first microinstants of the big bang.) But in between these two extreme size ranges, which it covers tolerably well, the details—even major details—of the two dozen or so orders of magnitude of size and time that interest us the most are left almost untouched.

But we do not really want a theory of everything. The ideal Peircean community will not "asymptote" to one big theory that explains everything in all of its details. Such a theory would be unmanageable, untestable, and incomprehensible, and it would have to mimic the detailed structure of the world itself as one big historical entity. The theories of the very large and very small can have simple structures because the middle range theories have to deal in detail with the largest range of types of entities. What we want is a number of partial theories of selected aspects of classes of things, which we can pick up and carry around as portable templates to organize and explain a variety of systems, and which can be used together to make a multiperspectival montage of each event in most of its complexity and guide the articulation of these different pictures, together with those uncommon, peculiar, and particular causal linkages that are easier to account for piecemeal. We can explain everything, but to do so we customize each explanation out of a bunch of adaptable standard pieces, tied together with selections from our junk box collection of tinkerable widgets. In doing so, we try to avoid in our theories the uninformative, abstract sterility of mass production, the epicyclic decadence of too much unconstrained curve fitting, and the disorganized urban sprawl of totally particularistic conceptual tinkertoys gone wild.

In this activity, we have learned about the danger of "single cause" explanations, but we still need to resist the temptation of "single discipline" explanations. (Witness the claims of all we are supposed to learn from the human genome project—as if the production of an untranslated Book of Nature, but one volume of a library-sized encyclopedia, would solve all of our problems.) Dave Raup has claimed that perhaps the biggest problem with the emerging investigations surrounding the astrophysical, geophysical, and biotic dimensions of large body collisions (descendants of the Alvarez hypothesis) is that no one is well placed to evaluate the good of work in the myriad of other disciplines that they must draw upon. If the probative force of evidence requires seeing how it fits into a network of other theory and data offered by a variety of other agents, we have to find ways both of bounding that network and of evaluating the heterogeneous mix of characters within those bounds. The same kind of problems affect the analysis of development: the relations between ontogeny and phylogeny, the causes of macroevolution, the analysis of culture, and—that classic gordian knot—the "mind-body" problem.

In these tasks, our concept of evidence would predictably be much more contingent, contextual, and historicist—complex, relational, and sensitive to context, but that is not to say relativistic. Because we cannot place clear bounds in general and in advance on what could be relevant considerations in weighing evidence in a particular case does not mean that there aren't any—that anything goes. There are some things that no one would defend and some defenses you do not have to accept just because they are offered by someone with good stature and good intentions. So we do not have a general theory of evidence. So what? Who thought the world was that simple? All of the cases Lewontin discusses have this character, and this seems likely as a pivotal source for many of their problems. But if so, so describing them is not yet solving them. There are many problems of evidence yet to come.

A Rejoinder to William Wimsatt

R. C. Lewontin

Bill Wimsatt's "Lewontin's Evidence (That There Isn't Any)" (pp. 492–503) made me think about a lot of questions in my paper. I would like to point out that the rhetoric of this conference has undergone a sudden change. Up until Bill's presentation and mine, everyone read his or her paper. In the tradition to which I belong, that would be considered very bad form. That rhetorical difference is a mirror of the differences that I want to talk about. The words that all of the rest of you use are conceived of as being the matter, and so you must choose them carefully, and, therefore, you have to compose your papers and read them. I, on the other hand, and perhaps Bill as well, but especially I, as a natural scientist, am nothing but the oracle of Delphi, sitting here on my stool with eyeballs rolled upwards, and through me Nature speaks. That explains, in my view, the difference in rhetorical tradition between a meeting like this and the ones at which I spend my time. No one in my tradition believes that the words are very important. After all, if I misspeak, someone else will say the right thing because we are both talking about the same things and ultimately the gods will speak through us. So words are not the matter. It is extremely important to understand the origin of that difference in rhetorical tradition because it represents a very great difference in what scientists believe to be the nature of evidence in natural science. A conference on the questions of evidence is really a conference on the questions of theory and metatheory. We cannot begin to talk about the evidence until we talk about what it is we are trying to produce evidence of. And the very method which we use is itself a form of evidence. My paper is very naive and unnuanced as compared with everyone else's for that reason. While it is called "Facts and the Factitious in Natural Sci-

504

ences" (pp. 478–91), it is really about facts and the factitious in biology, which has a very different history and structure than physics.

It is not the purpose of biology, no matter what biologists sometimes like to make you believe, to give explanations like the laws that govern the solar system. We have no Keplerian laws. On the contrary, although biologists suffer severely from physics envy, they do not in fact operate like physicists because everything they do, although beginning in an attempt to produce universal statements about the world, ends, in fact, in nothing but a wealth of detail about particular cases. Biology is all about unique historical events, unique nexuses of causal patterns of objects. It is about whether or not all persons who have AIDS are, indeed, infected by the AIDS virus, a quite specific question. It does not have the kind of universality of which physicists speak. The fact of the matter is that what appear in biology as grand universals, or at least grand generalizations, are what I would call organizing metaphors. They are not of the same status as, All planets move in ellipses. The best examples come, again, from evolutionary biology, which is essentially a form of history. An example is the difference between the metaphor of adaptation and the metaphor of construction. When people say that natural selection is universal, it is believed that Darwin has given us one of the great universals or, at least, generalizations about the history of life. But that is not true. What Darwin did was extremely important and progressive at its historical moment. He alienated the inside from the outside, the organism from the environment, the subject from the object—an act of alienation that completed the mechanistic program of nineteenth-century biology and that was needed because the failure to alienate the organism from its environment at that particular historical juncture made it extremely difficult to make any explanations of species formation and evolution. But this alienation depends upon a particular metaphor, a particular way of organizing the knowledge about the history of organisms. It is to say that organisms are *adapted* to their environments. The word *adaptation* means precisely that there is a preexistent model towards which something has moved and changed, just as you adapt a key to a lock or you adapt your hair dryer to the voltage in England. Adaptation means that there are problems set by an autonomous nature, and organisms either solve those

---

R. C. Lewontin is Alexander Agassiz Professor at Harvard University. He is an experimental and theoretical evolutionary geneticist who has also worked extensively on epistemological issues in biology. He is the author of *The Genetic Basis of Evolutionary Change* (1974) and, with Richard Levins, of *The Dialectical Biologist* (1985). His current research concerns the nature of genetic variation among individuals within species.

problems or die. Nature: Love it or leave it. It is this metaphor that is used to explain what appears to be the remarkable fit of the keys in the locks, the objects and nature. But, in fact, one can organize one's knowledge about organisms and the world in a completely different way by using a metaphor of *construction*. To do so, one needs to abandon the alienated view of the organism and the environment, to say that it is not the case that environments have an autonomous set of laws, and organisms discover them, meet them, and have to cope with them but that, in fact, environments are a consequence of what Marx called "the sensuous activity" of organisms.

The metaphor of construction replacing the metaphor of adaptation would completely change the problematic and the nature of evidence because many of the problems are the provision of evidence of adaptation, looking for ways to show that an adaptation has occurred. But if we deny in the first place that an adaptation has occurred and change the metaphor to one of construction, how organisms have constructed the world in which we live, then we look for totally different kinds of observations. We perform quite different experiments. Everything changes. So, I want to propose that, in general, what we have are organizing metaphors, powerful ones that enable us to talk about organisms and talk about the world in particular ways but which guide the direction of our search for evidence.

Bill Wimsatt has asked the question, When do we "jump ship" (p. 495)? How do we know? If nothing is evidence, how do we decide? The answer is that we don't "jump ship" in biology. Physicists jump ships; biologists never. What biologists do is give up the domain of the original assertion and narrow it. Because most of biology is, in fact, a form of taxonomy of nature, biologists say, Well, sometimes this happens and sometimes that happens, and sometimes *that* happens but less frequently than I had supposed. Let us take two examples. In the early attempt to understand how genes controlled—or determined, as people would have said—the development of organisms, there was a model that we owed to the French scientists, François Jacob and Jacques Monod. The Jacob-Monod model was a particular model of the way in which DNA interacts with proteins in the organism in order to control which genes were turned off and turned on. The details of the models are not important. As people began to work on the actual molecular details of protein manufacture using this model, they immediately discovered the model had to be "enriched" by yet other models. The model, in fact, fell almost immediately as a universal description, and we now have a list of some twenty-five different mechanical devices equivalent to that model for an explanation of the way genes are activated. It is well recognized that there are a lot of genes that do not match any of these. That is, molecular biologists are engaged in describing factories. And what they have discovered is that they are not all built on the same pattern. Different machines in different factories are designed in different ways, and this aspect of molecular biology is nothing but taxonomy. At one time it was exciting. Every time one found a new method of gene control, that was something wonderful, but by now this aspect of molecular biology is a great deal more run-of-the-mill. Every time one looks at a new gene, there may be some other wrinkle in the way in which the gene is controlled, and there are no universal signals nor are there universal rules about the decoding of DNA. DNA is a language with unknown hermeneutics. Particular DNA sequences may signify one thing at one time, and other things at other times, one thing in one context, other things in other contexts. We have periphrastic words in the DNA language like the periphrastic *do* in English, which do not seem to mean anything but are placeholders or syntactic functions.

Another example from evolutionary biology is the theory of speciation: How do species form? Darwin did not tell us a great deal about that problem. The great modern exponent and developer of the Darwinian theory of species formation is Ernst Mayr whose theory of so-called allopatric speciation is learned by all students. But the fact is that a lot of biologists are engaged in accumulating speciation events that do not fit Mayr's model. It is not the case that all speciation is allopatric speciation, and whole books have been written on other modes of speciation. So, again, rather than falsifying the theory of allopatric speciation, one simply adds to the list of models. Biologists are involved in creating lists of model historical scenarios. Biology is, in fact, just like history.

Bill Wimsatt asked, When do we change the models and the metaphors? Are there cases when we abandon, for example, the adaptationist metaphor and decide to take the constructionist one? This is a question that deserves a great deal of attention, attention that has not been given to it precisely because theorists, philosophers, and historians of biology have not seen biology as having these organizing metaphors. The answer to Wimsatt's question is that we change organizing metaphors when it is ideologically important and convenient to do so. When the notion you can't fight city hall, which is the notion of adaptation (they make the rules, and you either live by them or get out), ceases to be a political and social imperative, and the issue is no longer how to adapt but how to change the world, then we will change our congenial metaphors in biology from adaptation to constructionism. Either you take the Eleventh Thesis on Feuerbach seriously or you don't. There are undoubtedly other reasons besides political and social world views for changing metaphors in biology. I propose that as a subject of research in intellectual history, we ask not, How do we reject universal hypothesis in biology? but, What are the causes of the change in the general metaphors by which biology is organized?

Wimsatt also asked, Does anything go, then? How about creationism? Why do we say we don't believe in creationism? We don't believe in creationism, but not because the evidence prevents us from doing so. It is a mistake to try to struggle against creationism by getting into debates about radioactivity, the age of the earth, speciation rates, and the fossil record. There is no evidence that can reject creation. One rejects creationism because it is a general weltanschauung that would disturb everything else in our explanation of the physical world. Lewis Beck used to say, "Anybody who believes in God can believe in anything." If you want to be a natural scientist, you are not allowed to have a belief structure that includes miracles because then we would live in a world in which causation can be ruptured at any instant. After all, causation was ruptured several times according to religious belief. We have had virgin births, creations of all kinds, the sun has been stopped in its course, anything goes. So, creationism is not challenged by evidence. It is challenged by the totality of an intellectual stance.

Bill asked the question of whether realism is at issue or whether we are engaged simply in curve fitting. Realism is involved when one is giving descriptions of specific mechanisms of time-local and space-local events. That is to say, if I wanted to describe the machinery of the replication of DNA, the issue of curve fitting does not arise because I am describing the gears and levers of a machine, and a large fraction of science is nothing but the description of the gears and levers of particular machines. There are no very deep epistemological issues involved here. When we come to what I call the informing metaphors, then the issue of realism disappears for a quite different reason. Once you admit that they are nothing but organizing metaphors, then where does "realism" even enter into one's question? Thus the issue of how we decide whether we are doing curve fitting is irrelevant for most biological problems because either we are dealing with the dirty details of how many teeth are in the gears, or we are dealing with organizing metaphors, and neither case presents a serious problem for realism, but for very different reasons.

Finally, Bill suggests that we really should not be interested in making great generalizations and the way evidence can contradict or support them but rather in using evidence that appears to contradict a generalization in order to further refine that generalization, and also to suggest to us the conditions under which it might or might not be true. One might say that the purpose of disconfirming evidence is not to reject the hypothesis but to suggest those conditions under which the hypothesis might be applicable as opposed to the conditions under which it is not. What we might want to do in science is to make conditional statements of the form if A and B and C and D, then E, and then to claim that the reason we did not get E is because we did not have either A or B or C or D. But the problem with that approach in biology, unlike in physics, is that the list of conditions is extraordinarily large, the action of each causal pathway is extremely weak, and nonadditive interactions among pathways are extremely important. What I need to know about a heavenly body to know the rate at which a space capsule will be attracted to it is only its mass and perhaps something about the x-, y-, and z-coordinates of its motion. I do not know of any nontrivial biological question in which some four facts will be a sufficient conditioning of the outcome of the process. The conditioning facts for any nontrivial biological process form an immensely long list, any one of these facts may be debilitating. For that reason, I do not think the conditional mode is very useful. It is not very useful to say our job in biology is to write down the menu of conditions under which this will happen or that will happen because the menu will be just too long. We do not have world enough and time. The proper subtitle of my paper is "World Enough and Time." We cannot wait until the conversion of the Jews to disentangle the extraordinary complexity of specific biological circumstances. The number of things to be said about the specific history of specific biological organisms, species, and so on, and their diversity is so great that it cannot be the project of biological science to marshal that evidence which will give a satisfactorily detailed explanation of an arbitrary list of actual biological events. There are too many of them, and they are historically contingent.

So, what is biological evidence good for? What is the status of evidence? We come back to my original remarks that we only know the answer to that when we know what we are trying to do. If biologists are trying in specific useful cases, as in the case of the AIDS virus, to describe possible interventions, for example, then evidence has its very simplest relationship to the hypotheses that are made. Already in the nineteenth century Robert Koch told us how to use evidence to decide whether a disease is infectious or not. There are no very serious epistemological problems associated with that problem. To the extent that biology wants to live up to the claim that any decent science makes general, if not universal, statements about the world, then I come back to my original point that biology at that level of general laws is nothing but a small set of informing and organizing metaphors. The role of these metaphors is to bring order into the confusion. Evidence, then, has a very different relation to theory than it does in the classical view of the philosophy of science that comes from physics. To the extent that philosophy of science was becoming the philosophy of biology, the old problematic of justification in the philosophy of science in the continuum from the positivists, through Kuhn, through Feuerabend is no longer the problematic for us. We were much closer to the problematic of historiography and literary criticisms.

Index